IMPOSING VALUES

OXFORD POLITICAL PHILOSOPHY

General Editor: Samuel Freeman
University of Pennsylvania

Oxford Political Philosophy publishes books on theoretical and applied political philosophy within the Anglo-American tradition. The
series welcomes submissions on social, political, and global justice, individual rights, democracy, liberalism, socialism, and constitutionalism.

N. Scott Arnold
Imposing Values: An Essay on Liberalism and Regulation

IMPOSING VALUES

An Essay on Liberalism and Regulation

N. Scott Arnold

OXFORD
UNIVERSITY PRESS

OXFORD
UNIVERSITY PRESS

Oxford University Press, Inc., publishes works that further
Oxford University's objective of excellence
in research, scholarship, and education.

Oxford   New York
Auckland   Cape Town   Dar es Salaam   Hong Kong   Karachi
Kuala Lumpur   Madrid   Melbourne   Mexico City   Nairobi
New Delhi   Shanghai   Taipei   Toronto

With offices in
Argentina   Austria   Brazil   Chile   Czech Republic   France   Greece
Guatemala   Hungary   Italy   Japan   Poland   Portugal   Singapore
South Korea   Switzerland   Thailand   Turkey   Ukraine   Vietnam

Published by Oxford University Press, Inc.
198 Madison Avenue, New York, New York 10016
www.oup.com

First issued as an Oxford University Press paperback, 2011

Oxford is a registered trademark of Oxford University Press

Library of Congress Cataloging-in-Publication Data
Arnold, N. Scott.
Imposing values : an essay on liberalism and regulation / N. Scott Arnold.
p.   cm.
ISBN 978-0-19-979568-0
1. Liberalism.   2. Deregulation.   I. Title.
JC574.A75 2009
320.51'3—dc22   2008029351

Printed in the United States of America
on acid-free paper

To My Father

There is, in fact, no recognized principle by which the propriety or impropriety of government interference is customarily tested. People decide according to their personal preferences. Some, whenever they see any good to be done, or evil to be remedied, would willingly instigate the government to undertake the business, while others prefer to bear almost any amount of social evil rather than add one to the departments of human interests amenable to governmental control.

—John Stuart Mill, *On Liberty*

Preface

Perhaps the most basic and fundamental question of political philosophy concerns the moral justification for the state. Why should there be government? And if there should be government, what kind of government should it be, and what should be its proper scope? The question of the proper scope of government is an enduring one in liberal polities and has a salience that it does not have in societies where the line circumscribing the legitimate role of the state is drawn as an afterthought. This is because liberals of all persuasions believe that there are certain areas of social life that are and ought to be off limits to government.

A philosophically adequate response to the question of the proper role of government would seem to require an argument from first principles. In *On Liberty*, John Stuart Mill argues for the Harm Principle, which says that the only legitimate grounds for social coercion is to prevent harm to others. The argument of that book is of course utilitarian. If Mill were asked why utilitarian considerations should be determinative, he would refer the questioner to *Utilitarianism*, specifically chapter 4, "Of What Sort of Proof the Principle of Utility Is Susceptible." In this way, his answer to the question of the proper scope of government is rooted in deeper political, and ultimately moral, principles. As a philosopher, my first inclination was to approach the subject matter of this book in this way. I soon recognized, however, that whatever answer I gave to any of these deeper philosophical questions would be unlikely to be persuasive to those inclined to disagree with me about the proper scope of government. Another strategy suggested itself, but it required that I resist the impulse to try to answer fundamental philosophical questions. Instead, a more modest goal might be to seek agreement among my fellow liberals, leaving to others the task of justifying more fundamental principles.

As I understand it (and as defended in chapter 1), to be a liberal involves a commitment to limited constitutional government, which in turn involves a belief in equal liberty, democratic governance, and a more or less free market in which most of the means of production are privately owned. Although many parts of the world are ruled by illiberal governments, Western (and some Asian) societies are not, and it is for members of these societies that this book is written. Furthermore, although there are many immigrants from nonliberal political traditions living in contemporary Western societies, liberalism remains, in one form or another, the dominant ideology in the West. There is an important sense in which "there's no one here but us liberals," though that may change in the future. This in turn permits a useful discussion about the proper scope of a liberal state, which would not be possible if first principles were up for discussion. Besides, the resolution of the deepest disputes in political philosophy are, how shall we say, a long way off.

As I began to write this book, I cast it in terms intended to cover all liberal societies but soon recognized that this would not work. I had to come down from the level of philosophical abstraction at which I am accustomed to writing and talk at the level of particular policies and laws. Since I know U.S. society best, that became my topic, though it should be accessible and (I hope) of interest to non-Americans as well. Still, this is a very ambitious project.

The first four chapters are intended to be a comprehensive survey of the differences between classical liberalism and modern liberalism regarding the proper scope of government. Chapter 1 offers a preliminary characterization of classical liberalism and modern liberalism and explains the main areas of agreement between them. Although all liberals believe in limited constitutional government, classical liberals are inclined to favor a more limited role for government, whereas modern liberals are inclined to favor a more extensive role for government. This is aptly captured in the epigraph to this book from Mill's *On Liberty*. Chapter 2 begins a discussion of these differences. Classical liberals and modern liberals differ on the extent to which the state should own productive assets in an essentially private enterprise economy. It turns out, however, that these differences are not deep: classical liberals do not oppose all state ownership of productive assets, and modern liberals are open to privatizing government-owned assets and indeed have supported the latter. Deeper (philosophical) differences are to be found regarding tax policy and transfer programs, however. I argue that modern liberalism presupposes a form of social ownership of productive assets even though, at the end of the day, they favor private property in (most) of the means of production.

A presupposition of social ownership best explains modern liberal attitudes and beliefs about tax policy and transfer policy. These include, but are not limited to, redistributive taxation and transfer programs. Classical liberals, by contrast, believe that property rights in the first instance reside with private parties, either on grounds of natural rights or on utilitarian grounds. Government has the right to take some of that property—classical liberals are not anarchists—but government is much more constrained in what it may legitimately do in the name of tax policy and in transfer programs than in the modern liberal vision. In keeping with my methodology, I make no effort to resolve this philosophical difference.

Chapter 3 outlines the points of agreement and disagreement between modern and classical liberals on the extent to which ownership rights should be restricted by the state through regulation. Property is a complex of rights, terms, and conditions, and there are major and systematic differences between classical liberalism and modern liberalism about what regulatory restrictions they will countenance. Chapters 1 through 3 constitute a comprehensive statement of the points of agreement and disagreement between classical liberals and modern liberals about the proper role or scope of the government in modern U.S. society. One of the purposes of this book is to articulate a range of plausible forms of classical liberalism. It is unfortunate that classical liberalism has typically been identified with libertarianism. Libertarians believe that the sole legitimate function of government is to protect and enforce people's rights to life, liberty, and property. Some libertarians also allow that the state can legitimately supply some public goods. Classical liberalism need not be so narrowly understood, however. Indeed, historically, it has not been. There are versions of classical liberalism that do not presuppose the extremely stringent rights to private property and freedom of contract favored by contemporary libertarians, which their critics have used as a stick to beat them with. One purpose of this book is to outline a more moderate version of classical liberalism.

Chapter 4 identifies what I call "the modern liberal regulatory agenda," which consists of the various regulatory regimes that modern liberals are inclined to favor and classical liberals are inclined to oppose. The first section of this chapter distinguishes economic from noneconomic regulation. The former includes rate regulation, regulation of entry and exit, antitrust law, and wage and price controls. It is argued that the traditional disputes between modern liberals and classical liberals about economic regulation have become significantly attenuated over the past few decades, and the disagreements that remain are relatively narrow. By contrast, differences about noneconomic regulation remain profound. For this reason, the modern liberal regulatory agenda, as I define it, is about noneconomic regulation. That agenda is culled from the discussion in chapter 3 about classical and modern liberal attitudes regarding restrictions on property rights, and it covers three broad areas: (1) the employment relation, (2) health and safety regulation, and (3) land use regulation. The first four chapters, then, provide an accessible and comprehensive account of the differences between modern liberalism and classical liberalism concerning the proper scope of government.

Chapters 5 and 6 are about what I call in chapter 1 "common ground arguments." These are arguments that modern liberals might use to persuade classical liberals to support their regulatory agenda (or vice versa). They are based on shared liberal beliefs about the presuppositions of a market economy, fundamental rights, negative externalities, and public goods. I show that none of these arguments succeeds in providing a basis for reasoned agreement in support of the modern liberal regulatory agenda.

Chapter 1 identifies a common type of argument deployed by modern liberals in support of various government regulations—a type of argument that makes no appeal to abstract principles about the proper role of government but instead appeals to lower-level moral principles about how people ought to be treated. I call these "conversion arguments," since they are directed at converting classical liberals to the modern liberal faith (and vice versa). These arguments are also directed at those without firm commitments regarding the proper scope of government on a range of issues—moderates or pragmatists, as they style themselves. So, for example, instead of arguing for antidiscrimination law on the basis of some abstract principle about equal concern and respect, one might argue from a lower-level principle to the effect that discrimination on the basis of race in the workplace is wrong, and that these laws are the most effective means to prevent it. These conversion arguments reflect a kind of moral pragmatism characteristic of modern liberalism.

Chapters 7 through 10 canvass conversion arguments for each of the elements on the modern liberal regulatory agenda. It finds that, with a few exceptions, all such arguments can be reasonably challenged by classical liberal counterarguments of the same type. Such challenges typically involve explaining how the range of social problems identified by modern liberals could be or would be handled by a private ordering. The conclusion of these chapters is that, for nearly all items on the modern liberal regulatory agenda, there is persistent reasonable disagreement about these government interventions into a private ordering because there are opposing conversion arguments that each side can offer.

Chapter 11 considers what is to be done when reasonable disagreement persists among liberals about the proper scope of government, and when one or the other side has the political power to impose its vision—its values—on society. I argue for a number of procedural requirements that must be satisfied if the imposition of the values in question is to be morally or politically legitimate. Specifically, the imposition must be done by the elected branches of government and publicly justified. That justification must be transparent, which demands identification of both the intended and unintended beneficiaries and the intended and unintended "victims" (i.e., those whose interests are negatively affected) of the legislation. These requirements are rooted in certain values to which all liberals are committed.

Chapter 12 applies the requirements identified in chapter 11 to selected items on the modern liberal regulatory agenda, specifically the prohibition on race and sex discrimination, occupational health and safety regulation as embodied in OSHA, and medical products regulation as overseen by the FDA. In this chapter, I conclude that, with the exception of one form of race discrimination, the imposition of these elements of the modern liberal regulatory agenda has not been morally legitimate because one or more of the requirements articulated in chapter 11 has been violated. Those elements could have been legitimately imposed, but they were not—and this is because of the way it was done. In closing, I reexamine the requirements for legitimately imposing values. I am sensitive to the charge that these requirements are impossibly stringent and ignore the rough and tumble nature of politics. At the end of the book, I make some effort to rebut that charge.

There are many people and organizations I have to thank for help on this project. First and foremost is the Social Philosophy and Policy Center at Bowling Green State University in Bowling Green, Ohio. They have once again generously supported my work. This project stalled out a few years ago, and their assistance was instrumental in seeing it through to completion. Thanks are owed to the executive director, Fred Miller, and associate directors, Ellen Frankel Paul and Jeffrey Paul, and to the staff at the Policy Center, especially Mary Dilsaver.

They have always made me feel welcome there. While working on this project in the summer of 2006 at the Policy Center, I presented the results of some of my work to other visiting scholars and graduate students. Their feedback was most helpful. Some of the material in chapter 10 will appear in "The Endangered Species Act, Regulatory Takings, and Public Goods," which is forthcoming in *Social Philosophy & Policy* 26:2 (Summer 2009).

Further financial support came from a Faculty Development grant from the University of Alabama at Birmingham and from a grant from the Earhart Foundation. These grants allowed me to work undisturbed for a summer at the Hoover Institution at Stanford University. I am grateful for the support provided early in the project from all of these institutions. I also benefited from release from other duties by means of a sabbatical leave at the beginning of this project.

The Internet is an amazing research tool; it permits scholars to sit at their desks and download almost anything. It has another benefit that has proved almost equally valuable for me: because of the broad range of topics discussed in this book, I have been able to tap into the expertise of a wide range of scholars and experts through e-mail exchanges, and in a few cases, telephone conversations. I should like to take this opportunity to thank some of them by name. There are many others who answered a question or two or directed me to a reference, but there were a few who gave generously of their time and expertise to help me understand how laws and government bureaucracies actually work. Henry Perritt patiently explained the burdens of proof in disparate impact discrimination lawsuits and rescued me from a major confusion. A long phone conversation with Stanley Greer of the National Right to Work Foundation helped me to understand the National Labor Relations Act and some related Supreme Court decisions. Alex Tabarrok proved to be an invaluable resource about the Food and Drug Administration. Jonathan Miles provided research assistance on the Occupational Safety and Health Act of 1970. Daniel Shapiro, David Schmidtz, Gerald Gaus, Maureen Kelley, and Greg Pence provided useful feedback on different parts of the book. Thanks also go to two anonymous reviewers for Oxford University Press. Special thanks go to Samuel Freeman, who read the entire manuscript and provided very valuable feedback on all of it. This book is much improved owing to his efforts. Thanks also to Jennifer Stitt for help with proofreading.

More general debts are owed to W. Kip Viscusi, whose extensive writings on health and safety regulation have informed much of my thinking on these topics, and to Richard Epstein, who has similarly influenced my thinking about antidiscrimination law. A long time ago, James Cornman taught me to give the other side in any dispute the best case I could before criticizing it. I have tried my very best to do that in this book, though I have probably fallen short. Finally, I am pleased to acknowledge the assistance of my father. As a retired pharmacist, he was able to help me understand some things about the workings of the Food and Drug Administration. This book is dedicated to him.

Contents

IMPOSING VALUES

ONE

Rights, Public Goods, and Externalities

Two Views of the Proper Role of Government

The quotation from Mill that serves as an epigram for this book raises a question that is still with us. What is the proper scope of government activity? In Western liberal democracies, two prominent alternatives have been debated and defended: modern liberalism and classical liberalism. Though each would object to Mill's way of framing their respective positions, modern liberals do believe that the state should take an activist role in addressing a wide range of society's problems, whereas classical liberals deny this. It is arguable that in one form or another, this has been the central dispute among liberals since the time of Mill.

Modern liberalism occupies the left-of-center in the traditional political spectrum and is represented by the Democratic Party in the United States, the Labor Party in the United Kingdom, and the mainstream Left (including some nominally socialist parties) in other advanced democratic societies. Perhaps the two most important modern liberal political figures in recent U.S. history were Franklin Delano Roosevelt and Lyndon Johnson. They epitomized the modern liberal mindset and did more to implement the modern liberal vision of the proper role of government than any other political figures. Leading contemporary modern liberal political theorists include John Rawls, Ronald Dworkin, Joel Feinberg, and Bruce Ackerman. The most famous economist of modern liberalism is John Maynard Keynes, though Paul Samuelson might well be equally influential. John Kenneth Galbraith was an important semipopular figure in the modern liberal pantheon. From the Progressive Era until the early 1980s, modern liberalism dominated the political and intellectual landscape of Western democracies in general and the United States in particular.

Classical liberalism was less of a factor, both politically and intellectually, in the twentieth century until about the 1980s. The ascendancy of Margaret Thatcher in Great Britain and Ronald Reagan in the United States gave political voice to a set of ideas that trace their roots to the seventeenth and eighteenth centuries and the writings of Locke, Hume, Smith, and the Founding Fathers. It is at most a slight exaggeration to say that the rebirth of classical liberal ideas in the twentieth century can be traced to one man: F. A. Hayek. Two of his works, *The Road to Serfdom* (1944 [1972]) and *The Constitution of Liberty* (1960) inspired a relatively small number of thinkers who were profoundly dissatisfied with modern liberalism but who also believed that conservatism in its European and American incarnations constituted an inadequate political philosophy for the twentieth century. Two political economists, Milton Friedman and James Buchanan, each of whom was awarded the Nobel Prize, raised the profile of classical liberalism among economists, political scientists, and, in the case of Friedman, among the general public. The libertarian wing of contemporary classical liberalism was inspired by Robert Nozick in his early work *Anarchy, State, and Utopia* (1974), and libertarian political ideas have been further defended in the works of legal theorists Richard Epstein (1985; 1998) and Randy Barnett (1998; 2004) and in the writings of philosophers such as Loren Lomasky (1987), Jan Narveson (1988), Tibor Machan (1989), and Douglas Rasmussen and Douglas Den Uyl (1990). Other than the Libertarian Party in the United States and small libertarian parties in other countries (e.g., Costa Rica, Canada), there is no political party that could be characterized as classical liberal, though there are classical liberal elements in the Republican Party in the United States, the Conservative Party in the United Kingdom, and in various other political parties in democratic countries around the world. Over the past forty years or so, classical liberal think tanks have sprouted like mushrooms, especially in the United States, but elsewhere as well.

Though contemporary Western democracies largely embody the institutional framework of modern liberalism, challenges to that framework have come from classical liberal thinkers, and some changes in that framework have been inaugurated by politicians with classical liberal sympathies. The dispute between classical and modern liberals has been largely a dispute about the proper role of government that Mill calls attention to in the epigram for this book. The purpose of this book is to characterize that dispute accurately and to make some progress toward resolving it.

How might one proceed? Mill's approach in *On Liberty* was to articulate a relatively abstract principle, the Harm Principle (sometimes called "the Liberty Principle"), which addresses this question. This principle holds that "the sole legitimate grounds for social coercion is to prevent harm to others" (Mill [1859] 1978, 9). He argued for this principle on utilitarian grounds in the first four chapters of *On Liberty* and worked out some of its policy implications in the final chapter of that classic work. Jonathan Riley (1998, 46, 191–93), among others, has argued that Mill should be understood to be asserting that preventing harm to others is a necessary but not a sufficient condition for the justified use of social coercion. This seems obvious in light of the fact that an action may cause harm to others, but using social coercion to try to prevent actions of that kind might ultimately cause even more harm. While not a sufficient condition, the principle does tell us something about spheres or areas where government should not interfere. At the very least, it rules out most instances of state-sponsored paternalism.

It is worth noticing that Mill approaches this problem the way one would expect a philosopher to approach it, namely, by articulating a general principle about the proper role of government, which he then applies to policy questions. Indeed, the last chapter of *On Liberty* is titled "Applications." The principle itself is justified by reference to a deeper principle of moral or political philosophy, namely, the Principle of Utility, which says that a right action or social policy is one that maximizes utility. It is this principle that makes a policy's consequences for human happiness and unhappiness the decisive moral consideration. Ultimately, then, Mill's answer to the question of the proper scope of government activity depends on the case for this important principle in moral philosophy. Mill makes the case for the Principle of Utility in other of his writings, but not in *On Liberty*.[1] Other philosophers defend other answers to the question of the proper scope of government on the basis of equally fundamental principles, including principles of justice. In either case, the case for the proper role of government ultimately depends on the resolution of deeper disputes in moral or political philosophy. Unfortunately, however, because of the intractable nature of such disputes, this approach seems unlikely to produce agreement among those who care about the issue.

Philosophers might not be dismayed by this observation. After all, they might say, the central issue is truth, not agreement. If the truth depends on principles that are recondite, difficult to understand, or not subject to clear and convincing proof, then that is the way it is, and we must learn to live with our doubts. This attitude—dare we say philosophical attitude—will not do, however, for the simple reason it does not tell us *how* to live with our doubts. There are real-world problems in civil society for which government intervention may or may not be the best solution. Those in a position to address those problems—politicians, policymakers, and those who directly influence them—are seeking advice about what to do, to the extent that they are fair and open-minded. Or at least they are wondering whether they should follow a set of instincts or prejudices they bring to these problems. They do not really want to know what Mill or Kant or Aristotle would say, and they care even less about which of these thinkers comes closest to the truth about moral or political philosophy. Moreover, even if they are not seeking advice, and we are only contemplating what unsolicited advice to give them (in truth, a more likely scenario), it behooves us to offer arguments that do not depend on controversial philosophical principles and the easily controvertible and usually question-begging arguments that have been offered for them. Philosophers' penchant for arguments that depend on the deepest principles of political or moral philosophy might explain why they are rarely called upon to testify about impending legislation. The characteristic inconclusiveness of disputes about philosophical principles leaves those who shape public policy stranded on the shoals of uncertainty with only the special interests willing to tow them back out to sea and set their course. Or—even worse—it leads them to think that this inconclusiveness at the deeper, philosophical level licenses them to decide, in Mill's words, "according to their personal preferences," that is, their prejudices. How then to proceed?

If proof—and thus knowledge—of the ultimate truth about these matters is too ambitious a goal, reasoned agreement among the contending parties is not. There are four ways this agreement might be reached. First, classical and modern liberals do agree on a number of important matters of principle concerning the proper role of government. Those matters will be explored shortly, but the idea is that sometimes a proponent of one side can make a successful case for his point of view on some particular issue concerning the proper role of government by showing that his position is an implication of some lower-level shared principle. For instance, a modern liberal might successfully argue that a certain public good can best be secured or a certain negative externality (externalities are negative or positive spillover effects involuntarily incurred by third parties) can best be dealt with by government regulation. Since securing public goods and dealing with negative externalities are proper functions of government on both modern liberal and classical liberal views, classical liberals

could join in supporting this regulation. The regulation of air pollution would be an example. On the other side, a classical liberal might
successfully argue that financing political campaigns by tax dollars
would force people to subsidize speech they disagree with and that
this would violate a fundamental right of freedom of association.
Since both sides agree that people have such a right, modern liberals
should oppose such a scheme, supposing this argument to be a good
one. Philosophical disputes will remain about the justification for the
relevant principles about public goods, externalities, and fundamental rights, but in spite of those disagreements, reasoned agreement
could be reached on particular questions—policy questions—about
the proper role of government in civil society. For future reference,
call these *common ground arguments*.

One might wonder, why does the principle to which one side
appeals have to be shared by both sides? For example, why could not
a modern liberal try to persuade a classical liberal by appeal to a principle that the latter accepts but that the former does not (or vice versa)?
Indeed, this is possible, subject to an important qualification. The policy prescription in question has to be something that could also be
justified on the basis of some other principle that the modern liberal
accepts. Otherwise, support for it is unprincipled for the modern liberal, and the argument for it is insincere.[2] It would be as if an atheist
had an ungrounded prejudice against abortion and offered a religiously
based argument against abortion to a believer. If this sort of argument
succeeded in persuading the believer, it would not result in reasoned
agreement, at least on the part of the atheist, because the source of the
latter's belief is an ungrounded prejudice. If a modern liberal can support the policy prescription based on her own principles, as well as
classical liberal principles, then it would be justified in the context of
this debate. Let us call this a *convergence argument*. This sort of argument attempts to show that, contrary to what one's opponent believes,
a policy the latter is inclined to oppose is actually supported by some
principle he accepts. In such cases, both sides' principles converge
in supporting the policy in question.[3] Since people are not unerring
in their beliefs about the implications of their principles, one should
expect that this strategy would sometimes succeed.

A third possibility appears if one conceives of classical or modern
liberalism as consisting of something other than exceptionless rules or
principles that crank out answers to questions about when or where
the state should intervene in civil society. Instead, the rules or principles about the proper role of government that each side is inclined to

support could be conceived of as rules of thumb or as heuristic devices that serve as fallible guides for thinking about questions of social policy. This view is clearly expressed in the following quotation from Aaron Director about the meaning of laissez faire: "*Laissez faire* has never been more than a slogan in defense of the proposition that every extension of state activity should be examined under a presumption of error" (Director 1964, 2). Alternatively, the linguistic expression of these principles could be conceived of not as expressing one or more propositions but as giving voice to attitudes—attitudes that can be understood in terms of a disposition to defend one or the other side in a debate about the proper role of government. Indeed, this is nicely captured in the epigram from Mill wherein he describes the respective mindsets of modern and classical liberals, though not by those names. Few modern liberals would affirm that "whenever they see any good to be done, or evil to be remedied, [they] would willingly instigate the government to undertake the business," nor would classical liberals aver that they would willingly "bear almost any amount of social evil rather than add one to the departments of human interests amenable to governmental control." Though their opponents would describe them in exactly that way, they themselves would not. The quoted passages, however, do seem to characterize, with only a touch of exaggeration, their respective attitudes—attitudes which can be cashed out in terms of dispositions to argue for or against government intervention across a range of cases. Whether lower-level classical and modern liberal principles about the proper role of government are conceived of as rules of thumb, heuristic devices, or expressions of attitudes, by their very nature they invite exceptions. One way reasoned agreement could be achieved is to convince reasonable persons on the other side to make an exception to their favored view about the proper role of government.

This way of conceiving of classical and modern liberals' views about the proper role of government does not apply to all participants in this dispute. Most famously, libertarians in the natural rights tradition hold that people have natural rights, which, they maintain, have fairly direct implications for the proper role of government. These rights are themselves logical implications of deeper philosophical views about the nature of persons, the social contract, and so on, to which they subscribe. This would make them resistant to the sort of argument under discussion here. Some modern liberals have correspondingly principled views, especially as it pertains to principles of justice and the associated policies to assist the least advantaged. Many participants in the debate, however, lack that kind of confidence in the foundations of their views about the proper role of government and are thus willing to consider exceptions to whatever principles to which they tentatively subscribe.

To illustrate, classical liberals such as Hayek believe that the distribution of wealth and income is not the proper object of government policy, and people should be allowed to keep what they earn in the market, subject to a scheme of just taxation. Despite these beliefs, Hayek also maintains that there is a role for government in assisting the poorest members of society. In *The Constitution of Liberty* he says:

> All modern governments have made provision for the indigent, unfortunate, and disabled....There is no reason why the volume of these pure service activities should not increase with the general growth of wealth....It can hardly be denied that, as we grow richer, that minimum of sustenance which the community has always provided for those not able to look after themselves, and which can be provided outside the market, will gradually rise, or that government may usefully...assist or even lead in such endeavors. (1960, 257–58)

Hayek would not justify this intervention on the grounds of distributive justice. Indeed, he believes that the notion of distributive justice makes no clear sense.[4] Clearly, however, he has persuaded himself of the desirability of some government assistance to the most vulnerable members of society on some grounds—perhaps on the basis of some relatively abstract moral principle or, more likely, on the basis of something much less abstract, for example, the simple proposition that, left entirely to the vagaries of civil society, the well-being of some members of society would be seriously compromised and that government can and should prevent that. Whether there is a way to render this set of beliefs consistent with Hayek's general views on the proper role of government can be left open at this point; presumably, there would have to be some way of building (what would appear to be) an exception into a more general principle, and that would have to be shown to be not ad hoc.

For an example on the other side, modern liberals are inclined to favor government regulation of industries dominated by one or a few firms. Modern liberals might be persuaded by public choice arguments, however, that government regulation of emerging technologies in telecommunications has made consumers worse off, in terms of rates, choices, and product and service innovation than they would be in a completely unregulated environment.[5] The classical liberal might successfully argue that, whatever the deficiencies of unregulated markets generally, those deficiencies are milder or less severe than the deficiencies of government regulation in the rapidly changing environment of modern telecommunications. If this argument is rationally compelling, or at least rationally persuasive, modern liberals could make an exception to their general principle about the need for government regulation of industries dominated by one or a few firms and could support deregulation of the telecommunications industry.

This sort of argument can be made especially persuasive if it appeals to values or goals cherished by the other side. For example, as a matter of general principle, classical liberals are inclined to oppose government regulations of transactions that do not aim at preventing force or fraud. It might be argued, however, that they should make an exception in the case of current labeling regulations for consumer and industrial products on the following grounds: in recent years, a common strategy among plaintiffs' attorneys has been to initiate tort actions, often class action suits, against manufacturers of toxic substances for injuries and illnesses associated with the use of the latter's products. A lawsuit is launched on the grounds that the defendant failed to warn the plaintiff of safety hazards involved in using the product. Some courts have been moving toward the view that these "failure to warn" cases should be dismissed if the defendant has complied with federal labeling regulations, which, among other things, require that users be warned of the dangers of the product.[6] Arguably, classical liberals should support these regulations and the associated court rulings, which could be codified by statute, on the grounds that they remove a cause of action from a legal system that has in recent years rendered property rights in productive assets increasingly unstable or insecure. Classical liberals believe that it is vitally important that property rights be secure, and developments in the past few decades in tort law have jeopardized this. Companies' assets are increasingly up for grabs, as plaintiffs' attorneys have pressed tort actions against corporations for mishaps that could not be foreseen, prevented, or insured against. In this way, classical liberals could see their way clear to make an exception to a general principle about regulation on the grounds that, in the current legal environment, government regulation enhances security of possession, an important element of the classical liberal vision of the good society—and it does so at an acceptable cost in terms of the restrictions on contractual freedom that labeling regulations entail. In making this argument to classical liberals, an appeal is made to values or goals they endorse, though a modern liberal making this argument might endorse this policy on entirely different (e.g., paternalistic) grounds.

It might be thought that because of its appeal to stability of possession, this is really a convergence argument that runs from classical liberal principles to policy conclusions, but that would be incorrect. Although it is safe to say that all classical liberals agree that stability of possession is important (indeed all liberals could agree on that, since it is the primary reason to leave the state of nature, for those who think in those terms), they could reasonably disagree about its importance in this instance, either because they believe that the deficiencies of the tort system are overblown and that system in its unvarnished state is the best way to handle "failure to warn" cases, or they might disagree because they simply brook no exceptions to this principle of freedom of contract in light of their deeper philosophical commitments. Appeals to values (here stability of possession) as opposed to principles, have an indeterminacy about them, perhaps because the former can be traded off against other values at the margin or even against other principles (witness Hayek's views on government assistance to the disadvantaged), and there may be no unique rationally persuasive trade-off schedule that all classical liberals would be constrained to accept. In short, classical liberal principles and values do not point unambiguously to policy conclusions, at least in this case.

What is distinctive about all these arguments is that they are limited in scope and do not require settlement, once and for all, of the general question about the proper role of government. Nor do they require those on the other side to give up their general principles, at least as fallible heuristic devices or rules of thumb, since those who offer them seek only limited agreement on a particular issue. Philosophers are inclined to look for some comprehensive principle or principles under which all policy prescriptions could be subsumed (e.g., Mill's Harm Principle), but that is extraordinarily difficult to do. Reasonable people, when faced with decisions about what policies to support, will make exceptions to general rules they subscribe to and leave unresolved the difficult philosophical question of whether the totality of their views can be rendered coherent and consistent. It is not as if acceptance or advocacy of these policies is an ungrounded prejudice; after all, reasons for them can be given. It is just that those reasons do not in any obvious way appeal to deeper (and exceptionless) philosophical principles. More will be said about these arguments in chapter 7, but for now we need a name for them. They could be called "unprincipled exception arguments" or "ad hoc arguments," but a more neutral and instructive term would be "conversion arguments," since they aim at converting those on the other side or those who have no firmly held beliefs about the proper role of the state in this particular area. "Conversion arguments" is an apt term for another reason, namely, if one can pile up enough arguments of this sort on enough issues, then (most) reasonable people on the other side will have been effectively converted to the one's point of view, and the larger debate about the proper role of government between the two sides will have been essentially resolved. Modern liberals and classical liberals could then quit the field in comity if not in complete harmony, leaving only the socialists and the Randians glowering at each other.

There is another possible denouement: reasoned agreement on what had been the major points of disagreement might be reached on the classical liberal side on some issues and the modern liberal side on others, in which case it would be fair to say that neither side (or both sides) had been vindicated in the debate. "Moderates" or "centrists," as they describe themselves, firmly believe that this is where the truth lies or at least where reasoned agreement is to be found. After all, not all liberals are classical liberals or modern liberals. On the other hand, men and women of principle (as they like to call themselves) or ideologues (as their opponents call them) scoff at those who would make Swiss cheese out of whatever principles they bring to the table or who have no determinate views on the proper role of the state across a range of issues. But before the arguments have been deployed and evaluated, no one can say where the truth lies or even where reasoned agreement is likely to be found.

On the face of it, it is far from evident how many of the differences between classical liberalism and modern liberalism could be resolved by common ground, convergence, or conversion arguments. If some differences remain, how might they be resolved? Each side would presumably have their reasons for their respective views, but they would not be the sort of reasons the other side could accept, or at least would find rationally compelling. Under the circumstances, progress might be made if both sides could agree on some procedural principle(s) to follow in evaluating existing policies, or proposals for policy change, when they face persistent reasonable disagreement. This has to be done in a way that is consistent and coherent with liberalism, broadly understood. Otherwise, the question of the proper role of the state is answered, as Mill suggests in the epigram, by appeal to personal preference—and ultimately by sheer political power. What distinguishes these arguments from all the others canvassed above is that they are arguments not so much about what is reasonable for liberals to believe (in this case, about the proper role of government) as they are about what liberals who have the political power should *do* in the face of failure to achieve reasonable agreement with their liberal opponents about what to believe. More will be said about these arguments in chapter 11; for now let us call them *practical liberal arguments.*

It might be objected that the multifaceted approach to the question of the proper role of the state outlined above reads out of the debate those with more radical views. For example, some radical thinkers, such as Murray Rothbard (1978), believe in a form of anarchocapitalism in which there is no room for legitimate state intervention because the state itself is morally illegitimate. On the other side of the political spectrum, there are socialists, some of whom even describe themselves as liberals, who believe that role of the state in the economy should be so large or pervasive that it is not really accurate to think of the state as intervening in the economy. They believe that a private property market economy, as traditionally conceived, should be abolished (Schweickart 1993; Roemer, 1994a; 1994c). This is a necessary, though not a sufficient, condition for being a socialist (Arnold 1994, 7–8). What can be said in response to these and other radical critics of the existing order? After all, the mere fact that they are radical does not mean their views are mistaken.

The short answer is that this is another debate, or more exactly, these views involve other debates between liberals and their critics. Moreover, in these debates the critics bear substantial burdens of proof that they have not borne. In other writings, I have explored these burdens as they arise in Marx's and market socialists' critiques of (liberal) capitalist society (Arnold 1990; 1994). I have argued that radical critics owe us an account of property rights in a socialist system and an explanation of how a socialist economic system could overcome the perceived deficiencies of the existing order without creating problems that are worse—even from their own perspective. In both of these works, I have also argued that these burdens cannot be successfully discharged.[7] Even if they could, however, the radical critic would have yet another burden: he must explain, at least in general terms, how it is possible to inaugurate social change to bring about the new order and to do so in such a way that the costs of the transition, however those costs are assayed, do not outweigh the benefits. The apparent stability of the existing order makes the project of radical criticism appear to be, at least for now, merely an academic exercise in the pejorative sense of the term. For the foreseeable future, modern Western societies are liberal democratic capitalist societies with market economies characterized by private ownership of the means of production—economies in which the state intervenes in a variety of ways. When times change, the terms of the debate will change. As for now, there is a real and important debate about the circumstances under which state intervention in civil, capitalist society should take place, and radical critics' admonitions to tear down the system and replace it with something else seem largely irrelevant. Those who make or directly influence government policy are not likely to get useful advice from radical critics, whatever their persuasion, at least at this time. For all these reasons, in what follows, I shall assume that modern liberals all favor an economic system in which most productive assets are privately owned, thereby reading socialists out of the debate. In other words, I shall assume in what follows that modern liberals are not socialists.[8]

What about others who reject the liberal label, for example, communitarians, feminists, and civic republicans?[9] The policy implications of their principles, however, are very often versions of policies favored by modern liberals. They are, after all, on the left side of the political spectrum insofar as they are inclined to favor governmental solutions to a large array of social problems. There may be a range of issues on which their principles are silent, but on many policy questions their views coincide with those of modern liberalism. For these reasons, they will be included in the discussions that follow, as a matter of courtesy, as it were.

There are a number of different ways to characterize classical liberalism and modern liberalism. Philosophers seeking to chart intellectual territory typically look to philosophical principles as the obvious natural boundaries to use in drawing their maps. This is likely to be unhelpful in the present case, however, since some philosophically allied thinkers are on opposite sides of the ideological fence on policy questions, and some thinkers who are at odds philosophically nevertheless substantially agree with one another about the proper role of government. For example, one can find both classical liberals (e.g., Epstein 1998) and modern liberals (e.g., Goodin 1988) among those who confess the Utilitarian faith. Similarly, both kinds of liberals can be found among those for whom Kant's writings are the sacred texts (e.g., Lomasky (1987) among classical liberals and Rawls (1971) among modern liberals). Although it is possible that those who line up politically on one side or the other have drawn the wrong implications from philosophical principles of morality or rationality that they share with some of their counterparts on the other side, it is more likely that the route from abstract philosophical principles to policy conclusions is not direct and requires less abstract, ancillary principles, as well as empirical propositions, about which there is considerable disagreement.

Where classical liberals do largely agree among themselves and where they do largely disagree with modern liberals is on a range of questions about the proper role of the state in civil society, especially as it pertains to property rights and freedom of contract. How, then, should modern liberalism and classical liberalism be characterized? As suggested earlier (see pages 7–8), perhaps the most useful way is in terms of a propensity or disposition to argue in favor of, or against, government intervention in civil society. Of course, "intervention" must be defined relative to a conception of property rights. For present purposes, that conception can be understood as full, liberal ownership, which in turn is defined in terms of a complex of rights, terms, and conditions.[10] This means that there will be some indeterminacy about what the classical or modern liberal perspective is on some issues, which is as it should be, for there are those on both sides who are willing to make exceptions to whatever general principles about the proper role of the state to which they are inclined to subscribe or who do not claim to have a comprehensive answer to the general question of the proper role of the state in civil society. This way of characterizing modern liberalism and classical liberalism takes no stand on the deeper questions about philosophical foundations, but for the reasons just indicated, distinctions based on philosophical commitments are likely to prove unhelpful anyway. This means that classical liberalism and modern liberalism are not, strictly speaking, positions to be defended or, for that matter, attacked. They are instead inclinations or attitudes—instincts as Hume might call them. This way of characterizing modern liberalism and classical liberalism also papers over disagreements within each camp—disagreements that are typically rooted in internal disputes about moral and political principles and/or their implications. These disagreements are strictly parochial and only acquire independent importance when one side in the larger debate has decisively defeated the other, either on the intellectual battlefield or in the struggle for control of the levers of political power. Because neither event has occurred nor is likely to occur in the foreseeable future, a discussion of these internecine battles can be profitably postponed.

Marking the points of agreement between classical and modern liberals is as important as marking the points of disagreement, since it can assist in identifying some common ground that might serve as a touchstone for arriving at even greater agreement about the proper role of the state or at least can help identify the sorts of arguments that might be used to justify such claims. A limited conceptual geography of the sort to be undertaken here might also provide some hints about how to deal with the remaining differences between classical and modern liberals.

The balance of this first chapter details some broad areas of agreement between classical and modern liberals about the proper role of the state in civil society. Specifically, both sides agree that the government should enforce and respect fundamental personal and political rights, though there is some disagreement about what fundamental rights there are. Classical and modern liberal views on fundamental rights are discussed in the next section. Classical and modern liberals further agree that there is a role for the state in providing public goods and dealing with problems caused by externalities, though this way of putting it conceals some important disagreements between (and indeed within) each camp about the scope of these problems and what the state should do about them. The third and fourth sections of this chapter explore the points of agreement—as well as the points of disagreement—between classical and modern liberals on the related subjects of public goods and externalities.

As was hinted at earlier, perhaps the most striking disagreements between modern and classical liberals have to do with the extent of, and restrictions on, private property rights. Some questions this raises include: To what extent should productive assets be owned by the state in an essentially private enterprise system? Does the state have some sort of prior ownership claim on a portion of what is otherwise private property? What sorts of limitations on the exercise of private property rights—and its corollary, freedom of contract—are justifiable? Though there are points of agreement between modern and classical liberals on these questions, there are large and important areas of disagreement as well. Chapters 2 and 3 detail the positions of modern and classical liberals on these questions. Together, these first three chapters provide a comprehensive overview of the points of agreement and disagreement between modern and classical liberals and set the stage for the rest of the book, wherein an attempt is made to make some progress in the dispute between the two sides about the proper role of the state in one important area: government regulation.

Fundamental Rights

As a first approximation, it is fair to say that all liberals believe in equal liberty, democratic governance, and a market economy in which most productive assets are privately owned.[11] The commitments to equal liberty and democratic governance take the form of a belief that there should be fundamental legal rights of the sort found in the U.S. Constitution and guaranteed to all citizens, and in some cases, to all persons. They include what might be called "personal rights": the right to be secure in one's life, liberty, and property, which can be read to entail the right not to be deprived of any of these things without due process of law, the right to equal protection under the law, the right to freedom of thought and expression, and the right to freedom of association. Fundamental rights also include political rights: the right to vote, the right to hold public office, and the right to freedom of speech and of the press. The latter two rights include the right to petition the government for redress of grievances. To call these and other rights "fundamental" is to say that they are immune from legislative revocation or manipulation and can only be changed at the constitutional level. In this sense, liberal government is always constitutional government. Furthermore, these rights are rights against the state, that is, they impose duties of noninterference on the state. For this reason, liberal government is always limited government.

Although all liberals believe in these fundamental legal rights, they do so on different grounds. Natural rights theorists believe that these legal rights are grounded in natural (i.e., prepolitical) rights, and a central task of the state is to give legal expression to these rights. Liberals with utilitarian sympathies reject natural rights, but they believe that these fundamental legal rights should exist because a regime incorporating such rights maximizes utility. There are other possible philosophical defenses of these rights (e.g., social contract theories and even virtue ethics). There are, of course, important disputes about their content and implications and about the role of the judiciary in settling these disputes. Modern liberals in the United States have been in the forefront of far-reaching reinterpretations of fundamental personal and political rights, especially in the latter two-thirds of the twentieth century. Some of these reinterpretations have been contested, but conservatives have been the main opponents of modern liberalism on most of these issues, whereas (the libertarians excepted) classical liberals do not seem to have had a dog in these fights. Prominent twentieth century classical liberals such as F. A. Hayek, Milton Friedman, and James Buchanan have had little to say about issues such as one man-one vote, criminal procedure, free speech, and the separation of church and state. It is primarily when state power has been expanded at the expense of economic freedom that classical liberals have joined the debate to oppose the modern liberal judicial agenda. We shall return to these disputes in due course, but for now it is sufficient to point out that there is broad consensus among liberals that there should be fundamental (i.e., constitutionally guaranteed) personal and political rights. Disputes about the exact content and implications of these rights are not at the center of the debate between classical liberals and modern liberals.

There is one complication that must be added to this picture, at least in the case of personal rights, and that concerns the right to privacy, most famously articulated in *Roe v. Wade,* 410 U.S. 113 (1973). According to the majority opinion in this case, the right of privacy is an unenumerated fundamental right implicit in the due process clause of the Fourteenth Amendment to the Constitution. This imposes a major restriction on government power, and its policy implications have been embraced not only by modern liberals but also by some classical liberals of a libertarian persuasion. Other classical liberals are less sanguine about this right for essentially the same reason that conservatives are, namely, that it is unwise for judges to issue themselves drilling rights to extract whatever moral or political truths they might find in the Constitution.

There are two additional points of disagreement between modern and classical liberals about fundamental rights that warrant some mention. Classical liberals are inclined to believe that property rights are, or should be treated as, fundamental. That is, they believe property rights should be accorded approximately the same constitutional status as personal and political rights. A recurring theme in classical liberal thought has been that political and economic freedom are inextricably intertwined and that unless property rights are secure against majoritarian manipulation and expropriation, political freedom will be threatened as well. The classic statement of this view is of course Hayek's *The Road to Serfdom* ([1944] 1972), though there are suggestions of this view as far back as Adam Smith ([1776] 1976). Modern liberals flatly deny this and believe that private property rights can and should be much less insulated from the political process than other rights. On the key empirical question about the consequences of the growth of government, modern liberals seem to have been right. The liberal democratic state has grown dramatically over the past century and a quarter by almost any measure—property rights have been subject to almost continuous erosion by the state, and yet personal and political rights and the democratic freedoms they ensure have remained largely intact. Whether or not property rights should have the same level of constitutional protection as personal and political rights is a legitimate question, but it cannot be answered by a straightforward appeal to the threat of totalitarianism that was voiced by Hayek in 1944.

As an aside, however, it is worth noting that there may be a version of Hayek's claim about the consequences of the growth of government that is not so easily dismissed and for which there is some real evidence, namely, that the erosion of private property rights that characterizes modern welfare states leads to the delegation of significant power to unelected government officials, who will inevitably act arbitrarily in the exercise of that power. The arrogation and exercise of arbitrary political power is one of the chief evils of socialism Hayek identified in *The Road to Serfdom* and is deplored by liberals of all persuasions. So, if Hayek's main prediction is construed to mean that we are headed into a world in which the state increasingly exercises arbitrary power, that book retains it topical appeal—even if the arbitrary power is exercised over people's property and not their liberty.

A second point of disagreement about rights concerns welfare rights. Some modern liberals believe that people have a right to a certain standard of living or a certain level of well-being.[12] For these modern liberals, this undergirds the belief that the state should provide for the basic needs of those members of society who, for whatever reason, have not provided for themselves. Whether from a modern liberal perspective this right should be accorded the same fundamental status as other rights is less clear. The notion that people have welfare rights is, in some form, an important strand in modern liberal thought, however. Classical liberals dissent; even those who countenance some role for the state in helping the poor are unwilling to affirm that there is a right to a certain standard of living or level of well being. A comprehensive evaluation of the debate between modern liberals and classical liberals would have to explore these differences.

Besides a commitment to fundamental rights, a second point of basic agreement between classical and modern liberals has been about the indispensability of private property in the means of production, which in turn presupposes a market economy based on voluntary transactions—in a word, "capitalism." Central planning, which presupposes state ownership of the means of production, has been abandoned worldwide, and no serious thinker believes that this is a good way to organize economic activity. Moreover, attempts at articulating a "third way" that is neither a form of central planning nor markets have not been promising.[13] Despite agreement among all, or nearly all, liberals in favor of a capitalist economic system, there are three important areas of disagreement about the contours of such a system. One concerns the scope of private ownership. All liberals believe that the state should own at least some means of production. Even libertarians believe that the state should own (most of) the capital goods needed for national security. There are disagreements, however, about state ownership of other means of production, including, but not limited to, educational establishments, public utilities, and some land and natural resources. These disagreements will be discussed in the first section of chapter 2. There are also disagreements about the proper form(s) of taxation, specifically, whether taxes should be proportional or progressive and, if the latter, how progressive they should be. This will be discussed (briefly) in the second section of chapter 2. Finally, there are disagreements about the restrictions or limitations the state should place on private ownership rights. These will be discussed in parts of chapter 2 and all of chapter 3.

Although there is widespread agreement among liberals about the desirability of a market economy in which most of the means of production are privately owned, there is disagreement about the proper role of government in assuring the proper functioning of the economy. Throughout much of the twentieth century, modern liberals and classical liberals have been at odds over the extent to which government should intervene in a market economy to promote efficiency, economic growth, and stability through monetary, fiscal, and tax policy. Roughly, classical liberals have advocated little or no intervention in the economy, whereas modern liberals, following the lead of Keynes and the neo-Keynesian economists, have advocated a much more activist role for the state in macroeconomic policy. These debates have been complex and multifaceted, but an accurate summary and nuanced appreciation of them goes far beyond the scope of what can be attempted here. To some extent, however, the differences between classical and modern liberals at the level of macroeconomic policy have narrowed lately. A renewed appreciation for the workings of free markets has led to widespread acceptance among modern liberals of some views that were once closely associated with classical liberalism. For example, the inefficacy of wage and price controls, the need for restraint in monetary and fiscal policy, and the presumption in favor of free trade are today widely accepted among modern liberals, even if their acceptance of these ideas is attended with choruses of "Yes, but..." and a predisposition to poke the logs in the economic fireplace.

Indeed, it is fair to say that these positions are no longer identified with classical liberalism, though this was not always the case. Hayek's insights about the signaling function of prices and the role of the entrepreneur, Friedman's views on the relationship between inflation and the rate of growth in the money supply, and Buchanan's explanations of the sources of unwanted growth of government and deficit spending were all viewed as decidedly "right-wing" at the time they were first articulated, whereas now these views are, in one form or another, mainstream. Hardly any responsible thinkers now believe that a handful of companies control the economy of a nation, necessitating countervailing government control, or that (the quantity of) "money doesn't matter" or that the growth of government and government spending is a matter of no real concern, though all three of these views were widespread among modern liberals at various times in the twentieth century. This is not to deny that important disputes about macroeconomic policy remain, but their character as left-right disputes has become attenuated in the past two decades. As evidence for this, notice that free trade across international boundaries, which has always been supported by classical liberals, has garnered qualified support from many modern liberal politicians that simply was not there a half century ago. The disputes about free trade that remain are all about details, and indeed very often the differences are about which strategy would be most effective in opening borders to the free flow of goods and services.[14] To take another example, consider the dispute about supply-side economics that flared in the 1980s. It is true that the tax cuts supply-siders favored were generally perceived as classical liberal measures, especially to the extent that such cuts favored the most advantaged. However, everyone in this debate favored increased incomes and increased tax revenues; it is just that doubters, who, incidentally, could be found on both sides of the political spectrum, questioned the potential for tax cuts to bring about the

Pareto improvements for both the public sector and the private sector that supply-siders promised.[15]

Public Goods

The provision of some public goods is a state function that classical and modern liberals can agree on, at least in principle.[16] Public goods are defined by reference to two criteria: (1) nonrivalrous consumption, and (2) nonexcludability.[17] To say that consumption of a good is non-rivalrous is to say that consumption by one member of the group does not inhibit or diminish its consumption by others. Nonexcludability is defined in terms of the infeasibility of excluding from consumption those who did not pay for the good or who would not pay for it, if con-tribution were voluntary. These two conditions are logically distinct—a good can be nonrivalrously consumed and yet excludable. Seeing a movie in a theater in which there are empty seats would be an example of this, since one person's consumption of the good does not inhibit consumption by others, but theater owners can keep out nonpayers. On the other hand, a good can be nonexcludable and yet rivalrously consumed. A Peeping Tom may not be able to exclude other Peeping Toms from enjoying his view, but consumption of that good (enjoying the view) by other Peeping Toms would inhibit his consumption of the good. So, the two conditions are logically distinct.

National defense is the classic example of a public good meeting both conditions. It meets the first condition since consumption of the good by one citizen of a nation does not inhibit or diminish its con-sumption by other citizens. It meets the second condition because if contribution to national defense were voluntary, there would be no way to exclude noncontributors from benefiting from it. Briefly, the rationale for having the state provide some public goods is this:[18] There are some public goods people would prefer having to not having at a certain price, but they are so costly that no one's contri-bution would be sufficient to pay for the good and indeed would be negligible relative to the total cost of the good. In the absence of com-pulsory contribution, each person reasons as follows:

> Either enough others will contribute to the provision of this good or they will not. If enough others do contribute, my con-tribution will be wasted, assuming, as is often reasonable, that it is not the marginal contribution that would make or break the

deal with any potential supplier of the good. On the other hand, if enough others do not contribute, my contribution will also be wasted, since the good will not be provided. Even if my aims or goals are not selfish, it would still be a wasted contribution. After all, I could have spent any amount I might have contributed on something else, including giving it away to charity.

The problem is that everyone reasons like that, no one contributes, and the good does not get provided, even though it is worth the cost for each person. A *public goods problem,* then, is characterized by a kind of collective irrationality resulting from each person acting rationally, where rationality is defined, following Olson (1965, 64–65), as acting effectively to meet one's ends, whatever those ends happen to be. The state can solve a public goods problem by providing the good and making contribution nonvoluntary, that is, coerced. By a series of forced exchanges, then, people get the good (e.g., national defense) at a price they are willing to pay (e.g., a certain portion of their income paid as taxes).

Though the state can provide public goods, it does not follow that this is the only way to provide them.[19] Sometimes, public goods can be provided in ways that do not involve coercion. One way is to tie the production of the public good to nonpublic goods whose consumption is excludable. For example, those who organized antiwar protests in the early 1970s were able to persuade popular musical groups to give free concerts at the site of rallies. Though the protestors who attended the rallies probably recognized that their individual contributions to ending the war (the public good) through protest would be negligible, they also saw that they would get the benefit of the free concert (a private good not readily available to noncontributors) if they attended the rally. Other goods that were tied to production of the public good of ending the war through political protest included plentiful opportunities to buy illegal drugs and to meet members of the opposite sex. Both of these goods were not as readily available to those who did not show up for the rallies. (There is also some intrinsic, expressive value involved in giving voice to strongly held political feelings.) Sometimes these tying arrangements are infeasible, however, and the only way the public good can be provided at a price people would be willing to pay is by coercing everyone in the group to contribute.

It is important to understand that not all public goods give rise to public goods problems as that term has been defined here. There are cases in which it is worth it for one individual to pay the entire cost of the good, even if others free ride on her contribution.[20] In addition, there are some public goods for which people in the relevant group are not willing to pay their share because it is simply not worth it to them. Consider, for example, the public good that would result from doubling the yearly output of postmodernist literary criticism (viz., a modest increase in postmodernist insights into the human condition). Though undoubtedly postmodernist literary critics, most of whom are university professors, could quickly gear up production to that level, the associated public good is simply not worth it to those who would have to pay for it, namely, those who pay for higher education and those who buy books of postmodernist literary criticism. Finally, in some cases, an individual's contribution might be large enough, relative to the total cost of providing the good, that his decision to contribute would have a noticeable effect, or at least might have a noticeable effect, on whether or not the good is provided. In other words, the act of one person's contributing might have a demonstration effect that induces others to contribute. Under the circumstances, it may be rational for her to go ahead and make the contribution if that makes a real difference in the probability that others will contribute and the good will be provided. Charitable organizations and not-for-profit institutions often get big contributors to make their donations at the outset of a fund-raising campaign and in a highly public way to induce this demonstration effect. To summarize, for there to be a genuine public goods problem, four conditions have to be met: (1) contribution to the provision of the good is, or would be (absent state coercion), voluntary; (2) each individual in the population in question believes that the benefits of having the good outweigh her share of the costs; (3) the good must be so costly that no one individual could provide the good himself (or find it worth his while to so provide it), and (4) each individual's contribution is so small, relative to the costs of providing the good, that one person's failure to contribute would not have a noticeable effect on whether or not the good is provided.

There are some genuine public goods problems and modern liberals are quick to embrace statist solutions to them. Classical liberals are also willing to accept statist solutions to public goods problems, at least if there is no way to solve them through tying arrangements. Chief among these goods is the provision of peace and domestic tranquility, that is, national defense and criminal justice. Other apparent public goods problems for which classical liberals are inclined or willing to accept statist solutions include the administration of a civil justice system, clean air, and the construction and maintenance of local streets and highways, though some libertarians are dubious about the need for state provision even in these areas. Indeed, one way of characterizing the main difference among classical liberals is in terms of their willingness to embrace statist solutions to apparent public goods problems or, alternatively, their interest in finding noncoercive, nonstatist solutions (e.g., tying arrangements) to these problems. Those on the libertarian wing of classical liberalism are more reluctant to accept statist solutions to apparent public goods problems and are correspondingly more eager to find other solutions to these problems than their nonlibertarian classical liberal counterparts. The latter more readily accept the need for state provision of national defense, criminal and civil justice, and the solution to other public goods problems that apparently cannot be solved in any other way.

Anarchists with classical liberal sympathies, such as Rothbard (1978), might object that full respect for people's natural rights prohibits coerced provision even in these cases. This just shows, however, that whatever their sympathies, these anarchists are not classical liberals because they are not liberals. By definition, all liberals believe in at least the minimal state. What is in dispute among liberals is whether anything more extensive than the minimal state is justified. As I am using the term (and this is not precisely in accordance with how the term is sometimes used in the literature), libertarians are classical liberals who believe in the minimal state and nothing more extensive than the minimal state. This definition follows Nozick's usage in *Anarchy, State, and Utopia* (1974), which is a model of clarity on this point.

Just as there are public goods, so too are there public bads.[21] The criteria for public bads, like those for public goods, are nonrivalrous consumption and nonexcludability. To say that something is a public bad for a group is to say that one member of the group's suffering or enduring it does not hinder or interfere with the suffering or enduring of it by other members of the group. To say that the consumption of a public bad is nonexcludable means that it is not feasible for a member of the group to escape suffering it. The effects of high inflation and rampant official corruption would be examples of public bads for large subsets of natural populations, (e.g., subsets of populations of nation-states). The effects of these social conditions are nonrivalrously suffered and, for all practical purposes, inescapable.[22] Of course, not everyone who lives in a society in which there is high inflation or rampant official corruption suffers. Those who are net debtors and those with large

holdings of real assets tend to be net beneficiaries in a high inflation environment; corrupt public officials, their friends, and their
families benefit from rampant official corruption. This just means
that one must draw the lines that define the relevant group properly. Public goods and bads are always defined relative to a group,
and in these cases, the groups are large subsets of natural populations. For these subsets, high inflation and rampant official corruption are indeed public bads because these harms meet the two
criteria of nonrivalrous consumption and nonexcludability.

As in the case of public goods, not all public bads pose public bads
problems. One reason is that not all public bads are worth trying to
eliminate or solve. Some are small enough relative to the costs of solving them that not enough people in the group that suffers from them
would be willing to contribute to their solution. Removal from the
cultural or political scene of various public nuisances (e.g., narcissis-
tic celebrities, sanctimonious politicians) would benefit large subsets
of a national population, but the benefits of getting them to leave the
public stage are outweighed by the enormous costs that would have to
be incurred to make them go away. At the other limit, some problems
are so intractable that no feasible level of contribution from everyone
in the relevant group would solve them. For a public bad to pose a
genuine public bads problem for a group, additional conditions must
be met—conditions that exactly parallel conditions for a public goods
problem, to wit: (1) contribution toward the removal of the public bad
is, or would be (absent state coercion), voluntary; (2) each individual
in the group believes that the benefits of addressing the evil outweigh
her share of the costs; (3) addressing the evil is so costly that no one
person can afford to pay the entire cost; and (4) each person's contribution is so small relative to the costs of dealing with the evil that
one person's failure to contribute would not have a noticeable effect
on whether or not the evil is eliminated or significantly ameliorated.
A public bads problem exists with respect to some group and some
public bad if and only if these four conditions are met.

Although the concept of a public bad has not received the sustained attention from liberals of all persuasions that the corresponding concept of a public good has, it is not difficult to sketch the
classical and modern liberal positions on public bads. As in the case
of public goods, both modern and classical liberals would be open
to state action to address genuine public bads problems. After all,
whether or not something is counted as a public good or public bad
often seems to depend on nothing deeper than a choice of words.

For example, peace and domestic order are public goods, whereas a Hobbesian state of war is a public bad. Both are legitimate objects of state attention for liberals of all persuasions.

The concepts of public goods and public bads have very broad reference classes. Many macroeconomic problems can be thought of as public bads, as can a host of other social and economic ills, notably those associated with poverty. Alternatively, one can conceive of the elimination of these social evils as public goods. These concepts give us a handle on how to characterize some important differences between modern liberals and classical liberals. It is fair to say that modern liberals tend to favor state action to deal with a wide range of public goods and bads. The crucial question for classical liberals, however, is whether or not these public goods or bads rise to the level of genuine public goods or bads problems.[23] Otherwise the failure to deal with them cannot be characterized as preventing people from getting something that they all really want at a price they would all be willing to pay.

More needs to be said about classical liberalism's attitude toward public bads. There seems to be no unified classical liberal view about social problems that can be characterized in this way. Sometimes, one gets the impression that classical liberals believe that the free market, or more generally, a private ordering, can eliminate any social evil (other than the state itself!), except those for which there are obvious free-rider/assurance problems, such as the evils associated with a state of nature. Included in this is the belief that macroeconomic problems and most of the problems associated with poverty are actually caused by the state and that if the state were to stop trying to solve them, they may not immediately go away, but over time they would be all but extinguished by noncoercive social processes and institutions such as the market, private insurance, and private charities. This view seems to characterize the libertarian wing of classical liberalism. On the other hand, there is what might be called a conservative classical liberal outlook, which holds that many social evils (public bads) have no real solution; at most, these problems can be ameliorated at the margins, either by the private sector or through very limited state action. But, in the interests of realism, modest amelioration, not elimination, should be the goal and that at some point, often reached relatively quickly, the marginal costs of amelioration (understood broadly to include nonfinancial as well as financial costs) outweigh the marginal benefits. This classical liberal outlook—one is tempted to refer to it as the classical classical liberal view—is in tune with the more pessimistic views of the human condition found in the writings of Hobbes, Hume, and the Founding Fathers than it is with the optimism one finds in the writings of modern libertarians. As a general proposition, genuine pessimism about what are commonly called "social problems" is rare in mainstream political philosophy in the twentieth century, at least outside of the writings of thoroughgoing conservatives such as Russell Kirk.[24] It is, however, an important though forgotten strain in classical liberal thought. By contrast, this strain of pessimism is largely absent in modern liberalism. It is not that modern liberals believe that all social problems can be solved by state action, but it is fair to say that they do not dwell on the limited ability, or the record of at best limited success, of the state in dealing with social problems. Moreover, they are inclined to believe that there is considerable useful work, much of it yet to be done, that the state can do to address these problems. On their view, we are nowhere near the point where the marginal costs of state action outweigh the marginal benefits.

Externalities

Closely related to public bads and public goods are negative and positive externalities. Standardly, externalities are defined, relative to a transaction between two parties, as negative or positive spillover effects involuntarily incurred by third parties. (The definition varies slightly, depending on the source.) Air and water pollution are the classic examples because they are spillover effects onto third parties of transactions between manufacturers and their customers, which are not taken into account unless the state intervenes in some way. The state has a variety of mechanisms at its disposal to address problems of pollution. Until fairly recently, the main way it did so, if it acted at all, was by enforcing the common law, especially the common law of nuisance or trespass against polluters. Common law courts could issue injunctions and require compensation. With the rise of the modern regulatory state, however, the common law has been superseded by statutory law, which uses a variety of instrumentalities to address problems of pollution. To prevent the pollution from occurring at all, the state can impose an outright ban on the production of certain goods or the use of certain production processes. Another alternative is to impose a tax on pollution as a way of forcing the transactors to take into account (i.e., to internalize) the costs of the polluting activity. The proceeds of this tax can then be used to clean up the pollution or to compensate those who suffer it, though there is no assurance that the state will actually do either of these things. Even if the tax receipts are simply stuffed into the politicians' pockets, however, the company has to take account of its polluting activities in a way that it does not in the absence of these taxes. As a result, prices are higher, and production is lower. Pollution control devices might become economical to install. In the case of pollution whose outright prohibition would be too costly, the state may limit it by restricting the amounts that may be emitted or by creating tradable emission (pollution) rights that impose a regional upper limit on the amount of pollution created. These rights, which may then be bought and sold, create incentives to reduce pollution by those who can do it most efficiently. Finally, the state may discover that it is technologically feasible to define and assign private property rights in such a way that polluters can be identified and victims can sue them on the basis of common law principles.

It is generally true that classical liberals favor solutions to problems of air and water pollution that involve private property rights in some way (e.g., by invoking the common law, by defining and assigning property rights, or by creating tradable rights to pollute under a certain ceiling). Classical liberals in the free-market environmentalist movement regard the Environmental Protection Agency as a heavy-handed and inept purveyor of command and control regulations; they favor a more flexible approach to the problems of pollution that minimizes the use of such regulations and devolves pollution control responsibilities to lower levels of government.[25] By contrast, modern liberals are inclined to favor more direct national governmental action, such as mandated pollution control devices, restrictions or outright bans on products or production processes simply because they believe this is the best way to achieve a certain level of environmental protection. Nevertheless, there is, or at least there need be, no deep issue of principle involved in most debates about pollution. Modern liberals could agree with free-market environmentalists that some pollution is most effectively dealt with through the definition and enforcement of private property rights or through the creation of tradable emission rights. On the other side, classical liberals could accept top-down government regulation of air pollution caused by automobiles and trucks, for example, since there is no technologically feasible way to assign and enforce clean air rights nor is it feasible to create tradable emission rights in motor vehicle exhaust. The issue between the two contending sides is not, as it is in other areas, about whether the government should be involved in pollution control; rather it concerns the types of instrumentalities it should employ and the unit of government that should take the lead. It is easy to see how convergence arguments might be offered by each side in support of their respective views.

What about negative externalities other than pollution? Classical liberals cannot allow the concept of negative externalities to be infinitely elastic. To put in another way, they do not believe that it is appropriate for the government to be involved in regulating the production of everything that has negative spillover effects on someone or other. Consider, for example, competitive harms, that is, harms a business suffers because competitors have garnered some of its trade. Classical liberals oppose the typical statist solutions to competitive harms, namely, rate regulation and regulation of entry or exit, even if these forms of regulation do in fact prevent competitive harms from befalling existing firms. If the state acts to prevent competitive harms, it is simply overriding the verdict of the market in a way that classical liberals could never approve. How, then, do classical liberals draw the line between negative effects on third parties that count as externalities, which are to be remedied by the state, and negative spillover effects which call for no state action? Alternatively, which negative externalities do they think government should deal with in some manner and which do they think government should ignore? (This is the classical liberal version of Mill's problem of defining harm to others.) One way of characterizing the difference is by reference to the boundaries that surround a person and his property. Sometimes those boundaries are reasonably clear, but sometimes they are not. When they are clear, classical liberals are inclined to believe that it is appropriate for the state to prohibit or regulate (by statute, if necessary) actions that infringe on, or might infringe on, common law property or personal rights of third parties.[26] Because it is a boundary crossing, dumping raw sewage on someone else's land is a clear and unambiguous example of an externality that is the proper subject of government action on the classical liberal view. By contrast, it is a mistake to describe a competitive harm as a boundary crossing. There are, however, nontresspassory boundary crossings, which are also dealt with under the common law of nuisance. Noise pollution comes under this heading, as do such arcana as air and light easements, the duty of lateral support (which forbids excavation that undermines structures on the property of others), and spite fences.[27] Finally, there are low-level boundary crossings that individually do not amount to much and would not be actionable under the common law, but when aggregated to certain levels, become nuisances. Air pollution from motor vehicles and certain forms of water pollution (e.g., pesticides leaching into groundwater, rivers, and estuaries) fall into this category. These are cases where the boundaries around a person and his or her property are not clear, and classical liberals can accept, and indeed would insist upon, a role for the state in defining those boundaries. These and other complications present some interesting intellectual challenges in sorting out the proper scope and application of the common law of torts, but they should not obscure the main idea that classical liberals want to limit the negative externalities that might warrant government intervention to boundary crossings of third parties as defined by the common law. Whether these boundary crossings should be handled by the common law or by statutory law is an open question for classical liberals, though they typically favor a common law approach because the common law evolves in a way that is more sensitive to realities on the ground; they nevertheless believe that this is the sort of thing the state ought to be doing. For future reference, let us call these "common law negative externalities."

Modern liberals, by contrast, take a more capacious view of which negative externalities should be the subject to government regulation. They accept those that violate the common law rights of individuals and much more. The only regulations that are ruled out in principle are those that would infringe on people's fundamental political and personal rights. So, for example, hurt feelings cannot justify speech prohibitions, and those on the left who favor speech codes have strayed off the modern liberal ranch. Otherwise, any negative effects of a certain type of transaction that do not implicate fundamental rights would make that type of transaction at least potentially a proper subject of government regulation. So, for example, modern liberals are disposed to move the state to action when large numbers of workers in domestic firms suffer at the hands of foreign competition because they conceive of this harm as a negative externality (or a public bad) that government should presumptively address. There is clearly no justification for considering this to be a common law tort perpetrated by competitors. The same is true of job losses occasioned by technological innovation that, modern liberals believe, could be ameliorated by a wise industrial policy. In delimiting the proper scope of government activity in these areas, modern liberals adopt the basketball adage, "No Harm, No Foul," where harm is interpreted very broadly. By contrast, classical liberals follow the common law precept, "No Tort, No Foul."

Positive externalities are beneficial spillover effects of exchanges. When positive spillover effects occur, parties to the transaction are unable to capture all the benefits of the transaction for themselves. A commonly cited example of a positive externality is the beneficial spillover effects of mass inoculation against communicable diseases. As the number of people who receive vaccinations increases, the probability that others who have not been vaccinated would contract the disease decreases. Those others, who remain unvaccinated but whose risk of contracting the disease has diminished, do not pay for that positive spillover effect. Another commonly cited example of positive externalities are the benefits associated with the production of some forms of human knowledge, especially basic scientific research. The latter can have enormous long-term benefits for large numbers of people, but since the efficient production of scientific knowledge requires free and open communication of ideas, there will often be substantial positive spillover effects, which are not capturable by those who pay for the production of that knowledge.

What are the classical and modern liberal positions on positive externalities? Modern liberals tend to favor the state taking a hand in the production of goods and services that have substantial positive spillover effects, either directly, or through subsidies to private producers. One common argument for this appeals to the standard neoclassical model of perfectly competitive markets, which assumes the absence of positive (as well as negative) externalities. Under this and other very strong assumptions, a Pareto Optimal distribution of income, wealth, and resources will be realized. The existence of positive externalities in the real world is conceived of as a market imperfection, which translates into an inefficiency. Specifically, because the positive spillover effects are not captured by those who pay for the production of the associated good, the latter tends to be underproduced relative to the level of production that would exist in a perfectly competitive market, and underproduction of this sort is defined in the model as an inefficiency. This forms the basis for a standard modern liberal argument for state production of the associated good or service or subsidization of private producers.

By contrast, classical liberals are inclined to reject this broad view of the proper role of government concerning positive externalities. One reason is that many classical liberals are not enamored of the neoclassical model of perfectly competitive markets and thus reject the idea that there is any useful sense in the assertion that the relevant good is "underproduced" because less of it is produced than one finds in the model of perfect competition. Others believe that if the government is involved in the good's production in any manner, it will be overproduced at too high a cost and underpriced to boot. In this way, a free-market inefficiency is replaced by an even greater government inefficiency. More generally, if any positive spillover effect counts as a positive externality and if it is appropriate for the state to get involved in the production of goods that have positive externalities, that would give the state carte blanche to involve itself in almost any type of transaction. That is one credit card classical liberals want to deny to state officials. Are there, then, any positive externalities that the state should be involved in producing, according to the classical liberal perspective?

This question can be approached indirectly by considering a related question: What is the nature of the twin relationships between public bads and negative externalities on the one hand, and public goods and positive externalities on the other? Specifically, are the former equivalent to the latter in each pair? On the face of it, it would seem so, if the populations are properly defined. Consider first negative externalities and public bads. Pollution fits the definition of a negative externality for anyone who involuntarily suffers from it, and it is a public bad for the members of a group who cannot readily avoid it. That said, it seems more natural to use the language of externalities (both positive and negative) when both the person or firm causing the benefit or harm and the affected third parties are readily identifiable. Consider, for example, a pulp and paper mill that pollutes the air. The polluter is easily identified, as are those who are negatively affected by the foul smells, namely, the residents of the immediate area and passersby; consequently, it would be most natural to think of this as a negative externality. On the other hand, the language of public goods and public bads seems most appropriate when one or the other set of relevant parties are harder to identify. For example, global warming is more naturally conceived of as a public bad, since the set of individuals and firms producing the harm is difficult to identify, as is the set of victims. On the other hand, in cases of acid rain, high inflation, and pollution due to motor vehicles, although the perpetrators are readily identifiable, those who are negatively affected within any natural population are difficult to identify with any precision. In general, the reason that the set of victims is difficult to identify is that, within any natural population affected by the public bad, there will be some net beneficiaries. Some Canadians may prefer milder winters caused by global warming, net debtors benefit from high inflation, and there are countless net beneficiaries of motor vehicle pollution. For the subset of natural populations who suffer net harm from the bad, however, the evil meets both criteria for a public bad: nonrivalrous consumption and nonexcludability.

The same distinction seems to hold for positive externalities and public goods. The language of positive externalities seems most appropriate when the benefactors and the beneficiaries of those spillover effects are easily identifiable. Suppose that most of my neighbors remodel their homes to the extent that real estate values in the entire neighborhood go up. Increase in the values of the homes in the neighborhood that were not remodeled would count as positive externalities, since both the benefactors (the remodelers) and the beneficiaries (the rest of the neighborhood) can be easily identified. By contrast, public goods are best thought of as benefiting more or less large subsets of natural populations, where exactly who belongs to the subset is not easy to identify empirically, or where those responsible for the benefit are hard to identify. Even national defense is a public good on this account because there is a hard-to-specify group of people outside the nation's boundaries who also benefit from the good. In the cold war, the U.S. military provided protection from Communism for an indefinitely large group of people. It was in the U.S. national interest that some people be provided with this good, but there were others whose protection was not clearly or not necessarily in the U.S. national interests but who got protected anyway as a result of spillover effects. Since the exact set of beneficiaries is hard to identify, national defense is a public good, according to this criterion. What about the traditional examples of positive externalities, namely, the benefits associated with vaccinations and basic scientific research? These would be counted as public goods on the criterion being advocated here, since the beneficiaries are, in both cases, hard to identify with any precision. Whether there is a public goods problem in either example is another question, the answer to which depends on the particulars of the situation.

With these distinctions in hand, it is possible to summarize more clearly the classical liberal view on both externalities and public goods, as those terms have been defined here. Consider, first, the classical liberal view of negative externalities. They favor government action to deal with common law negative externalities, either through enforcing private property rights or creating such rights, including, for example, tradable rights to emit certain pollutants. These property rights solutions are implicit in the framework of common law. Sometimes, however, these options are unavailable because existing technology does not permit exact or precise identification of those causing the harm or those suffering from it (e.g., global warming), in which case there are public bads involved. Classical liberals would favor, or could be persuaded to favor, direct state regulation up to and including prohibition, if there is a genuine public bads problem.

In the case of positive externalities, classical liberals do not believe the government should be involved in the production of a good or service merely because it has positive spillover effects. The neoclassical economists' rationale for government involvement is unpersuasive for the reasons indicated above. Sometimes, however, the positive spillover effects have the character of a public good, and a genuine public goods problem presents itself. Under those circumstances, classical liberals typically favor state provision, though libertarians often do not. For instance, except for the anarchists (who, as noted above, are not, strictly speaking, liberals), classical liberals typically believe that statist solutions are the only effective solution to providing the public goods of peace and domestic order or avoiding the public bads associated with a state of nature. As was suggested earlier, one way of characterizing the main dimension along which classical liberals differ among themselves is in their willingness to acknowledge public goods problems in civil society and to countenance state action to deal with them. The more libertarian types are slow to concede any legitimate area for state involvement, beyond the protection of life, liberty, and property and sometimes then only reluctantly or grudgingly.[28] For any other public good, they believe that either (1) it does not pose a genuine public goods problem (i.e., one or more of the four conditions is not met) or if there is a genuine public goods problem, (2) it could be obviated by a better definition and enforcement of private property rights or (3) that a tying arrangement to solve the problem could be found by the private sector. By contrast, nonlibertarian classical liberals are more comfortable with the existence of the state—they are more ready to endorse statist solutions to public goods problems and to concede that alternative solutions are impracticable.

For public goods that clearly do not constitute public goods problems, however, classical liberals are inclined to oppose state provision. This opposition could be grounded in the belief that citizens of the state in question are not willing to pay the price, or alternatively, they believe enough citizens would be willing to contribute voluntarily so that the public good would be sufficiently provided, or the public bad sufficiently ameliorated, without state action. Another ground for opposing state action on public goods that do not constitute genuine public goods problems is a belief that the state is incompetent to solve them, even if, in some abstract sense, it is possible for them to do so. It is a commonplace among classical liberals that, even with the best of intentions, the state is unable to solve a host of problems it has attempted to solve, and indeed in attempting to solve them, it often makes things worse. Under the circumstances, they prefer to live without the public good (or to live with the public bad) rather than to let the state try to provide it.

Where do modern liberals stand on the question of the proper role of the state in dealing with externalities and public goods and bads, as defined here? Modern liberals are inclined to seek statist solutions to as many of the problems about externalities, both positive and negative, as is practicable and are inclined to favor state action to deal with public goods and bads that reach a certain level of political salience, whether or not they constitute genuine public goods or bads problems as here defined. Because of their commitment to the market as the basic framework for economic activity, however, they are willing to entertain property rights solutions to any of these problems. However, they have about as much confidence in markets as classical liberals have in the state and indeed are inclined to believe that markets, and the culture of markets, are responsible for a whole host of public bads, whether or not the latter constitute genuine public bads problems. State solutions are typically preferred.

These differences between modern liberals and classical liberals about externalities and public goods are real and important, but they do not exhaust the differences between the two camps. More salient are differences about private property itself. A complete picture of the two sides' positions on the proper role of government can emerge only when their respective views on the extent of, and restrictions on, private property rights have been fully articulated. This is the subject of chapters 2 and 3.

Private and Public Property

As indicated in chapter 1, both modern liberals and classical liberals believe in a regime of private property. This statement conceals some important differences, however. There are two dimensions along which classical and modern liberals differ about private property: its extent and the restrictions that may be placed on it. Regarding the former, there are disputes about what productive assets should be owned by the state and what should be privately owned. For example, should monopolies be owned by the state or privately owned but state-regulated or even unregulated? To what extent should the state own firms that compete with private firms (e.g., in education)? What assets (if any) that the state currently owns should be privatized? There are points of agreement and disagreement between classical and modern liberals on these questions.

In a related vein, there is also a question about the nature of the state's claim on a portion of citizens' income and wealth in virtue of its taxing authority. If the state has a prior ownership claim on a portion of citizens' income and wealth—and this chapter argues that on the modern liberal view it does—then it has considerable discretion in how it exercises its taxing authority. It can use the tax code for a variety of purposes other than raising revenue, such as changing the distribution of wealth and income. If, on the other hand, the state does not have this priority of ownership, it is more constrained in what it can do through tax policy. This question about the priority of ownership also has implications for spending policy, including the propriety of state-mandated transfers from some citizens to others through various entitlement or transfer programs, such as those that provide welfare, old-age insurance, and health insurance. Questions about the extent of private versus public property, broadly understood to include tax policy and transfer programs, are among the most important questions facing modern Western societies today. Modern liberals and classical liberals have largely, though not entirely, divergent views on these questions.

When one turns to the question of restrictions on private property in a liberal society, there are a host of important issues that divide classical liberals from modern liberals. Specifically, there are important disagreements about the proper scope of government regulation of private property. Private property is a complex of rights, terms, and conditions, including the right to possess, the right to manage, and the right to dispose of the thing owned. Much of the modern regulatory state is devoted to limiting the latter two incidents of private ownership, and it is here where some of the most important disagreements between modern liberals and classical liberals are to be found.

This chapter concerns the extent of private property, broadly understood. It is divided into three sections. The first deals with the question of the extent to which productive assets should be owned by the state in the context of an essentially private enterprise market economy. The second section concerns the differences between classical and modern liberals on tax policy, which, it shall be argued, reflect differing views about the ownership of income and wealth generated in the market by the use of private property. These differences are further reflected in modern and classical liberal views of the propriety of government-run transfer programs, which is the subject of the third section. These three sections together provide a comprehensive overview of the positions of classical and modern liberals on the question of the extent of private versus state ownership of property in productive assets and the wealth those assets represent. Chapter 3 deals with classical and modern liberals' views about limitations on the incidents of private property rights, most notably though not exclusively, the right to manage and the right of disposition. Essentially, this is the question of the proper scope of government regulation.

Ownership of Productive Assets

"Creeping socialism" was a strategy by which those on the left in Western Europe hoped to transform a capitalist society into a socialist society. The idea was for the state to seize first the commanding heights of the economy by nationalizing monopolies and other large firms in strategic industries. The nationalization of coal mines, railroads, and telecommunications in Western European countries are all examples of this phenomenon. Though the ultimate goals of this process were never completely clear, its direction was—increasing state ownership of the means of production. For a variety of reasons, Western European polities eventually became disillusioned with this process; a backlash set in, and many of these firms and industries were wholly or partially privatized, perhaps the most famous instance being the ambitious privatization campaign of Margaret Thatcher in Great Britain in the 1980s.

Creeping socialism, as practiced in Western Europe, never had much currency in the United States. In its stead, the state imposed an increasingly stringent regulatory regime on the private sector, especially in industries dominated by the kind of firms that were nationalized in Western Europe. This started in the late nineteenth century and continued into the first half of the twentieth century. This regulatory regime was composed of two elements: (1) rate regulation in certain industries, beginning with the Interstate Commerce Commission's regulation of the railroads in 1887; rate regulation was subsequently extended to other industries such as insurance, electricity, and telecommunications,[1] and (2) antitrust law. Both can be conceived of as a response to the problem of monopoly: rate regulation was intended to prevent natural monopolies from gouging consumers and antitrust law aimed at preventing any one firm in an industry from becoming so dominant in a market that it could behave like a monopolist.

Rate regulation began in the 1870s when the state of Illinois regulated what grain elevator operators could charge farmers for storing grain. The relevant statute was subsequently upheld by the Supreme Court in *Munn v. Illinois,* 94 U.S. 113 (1876). The legal significance of this decision is that it permitted the government to restrict freedom of contract on the terms and conditions of trade. The Interstate Commerce Act of 1887 created the Interstate Commerce Commission, which had some authority over shipping rates for railroads, though full authority to set rates was not granted until 1920.[2] *Nebbia v. New York,* 291 U.S. 502, 525 (1934) established that the states could impose pretty much any form of regulation they believed was in the public interest. This sanctioned rate regulation in industries that were not monopolies, ranging from insurance to air travel to oil and natural gas. Starting in the 1970s, a wave of deregulation swept the nation, and rate regulation was abolished in industries as diverse as air transport, oil, natural gas, telecommunications, and electricity at the wholesale level. It remains, however, in some industries, such as insurance and electricity at the retail level.

The three most important pieces of antitrust legislation were the Sherman Antitrust Act (1890), the Federal Trade Commission Act

(1914), and the Clayton Act (1914, as amended in 1950).[3] The Sherman Act prohibits monopoly pricing, either by a single firm or through collusion among a number of firms. The Federal Trade Commission Act created the FTC and outlawed "unfair" competitive practices, a concept that the statute left undefined. The Clayton Act remedied this to some extent by identifying a number of specific practices that would count as unfair competition (e.g., price discrimination, exclusive dealing), but this list was not exhaustive. The 1950 amendment to the Clayton Act allowed the FTC to prohibit mergers under certain circumstances. All this legislation was motivated by the belief that, left without government supervision, corporations would amass economic power that would then be exercised against the public interest, typically through monopoly pricing. The commanding heights of the economy were to be left in private hands, but, through rate regulation and the enforcement of antitrust law, the state would watch what those hands were doing.

Despite the fact that there has been little support in the United States for nationalizing privately owned firms and entire industries, the state has nevertheless owned considerable productive assets, including, notably, land. The U.S. government owns vast amounts of land, especially in the West. For example, about 45 percent of the land in California, 62 percent of the land in Idaho and 80 percent of the land in Nevada are owned by the federal government.[4] Much federally owned land, especially in the West, is subject to various leaseholding arrangements with private interests for timber, minerals, and grazing. In addition, the federal government claims ownership of coastal waters (including the oil deposits under those waters) and of inland waterways. In that connection, it has been directly involved in the production of electricity in the Tennessee Valley and in the West, where it has also been involved in the creation and distribution of water supplies in the form of dams and aqueducts. The state has also claimed ownership of the electromagnetic spectrum, which it leases to broadcast and wireless telecommunications companies. This ownership serves as the predicate for much government regulation of these industries.

Government has also owned public parks at the national, state, and local level. Local water and sewer service, garbage collection, and like services have also been provided by directly by the government or by government-owned entities in many municipalities, though some of these services have been privatized in recent years. The postal service is also government-owned, though their monopoly has been eroded in recent years by e-mail and private package delivery and express mail services. One service for which the state has been the dominant but not sole provider from the nineteenth century down to the present is education. It has provided a large percentage of educational services from grammar school through postgraduate and professional education, though it has never been a monopoly provider.

One other productive asset the state owns that warrants mention in passing is the monetary system. Ownership of the monetary system is exercised through government control of the money supply and legal tender laws, which make government currency legal tender for all debts, public and private. Control of the money supply, along with taxation and government spending, are the primary vehicles by which the state sets macroeconomic policy.

What is the modern liberal view on the extent of state ownership of productive assets as it currently exists and about rate regulation and antitrust law? By and large, they have favored the current system. This is not to say that modern liberals are entirely satisfied with how this has worked out. Among their most important criticisms is that the state has not been a good steward of public property and that government agencies that are charged with setting rates for regulated industries and enforcing antitrust laws have frequently not acted in the public interest. Modern liberals have charged that timber, mining, ranching, and farming interests have gotten sweetheart deals from the government in their respective leasehold arrangements for government-owned land; regulatory bodies have been captured by the industries they are supposed to regulate; officials who are skeptical of the wisdom of antitrust laws have been put in charge of enforcing them. And so on. In sum, the modern liberal view is that, while rate regulation and the enforcement of antitrust law are vital government functions, in practice government has often failed to discharge its duties in the public interest. One of the main unsolved problems in the modern liberal agenda is how to make the state less responsive to private interests and more responsive to the public interest, both in its stewardship of publicly owned property and in its various regimes of rate regulation.

Partly for these reasons, modern liberals have been skeptical of the drive to privatize state-owned assets, as well as the impulse to deregulate certain industries such telecommunications. Privatization and deregulation, they fear, would only exacerbate the outstanding problems with the current regime of state ownership and regulation. Finally, modern liberals fear that the repeal of, or a less than vigorous enforcement of, antitrust laws would result in the creation of new and dangerous centers of private economic power unchecked by counter-vailing public power.

These concerns have not made modern liberals dogmatic in their opposition to deregulation and privatization, however. Few modern liberal politicians or their policy advisers want to bring back the Civil Aeronautics Board or the Interstate Commerce Commission, which comprehensively regulated routes and prices in domestic air travel and rail and truck transport, respectively. Indeed, it was under the modern liberal regime of President Jimmy Carter that airline deregu-lation took place, and Senator Edward Kennedy, a prominent mod-ern liberal politician, was a leading force behind deregulation in the trucking industry.[5] Modern liberals do believe, however, that the threat of reregulation should never be taken off the table and are inclined to reach for the regulatory club at the first sign of what they consider to be private-sector abuses. As for outright privatization of productive assets, while there are few cases that modern liberals have greeted with genuine enthusiasm, there is little support among them for increasing government ownership of the means of production. That might be purely a matter of practical politics, but it might also reflect a disenchantment with state ownership of productive assets, comparable to what has happened in Western Europe.

There is nonetheless at least one area in which modern liberals have been more resistant to privatization and correspondingly more supportive of public ownership, and that is education, especially at the primary and secondary levels. Modern liberal politicians have repeatedly thwarted privatization efforts and have been strong sup-porters of public education. Some of this is no doubt explainable in terms of political support from teachers' unions, but there are a num-ber of more or less legitimate reasons that have been, or might be, offered for this.

One rationale, popular among economists, is that there are positive externalities or public goods associated with the provision of edu-cational services. It is often argued that an educated public makes for better citizens and more informed voters. While there may be some truth to this, there is a point—more quickly reached than many would like to admit—at which the marginal returns of good citizen-ship to additional units of educational inputs are vanishingly small and indeed possibly negative. William F. Buckley is supposed to have once said that he would rather be governed by the first 100 people listed in the Boston telephone directory than by any 100 members of the faculty of Harvard University. Buckley's preference is probably reasonable, even if one does not share his classical liberal sympathies—and even if one excludes those faculties least suited to govern (viz., those of the Kennedy School of Government and the Harvard Law School). At considerably lower levels of education, however, the proposition that an educated populace improves the quality of public life seems more plausible.[6] Modern liberals with communitarian leanings have seen public education as a key instrumentality in securing widely shared communitarian values among the citizenry (e.g., tolerance for diversity), which they believe is essential for the proper functioning of a liberal democracy.[7]

A final reason why modern liberals favor state provision of educational services is that it a way to realize equality of opportunity, or, to be more realistic, to reduce the range of inequality of opportunity among its citizens. The belief seems to be that if the responsibility for educating children were left entirely to their families, the resultant inequalities in educational opportunities, and the consequent inequalities of other opportunities, would be so severe as to permanently handicap the children of the worst off, thereby further diminishing their life prospects, even if only in relative terms. This rationale for public provision of education bears an important similarity to the modern liberal rationale for a steep inheritance tax. Traditionally, the latter has been viewed as an important modality for reducing the unfair advantages associated with being born to a family of great material wealth.[8] As human capital has become a more important source of wealth and well-being, modern liberals have paid more attention to educational inequality and less attention to the inheritance of material wealth. In the United States, a growing movement in favor of limitations on, or even abolition of, estate taxes has not met with the concerted opposition from modern liberals that it would have a generation ago.[9] Instead, modern liberals seem to be more concerned that the better off are securing an unfair competitive advantage for their children through private education or through locally funded public education in wealthy communities. This might partly explain their otherwise puzzling defense of a failing public education system and modern liberal hostility to privatizing primary and secondary education. The worry is that privatization would make educational inequality—and all the other inequalities that would follow in its train—much more pervasive than they already are.

Finally, modern liberals support state control over the money supply. No doubt part of the reason for this is that this control is an essential tool of macroeconomic policy. This tool has proved difficult to use effectively, however, in part because of the difficulty in controlling the responses of millions of individuals and firms to changes in the money supply.

To summarize, then, modern liberals favor the basic contours of the existing balance between state and private ownership of productive assets and the existing regime of rate regulation and antitrust law. There is no deep or principled opposition to adjusting the boundaries between the public and the private sector in either direction or to rate deregulation, though there is a persistent concern about the dangers of concentrations of private economic power. The state is seen as an often not very effective counterweight to private power. The main unresolved problem is to make the state less accountable to private interests and more accountable to the public interest.

Classical liberals have a very different take on all these questions. They have been the principal advocates of privatization and deregulation. Let us consider privatization first. There are essentially two forms that privatization can take: (1) privatization of the provision of goods or services that have been provided by the state but not their funding (call this "partial privatization") and (2) privatization of both the provision of goods and services and their funding (call this "full privatization"). Classical liberals have favored full privatization in cases such as the delivery of first-class mail and the provision of basic utilities (e.g., electricity and water) where the latter are publicly owned. They also believe that the state should drastically reduce its land holdings by auctioning them off to the highest bidder. On their view, these are all cases in which there are no obvious public goods problems involved (with the possible exception of some parks). In the libertarian wing of classical liberalism, one finds enthusiasm for selling off entire government agencies (or disbanding them and selling their assets) used for traditional government functions, including elements of the criminal and civil justice system, such as prisons, and elements of the transportation infrastructure, such as airports and toll roads. Some libertarians also favor privatizing the monetary system, either in part (e.g., through repeal of the legal tender laws) or entirely, as a way of preventing the state from manipulating the money supply. They believe that the latter is responsible for many of the macroeconomic problems (e.g., the Depression) traditionally ascribed to the free enterprise system.[10] On the other hand, sometimes classical liberals favor only partial privatization of state services. This might be seen as a useful first step to full privatization, but in some cases, there could be a public goods justification for leaving funding in the hands of the state. An example of this would be the operation of prisons. Though the private sector might be better at running prisons than is the state, it is hard to see how to privatize their funding.

Another area in which classical liberals have favored at least partial privatization is in education. Classical liberals have been especially keen to break the near monopoly that the state has in the provision of primary and secondary education. They believe that public schools do a poor job in educating children, largely because these schools are insulated from market forces. What is their alternative? It is difficult to find classical liberals outside of some libertarian circles who advocate full privatization of education, which would require parents to bear full financial responsibility for their own children's entire education.[11] Most have favored state-funded educational vouchers or tax credits for educational expenditures (e.g., Friedman 1962, 83–107). Why is this? Arguments for state funding or tax credits typically appeal to the positive externalities associated with education discussed above.[12] Without some further premises, this cannot be a compelling argument from a classical liberal perspective, since classical liberals do not believe in state funding for any activity simply on the grounds that it has positive externalities associated with it. Perhaps the appeal to positive externalities is part of an attempt to argue on the basis of what modern liberals would accept, or perhaps it represents a conflation of positive externalities and public goods. In any case, classical liberals are in agreement that the entities that actually provide educational services should be privately owned or managed because the quality of the product will be higher, dollar for dollar. They need not be profit-making firms (e.g., in the case of church-run schools), but at the very least, privately managed schools should be able to compete on an equal footing with state-owned schools.

Indeed, on education, the differences between classical and modern liberals might not be as great as they appear. Modern liberals are most interested in seeing to it that the least advantaged have decent educational opportunities (or in dampening inequality of educational opportunity) and, not unrelatedly, that some common standards are maintained. They need not oppose expansion of private sector education through vouchers and tax credits, at least as long as the state retains some regulatory authority over the schools and backstops the private sector in some manner. In fact, some modern liberals have openly advocated such a regime (e.g., Jencks 1966). Classical liberals, on the other hand, have been willing to accept a mixed public-private regime in which there is some—or even considerable—state funding. In view of their confidence in the private (profit and not-for-profit) sector, they even accept allowing state-operated schools to remain open, so long as the latter compete on equal footing with privately operated schools. It might turn out, then, that for different yet overlapping sets of reasons, both sides could support increased partial privatization of education, though much depends on the details of any concrete proposal.

Let us turn now to the classical liberal view of deregulation, understood broadly to include rate deregulation and a narrow reading of antitrust law that only prevents collusion. The standard justification for rate regulation is that it prevents monopolies from charging supracompetitive prices.[13] In his classic article "Is Government the Source of Monopoly?," Yale Brozen (1980) argued that nearly all monopolies in contemporary capitalist societies are creatures of the state in one way or another. Sometimes, the state provides the service in question and legally prohibits competition, as in the case of the delivery of first-class mail, or it guarantees a private firm a legal monopoly within a certain geographical area through a franchise arrangement, in exchange for a franchise fee and submission to regulation. Some utilities, such as cable television firms and local telephone and electric companies, maintain their monopoly position in this way, and because they are granted exclusive rights of condemnation for easements and the exclusive right to avail themselves of public rights of way. Rate regulation is often a vehicle that permits private firms to charge supracompetitive prices (Brozen 1980, 8–19). For example, Congress gave the Interstate Commerce Commission explicit authority to impose price *floors,* as well as ceilings, which indicates that concern about monopoly pricing was not the only consideration that led to the formation of the ICC. Price floors are a response to too much, not too little, competition.

More generally, it has been widely observed that rate regulation, as it has actually worked in practice, has been primarily for the benefit of firms that are being regulated. This "capture theory" of regulation has been most fully articulated and generalized by Stigler and others into what has been called the "economic theory of regulation."[14] This theory holds that the firms to be regulated and other interest groups influence the political process that shapes regulation so as to further their own interests at the expense of consumers. The relative ineffectiveness of rate regulation in achieving its stated aims has fortified classical liberal opposition to this form of intervention in the economy.

A second problem with rate regulation from a classical liberal perspective is that it has often been a necessary accompaniment of redistributive programs. For example, until recently, regulation of telephone rates was used to shift costs from residential customers to business customers; this meant that the former's rates were artificially low and the latter's artificially high, and regulation was necessary to keep the market from sorting out this inequity. In addition, a universal service mandate still requires users of telecommunications services in more densely populated areas to subsidize users in more sparsely populated areas (Viscusi et al. 2005, 540). Classical liberals have opposed these redistributive policies, which could not survive in an unregulated environment.

This does not mean that classical liberals must oppose all rate regulation. Natural monopolies do exist, even if there is a tendency for technological developments to break them down, as in the case of the railroads (with the advent of interstate trucking), telephone service (with the advent of cellular phones), and cable television service (with the advent of satellite TV). In many localities, electricity at the retail level and water and sewer services are still natural monopolies and are likely to remain so for the foreseeable future. Common law principles have always recognized exceptions to the freedom of contract principle in cases like these and have prohibited discriminatory pricing and price gouging by so-called common carriers (Epstein 1998, ch. 10). Once technology has developed to the point where competitors can enter the field, however, classical liberals favor abolishing rate regulation in any form and letting the market take its course. And, of course, classical liberals have consistently opposed rate regulation in industries in which there are no natural monopolies, such as insurance and fossil fuels.

Classical liberals, at least in the United States, have also been inclined to disagree with antitrust policy throughout most of the twentieth century. Recall that the Sherman Antitrust Act outlawed monopoly pricing (either directly or by collusion), while the FTC Act and the Clayton Act were supposed to prevent monopolies from forming by prohibiting so-called "unfair competition" and at least some mergers. Underlying all three acts, especially the latter two, is the presumption that dangerous concentrations of economic power are incipient in every industry in which consolidation takes place and in every firm that significantly outperforms its rivals in the marketplace. Unless these practices are outlawed, so this conventional wisdom holds, competition will be eliminated and replaced by a monopoly.[15]

Economists with classical liberal sympathies have maintained that these consolidations and the so-called monopolistic practices of successful firms have actually benefited consumers and harmed only, or mainly, less efficient competitors. Business practices that raise red flags for antitrust lawyers, such as retail price maintenance agreements and vertical integration, have unobvious efficiency advantages that these economists have tried to elucidate. If they are correct, enforcement of antitrust laws has actually harmed consumers by penalizing firms that have more successfully met their needs through technological, marketing, and organizational innovation than their rivals.[16] The stated goal of antitrust policy—protecting competition—has, on their view, been nothing more than a policy of protecting competitors at the expense of consumers. The policy prescriptions that have emerged from this critique of antitrust law include dropping legal barriers to entry for new firms, removing legal privileges for existing firms, and enforcing only those portions of antitrust law that prohibit collusion.

Tax Policy

Both classical liberals and modern liberals believe that the state has some sort of legitimate claim on a portion of the wealth and income people get through their participation in the market. The state cannot operate without revenues, and if the state is indeed legitimate, it has the right to take a portion of people's income and/or wealth in the form of taxes to meet those revenue needs. However, the two sides have different conceptions of the nature of that claim. The difference is revealed at the policy level and at the philosophical level. Let us consider these two conceptions of the nature of the state's claim on social wealth in turn, focusing first on the modern liberal view.

Modern liberals believe that it is perfectly appropriate for the state to manipulate the tax code for various social purposes, that is, for purposes other than raising revenue to fund the state's operations. They believe that the tax code is an important vehicle by which government can achieve a variety of objectives. Changing the distribution of wealth and income, usually in the direction of equality through progressive income and estate taxes, is one such objective that immediately comes to mind, but it is probably not the most important one, in part because it is difficult to accomplish. Some economists have argued that the state is much more limited in its ability to change the distribution of income through progressive taxation on income than one might suppose. Roughly, the idea is that labor markets tend to adjust to offset the degree of progressivity of an income tax to establish income differentials to the level or degree that would exist in the absence of the progressive tax.[17] In addition, it has long been observed that estate taxes are not very effective at changing the distribution of wealth.[18] Finally, there is the familiar public choice argument that once the tax code is open to manipulation through the political process, the powerful and the organized will benefit at the expense of the powerless and the unorganized and that redistribution from the rich to the poor will be at best incidental.

There is, however, one sort of distribution that the state can clearly affect, and that is the distribution of the tax burden itself. Although the top marginal tax rates have declined dramatically since the heyday of socialist influence on liberal polities, changes in the tax code and the economic response to those changes have occasioned an important shift in the percentage of the total income tax burden borne by the very rich. In the United States, twenty years ago the top 1 percent of all income earners paid 19 percent of all federal income taxes, but by 1999, they were paying 36 percent of all income taxes. In 1991, the top 5 percent of income earners paid 43 percent of all federal income taxes, but by 1999 they paid 55.5 percent. This means that 5 percent of taxpayers are paying over half the income taxes—welcome news, one would suppose, from a modern liberal perspective. Percentage-wise, the burden has been shifted in recent years from the lower to the upper reaches of the top 50 percent of income earners. According to the IRS, this is the breakdown for total adjusted gross income (AGI) and taxes paid by various percentiles in 1999 and in 2005:

Table 2.1. Federal Income Tax Payments, 1999 and 2005

Percentiles	% of Federal Personal Income Tax (1999)	% of Federal Personal Income Tax (2005)
Top 1%	36.2%	39.38%
Top 5%	55.5%	59.67%
Top 10%	65.5%	70.03%
Top 25%	83.5%	85.99%
Top 50%	96.0%	96.93%
Bottom 50%	4%	3.07%[19]

Of course, income taxes are not the only taxes paid; there are also excise, payroll, and sales taxes, which are generally regressive, and there are state income taxes, as well as property taxes, both of which are somewhat flatter than the federal income tax. Of course, this change in the percentage of the tax burden shouldered by the rich reflects significant growth in income inequality in recent years. That is, the rich have gotten richer relative to the middle class, whose incomes have been more or less stagnant for quite some time. Still, these are remarkable figures, and the tendency for the wealthy paying a greater and greater share of the income tax burden continues. If this trend persists, at some point the rich will finally be paying their fair share.

Redistribution, either of after-tax income, or of the tax burden, has not always been an explicit aim of changes in tax policy. Frequently, especially in recent years, the manipulation of the tax code has been a tool of macroeconomic policy. Tax cuts are instituted in an attempt to stimulate economic activity; tax increases are used to attempt to lower government deficits and thereby lower interest rates; adjustments in depreciation schedules are used to try to stimulate investment. Tariffs and "voluntary" import quotas are instituted to protect jobs from foreign competition. In addition, political leaders change the tax code to encourage behaviors they think should be encouraged and discourage behaviors they believe should be discouraged. For example, "tax shielding" for funds spent on medical care or on higher education is designed to encourage spending on medical care and education, respectively, at the expense of spending on other things.[20] On the other side, increases in taxes on tobacco are seen as a useful vehicle for discouraging smoking, as well as for allocating the alleged social costs of smoking to smokers. The use of the tax code to change the distribution of income or of the tax burden, to promote macroeconomic goals, and to encourage or discourage certain forms of spending are reflective of the attitude that a portion of citizens' income fundamentally belongs to the society at large, for which the state acts as agent.

Further evidence for this conception of ownership can be found in a widely shared attitude among modern liberals toward proposed tax cuts and toward how resources are allocated by the market in a society. Many modern liberal politicians and policy analysts label proposed tax cuts as "tax expenditures," which are conceived of as fully equivalent to government subsidies. When tax cuts (especially for those with high incomes) are under discussion, they are viewed as subsidies to their beneficiaries, and the question then becomes whether such subsidies are a better use of society's wealth than other things these funds might be spent on. (This conception of tax cuts does not preclude a "yes" answer to this question.) For example, in 2001 the U.S. government was trying to determine what to do with actual and projected budget surpluses. For modern liberals, the question was how best to spend this money—society's money. One way to spend it is to give tax cuts, preferably targeted to those with lower incomes or to a more narrowly delimited segment of the population to achieve some worthy objective. On the other hand, some classical liberals argued in favor of tax cuts that disproportionately benefited the well off and did so on macroeconomic grounds, namely, that such cuts would spur investment and economic growth that would benefit everyone. This appears to be a convergence argument in which classical liberals adopt the modern liberal assumption that this money antecedently belongs to society; they then went on to argue that these tax cuts would be the best use of society's wealth, since it would increase the size of the pie, as well as the government's take.

Negative pronouncements about how society allocates its wealth or income abound among those with modern liberal sensibilities. Consider the follow quotation from Arthur Caplan, in which he reflects on the wisdom of using society's resources to treat infertility:

> assisted reproduction, unlike sexual reproduction, is a social enterprise. It requires the involvement of many third parties as well as significant amounts of social resources.... What level of help society is willing to tolerate, provide or pay for moves assisted reproduction beyond the boundaries of personal choice and individual liberty. (1997, 7)

What is especially telling about this example is that infertility treatments are not only not paid for by the government, they are normally not even covered by private insurance plans, a fact Caplan surely knows. To say that the amount of "social resources" that are allocated to assisted reproduction should be subjected to "society's" (i.e., the state's) judgment about what it "is willing to... pay for," implies pretty clearly that Caplan regards the funds infertile couples might spend on infertility treatment out of their own pockets as belonging in the first instance to society, in which case society must consider other goods or services on which these funds might be spent, that is, the opportunity costs. To this it might be objected that the source of Caplan's observation is the fact that the state directly and indirectly heavily subsidizes medical care. It is not that the state is claiming ownership over the resources private couples would spend on infertility treatments but that it is simply exercising its ownership rights over the resources that it has provided to the medical community. This reply, however, will not do, since it assumes that in any arena in which public and private funds are used, the state should determine what private resources can be spent on in the course of deciding how "its" resources can be used. If the state is big enough and ubiquitous enough (as indeed it currently is), almost anything a person spends his or her money on will be in a place where public and private funds mix. This reduces to the view that the state has an ownership stake in the resources people use to purchase just about anything. More precisely, what stands behind the view of Caplan and countless others who question how scarce resources are being allocated in a market society is a conception of ownership in which that society has, through the state, a kind of priority claim on an indeterminate portion of all wealth and income.

This conception of the priority of society's claim on a portion of social wealth is given further expression in the writings of leading modern liberal political philosophers' conception of the fundamental problem of distributive justice. This is clearest in John Rawls's *A Theory of Justice,* where he defines the problem of distributive justice as the problem of how the benefits and burdens of social cooperation should be distributed (1971, 4). Given that it is the state's job to ensure (distributive) justice, this assumes without argument, as Robert Nozick has pointed out (1974, 185–86), that the state has the right to determine how these benefits and burdens are to be distributed. Moreover, Nozick has charged (1974, 228) that Rawls also maintains that people's talents and abilities—their human capital from which much of their income flows—are common assets. Many liberals—both classical and modern—have found this conception of the ownership of people's talents and abilities arresting and troublesome, and indeed Nozick has ascribed to Rawls the view that individuals are (partially) owned by others. In point of fact, however, Rawls never claimed that people's talents and abilities are owned by others. What he actually says is "we see then that the difference principle represents, in effect, an agreement to regard the *distribution* [my emphasis] of natural talents as a common asset and to share in the benefits of this distribution, whatever it turns out to be" (Rawls 1971, 101).[21] A more modest and more liberal interpretation of Rawls's claim is that society has a prior claim on a portion of the income and wealth that people's talents and abilities generate. Society has partial income rights in these talents and abilities, and only in that limited and tendentious sense may they be said to own the people who possess those talents and abilities. People are not forced to labor for one another; it's just that if they put their human capital to work, society has a claim on a portion of the income thereby generated, just as it has a claim on the income generated by nonhuman capital. This misinterpretation of Rawls comes from treating ownership as a simple relation between the owner and the thing owned; as we shall see in the next chapter, ownership is actually a complex of rights, terms, and conditions.

Rawls is not the only modern liberal theorist who believes that society has some sort of antecedent claim on assets found within a state's borders. In Ronald Dworkin's exposition of his views on distributive justice, he asks us to consider a hypothetical auction in which all of society's (nonhuman) resources are to be bid upon by people with equal wealth (Dworkin 1981b). Bruce Ackerman poses the problem of distributive justice in the context of a story about people in a spaceship trying to decide how to divide up a valuable commodity that they are about to acquire on a planet they are approaching (Ackerman 1980, ch. 2). All of these conceptions of the problem of distributive justice clearly presuppose that the community, for which the state acts as agent, has some sort of prior ownership claim on all natural resources and productive assets, which it then has to decide how to distribute.

To articulate further this view about the modern liberal conception of ownership, more needs to be said about the notion of priority. What does "priority" mean in this context? What does it consist of? Two things. First, in the language of social contract theory, it means that society, or the community, would have an enforceable morally legitimate claim on some of people's income and wealth in a state of nature. This does not mean that the community would have full liberal ownership of all productive assets in a state of nature. (That might be one conception of communism.) The claim only extends to a portion of the income the assets generate or to a portion of the wealth those assets represent, not to control of the assets themselves nor even to all of the income or wealth associated with the asset. Second, and perhaps more importantly, it means that the extraction of revenue from individuals by the state need not be conceived of as an exchange for which the state must provide something of comparable value in return to that individual, since that revenue did not belong to the individual in the first place. On this conception, if the state takes from Peter and gives to Paul, Peter has no legitimate complaint that he does not benefit. The state, acting as an agent for the community at large, is simply taking what antecedently and rightfully belongs to its principal—society—and using it in the way that it sees fit.

A modern liberal might object that favoring tax policies that change the distribution of wealth and income presupposes no such conception of social ownership because his reasons are purely pragmatic. He might point out that there is a whole range of social problems the solution to which government can make a major contribution. Income taxes, especially progressive taxes that fall more heavily on the wealthy, are simply the most effective vehicles by which to raise the funds to address these problems. As the bank robber Willie Sutton once observed about banks, "that's where the money is." A modern liberal may proclaim no particular beliefs about ownership rights or a theory of the demands of justice. He simply wants to solve certain social problems for which large amounts of revenue are required, and such revenue is not to be found among the least advantaged, and those in the middle class are not likely to be persuaded to bear a proportionate share of the burden. Increasing taxes on the well-to-do has the complementary advantages of being a fiscally and politically effective vehicle by which these revenues can be raised. Alternatively, a modern liberal might maintain that there are a multitude of claims on the wealth found in a community, and the central political problem is to determine a method by which to adjudicate these claims. For a variety of reasons, democratic decision-making, within broad limits, is the preferred method, and so whatever emerges from this process should be accepted as a suitable compromise. One need not suppose any particular theory of ownership to endorse this solution.

But is this true? Can one maintain skepticism about the nature of ownership rights in productive assets (natural resources, nonhuman and human capital) and yet have substantial and consequential views about the legitimacy of certain forms of taxation or the distribution of the burdens? Alternatively, do not the latter presuppose something about ownership rights in productive assets? The question at issue is whether modern liberalism is committed to the view that the state, or society as a whole, has a prior ownership claim on (part of) the income associated with productive assets. It seems that an affirmative answer to this question cannot be avoided as long as modern liberals maintain that the state has wide discretionary taxing and spending authority. This assumption or presupposition of social ownership best explains the modern liberal attitude that it is up to the state to decide within fairly broad limits what proportion of the total wealth and income of a society to take in the form of taxes, how those tax burdens should be distributed, and how the revenues collected should be spent. That "spending" can include selective tax cuts, as well as government spending. In light of these observations, it is hard to deny that modern liberalism is committed to the view that the state has income rights and rights of disposition in productive assets, including human capital.

On what grounds might this presumption of social ownership be based? One might take the view that there is a primordial social obligation to share the fruits of one's labor, land, and capital with the community at large. This might in turn depend on deeper views in moral philosophy, which take a presumption of equal treatment as fundamental to the moral point of view. Alternatively, as Hobhouse (1964, 99) has argued, society contributes in innumerable ways to the value of productive assets and to what entrepreneurs and capitalists earn in a market economy. A more direct argument, also suggested by Hobhouse (1964, 98), drops the presumption that the state acts as agent for society as principal. The state itself is responsible for a substantial portion of the value of land, labor, and capital, since it provides a stable framework within which its citizens can use their property to further their own ends. It defines and enforces property rights, which involves expensive and complex criminal and civil justice systems. After all, it is the state that allows us to pass from a state of nature into civil society. It might be argued that the marginal difference the state makes in the value of all forms of property is substantial enough to justify the partial ownership claim the state makes on these forms of wealth. The state also directly provides its citizens with human capital in the form of publicly funded education.

Classical liberals have a very different way of conceiving of taxation. They believe that individuals have priority of ownership of productive assets, which means that in a state of nature, others would have no enforceable claim to a portion of the income derived from those assets, though there might be a noncoercively backed moral obligation to help those in dire need. It also means that taxation and the provision of government services have to be conceived of as a form of exchange. Familiar classical liberal attitudes toward taxation and government spending follow from this conception. Classical liberals believe that it is inappropriate for the government to manipulate the tax code for purposes other than raising revenue, including notably redistributing wealth and/or income, though it is unclear whether they are committed to ignoring the macroeconomic consequences of tax policy and changes thereto. In addition, they oppose the use of the tax code to encourage some behaviors and discourage others. Finally, for classical liberals, there can be no such thing as a tax expenditure; there are only larger or smaller, broader or narrower tax cuts, though this does not imply that they always favor tax cuts. On the spending side, they believe that the government legitimately has very little discretion about the kinds of things on which it spends tax revenues because they believe the proper functions of government are relatively few and limited.

All of these views at the policy level reflect and presuppose the ascription of priority of ownership to individuals as suggested above. This priority can be further unpacked by one or another philosophical theory of property rights. Perhaps the clearest and most obvious way is in terms of Lockean natural rights. The Lockean tradition holds that people have full liberal ownership rights in property independent of the state. The state has a right to take what antecedently belongs to private individuals only as part of an ostensibly forced exchange wherein it provides certain services to those from whom it extracts a fee in the form of taxes. What justifies this forced exchange is only one of a number of questions this account raises. The most basic or fundamental question of course is the justification of these natural rights themselves. How might that be done? Locke's theory clearly will not do because of its theological basis. In answer to the question, "Where do natural rights come from?" Locke says, "God. Next question." Loren Lomasky (1987) has tried to justify such rights by appeal to the concept of persons as pursuers of what he calls "projects." This metaphysical fact is supposed to ground personal, political, and property rights, though whether he succeeds in this attempt is another matter. Another way these rights might be supported is by appeal to utility, which is the hallmark of the Law and Economics movement. This approach is programmatic, however, in the sense that justification for (common law) property rights has to be piecemeal and on a case-by-case basis. Further support for this justificatory strategy comes from public choice. Public choice economists with classical liberal sympathies maintain that once the state takes as a proper object of government policy the distribution of wealth and income—or for that matter, any other objective not on their list of approved government purposes—it opens the door, or opens the door more widely, for the redistribution of wealth from the unorganized taxpayers to organized special interest groups. On this view, tax revenues in the modern liberal state are a commons looking for a tragedy. Preventing this tragedy requires privatizing as much of the commons as possible. What all classical liberals seem to agree on is that a firewall between the state and its citizens' property is necessary to stop this ostensibly unintended redistribution—a firewall which cannot exist if a portion of citizens' wealth and income is antecedently regarded as belonging to society or the state. What that firewall would look like remains an unsolved problem for classical liberalism, though some form of constitutional limitation on the state's power to tax or to spend (or both) seems to be part of the preferred solution.[22]

As suggested above, classical liberals' views on taxation are conditioned by their belief that the legitimate functions of government are few and are largely, if not entirely, exhausted by the protection of people's rights, solving public goods problems, and dealing with common law negative externalities. Perhaps because of this and because they believe that the notion of equal treatment under the law extends to property rights, they favor some form of tax neutrality, though there are disputes about how tax neutrality should be understood. Typically, they favor a flat (i.e., a proportional) tax, perhaps with an exemption for the poorest members of society so that the latter pay no tax at all (Hayek 1960, ch. 20; Friedman 1962, 174–75). Though almost any workable tax system will have some effect on the distribution of wealth and income, the latter is not the proper object of government concern on the classical liberal view, which means that redistributive consequences of tax policy have no justificatory weight.[23] These views on taxation are buttressed by a variety of different classical liberal theories of justice. While there are important differences among these theories, they have in common the view that the proper role of the state in assuring justice is limited to enforcing contracts and protecting people's fundamental rights, among which they include property rights.

Though income and consumption taxes (value added taxes, sales taxes) are the main forms of taxation, there are other forms as well. Taxes on wealth in the form of estate taxes raise the same issues as income taxes. Another type of tax is user fees. Gasoline taxes, for example, are used (in part, anyway) to fund new highway construction and to maintain existing roadways. They are paid by the people who use the service and approximately in proportion to how much they use it. Though user fees are the sort of tax classical and modern liberals could in principle agree on, some economists have shown that user fees are systematically misappropriated.[24] What they have demonstrated is not the familiar observation that politicians "bring home the bacon" by getting, for example, large and dubious high-way projects for their districts. Instead, the problem is that user fees are routinely diverted to completely different purposes, including diversions into the general fund to pay for anything the state pro-vides, which in turn systematically misleads the public about the costs of the services for which they are being charged user fees. It also misleads the public about the extent of general purpose taxa-tion and the costs of other government activities funded by these revenues. A full airing of the points of agreement and disagree-ment between modern liberals and classical liberals on all forms of taxation goes beyond the scope of what can be accomplished here. The main point of this section has been to highlight the most important differences between the two sides on tax policy and to show that these differences reflect different conceptions of owner-ship rights in the income and wealth that people earn in the market or get through other forms of voluntary transfer. Those differences are fairly deep.

Transfer Programs

To some extent, the distinction between tax policy and transfer pro-grams is artificial. A theme in the last section is that tax policy is a major vehicle by which income and wealth can be transferred from some individuals and groups to others. Nevertheless, for analytical pur-poses, it is useful to distinguish the two. Tax policy affects economic decisionmakers in such a way that they alter their private economic activity to minimize or at least reduce their tax burden, and income or wealth is diverted into some uses rather than others. Transfer pro-grams, by contrast, involve the transfer of resources through the inter-mediary of some type of government organization or program. These programs can be divided into three categories: (1) welfare programs intended to help the poor, (2) transfer programs designed to help more or less narrowly defined segments of the nonpoor, and (3) social insur-ance programs. Welfare programs include those that involve straight cash transfers to the disadvantaged, as well as those that provide enti-tlements to food (food stamps), health care (Medicaid), and housing (public housing). Other, more narrowly targeted transfer programs for the nonpoor include farm subsidies, government participation in the home mortgage market, subsidies targeting rural areas, urban areas, mass transit, and so on, and various forms of so-called "corporate welfare." By any measure, the largest transfer programs are the social insurance programs, in particular, those that provide health insurance for varying percentages of the population and old-age insurance for nearly everyone. Other forms of social insurance include disaster (e.g., flood, crop, and earthquake) insurance, unemployment insurance, and workers' compensation insurance. Deposit insurance for commercial banks and savings and loans is also a form of social insurance. Social insurance programs have three distinctive features: first, rates are not determined by actuarial considerations alone, which means that some participants in these programs are subsidized by others and/or by the taxpayers at large; second, shortfalls are insured against by the state's power to tax; third, with the exception of some of the disaster insurance programs, persons in the targeted group are not permitted to opt out of participation. All transfer programs involve the forced transfer of wealth and/or income from some citizens to others, though this is to some extent disguised in social insurance programs by the requirement that recipients pay nonactuarially determined premiums in exchange for coverage.

Putting aside for now the more narrowly targeted transfer programs, it is uncontroversial to say that modern liberal politicians have been responsible for transfer programs intended to aid the disadvantaged and for health and old-age social insurance programs. They were able to forge a political consensus that these are appropriate tasks for the state to undertake, though there has always been dissent from those with classical liberal sympathies. Lately, welfare programs for the poor have come under broad attack as counterproductive in that they encourage dependency on the state, which is bad for both recipients and the taxpayers who have to foot the bill. In recent years, significant reform in these programs has taken place based on this criticism, and the debate has been carried on in about as nonideological a spirit as one could reasonably hope for. Despite these reforms, there has been no real challenge to the modern liberal view that the state has an important role to play in providing for the worst-off members of society. The only question is how best to do it.

In the case of some social insurance programs, most notably health insurance, modern liberals have favored state funding, at least for the elderly and in many cases for the entire population.[25] They have been divided, however, on the question of full socialization of health care.

The creeping socialists in Great Britain have carried the day on these questions, but modern liberals in the United States have not spoken with a unified voice. Though virtually all favor some form of national health insurance (so-called single-payer plans), there is no consensus on the question of whether health care should be fully nationalized so that most physicians work for the government, and the government owns most hospitals and clinics. What has emerged in practice in the United States, and in other Western democracies to a lesser extent, are mixtures of public and private systems. Much of the funding comes from the government, but most health care providers are not government employees, and productive assets used to deliver medical care are largely in private hands. Full nationalization does not seem to be on the modern liberal agenda, though that may be merely a matter of practical politics. As consequential as the government's involvement in health care is, the largest transfer program by most measures is the provision of old-age insurance, either as a basic minimum or as a supplement to private pensions. Modern liberals pioneered and continue to support with great tenacity state provision of this good. Finally, workers' compensation, unemployment insurance, bank deposit insurance, and disaster insurance programs in the United States were first offered in the twentieth century as part of government's response to unchosen adverse conditions (injuries on the job, involuntary unemployment, banking disasters, natural catastrophes) that were insufficiently addressed by the market, or in the case of workers' compensation, by contract law and tort law, though whether these programs should be credited exclusively to modern liberal politicians and their supporters is doubtful.[26]

Why do modern liberals favor welfare and social insurance programs? As in the case of tax policy, one answer is redistribution. Especially among the more philosophically minded, many modern liberals believe that inequalities in wealth and income beyond a certain limit, or inequalities in some of the things that can be bought with wealth and income, such as health care, are unjust or otherwise morally objectionable, and it is the state's task to ensure a more equitable—which is understood as a more equal—distribution of wealth and income or of some things that wealth and income can purchase, such as the basic necessities of life.[27] Welfare programs and some social insurance programs appear to do just that, especially insofar as they are funded by progressive taxation on income and wealth. However, this justification for transfer programs has probably been given more prominence by both sides in academic disputes than it has had in the real world of politics. This is evident if one considers state-provided health insurance and pensions for the elderly. Though the lower-income elderly benefit in the intended way (i.e., at the expense of the nonpoor) in the case of health care insurance and possibly in the case of old-age insurance (though this is uncertain),[28] much of the redistribution goes from relatively less well-off younger working people to relatively better-off retired senior citizens, which is not the sort of redistribution philosophers and social theorists typically defend. Similarly, subsidized disaster insurance often covers relatively prosperous farmers (crop insurance) and upper-income individuals with first or second homes in flood plains, on beachfronts, or near earthquake fault lines (catastrophe insurance). Bank deposit insurance covers depositors up to a set limit, regardless of the wealth of the depositor.

How could these nonprogressive transfers be justified? A commonly voiced alternative justification for state-mandated pensions and state-funded health care, which is consistent with the above-noted regressive intergenerational wealth transfers, is more communitarian in spirit. It is based on the idea that these programs express a generational bond, promise, or commitment between the young and the elderly—a bond that is constitutive of community. In other words, this is a sacred bond that in part defines who we are as a community; as such, it is a promise that would be broken by abandoning (i.e., privatizing) the system. As Amitai Etzioni and Laura Brodbeck, two leading communitarians who have discussed Social Security, put it, "*these commitments ought to be honored* [their emphasis], because it is the ethically appropriate thing to do, because if one violates such commitments the social and moral order of a society is diminished."[29] These obligations based on community values need not be conceived of in terms of doing what justice requires, even if they are "ethically appropriate."

Poverty in the United States became an important item on the public agenda and a matter of public debate and discussion in the early 1960s. Books such as Michael Harrington's *The Other America* (1962) called attention to the plight of the poor in the midst of general economic prosperity. General welfare programs designed to address these problems have had a mixed record, in part because they have created a culture of dependency that is hard to replace. Whatever their problems, however, these programs have been a success by some measures. Social evils, such as hunger and malnutrition, and to a lesser extent, the lack of health care and inadequate housing, have been addressed in a substantial way, even if many of the collateral problems of poverty remain.[30] Whether or not these programs have been, or continue to be, desirable, the key point for present purposes is that, as in the case of health insurance and old-age insurance, one need not believe that distributive justice requires a more equal distribution of wealth and income to support the view that the state should help to provide some or all of the basic necessities of life for some of its citizens. Communitarian arguments could be offered for these programs, as could arguments that appeal straightforwardly to altruistic principles.

Modern liberal politicians and their academic supporters are firmly committed to the defense of the broadly based transfer programs of the modern welfare state, especially those whose intended beneficiaries are the poor and the elderly. The depth and nature of that commitment is reflected in the fact that many of these programs are open-ended in the sense that they have no fixed budget. Whoever meets the eligibility requirements is entitled to the benefits. The open-ended character of these programs is best justified and explained by the presupposition that the state, or its principal, society, has ownership rights in a portion of society's wealth and income, which state officials then claim, subject only to the constraints imposed by fundamental rights and basic political prudence.[31]

Communitarian arguments and arguments based on considerations of justice might also be given in the case of other social insurance programs such as disaster, unemployment, workers' compensation, and deposit insurance. All of these are typically seen as appropriate responses to actual or prospective private-sector failures to provide the type of insurance in question. In all cases other than workers' compensation, the fundamental problem is alleged to be one of correlated risks. In a typical insurance policy, the risks of adverse events for one policyholder are independent of the risks facing other policyholders. Not so in the case of unemployment, natural disasters, and banking catastrophes. At certain levels of unemployment, or when a natural disaster strikes or when a run on the banks occurs, damages are so broad and deep that the ex ante risks of these types of adverse events are not independent for policyholders, that is, they are correlated risks.[32] It has been argued that private insurance cannot handle these correlated risks, which is why the state has to step in. Government-mandated workers' compensation programs, on the other hand, have a fundamentally different rationale. They were instituted around the turn of the twentieth century not so much in response to failures of the free market, but instead to failures in the legal system that frames it. Four common law principles contributed to immunizing employers from responsibility for most workplace injuries (Rothstein et. al 1994, 403–4). The first is the fault requirement. Employers were liable only if they were at fault, and proving that was often difficult. Second, the fellow servants' rule allowed employers to escape responsibility when other employees were partly to blame. Typically, the latter were the proverbial turnips, from whom blood cannot be gotten. Third, two legal defenses available to firms further vitiated employer responsibility for workplace injuries: the doctrines of contributory negligence (employers escape responsibility when the plaintiff has been negligent), and assumption of risk (employee assumes risks inherent in the job). Fourth, factual issues were often difficult and expensive to resolve. All these factors conspired to make the common law in this area cumbersome and unresponsive. The legislative response to these problems was a mandatory no-fault insurance system, regulated or owned outright by the states, in which fault need not be proved. Payouts were somewhat less generous than under the common law, but claims were settled less contentiously and more expeditiously.[33]

Finally, there are the more narrowly defined transfer programs, which are for the most part direct subsidies to the nonpoor, though originally many of these programs, such as agricultural subsidies, were designed to help groups who were genuinely hurting because of economic forces beyond their control. Today, these programs, which include various forms of corporate welfare, are justified on grounds of national economic policy. They are represented as complex nautical maneuvers of highly skilled politician-sailors trying their best to sail the nation's economy smoothly on the high seas of global markets. Most economists and many laypersons recognize, however, that these politicians fly the flag of the Jolly Roger and that these programs are nothing more than the piratical depredations of their special interest crews on polities at home and abroad. Despite the political invulnerability of these programs, and despite the fact that principled modern liberals have become disillusioned with them, many modern liberals nevertheless remain powerfully attracted to industrial policy schemes that hold out the promise of state management of economic change in ways that minimize the attendant social costs.

Classical liberals differ sharply with modern liberals about government transfer programs: they oppose nearly all of them. The classical liberal view on welfare for the poor, however, is in some respects indeterminate. On the one hand, there is a principled rejection of the view that it is a proper task of government to redistribute wealth and income in the direction of equality (or indeed in any direction as a matter of explicit government policy), as well as rejection of any welfare rights doctrine. On the other hand, the proposition that some level of government has some role to play in helping citizens most in need has been accepted, or at least has not been summarily rejected, by most classical liberals, once again with the exception of the pure libertarian wing of classical liberalism.[34] Classical liberals such as Charles Murray have been in the forefront of the ranks of critics of welfare. They have charged that welfare programs discourage individual responsibility and encourage an entitlement mentality that fosters dependency, thereby crippling recipients' lives (Murray 1984; 1988). Classical liberals have also favored the devolution of welfare responsibilities to lower levels of government, both because they believe that officials at lower levels of government are better situated to understand and meet the needs of the desperately poor and because they believe that state and local funding impose important constraints on the generosity of these programs. Under devolution to smaller units of government, relatively generous programs would tend to attract, and subsequently be overwhelmed by, recipients from other political subdivisions. Geographical division of responsibility, then, provides an important check on government generosity; that generosity is what classical liberal critics such as Murray see as the most important causal agent in perpetuating poverty and dependency. Finally, classical liberals are inclined to believe that private charities and voluntary mutual aid societies are much more efficient vehicles for delivering services to the needy than is the state.[35] However, except for libertarians, it is difficult to find among classical liberals categorical denials that the state has any legitimate role to play in helping society's neediest members, especially its children.

In the case of health insurance, classical liberals have been less compromising. Their view is that massive government involvement in the funding and delivery of medical services is behind most of the problems in that industry today.[36] The chief modes of government involvement are state provision of health insurance for the elderly and the poor and tax breaks for employer-provided health insurance premiums for workers. Because they pay little or nothing out of pocket for health care, the elderly and the poor have little incentive to economize on health care expenditures; the nonpoor also lack this incentive because tax breaks for employer-provided health insurance have encouraged almost all health care to take place under the umbrella of insurance, which means that third parties pick up most of the tab.[37] This has led to an overutilization of health care services, which drives up prices. This in turn induces government attempts to hold prices down, which invariably has a variety of unintended negative consequences. Classical liberals favor reforms, such as Medical Savings Accounts, that force people to make trade-offs between health care and other goods and to take full operational and financial responsibility for their health care (Goodman and Musgrave 1992). Is there any role for government, aside from enforcing contracts, in the classical liberal vision of the provision of health care services? In principle, there would seem to be none, but it is difficult to find categorical affirmations of this claim in their writings, again with the exception of some libertarians. As in the case of welfare, most classical liberals are conservative enough that they are unwilling to commit themselves to a complete and relatively rapid withdrawal of government from the funding of health care. In a manner reminiscent of the creeping socialists in Western Europe, they favor a change in a certain direction, namely, increasing reprivatization of the funding and delivery of health care services, but they are reluctant to be pinned down on the question of the ultimate goal of their reforms, specifically, whether or not the state has any ultimate financial responsibility for health care, at least for the poor and the elderly. Maybe they are genuinely uncertain about the effects of reprivatization. Or perhaps the explanation is political, namely, that state funding of health care for the elderly and the poor are so deeply woven into the fabric of the modern United States (as well as other democratic societies) that it is difficult to envision politically viable alternative funding mechanisms. Finally there is a moral argument—undoubtedly a conversion argument—for creating a soft landing for people who have come to rely on these programs as society transitions away from public provision.

In the case of old-age insurance, however, classical liberals have taken a harder line and favor almost complete privatization—and sooner rather than later. They believe that the Social Security system in the United States and like systems in other countries should be dismantled. People should be put in charge of saving for their own retirement, though all advocates of privatization countenance both practical and moral problems in the move from current systems to more privatized systems. A privatized system with forced participation has been tried in Chile, and the experiment has been hailed by some classical liberals as a model for other developed countries.[38] Some classical liberals might allow that it would be acceptable for the state to force people to save for their own retirement through contributions to an approved investment fund. Since we live in a society that is simply not going to allow destitution among the elderly, forced participation might be the least intrusive alternative that the state could deploy (see, e.g., Hayek 1960, 286). As with health care and health insurance, there are practical political problems with privatizing old-age insurance, genuine uncertainty about the effects of proposed reforms, and moral arguments for helping those who have come to rely on these programs. What is not uncertain, however, is the direction that reform should take, according to classical liberals.

What about redistribution? Although most redistribution in existing old-age insurance programs is intergenerational and not at all in an egalitarian direction, there is at least one egalitarian redistributionist element in the current U.S. system: the benefit formula is mildly progressive so that those with lower earnings get more in benefits, relative to their contributions, than high earners. As noted above (see note 28), however, this mild progressivity may be canceled out by the fact that the poor tend to be in the system longer and die younger than the wealthy, so whether or not the current system is redistributive in the usual sense is unclear at best.[39] Could classical liberals favor retaining some redistribution in a privatized system? Perhaps. As in the case of health care, it is hard to find categorical denials from classical liberals of the legitimacy of any redistribution, no matter how slight, to the elderly poor, again with the exception of hard-line libertarians. Assuming some redistribution to the elderly poor is inevitable, an additional benefit of a privatized system with forced participation is that it minimizes the need for this form of redistribution, since only the unlucky and not the improvident would have to be subsidized.

Other social insurance programs have not been subject to a great deal of attention by classical liberals, though in general they oppose them. Compulsory unemployment insurance is tied up with government responses to poverty, recession, and depression, and it has not received sustained independent attention from classical liberals. It might be possible for classical liberals to support compulsory unemployment insurance (though not government-controlled insurance), if it is conceived of as a prophylactic against people becoming charges of the state when bad times befall individuals, entire industries, or geographical regions. State-provided disaster insurance has also not attracted much attention from classical liberals, though arguably it is something they should oppose, since the problem of correlated risks, which only government is supposed to be able to solve, can be solved through the private sector.[40] Similar observations apply to workers' compensation insurance, which, as noted earlier, might have had a private sector solution early in the last century. The case of insurance for bank deposits is more complex, since it is inextricably intertwined with an array of banking regulations that are not part of any transfer program. These regulations, and the place of deposit insurance in them, will be discussed in the next chapter.

As for the more narrowly focused transfer programs justified by reference to economic policy goals, classical liberals, especially those in the public choice school, have been in the front ranks of their critics. They have an elaborate story to tell about how economic policy is routinely hijacked to serve special interests and how the resulting rent-seeking frenzy causes deadweight welfare losses all around.[41] On their view, the fact that special interest snouts are deep in the public trough is a completely foreseeable consequence of the government's decision to try to manage the economy, especially through various forms of "managed competition" and trade policy. Other economists, notably those of the Austrian school, have buttressed the public choice perspective with arguments to the effect that macroeconomic problems, especially those associated with the business cycle, are in fact caused by other forms of state intervention.[42] There is no suggestion in the writings of classical liberal thinkers that the state has a prior ownership claim on a portion of society's wealth and income, which allows the state to transfer wealth to wherever they think it might do the most good. They view this income and wealth as belonging to individuals, who can be forced to give up some of it to support the legitimate functions of government. The latter might conceivably include some modest transfers to their less fortunate fellow citizens, but it does not include transfers to support whatever policies and programs state officials believe would be good economic policy.

This concludes the discussion of modern liberalism's and classical liberalism's positions on the extent of public versus private property. The main point of agreement is that it is appropriate for the state to own some productive assets and to fund the delivery of some goods and services through taxation, though there are important disagreements about the details. The main point of disagreement can be framed by reference to the question of partial state ownership of the wealth and income associated with productive assets (natural resources, human and nonhuman capital). Modern liberals believe that the state (or society) has a prior ownership claim on some portion of social wealth and income. Classical liberals deny this. This explains the systematic differences between the classicals and the moderns on both tax policy and transfer programs. Classical liberals favor rather severe limitations both on the kinds of taxes governments can impose and on the kind and extent of programs it can fund with tax revenues. John Gray captured nicely the classical liberal attitude when he said,

> Common to all contemporary classical liberals is the goal of a form of limited government under the rule of law in which...the central economic powers of government—powers of taxation, spending, and the issuance of money—are subject to rules no less stringent than those which protect the basic personal liberties. (1995, 76)

Modern liberals, by contrast, have a more open-ended view about the purposes for which the tax code and tax revenues can be used. This translates into support for a wide variety of transfer programs run by the state from welfare to subsidized insurance to outright subsidies to the nonpoor. This is a fairly direct implication of the modern liberal view that the state has at least a partial ownership claim on the wealth and income of a society.

THREE

Liberal Conceptions of Private Property

Both modern liberals and classical liberals believe in a regime of private property rights, though as the last chapter demonstrates, the extent of private versus state ownership of productive assets is a matter of contention. But how is private ownership, for those things that are privately owned, to be understood? Ownership is a complex notion involving a number of rights, terms, and conditions. A. M. Honoré (1961, 112–28) defines full, liberal ownership, which serves as a kind of benchmark in these discussions, in terms of the following incidents:[1]

1. The right to exclusive physical possession.
2. The right to manage, which includes the right to use or modify, as well as the right to enter into contractual relations with others to use or modify.
3. The right of disposition, which includes the right to alienate or destroy.
4. The right to the income and to the capital value.
5. The right to bequeath.
6. A prohibition on harmful use.
7. The right to security, that is, immunity from expropriation.
8. Absence of term, that is, the other incidents of ownership do not automatically expire at a specified time.
9. Liability to execution of debt, that is, the right to pledge as security for debt.

These incidents may be held singly or jointly with others. The types of things that might be so owned are productive assets (including a firm or a business), personal property, one's labor, and oneself, at least in principle. Putting aside the latter, it is fair to say that all liberals favor some form of private (i.e., nonstate) ownership of all these types of things, though not all liberals favor full liberal ownership of same. In particular, modern liberals favor a host of restrictions and limitations on these incidents of ownership for each type of thing that might be owned. Classical liberals, on the other hand, favor full liberal ownership of all of these types of things, subject to some exceptions noted below. This chapter explores all the points of disagreement, as well as points of agreement, among modern and classical liberals about these incidents of ownership for each type of thing that might be owned, starting with three sections on the ownership of productive assets and personal property. Following this will be sections on the ownership of labor and of human capital. Finally, there is the question of whether people own themselves. This will be the venue in which to discuss the question of the proper role of the state in regulating people's ostensibly private behavior and their lifestyle choices; this turns out to be a complex question on which there are points of agreement and disagreement between and among classical and modern liberals.

Ownership of Productive Assets and Personal Property: Some Traditional Incidents

Productive assets and personal property include land (broadly understood to include natural resources), buildings, machinery, and chattels. They are the sorts of things that people usually think of when they think of property. There are more esoteric objects that fit under this heading as well, such as intellectual property and businesses or firms themselves. Let us proceed by considering what each of the traditional incidents of ownership amounts to for all these forms of property and what the classical and modern liberal views are on each of them.

Incident #1: The right to exclusive physical possession. The right to exclusive physical possession is the sine qua non of private ownership of tangible property. The corresponding rights in intellectual property would be the right to use (a subincident of the right to manage). Focusing for the moment on tangible property, there is at least one widely accepted limitation on the right of physical possession, namely the one embodied in the eminent domain clause of the Fifth Amendment, which permits the state to take private property—here understood as taking physical possession—for public purposes provided that just compensation is paid.[2] Because of the centrality of the right of physical possession to ownership, there seems to be widespread agreement among liberals that if this right is negated by the state taking physical possession of one's property, it is compensable, barring special circumstances. Otherwise, there would be no security of possession (incident #7) because there would be no effective immunity from expropriation. Similar considerations apply to the right to manage (i.e., use) intangible property. If, for example, the state prohibited a private individual from using a computer program she created (e.g., encryption software), compensation would prima facie be owed.

The nature and extent of incidents #2 and #3 (management rights and disposition rights) go to the heart of the question of the proper role of government, since they concern the proper scope of government regulation. Because the issues raised by these incidents constitute such an important part of the overall disagreement between classical and modern liberals, a discussion of them can be usefully postponed until the other incidents have been discussed. Accordingly, let us next consider incident #4, income rights.

Incident #4: The right to the income and to the capital value. One way of characterizing the difference between modern and classical liberals concerning this right is that modern liberals favor a much more extensive limitation on this right by the state than do classical liberals. However, for the reasons given in the last chapter in the discussion of the implications or presuppositions of tax policy and transfer programs, it is more accurate or more perspicuous to characterize the modern liberal position not in terms of a limitation on private ownership but instead in terms of a division of ownership between the state and private parties. In the modern liberal view, the state has a prior ownership claim on an ill-defined portion of the income from productive assets that it does not directly control.

Other considerations, which expand on some remarks made in the last chapter, support this notion that the state has a prior ownership claim on a portion of income attributable to otherwise private assets. Notice that private individuals, who have at least some income rights in productive assets, are relatively unconstrained in how they can acquire income from employing those assets and what they can spend that income on. The state is similarly unconstrained: it can exercise its income rights in productive assets through myriad forms of taxation and even more multifarious forms of spending. Of course, private individuals, unlike the state, cannot exercise their income rights through coercion. In a corresponding manner, the state faces some modest legal constraints (as well as more substantial political constraints) on its taxing and spending authority. For these reasons, and for the reasons detailed in the last chapter, it is useful to characterize the modern liberal view as one which assigns income rights in productive assets in part to private individuals and in part to the state.

The capital value of an asset is standardly defined as the present value of the future income streams associated with that asset. On the modern liberal view, just as in the case of income, ownership of capital value is similarly divided between the state and the private parties who possess the asset; the state asserts its ownership rights through capital gains taxes that must be paid when the asset is sold and through estate taxes when the possessor dies. This is as it should be, on the modern liberal view, for reasons discussed in chapter 2 regarding the priority of ownership of productive assets.

For classical liberals, on the other hand, the power to tax is best conceived of as imposing a limitation on income rights that antecedently reside entirely with private parties. The justification for that limitation is to be found in whatever justification classical liberals accept for the existence of the state and its legitimate functions. Of course, these functions are much more narrowly circumscribed for classical liberals than for the moderns.

Incident #5: The right to bequeath. The right to bequeath productive assets and personal property was mentioned in passing in the last chapter. Modern liberals have favored more or less severe limitations on this right, or more accurately, they believe that there is a partial residuary state ownership claim on the asset that it exercises when the individual who (also) partially owns it dies and bequeaths it to his or her heirs. At that point, the state asserts its partial ownership right to the thing through the imposition of an inheritance tax. Modern liberals believe that policies on inheritance should be governed by the same considerations that govern income taxes. Rates should not be so high as to severely compromise investment and saving, but individuals have no presumptive moral claim on the right to bequeath whatever productive assets and personal property they control.

By contrast, classical liberals have been opposed to inheritance taxes, at least to the extent that they fall disproportionately on the better off. Their position also parallels their views on income taxes, which was discussed earlier. If estates are to be taxed at all, some sort of neutrality is the favored view, either on Lockean grounds or on the grounds of incentive effects. As previously noted, the question of the legitimacy of inheritance taxes, at least at confiscatory levels, used to be much more contentious than it appears to be today. Perhaps inherited wealth is thought to be a less important source of wealth in the dynamic conditions that characterize the current world economy. It may also be that the tax loopholes, distorted incentives, and downright disincentives created by steep inheritance taxes have persuaded modern liberals that chasing down large percentages of the wealth of the dead is not worth the effort. The left wing of modern liberalism remains undeterred, but it seems fair to say that those concerned with inequality of material condition have turned most of their attention in recent years to inequalities in human capital formation and away from inequality in inherited wealth in real assets; hence the emphasis on education and equal educational opportunities. We shall return to this concern in discussing the ownership of labor in the fourth section of this chapter.

Incident #6: Prohibition on harmful use. A prohibition on harmful uses of productive assets and personal property is widely agreed to among liberals of all persuasions. Tort law (and for a certain class of harms, criminal law) deals with violations of this prohibition. The current crisis in tort law finds liberals across the spectrum favoring different theories about how to assign liability for various harms relating to the use of productive assets and personal property.[3] If the other disputes detailed in this and the preceding chapters can be thought on analogy to the cold war, where participants have lined up on one of two sides, the crisis in tort law is more like World War II in the Balkans: unlikely alliances have formed to fight a common enemy (viz., contingency fee plaintiffs' attorneys), though as in the Balkans, the parties are fighting each other, even before the common enemy has been vanquished. The crisis will likely continue until a modern-day Tito of Torts emerges. Though classical and modern liberals have taken part in this debate, it has not broken down cleanly along left-right lines: no "party line" has clearly emerged on either side. This dispute, however, does have some indirect bearing on the question of the proper scope of government regulation, insofar as tort law is conceived of as an alternative to government regulation—an alternative often favored by classical liberals. More on this later.

Incident #7: The right to security. The right to security, or immunity from expropriation, has already been briefly touched on in connection with the right to physical possession. This immunity must be held against both private parties and government. The criminal and civil justice systems are supposed to enforce a right against expropriation by private persons. But what about the government? Since all liberals favor limited constitutional government, all favor, or should favor, some sort of constitutional prohibition on uncompensated takings by the state—at the minimum, uncompensated physical seizure of assets, subject to the exceptions provided by tort law. However, liberals of different persuasions have understood uncompensated takings more or less broadly. In his influential book *Takings,* the classical liberal legal theorist Richard Epstein (1985) has argued that much of the modern welfare-regulatory state is incompatible with the takings clause of the U.S. Constitution, which says that private property shall not be taken for public use without just compensation. For Epstein, forced one-way transfers and state-imposed regulations amount to the effective taking of private property, often not for public use and often with no compensation. Epstein's analysis (1985, 11–13) gets traction from two Lockean postulates: (1) private individuals have full, liberal ownership rights in their labor, productive assets, and personal property, and (2) the state derives all its powers from those whom it governs; number (2) implies that the state cannot do through public law what individuals cannot do through private law (the law of contracts and torts). Whatever the merits of Epstein's analysis of the Constitution, these Lockean postulates are contestable and would be rejected by modern liberals. The latter would claim that the state has prior partial claims on many of the incidents of ownership. This means that most of what Epstein regards as a taking for which compensation is owed is simply not a taking at all. Instead, the state is simply exercising its ownership rights. Only if it oversteps the bounds of its ownership rights, as in the case of taking physical possession, would compensation be owed.

Wherever the truth about takings lies, there is an important issue of principle at stake in this incident of ownership that is not reducible to the question of whether individuals have Lockean private property rights. Going back to Hume, and possibly to Hobbes, a common theme in the writings of classical liberals is that private property rights should be secure or stable and not open to constant redefinition by the state. In the twentieth century, this theme is never far from the surface in the works of classical liberals, whether in the worries about inflation voiced by Hayek (1972) and Friedman (1962, 51–55; 1978), Buchanan and Wagner's (1977) concerns about deficit spending, or in Epstein's (1985) analysis of the takings clause of the Fifth Amendment. All of the problems these authors call attention to can be seen as sources of instability of possession, or a diminution of security of possession, for owners of private property. Classical liberals believe that instability of possession is one of the truly great social evils. Paradoxically, it is one that government is supposed to solve and yet government is the main source of it, at least in the modern world. This of course is the modern version of the Hobbesian dilemma. On the other hand, modern liberals do not seem to take these concerns about instability of possession as seriously, perhaps because they believe that the political process, as it usually works on the ground, does not destabilize private property rights to the extent that it imposes significant social costs and burdens. They might argue that property owners have enough political power to keep the state in check. Moreover, they might argue, whatever costs it does impose are more than compensated for by the benefits of additional flexibility the government gets by eschewing adherence to the more stringent standards of stability of ownership rights that classical liberals favor. It is hard to characterize precisely the difference between the two camps on this issue except to say that classical liberals affirm, and modern liberals deny, that the modern welfare-regulatory state, conceived of as the sum total of encroachments or usurpations of the incidents of private ownership—or the exercise of public ownership rights—seriously compromises security of possession.

Incidents #8 and #9: Absence of term and liability to execution of debt. There is not much to be said about these two incidents of ownership. It is hard to see how any liberal could oppose either. If the other incidents of ownership were to be held for only a determinate length of time, owners of productive assets would have a strong incentive to consume the capital value of those assets before the latter reverted to the state or were otherwise reassigned.[4] Similar observations apply to personal property. Liability to execution of debt is an incident of ownership of productive assets and personal property. Whether they are owned by individuals or corporations, productive assets can be seized to satisfy debt obligations. On the other hand, liability to execution of debt is limited to the assets in question for the owners of corporations and thus serves to protect their personal property, as well as assets they own that are part of other limited liability organizations. If a corporation in which a person owns stock goes bankrupt, neither stock in other corporations nor the personal possessions of the owners can be seized. Indeed, it might be more perspicuous to characterize this incident as the right to pledge as security for debt. In any case, the reasons for having a system of limited liability are straightforward and widely accepted, at least since the late nineteenth century: if liability were unlimited, it would be extremely difficult to raise the huge amounts of capital required for some production processes, since investors would be exposing their entire wealth to the vagaries the marketplace and the competence of their hired hands. The efficiencies of bringing together large amounts of capital are manifest, and while there might be disagreements about some of the details of limited liability, there is no dispute between modern and classical liberals about the desirability of a regime of limited liability. Indeed, paradoxically, a system that allows large amounts of capital to be brought together under one legal roof provides better security for both creditors and potential tort plaintiffs than a system of unlimited liability, since, as just noted, in the absence of limited liability, it would be harder to amass the large amounts of capital embodied in large corporations—capital that serves to secure debt and that can be seized to execute adverse tort judgments. Also, in the absence of limited liability, creditors would have to go after personal assets, which are usually easier to hide.

The Right to Manage

The right to manage and the right of disposition are perhaps the two most important and contentious incidents of ownership. There are only a few disagreements between classical liberals and modern liberals about the right to manage personal property (which includes the right to use it), and there are no substantial disagreements about the right of disposition with regard to personal property. But, though there are some points of agreement about restrictions on each of these rights when it comes to productive assets, their differences are more consequential and systematic. Let us turn now to the first of these two important incidents of ownership of productive assets, the right to manage.

Management rights in productive assets can be defined as the rights exercised over productive assets in the production of goods and services. The exercise of these rights includes decisions about how to organize production, what production processes to use, and what contracts to enter into with suppliers, including labor contracts. Management rights in personal property, including land held for personal use, are essentially use rights. Both are constrained by the prohibition on harmful use, which was discussed above (incident #6). A general prohibition on harmful use is agreed upon by all sides, though as noted, there is a multisided dispute about how this prohibition should be understood in the context of tort law.

The twentieth century witnessed the dramatic growth of restrictions on the right to manage productive assets, restrictions that have typically taken the form of government regulations. Most of these restrictions fall into two categories: (1) regulations governing the employment relation and (2) environmental regulations.

Regulation of the Employment Relation

Up until the twentieth century, the employment relationship was pretty much at will, which meant that the employment contract was formed if and only if both sides voluntarily agreed to it, and either side could terminate the contract for good reason, bad reason, or no reason at all.[5] Employers—or more accurately, the market—set the terms and conditions of employment, which workers were at liberty to accept or reject. Since the early twentieth century, however, the state has imposed four basic kinds of limitations on freedom of contract in the employment relation: (1) mandatory terms or conditions of employment, (2) antidiscrimination laws, (3) occupational health and safety regulations, (4) regulations governing interactions among employers, workers, and unions. Let us consider each of these types of restrictions on the employment relation in turn.

Mandatory Terms or Conditions of Employment

One of the first modern limitations on the employment relation was instituted in 1913, when the first mandatory minimum wage law was passed at the state level. Legislation of this sort proliferated at the state level until in 1938 the Fair Labor Standards Act (29 U.S.C. § 201–219) established a minimum wage and required time and a half for overtime for all companies engaged in interstate commerce; it also restricted child labor. Over the years, the scope of the minimum wage laws has been broadened to cover an increasing percentage of the workforce, though the law still lists eleven categories of workers who are exempt from minimum wage laws, the most important of which includes most agricultural workers (29 U.S.C. § 213). Also over the years, the statutory minimum has been repeatedly raised. Other state-imposed limitations on the terms and conditions of employment are the Equal Pay Act of 1963 (29 U.S.C. § 206(d)), which mandates equal pay for equal work between men and women, the Family and Medical Leave Act of 1993 (29 U.S.C. § 2601 et seq.), which requires employers to grant workers family and temporary (unpaid) medical leave under certain circumstances, and the three main social insurance programs: unemployment insurance, Social Security, and workers' compensation.[6] Aside from Social Security, there are no other mandatory pension programs nor must employers provide employees with health insurance. However, in 1974, ERISA, the Employee Retirement Income Security Act (29 U.S.C. § 1001–1461) was passed. It imposed a host of reporting requirements and minimum standards on benefits of this sort that employers may choose to offer (Rothstein et al.1994, 635).

Antidiscrimination Laws

Beginning with the Civil Rights Act of 1964 (42 U.S.C. §2000e), the state began to regulate other aspects of the employment relationship. This was in large part motivated by heightened awareness of racial discrimination throughout society, particularly in employment. The act prohibited discrimination on the basis of race, color, religion, gender, or national origin. The law was later interpreted to prohibit sexual harassment in the workplace (*Meritor Savings Bank v. Vinson*, 477 U.S. 57, 65 (1980)). Other protected classes (older workers, disabled workers) were added later by the passage of additional laws, specifically the Age Discrimination in Employment Act of 1967 (29 U.S.C. § 621 et seq.) and the Americans with Disabilities Act of 1990 (42 U.S.C. § 12101). Nominally, the current state of the law continues to allow employment at will (or more articulated contractual arrangements), provided that employers make no decisions on the basis of "forbidden grounds," to use Epstein's apt phrase (Epstein 1992).[7] In practice, however, something like a doctrine of "just cause" has taken root for most workers. Decisions to hire, fire, demote, or reassign are subject to judicial review if an employee chooses to contest a decision on the basis of the many prohibitions stated in the various antidiscrimination statutes and articulated in case law. This means that most people who are terminated and/or believe they are otherwise ill-treated can initiate a lawsuit on the grounds of discrimination. To protect themselves from these suits or to prevail if they go to trial, firms have instituted policies and procedures designed to ensure that adverse actions taken against employees can be justified to third parties (viz., juries), which is essentially what a doctrine of just cause requires. Of course, injustices take place on both sides: unfit employees use the threat of lawsuits to practice extortion of employers, and employers successfully violate the explicit provisions of the law in their treatment of some of their employees, as well as the implicit requirement not to fire workers without just cause. The relative frequency of the opposite types of injustices is hard to estimate, since the law has shown almost no interest in employee abuse of antidiscrimination statutes, nor is it easy to see how it could.

Occupational Health and Safety Regulation

Originally, workplace injuries were handled through the tort system, but, as explained in the preceding chapter, that system became unworkable. In the early twentieth century, the political response to this problem was the introduction of various compulsory no-fault workers' compensation insurance programs. Workers' compensation programs have all the indicia of a social insurance program: rates are not determined by actuarial considerations alone, shortfalls are insured against by the state's power to tax, and participation is mandatory.[8] Risks to workers' health and safety were further addressed in a more purely regulatory manner by the Occupational Safety and Health Act of 1970 (29 U.S.C. § 651), which created the Occupational Safety and Health Administration. This agency had as its legislative mandate "to assure as far as possible every working man and woman in the nation safe and healthful working conditions" (29 U.S.C. § 651). Clearly, the primary purpose of the law was to protect the health and safety of workers, and it placed the burden of that protection squarely on employers. There is a separate agency, the Mine Safety and Health Administration, to deal with workplace health and safety issues in the extractive industries.

Regulations Governing Interactions among Employers, Workers, and Unions

Throughout the nineteenth century, the judiciary was hostile to "combinations" of workers, and employers used both the criminal law and civil law to thwart attempts at unionization. Beginning in the early twentieth century, however, the legislative and executive branches began to take a more favorable view of unions. The Norris-LaGuardia Act of 1932 barred the judiciary from issuing injunctions against unions and permitted workers to unionize and bargain collectively. The National Labor Relations Act of 1935, arguably the most important piece of labor legislation of the twentieth century, explicitly granted workers the right to unionize through secret ballot elections, and it prohibited various unfair labor practices by employers that could impede labor organizing. The act also created the National

Labor Relations Board, which was empowered to enforce the law and to oversee the process by which employees selected their collective bargaining representatives, if any. More generally, these laws defined the rights and responsibilities of employees, unions, and employers in their dealings with one another. Both of these acts were premised on the assumption that workers and the unions that might represent them were disadvantaged relative to employers because of differences in bargaining power. Through these statutes, the state used its power to level the playing field, so to speak, between labor and capital.[9]

What are the modern liberal and classical liberal attitudes toward the varied regulations of the employment relation? It is fair to say that the major regulatory initiatives in this area have been viewed favorably by modern liberals. These regulations have for the most part been created by modern liberal politicians in response to perceived problems with labor markets. It would be uncharitable to these politicians or their academic defenders, however, to attribute to them carte blanche support for each and every regulation and enforcement action that pours out of the vast regulatory bureaucracies charged with enforcing these laws. No serious modern liberal believes all such regulations are wise and sensible.[10] But, as a general proposition, modern liberals want to defend a system in which the state is a countervailing power to private interests and can intervene selectively to protect workers against perceived abuses by those who manage productive assets. Not every regulation will have its intended effects, and some will produce unintended negative consequences that outweigh their benefits, however costs and benefits are calculated. Moreover, modern liberals worry about the influence of private interests on the political process that produces regulation. Two forms of influence are particularly pernicious from their perspective: (1) campaign contributions from those who are regulated to politicians who can affect the regulatory environment, leading to regulatory capture, and (2) employment opportunities for regulators and the politicians who oversee them after their stint in government ends. From a modern liberal perspective, a crucial unresolved problem is how to limit these forms of influence in the context of a democratic system in which government regulation presents both enormous risks and lucrative opportunities for private interests. In this way, the same issues discussed in the last chapter concerning rate regulation and public ownership also come up in this type of regulation.

What about classical liberals? In general, they have opposed current regulatory limitations on management rights in the employment relation, though there are some exceptions. Classical liberals support the right of workers to organize and bargain collectively: this is simply a matter of freedom of contract. Whether they could support other elements of labor law governing firms and unions is doubtful, however, since they are reflexively suspicious of government attempts to "level the playing field" in any sport. The main classical liberal concern with unions is their sporadic use of violence and the threat of violence against employers and workers, both members and nonmembers. In principle, all liberals oppose the use of violence, so this can hardly be counted as a difference between the two forms of liberalism. Indeed, employers have also used violence against employees, and liberals of all persuasions would oppose that as well. As for child labor laws, they pose no particular problem for classical liberals, since children are incapable of consent, which is required for a labor contract. Classical liberals could also accept, at least in principle, regulations mandating the disclosure of known workplace health and safety hazards as a way of ensuring that the employment contract is genuinely voluntary, though this falls far short of what the Occupational Safety and Health Administration (OSHA) requires. Some of the regulations imposed by ERISA (e.g., reporting and funding requirements relating to employers' fiduciary obligations to employees) are designed to prevent fraud on the part of companies or pension managers and thus could conceivably be supported by classical liberals. Other elements of this complex act are intended to prevent harsh qualification and forfeiture rules and to prevent plan amendments that go back on previously made promises (Rothstein et al. 1994, 635). It is less clear that classical liberals could support these limitations on the terms and conditions of employment, except to the extent they could be conceived as preventing fraud or breach of contract.

However, classical liberals are inclined to oppose the rest of the modern liberal regulatory agenda on the employment relation, from mandated health and safety standards to antidiscrimination laws to minimum wage laws. Many economists with classical liberal sympathies and neoclassical methodological commitments see any regulation of the employment relation as a loss for both sides for the simple reason that it restricts bargaining on some of the terms and conditions of employment, which has the effect of prohibiting the consummation of mutually beneficial exchanges that might otherwise occur. For example, if some workers want the kind of job protection a just cause dismissal policy provides, they will gravitate to firms that offer it, and those who do not want it—at least at the price they would have to pay—receive a relative wage premium to do without it. For some firms, offering a just cause dismissal policy makes sense. Their workers acquire firm-specific human capital that would be at risk if the employer or his agents could act capriciously. Instituting such a policy would diminish the risks employees face in acquiring that capital, and this could be done at an acceptable cost (both financial and otherwise) to the firm, which makes it an efficient response to the situation. And, of course, unions frequently win some form of a just cause dismissal policy in negotiations with firms. But, some firms may find such a policy too costly to implement, if, for example, they hire workers with little human capital, bad work habits, and/or high turnover rates. By firing at will, they are able to offer more jobs at better pay than they otherwise would be able to do. What would emerge in labor markets not encumbered by a legal system that effectively requires a just cause dismissal policy is hard to predict in the abstract, but it would likely be quite variegated in regard to dismissal (as well as hiring and promotion) policies and the protections they afford against abusive or unjust treatment by management. Similar considerations apply to other restrictions on the employment contract mentioned above, such as family leave. At the end of the day, for these classical liberals, eliminating restrictions on the employment relation would bring a round of Pareto improvements for all at the Public Policy Tavern.

A more subtle basis for this classical liberal criticism of regulation of the employment relation starts with a definite, but usually unstated, skepticism about the large bargaining power differentials that modern liberals believe exist between businesses and workers. Bargaining power differentials are a function not of the absolute wealth of either party but of the relative opportunity cost of finding other trading partners. With the demise of the company town and with the increasingly extensive and intensive development of labor markets, bargaining power differentials have diminished compared to what they were in, say, the nineteenth century. Competitive pressures significantly constrain the range of terms and conditions within which companies can offer employment. What appears from the outside to be a take-it-or-leave-it offer by employers is in reality at most a minor modification on terms and conditions of employment dictated by market forces. On the classical liberal view, when labor markets are in approximate equilibrium, the market dictates to both employers and employees the terms and conditions of employment within a relatively narrow range. Both sides are free to propose, and actually do make, adjustments within that range along any of the relevant margins (e.g., pay, working conditions, job security, benefits), though it is usually the employer who proposes the adjustments because of the latter's more intimate knowledge of the market for labor. In conditions of labor market disequilibrium, however, more radical changes in pay, benefits, and working conditions are possible, changes that can be on balance positive or negative for workers, depending on the nature of the disequilibrium. In a recession or depression, the terms and conditions of employment will tend to deteriorate from the perspective of employees, whereas in boom times, employers will have to make concessions along various margins. In both cases, the market process forces adjustments in the employment relation, but those adjustments will vary along different margins and across firms and industries. On Hayek's view (1945; 1978), the benefits of this process are not limited to the satisfaction of preferences; the process itself is a "discovery procedure," which produces new social knowledge about what works and what does not, in this case, in the employment relation. Regulation that forecloses bargaining on these dimensions closes off a valuable source of experimentation and with it, the social knowledge that can be generated. In short, more is at stake than satisfying preferences.

Environmental Regulation

Another type of restriction on management rights is environmental regulations. Many of these impose restrictions on airborne emissions and effluents. They supplant traditional tort law dealing with environmental common law negative externalities (Morriss 2000, 130). Not all environmental regulation is intended as a codification of or supplement to the common law, however. There is also land use regulation. The most important land use regulatory regimes at the national level are wetlands regulation under section 404 of the Clean Water Act of 1977 (33 U.S.C. §1344) and regulation under the Endangered Species Act of 1973 (16 U.S.C. §1531 et seq.) both of which are intended to protect and enhance biodiversity.

Section 404 of the Clean Water Act has been interpreted to require landowners to get a permit from the Army Corps of Engineers if they intend to modify any wetland. This permitting process imposes an important limitation on private ownership rights, since the government can refuse to issue a permit for any use of the land at its discretion, or it can require expensive mitigation measures if the proposed modification of the property is to go forward (33 U.S.C. § 1344(c)). The Endangered Species Act does essentially the same thing for land on which endangered species of plants or animals are found. It prohibits "takings" of endangered species, though there are various exceptions, in particular, one that allows for "incidental takings." Getting approval for incidental takings is quite demanding, however.[11]

As noted in chapter 1, modern liberals are inclined to favor direct government regulatory action to restrict pollution, whereas classical liberals tend to believe that the problems to which regulation is offered as a solution can often (though not always) be more satisfactorily dealt with by better definition or enforcement of private property rights, or by the creation of structures that simulate the market, such as tradable emission credits. A second characteristic difference is that classical liberals are inclined to believe that most environmental regulation is best undertaken at the state, regional, and local level and not the national level, since the environmental problems they believe the government should deal with are mostly localized or tend to exhibit significant variation across the nation. These are not deep differences, however, but are merely differences about the best instrumentality to deal with pollution and the problems it causes.

Yet classical liberals are deeply skeptical of environmental regulations that cannot be construed as codifications of the common law (viz., the Endangered Species Act and section 404 of the Clean Water Act). They are inclined to see such regulations as nothing more than an attempt by some people to impose their values on others by partial confiscation of the latter's property rights. Modern liberals, by contrast, see this legislation as a way to realize important social values that cannot be realized through the market, or more generally, through a private ordering.

To summarize, there are profound and important disagreements between classical liberals and modern liberals about the extent to which government should limit management rights in productive assets. These differences could in principle be narrowed to the extent that freedom of contract, including the voluntariness of transactions, is at stake, or if the negative externalities would violate the common law or if genuine public goods problems are involved. Some of these ways to narrow the differences will be discussed in more detail in subsequent chapters. Many of the differences about this incident of ownership, however, appear to go deeper and to be more difficult to resolve. Modern liberals think there is a host of important problems that a private ordering simply cannot handle. At the deepest level, these differences about management rights reflect the same sort of difference discussed in the last chapter about who has a prior ownership claim on the income generated by property: the state, in its capacity as a representative of society as a whole, or private parties. If one believes, as modern liberals are inclined to believe, that the government has broad discretionary power to impose limitations on management rights without compensation, or if compensation is entirely a matter of legislative discretion, then they appear to be committed to the proposition that management rights in productive assets and personal property effectively reside with the state, at least in part and in the first instance. Of course, the state may choose not to arrogate those rights to itself or may choose to delegate the latter to private parties, but it also reserves the right to assert its rights, at its discretion, at any time, and without compensation. By contrast, classical liberals are inclined to believe that private parties, not the state, have these rights in the first instance, which means that so-called regulatory takings are prima facie illicit or at least compensable.

As an aside, it is worth pointing out that the modern liberal view about the locus of management rights (and the corresponding view about income rights) provides a philosophical justification for using cost-benefit analysis in government regulation. If society has management and income rights in productive assets in the first instance, cost-benefit analysis provides a good first approximation of what should be done. Suppose the government calculates that a workplace safety regulation R yields a benefit of $\$X$ and imposes a cost of $\$Y$, where $X \gg Y$. Though this may not be a conclusive reason for mandating R (other considerations may countervail), it would be a good prima facie reason for doing it. After all, it is a rational use of society's resources. Classical liberals, by contrast, are more suspicious of regulations based on cost-benefit analysis, since that approach assumes a position on the priority of management and income rights that they are not inclined to accept.[12]

The Right of Disposition

The right of disposition includes the right to alienate the thing, or more accurately, the right to alienate the *rights* to the thing, severally or jointly, on whatever terms are mutually agreeable with a buyer. It permits leases, mortgages, pooling of assets for business or personal use, as well as outright sale or gift, which transfers all the incidents of ownership to another party. Though there cannot be private ownership without some right of disposition, there are numerous disputes among liberals about what limitations should be placed on this right. The state imposes a host of limitations on the right to alienate consumer products and services. These limitations fall naturally into two categories: (1) regulation of the characteristics of consumer products and services, (2) regulation of the terms and conditions of trade. Let us consider each of these in turn.

Regulation of the Characteristics of Consumer Products and Services

Much health and safety regulation outside of the employment context comes under this heading. The safety characteristics of consumer automotive products and aircraft are regulated by the National Highway Traffic Safety Administration and the Federal Aviation Administration, respectively. The Food and Drug Administration (FDA) heavily regulates medical products and devices, and the Consumer Product Safety Commission (CPSC) regulates the safety characteristics of other consumer products. Food production and distribution are regulated by the Agriculture Department and the FDA. The characteristics of goods judged to be inherently dangerous, such as firearms, explosives, pesticides, tobacco, and alcohol, have also been subjected to extensive regulation by various government agencies. Occupational licensure could also be conceived of as a form of regulation of the characteristics of consumer services in the sense that providers of many professional services cannot sell those services without the blessing of the state in the form of an occupational license. Occupational licensure will be discussed in the second following section of this chapter as a restriction on the ownership of labor.

Other consumer product regulations are not directly health or safety related. Health insurers have to offer coverage of certain conditions and procedures, and health maintenance organizations are subject to an increasing array of government-imposed mandates on their policies and procedures.[13] Banks are required to insure deposits up to $100,000 through the Federal Deposit Insurance Corporation (FDIC); motor vehicles have to meet fuel economy standards, and so on.

Regulation of the Terms and Conditions of Trade

Very often the government does not mandate or prohibit the characteristics of certain consumer products and services, but it does specify the terms or conditions under which they may be sold. This encompasses a broad array of government regulations, which can be grouped under three headings: (1) regulation of advertising, (2) regulation of marketing, and (3) price controls.

Regulation of Advertising

Although the Federal Trade Commission was originally created to prevent businesses from unfairly competing with one another, passage of the Wheeler-Lea Act in 1938 (15 U.S.C. § 41–58) gave the FTC regulatory authority to act directly on behalf of consumers by prohibiting deceptive advertising. The FTC also has other duties, such as scrutinizing potential mergers for compliance with antitrust laws, which it shares with the Justice Department, but it is the primary agency responsible for policing advertising at the federal level. State attorneys general also have a role to play in regulating advertising through their consumer affairs divisions.

Regulation of Marketing

Marketing regulation includes a variety of mandatory disclosure requirements, that is, requirements that demand that sellers disclose certain information about a company or its products to buyers. The FTC was also given the authority to enforce laws requiring "truth in packaging" and other labeling requirements (15 U.S.C. § 1451–1461), except for food and medical products, which are handled by the FDA (21 U.S.C. § 343, 352). In 1975, the Magnuson-Moss Act (15 U.S.C. § 2301–2312) gave the FTC regulatory authority over warranties, and it also gave the FTC the authority to issue trade regulations for specific industries, that is, it can write rules designating certain marketing practices as unfair and/or deceptive and thus prohibited (15 U.S.C. § 45). Securities regulation is mostly about disclosure. The two main pieces of legislation are the Securities Act of 1933, which mandates reporting and disclosure requirements for companies issuing stock (either existing publicly traded companies or IPOs), and the Securities Exchange Act of 1934, which regulates what happens after stock is issued.[14] It requires that the financial statements of publicly traded firms be periodically audited, controls the solicitation of proxies, prohibits market manipulation and insider trading, regulates the stock exchanges, and gives the Securities and Exchange Commission the authority to oversee brokers. The Trust Indenture Act of 1939 provides parallel regulations for debt instruments. Firms cannot market their products without abiding by the rules specified in all of the applicable laws. The overarching purpose of nearly all securities regulation is to maintain the integrity of the fiduciary relationship between a firm and its clients, especially individual investors, by forcing providers to disclose materially relevant information to their clients.[15]

Marketing regulations can also be taken to include other regulations intended to ensure the soundness or solvency of businesses that have a fiduciary relationship with their customers, notably, banks and insurance companies. Banks and insurance companies are in the business of selling promises, and banking and insurance regulations are intended to ensure that those promises are kept. The cornerstone of banking regulation is federally guaranteed deposit insurance. It was introduced in the aftermath of the Great Depression, during which bank runs resulted in the failure of approximately 4,000 banks (Hall 1993, 55). Because their deposits are insured, depositors are less likely to panic and start a run on the banks in response to some exogenous shock (e.g., war, depression, or severe recession). Other regulations in the banking industry include chartering, capital requirements, periodic examination by bank examiners, audit requirements, lending restrictions (on, e.g., risky investments, loans to bank officers), and liquidity requirements (Hall 1993, 61–70). All are designed to ensure the soundness or solvency of banks, which in turn is supposed to prevent runs on banks and to minimize the chances that the FDIC will have to bail out depositors.

A similar rationale lies behind regulation in the insurance industry. The main purpose of insurance regulation is to ensure the financial solvency of the firms so that they can pay claims to policyholders who suffer losses.[16] To this end, firms must meet certain capital requirements, and their investment portfolios are subject to regulatory scrutiny. Rate regulation, which is more concerned with imposing floors rather than ceilings, is also justified in these terms.[17] The theory behind rate regulation in the insurance industry is that unrestrained price competition (on the price of premiums) would lead insurance companies to take unacceptable risks of insolvency in their portfolio management, which could effectively leave consumers without coverage when an adverse event occurs.

Price Controls

Price controls are localized or general restrictions on the movements of prices and wages. They may be temporary or relatively permanent.[18] Sometimes, these controls take the form of price floors, as is often the case when the favored group is some assemblage of producers, such as farmers. Other times, they take the form of price ceilings, which prohibit vendors from selling their products for more than a state-mandated maximum without the government's consent. Rent control is a classic example of the latter. Comprehensive price controls, while they may not include every product or service for sale on the market, typically control wages as well as prices of most consumer and producer goods.

What are modern liberal attitudes toward these regulations of the right of disposition? Modern liberals tend to favor regulation of the characteristics of consumer goods and services. Consumers are thought to be unable to make an informed judgment about the health and safety characteristics of pharmaceuticals and a wide array of other consumer products, which puts them at a disadvantage in dealing with purveyors of these goods. As is customary in situations like this, modern liberals favor calling in the regulatory road graders and bulldozers to level the playing field. "Leveling the playing field" is an important concern of modern liberalism, which finds philosophical expression in the latter's extended encounter with equality as a moral and political concept. What they seek in this context is rough or approximate equality of bargaining power. Bringing about equality of bargaining power, or more accurately, a reduction in the inequality of bargaining power, between consumers and purveyors of goods and services serves a more straightforward utilitarian end for modern liberalism. To put that end in the language of interpersonal comparisons of utilities (which for orthodox economists is the equivalent of Jews or Muslims eating pork), some government interventions are a means by which the interests of consumers can be advanced more than interests of producers or vendors are set back. Consumer product regulation, then, can be seen as a way of preventing or ameliorating what might be called "relative harm" to consumers, typically by constraining options that vendors may offer consumers. This way of thinking, of course, leaves the door open for interventions that advance the interests of vendors or producers more than they harm the interests of consumers, and liberal politicians sometimes support such interventions on behalf of vendor or producer groups to correct some perceived imbalance in the other direction. These reasons for regulation, whether or not they are expressed in terms of interpersonal comparisons of utilities, are not of course reasons that classical liberals could accept, but they are often what modern liberals say to each other when their economist friends are not in the room.

Modern liberals also favor consumer product regulations that are intended to ameliorate large-scale social problems that the market creates, or at least cannot solve. For example, fuel economy standards for motor vehicles are defended on the grounds that they ameliorate the problem of dwindling petroleum reserves or the problem of undue dependence on foreign suppliers, or environmental rapacity. More will be said about these reasons in chapters 5 and 6 under the heading of public goods.

What about the regulation of advertising and marketing? Here, too, modern liberals are inclined to favor these types of regulation and for the same range of reasons they support mandating or prohibiting the characteristics of consumer goods and services: regulation can level the playing field by ameliorating information asymmetries between businesses and consumers, and/or it can prevent relative harm to consumers. As in the case of employment regulation, it is not necessary to ascribe to modern liberals support for each and every regulation the government promulgates; instead, they believe that, as a general proposition, the state should be able to intervene in transactions between consumers and businesses for a wide variety of purposes; indeed, it seems that the only constraints on reasons for regulation would be those imposed by respect for fundamental political and personal rights. This suggests that the right of disposition is held by the state in the first instance, which it delegates to particular government bureaucracies and to the nominal owners as it sees fit.

The modern liberal attitude on price controls is more difficult to discern. They have supported sporadic or isolated limitations on the terms of trade, as in rent control, usury laws, and excess profits taxes on industries (such as the oil industry in the 1970s) where extraordinary profits accrue because of exogenous shocks to the economic system that harm consumers. The most important price control for modern liberals is undoubtedly the minimum wage law, which sets a floor on the price of wages. Modern liberals have generally favored all these measures on the grounds that the state is serving as a check on private economic power or perhaps because such measures prevent or diminish what they regard as unjust enrichment. Comprehensive wage and price controls are another matter, however, and for reasons to be explained below, it is hard to find support for them among either modern liberals or classical liberals.

What is the classical liberal attitude toward the various forms of regulation of the right of disposition detailed above? The answer is not straightforward. As a general proposition, they have opposed the regulation of the characteristics of consumer services and products on the grounds that such regulations close off avenues of mutually beneficial exchange, unjustifiably cause transfers of wealth from some groups to others, or violate natural rights. Consumers cannot purchase many products without a host of safety devices they may not want at a price they may not otherwise be willing to pay. Mandated coverage of politically popular medical conditions raises the cost of health insurance to levels that prevent some people from purchasing insurance coverage who otherwise would get it, and it enriches provider groups by increasing the demand for their services. If firms offering pensions are forced to use the same payment schedules for men and women, despite the fact that women live longer than men, this forces a wealth transfer from men to women (Epstein 1985, 312–14; 1992, 320–21). If the state of Florida forbids insurance companies from canceling homeowners' insurance policies in areas vulnerable to hurricanes, as it did in the aftermath of Hurricane Andrew in 1992 (LeComte and Gahagan 1998; Moss 1999), rates have to be raised to other homeowners or to policyholders in other lines of insurance the company offers, or resources are taken from shareholders, thereby causing some people to subsidize the housing decisions of others. These and countless other regulations are thinly disguised redistributive programs in which the government plays musical chairs with wealth and income created in the private sector. As for consumer product health and safety regulation, classical liberals tend to oppose both on the grounds that the market would produce a better package of health and safety characteristics, attractively priced, than the state-mandated alternative.

Let us turn now to a consideration of classical liberal attitudes toward the regulation of advertising and marketing, and toward price controls. In principle, classical liberals could agree with modern liberals about much of what the FTC is supposed to do, though perhaps on different grounds. Modern liberals see this type of regulation as a counterweight to the power of business vis-à-vis consumers. Classical liberals, by contrast, could support at least some of this regulation on the grounds that deceptive advertising and marketing practices are fraudulent. The problem is that this agency has been notably ineffective in fulfilling its mandate for a variety of reasons (Stone 1977, 206–8). One is that its major enforcement tool—the cease and desist order—has little deterrent effect, especially if the firm can stop the offending practice and introduce a new and different version of the product or service in short order or if the firm is a small operation that can flee by night. A more robust enforcement tool, however, would require even more procedural safeguards than currently exist, further slowing down the process. A second problem is that the fact-finding necessary to enter such an order can be a drawn-out and complex affair, which can be challenged by the respondent at virtually every phase. Finally, there is an inherent problem in determining what counts as deception for at least two reasons. First, deception is a relative notion, in other words, who must be judged deceived for a practice to be counted as deceptive? Is it the knowledgeable consumer, the reasonable person, the person of average intelligence, or the real dolt? The FTC has taken the attitude, affirmed by the Supreme Court, that no child-like person should be left behind.[19] Consequently, they have opted for what in the business is sometimes called the "Mortimer Snerd Standard" that protects the least advantaged in the related categories of intelligence and good sense (Stone 1977, 181). Second, even if a more defensible standard could be spelled out, the terse, attention-grabbing character of modern advertising makes it easy to find something deceptive in almost any advertisement. Since enforcement authority must be exercised with discretion, this implicitly gives the bureaucrats who enforce the law coercive power that can be, indeed must be, exercised arbitrarily—always a bad thing from a classical liberal perspective.

It may be that there is no "party line" among classical liberals regarding government regulation of advertising. The relative ineffectiveness of the FTC in curbing deceptive practices is beyond dispute. Where differences emerge is on the question of what should be done about that. Classical liberals might favor abolishing the FTC and allowing state and local enforcement of the fraud statutes to handle most of the problems the FTC is supposed to address, leaving only a fragment of the former agency to deal with interstate fraud. Modern liberals, however, might favor giving the agency more powerful enforcement tools, an infusion of new resources, and fewer procedural safeguards to protect respondent firms. But these speculative differences are fundamentally pragmatic and do not reflect any principled difference on either side about the proper role of government in dealing with the problem of deceptive practices. Both believe that there is in principle a role for the government in dealing with deceptive practices, but both should be able to recognize that there are important limitations on what the government can do. This might be as far as reasoned agreement can go.

The regulation of marketing practices presents a mixed bag for classical liberalism. Numerous government agencies enforce a variety of mandatory labeling requirements for consumer and producer goods, from prescription drugs and hazardous chemicals to that infamous tag on mattresses that cannot be removed under penalty of law. It might be thought that classical liberals could support such laws on the grounds that ensuring the disclosure of this information is a necessary condition for the transactions in question to be voluntary, but matters are not that simple. The development and dissemination of information has costs, and in principle more information can always be provided. Consumers may rationally choose (i.e., voluntarily choose) to remain ignorant of some features of products if it costs too much to get that information. The strict libertarian view is that of caveat emptor, which means that as long as the seller does not misrepresent the characteristics of what he or she is selling, the transaction should be counted as voluntary. Of course, determining what counts as misrepresentation in advertising is not straightforward, especially since there can be misrepresentations of omission as well as commission. So the question recurs: How much and what kind of information must be provided for a purchasing decision to be truly or genuinely voluntary? One plausible classical liberal standard would be the buyer's reasonable expectations about what the seller should disclose. Those expectations are in turn shaped by the common law and by statutory law. However, the common law is the source of the charge of "failure to warn" that plaintiffs' attorneys have used to dynamite the vaults of corporations and their insurance companies when consumers exercise their right to act foolishly. Statutory law is clearer about what is required, but what is at issue is whether classical liberals could or should support statutory laws that mandate product labeling, at least in the case of health and safety information. A case can be made that they should. As was noted in chapter 1, some federal courts have been moving toward the view that common law tort cases based on a claim of "failure to warn" should be dismissed if the defendant has complied with federal labeling regulations. Widespread adoption of this rule would enhance the stability of property rights in corporate assets, since it would greatly reduce the effectiveness of one of the main tools used by corporate safecrackers from the plaintiffs' bar.

Continued enforcement of non-health and safety-related labeling requirements (e.g., truth in lending laws, regulations of warranties, etc.) might be justified to classical liberals on the grounds that these laws have shaped people's reasonable expectations about what information they will be given, so that if these laws were repealed and subsequently corporations failed to provide the information that they had previously provided, that would make the affected transactions nonvoluntary in some way. Or at least that would be arguable in a common law court, which creates the same type of problem that can be avoided by health and safety-related labeling regulations. In other words, whether or not any of these labeling regulations were a good idea in the first place, there is a case for retaining them that classical liberals could accept: they set the standard for what information sellers can be expected to reveal about their products to make the transactions voluntary and thus (in theory, anyway) to diminish the number of legal claims that may be brought against manufacturers and vendors. This, of course, leaves open the question of the basis on which such laws might be modified, that is, what additional requirements might be imposed or what existing requirements might be dropped. Those problems, however, would seem to be addressable outside of the confines of the debate between modern liberals and classical liberals; here might be a useful place for cost-benefit analysis.

It might be thought that a parallel argument could be made for mandating not just health and safety information but health and safety characteristics of consumer products themselves. On this proposal, if consumer products met government-specified health and safety standards, then the courts could dismiss common law tort actions brought on the grounds of defect in design. The problem with this proposal is that classical liberals would reasonably object that constraining product design by government safety standards would impose too high an opportunity cost, in terms of lost innovations, for the marginal benefit of increased safety for consumers and increased security of possession that would come from restraining the pillaging of the Cossacks of the plaintiffs' bar. Besides, it is impractical for the government to develop health and safety standards for all consumer products. The Consumer Product Safety Commission is essentially a reactive body, which responds to safety problems after the fact. The only consumer products that require prior approval are prescription drugs. The idea that one could require that all consumer products meet the same sort of safety standards that prescription drugs meet is pure fantasy.

What about disclosure requirements in the securities industry? Once again, a simple appeal to requirements of voluntariness will not suffice. Purchasers may choose to be rationally ignorant of some of the details of an investment venture that its promoters do not want to reveal, perhaps because it would alert competitors to the details of a business plan. Edward Soule clearly articulates (without endorsing) the libertarian case against disclosure requirements:

> The libertarian objection could champion the issuer and note the risks, competitive or otherwise, of publicly disseminating proprietary information. Such risks could discourage otherwise qualified companies from accessing the public capital markets... it imposes the costs of compliance on businesses without regard to their wrongdoing or the exigencies of individual cases. (2003, 114–15)

What makes this case more difficult than consumer product labeling is that the financial and opportunity costs of disclosure in the securities industry are not trivial. The disclosure requirements of the Securities Act of 1933 are quite burdensome and expensive and, as Soule points out, public disclosure of proprietary information may prevent successful ventures from getting off the ground. But, if disclosure requirements were eliminated, the number of shareholder suits against promoters of investment ventures would likely explode, as disaffected investors sought to recoup their investments from failed ventures through the courts. Similar considerations apply to the disclosure regulations imposed by the 1934 Securities Exchange Act. Libertarians tend to ignore the civil litigation opportunity costs of more free-wheeling securities markets. In light of all of these considerations, it is easy to see how classical liberals might reasonably disagree among themselves about the wisdom of securities regulation. On the one hand, securities regulation might be justified preemptively, that is, on the grounds that it preempts more violations of rights than it causes. On the other hand, that might not be the case. Sophisticated institutional investors might set the standard for disclosure, without the force of law, at a level close to what currently exists, and it is likely that intermediaries would help the individual investor evaluate investment risks, as they currently do. Another alternative, canvassed by Romano (2002), would allow the various states to compete in a market for securities regulation.

Banking and insurance regulation have slightly different rationales, both from securities regulation and from each other. Both aim at ensuring the solvency of firms in the respective industries, though the ultimate rationale for ensuring solvency is different in the two cases. On the face of it, the deposit insurance requirement looks to be the kind of rank paternalism that sets libertarian teeth on edge. Consumers cannot be trusted to make decisions about where to deposit their money and what level of insurance, if any, they should have for those deposits. However, while consumer protection is one reason for state-provided deposit insurance, it is not the only one nor indeed is it the one most insisted on by its proponents. The most important rationale for deposit insurance, and by implication for most of the rest of the current banking regulatory regime, is the avoidance, or better, the management of, *systemic risk*. Allen and Herring define systemic risk in this context as

> the risk of a sudden, unanticipated event that would damage the financial system to such an extent that economic activity in the wider economy would suffer. Such shocks may originate inside or outside the financial sector and may include the sudden failure of a major participant in the financial system; a technological breakdown at a critical stage of settlements or payments systems; or a political shock such as an invasion or the imposition of exchange controls in an important financial center. Such events can disrupt the normal functioning of financial markets and institutions by destroying the mutual trust that lubricates most financial transactions. (2001, 6)

Successful management of systemic risk has the characteristics of a public good in that it is jointly consumed and nonexcludable. Since classical liberals can accept a role for government in providing public goods, state-provided deposit insurance (and the other banking regulations that go with it) may be justifiable on these grounds for many classical liberals. But, though classical liberals admit that there is a role for the state in providing public goods, they maintain that the state should take on this task only if it cannot be provided in some way through the private sector. For these classical liberals, then, the crucial question is whether systemic risk could be effectively managed by the private sector, that is, by private deposit insurance. The answer is unclear.

Fundamentally, the problem is one of correlated risks, that is, situations in which the risk of an adverse event for one policyholder is not independent of the risk of that adverse event for other policyholders. Floods and earthquakes are held up as the classic examples in casualty insurance of correlated risks. In regard to banking, the worry is that there could be some exogenous shock to the financial system, such as a deep recession, which would cause a run on banks and consequent bank failures that private deposit insurance could not staunch. This in turn would exacerbate the very problems that caused the bank runs in the first place, as depositors lunge for their funds.

But is this really true? Is the private sector incapable of handling correlated risks in the banking industry?[20] Although risks are often described as correlated relative to a particular kind of adverse event (e.g., a flood, an earthquake, a depression), that is not really accurate for insurance purposes. A correlated risk is defined relative to an adverse event *and* a set of policyholders whose policies are held by a particular company. If there is only one private insurance company for that sort of adverse event, the problem would indeed be difficult to avoid. Assuming that there would be a number of private deposit insurance firms, the problem of correlated risks is for each such firm to find a way to limit its exposure to bank runs for the set of depositors they insure. This might be accomplished in a variety of ways: reinsurance is an obvious first step in mitigating risk. In a reinsurance contract, an insurance company buys insurance from another company to cover their obligations to policyholders over a certain amount. Also, and perhaps more importantly, private deposit insurance companies might limit the number of policies they write for banks in certain geographical areas (up to and including countries) or they might limit lending by member banks in certain sectors of the economy, or they might impose other requirements on member institutions that make them less vulnerable to exogenous shocks to the financial system.

Whether or not a system of private deposit insurance would work is hard to say in the absence of a more detailed model and indeed empirical observation of a functioning system. One would have to know if regulations comparable to what currently exists might be imposed on banks by private deposit insurance policies. Arguably, they would be. Under the current system, the fact that taxpayers are liable to cover deposits in the event of a bank failure is responsible for the proctological character of current banking regulation (e.g., chartering, periodic examination by bank examiners, liquidity and capital requirements, etc.). It is likely that private deposit insurance companies would impose similar demands on banks whose deposits they insure. The state of the U.S. banking system on the eve of the Great Depression is of limited predictive value as a model because of the enormous changes that have occurred in the banking industry in the intervening years. Indeed, it is likely that the current international banking system (conceived of in abstraction from U.S. government regulation) is more robust than the U.S. banking system was on the eve of the Great Depression, and it is not obvious that the private sector could not successfully manage systemic risk via private deposit insurance.

However, state-mandated deposit insurance has a number of advantages that their private counterparts would not have. Most importantly, they have—or have access to—the power to tax and the power to print money to make up for shortfalls. Libertarians would find this outrageous, since, from their perspective, it would be like saying that one's insurance company is on a firmer financial base than its rivals because it employs bank robbers and counterfeiters who can make sure that all claims are paid. But, an advantage is an advantage, and state-backed deposit insurance has it. In addition, the FDIC does not itself pay taxes, which a private deposit insurance company would have to do. Taken together, these are not insignificant advantages, and on the face of it, they appear to make systemic risk more manageable by state-owned and operated entities. However, state-run deposit insurance has its own problems. As with all "last resort" government programs, there is a moral hazard problem in encouraging the very behavior one is insuring against. Some banks are too big to fail, and those who manage those banks know that—and they know that the government knows that. As the savings and loan debacle of the late 1980s made clear, moral hazards can be quite expensive. In sum, for classical liberals, deposit insurance and the rest of the current banking regulatory regime is like securities regulation in the sense that there would be reasonable (internal) disagreement about whether or not this is a form of government regulation they can accept.

Insurance regulation is more strictly a consumer protection measure and raises no new issues that do not come up in securities regulation. The proximate purpose of insurance regulation is to ensure the solvency of insurance companies so that claims can be satisfied even if the companies' investments are not performing well. The worry is that if rate regulation and reserve and portfolio requirements were removed, a combination of adverse selection and moral hazard problems would lead to a crisis in the insurance industry. Firms that take big risks with their level of reserves and their investment portfolio would be able to charge significantly less in premiums. This would cause other firms to follow suit; sooner or later, and probably sooner, a crisis would ensue. Classical liberals might object that private sector solutions to these problems would emerge, for example, reinsurance companies could take the place of regulators or independent bodies could rate insurance companies (which they currently do anyway). Then the issue turns on a comparative evaluation of state regulation and private regulation. As public choice scholars have taught, it is naive to suppose that government regulators act in the public interest whereas private companies would readily sacrifice the public interest on the altar of greed. But, the state does have the power to tax, which could be used to bail out policyholders and/or tighten requirements, if push comes to shove. The ultimate question for classical liberals, then, is whether or not this is a good thing overall. This seems to be a matter about which classical liberals could reasonably disagree among themselves. One possibility, which cannot be explored in any detail here, is that the extant securities, banking, and insurance regulatory regimes were a good idea at one time but are no longer necessary or desirable, as these industries have become more complex, sophisticated, and capable of self-regulation. Correspondingly, government regulation is fraught with problems of regulatory capture and moral hazard. So, maybe it is time to pull the plug on these regulatory regimes. But maybe not.

Classical liberals have consistently opposed price controls, either on Lockean grounds or the more consequentialist grounds implicit in Hayek's groundbreaking articles on the information-transmitting properties of prices (Hayek 1937; 1945; 1978). Basically, Hayek's idea is that the price system is a decentralized information processing network that informs disparate actors of supply and demand conditions that affect them. When prices change, that signifies changes in underlying economic conditions that economic actors must adjust to. Moreover, changes of greater or lesser significance are occurring all the time. Entrepreneurial profit comes from being among the first to recognize and act on these changes. The price system, activated by myriad entrepreneurs seeking to move resources from lower valued uses to higher valued uses, plays a central role in coordinating activities among all participants in a market economy. The imposition of wage and price controls amounts to pulling the plug on this very complex and sophisticated information processing system. Economic actors stumble around in the dark, since they are deprived of the information needed to coordinate properly the production and distribution of goods and services in a changing world. The inevitable consequences include shortages, queuing, and other logs, boulders, and even dams in the stream of commerce. Moreover, once in place, price controls are very hard to remove because of political pressures from those who would be hurt in the short term if controls were to be lifted. As time passes, resource allocation of inputs, as well as the price of goods subject to price controls, becomes increasingly irrational. Furthermore, on the classical liberal view, price controls effect an illegitimate transfer of income or wealth from some groups to others and, more ominously, enhance the power of state officials charged with administering the relevant rules and regulations; this in turn leads firms to make substantial investments in the political process as a form of rent-seeking.

In recent decades, the classical liberal point of view on the inadvisability of comprehensive wage and price controls seems to have carried the day. There is about as much unanimity in the economics profession as one can reasonably expect that the remedy of wage and price controls in a market economy is the modern counterpart to the bloodletting protocols that used to be practiced by physicians. Like bloodletting, wage and price controls might have beneficial short-term psychological effects, but they always inflict a variety of serious iatrogenic maladies on the economy that far outweigh whatever benefits they might provide. This fact now seems to be more widely recognized among modern liberal elites beyond the economics profession (though it is usually forgotten in a crisis), and of course there is the exception for the minimum wage law noted above. It is difficult to find support for comprehensive wage and price controls among liberals of any stripe these days.

Antitrust law seems to fall between restrictions on management rights and rights of disposition and could be counted as either type of regulation. Recall from chapter 2 that antitrust law attempts to prevent monopoly pricing and unfair competitive practices, and it gives the government (the FTC and the Department of Justice) the authority to regulate mergers and acquisitions. Unfair competitive practices can be grouped under the headings of exclusionary practices and collusive practices. Firms engage in exclusionary practices (volume discounts, tie-in selling, etc.) as a way of binding themselves to their suppliers or customers. Collusive practices include collusion on prices (price-fixing, which is a form of monopoly pricing) and price maintenance agreements, which require retailers to sell a product at a certain price.[21] Mergers are of three types: horizontal (merging of firms that sell the same product), vertical (either backward into supply or forward into distribution or retail), and conglomerate (where divisions have no apparent relation to one another). The rationale for regulating mergers is a theory whose central idea is that the degree of concentration in an industry is positively correlated with monopoly pricing. As noted in chapter 2, modern liberals have been inclined to favor all the antitrust laws, whereas classical liberals have been inclined to oppose them, though the latter sometimes accept a prohibition on collusion.[22]

As this section has demonstrated, some regulations of the right of disposition, such as those designed to reduce the incidence of fraud, are arguably consistent with classical liberal principles, but most are not. As in the case of management rights, the modern liberal view seems to be that the state antecedently has the right of disposition, or at least a limited or partial right of disposition, with respect to what is otherwise private property. On this view, government regulation of the right of disposition is in reality the exercise of the state's rights, or more exactly society's rights, to determine the conditions under which things are alienated. What this means in concrete terms is that the government has broad discretionary power over the terms and conditions of disposition, which it can exercise without compensation. One of the clearest examples of this is rent control, which is always imposed without compensation. Classical liberals, of course, deny this priority to the claims of the state, acting as agent for society. Two of their complaints about this broad discretionary power are that it permits, and indeed requires, that state officials exercise arbitrary power, and second, by making property rights relatively ill-defined, the affected parties have strong incentives to influence government policy in ways that all liberals find objectionable. This, of course, is a key element in the public choice critique of the modern welfare-regulatory state.

Ownership of Labor and Human Capital

From an analytical point of view, the restrictions on the employment relation discussed in the section on the ownership of productive assets can equally well be conceived of as restrictions on individuals' ownership of labor and/or one's human capital. Workers are legally forbidden from entering into labor contracts that require them to accept risks or any other terms and conditions of employment that the government has deemed unacceptable. However, it is more useful to conceive of these as restrictions on management rights and rights of disposition with respect to (nonhuman) productive assets because enforcement actions are directed at employers, not employees. Are there any restrictions on the labor contract that are directed at workers?

Perhaps the main one is occupational licensure. This is direct state control over one's capacity to labor. Unless one has been licensed by the state, one cannot practice many professions. Modern occupational licensure has its roots in the medieval guild system of England and Western Europe.[23] Except for a brief period in the early nineteenth century, the state has typically conceived of the practice of professions as a privilege it grants and not a right individuals antecedently have. In the second half of the nineteenth century, modern occupational licensure as we know it was born. The American Medical Association was a driving force in getting states to enact mandatory licensing laws for physicians. By 1900 every state had some form of licensure for physicians. Occupational licensure continued to grow throughout the twentieth century as more specialized professions came into existence, and professional associations lobbied states to pass licensure laws that would be overseen by these very associations. Attorneys, accountants, engineers, architects, hairdressers, plumbers, and electricians, to name just a few, now all require licenses. Specialties within professions, notably medical specialties, are also highly regulated by a form of occupational licensure. To be sure, not all professions are regulated. Journalism and the ministry, for example, could not be regulated professions without violating the right to freedom of speech and the right to freedom of worship, respectively. The same is true of teaching and research careers in higher education, though most primary and secondary school teachers are licensed. One need not have a master's of business administration to run a business, but entry into the upper levels of management in corporations of any size is often through regulated professions such as engineering, finance, law, or accounting. According to Morris Kleiner, "data from the Labor Market Information Survey and the 2000 census showed that the number of workers in occupations licensed by states in 2000 grew by 11 percent during the past 15 years to approximately 20% of the workforce" (Kleiner 2006, 1).

As in most other restrictions on property rights, modern liberals have supported occupational licensure, though this support has been more prominent among practicing politicians than academic theorists. The usual proffered rationale is that it is hard for consumers of professional services to evaluate the skills and training of providers. In an unregulated environment, so the argument goes, the informational asymmetries between professionals and consumers would translate into power differentials that would systematically disadvantage consumers at the expense of providers. Bad outcomes can be catastrophic, ranging from death in the case of physicians to multiple bad hair days in the case of hairdressers. Even though the state cannot eliminate bad outcomes, it can reduce them by correcting the informational asymmetries and diminish the consequent power imbalances by means of licensing requirements, which, in theory at least, assure minimum standards of competence.[24]

Classical liberals have generally opposed occupational licensure and not merely on the grounds that the state puts the professions in charge of disciplining their own. Economists with classical liberal sympathies have made a case that occupational licensure has been essentially a barriers-to-entry device that the professions have persuaded the state to erect to restrict the number of practitioners so as to drive up the cost of the service and thus the income of providers.[25] Another theme in this and related literature is that the market can produce institutional mechanisms to deal with informational asymmetries between providers and consumers. For example, as managed care has become the norm in medical practice, consumers no longer hire physicians. HMOs serve as their agents and are fully capable of evaluating the credentials of their physician-employees. Private certification agencies, classical liberals believe, could also take up some of the slack that would exist if government got out of this business. The basic idea is that if there is a need for a (nonpublic) good or service, the market can and would provide it—if not right away, then after a time, through a trial-and-error process whose ultimate outcome is hard to predict but that will likely produce a better product (service) than state regulation. Classical liberals are correct to insist that the question is always one of comparative institutional analysis, so that it is not enough to point to some need that government regulation meets; it is also necessary to explain how or why that need is better met through government regulation than through the market, or more generally, through a private ordering. This puts a burden of proof on modern liberal supporters of occupational licensure, but the burden is the same for classical liberal opponents of existing occupational licensure regimes.

The above account of occupational licensure covers restrictions on management (use) rights and the right of disposition with respect to the ownership of labor and human capital. What about the other incidents of ownership of labor? With whom do they reside and what sort of restrictions on them are viewed as legitimate by modern and classical liberals? There is no serious dispute about the right of exclusive physical possession, prohibition of harmful use, and the right to security of possession; these reside with the person in question and are understood in the same way as they are in regard to other forms of property. Nor is there any dispute about the proposition that, in general, people should be able to pledge their labor to secure debts, which is what physicians or soldiers do when they promise to work for the state, or to work subject to conditions imposed by the state, in exchange for state assistance with payment for their education. In the case of ordinary labor contracts, typically the labor is performed prior to payment, in which case the other party's asset secures a debt owed to the person providing the labor. As for the right to bequeath, there is no way one can literally pass on one's labor to another. One's knowledge and skills—human capital—are another matter. These may be transferred to others via education, as when parents train their children in the family business. No one seriously objects to people passing on their knowledge and skills to whomever they choose, and indeed there seems to be no practical way to prevent it, except insofar as training is regulated by occupational licensure. This leaves only the right to the income from labor or human capital.

It was argued in the second section of chapter 2 that modern liberals believe that the state has a prior ownership claim on at least part of people's income. Since much of people's income comes from their labor and since much of people's wealth, nowadays at least, resides in their human capital, this would mean that the state has a partial ownership claim, in the form of limited income rights, in people's capacity to labor. One need not go so far as Nozick, who claims that this means that people are partially enslaved by others.[26] Nevertheless, it is difficult to see how one can maintain the modern liberal view about taxation of labor and the purposes for which tax revenues can be used without assuming a partial ownership claim (here understood as a partial income right) in people's labor and/or the human capital that supports that labor. Classical liberals deny this. They believe that people own—in the sense of full liberal ownership—their labor and their human capital outright. This coheres with, and indeed may even be a presupposition of, their view of the highly limited purposes for which tax revenue may be used.

Self-Ownership

Few liberals would claim that people own their bodies in the same manner that they own other property. Consider first the right of disposition. If one had this right in the way one has it with respect to other forms of property, it would be permissible to sell oneself into slavery, which most liberals would deny, believing as they do that some rights are inalienable or that some contracts should not be enforced. There is less agreement among liberals about whether people ought to be able to sell their body parts or rent their bodies (organ sales and prostitution or surrogacy arrangements, respectively). Some modern liberals have expressed doubts about the voluntariness of these transactions, given their nature. Worries have also been expressed about the wider social ramifications of the "commodification" of human body parts and functions.[27] But, modern liberals with strong civil libertarian sympathies have been inclined to see state involvement in these areas as an unwarranted restriction of personal freedom.[28] Classical liberals with conservative sympathies see a role for the state in prohibiting or regulating these transactions, whereas the libertarians among them have consistently supported people's right to enter into these contracts, with no interference from the state.[29]

Consider now the other incidents of ownership. People do have the right to exclusive physical possession of their bodies, unless they have been convicted of a crime. Management (use) rights and rights of disposition over one's body would be the right to do what one wants, subject to the prohibition on harmful use. This is the general right to liberty of the person that all liberals endorse. The right to the income is usually understood in connection with ownership of human capital, which was discussed above, though there are also cases in which people have claims to income in virtue of who they are (their fame or notoriety) or their appearance.

What about the prohibition on harmful use? Just as in the case of inanimate objects, people are prohibited from using themselves to harm others. In the case of harms that involve violating people's rights to physical security and security of possession, this prohibition is embodied in the criminal law and tort law and is unproblematic. But what about when others' rights are not violated? This raises two important questions: (1) Should people be prohibited from harming themselves? and (2) How broadly is harm to others to be understood? As previously noted, both questions were initially raised by Mill. The first question concerns the legitimacy of state-sponsored paternalism. Few liberals of any stripe favor government restrictions on behavior that literally affects no one but the person who does it. However, it is often alleged that what might be called "ostensibly private behaviors" (i.e., lifestyle choices) have broader social ramifications that potentially render it a fit subject for government attention. These ramifications, if they are negative, can count as harms to others under a suitably broad conception of harm. What are the modern liberal and classical liberal attitudes toward government regulation of this type of behavior?

There is one point on which classical and modern liberals can agree: the state cannot restrict ostensibly private behavior if that would violate citizens' fundamental personal and political rights. There is agreement between modern liberals and classical liberals about the existence and importance of fundamental rights. So, for example, restrictions on freedom of expression could not be justified on the grounds that certain forms of expression harm others. But, there is a dispute about how some fundamental rights are to be understood. One of the most controversial elements of the modern liberal view concerns the existence of a right to privacy, most famously articulated in *Roe v. Wade,* 410 US 113 (1973). According to the majority opinion, this right of privacy is an unenumerated right implicit in the due process clause of the Fourteenth Amendment. What is the classical liberal position on the existence or scope of this right? On the one hand, there is sympathy for the general proposition that the state should not be involved in regulating ostensibly private or self-regarding behavior; on the other hand, there is also sympathy for the conservative worry about the power of the judiciary to discover—some would say invent—unenumerated constitutional rights lurking in the penumbras of the enumerated ones. Setting aside the abortion issue (about which there is no canonical position on either side), it is probably fair to say that classical liberals favor most of the protections a right of privacy affords while being skeptical of the manner in which these protections have been read into the Constitution by modern liberal jurists.

What about ostensibly private behavior that is not protected by personal and political rights, however those rights are to be understood? From the birth of modern liberalism in the writings of John Stuart Mill (notably, *On Liberty*) to Rawls's *A Theory of Justice,* modern liberals have held that the state should not interfere in people's lifestyle choices as a matter policy, unless these choices infringe on the rights of others. The way this is sometimes expressed is that the state should be neutral with respect to different conceptions of the good life. In the past two decades or so, however, some modern liberals have begun to question this ideal of liberal neutrality.[30] These modern liberals do not believe it is desirable or even possible for the state to maintain neutrality among different conceptions of the good life. Though the state cannot force people to adopt a certain lifestyle and cannot violate fundamental rights, it can—and indeed inevitably will—promote certain lifestyle norms and values and discourage others, since many of the laws it passes (or fails to pass) and many of the policies it institutes (or fails to institute) will affect people's norms and values. Cass Sunstein calls this "norm management" (1996, 2023–28). Given that the state cannot avoid some norm management, it might as well do it intelligently, which means, according to these modern liberals, that the state should promote good lifestyle choices, or at least discourage bad choices—as state officials judge those choices.

Further impetus toward this view of the state as norm manager for lifestyle choices comes from what might be called (with apologies to Ronald Coase) "the problem of expanding social costs." Throughout the twentieth century, the government took an increasingly active role in providing the basic necessities of life for the poor and the elderly, including most notably health care. Even those who are not currently beneficiaries of these programs will eventually depend on the government as they come to participate in retirement and health care programs for the elderly. What this means is that the government has to clean up when people make a mess of their lives. Because the government has to bear some of the burdens of these bad choices, it is not surprising that politicians, who bear ultimate responsibility for these programs, have taken an increased interest in what people are doing with their lives in general and with their health in particular. Although what people are doing, in terms of their lifestyle choices, may seem to be purely private behavior, in point of fact it is not. Aside from demonstration effects, lifestyle choices inevitably have a public component because the public, as a provider of social insurance against poverty and illness (at least in old age), bears ultimate financial responsibility for what happens. Herein lies a rationale, though not the only rationale, for what critics call "the nanny state." The modern state invests considerable resources and effort in advising, cajoling, and pressuring people to lead what state officials believe to be better lives—better both for the people themselves and for society at large. Regarding the latter, these days social problems, especially health problems, have dangling from them a price tag that quantifies the lost wages and lost tax revenues traceable to that problem, and this price tag is offered as part of the argument for state action. Perhaps the most dramatic recent illustration of this struggle for healthy bodies and souls is the escalating twin wars on tobacco and recreational drugs. The drug war in the United States has continued unabated from early in the last century and has even intensified in the past generation. In the newer war on tobacco, smokers are being hounded by state and local governments from public places, and the various states have sued tobacco companies to recover what they claim to be the costs of smoking-related illnesses that they have borne for the elderly. Arguably, these suits are a mere pretext for extortion from a politically vulnerable tobacco industry. The best studies indicate that previous levels of taxation more than covered the additional costs states have borne in this connection.[31] The general direction of tobacco regulation is toward prohibition, even if that endpoint will never be reached. In these and many other ways, the government is actively trying to manage norms by discouraging the use of recreational drugs and tobacco, and to a lesser extent, other harmful behaviors, such as overeating. Though many modern liberals question the effectiveness of these wars, especially the war on drugs, they do not question the propriety of the state taking an interest in these matters.[32] The government also regulates a whole host of other activities through its power to restrict or prohibit the sale of certain consumer goods and services or to mandate a certain level of safety in various products and activities.

This proprietary interest in people's health and well-being gets further impetus from a widely shared belief in the general culture that various bad outcomes that people suffer as a result of their choices are best conceived of and dealt with on a medical model. On this model, people who have bad things happen to them as a result of their choices are suffering from something like an illness.[33] If this is the case, and if the state bears some responsibility for health care, then it is natural to suppose that it bears some responsibility for discouraging and otherwise treating the behaviors that produce these bad outcomes. The fact that taxpayers must subsidize bad outcomes to risky behavior makes it seem natural and appropriate for the state to try to influence more broadly and deeply people's lifestyle choices than it used to.

Another rationale for the state to involve itself in a systematic way in people's lifestyle choices can be found in communitarian values that are alleged to be widely held in modern societies. Many Americans, it is alleged, want to live in a society which, for example, condemns the use of recreational drugs, alcohol, and tobacco. The state is seen as an important vehicle to express these values. Failure to "make a statement" evinces a lack of compassion for fellow citizens or an indifference to the kind of society in which we live. Besides, the law inevitably has an expressive function as Sunstein and others have pointed out,[34] and it is important that the law "say the right thing," where saying the right thing is understood as expressing widely shared values that people actually have. This is to be distinguished from "norm management," where state officials try to change people's values in what state officials judge to be desirable ways.

Much of the state's attempts to influence ostensibly private behavior does not involve the direct regulation of this behavior by government edicts. Modern governments use tax policy (e.g., tobacco taxes) and consumer product health and safety regulation (e.g., automobile safety regulations) to encourage or discourage various types of ostensibly private behavior. Transfer programs are also pressed into service, as when the government subsidizes public transportation to make it more financially attractive. Finally, there are some things the government does to influence people's behavior that do not seem to fit easily into any of the three main categories of government intervention (taxation, transfer programs, regulation), such as when it creates and funds programs whose intended aims are to get young people to live chaste lives that are free of drugs, tobacco, and alcohol.

Whether these forms of government attempts to influence ostensibly private behavior are imposed in the name of inevitability (the state cannot help but promote some values at the expense of others), risk management (as part of the state's role as society's major insurer), or on the basis of widely shared communitarian values (about the kind of society in which we want to live), there is no denying the paternalistic thrust of the modern state. Whatever their ultimate goals, the proximate goal of these laws and regulations is to get people to do what is in their best interests, as state officials see it. Supporters of these laws, programs, and regulations and the statements those laws, programs, and regulations make—"postmodern liberals," as they might be called[35]—need not endorse everything the government does that is designed to foster healthy lifestyles, other forms of self-improvement, or communitarian values. Nevertheless, they do believe that there is a role for the state in using its authority to promote certain lifestyle choices and discourage others. The further consequences or broader ramifications of ostensibly private behavior have, on this view, rendered obsolete the terms of the older debate about the propriety of government-sponsored paternalism. Perhaps the best way to characterize the emerging view among many modern liberals about state-sponsored paternalism is that the latter can be justified if and only if it promotes worthy social goals and does not violate fundamental rights. The costs of these programs, whether conceived of in financial terms or in terms of the potentially deleterious effects of government-sponsored paternalism on individuals or on society as a whole, seem not to be seriously assayed.

However, it is not clear that all modern liberals would take this line. Those with strong civil libertarian sympathies retain a reflexive hostility toward the state in matters of ostensibly private behavior. In support of this, they might maintain that the sphere of freedom guaranteed by fundamental rights, notably the right to privacy, is so large that most of the state's attempts to promote or discourage lifestyle choices will inevitably infringe on these rights.[36] If this is correct, there may be no canonical modern liberal position on the propriety of the state trying to influence ostensibly private behavior. Even so, modern liberal thought (perhaps in response to communitarian ideas and to feminist critiques of the public/private distinction) seems to be moving in the direction of the postmodernist position identified above.

Classical liberals have generally opposed this growing intrusion into lifestyle choices. As usual, libertarians object on the grounds that these measures are straightforward infringements on people's natural rights to liberty and property. Classical liberals whose views are not anchored in natural rights have opposed attempts to influence lifestyle choices on more consequentialist grounds. Essentially, they follow Mill's own reasons for opposing paternalism: "But the strongest of all the arguments against the interference of the public with purely personal conduct is that, when it does interfere, the odds are that it interferes wrongly and in the wrong place" (1859 [1978], 81). Of course, postmodern liberals would deny that the conduct is purely personal or self-regarding because of the problem of expanding social costs and the nature of social meanings, but Mill's basic claim, which many classical liberals would echo and indeed would insist on, is that when the state seeks to guide people in their lifestyle choices, whatever their ultimate aims, they tend not to do a very good job at enhancing well-being. Their general critique of government-sponsored paternalism starts with the observation, familiar from public choice theory, that the political process as it actually operates in the real world is not a particularly good vehicle for transmitting preferences or values from the people to their elected leaders. Most people are rationally ignorant and rationally apathetic about the political process. Consequently, politicians are not sensitive to their values and interests but are instead sensitive to the values and interests of organized groups, who are often seeking merely to impose their values on others with the force of law, or who are looking for an angle from which they can winkle resources out of the state. There is also an adverse selection problem (not remarked on by Mill) in staffing the agencies of government charged with influencing people's lifestyle choices. Specifically, those who are most attracted to the job of formulating policy to regulate people's lifestyle choices tend to be least suited to do it in a way that reflects either broadly held communitarian values or values that are, in some objective sense, "best." In light of this adverse selection problem, some classical liberals worry that we have already arrived at a society ruled by those drawn from the same talent pool that produces junior high school vice principals and college student government leaders. The case of Prohibition (of the sale of alcoholic beverages) in the 1920s can be used to illustrate all these points. The main beneficiaries were police thugs, temperance crusaders, and members of organized crime. The new beneficiaries of lifestyle regulation closely, indeed exactly, parallel the beneficiaries of Prohibition: police departments (civil forfeiture laws encourage asset seizures), lifestyle scolds, and the plaintiffs' bar. For all these reasons, classical liberals believe that it is inappropriate for the state to undertake as its deliberate policy the inculcation of values that shape people's lifestyle choices. This is so even though state policy inevitably influences lifestyle choices. On their view, the fact of that influence simply carries no justificatory weight. On the problem of expanding social costs, classical liberals have viewed as illegitimate most of the government programs that have been the source of this problem. For example, they believe it is not the job of the state to guarantee health care to the poor and to the elderly. Indeed, one reason for opposing these programs is that it encourages the state to scrutinize people's personal habits that impinge on their health and safety.

This does not mean that classical liberals must oppose all attempts to influence ostensibly private behavior. Classical liberals of a conservative bent favor laws that prohibit recreational drugs, prostitution, and gambling and laws that regulate or discourage various forms of so-called adult entertainment. Is this a position that they should feel comfortable taking? It depends. They are on firm classical liberal grounds to the extent that they can justify these laws by reference to potential violations of the rights of others. For example, zoning ordinances directed against adult entertainment establishments have been defended on the grounds that these establishments create a nuisance (as understood by the common law) by serving as a magnet for the criminal element. The prohibition on recreational drugs has been defended on the grounds that legalization would lead to an increase in crime. The war on smoking has been publicly justified by appeal to the putative negative health effects of second-hand smoke. Without passing judgment on the merits of these claims (most of which are quite dubious), they are clearly of the type that could figure in an argument for regulation of ostensibly private behavior that classical liberals could make or could accept.[37]

Some conservatives, however, favor regulating ostensibly private behavior because they believe there is a role for the state in discouraging vice and promoting virtue.[38] The question then becomes whether or not these conservatives have wandered off the classical liberal ranch.[39] No definitive answer may be possible, since classical liberalism, as it was defined in chapter 1, is more a mindset than a set of propositions. Consistent with that definition, however, it is worth noting that central to the classical liberal tradition is a broad and deep streak of skepticism toward the state—a skepticism that makes it hard for classical liberals to say, without feeling hypocritical or foolish, that the state should promote virtue and discourage vice in lifestyle choices—at least if this implies anything very ambitious and beyond the criminal law. Even classical liberals who reject the easy skepticism and tolerant relativism that some libertarians exhibit toward lifestyle choices have deep misgivings about justifying state action on the grounds that it promotes "appropriate" values, if only because they fear that as the state gets into that line of work, the wrong people would inevitably take charge and promote inappropriate values. For example, from a classical liberal perspective, the costs of drug prohibition laws, which are often explicitly justified by appeal to what is best for the character of those affected, must be taken to include over 170 statutes at the state and federal level that seek to protect or enhance self-esteem, particularly among school children (Nolan 1998, 157–61). Even classical liberals from California must view these intrusive and dubious programs with dismay.

So, although there seems to be no canonical modern liberal or classical liberal position on the question of whether the state should try to influence ostensibly private behavior, perhaps it is fair to say that these days modern liberals are more inclined to support this sort of thing and classical liberals are more inclined to oppose it. One way of characterizing the difference between the two camps is by reference to the kinds of arguments each side is willing to make or accept in favor of this form of state action. On the one hand, modern liberals who favor of this sort of thing typically appeal to the inevitability of norm management, to the state's role as a risk manager and/or to communitarian values that laws or regulations express. On the other hand, classical liberals are inclined to dismiss these sorts of arguments, though they can in good conscience endorse state action that aims at influencing ostensibly private behavior, if that behavior has the potential to violate the common law personal or property rights of others.

This completes the overview of classical liberalism and modern liberalism and the associated foray into conceptual geography. The basic strategy has been to conduct a comprehensive review of the points of agreement and disagreement between classical liberals and modern liberals with special attention to the forms in which government intervenes in civil society. This was Mill's original concern in *On Liberty* and remains an outstanding problem for liberalism today. One thing that emerges very clearly from this overview is that modern liberalism is the political philosophy of the contemporary welfare-regulatory state. Modern liberals are by no means committed to defending each and every program dreamed up by legislators and bureaucrats. They can admit, even insist, that some of these programs have outlived their usefulness (agricultural subsidies), are poorly conceived or poorly run (federal job-training programs), or have been perverted in their function to serve ends other than their original purpose (subsidies for marketing U.S. products overseas). However, modern liberalism is committed to defending certain types or modes of government intervention in civil society. Though modern liberals need not defend OSHA regulations requiring port-o-potties for cowboys or life vests for bridge workers working over dry riverbeds (Viscusi 1983, 11), they do defend the appropriateness of the state regulating working conditions that affect health and safety through an

OSHA-like agency. Welfare programs for single mothers that penalize them for getting married are difficult for anyone to defend, but modern liberals do want to defend the proposition that the state should guarantee that no one, especially no child, goes hungry or without shelter or without basic medical care. And so on.

In the broadest terms, there are three basic types of intervention about which modern liberals and classical liberals differ: (1) taxation, (2) transfer programs, and (3) regulation. The distinctions between these categories are to some extent arbitrary. For example, some forms of taxation (e.g., tariffs) and some regulations (e.g., minimum wage laws) could be conceived of as transfer programs.[40] Although it is somewhat arbitrary where to draw the lines between these various forms of government involvement, some ways of categorizing various forms of intervention seem more natural than others; the rest can be settled by stipulation. That caveat noted, let us review briefly each of these categories of government intervention.

Taxation. Modern liberals have supported tax policies that attempt to place a proportionately heavier burden on the more advantaged. Historically, progressive income and estate taxation are the main vehicles for this. Although changing the distribution of after-tax income has often been an explicit goal of modern liberal tax policy when taxes are to be increased or cut (in the guise of claiming the mantle of fairness) such tax policies need not be, and have not always been, advocated on grounds of fairness or distributive justice. They have also favored using the tax code to achieve various macroeconomic goals and to achieve various social goals by influencing how citizens spend their money. Modern liberalism presupposes that society has a prior claim on a portion of citizens' income and wealth, though how great a portion seems to be indeterminate or variable. That assumption best explains the wide discretionary power they believe public officials should have when it comes to imposing taxes and spending the revenue those taxes generate. Classical liberals, on the other hand, favor some form of tax neutrality, typically some version of a flat income tax, as well as user fees, and they oppose the use of the tax code for purposes other than raising revenue for legitimate (as they see it) government activities.

Transfer programs. Modern liberals have also consistently favored the major transfer programs of the welfare state, ranging from welfare (broadly understood to include various forms of in-kind assistance) to pensions and health insurance, at least for the elderly and at most for everyone. Modern liberals have also favored some more narrowly targeted transfer programs as a way of addressing various social problems, though they recognize that some of these programs are ineffective or unjust. Classical liberals have opposed most of the transfer programs of the modern welfare-regulatory state. There is, however, qualified support among some classical liberals for a not very strong safety net hanging close to the ground to address the most serious and intractable problems of the least advantaged that a private ordering might not be able to handle.

Regulation. Regulation can be thought of as state restrictions on the incidents of private ownership, other than restrictions on income rights imposed by the tax code. (A more formal definition will be offered at the beginning of the next chapter.) Though there are disagreements of greater or lesser moment about many of the incidents of ownership, the most significant disagreements between classical and modern liberals have been about management rights and disposition rights. Modern liberals have consistently favored a large array of restrictions on the rights of management and disposition, whether those rights be in productive assets, personal property, labor, or human capital. In addition, modern liberals have increasingly favored state action to shape or influence ostensibly private behavior, either as risk managers for various social insurance policies run by the state or on the basis of widely shared communitarian values or simply as an attempt to carry out intelligently what they believe to be an inevitable activity of the state. With some important exceptions, classical liberals have opposed virtually the entire regulatory agenda of the modern state and its modern liberal supporters.

Disputes about taxation, transfer programs, and regulation are at the heart of the debate between classical and modern liberals. However, it would be inaccurate to suppose that these three topics exhaust the dispute. There are other differences between the two camps, which have been noted in passing. For example, there remain some disputes in macroeconomic policy that cannot easily be brought under any of these headings. And, there are disagreements about the extent to which the state should own productive assets, such as land and educational institutions, and the related question about which assets the state currently owns which should be privatized. There are also disagreements about how the state should manage the assets it owns. Historically, differences about taxation and transfer programs have dominated the debate among philosophers and economists. Perhaps because of the explosive growth in regulation, recent years have witnessed increased attention to regulation, especially by economists but also by philosophers. The remainder of this book is about regulation, or more exactly, about the dispute between modern liberals and classical liberals about the proper scope of government regulation. Drawing on the preceding discussion in this chapter, the next chapter spells out more explicitly and more precisely the main points of disagreement between modern liberals and classical liberals on the question of the proper scope of government regulation.

FOUR

The Modern Liberal Regulatory Agenda

Thus far it has been possible to operate with only an intuitive under-standing of the concept of regulation, but at this point a more explicit definition would be helpful. Alan Stone (1982, 10) gives the follow-ing standard definition: a regulation is "a state-imposed limitation on the discretion that may be exercised by individuals or organizations, which is supported by the threat of sanction." Call this Definition D_1. There are a number of problems with D_1. One very minor one is that the term "limitation on the discretion" suggests that the conduct that is being restricted is presumptively legitimate; a somewhat more neutral term would be "limitation on the freedom of." Another prob-lem with D_1 is that it neglects to mention that the sanction has to be coercively backed by government to be a regulation. Though some regulations (e.g., of behavior in private organizations) are not backed by a coercive sanction, Stone's topic—and ours—is government reg-ulation, and if the sanction is not coercive, it is not a government regulation: it is merely an admonishment or recommended behav-ior. Revising Stone's definition to take account of these observations yields definition D_2:

> D_2: x is a government regulation $=_{df}$
>   (1) x is a government-imposed limitation on the freedom of an individual or organization,
> & (2) x is backed by coercive sanction.

The main problem with D_3 is that nearly any law fits this defi-nition of "regulation," including the criminal law. For example, the law against battery limits people's freedom ("discretion," in Stone's terminology) and is backed by coercive sanction. Such laws are not normally thought of as regulations, however. How, then, does one distinguish government regulation from all the other laws that restrict freedom? Chapter 3 suggests an obvious answer: government regula-tions are all restrictions on the incidents of full, liberal ownership rights in private property. As a first approximation, this is a promising approach to delimiting the realm of regulation, but it cannot be the last word. Tort law limits the freedom of private property owners but should not count as regulation, despite some functional similarities between regulations and the law of torts. Indeed, the very definition of property rights implies government limitations on the freedom of nonowners backed by coercive sanction. To rule out the criminal law, tort law, and property rights themselves as regulations, the following revised definition might be proposed:

> D_3: x is a government regulation of O's private property $\phi =_{df}$
>   (1) x is a government-imposed limitation on the freedom of O
>   (where O is a natural or artificial person) with respect to
>   the incidents of full, liberal ownership of ϕ by O
> & (2) x is not grounded in the common law,
> & (3) x is backed by coercive sanction.

Note that the definiendum presupposes that O does in fact own ϕ, which is reflected in the first condition; this implies that property rights themselves are not regulations. The second condition removes both the criminal law (or at least most of it—see below) and tort law from the realm of regulation, since both are rooted in the common law. Condition (2) also gets around the problem of the different conceptions of private property held by modern liberals and classical liberals. Recall that modern liberals believe that some of the incidents of ownership reside in the first instance in the state, whereas classical liberals deny this. Wherever the truth about this dispute is to be found, the common law is clearly on the side of the classical liberals. Regulations, whether or not they are justifiable, are clearly restrictions or limitations on the standard incidents of common law private property rights (not grounded in torts) as they are held by private individuals. Notice also that condition (2) does not rule out all of the criminal law, nor should it. For example, drug prohibition laws and other ostensibly paternalistic laws of the modern regulatory state are not grounded in the common law but they do have criminal penalties attached to them. They are also regulations because they are most naturally conceived of as restrictions on self-ownership rights, as are laws (with criminal penalties attached) prohibiting people from entering into certain contractual relations, such as laws against prostitution. But, the part of criminal law that is grounded in the common law are those laws that protect fundamental rights such as the right to life, the right to be free from assault, and so on; according to D_2, these laws are not regulations, which is at it should be. Finally, condition (2) makes clear that an important bone of contention between classical liberals and modern liberals about regulation is the extent to which the common law of torts is adequate to deal with the social evils associated with private property. Classical liberals are inclined to believe that the common law can do the job, whereas modern liberals think that the state should deal with these evils via various regulatory bureaucracies—mostly because the common law offers no solution to these problems. For these reasons, it is not misleading to characterize modern liberals as favorably disposed, and classical liberals as unfavorably disposed, toward government regulation.

D_3 is an improvement over D_2, but it remains problematic for reasons suggested by some remarks made toward the end of chapter 3 about the distinction between taxation and regulation. This distinction, like the distinction between taxation and transfer programs, is somewhat artificial, but it is useful for analytical purposes to keep these categories distinct. According to D_2, taxation would count as a form of regulation (but it should not), since it is a limitation on a person's freedom backed by coercive sanction but not grounded in the common law. Consequently, a clause should be added to exclude from the extension of "regulation" restrictions on income rights, the right to the capital value, and the right to bequeath. In common parlance, all of these restrictions on full, liberal ownership are taxes, not regulations. These considerations are incorporated into our final version of the definition of "regulation":

D_4: x is a government regulation of O's private property $\phi =_{df}$
    (1) x is a government-imposed limitation on O's freedom (where O is a natural or artificial person) with respect to the standard incidents of full, liberal ownership of ϕ by O, except for:
    (a) the right to the income,
  & (b) the right to the capital value,
  & (c) the right to bequeath,
& (2) x is not grounded in the common law,
& (3) x is backed by coercive sanction.

This includes, most notably, state-imposed limitations on the exercise of management rights and disposition rights with respect to private property. It also includes sanction-backed restrictions on personal behavior not related to the fundamental legal rights mentioned above.

These can be thought of as regulations of (i.e., restrictions on) the right of self-ownership.

Among the various regulations imposed by government on the private sector, some are justified primarily or exclusively by efficiency arguments of the sort offered by economists. These include rate regulation, regulation of entry and exit, and antitrust law. In the European Union, the latter goes under the heading of competition policy.[1] Let us refer to these forms of regulation as "economic regulation." By contrast, other kinds of regulation are more commonly justified by moral arguments or even by appeal to considerations of justice. These include environmental regulation, health and safety regulation, and regulation of the employment relation (e.g., antidiscrimination law). For future reference, let us refer to these types of regulation as "noneconomic regulation." This way of drawing the distinction is somewhat misleading, since efficiency arguments for noneconomic regulation are commonplace. For example, cost-benefit analysis has been used in all so-called noneconomic types of regulation, especially environmental regulation. Dollar values are assigned, costs and benefits are calculated. More generally, because of their imperialistic tendencies, economists have tried to horn in on discussions of noneconomic regulation, peddling formal apparatuses that model, for example, environmental, consumer, and workplace health and safety regulation.[2] It nevertheless remains true that moral arguments are offered for what I have called "noneconomic regulation" but are rarely offered for rate regulation, regulation of entry and exit, and antitrust law. Although historically modern liberals have generally favored economic regulation while classical liberals have generally opposed it, in the next section we shall see that this aspect of the dispute has been attenuated over the past few decades. By contrast, the differences between modern liberals and classical liberals regarding noneconomic regulation remain sharp and show no signs of diminishing. This will be the subject of the second following section. Let us begin with economic regulation.

Economic Regulation

From the inception of the Interstate Commerce Commission in 1887 up through the post–World War II years, most government regulation was economic regulation. The standard account of the origins of this form of regulation is that growing public concern about increasing concentrations of economic power, especially in industries such as railroads, steel, telecommunications, and electricity, led to the creation of regulatory bodies that oversaw these industries. Rate regulation was intended to prevent these firms from gouging consumers. Antitrust laws were intended to deter firms with market power from charging monopoly prices, punish those that did, and prevent monopolies from forming in the first place by preventing mergers and acquisitions that threatened competition and by curbing so-called unfair business practices (e.g., price discrimination and vertical integration) that could be used to drive competitors from the field.

These political and economic developments were mirrored by developments in economic thought. The 1920s witnessed the rise of neoclassical economics and with it the articulation of the model of perfect competition. In a perfectly competitive market, all firms are small enough so that they are "price-takers," that is, no firm can exert market power by raising prices on outputs or lowering bids on inputs. Real world markets, of course, are not perfectly competitive. In a subsequent move toward greater realism, leading economists such as Edward Chamberlin (1938) and Joan Robinson (1933) developed models of imperfect or monopolistic competition. Ellis W. Hawley has described this as,

> a new technique of economic analysis, one that regarded monopolistic conditions as ubiquitous and determining, not exceptional and inconsequential, and one that treated the typical seller as a partial monopolist.... The term [i.e., "monopoly"] now came to include all behavior that departed from the concept of pure competition, including a good deal of the oligopolistic rivalry that businessmen regarded as "competition." (1966, 297–98)

Jack High and Thomas DiLorenzo (1988) have argued that economists were lukewarm at best in their support for the Sherman Act when it was originally passed in 1890. It was only in the 1920s that the profession began to support antitrust law more strongly. On their view, the rise of neoclassical economics was an important factor in this sea change in economists' opinions about the Sherman Act.

The standard account of the rise of the regulatory state as a response to concerns about the economic power of big corporations has been forcefully challenged by, among others, Gabriel Kolko. Kolko argued that economic regulation was in fact a creation of big business. The merger movement in the early twentieth century was intended by big business to prevent competition, but it failed to achieve that aim. Rate regulation and regulation of entry, instigated at the behest of big business, were responses to that failure and were intended to ensure the profitability of the participating firms. The prohibition in antitrust law on so-called "unfair" business practices was a way of preventing the introduction of innovations by upstart firms that would benefit consumers and harm competitors. As Kolko has said,

> Despite the large number of mergers, and the growth in the absolute size of many corporations, the dominant tendency in the American economy at the beginning of [the twentieth] century was toward growing competition. Competition was unacceptable to many key business and financial interests, and the merger movement was to a large extent a reflection of voluntary, unsuccessful business efforts to bring irresistible competitive trends under control...internal problems that could be solved only by political means were the common denominator in those industries whose leaders advocated greater federal regulation. Ironically, contrary to the consensus of historians, it was not the existence of monopoly that caused the federal government to intervene in the economy, but the lack of it. (1963, 4–5)[3]

From the perspective of Kolko, the phrase "regulatory capture," is a misnomer; these regulatory bodies could not be captured by the industries they regulate, since that would imply they were once free. Rather, these agencies were born and raised in captivity, that is, they were created by the very corporations, or their predecessors, that they have been charged with regulating. Classical liberals, especially the economists, are inclined to support Kolko's interpretation, since it dovetails nicely with the public choice analysis of the relationship between interest groups and the state.[4] On that analysis, interest groups (in this case, trade or industry groups) "buy" influence on the regulatory process via campaign contributions to politicians, employment offers to regulators when the latter's government service ends; this gives these industries or trade groups the stability they seek, either directly by state-mandated price-fixing or indirectly by various measures designed to keep out competitors. The benefits of regulation to regulated industries are concentrated and substantial while the costs to the public (who are rationally ignorant) are highly diffuse and individually insignificant—a perfect hothouse environment for the growth of government, just as public choice theory predicts.

Beginning in the 1970s, however, a wave of deregulation swept over the U.S. economy.[5] AT&T was broken up, and long-distance service became competitive as new firms, such as MCI and Sprint, came into being. Local telephone service remained a regulated monopoly of the regional Baby Bells, though even here competition has begun to emerge as cellular phone service has become more widespread and as cable companies offer phone service. Deregulation following the breakup of AT&T in the 1970s occurred in air transportation, trucking, oil and natural gas, cable television service, and wholesale electric power. All that remains of rate regulation is what is done at the state or local level: local telephone service, some cable television service, retail distribution of electric power, and insurance.[6] Some thorny issues remain in the deregulation of retail electrical power and telecommunications because of the respective companies' monopolies on local telecommunications and power lines (the so-called "last mile"). The central question of the day is whether they should be required to supply the services of their equipment to competitors and at what price.[7] There are some other issues regarding telecommunications, such as rules that mandate that cable companies carry local television stations (must-carry rules). Although these rules seem like regulations, they are more accurately described as operating conditions for state-owned assets (the airwaves) that are leased to private telecommunication firms.

Classical liberals have welcomed, and modern liberals have come to accept, rate deregulation in these various industries. Indeed, as noted in chapter 2, modern liberal politicians have sponsored some of this deregulation. There no longer seems to be any deep dispute about rate deregulation in industries that are not natural monopolies (of which there are few),[8] and the disputes about local telecommunications and power lines seem relatively narrow.[9] The key question is how best to foster competition and make deregulation work. All of the relevant arguments take place on common ground.

There has also been rapprochement between modern liberals and classical liberals on antitrust. In a recent article, mainstream economists Robert W. Crandall and Clifford Winston (2003) made a sustained effort to evaluate the evidence regarding the effect of antitrust policy on consumer welfare since the passage of the Sherman Act. They found that there is little evidence that antitrust actions undertaken by the Department of Justice or by the Federal Trade Commission have had beneficial consequences for consumers. Their conclusion is worth quoting at some length:

> The apparent ineffectiveness of antitrust policy stems from several causes: 1) the excessive duration of monopolization cases, which portends that the particular issue being addressed will evolve into something different—often of less importance—by the time it is resolved; 2) the difficulties in formulating effective remedies for monopolization and effective consent decrees for proposed mergers; 3) the difficulties in sorting out which mergers or instances of potentially anticompetitive behavior threaten consumer welfare; 4) the substantial and growing challenges of formulating and implementing effective antitrust policies in a new economy characterized by dynamic competition, rapid technological change and important intellectual property (Carlton and Gertner, 2002); 5) political forces that influence which antitrust cases are initiated, settled or dropped (Weingast and Moran, 1983; Coate, Higgins and McChesney, 1995), including situations where firms try to exploit the antitrust process to gain a competitive advantage over their rivals (Baumol and Ordover, 1985); 6) the power of the market as an effective force for spurring competition and curbing anticompetitive abuses, which leaves antitrust policy with relatively little to do. (Crandall and Winston 2003, 23)

Of course, this does not mean that the Department of Justice is closing down its antitrust division or that the FTC is about to announce that it has no useful work to do in this area. Sparring over this issue continues for some political actors, but whatever changes occur in antitrust policy from one administration to the next seem to be relatively minor.

There is one other form of economic regulation that merits brief mention: wage and price controls. As was pointed out in chapter 3, comprehensive wage and price controls are supported by almost no liberal, classical or modern. Indeed, such controls should probably not be categorized as "economic regulation," since they are not supported by efficiency arguments, even spurious or disingenuous ones. Their motivations are purely and overtly political; they are, in effect, economic amputations on the body politic designed to prevent gangrene in someone's political career. Modern liberals do, however, favor specific price controls on some goods or services in the face of exogenous shocks (e.g., prohibitions on price-gouging by retailers

in areas struck by natural disasters) or when industries such as the
oil industry reaps "undeserved" windfall profits. Classical liberals
are inclined to oppose such regulations because they interfere with
the market response mechanism to changed conditions. For example,
if the price of plywood doubles in an area hit by a hurricane, lum-
ber yards distant from the scene have a strong incentive to rush as
much product as soon as they can to the affected area. Absent the
lure of extraordinary profits, the motive to move heaven and earth
to get product to the affected area must be altruistic; such motives
are present and do work, especially in the immediate aftermath of
a natural disaster, but they are more uncertain in their extent and
operation as time goes on. As Adam Smith once noted, one of the
advantages of a market economy is that it economizes on altruism.
Moreover, outside of the context of natural disasters, the imposition
of selective price controls is, in effect, a signal from politicians to
the business community that, just like the Mafia, they might be willing to sell protection (i.e., an exemption) from the controls they are
considering imposing. In other words, they are, in classic Mafia style,
offering protection from themselves. However, sometimes the market
cannot respond quickly enough to do any good (e.g., out-of-state lum-
ber yards may not be able to get business licenses to sell plywood)
and the opportunities for fraud might be so great that the precedential
significance of temporary selective price controls is inconsequential;
classical liberal opposition to them may seem stiff-necked and ideological. Finally, there is economic regulation in the service of various macroeconomic goals through instrumentalities such as control
of the money supply, tax policy, and fiscal policy; these were briefly
mentioned in chapter 2.

Noneconomic Regulation and the Modern
Liberal Regulatory Agenda

Let us turn now to noneconomic regulation. Beginning in the 1960s
and through the middle of the 1970s and beyond, a regulatory agenda
took shape which resulted in the creation and empowerment of a
number of new regulatory agencies. Unlike economic regulation, noneconomic regulation was motivated more by explicitly moral considerations than by considerations of efficiency. According to those who
championed this regulatory agenda, morally unacceptable business

practices were far too common. African Americans, other minorities, and women were routinely discriminated against in employment and in other markets; companies regularly polluted the water and air with impunity; workers' and consumers' health and safety were systematically ignored by businesses, large and small. And so on. The claim was not that any of this was new; rather, the idea was that for the first time, consciousness had been sufficiently raised and the political forces had become properly aligned so that something could be done about these long-standing problems, and this could be done without imposing unacceptable costs on people's standard of living. Noneconomic regulation was intended to stop or diminish the frequency and severity of these morally objectionable practices. It includes antidiscrimination law in all its manifestations, environmental regulation, health and safety regulation, indeed most of the restrictions on management rights and disposition rights discussed in the last chapter.

Because disputes about rate regulation and other forms of economic regulation seem to be effectively over, or at least reduced to haggling over details, debates about economic regulation will not be further discussed in this book. Our attention will be restricted to the disputes between modern liberals and classical liberals about noneconomic regulation. On the face of it, they are significant. Modern liberals are not impressed by classical liberals' claim that occupational safety regulations preclude workers from choosing wage and safety packages that the latter would prefer to what they currently have. Classical liberals are inclined to believe that antidiscrimination laws (including, most famously, the Americans with Disabilities Act) have collectively become a Bermuda Triangle for sensible ideas about dealing with race, gender, ethnicity, and disabilities in the workplace.[10] Modern liberals distrust the ability of the market and tort law to protect consumers from dangerous products, especially from dangerous medical products, but classical liberals tend to believe that the health and safety paternalism practiced by the modern regulatory state is occasionally harmful, often ineffective, and always incompatible with the dignity of a free people. Modern liberals believe that the Endangered Species Act is essential for preserving the biodiversity of the planet; by contrast, classical liberals believe that state-sponsored efforts to save endangered species are, with the exception a few celebrity megafauna species, pointless, ineffective, or merely a pretext for environmentalist "watermelons" (green on the outside, red on the inside) to impose their dubious values on the population as a whole.

And so on. In these debates, no narrowing of differences or emerging consensus is apparent, as is the case with, say, rate regulation. But perhaps this pessimism is ill-founded, and there may be much useful work to be done in the search for reasoned agreement about noneconomic regulation. In the next chapter, we begin that search. Before doing so, however, it is necessary to clarify more exactly the nature and extent of the multifaceted dispute between classical liberals and modern liberals about noneconomic regulation.

Perhaps the most natural way to proceed is to construct what might be called "the modern liberal regulatory agenda" from the points of disagreement between modern and classical liberals about restrictions on the incidents of ownership discussed in chapter 3. This agenda seeks to identify the types of regulation favored by all, or nearly all, modern liberals and opposed by all, or nearly all, classical liberals. Based on that discussion, it is fair to say that near unanimity within each camp, and near total disagreement between the two sides, can be found in three broad categories of regulation: (1) regulation of the employment relation, (2) consumer products and services regulation, and (3) some forms of environmental regulation, specifically land use regulation. The first and third categories involve truncation of management rights in productive assets, and the second involves truncation of disposition rights in goods and services. Let us restate the modern liberal point of view on each of these types of regulation in a bit more detail.

A. Regulation of the employment relation. Modern liberals are inclined to favor extensive regulation of the employment relation, that is, government-imposed restrictions on freedom of contract between employers and employees. These include:

(1) *Mandatory terms or conditions of employment, other than child labor laws.* This includes a federally mandated minimum wage, mandatory time and a half pay for overtime, and employment policies such as the statute requiring equal pay for equal work and mandated family leave for employees with young children or sick dependents.[11]

(2) *Antidiscrimination laws.* These laws prohibit discrimination in hiring, promotion, and termination based on race, ethnicity, religion, gender, age, and disability status.

(3) *Occupational health and safety regulation.* This is government regulation of the workplace that affects worker health and safety, with almost the entire burden falling on employers, not employees.

(4) *Laws regulating the interactions of firms, individuals, and labor unions, other than those that the guarantee of the right of workers to organize and bargain collectively.* The laws in question forbid companies from engaging in specific unfair labor practices, limit the activities unions can engage in (prohibitions on secondary boycotts, common situs picketing, etc.), and define in detail the framework within which collective bargaining is to take place. All these are limitations on freedom of contract that classical liberals are inclined to oppose.

The exceptive clauses in numbers 1 and 4 warrant a brief comment. As noted in chapter 3, classical liberals could agree to restrictions imposed by child labor laws on the grounds that minors are incapable of consenting to labor contracts. The right to organize and bargain collectively are simply instances of the right to freedom of contract and thus would be supported by classical liberals.

B. Consumer products and services regulation. Modern liberals favor extensive government regulation of the characteristics of consumer products and services. That is, the government mandates or forbids that an array of products and services have certain features. Most of these regulations concern characteristics that affect consumer health and safety, especially in connection with prescription drugs. Modern liberals need not be saddled with a position that implies a favorable judgment of all regulations that fall under this heading. They are committed, however, to the view that regulation of the characteristics of consumer products and services are properly within the scope of government activity. Classical liberals, by contrast, are inclined to oppose all, or nearly all, attempts on the part of the government to dictate the health and safety (or virtually any other) characteristics of consumer products. On their view, this is something that should be determined by the interplay of market forces, as well as tort law—not by state edict. Occupational licensure laws should also be included under this heading. These laws are typically favored by most modern liberals and opposed by most classical liberals.

C. (Some) environmental regulation. Essentially there are two kinds of environmental regulations: those that deal with preventing or cleaning up messes and those that aim at enhancing or preserving certain features of the environment. The former consists of regulations that attempt to limit air, water, or noise pollution and those that deal with hazardous wastes. Regulations of this sort can in principle be supported by both classical and modern liberals. Classical liberals, however, are inclined to favor a common law approach, as opposed to regulation by statute, to most problems of pollution. This is so for a number of reasons.[12] First, the common law enforces existing norms instead of imposing norms generated by intellectuals and bureaucrats in the state apparatus. The former are likely to be reasonably close to common-sense morality and thus are more likely to be observed. In a related vein, under the common law, liability tends to fall upon those who engage in conduct regarded as unjust or immoral, whereas under a regulatory regime, liability resides wherever the state judges it most convenient to place it. For example, the Comprehensive Environmental Response, Compensation, and Liability Act of 1980 (42 U.S.C. § 9601) (the so-called "Superfund Act") contains a provision for joint and several liability. This means that PRPs ("potentially responsible parties," as they are designated in the law, or "perps," as they are ironically called in the business community) who generated or even transported a tiny fraction of the toxic wastes at a site can be held liable for the entire clean-up costs.[13] Under these circumstances, legal responsibility does not track moral responsibility in any meaningful way. A second reason classical liberals favor a common law approach is that the common law evolves over time, constrained by precedent, whereas the administrative state works through spasms of legislative authorization, which set out unattainable goals and timetables, which then must be adjusted by the bureaucracy. This requires that unelected bureaucrats be given considerable discretionary authority—always problematic from a classical liberal perspective. Fourth, common law decisions are limited in scope, and mistakes can be confined to a particular jurisdiction if the precedent is not applied in other jurisdictions; statutory law lacks these characteristics. For these and other reasons, classical liberals are inclined to prefer the common law to statutory law as a way of dealing with problems associated with pollution.

That said, there are a number of reasons why the common law is sometimes ill-suited to deal with such problems (Schoenbrod 2000, 4–6). The common law cannot always (1) judge liability, (2) provide remedies, or (3) secure sufficient enforcement. Regarding (1), liability issues arise because it is impossible to carry on modern life without crossing the boundaries of someone's person or property. The common law cannot and will not prohibit an action based on the mere fact that particles of pollution invade someone's airspace or seep into groundwater. The law of nuisance requires actual injury, but then the problem becomes one of delimiting what counts as an injury. It used to be that custom or tradition determined this, but that will not suffice in a dynamic society where technology and scientific knowledge (especially medical knowledge) are continuously improving. Regarding (2), the problem about providing remedies comes up because some activities only risk harming others, and those risks do not always eventuate. Storage of hazardous waste is an obvious example. What are the appropriate remedies, if any, for exposure to risks that do not eventuate? The common law provides no clear guidance. Finally, (3) there is the matter of securing enforcement. If millions of automobile owners are polluting the air that millions of people are breathing, who should compensate whom and for how much? Someone would have to undertake the difficult and maybe practically impossible task of sorting out the victims and the perpetrators in order to assign liability and determine compensation. Attorneys from the plaintiff's bar would undoubtedly volunteer for this morally hazardous duty, which would have foreseeably disastrous consequences. In these and like cases, regulation by statute makes sense and can be conceived of as supplanting or superseding the common law—and as doing so in ways that classical liberals could accept.

Not all environmental regulation can be represented in this way, however. Federal land use regulation appeals to values not easily accommodated by a private ordering and thus not reflected in the common law.[14] Rationales for the Endangered Species Act of 1973 (16 U.S.C. § 1531 et seq.) appeal to the interests of future generations or to the independent value of biodiversity as a justification for imposing restrictions on what landowners can do with their property.[15] Section 404 of the 1972 Clean Water Act is intended to preserve wetlands, which perform a variety of useful environmental functions. These regulatory regimes are intended to realize values that, for one reason or another, are unlikely to be realized by a private ordering. Modern liberals are inclined to favor such regulations, but classical liberals are inclined to oppose them. To summarize, then, the modern liberal regulatory agenda consists of environmental regulations that cannot be represented as substituting for the common law, most regulation of the employment relation, and the regulation of consumer products and services.

The modern liberal regulatory agenda identifies all and only those regulations, or types of regulations, that modern liberals are inclined to favor and classical liberals are inclined to oppose. Accordingly, there are a number of different kinds of regulation that do not show up on this agenda, either because there is already some agreement between modern liberals and classical liberals about that form of regulation or because there is disagreement among classical liberals or disagreement among modern liberals about the type of regulation in question. The regulation of air pollution is an example of the former that was just discussed. It may also be possible to get agreement between classical liberals and modern liberals about the regulation of deceptive advertising and marketing practices. The arguments here would likely be common ground arguments. Because of the lack of deep disagreement between modern liberals and classical liberals about these forms of regulation, they do not appear on the modern liberal regulatory agenda.

In addition, there are types of regulation that are not on the agenda because there is no consensus, or even near consensus, about them among classical liberals or among modern liberals. For instance, in chapter 3 a case was made that such disagreement might exist among classical liberals about banking regulation, insurance regulation, and regulation of capital markets. Modern liberals are inclined to favor all three forms of regulation but so too might some classical liberals. Because classical liberal opinion is divided, these forms of regulation cannot form part of the modern liberal regulatory agenda that constitutes the heart of the disagreement between classical liberals and modern liberals about the proper scope of government regulation.

Consider also the regulation of ostensibly private behavior. Although much of what the state attempts to do in this area is done through the tax code and transfer programs, there are some laws that directly regulate this behavior. These include mandatory seat belt laws, motorcycle helmet laws, laws prohibiting or limiting gambling, prostitution, surrogacy contracts, and laws forbidding the use of recreational drugs. As was suggested in chapter 3, there appears to be no hard and fast classical-modern liberal divide on these issues either. On the one hand, some modern liberals and some classical liberals with strong civil libertarian sympathies are inclined to oppose such laws on the grounds that these prohibitions violate fundamental rights— though different fundamental rights: a right to privacy in the case of modern liberals and a right to liberty (or autonomy) or freedom of contract in the case of classical liberals. And, as noted, some classical liberals and some modern liberals of a more consequentialist bent oppose some or all of these restrictions because they believe these prohibitions do more harm than good. On the other hand, some modern liberals favor these restrictions on self-ownership rights, but they do so on grounds classical liberals could not accept (e.g., risk management for social insurance programs, communitarian values they believe the state should impose, the inevitability of state influence on lifestyle choices). Classical liberals who favor these laws sometimes do so on the grounds that the prohibited activities cause the sorts of harms that government should prevent (viz., crimes or torts), as when it is claimed that legalizing gambling or prostitution would attract organized crime[16] or that legalizing recreational drugs would lead to an increase in property crime or violent crime. These observations are not meant to endorse these arguments for the relevant laws and prohibitions. The point is simply that classical liberals have favored these laws on grounds consistent with their understanding of the proper role of government. Because there is reasoned disagreement within each camp and reasoned agreement between some modern liberals and some classical liberals (though not necessarily on the same grounds) about the regulation of ostensibly private behaviors, direct attempts to regulate ostensibly private behavior do not appear on the modern liberal regulatory agenda.

To summarize, then, the modern liberal regulatory agenda that is the focal point of this facet of the dispute between modern and classical liberals about the proper role of government is constituted by the following three categories of regulation:

A. Regulation of the employment relation.
1. Mandatory terms or conditions of employment, specifically, laws mandating a minimum wage and overtime pay, the law requiring equal pay for equal work, and the law requiring firms to grant family and medical leave
2. Antidiscrimination laws
3. Occupational health and safety regulation as imposed by OSHA
4. Laws regulating employer and union behavior in the collective bargaining process

B. Consumer products and services regulation.
1. Mandated or forbidden features of consumer products and services, especially medical products
2. Occupational licensure laws

C. Some environmental regulation

Included in this category are regulations designed to enhance environmental quality in ways that cannot be construed as required by respect for the common law rights of existing individuals. Specifically, this includes:

1. The Endangered Species Act (16 U.S.C. §1531 et seq.), which is intended to preserve and protect biodiversity,
2. Section 404 of the Clean Water Act (33 U.S.C. §1251 et seq.), which gives the government extensive powers to regulate wetlands.

How might reasoned agreement on this agenda be reached? Recall from the beginning of chapter 1 the various ways this might happen:

(1) Common ground arguments appeal to a principle or principles that both sides share about the proper scope of government. If, for instance, modern liberals could argue that an item on the modern liberal regulatory agenda solves a genuine public goods problem that cannot be solved by the private sector, that would be a common ground argument, since both sides agree there is a role for the state in solving public goods problems that cannot be solved by the private sector. Assuming the argument is a good one, classical liberals could then accept this item on the agenda.

(2) Modern liberals might also persuade classical liberals to support some item on their regulatory agenda through a convergence argument. Recall that convergence arguments are those based on disparate principles that converge on the same policy conclusion. A modern liberal might argue that, despite appearances to the contrary, a regulation is actually required by some classical liberal principle. For instance, classical liberals might be persuaded that a proposed consumer privacy law that would prohibit Internet service providers and online advertisers from collecting information from subscribers without their permission can be justified on the grounds that what the former do violates the latter's property rights in information about themselves or their property rights in their personal computers. Modern liberals may have no particular fidelity to this conception of property rights and may favor this regulation on other grounds (e.g., it protects what they see as a fundamental right to privacy), but the former is the sort of argument classical liberals could accept. However, although it is easy to see how laws defining or articulating property rights could be supported by convergence arguments

classical liberals could accept, it is doubtful that any of the items on the modern liberal regulatory agenda could be supported by a convergence argument from classical liberal principles not shared by modern liberals. There are a couple of reasons for this. One is that all the items on the agenda are restrictions on Lockean property rights, specifically, restrictions on management rights and rights of disposition. Or, what comes to the same thing, they are restrictions on freedom of contract. Though it cannot be proved outright, it is difficult to see how restrictions on such rights could themselves be justified by appeal to full liberal ownership rights or rights to freedom of contract. Second, to the extent that there is a classical liberal alternative to any item on the modern liberal regulatory agenda, it argues against the possibility of a convergence argument on grounds of consistency. In other words, assuming classical liberal principles are internally consistent, they cannot imply both an item on the modern liberal regulatory agenda and its classical liberal counterpart. For this reason, the set of convergence arguments from classical liberal principles that modern liberals do not accept to items on the modern liberal regulatory agenda is probably the empty set, or something close to it.

(3) A third way to argue for various elements on the modern liberal regulatory agenda is to argue that classical liberals ought to make an exception to a general rule (a rule of thumb) about the proper scope of government that they subscribe to. The appeal might be to some lower-level, easily agreed upon moral principle or to efficiency or to the sheer impracticality of any alternative, but there is no pretense that the exception is in some way required by, or even is consistent with, any particular classical liberal principle about the proper scope of government, if that principle is conceived of as an exceptionless rule. These "conversion arguments," as they were called, are intended to persuade classical liberals to reject the implications of a more austere version of classical liberalism (viz., libertarianism) on a particular issue, that is, to make an exception. Conversion arguments get their traction from conceiving of classical liberalism, not as a set of principles (propositions) but instead as a propensity to advocate a very limited role for government—a propensity that can be stayed in particular cases, if compelling or at least persuasive reasons can be offered in support of government intervention. Other intended targets of conversion arguments are those who identify themselves as neither modern liberals nor classical liberals.

Chapters 5 and 6 explore common ground arguments for the modern liberal regulatory agenda. The guiding question is "How might modern liberals argue for elements of the modern liberal regulatory agenda in ways that appeal to classical liberal principles about the proper role of government?" Chapters 7 through 10 consider conversion arguments for the items on the modern liberal regulatory agenda. These arguments make no pretense of appealing to classical liberal principles but are intended to be compelling, or at least persuasive, to classical liberals not lashed to the mast of exceptionless libertarian principles about the proper role of government. The general conclusion of these chapters is that, with a few minor exceptions, attempts to reach reasoned agreement between classical liberals and modern liberals on the modern liberal regulatory agenda fall short or fail. En passant, it will be argued that classical liberals have good reasons to disagree with this agenda. Chapter 11 considers what is to be done in light of this persistent, reasonable disagreement about the modern liberal regulatory agenda. Specifically, although reasoned agreement about what to believe about the proper role of government may be unachievable, reasoned agreement about what the government should do in the face of this stalemate may be possible. I shall argue that modern liberals (and, for that matter, classical liberals) are justified in imposing on society elements of their vision of the proper role of government only if they go about it in a certain way. These procedural requirements laid down in chapter 11 are justified by appeal to liberal values and ideals shared by both modern and classical liberals. In spite of persistent reasonable disagreement, then, imposition of elements of the modern liberal regulatory agenda would be politically or morally justifiable, provided that these conditions are met. Chapter 12 investigates whether these requirements have actually been met in the case of a few selected items on the modern liberal regulatory agenda. For now, however, let us turn now to a consideration of common ground or convergence arguments that modern liberals might employ to persuade classical liberals to accept the types of regulation that constitute their regulatory agenda.

Common Ground Arguments

Presuppositions of a Market Economy

Chapter 1 notes that one of the points of agreement between classical liberals and modern liberals is that the economic system should be a market economy in which most of the means of production are privately owned. As chapters 2 and 3 show, however, there is much that modern liberals and classical liberals have to disagree about regarding private ownership. But what about the market? Specifically, are there any presuppositions of a market economy that might serve as a basis for reasoned agreement for elements of the modern liberal regulatory agenda? One possibility is that it might be argued that some types of regulation serve to ensure that some range of transactions is voluntary. A market economy presupposes that transactions are voluntary, and it might be argued that minimum wage laws, occupational health and safety regulation, and consumer product and service regulation are necessary to ensure that transactions between firms and their employees or between firms and their customers are truly voluntary.

Traditionally, there are two grounds on which a transaction may be said to fail to be voluntary: ignorance and coercion. Coercion is one of those philosophically difficult concepts whose meaning and reference have been the subject of much controversy.[1] Are workers coerced into taking low-paid jobs or unacceptable health and safety risks if their alternative is penury or some inadequate standard of living provided by a government-sponsored safety net or private charity? Charges that low wage offers or offers to work under undesirable health and safety conditions are coercive might be used to justify minimum wage laws and occupational health and safety regulation, respectively. The problem with an argument of this sort, however, is that it would have to appeal to a conception of coercion that classical liberals would reject. The classical liberal conception of coercion has as its core the notion of the use or threat of violence as an inducement to action.[2] Coercion in this sense (or in these senses) is not routinely practiced in the private sector, except in some criminal enterprises, as when the Mafia extorts protection money from businesses. When a person accepts a dangerous or low-paid job, however, he or she is typically not coerced, on any conception of coercion classical liberals would accept.

An obvious modern liberal reply questions this conception, however. Why could not the argument proceed on the basis of a different, perhaps broader, conception of coercion? After all, it could be that the most philosophically defensible conception of coercion, together with facts about the situations in which workers find themselves, justify the proposition that workers would be routinely coerced to accept subminimal wages and/or unsafe working conditions, absent state intervention.[3] Thus, it might be argued, classical liberals should favor these types of regulations because they believe the state should prohibit coercion. This would be a common ground or convergence argument for these forms of government regulation.

This will not do, however, for at least two reasons. First, it is hard to see how one could know, or reasonably estimate, what the lowest typical wage would be, absent minimum wage laws; similarly for workplace risks. These are very large counterfactuals that would be very hard to substantiate without actually implementing the policies in question. Second, and perhaps more importantly, an argument in favor of regulation based on a claim about coercion has to appeal to a conception of coercion that classical liberals could accept. The reason for this is to be found in the nature of a common ground or convergence argument: either type of argument must appeal to a principle accepted by the other side. The principle that the state should prevent coercive transactions between private parties is such a principle only if the reference of the term "coercion" is the one that can be endorsed by classical liberals. One might introduce two terms to mark more accurately the distinction between different conceptions of coercion and to spell out the points of agreement and disagreement by reference to these terms. For example, one could say that modern liberals and classical liberals agree that the state should prevent "narrowly coercive" exchanges between private parties, but they disagree that the state should prevent "broadly coercive" exchanges between private parties. The situation closely parallels the long-running debate in political philosophy between advocates of positive freedom and advocates of negative freedom about the "real meaning" of freedom. This debate is perhaps more usefully characterized more substantively. One can define terms in any way one chooses, so long as the definitions are clear and do not depart too far from common usage. It is then possible to restate the philosophical disputes in the new, clarified language.

In the case of negative and positive freedom, one can reframe the traditional debate about the "real meaning" or the "true nature" of freedom by reference to the question of whether the state should ensure or maximize people's positive freedom, negative freedom, or both. There are arguments on both sides, but this is a more fruitful way of characterizing the debate—as opposed to conceiving it to be a dispute about the true nature of freedom or the real meaning of the term. In the case of coercion, one can ask whether the state should prevent narrowly coercive exchanges, broadly coercive exchanges, or both. However, if a common ground or convergence argument is to be made that government regulation is necessary to prevent private-sector coercion, the conception of coercion must be a narrow one (or one among a number of narrow ones) endorsed by classical liberals. The modern liberal may have a better account, philosophically speaking, of coercion, but because of their reliance on philosophically contentious concepts, arguments based on such an account are not common ground or convergence arguments.

What about ignorance? Could it be argued that elements of the modern liberal regulatory agenda are necessary to prevent transactions done in ignorance—ignorance that would mark such transactions as involuntary? This idea would have its most natural application in consumer product regulation and occupational health and safety regulation. Various health and safety regulations mandate the disclosure of information about workplace hazards and consumer product hazards. In addition, part of the Occupational Safety and Health Act of 1970 created an agency responsible for producing knowledge about workplace health and safety: NIOSH—the National Institute of Occupational Safety and Health. Moreover, some economists have argued that information has the characteristics of a public good.

If this sort of information is a public good, that by itself would be insufficient to justify state provision of it. Classical liberals believe that only genuine public goods problems are candidates to be solved by state action. They would, therefore, be willing to consider arguments to the effect that the state could solve a genuine public goods problem regarding the provision of occupational and consumer product health and safety information. The problem is that this is insufficient to justify these two elements of the modern liberal regulatory agenda. There is much more to this agenda for consumer and occupational health and safety regulation than the production and dissemination of information about risks and hazards. In both areas, there are mandatory standards that firms must follow, as well as significant reporting requirements and fines for noncompliance. While it might be that mandatory provision of health and safety information could be justified by a public goods argument, that is not the key point of contention between modern liberals and classical liberals. Instead, it is about forcing people not to take jobs or to buy products that have or lack certain characteristics the government deems important.

It might be noted in passing that there is another argument that classical liberals might accept for the mandatory provision of health and safety information, which was suggested in chapter 1 and again in chapter 3. The idea behind this argument is that labeling and other regulations designed to warn users of various consumer products or occupational equipment might be used to preclude tort actions against manufacturers on the grounds of "failure to warn." The consequent gain in security of possession that would come from precluding these suits, especially the class action suits, would arguably offset the (relatively minor) infringement on freedom of contract that labeling regulations represent. This is a conversion argument, however, since it does involve making an exception to allow for this infringement.

Fundamental Rights and Negative Externalities

Aside from the presuppositions of a market economy, there are three broad areas of agreement between classical liberals and modern liberals about the proper role of the state. Both sides agree that the state should (1) enforce and respect fundamental personal and political rights, (2) prohibit or regulate common law negative externalities, and (3) solve public goods problems that cannot be solved via tying arrangements. Could any of these agreed-upon types of government activity be construed to include elements of the modern liberal regulatory agenda?

Fundamental personal rights include the right to be secure in one's person and one's possessions, the right to freedom of thought, expression, and worship, the right to freedom of association, the right to due process, and the right to equal protection under the law. Political rights include the right to vote, the right to run for public office,[4] and the right to freedom of speech and of the press. How might modern liberals argue for elements of their regulatory agenda on the grounds that the latter are needed to secure these agreed-upon fundamental rights? It is hard to see how one might get environmental regulation or consumer product regulation out of any of these rights. The most promising venue for deploying arguments from fundamental rights is in the area of employment law. Perhaps antidiscrimination law could be justified by reference to equal protection or due process rights insofar as the cumulative effect of antidiscrimination law is to require a just cause dismissal policy for protected groups (e.g., women, minorities, the disabled, the elderly). Laws regulating how companies must deal with unions might be justified by reference to a right of free association.

Classical liberals are likely to dismiss any attempt to make an argument of this sort on the grounds that fundamental personal and political rights are rights against the state, not against private parties.[5] On their conception of these rights, the latter secure a sphere of civil society that the state may not invade. The state cannot, for example, order the Catholic Church to ordain women priests, no matter how strong the theological and practical arguments are for doing so. Fundamental rights are a shield against the state, not a sword wielded by the state on behalf of some private parties—or on behalf of society at large—against other private parties. Classical liberals would say that for the state to use these rights against private parties as a way of achieving desirable results in civil society involves a profound misunderstanding of their proper role. Fundamental legal rights are intended to shackle the state and to ensure limited government vis-à-vis civil society. The state may be justified in its regulatory interventions in civil society but not under color of enforcing fundamental rights.

Modern liberals (e.g., Sunstein (1993)) might disagree with this constrained conception of rights and their role in liberal society. They might argue for a broader conception of fundamental rights in which rights can and should be conceived of as a sword against private parties as well as a shield against the state, perhaps on the grounds that the ends that fundamental rights secure are so important. The problem with this sort of move should be self-evident, however. A common ground argument based on claims of fundamental rights requires a shared conception of these rights, and an appeal to a broader conception of fundamental personal and political rights as involving claims against private actors as well as the state means that modern liberals have effectively abandoned an attempt to make their case on common ground. They have turned their backs on the classical liberal sinners in their congregation and are preaching to the choir. Classical liberals would point out that their common ground with modern liberals about fundamental personal and political rights is limited by an understanding of these rights as rights against the state, not as rights that private parties have against one another that the state enforces. Essentially, what the modern liberal is asking for is an expansion of fundamental rights. Justifying this would seem to be an inherently difficult task, more so if the goal is reasoned agreement with classical liberals and not truth, as it appears in the mind's eye of a modern liberal. To the extent that elements of the modern liberal regulatory agenda are grounded in deeper or more abstract philosophical principles, classical liberals will be rightly skeptical of modern liberal excavations of those principles.

What about arguments that appeal to externalities? Classical liberals accept that it is appropriate for the state to regulate some negative externalities, such as pollution. Negative externalities—or to be more precise, negative externalities that classical liberals believe are the appropriate subject of government regulation—are not to be construed so broadly as to include any negative effect on third parties, however. Instead, they are limited to negative effects on third parties that would count as boundary crossings according to the common law—"common law negative externalities" in the language of chapter 1. The kinds of harms that elements of the modern liberal regulatory agenda could prevent, however, do not appear to fall into that category. Competitive harms, for example, are not common law negative externalities and thus could not justify rate regulation and regulation of entry and exit for classical liberals. Nor could antidiscrimination law be justified on the grounds that allowing employers to discriminate against African Americans when they make hiring decisions is a negative externality (spillover effect) of hiring only whites, since this too is not a common law negative externality. As for positive externalities, classical liberals deny that the mere existence of positive spillover effects on third parties warrants government involvement.

The short shrift given to appeals to both positive and negative externalities is in part justified by some stipulations introduced in chapter 1 regarding the twin distinctions between public goods and positive externalities on the one hand and public bads and negative externalities on the other hand. It was suggested there that it is more natural to use the language of externalities (both positive and negative) when both those causing the benefit or harm and the affected third parties are readily identifiable, whereas the language of public goods and bads is more appropriate when either party is harder to identify empirically. If my neighbor were to dump raw sewage onto my land, a common law negative externality would exist, and my lawyer could be unleashed to gnaw on his leg. When thousands of farmers use pesticides that leach into the soil in minute quantities that eventually add up to something substantial, a public bad is created in downstream waterways, and classical liberals can agree that this is a job for the Environmental Protection Agency.

As should be clear from the above discussion, for a common ground argument to be deployed, it has to appeal to understandings of key concepts that classical liberals accept. It is of course possible for modern liberals to argue for the modern liberal regulatory agenda on the basis of their own understandings of ancillary philosophical concepts and principles—understandings that classical liberals would not accept, and indeed that has been the pattern on both sides and on many fronts in the larger dispute between modern liberals and classical liberals about the proper role of government. This, however, is a form of preaching to the converted. These are not common ground arguments, and for that reason they do not reach classical liberals who are willing to be convinced that their principles should lead them to convert to the modern liberal faith. They also violate the methodological precept laid down in chapter 1, which is richly supported by inductive evidence: arguments that ascend to the level of philosophical principle are likely to be inconclusive or to ascend into even more abstract realms of philosophy where the disputes are even more inconclusive, if that is possible. What starts out as an attempt to justify laws regulating the employment relation, for example, ends up as a dispute in moral theory or, even worse, in metaphysics. Hobbes, Spinoza, and Hegel, to name three famous examples, all attempted to justify some fairly specific normative political claims by reference to a comprehensive metaphysical vision of humanity's place in the universe, but the days of that sort of grand theorizing are over—or at least they should be. Such pretensions have been unseemly ever since Hume rediscovered the ancient skeptics' insight that reason's most becoming virtue is modesty.

Agreement between classical liberals and modern liberals on the presuppositions of a market economy, fundamental rights, and externalities is actually quite thin, at least in ways that might be relevant to the dispute at hand. What about public goods and public bads? Are prospects for reasoned agreement any better there? Indeed, they are. The remainder of this chapter and the next examine this possibility in detail.

Public Goods Problems and Public Goods Arguments

Recall that a public good is defined by two conditions: nonrivalrous or joint consumption and nonexcludability. To say that a good is jointly consumed is to say that its consumption by one member of the group does not impede consumption by others in the group. To say that a good is nonexcludable is to say that, were contribution toward funding the good voluntary, noncontributors could not be feasibly excluded from getting it; similarly for public bads. Both joint consumption and nonexcludability are matters of degree. Consumption by one person might only very slightly diminish the ability of others to consume the good. Nonexcludability is even more clearly a matter of degree, depending as it does on the state of technology and the legal system. Both joint consumption and nonexcludability gradually fade away, as it were, and the public goods intellectual apparatus becomes increasingly ill-suited to the subject matter at hand.

For present purposes, however, it is important to press this apparatus into service as much as is feasible, since it appears to have the potential to bring classical and modern liberals together. The reason is that classical liberals allow that it can be appropriate for the state to provide public goods. But not just any public goods. They believe that state provision is appropriate only if it solves a genuine public goods problem, which requires four conditions: (1) contribution to the provision of the good for a given population would be voluntary, absent state coercion; (2) each individual in that population believes that the benefits of having the good outweigh her share of the cost; (3) the good is so costly that no one individual could afford to provide it herself, or find it worth his or her while to provide it; (4) each person's share of the cost of the good is so small, relative to the total cost of providing the good, that any one person's failure to contribute her share would not have a noticeable effect on whether or not the good is provided.

There are two complications associated with condition (2) that were glossed over in chapter 1: first, in describing people's states of mind, the beliefs in question must be understood dispositionally (i.e., in terms of judgments a person would make if he or she were asked), since not every member of the group explicitly considers the issue. Second, notice that this formulation defines public goods problems in terms of people's judgments about whether the benefits outweigh the costs, instead of whether the benefits actually do outweigh the costs.

In other words, this is a preference conception, not a welfarist conception, of public goods. The typical statement of what constitutes a public goods problem is ambiguous between these formulations. The reason for adopting a preference formulation of public goods problems will become apparent shortly.

The existence of a public goods problem does not, for classical liberals, entail that the government should solve it by providing the good or by providing it in whatever way it chooses. Other conditions must be met. One is that there must be no feasible tying arrangement, that is, no feasible way to tie the provision of the public good to a private good. Finally, there is the presumption that if the state does provide it, it does so by purchasing the good with tax revenues. This is justified by the basic idea behind state solutions to public goods problems, namely, that the state is giving people what they want for a price they are all willing to pay. State provision is supposed to result in a Pareto improvement, just like the market. This introduces yet another complication into the conception of a public goods problem: it is necessary to suppose that everyone would agree that the value of the good is greater than the value of his or her share of the costs, where the latter is determined by the tax system. If the goods in question (e.g., national defense, the criminal and civil justice system) are sufficiently important, that is a reasonable supposition, but in the case of other public goods, that may not be so.

A *public goods argument,* then, has a number of different premises: it establishes that the provision of a certain good involves a genuine public goods problem, that there is no solution to that problem involving a tying arrangement, and that the state provides the good by purchasing it and paying for it with tax revenues. Such an argument, then, could be a common ground or convergence argument that a modern liberal might offer to persuade classical liberals to accept some element of the modern liberal regulatory agenda.

But can all classical liberals be persuaded by public goods arguments? Probably the economists can, since economists have never met a Pareto improvement they did not like. More generally, public goods arguments are attractive to those who are inclined to believe that the proper role of government includes providing goods and services that people want at a price they would be willing to pay but cannot get directly through the market. The notion that government should solve genuine public goods problems by making contribution nonvoluntary and purchasing the good with tax dollars is one way of making that inclination more precise. However, it seems reasonably clear that not all classical liberals would be willing to accept these arguments. Libertarians such as Jan Narveson (1988, 235–240) reject them, as does the early Nozick, who rejects public goods arguments in his discussion of the Principle of Fairness. The Principle of Fairness says that "when a number of people engage in a just, mutually advantageous cooperative venture according to rules and thus restrain their liberty in ways necessary to yield advantages for all, those who have submitted to these restrictions have a right to similar acquiescence on the part of those who have benefited from their submission" (Nozick 1974, 90). Nozick rejects both this principle and the claim that it could be enforced against someone's will.[6]

Nevertheless, it is worth investigating how public goods arguments might be used to justify elements of the modern liberal regulatory agenda to classical liberals who are willing to accept them. On the face of it, however, appealing to public goods problems is an unpromising approach to justifying any part of the modern liberal regulatory agenda. A necessary condition for a public goods problem is that each person believes that the benefits of having the good outweigh his or her share of the costs. It is hard to see how the ends for which elements of the modern liberal regulatory agenda are pursued could be thought of as having this characteristic. Any of those items is going to be opposed by people who believe (some quite correctly) that they are on balance negatively affected by it. Indeed, if this requirement is interpreted strictly, it may be that there are no genuine public goods problems when the reference group is any natural population, such as the population of a nation-state. The reason for this is there will almost always be what David Schmidtz (1991, 84) has called "honest holdouts." These are people who really do not want the good in question, or do not want the state to provide it. They are typically ignored in the economics and social philosophy literatures by a kind of definitional sleight of hand. Public goods are always defined relative to a group, and something is a public good for a group only if every member of the group wants it at some presumed cost. Honest holdouts are simply defined out of the problem and its solution because they are not in the relevant group. However, if this conceptual apparatus is to be applied to the real world, that is, to natural populations such as populations that compose modern nation-states or federations of nation-states, the existence of honest holdouts and the complications they raise must be addressed.

Consider the case of national defense, which is the paradigm of a public goods problem that the state is supposed to solve. In any sufficiently large society, there will very likely be people who do not want national defense at all or do not want it provided by the state. Some might believe that adequate defense services will be provided anyway by other, larger states, so that any contributions they might make are wasted. Call these individuals "international free riders" (or "Europeans," for short). There are also anarchists. Anarchists believe that the state should be abolished, so they do not want what the state is offering in any department. Many of them believe that the state is the source of most of society's evils.[7] The philosophical foundations of anarchism are various: some forms of anarchism, such as Emma Goldman's, are rooted in pacifism, and those anarchists would thus want no defense services at all.[8] Not all anarchists are pacifists, however. Some believe that coercion is sometimes justified, but no person or group is entitled to be the sole authorizer of the use of coercive power—a defining condition of a state. For example, the individualist-anarchist Murray Rothbard believes that when the state takes on this role (as it must, if it is to be a state), it necessarily violates people's natural rights. Rothbard (1978, 237–41) believes that whatever security from external aggressors is needed could be purchased on the market from private companies or, failing that, through spontaneous armed resistance. In general, anarchists believe that whatever defense is needed against external aggressors could be provided by the people themselves through passive resistance, deft argumentation, spontaneous armed resistance, or privately funded armed forces. Whatever their favored alternative, in their judgment they would be better off with that alternative than they would be having defense services provided by the state. For the anarchists, the basic problem is not that the financial cost is too great. Rather, what is too high is the opportunity cost, which is simply the value of the next most preferred alternative.[9] For them, this includes some form of nonstate provision of defense services or even no defense services at all. The opportunity costs might also be taken to include the myriad beneficial side effects that anarchists believe would flow from the elimination of the coercive apparatus of the state. Let us suppose, as seems reasonable, that every natural population (e.g., the population of nation-states) has some anarchists in it, or at least some other honest holdouts who do not want the good in question. How might their situation be addressed within the public goods framework?

One way is to argue that the status quo provision of the good at the stipulated cost really is in their interests and that their actual preferences (or, what comes to the same thing, their beliefs about their interests) do not track their true interests. It might be argued that, contrary to what the anarchists think, there is no effective alternative to state provision of this good. They are simply being naive about the pervasiveness and seriousness of potential threats and/or about what must be done to meet those threats. Whether they recognize it or not, having a state-financed military establishment is in their own interests, all things considered. Perhaps what one needs to consider here are not the preferences that people actually have but rather the preferences they would have if they saw their interests rightly, "idealized" or "considered" preferences, if you will. As attractive as this approach might appear to be, however, it shall not be pursued here for at least two reasons.

First, while anarchists may have a faulty appreciation of their national security interests, they may not have, and for present purposes it is worth investigating the consequences of their having an accurate appreciation of their interests when those interests conflict with the interests of others who want the good at the stipulated price. This has important implications for conceiving of regulatory public goods as presenting public goods problems. Second, suppose that the anarchists are not right and that their preferences, or the beliefs that undergird them, are unreasonable or false. Whatever the truth about the real interests of these groups, it is clear that making a public goods argument on the basis of idealized preferences (or on the basis of people's "true interests") is not the sort of move that classical liberals can easily make. Classical liberals are committed to the proposition that people should be treated as if they are the best judges of their own interests. This does not mean, as some critics seem to think, that classical liberals believe that people actually *are* the best judges of their own interests—invariably. It does, however, require a respect for people's actual preferences that would prevent classical liberals from dismissing the expressed preferences of anarchists on the grounds that classical liberals and their friends (who, we are supposing, have the collective power to enforce their views) are really doing what is in the dissenters' best interests, and indeed everyone else's, whether these others know it or not.

This raises a more general question that warrants a brief aside: why are classical liberals so reluctant to accept the proposition that people are sometimes faulty judges of their true interests, and, correspondingly, why are they so reluctant to appeal to idealized preferences (or "true interests") as a basis for public policy? After all, the thrust of their arguments is that the institutions they favor (e.g., the minimal state, the free market) are what people would prefer if they were to judge their interests accurately. One reason is the obvious rule utilitarian argument that usually people are the best judges of their own interests, but it is too difficult for public policy purposes to identify the range of cases in which they are not. Perhaps more importantly, however, classical liberals worry that an appeal to idealized preferences or true interests as a justification for government policy would be, or would become, merely a pretext for state officials to impose arbitrarily their own values—their own vision of the good society—on others. Personal wisdom, like consumer sovereignty, is a convenient fiction that classical liberals cling to, not out of a misplaced individualism or a belief in each person's infallibility about his or her own values but instead out of a deep and abiding concern for what happens when state officials take it upon themselves to discern and act upon people's true interests. These observations also explain why classical liberals cannot dismiss the actual preferences of those who disagree with government policy as not reflective of the latter's true interests, even on something as basic as national defense—and even if the latter's judgment is incorrect. If a public goods argument is to be part of a common ground or convergence argument to persuade classical liberals, it must be formulated in terms of what people think is in their best interests, that is, their preferences and not in terms of what is in their best interests, that is, their welfare. This explains why, for present purposes, public goods problems—and public goods arguments—have to be framed in terms of actual preferences and not welfare.

This means that ultimately, classical liberals who are attracted to public goods arguments as a justification for state activity, must face squarely the fact of real disagreement about what public goods the state should supply. That disagreement needs to be distinguished from disagreement about the level of provision of the public good, (e.g., national defense). In the United States, many liberals of various persuasions believe that, although it is appropriate for the state to provide national defense, they also think that it is providing too much of the good either absolutely or relative to its cost. They would prefer less of the good at a lower cost. These liberal dissenters from the status quo accept the legitimacy of the liberal state, however, which means they have bought into the basic democratic framework within which these problems are hashed out. They get to make their case in the political arena and have agreed, either explicitly, tacitly, or hypothetically (depending on their theory of state legitimacy) to accept whatever results emerge from that process. The disagreement with the anarchist is more fundamental in the sense that it goes to the question of the legitimate scope of government activity. Honest holdouts, as here understood, believe that the state should not provide the good at all. The question at issue is how to justify state provision of goods that not every member of the society believes the state should provide.

If classical liberals are willing to justify state action to solve public goods problems in the real world of natural populations and if they believe that national defense is a paradigm example of a public goods problem the state can and should solve, then they are going to have to modify their account of what counts as one of these problems. Specifically, unanimity cannot be required or presumed for something to create a public goods problem for a natural population, given the near certainty of honest holdouts. How much less of a consensus than unanimity is required for a public goods problem can be left indeterminate at this point, but clearly some relaxation of the unanimity requirement is necessary. Only by so doing will they be able to justify statist solutions (i.e., state provision) to the traditional public goods problems of national defense, clean air and water, the administration of the criminal and civil justice systems, the funding of local streets and highways, and any other public goods problems, as the latter come up in the real world. This modification might in turn provide an opening to justify some elements of the modern liberal regulatory agenda. The last section of this chapter and all of the next chapter investigate this possibility in detail, but for now, it is necessary to examine more closely the nature of the preferences or values that government solutions to public goods problems realize and how the honest holdouts are to be dealt with.

Public Goods and Collective Values

Recall that public goods are by definition jointly consumed, which means that consumption of the good by one individual does not impede or diminish its consumption by others. Following David Schmidtz (1991, 55) again, let us call any good that meets this condition a *collective good*. A public good is simply a collective good whose consumption is nonexcludable. Consider now the preferences people have for collective goods. Typically, these preferences are collective preferences in the sense that they refer to collective entities of which the individual in question is a member (e.g., one's nation or one's local community). To put it more precisely, collective preferences include collectivities as the subjects of their intentional objects.[10]

By contrast, an egoistic preference has only the person who has the preference as the subject of its intentional object, as when Smith prefers (for himself) six apples to five oranges. There are also altruistic preferences, which can be defined as preferences that have only others as subjects of their intentional objects. "Others" include both individuals and groups, as when I prefer that my son enter the priesthood rather than become an attorney or when a Boston Red Sox fan desires that the New York Yankees not win the World Series for the remainder of the millennium. What distinguishes a collective preference from a group altruistic preference is that in the case of the former, but not the latter, the person who has the preference is included in the collectivity that is the subject of the intentional object.

Public goods problems are typically formulated in terms of egoistic preferences. Supposedly, each individual prefers that he or she have the good at the associated cost to not having the good and having the money he or she would have spent for his or her share of the good. In this way, state provision of a public good, funded by forced contributions, can be represented as a Pareto improvement. This is perfectly accurate as far as it goes; people do have those egoistic preferences, at least dispositionally. However, it also seems that people have and consult collective preferences when asked—preferences whose intentional objects have as subjects groups of which they are members. To the extent that public goods—and public goods problems—are conceived of in terms of the realization of collective preferences, then what a person wants when it comes to, for example, national defense is not (merely or only) that he should be protected from extraterritorial threats; he wants it to be the case that *we* are secure from the predations of the various Mongols, Vandals, and Huns of the world. In other words, he wants collective security. Indeed, it seems more plausible, more psychologically realistic, to suppose that people consult their collective preferences when they think about things like defense from extraterritorial threats. Members of our society want *us* to be protected from these threats, and it is in the language of collective preferences that people think about public goods such as national defense, to the extent that they give the matter any thought at all. Of course people also want themselves and their families to be protected from external threats, but these egoistic and altruistic preferences are typically satisfied when and only when the corresponding collective preference is satisfied.

It is worth noting that this collective way of thinking also pervades how people are disposed to think about the costs of public goods. This is true whether those costs are conceived of in financial terms or in terms of opportunity costs. To the extent that they give the matter any thought at all, people typically do not consider whether their individual financial contributions to national defense are worth it. In fact, they usually do not know what that contribution is, since only a trivial fraction of the population has any idea what percentage of their taxes goes to national defense. Indeed, thanks to the complexity of the tax laws, only a trivial fraction of citizens know even approximately what percentage of their income they pay in taxes! Typically those who do give the matter some thought ask, "Is the total financial cost of the good that we bear worth it?" (relative to the alternative of keeping those tax dollars and having no defense services provided by the state), where the costs as well as the benefits are construed collectively. Certainly their elected representatives think of both the costs and the benefits in collectivist terms. It is even more natural to conceive of opportunity costs collectively. Reasoned persuasion, passive resistance, and private armies are all alternatives to state-provided national defense that a society (i.e., we, as a society) could adopt. As in the case of the financial costs, most people do not even consider the opportunity costs of state provision of national defense; that is, they do not consider alternative ways of providing—alternative ways we might provide—security from external threats. It is likely that if they were to consider these alternatives, they would reject them out of hand as utterly unrealistic, which is one reason why the national defense case is the most commonly cited example of a public goods problem that the state can solve. Even so, these opportunity costs are most naturally described in terms of what alternatives a society could adopt and not what individuals might do for themselves in the event that their state ceased to provide national defense or even ceased to exist.

Of course, the benefits of public goods accrue to individuals and the costs of public goods are borne by individuals, whether those costs are conceived of in financial terms or in terms of opportunity costs. Individuals get protected, pay taxes, and would live under the alternative institutional arrangements that would exist if the state did not provide the good. Indeed, the fact that individuals bear the costs of public goods is implicit in the conception of collective costs, since these are costs that accrue to individuals in virtue of their membership in the collectivity—the costs that we bear.

Returning to the notion of a collective preference, does it help liberals to conceive of public goods problems as problems about satisfying collective preferences? On the face of it, it would seem not. After all, there would still be honest holdouts. For example, anarchists have a collective preference that organized violence by the state not be used against external threats, either because they are pacifists or because they believe in the effectiveness of the private sector in handling whatever threats might emerge, or because they worry more about other things that a state would do when it holds a monopoly on coercive power, as it must, if it is to be a state. They judge that the benefits of the good do not outweigh the costs they would bear. What makes these anarchists honest holdouts is that they really do believe that they and the societies of which they are members would be better off without any national defense; they are not dissembling in order that they may free ride on others' contributions.

What, then, could be said to these honest holdouts? Those who believe in the legitimacy of the state in its role as a defender against external threats—including classical and modern liberals—can begin by pointing out that no matter what happens, someone's collective preferences about national defense are going to be realized, and others' collective preferences will be frustrated. In other words, satisfying the collective preferences of these honest holdouts necessarily frustrates the collective preferences of those who favor state provision of national defense and vice versa. The anarchists might object that they have no collective preferences in these matters, or perhaps their collective preferences extend no further than a relatively small circle of like-minded individuals. They are not, how shall we say, ideological in their beliefs. They say that they do not want to "impose their values" on others; they just want to be left alone. The preferences they consult, the costs and benefits they weigh, are either egoistic or include only a small group of like-minded individuals. The problem is that even if they are right about the content of their mental states, the satisfaction of their preferences to be left alone would realize a state of affairs indistinguishable from what realizes the collective preference for no national defense. In other words, their preferences are functionally equivalent to a collective preference that refers to the entire nation of which they are a part. The reason for this is that if principled anarchists and any other honest holdouts were to be permitted to realize their preferences, they would necessarily be freed of their obligation to contribute to state provision of national defense; that in turn would encourage the appearance of dishonest holdouts, that is, people who want the good at the specified price but would misrepresent their preferences in hopes of getting it for free. Furthermore, once the principle became established that people do not have to contribute to the provision of public goods that they believe the state should not supply, the state would collapse. Ideological anarchists would cheer this development, which is why those anarchists who claim no collective preferences for their society effectively want the same thing as their more ideological brethren.

Realizing anarchist or other honest holdout preferences, however characterized, would obviously frustrate the collective preferences of others by depriving the latter of a collective good they want at a collective and individual price they are willing to pay, since national defense cannot be provided for some without being provided for all. After pointing this out, those who believe in state provision of national defense can then ask, "Why should *your* preferences regarding national defense carry the day? Why should *your* preferences—however they might be characterized—be imposed on *us?*" This impasse, and the rhetorical questions each side might be prompted to ask the other side, suggest that at bottom public goods problems for natural populations are best conceived of as practical problems that cannot be avoided and that addressing them will inevitably involve imposing some people's collective preferences—values—on others. Some public goods problems will be solved by state provision, and those will be public goods that some people either do not want or do not want the state to provide. Once these facts are admitted, the most pressing question becomes how those who are in a position to have their way deal with those who dissent.

How, then, should honest holdouts be dealt with? As indicated above, they cannot be absolved of their responsibility to contribute. But their consent can and should be sought by liberals, as well as others who believe in state-provided national defense. Obviously, their consent should first be sought by argument and not by deceit or trickery. So, what kind of arguments should liberal defenders of state provision of national defense make to those who reject same, for whatever reason? Consider, first, the anarchists. Following the lead supplied by the discussion in the first section of chapter 1 about how classical and modern liberals should try to reach reasoned agreement among themselves about the proper role of the state, it seems that the liberal statists (as they might be called) should seek out principles they share with their interlocutors or appeal to principles their interlocutors already accept. For example, the anarchist Murray Rothbard has a great deal in common with libertarians and other classical liberals (so much so that he sometimes calls himself a libertarian), so it might be possible to make a case for state provision of protective services, including national defense, based on principles he accepts. Indeed, this is exactly the point of part I of Robert Nozick's *Anarchy, State, and Utopia,* in which Nozick argues on the basis of Lockean natural rights that the minimal state is justified and that the individualist-anarchist is mistaken in believing that the state is an inherently immoral organization.[11] Notice that Nozick, like Locke, begins with a discussion of the defects of a pure private ordering, that is, a state of nature (Nozick 1974, ch. 2). Locke calls these the "inconveniences" of a state of nature (Locke [1690] 1988, § 13, 124–126). Anarchists such as Rothbard believe these inconveniences can be overcome by the private provision of protective services, but at least by the end of part I of his book, Nozick denies this. In short, liberal statists of various persuasions could offer their anarchist opponents common ground arguments or convergence arguments for state provision of national defense. Conversion arguments might also be tried, but such arguments are not likely to be persuasive to stiff-necked (i.e., highly principled) anarchists.

None of these types of arguments may succeed, however, in the sense of rationally persuading the anarchists. What happens in that case? Under these circumstances, there may be some principle that liberal defenders of the status quo and their anarchist interlocutors could agree on for resolving deep disagreements that must, as a practical matter, be resolved. In the context of the debate between modern liberals and classical liberals, this sort of argument was called a practical liberal argument. Since anarchists are not liberals, another name is needed for the kind of argument that needs to be made here— call it simply a "practical political argument." There is of course the distinct possibility that there is no such argument because there is no such principle, in which case the problem has finally ceased to be one of seeking reasoned agreement—even about how to proceed; instead, it becomes entirely a practical problem—actually a moral problem—about how to treat this sort of person (whom, by this point, postmodern liberal statists would call…"the Other"). Under the circumstances, assuming that the liberal statists have the guns and the votes, they must determine what their principles permit and require them to do with their recalcitrant interlocutors. The latter will undoubtedly be forced to contribute, but do liberal principles require anything of those liberals doing the forcing? A version of this question will be systematically investigated in chapter 11. For now, it is enough to recognize that the search for reasoned agreement with the anarchists has come to an end, though not a happy one, and the only question that remains is Lenin's question: "What is to be done?" Unlike Lenin, however, liberals must answer this question in a way that is compatible with liberal principles and values. Whatever else is required under the circumstances, it is plausible to insist that liberals have made this effort to persuade the anarchists by appeal to principles, either substantive or procedural, that anarchists might be inclined to accept. This is a way of showing respect for them as reasoning beings.[12] To reiterate, at the end of the day, there may be no such argument, but liberal statists at least have to explore the possibility of such an argument.

The main points of this discussion can be summarized as follows: public goods can and should be conceived of as the realization of the collective preferences, as well as egoistic and/or altruistic preferences, where the collectivities are groups (typically nation-states) of which the individuals who have these preferences are members. The costs of a public good can also be conceived of individually or collectively, and that can be done either in terms of what members of the society think is a good use of their money or in terms of the value of forgone alternative ways of providing the good. In other words, the costs, both individual and collective, can be conceived of in financial terms or in terms of opportunity costs. These collective conceptions of costs and benefits more accurately capture how many people in the real world do think, or would think if they were asked, about public goods and their costs, though they also have the relevant egoistic and/or altruistic preferences. But, even if the latter are the only preferences they have, a state of affairs that satisfies them is, or would lead to, a nonexcludable collective good, together with the associated collective costs. This means that collective preferences can be effectively imputed to them no matter what their mental states. Recognizing the complications raised by conceiving of the costs and benefits both collectively and individually means that, as a first approximation, the second condition for a public goods problem should be restated to read: (2a) each person would judge that the collective benefits of the good to the society of which he or she is a member outweigh its collective financial costs and its collective opportunity costs and (2b) each person would judge that the individual benefits of the good outweigh his or her share of the individual financial costs (as determined by the tax system) and the individual opportunity cost of his or her living under alternative institutional arrangements.

This revised second condition is only a first approximation, however. Even if costs and benefits are conceived of collectively and the judgments about them are conceived of subjunctively, insistence on unanimity is too stringent. That would render sterile the concept of a public goods problem—at least if the natural populations are the groups for which it is provided. This is so because of the near certain existence of honest holdouts, that is, those who do not believe the state should provide the good, either because they do not want the good at all or because they want the good but do not want the state to provide it. So, the second condition must be relaxed so that unanimity is not required. How far it should be relaxed is unclear. Adding an undefined qualifier, such as, "the vast majority" will suffice for present purposes, at least if national defense is held up as the paradigm case of a public goods problem that the state should solve.

To summarize, then, the second condition for a public goods problem needs to be restated as follows:

> P is public good whose provision creates a public goods problem for population x if and only if:
> (2a) the vast majority of the members of x would judge that the collective benefits of the good to the society of which he or she is a member outweigh its collective financial costs and its collective opportunity costs
> AND
> (2b) the vast majority of the members of x would judge that the individual benefits of the good outweigh his or her share of the individual financial costs (as determined by the tax system) and the individual opportunity cost of his or her living under alternative institutional arrangements.

The other three conditions for a public goods problem remain unchanged:

> (1) contribution to the provision of the good for a given population would be voluntary, absent state coercion;
> AND
> (3) the provision of P for x is so costly that no individual member of x is willing or able to supply it himself or herself,

AND

(4) each individual's share of the costs of p is so small, relative to the costs of providing the good, that one person's failure to contribute his or her share would not have a noticeable effect on whether or not the good is provided.

Relaxation of the unanimity requirement has an important implication: it creates an opening for modern liberals to make public goods arguments for elements of the modern liberal regulatory agenda, as well as for elements of the modern liberal transfer agenda (though the latter possibility will not be explored in this book). Since public goods arguments are the kind of arguments some classical liberals can accept, this makes it possible for modern liberals to reach for reasoned agreement with them on elements of the modern liberal regulatory agenda. The next section explores in more detail how that might be accomplished.

Regulation and Collective Values

To see how this might work, recall that various social problems that modern liberals want the state to solve can be conceived of as public bads, the solutions to which can be thought of as public goods. This is evident if these goods are conceived of as answering to collective preferences that people have about the kind of society in which they want to live. These "communitarian values," as they might be called, are values people believe should characterize their society. For example, modern liberals might argue that, in response to the perceived problem of poverty among the elderly in the Great Depression, most Americans came to have a collective preference for some sort of assurance or a guarantee that senior citizens in their society (which ultimately includes themselves) not be impoverished. This collective preference was satisfied by Social Security, one of the main transfer programs of the modern welfare state. In a similar manner, a modern liberal might argue in favor of the existing medical products regulatory regime, which is administered by the Food and Drug Administration (FDA), by asserting that the vast majority of people in the contemporary United States want an independent assurance that medical products sold in their country are generally safe and effective. It is not just that people want safe and effective medical products for themselves and their families, though they do want that. Indeed, those desires might explain why they have this collective preference. People have a certain conception of the kind of society in which they want to live; while their conceptions undoubtedly vary in their particulars across individuals, arguably a widely shared part of that conception is that of a society in which there is an independent assurance that medical products are generally safe and effective. The collective origins of such preferences may be found in some particular highly publicized failure of a private ordering. For example, unintended deaths caused by the ingestion of elixir sulfanilamide in 1937 galvanized public opinion behind the Food, Drug, and Cosmetic Act of 1938, which required drug companies to prove to the FDA that new drugs are safe. Once in place, an agency like this comes to be accepted as a necessity, and people cannot conceive of a satisfactory alternative.

A state of affairs that satisfies this preference about medical products is a collective good because one person's consumption of this good does not impede the consumption of that good by others. In other words, it is jointly consumed. There are also private goods (e.g., consumption of particular medical products that are safe and effective) associated with this public good, but the public good is the independent assurance that medical products in that society are generally safe and effective, and that good—that assurance—is jointly enjoyed or "consumed." What about nonexcludability of potential noncontributors? The state does in fact provide this good through the existing regulatory regime, funded by tax revenues, but it could not allow people to opt out of their share of the costs that the state incurs, since it would be infeasible to exclude noncontributors. Thus the assurance that medical products are generally safe and effective meets both conditions for a public good.

Not all public goods involve genuine public goods problems, as that notion was defined in chapter 1. What about this good? There are four conditions that must be met for this to be the case. The first condition—that contribution to the provision of the good, in the absence of state coercion, would be voluntary—is satisfied. Postponing for a moment a consideration of the second condition, recall the third and fourth conditions: (3) the good must be so costly that no one individual could provide it herself, and (4) each individual's contribution is so small, relative to the total cost of providing the good, that one person's failure to contribute would not have a noticeable effect on whether the good is provided. The third condition is obviously met in this example. No one individual has the resources to see to it that people can be assured that medical products are generally safe and effective. The fourth condition is also met, since any one person's failure to bear her share of the costs associated with this good would obviously have only a negligible effect on whether or not the good is provided.

But what about the second condition? Recall that the unanimity requirement has to be relaxed, and this condition has to be formulated both in terms of collective benefits and costs and individual benefits and costs. How much should the unanimity requirement be relaxed? If national defense is the paradigm case that classical liberals accept, then it would have to be true that at least the vast majority of the people would judge that the collective benefits of the good to the society of which he or she is a member outweigh its collective costs. Is it really true that the ends or goals of the existing medical products regulatory regime are desired, even if only dispositionally, by the vast majority of people? On the face of it, it would seem so. If one looks to the stated or intended aims of this regulatory regime, they seem to be the sort of thing to which few people could object. The relevant section of the Food, Drug, and Cosmetic Act that created the FDA says:

> The [Food and Drug] Administration shall:
> (1) promote the public health by promptly and efficiently reviewing clinical research and taking appropriate action on the marketing of regulated products in a timely manner;
> (2) with respect to such products, protect the public health by ensuring that
> (A) foods are safe, wholesome, sanitary, and properly labeled;
> (B) human and veterinary drugs are safe and effective;
> (C) there is reasonable assurance of the safety and effectiveness of devices intended for human use. (21 U.S.C. § 393(b))

Notice that these aims are quite vague, and they have what might be called an aspirational component. In other words, they articulate an ideal that government policy (i.e., implementation of the enabling legislation) is supposed to approximate or approach, which in fact it does by closely regulating the introduction of new drugs and medical devices.

It is at this juncture that classical liberals are likely to raise two objections. First, they would charge that people's collective preferences are far too vague or ambiguous to justify the imposition of the ambitious regulatory regime that has been implemented by the FDA over the years. More exactly, the problem is that people have very different ideas, though not very determinate ones, about the collective good in question. This ambiguity and vagueness must ultimately be resolved by government policymakers at the point of implementation. But, the classical liberal charges, the resolution of that ambiguity and the associated indeterminateness cannot be said to reflect what people "really" want.

A second problem concerns the costs. There seems to be no determinate answer to the question of how people would weigh the collective costs of various regulatory regimes against their benefits or against nonstate alternatives. This is so for the simple reason that the vast majority of the people have not the faintest idea of the financial costs of these regulatory regimes, nor do they have the faintest idea about nonstate alternatives and the consequences of those alternatives as it pertains to health and safety. That is, they know neither the financial costs nor the opportunity costs of this regulatory regime. In consequence, it is pure fabrication or speculation to claim that most people would judge or affirm that the collective costs of some disambiguated end are worth it. In short, there seems to be no determinate answer to the question of whether the vast majority of the people would judge that having the collective good provided by the state at the associated collective cost is worth it, which is the stylized version of condition (2a) for a public goods problem that emerged from the discussion in the previous section. In the final analysis, classical liberals might charge, conceiving of elements of the modern liberal regulatory agenda as involving the production of collective goods that people vaguely want at a cost they are vaguely willing to pay is nothing more than a pretext for modern liberal politicians and their supporters to impose their own collective values on the societies of which they are members. The same problem faces the cost side of condition (2b): few people have even the slightest idea of how much of their own tax dollars go to support the FDA; nor do people have much of an idea of the opportunity costs to them of this regulatory regime.

To all these charges, modern liberals could justly reply that the case of national defense is exactly analogous. People have collective, egoistic, and altruistic preferences for national security. These preferences are as vague, ambiguous, and aspirational as those that inform elements of the modern liberal regulatory agenda. The vast majority of people do want the collective good of national security, and they do want themselves and their families protected from the various Huns in the world, but almost everyone has no clear idea of what this means in concrete terms, nor do they have any clear or determinate ideas about its collective or individual costs, whether those costs are conceived of in financial terms or in terms of opportunity costs.

These observations raise a deeper skeptical question about the applicability of the public goods model even to the paradigm case of national defense. Would the vast majority of, say, contemporary Americans judge that the collective and individual benefits provided by the U.S. military establishment—national security to the extent that it is offered—outweigh the total collective and individual costs, whether those costs are conceived of in financial terms or conceived of in terms of opportunity costs (i.e., the value of the forgone alternatives, viz., private provision of defense service)? While a "yes" answer to this question is speculative, it is neither purely speculative nor merely speculative. To see why, it is worth reflecting on the question of why the national defense case is always cited as the classic example of a public goods problem that the state can and should solve. The answer is straightforward, though loaded with qualifications: within fairly broad limits, almost any amount of the good of national defense above a certain minimum level is worth whatever it costs in treasure. As to the opportunity costs, it is a fair bet that most people would judge that nonstate alternatives are radically inferior to state provision of the good. That is why anarchists are widely regarded as, how shall we say, lacking in good judgment. If this sweeping, though qualified, judgment is correctly attributable to nearly anyone who would give the matter some thought (the few anarchists being screened out by the term "nearly"), then it is reasonable to affirm that the vast majority of Americans would judge that the collective and individual benefits of their defense establishment outweigh its collective and individual costs, in comparison with an alternative in which there is no state provision of this good. This is true even though most people have never explicitly considered the question. (The same could be said of the peoples of many other nations, though this may no longer be true of many citizens of the European Union, who have apparently joined the International Free Riders Brigade.) There is some indirect, though hardly conclusive, evidence for this proposition as well: few lawmakers called into question the need for national defense and, by implication, the military. It is reasonable to suppose if politicians' constituents contained many potential voters who thought otherwise (e.g., anarchists, international free riders), astute political entrepreneurs would have seized the opportunity those potential votes represent, and their voices would be heard.

It might be objected that these observations depends on rigging the question so that all the alternatives involve the abolition of the military. After all, many people favor having a military, but believe that, as currently constituted, the costs vastly outweigh the benefits. They would favor a much smaller military at greatly reduced cost. But that option is not on the table because of the nature of the question under discussion, namely, the rationale for state provision of national defense. The public goods apparatus answers the question of why the state should provide national defense. Principles of representative democracy explain—and ultimately justify—why we have the levels of defense spending that we do.

These reflections on the public goods problem of national defense and its implications are sufficient to turn back the classical liberal charge that the vagueness of the ends of particular elements of the modern liberal regulatory agenda and the cluelessness of the general public about its costs make it completely inappropriate to represent those regimes as providing solutions to various public goods problems. It remains to be seen, however, if this approach can actually be sustained for any or all of these elements of the modern liberal regulatory agenda.

It has been noted that not all public goods give rise to public goods problems and that one of the differences between modern liberals and classical liberals is that the former, but not the latter, believe that there is a role for the state in providing public goods that do not meet the defining conditions for a public goods problem. Because of the loosening of the unanimity requirement, however, it should be evident that what counts as a public goods problem should be more broadly construed than classical liberals have been inclined to allow or, alternatively, that the line between what is and what is not a genuine public goods problem is less clear than what was assumed in chapter 1. An implication of this discussion is that classical liberals who accept public goods arguments for national defense cannot reject out of hand the legitimacy of the modern liberal regulatory agenda, at least to the extent that this agenda can be represented as providing public goods that the vast majority of people want at a collective financial or opportunity cost they would be willing to pay. These classical liberals can, however, reasonably disagree with that agenda, as we shall see in the next chapter.

Regulatory Public Goods

The Private Provision of Regulatory
Public Goods

There is a general argumentative strategy open to classical liberals who do not want to succumb to the blandishments of modern liberals that allows classical liberals to maintain their virtue. They can begin by pointing out that the existence of a public goods problem does not entail, on their principles, that the state should solve it. In other words, the fact that there is a problem the state *can* solve (by making contribution nonvoluntary and purchasing the good with tax dollars) does not mean there is a problem the state *should* solve. It is open to classical liberals to argue that some public goods could be provided through a private ordering, as when the provision of the public good is a by-product of, or tied to, voluntary transactions and the provision of private goods (so-called "tying arrangements"). To secure the private provision of public goods in this manner might seem to be exceptional and exotic, but it is not. One need only look to the operating system that the vast majority of personal computers run on to find an example of a public good that is privately provided through a tying arrangement. The software that constitutes Microsoft Windows meets both of the defining conditions for a public good: it is jointly consumed in the sense that one person's consumption of this good does not impede the consumption of that good by others. As for nonexcludability, which is always a matter of degree, the program can be copied, although the Microsoft Corporation has some success in using features of the software, as well as copyright law, to fight this form of piracy. Perhaps their most important instrumentality for preventing pirates and free riders, however, is a tying arrangement that they have with manufacturers of new computers. The operating system is sold to manufacturers of personal computers, and the price is determined by the number of units a company ships, regardless of whether the Windows operating system is placed on the computer.[1] Because original equipment manufacturers (OEMs) pay for the Windows operating system for each unit they ship, whether or not it is installed, it makes little sense for them to purchase and install another operating system and add that to the price of the machine. The invention of a public good (the operating system) can, and in this case did, call forth creative efforts to tie it to an excludable nonpublic good (the computer). But, one might wonder, how could a tying arrangement work to produce a public good of the sort that is currently provided by the government through regulation?

Consider, once again, the independent assurance that the government provides that new medical products are safe and effective. How might this assurance be provided through a tying arrangement? Charles Murray (1997, 69–70) has suggested how this might be done.[2] The FDA would continue to exist but it would be stripped of its authority to prohibit the manufacture and sale of drugs and devices that it did not approve of. In other words, medical products manufacturers would be able to opt out of the FDA's regulatory regime by simply labeling their products as UNREGULATED (or, to be more accurate, "NOT APPROVED BY THE FDA"). Firms that want their products certified by the FDA could continue to have this done and would have to pay for it and could advertise that fact. The cost of the information about the product's safety and effectiveness would be included in the cost of the product itself, so that ultimately the consumers of the product would pay for the assurance that it is safe and effective, according to FDA standards. Under this scenario, there would be two kinds of drugs, those approved by the FDA and those not so approved, and people could choose to buy either kind. If the vast majority want drugs that are guaranteed safe and effective by the FDA, that is what they would purchase. Many firms would probably still seek certification and approval from the FDA for new drugs and devices, but they would not have to do so. Indeed, competitor private sector certifying agencies might spring up to evaluate new medical products. After all, such agencies are common for other products and services. (More on this in the next section.) Major research universities would likely be the natural seedbed from which these agencies would grow, since few corporate heads can match the presidents of research universities in what Marx called "the boundless thirst for surplus value."

The FDA, now stripped of its authority to prohibit the sale of drugs and medical devices it has not approved, might nevertheless provide a greater assurance of effectiveness than what is offered by other certifying agencies because, let us suppose, the manufacturers' claims authorized by the FDA would be backed by more extensive and elaborate clinical trials. But, competitor certifying agencies might guarantee only that certain safety standards had been met and would make only those carefully hedged claims about effectiveness that are necessary to indicate what a drug or device might be used for. That would allow them to make new drugs more quickly and less expensively available. One result would be that desperately ill individuals could get faster access to new or experimental drugs that would otherwise be held up in the FDA pipeline awaiting regulatory approval. Another result of the decline in approval costs would be stepped up R&D efforts to discover new drugs. It is of course possible that some drugs would be sold without any third party approval, as is now the case with dietary supplements. The latter routinely carry on their labels a statement to the effect that the claims manufacturers make on behalf of these products have not been evaluated by the FDA. As is the case with dietary supplements, the only protection consumers would have would be the manufacturer's reputation and tort law. There might be a role for the FTC in policing the advertising claims for uncertified products and/or prosecuting miscreants for fraud, though as the discussion of that agency in chapter 3 suggests, policing the marketing of goods and services is at best difficult and at worst unhelpful.

It is difficult to know what percentage of U.S. drug consumption would be uncertified by any agency. However, if a substantial majority of people really do want an independent assurance that a broad range of medical products is safe and effective, they would use almost exclusively those products approved by the FDA or by another reputable independent body. After all, the presumption that people want this assurance can be taken as given, since we are assuming that the existing medical products regulatory regime provides a public good that the vast majority of people want at a price they are willing to pay. Under the conditions specified in Murray's thought experiment, the public good of an independent assurance that medical products are generally safe and effective would emerge as a by-product of individuals seeking safety and efficacy in the course of individual transactions and without this public good being an explicit policy or policy goal of any one person or group.

As under the current system, tort law would have to deal with bad outcomes, and there might well have to be additional statutory reforms. A full comparative evaluation of the current regulatory regime and a classical liberal alternative goes beyond what is necessary for present purposes; it is enough to sketch a classical liberal alternative to the current regime in enough detail so that it is at least arguable that it would be adequate to the task of providing the public good the FDA provides and to do so at collective and individual financial and opportunity costs that are comparable, acceptable, or even superior. This is enough to make it unlikely that reasoned agreement between modern liberals and classical liberals could be reached about this part of the modern liberal regulatory agenda based on the proposition that only the existing medical products regulatory regime, in which the FDA can forbid the sale of medical products it has not approved, could produce the public good in question. That proposition can be reasonably doubted.

It is important to understand the claim being advanced here, namely, that it is possible that the public good in question could be provided as a by-product of individual transactions and that this way of providing the good is arguably as effective or more effective than government regulation, whether or not most people would be able to see that or would agree with that. It is of course an entirely different question under what circumstances classical liberals would be justified in imposing on society some alternative to the current medical products regulatory regime, assuming they had the political power to do so. That question will be taken up in chapter 11. All that is at issue here is whether there is a plausible alternative to the current regime that does not mandate the elaborate approval process currently overseen by the FDA. Given that there is such an alternative, reasoned disagreement between classical liberals and modern liberals can be said to persist about the proposition that only the current medical products regulatory regime can produce the relevant public good at an acceptable financial and opportunity cost.[3]

There are some larger lessons to be learned from this example, which may have application to other items on the modern liberal regulatory agenda. The discussion of public goods in chapter 5 stressed the similarities between national defense and the public goods that might be provided by government regulation. The preceding discussion suggests that there are some important differences as well. One is that it is difficult to imagine collective security emerging piecemeal as an unintended by-product of other activities that do not aim specifically at producing that public good. A situation would have to exist in which security could be provided for individuals or families against one threat but not others, and this could be done at an individually affordable price. Suppose further that if most individuals purchased security against enough different threats, reasonably good collective security against all threats would emerge as a by-product. National defense is clearly not like that, however. The problem is not spillover from contributors to noncontributors. Instead, it is that affordable units of the good cannot be provided to anyone, whoever supplies it. By contrast, the public good provided by government regulation of medical products—an independent assurance that medical products are generally safe and effective—could emerge as a by-product of discrete transactions in which units or "components" of the public good are provided and purchased piecemeal through the private sector. In short, what the FDA purports to provide differs in important respects from what the military provides—respects that would frustrate attempts to elicit classical liberal support for the current medical products regulatory regime on the grounds that only the government can provide the relevant public good or on the grounds that government can clearly do a better job in providing that good than can the private sector. Classical liberals would reasonably dissent from both of these claims.

Nonmedical Consumer Product Safety

The remainder of this chapter considers the other types of regulation that compose the modern liberal regulatory agenda: nonmedical consumer product safety regulation, occupational licensure, land use regulation, and regulation of the employment relation. Following the pattern of the discussion of the FDA in the previous section, the key questions are these: (1) Can the goals of these elements of the modern liberal regulatory agenda be construed as public goods that the vast majority wants? (2) Does the provision of the public good in question constitute a genuine public goods problem? (3) Is there no arguably effective private sector solution to the public goods problem in question? (4) Does the state solution to this problem require that the state pay for the good with tax revenues? It is possible for reasoned agreement between the two sides to be reached about a particular item on the modern liberal regulatory agenda by way of a public goods argument if and only if the answer to all of these questions is yes. Let us begin with nonmedical consumer products.

The Food and Drug Administration is a particularly important regulatory agency, but it is not the only regulatory body charged with protecting health and safety. Safety regulation of nonmedical consumer products is provided mainly by the Consumer Product Safety

Commission (CPSC), and to a lesser extent by the National Highway Traffic Safety Administration (NHTSA) and the Federal Aviation Administration (FAA), which regulate automotive and aviation products respectively. Not only are food, drugs, and cosmetics excluded from the CPSC's mandate; so too are food, alcohol, tobacco, firearms, pesticides, and boats. Putting all these other products aside for the moment, let us focus attention on what the CPSC does. According to the Consumer Product Safety Act, the agency's mandate is

(1) to protect the public against unreasonable risk of injury associated with consumer products
(2) to assist consumers in evaluating the comparative safety of consumer products
(3) to develop uniform safety standards for consumer products
(4) to promote research and investigation into the causes and prevention of product-related deaths, illnesses and injuries. (15 U.S.C. § 2051)

It is difficult to identify a public good that this agency can be said to produce. Regarding the first and third goals, it does not ensure that all new nonmedical consumer products are safe (whatever that might mean) because, unlike the FDA, manufacturers are not required to get CPSC approval before marketing their products.[4] Instead, the CPSC acts in more post hoc and ad hoc ways. For example, it gathers injury information through the National Electronic Injury Surveillance System (NEISS), which processes injury reports from a sample of hospital emergency rooms. The policy instruments by which it acts on this information are (1) standards, (2) recalls, (3) bans, and (4) seizures of products posing imminent hazards.

Let us suppose, to be generous, that the CPSC does in fact "protect the public against unreasonable risk of injury associated with consumer products" and that this is a public good that the vast majority wants, analogous perhaps to the public good provided by the FDA. Let us further assume that the state produces this collective good at an acceptable financial and opportunity cost, i.e., at a financial and opportunity cost most people would be inclined to think is worth it. Major assumptions to be sure.[5] Let us further assume that the other two conditions for a public goods problem hold, and so a genuine public goods problem exists, and the state can solve it. There is still the question of whether there are nonstate alternatives that are comparably successful in realizing whatever widely shared values regarding consumer product safety that the CPSC is supposed to realize.

There are already in existence numerous private standard-setting agencies for various classes of consumer (and producer) goods, and many of these standards are health or safety related. In his study of private standards, Ross Cheit says that "there were thirty-two thousand private standards in 1983.... The number infused with significant implications for the public interest is probably in the thousands. These standards aim to promote social goods such as fire safety and product safety" (Cheit 1990, 5–6). The four most important private standard setting agencies are the American National Standards Institute (ANSI), the National Fire Protection Association (NFPA), the American Society for Testing and Materials (ASTM), and Underwriters Laboratories (UL). ANSI is the trade association of the private standards writing industry. It "accredits" the groups that write the actual ANSI standards, of which there are at least 8,500, covering a wide variety of products (Cheit 1990, 26). NFPA essentially writes the nation's fire codes, many of which have the force of law. ASTM (now known as ASTM-International) was started over a century ago to address problems in the railroad industry, specifically the frequent breakage of steel track. Over the years, it has evolved into the premier source for materials standards and testing, ranging from steel to fiber optic cables. Underwriters Laboratories, which has been in business for over 100 years, is the major private provider of consumer safety certification for electronics products. Manufacturers pay for the testing, and if their products pass, they can display the UL seal. In this way, independent assurances that particular products are safe can be linked to the product itself through a tying arrangement by which manufacturers purchase the information from independent private suppliers and bundle it with the product as part of the selling effort.[6] Finally, consumer product information, which includes but is not limited to health and safety information, is also provided by Consumers' Union through its magazine *Consumer Reports,* as well as by an array of other, often more specialized, publications that evaluate consumer and producer goods. For example, the Emergency Care Research Institute evaluates many products used in hospitals.

For most consumer goods, perhaps the most important determinant of their safety characteristics is the tort system, which operates on some variation of a strict liability standard. Whatever the deficiencies of the current tort system, it has created significant incentives for companies to design and manufacture safe products. In their study of corporate responses to product liability law, George Eads and Peter Reuter found that

> of all the various external social pressures, product liability has the greatest influence on product design decisions. The other influences largely work through the product liability mechanism. In industries with potentially high-hazard products, but not subject to significant product-related regulation (e.g., industrial machinery), product liability probably dominates design decisions, in terms of safety considerations. In industries subject to moderate regulatory pressures (industries subject only to CPSC regulation, for example), the influence of product liability likely overshadows that exercised by the regulators. Indeed, regulatory actions in such industries may be perceived as important or unimportant depending primarily on their impact on a firm's liability exposure.... Only in a few highly regulated industries (drugs and aircraft, for example) does regulation likely exceed product liability as a design influence. Even here, the liability consequences of design decisions are seldom far in the background. (1985, 27–28)

It is reasonably clear that whatever public good might be provided by the CPSC (as well as NHTSA and the FAA) could also be provided through a private ordering, that is, through market mechanisms (including private standard-setting) framed by tort law and without the mandatory standards, bans, seizures, and recalls that characterize the modern liberal consumer products regulatory regime. Indeed, chapter 9 lays out the case for the proposition that the CPSC has had little to no effect on the safety of consumer products.[7]

Occupational Licensure

Occupational licensure is intended to assure purchasers of professional services that practitioners, especially in areas that impinge on health and safety, have a minimum level of competence. Consumers are thought to be unable to evaluate providers' credentials for themselves. Whether or not there is a public good provided by occupational licensure (e.g., an independent assurance that providers of professional services are generally competent) and whether or not there is a genuine public goods problem, it is reasonably clear that the private sector can address this issue.

For instance, the need for licensing physicians, as a way of protecting the public from incompetent practitioners, has greatly diminished in recent decades for the simple reason that many individuals do not hire their own physicians anymore. As indicated in chapter 3, physicians are mostly hired by third parties (e.g., insurance companies, health maintenance organizations) and patients are required to pick from a list of approved physicians. These third parties are certainly competent to judge the qualifications of physicians and are unlikely to pay for the services of the graduates of dubious Caribbean medical schools. In addition, hospitals have increasingly taken an interest in the qualifications of physicians, as the courts have made them liable for malpractice by physicians who have been granted staff privileges at their facilities (Svorny 1992; 2004). Private certification agencies could take up whatever slack remains. Indeed, this might be a task for the American Medical Association, or perhaps for consortia drawn from teaching hospitals. The only classical liberal requirement is that no such certifying agency should be granted the legal right to exclude competitors (i.e., a legal monopoly). Those who choose their own physicians, such as the uninsured, could seek out only physicians who advertise that they are properly certified or are members of well-known HMOs or who are approved by large insurance carriers. As a practical matter, doctors would probably have to get some sort of (private) certification in order to receive malpractice insurance, and it may be appropriate for the government to require such insurance, for the same reason that many states require automobile owners to carry liability insurance. (There should be a persuasive conversion argument classical liberals could accept for requiring liability insurance for professionals who deal with people's health or safety.) In this way, not just anyone could practice medicine, and insurance companies would have an incentive to ensure the qualifications of providers and to monitor their delivery of services.

If medical licensing were effectively privatized, less well-trained medical providers, who handle a limited range of less complex medical problems, would likely flourish. There is some of that happening now, as nurse practitioners have gone into private practice, though they have been kept on a short leash by doctors, and of course there have always been chiropractors, podiatrists, optometrists, and so on. To the extent that they do not already do so, these other professionals would also likely seek certification from private certifying agencies for the same reasons that physicians would, namely, that it would be required by providers of liability insurance, and it might make sense for the state to mandate that providers carry such insurance.

A final piece of deregulation has to do with prescription drugs. Currently, the U.S. government requires a prescription from a licensed physician for a vast array of therapeutic drugs. Many foreign countries have a much shorter list of drugs requiring a physician's prescription. If the list of therapeutic drugs requiring a prescription were eliminated or restricted to those drugs that are truly dangerous, pharmacists would play a more important role in health care delivery than they currently do, at least in the United States. However, there are liability issues here as well that would have to be explored, since it is easy to imagine customers looking to the pharmacist to diagnose their medical problems. These changes in the health care professions would lead to a decrease in demand for the services of highly trained physicians and an increase in demand for the services of less highly trained medical practitioners, which is why physicians would likely oppose them with all the political muscle they could bring to bear.

As in the case of medical products, it is easy to imagine ways in which private sector alternatives might not work very well. Health insurance companies might steer policyholders to less qualified (because less expensive) heath care providers, and the uninsured might be lured into purchasing inferior services—services that a regime of occupational licensure is supposed to prevent. Or, to be more accurate, it is possible that more unqualified or underqualified physicians would practice under a nongovernmental alternative than practice under the current regime.[8] Insufficiently capitalized liability insurance companies might write large numbers of malpractice policies for the physicians' equivalent of unmarried male drivers under the age of twenty-five. Bad outcomes are virtually certain—as they are under the current system, and the tort system is available to clean up the inevitable messes to the extent that it can. No system operates flawlessly, but it is by no means obvious that whatever assurance is offered by the current regime of occupational licensure for the health-related professions could not also be produced by the private sector, assisted by a liability insurance requirement for health care practitioners and the tort law system.

Similar private sector alternatives to occupational licensure would be feasible for other professions that impact public safety or health, for example, architecture and engineering. Consumers of these services may benefit from private certification agencies, though many of these consumers are probably better able to assess the competence of professionals on their own. For example, many businesses that hire engineering and architectural firms have in-house expertise that is sufficient to evaluate the credentials and the work of outside professionals, even if they cannot do that work themselves.

Private sector alternative to occupational licensure for nonhealth and nonsafety related professions is even more clearly feasible. Elementary and secondary education offers an interesting case study. Public school teachers typically must have occupational licenses, so that one cannot be a public school teacher without government certification. Private schools, however, do not require this credential,[9] nor are parents who homeschool their children required to be certified. While it is true that private schools have certain distinct advantages that make them attractive for well-qualified teachers, there is no evidence to suggest that their selection process is inferior to that used by the public schools, which relies on certification, and it is utterly and completely implausible to believe that private education would be improved if private school teachers had to have education degrees. Only education bureaucrats—and not even most of them—can say with a straight face that education degrees are necessary for quality instruction.

Higher education has essentially no occupational licensure requirements, and it is difficult to find anyone who affirms that the problems in higher education would be ameliorated by government-mandated licensing requirements.[10] With regard to other professions, many have strong professional associations that would be well-positioned to certify practitioners. Classical liberals demand only that they be denied the legal power to exclude competitor agencies and thereby to exclude from the profession those who do not meet their criteria. As long as no one has a legally secured monopoly, there is always the possibility of a competitor offering superior certification services, and modern universities, always hungry for funds, would be well-suited to offer such services. Indeed, assuming private accrediting bodies for professional schools continue to function, a degree from an accredited institution might be sufficient certification for most professions. The main classical liberal objection to government-required occupational licensure is that, whatever its historical justification, it has become little more than a barriers-to-entry device that practitioners have used to restrict entry into the professions to raise their incomes at the expense of the public. To the extent that people want independent assurances of professional competence, they maintain, the private sector can do the job. There may have been a time when occupational licensure did provide a public good at an affordable financial and opportunity cost, but the question at issue is whether, at the present time, there could be a private sector alternative that is superior, or at least not inferior to the current regime. Classical liberals believe that there is. This belief, while possibly false, is not unreasonable.

Land Use Regulation

The main forms of land use regulation at the national level are the regulatory regimes embodied in the Endangered Species Act and section 404 of the Clean Water Act (hereafter, the ESA and the CWA). Both restrict, sometimes dramatically, what property owners can do with their land. Their purpose is to promote environmental values that are not easily promoted through a private ordering. These values are arguably public goods. Randy Simmons summarizes (without endorsing) the public goods associated with the ESA in the following passage:

> In fact, each of the most commonly cited justifications for preserving species focuses on their character as public goods: (1) they serve ecological functions; (2) they are sources of knowledge that can be turned to consumptive and nonconsumptive human uses; (3) they are sources of scientific information, models, and theory; (4) all species have rights worthy of respect; and (5) a species-rich world is esthetically superior to a species-poor world. The first three justifications qualify on public-goods grounds—benefits flow to everyone, and no one's consumption of those benefits diminishes anyone else's consumption. The esthetic justification is also a public-good argument to the effect that if we allow species loss to continue, each of us is impoverished, or each person's soul is diminished. (1999b, 517)

There are well-known cases in which medicines have been derived from plants, some of which are endangered species.[11] Some animals are useful as scientific models. For example, the cheetah might hold the key to a better understanding cardiovascular function, since it can withstand severe oxygen deprivation when it quickly accelerates to and then sustains speeds up to seventy miles per hour over short distances. Species diversity can serve as a source of genetic information to make commercially grown crops resistant to disease or pests. For terminological convenience, let us bring all of these goods under the heading of "biodiversity," and let us grant for the sake of argument that biodiversity is jointly consumed and nonexcludable, that is, it is a public good.

Section 404 of the CWA is also intended to produce or sustain public goods associated with wetlands. Wetlands moderate the volume and velocity of water that enters them, including storm runoff and seasonal flooding. Wetlands permit spatial spreading of flow. In addition, by maintaining contact between groundwater and surface water, wetlands allow surface water to replenish groundwater and vice versa. Finally, water detention in wetlands reduces the kinds and amounts of dissolved and suspended substances in water. In this way, wetlands diminish eutrophication by removing part of the nutrient load from the water. The ecosystem stability that the ESA and section 404 of the CWA foster provides important ecological services such as maintenance of atmospheric air quality, soil regeneration, waste disposal, and pest control. All public goods.

Does the provision of this good constitute a genuine public goods problem? To answer this, it is first necessary to determine whether the vast majority would judge that the collective benefits outweigh the collective costs, which is condition (2a). Direct evidence on this question is hard to come by, but there is some indirect evidence that bears on it. The fact that the ESA passed unanimously in the Senate and by a 390 to 12 majority in the House (Hayward et al. 2001, 4) would seem to indicate indirectly that there was strong public support for protection of endangered species, at least at that time. Other indirect evidence comes from an analysis of public expenditures, which can be taken to reflect revealed public demand. These expenditures can then be compared to the results of contingent valuation surveys, which attempt to ascertain people's willingness to pay for various goods—in this case, species preservation—that have no market price.[12] If the latter is greater than the former, across a wide group of citizens, that would suggest that species protection is judged to be "worth it," at least at the collective level. In one study, Don Coursey found that "the evidence...supports the conclusion that Congress is buying protection of animals in a manner consistent with the median desires of the public" (Coursey 2001, 219). Let us grant, at least for the sake of argument, that support for this law is substantial enough to warrant the proposition that the vast majority judges that the collective benefits outweigh the collective costs. Condition (3) for a public goods problem is also met, since the benefits associated with biodiversity obviously cannot be provided by any one individual. Finally, it is clear that each individual's share of the costs of the goods associated with biodiversity is so small, relative to the total cost of providing the good (to the extent that it is provided), that any one person's failure to contribute would not have a noticeable effect on whether or not the good is provided.

What is not clear, however, is whether condition (2b) is met. This requires that the individual benefits are greater than the individual costs, at least for the vast majority. Whether or not this condition is met will depend on how many people are subject to a regulatory taking under these land use regulatory regimes. When someone's land is discovered to be a habitat for an endangered species under the ESA or is declared a wetland under the CWA, the value of that land can fall precipitously because its use is now subject to strict regulation; indeed, certain forms of development may be entirely prohibited.[13] Virtually the entire burden of this prohibition falls on the landowner. Whatever benefit she gets from an endangered species or a wetland being protected is swamped, so to speak, by the costs of having her property subject to a regulatory taking. For these individuals, the benefits of this regulatory regime clearly do not outweigh its costs. But, it might be that the number of people affected is small enough so that condition (2b) is met, and thus all the conditions are met for a genuine public goods problem. However, the current state solution to that problem is not one that classical liberals could accept. Recall that one of the requirements for a public goods argument is a premise to the effect that the state purchases the good and pays for it with tax dollars. That is not what happens in these regulatory regimes. No pretense can be made that other citizens are paying their share—they pay nothing for the taking and at most a trivial amount for their share of the enforcement costs. These takings would be defensible to classical liberals by reference to public goods arguments if the state were to compensate affected property owners.[14] If they were compensated for the value of the land diminished by the regulatory taking and were only required to contribute their share of the tax burden needed for compensation and enforcement, a public goods argument might succeed, but that is not what happens now in many of these cases, even in light of recent Supreme Court decisions that make some regulatory takings compensable.

In 1993, Rep. Robert F. Smith of Oregon introduced a bill before Congress titled "The Just Compensation Act of 1993," which proposed to do just that. Secretary of the Interior Bruce Babbitt thought that this was a bad idea. In his colorful description of this proposed bill he said,

> let's examine the implications of this proposed raid on the public treasury. The Kesterson National Wildlife Refuge in California is one of the great migratory bird stops on the Pacific flyway. But a few years ago, the waterfowl were dying, and they were deformed at birth. It turned out to be selenium poisoning running off into the refuge from nearby farm irrigation wastewater. Under the Endangered Species Act, I tell the farmers: Clean up the pollution or we'll sue you. But under this new proposal, I am undeniably causing a "diminution in value" of a property right—it will cost those farmers money to clean up. They'll comply, but then they'll send me the bill! The old legal maxim, "make the polluter pay," would be replaced by a new legal rule: "It pays to pollute; the government will reimburse your costs." (Babbitt 1994, 55; quoted in Simmons 1999b, 518)

There are a number of problems with this argument. Under the common law, pollution is a nuisance or a form of trespass that the state can prohibit without compensation under its police power.[15] The "polluter pays" principle is a well-established common law principle that classical liberals accept, and if private parties are polluting government land, they can be enjoined. If Babbitt had actually read the bill, he would have noticed that it does not provide compensation for polluters. Compensation is paid only for regulatory takings occasioned by enforcement of the ESA, section 404 of the CWA, the Surface Mining Control and Reclamation Act of 1977 (30 U.S.C. § 1201 et seq.), and subsections (c), (d), (e), and (f) of section 9 of the National Trails System Act (16 U.S.C. § 1248).[16] It leaves unimpaired the rights of private individuals and the government to enjoin pollution and to demand compensation for it.

There may be another way to construe Babbitt's objection to this proposed bill. He might be arguing that the real problem the ESA and CWA are supposed to prevent is habitat degradation (a diminution of biodiversity), which occurs as the result of residential, commercial, or agricultural development. This is *like* pollution in the sense that it is a negative externality for which compensation is not owed. The permitting process, as defined under these acts, is simply a way of preventing habitat degradation. Just as the government ought to be able to prohibit without compensation point source water pollution, so too should it be able to prohibit without compensation habitat degradation. Both are negative externalities for which compensation is not owed. But this will not do. Habitat degradation by individual landowners (including corporations) does not appreciably diminish biodiversity. However, enough instances of it do, and that is a reason to treat habitat degradation like air pollution from automobiles, which, as argued in chapter 1, is not an externality but a public goods/bads problem.

The problem is that habitat degradation is not treated as a public goods/bads problem in these regulatory regimes. Those who benefit do not pay, and those who pay do not benefit. This is not merely a case in which the benefits for a few individuals do not outweigh the costs imposed on them (which might be the case in minor regulatory takings). For any public good, it is virtually certain that there will be such individuals. Rather, the problem is in the distribution of the costs. Because these regulatory takings are uncompensated, there can be no pretense that, under these regimes, each citizen who benefits from the good pays his or her share of its cost. Possibly, one of the reasons the ESA and section 404 of the CWA have such broad support is that they are financed on the backs of a very small minority, namely, property owners on whose property endangered species or wetlands are found. It might be objected that the state could never afford to compensate all property owners who bear these regulatory burdens, but that just means that the public would not judge protecting wetlands and endangered species to be worth the full costs.[17] It would be as if only the anarchists were required to pay taxes to support the military, and everyone else had to pay only his or her share of what it costs to force these recalcitrants to pay up. Whether or not these forms of land use regulation are ultimately morally defensible, they do not fit the description of the state solving a public goods problem in a way that classical liberals could accept.

Regulation of the Employment Relation

Recall from chapter 4 that the modern liberal regulatory agenda contains four main types of regulations of the employment relation: (1) mandatory terms and conditions of employment, specifically, laws mandating a minimum wage and overtime pay, equal pay for equal work, and family medical leave, (2) regulations governing collective bargaining and union organizing, (3) occupational health and safety regulation, and (4) laws prohibiting discrimination based on race, color, national origin, religion, sex, age, and disability.

Mandatory terms and conditions of employment and regulations governing collective bargaining can be discussed together. Neither can be assimilated to the public goods model because of the distribution of the benefits and the costs. Consider first regulations governing union organizing and collective bargaining. Perhaps the main purpose of these regulations is to "level the playing field" between management and unions by prohibiting management from doing most of the things that make it more difficult for workers to organize and bargain collectively. More simply, these regulations are intended to enhance—and in fact do enhance—the right of workers to organize and bargain collectively. However, to the extent that workers regard "their" unions as parasites or believe that union representation diminishes their employment prospects, such workers would dissent from the proposition that the regulatory regime of the National Labor Relations Board (NLRB) produces a public good that the vast majority wants at a cost (including especially an opportunity cost) they are willing to pay, either individually or collectively. In addition, and needless to say, employers and managerial employees are also unlikely to take a positive view of the individual or collective benefits of this regulatory regime relative to its costs. Once again, this is a situation in which the state acts to benefit some at the expense of others. While this may be defensible (and indeed in chapter 7 I shall argue that parts of this regulatory regime are), it does not involve a society collectively imposing on its members the proportionate costs of a public good in exchange for the benefits, collective and otherwise, of that good.

The case of mandated terms and conditions of employment also fails to meet condition (2b) of a public goods problem for essentially the same sorts of reasons. The purpose of minimum wage law is to effect a transfer of income from employers who hire low-wage employees to those low-wage employees who would make less than the legally mandated minimum if there were no such law. Whether or not this is good policy, it is not solving a public goods problem for the same reason that many of the regulatory regimes discussed above are not solving a public goods problem, namely, those who benefit are not burdened and those who are burdened do not benefit. Those burdened by the minimum wage law include not only employers who cannot easily shift their capital to other lines of employment but also workers who are let go (or are never hired) because employers cannot economically justify paying them the mandatory minimum.[18] Mandatory conditions of employment, such as mandated family leave, have similar, though milder, effects: those who benefit do so at the expense of those who own or control the means of production (capitalists and managers, respectively)—and at the expense of workers who must take up the slack of those who are absent but would have been replaced. A further feature of mandated terms and conditions of employment is that they do not affect all workers. Most workers are not minimum wage employees, and some workers have no dependents or have dependents who never require the level of care that causes workers to avail themselves of family medical leave and who would not have gotten such a benefit in the absence of the relevant legislation. To the extent that these people support the imposition of these burdens on employers, it is essentially cost-free for them. This does not fit the model of a state solution to a public goods problem in which everyone, or nearly everyone, benefits and everyone, or nearly everyone, pays.

In 1970, Congress passed and the president signed the Occupational Safety and Health Act. The stated purpose of the Occupational Safety and Health Administration (OSHA), which was created by the Act, was "to assure so far as possible every working man and woman in the nation safe and healthful working conditions" (29 U.S.C. § 651). As with the other regulatory agencies, this mandate is remarkably vague. The agency has interpreted it very broadly so that it can regulate virtually any potential workplace hazard it sees fit to regulate. The most important policy tool it has at its disposal is the setting of mandatory standards for the workplace, violations of which result in a fine. Although it has impressive powers, it turns out that OSHA can inspect only a trivial percentage of the total number of workplaces it regulates, and the fines it imposes are typically small because the violations it uncovers are minor (Viscusi 1983, 24). For these reasons, the effectiveness of OSHA has long been questioned. Doubts about the effectiveness of OSHA translate into reasonable doubts that most people would judge that the benefits of OSHA outweigh the costs, which in turn would entail reasonable doubts that there is a public goods problem that OSHA solves. Modern liberals might agree with an adverse assessment of OSHA's effectiveness, but they might argue that more inspectors should be hired, more and tougher standards developed, and higher fines imposed. Also, the agency could "work smarter" by focusing less on trivial but easily identified safety hazards and focus more on subtle, long-term health hazards. It might turn out, however, that the total financial costs of making OSHA effective (both in terms of its budget and the financial costs it imposes on businesses, workers, and consumers) would be so great as to outweigh whatever public good OSHA purports to provide, in which case there is still no genuine public goods problem that OSHA solves. But all this is highly speculative.

There are further grounds for skepticism about the existence of a public goods problem that OSHA solves or addresses—grounds that parallel the objections to the ESA and section 404 of the CWA. As in previous cases, there is a problem about the distribution of the costs. Once again, the basic idea behind a state solution to a public goods problem that classical liberals could endorse is that there is some good that the vast majority of people want at a stipulated price, and they are using the state to impose on themselves the cost of providing that good as a way of overcoming the fundamental collective action problem, namely, the difficulty that would arise if each person were free to consider whether or not he or she should contribute to its provision, when his or her share of the total cost is trivial. A regulatory agency like OSHA, however, does not provide a solution to this sort of problem, because of the way the benefits and burdens of this regulatory regime are distributed. For example, many businesspeople would clearly prefer that OSHA be dismantled because of the financial, and especially the aggravational, burdens it imposes. As Eugene Bardach and Robert Kagan said in their study of OSHA,

> resentment and hostility from those who are regulated are direct effects of legalism and its attendant unreasonableness. Some businessmen we interviewed complained far less about the costs of complying with reasonable orders than about the arbitrariness of agency actions. Businessmen who think of themselves as trying to do a decent job are not likely to cooperate with an agency that in effect disregards their judgment and good-faith efforts or even denies...that they are to be trusted at all. (Bardach and Kagan 1982, 105)

For these reasons, they are inclined to disbelieve that the overall benefits of the agency outweigh the costs it imposes, or perhaps they want only to be left alone, that is, to opt out of this regulatory regime; the latter of course is not an option because of the enabling legislation. While such judgments are undoubtedly skewed by their personal experience with OSHA or by horror stories they have heard from other businesspeople, those judgments must nonetheless be respected by any public goods argument that would be acceptable to classical liberals.

The manner in which the benefits and burdens of OSHA are distributed does not parallel the distribution of benefits and burdens of national defense or any other clearly recognizable public good. This regulatory regime imposes costs on some persons to benefit others, whereas in the national defense case, those who benefit and those who are burdened are substantially the same sets of people. The imposition of these burdens may be defensible, but not because it provides a public good that the vast majority want at a price they are willing to pay.

Finally, even if these considerations were not conclusive against the public goods character of occupational health and safety, there are alternative institutional arrangements implicit in a private ordering that are arguably as effective as OSHA in producing adequate workplace health and safety conditions. First, there are obvious market advantages to operating a safe workplace: it makes it easier to attract and keep workers, it minimizes disruptions that inevitably accompany work-related injuries and illnesses, and it keeps insurance costs down. As explained in chapter 9 (see below, ch. 9, pp. 276–81), market forces, in the form of wage premiums for hazardous work, provide firms with a much greater incentive for workplace health and safety than do regulations and standards promulgated by OSHA.

As noted earlier, the tort system is an essential component of the free market alternative to government regulation. The tort system, however, has no impact on occupational health and safety because nearly all workers are covered by a no-fault workers' compensation insurance policy that does not allow lawsuits against companies for negligence. If OSHA were eliminated, classical liberals might favor reforms in workers' compensation laws. For example, in many states, there is rate regulation of workers' compensation insurance rates, something classical liberals would oppose.[19] The latter might be willing to accept a role for the government in seeing to it that workers are adequately informed about workplace risks, especially long-term health risks, on essentially the same grounds that classical liberals can accept labeling requirements for consumer products. (See chapter 1, pp. 10–11.) However, that is a far cry from the current regime at OSHA, which sets mandatory safety standards and does so at a level of detail to make it virtually inevitable that a firm is in violation of some regulation or other. Indeed, there is another government agency charged with developing and disseminating information about occupational health and safety, the National Institute for Occupational Safety and Health (NIOSH), and to the extent that the provision of this information can be represented as the solution to a public goods problem that cannot be solved by the private sector, classical liberals would be able to support it.

All of these considerations suggest that there is no compelling public goods argument for the regulatory regime imposed by OSHA that classical liberals would be constrained to accept, though this does not mean that OSHA cannot be justified by some other argument, perhaps by an (altruistic) conversion argument that appeals to the well-being of those whom it might protect as judged against the opportunity costs that both businesses and employees are forced to pay. We return to these issues in chapter 9.

Finally, there is antidiscrimination law. Taken individually, these laws appear to face the same problems as the other regulations of the employment relation. However justifiable they might be, they impose burdens on some to benefit others. Taken together, however, there is a case to be made that antidiscrimination laws do solve a public goods problem. To see why, recall from chapter 3 that antidiscrimination law covers race, gender, national origin, religion, age, and disability status. The vast majority of the workforce is currently covered by one or another of these laws. Though white males of European extraction are not explicitly covered and have often been unsuccessful in claims of discrimination on the basis of race or gender, some are covered under the Americans with Disabilities Act of 1990 (42 U.S.C. § 12101), and all are eventually covered under the Age Discrimination in Employment Act of 1967 (29 U.S.C. § 621). The public good that these laws taken together might be said to produce is difficult to characterize, in part because the goals of antidiscrimination law are rather vague—even more so than other public goods the state might be producing through its various regulatory and transfer regimes. Perhaps the most that can be said is that these laws express a widely shared social intolerance for certain forms of discrimination in the workplace. A societywide intolerance of certain forms of discrimination has the characteristics of a public good (joint consumption and nonexcludability). Does its provision constitute a genuine public goods problem? Perhaps. It may be something that the vast majority wants and for which they are willing to pay the price, the latter being understood in terms of the intrusiveness of the enforcement mechanism, the negative effects of keeping incompetent workers around who would otherwise be fired, and the opportunity costs of the enforcement machinery. Certainly a societywide intolerance of discrimination is not something that any one person or company could produce on its own, and anyone's failure to contribute to its provision would not make much of a difference as to whether or not it is provided. So, there may be a case for the proposition that antidiscrimination law solves a public goods problem.[20] However, there is arguably a private sector solution to the problem.

To see why, suppose that all antidiscrimination statutes were repealed. What would happen? Surely it is very difficult to know but some tentative speculations are possible. Preferential treatment programs in the business world would probably wither at many firms because of their negative effects on employee morale and on the bottom line. The employment prospects of the disabled may or may not diminish; repeal of the ADA might make it possible for employers to ignore the disabled when making hiring decisions. But, without fear of the burdens of compliance costs imposed by the ADA, employers might be more willing to hire disabled workers than they currently are, since compliance with the ADA can be a Dostoyevskian nightmare.[21] On the core categories of race, ethnicity, gender, and age, what would happen is much more uncertain. If discriminatory attitudes are powerful and commonplace (as some modern liberals seem to believe), there would be an upsurge in discriminatory hirings or failures to hire, promotions or failures to promote, and firings. However, it might be the case that the strength and pervasiveness of these attitudes has greatly abated, in part, it can be conceded, because of the educative effects of current laws. In consequence, much less momentous changes might occur; large corporations might still advertise, for example, that they do not discriminate on the basis of race, gender, and so on, and invite third parties to certify their claims. There might finally be some legitimate work for the "diversity industry," as Frederick Lynch (1997) calls it. Undoubtedly, some discrimination would still be practiced, as indeed occurs under the current clutch of antidiscrimination laws. To answer the question of how much would occur under alternative regimes, it would be necessary to know if these laws are currently making an appreciable difference in discouraging discriminatory practices and what would happen if they were repealed. On these questions, there could be reasonable disagreement.

Wherever the truth lies, however, the modern liberal faces an uncomfortable dilemma in arguing for antidiscrimination law on the grounds that it solves a public goods problem that cannot be solved by the private sector: it is difficult to see how he could simultaneously maintain that the vast majority of people oppose discriminatory practices and favor nondiscriminatory environments in the workplace—which must be assumed if there is a genuine public goods problem that the state can solve—and also that there would be an upsurge in such practices were these laws to be repealed. These two propositions are not logically inconsistent, but there is clearly some tension between them. One could hold, for example, that the stereotyping that results in discrimination in the workplace is largely a subconscious phenomenon restricted to those who make personnel decisions, and the latter constitute a fairly small minority of the total population. Empirically verifying such a claim would be very difficult, however, and it is hard to square with the idea that discriminatory attitudes are a pervasive phenomenon. However that tension might be resolved, classical liberals are still in a position to resist a public goods argument for the current antidiscrimination regulatory regime on the grounds that there can be reasonable disagreement about the effects of a repeal of these statutes. If social realities were to remain essentially or largely unchanged after repeal, whatever public good is produced by the current brace of antidiscrimination laws might well be produced and sustained piecemeal as the result of nondiscrimination policies and attitudes at individual firms across the society. If this sounds too optimistic, it is worth recalling that the public good the state is supposed to be producing now is an ideal which no one would claim has been even approximately realized. The outstanding question is whether the private sector would better or more fully realize this ideal over time by private action than would the public sector by the instrumentality of antidiscrimination law. This is a question about which reasonable people—classical liberals and modern liberals—may differ.

To summarize, it is difficult to construe many of the ends or goals of the modern liberal regulatory agenda as public goods that the vast majority want at a stipulated price or to construe state provision of these goods as a solution to a public goods problem that classical liberals could accept. For those elements of the agenda that can be represented as a state solution to a public goods problem, there is, or may well be, a way to provide the good through a private ordering. The medical products regulatory regime run by the FDA falls into the latter category; independent assurance of the safety and effectiveness of the medical products can be provided by a fundamentally different regulatory regime that contains important private sector elements. The same holds for whatever public good occupational licensure delivers. It is a common mistake to assume that if a regulatory regime were to be eliminated, nothing would arise in the private sector to take its place, though it is usually difficult to predict in any detail what institutional forms an alternative would take. As to nonmedical consumer product safety, it is doubtful that such safety as provided by the CPSC is something that most people want at the stipulated price. Waiving that problem, however, it is abundantly clear that a private ordering can provide the good in question. The much-maligned tort system is part of (or more exactly, the framework of) a private ordering that addresses these concerns, but so too are private certification agencies. Indeed, the multitude of such agencies discussed above suggests that the CPSC is essentially useless, and/or the private sector could immediately fill any gaps occasioned by the abolition of the CPSC and other agencies that regulate nonmedical consumer products.

Land use regulation at the federal level arguably provides a public good that the vast majority wants at a collective price they are willing to pay. Even so, classical liberals would object on the grounds that the benefits of the good and the burdens of its costs are distributed in such a way that, in effect, those who benefit do not pay and those who pay do not benefit. Laws governing collective bargaining and mandatory terms and conditions of employment face similar problems. In the case of occupational safety and health, there are private sector alternatives to government-mandated safety standards. The same holds true for antidiscrimination law, conceived of as forbidding certain grounds for employment decisions.

For many of these regulatory goods, there are simply too many citizens who are not net beneficiaries of these laws for any of these regulations to be represented as a state solution to a public goods problem. At one level, this should not be surprising. FDA and CPSC bureaucrats, plaintiff's attorneys who practice employment law, Fish and Wildlife Service (FWS) personnel who enforce the ESA and OSHA inspectors, these and other enforcers of the modern liberal regulatory agenda do not enjoy the broad popular support that, for example, the military has in liberal societies. They may be necessary functionaries in a liberal society but not because they are providing public goods that the vast majority of people want at a price they are willing to pay. The attempt to justify elements of the modern liberal regulatory agenda via public goods arguments fail. Since arguments from the presuppositions of a market economy and from fundamental rights are also unpersuasive, common ground arguments will not succeed in persuading classical liberals of the desirability of the modern liberal regulatory agenda. Other arguments must be found. It is to these arguments that we now turn.

SEVEN

Conversion Arguments

Employment Law

Conversion Arguments

The arguments canvassed in the preceding chapter are not the sort of arguments that one typically finds offered in public discourse by modern liberals or among academic defenders of the modern regulatory-welfare state. For a variety of reasons, modern liberals have not felt much need to try to convince those who are ideologically opposed to their view of the proper role of the state and even less need to do so on grounds the latter would find acceptable.[1] This is not particularly surprising; in political controversies, it is natural to suppose that those with whom one has important disagreements are intellectually or morally obtuse. It is not that modern liberals have no arguments for their various regulatory agendas; it is just that those arguments do not appeal to principles classical liberals accept and thus are not common ground or convergence arguments. Instead, they have relied either on arguments that appeal to modern liberal principles or on conversion arguments; the latter can be construed as directed to those without firm commitments about the proper scope of government on a range of issues (moderates or pragmatists, as they style themselves) or those on the other side who are open to persuasion because they wear their principles lightly. Arguments that appeal to abstract modern liberal principles are nonstarters for classical liberals, or more exactly, they require the substantiation of philosophical views about which there is persistent reasonable disagreement. For example, Rawls's principle of fair equality of opportunity arguably supports the affirmative action component of contemporary antidiscrimination law, but there is persistent reasonable disagreement about the intellectual edifice within which that principle is located and thus about the principle itself. If the goal is reasoned agreement with classical liberals about the proper scope of government, it is unlikely to be found by appeal to Rawls's Difference Principle or, more generally, by appeal to the abstruse writings of the theoreticians of modern liberalism.

Conversion arguments would seem to be a more promising way of securing reasoned agreement because they appear to carry with them so much less intellectual baggage. For example, to argue for antidiscrimination law as it applies to race, it is not necessary to establish some grand principle to the effect that the state should show equal respect and concern for all or that justice demands that the state guarantee fair equality of opportunity and that only antidiscrimination law can instantiate one or the other of these principles insofar as the employment relation is concerned. It is easier, and far more compelling, to argue from the widely shared lower-level principle that treating people differently in the employment context because of their race is wrong. Of course, more is needed than just that principle to warrant the conclusion that there ought to be an antidiscrimination law such as title VII of the 1964 Civil Rights Act, but some such principle is key to the argument and is much less abstract and much less controversial than any of the grander principles from which it might be derived. It is one of those "considered judgments" that might be entailed by a variety of more abstract philosophical principles—and if it is not, one's principles need straightening, perhaps by the chiropractic subluxations of the sort practiced by Dr. Rawls.

Conversion arguments have another virtue in that they seem to represent more accurately how modern liberals have thought about the proper role of the state. Modern liberalism has been characterized by a kind of moral pragmatism that is captured, albeit in caricatured form, by Mill's portrayal of it in the epigram for this book. Recall his description of the modern liberal mindset: "whenever they see any good to be done, or evil to be remedied, [they] would willingly instigate the government to undertake the business." This, of course, is inaccurate as a literal description of what modern liberals believe, since many thoughtful modern liberals have come to appreciate the limits of state action, especially in recent decades, and modern liberals have always opposed state action that trenches on individual rights. It is also inaccurate insofar as it suggests that modern liberals have no principles by which they assess government intervention in civil society. Those caveats noted, however, modern liberalism does seem to be driven less by abstract principle and more by particular social problems than classical liberalism—and the state is their favored instrumentality for dealing with these problems. Libertarianism, which serves as a point of departure by which classical liberals define themselves—and which not coincidentally has a rigorously defined view of the proper role of government—has no counterpart in the conceptual landscape of modern liberalism. One searches in vain for a comprehensive principle defining the proper role of the state in the writings of modern liberal theorists.[2] Of course, there are modern liberal principles that have implications for this question in particular areas, notably principles of distributive justice and their apparent implications for tax and welfare policy. But, modern liberal views on a range of issues, especially on regulatory issues, do not appear to be dictated by any such principles. In an attempt to reach reasoned agreement with classical liberals, therefore, eschewing appeal to abstract philosophical principles is not only good strategy but also seems to comport best with how modern liberals conceive of the proper role of government, namely, as the best instrumentality to deal with an array of social problems and evils that are caused by, or at least allowed to exist in the context of, a private ordering. It is these defects that drive the modern liberal regulatory agenda. The widespread practice of racial discrimination, for example, is what motivated the 1964 Civil Rights Act. The increased complexity and potency of modern prescription drugs was a key factor in the evolution of the current prescription drug regulatory regime. And so and so forth.

Contrariwise, when conditions change, modern liberals are willing to change their minds about the desirability of regulation, certainly in theory and occasionally in practice. This is clearly illustrated in the modern liberal view of economic regulation discussed in chapter 4. Rate regulation and antitrust law have been defended as correctives to the economic power of corporate interests. Modern liberals have no principled opposition to rate deregulation, and indeed some modern liberal politicians were responsible for rate deregulation in trucking and in the airline industry. Nevertheless, if it takes place, they believe that the regulatory club should be conspicuously on the table to threaten firms and industries that ignore (what state officials take to be) the public interest when firms are free to set prices. Similarly, in the area of antitrust law, modern liberals believe that the task of the Justice Department and Federal Trade Commission is to keep a watchful eye on business activities and practices, particularly mergers and acquisitions, to prevent abuses of economic power. When any of these activities appear likely to involve such abuses, they should be prohibited; otherwise, they should be permitted. The same sort of thinking applies in the three main areas of noneconomic regulation: (1) regulation of the employment relation, (2) consumer products and services regulation, and (3) land use regulation. Each of these types of regulatory regimes was put in place to deal with an array of problems caused by, or permitted to exist in the context of, a private ordering. Modern liberals are willing to concede that at some time in the future it may be appropriate to revisit these regulatory regimes, but for the present, the latter address real problems inherent in a private ordering.[3] In the remainder of this chapter and the next three, this picture will be filled in for each of these regulatory regimes, beginning in this chapter with regulation of the employment relation, exclusive of antidiscrimination law, which will be the subject of chapter 8. In each instance, the most obvious conversion arguments that modern liberals have offered or would offer in support of these regimes will be articulated, and classical liberal replies and counterarguments will be considered. In nearly all cases, it will be argued that classical liberals have good reasons to object to these regulatory regimes. The larger conclusion toward which these chapters are directed is that conversion arguments cannot produce reasoned agreement in favor of the modern liberal regulatory agenda. Together with the results of chapters 5 and 6, this points to the conclusion that there is persistent reasonable disagreement about the modern liberal regulatory agenda, in other words, epistemic stalemate.

The epistemological underpinnings of what follows in this chapter and the next three warrant a digression. Typically, philosophers seek to undermine an argument by showing either that its conclusion does not follow from its premises, that it begs the question, or that one of its premises is false or doubtful. This strategy cannot be used to undermine the modern liberal regulatory agenda in this context for the simple reason that demonstrating the failure of any particular conversion argument does not mean that all such arguments will fail. Absent a comprehensive critical discussion of all conversion arguments for any given item on the agenda, one would not be entitled to conclude that no such item can be substantiated by a conversion argument. This elementary point of dialectics means that a different strategy will be required to raise reasonable doubts about this agenda. The strategy to be employed in this chapter and the next three is a variation on a strategy that was first used by the ancient Greek skeptics, notably Pyrrho and his followers. The Pyrrhonians made their case for suspending belief about any given proposition by producing an argument in favor of it and then immediately presenting an entirely different argument against that proposition (that is, in favor of the denial of the original proposition). Both arguments use propositions that seem to be true and seem to support their respective conclusions. The ultimate goal of this procedure is to cause a suspension

of judgment about both the proposition and its denial. As one com-
mentator describes it,

> in general, Pyrrhonean [sic] arguments hold that it is impos-
> sible to choose between opposing views and appeal to various
> antitheses to show this to be the case.... The Pyrrhoneans' [sic]
> general strategy is summarized in Sextus' [i.e., Sextus Empiri-
> cus's] introduction to the older modes, which explains that they
> induce a suspension of judgment *(epoche)* on the question of
> what is ultimately true. (Groarke 1990, 82–83)

Pyrrho believed that this procedure of giving arguments and counterarguments on a wide range of fundamental propositions would
ultimately lead to a kind of equanimity (*ataraxia*) that would perme-
ate all aspects of one's life. In this way, skepticism is not a proposition
or set of propositions to which one subscribes, however diffidently.
Rather, it is a way of life for which one prepares by considering or
offering arguments pro and con for a variety of fundamental propositions.

The methodology of the remainder of this chapter and the next
three follows Pyrrho, but only up to a point. It articulates the most
obvious and commonly offered justifications in support of the various elements of the modern liberal regulatory agenda in the form of
conversion arguments. If good reasons can then be given (i.e., if an
argument can be given) for believing that some particular item on
the modern liberal regulatory agenda should not be in place, or if
good reasons can be given for doubting that it should be in place,
that implies that there is something wrong with the original conversion argument, and indeed with any conversion argument that might
be offered in support of that element of the agenda. In the spirit of
Pyrrhonian skepticism, these counterarguments should have the
same character as the ones offered on behalf of any given element
of the modern liberal regulatory agenda, namely, they too should be
(attractive) conversion arguments. Of course, the original modern liberal argument, to the extent that it is persuasive, implies that there
is something wrong with the classical liberal counterargument and
indeed with any classical liberal counterargument. *Epoche* should be
the result, at least in theory. In practice, of course, people will not
give up their modern liberal or classical liberal predilections; this
will manifest itself in the judgment that one of these arguments is
more rationally compelling or persuasive than the other.

Typically, casting doubt on an element of the modern liberal regulatory agenda, or arguing that that element should not be in place, will involve explaining how a private ordering would handle the problems any given regulatory regime addresses about as well as, or better than, the extant regulatory regime. These explanations are really predictions about what would happen if some regulatory regime were dismantled. There is no way to be completely confident about how things would work themselves out, since other factors may interfere, but for present purposes, that level of assurance is unnecessary. Any modern liberal conversion argument assumes, either explicitly or implicitly, that government regulation is the most effective way to deal with the deficiencies of a private ordering. If the classical liberal can cast doubt on that proposition, reasonable disagreement about that element of the modern liberal regulatory agenda can be said to exist.[4]

As an aside, it is worth noting that the classical liberal point of contrast is not "the free market" but instead "a private ordering." The contrast between these two notions has been implicitly appealed to on a number of occasions, but it warrants a brief, more explicit discussion. The term "the free market" connotes the set of for-profit business enterprises in an economic system, but classical liberals do not believe that all social problems would be solved by for-profit enterprises. For example, in dealing with the problems of the least advantaged, classical liberals favor a much larger role for private philanthropic organizations, which are nonprofit organizations. Less obviously, the common law of torts and contracts and/or the statutory law that codifies it, are important parts of a private ordering. Or, to be more accurate, it is the framework of a private ordering. As a first approximation, it presumes that people have legal rights that mirror Locke's natural rights, especially property rights, and freedom of contract. This means that the common law operates on a presumption in favor of the rights, terms, and conditions that constitute full, liberal ownership as specified in chapter 3. Tort law has evolved away from its Lockean roots to some extent (e.g., in products liability law), and some classical liberals believe that these developments are unwelcome. And, of course, statutory law has eclipsed the common law in many ways, most notably, in the implementation of the modern liberal regulatory agenda. The fact remains, however, that the common law frames private orderings, and enforcing those laws, including most especially the common law of torts, requires a state. Classical liberals, even libertarians, believe in the state; they are not anarchists. As to the philosophical foundations of the common law, which includes Lockean rights to private property, these of course have to be put on secure intellectual foundations. Various attempts have been made to do that, but those attempts have been about as successful as modern liberal attempts to secure their foundations, which is to say not very successful. But this sad chapter in the history of contemporary political philosophy need not detain us, since our concern at this juncture is with precisely those arguments for and against the modern liberal regulatory agenda that do not depend in any obvious way on those deeper principles. The basic idea behind conversion arguments is that their appeal should be both broad and shallow. These arguments might well depend on deeper principles in the final analysis, but these chapters are not the final analysis.

Moreover, under the terms of this part of the debate, the dispute between modern liberals and classical liberals about any particular item on the regulatory agenda cannot be resolved by appeal to more general principles about the proper role of the state, since conversion arguments do not ascend to that level of abstraction or generality. As has been pointed out repeatedly in this book, appeals to philosophical principles ultimately get bogged down in inconclusive philosophical arguments and counterarguments. There are, in addition, other principles or types of principles, explicit appeals to which are off limits in conversion arguments. The remainder of this section discusses some of them.

One of these is a quasi-methodological, quasi-substantive principle linking government intervention to market failure. Some modern liberals (and for that matter, some classical liberals), as well as many economists of whatever persuasion, seem to assume that market failure is a sufficient condition for government intervention, where the concept of market failure is defined precisely, that is, relative to what would occur in a regime of perfect competition. For example, in his book *Consumer Safety Regulation,* Peter Asch argues that consumer product safety information is a public good. He then says, "the argument for public intervention...is completely clear. We can improve social welfare either by subsidizing private firms to a point such that it becomes profitable to produce and distribute the information, or by having the government itself do the job" (Asch 1988, 51). Of course it is not completely clear. The argument obviously relies on a principle to the effect that government should produce or subsidize the provision of public goods. As chapter 5 demonstrates, that principle is something from which classical liberals would reasonably dissent. Not all public goods create public goods problems. For classical liberals, not only must there be a genuine public goods problem, as defined in chapter 5, it must also be the case that there is no effective way to solve it through a tying arrangement with the production of nonpublic goods. This quasi-methodological, quasi-substantive principle linking market failure to government intervention also assumes that government would produce this good or service in a quantity and at a cost that approximates what would be produced by the market (if that were possible) or that the government would subsidize private producers about enough to get that result. Neither assumption is at all plausible, and for that reason alone, no conversion argument should appeal to such a principle. However, if a specific market failure can be described in some nontendentious way, that is, in some way that does not require a cold start of all the associated neoclassical machinery, that description could form part of a conversion argument for regulation. Indeed, as we shall see on occasion, the formal and technical arguments of economists can be restated in simpler and more intuitive ways; such restatements are not appropriate for all purposes, but they are often perfectly suited as conversion arguments. Such arguments need not be simple, but they cannot rely in any obvious way on principles about the proper role of government that might be reasonably doubted or called into question.

Second, conversion arguments that explicitly appeal to some exceptionless principle of cost-benefit analysis will likewise be ruled inadmissible. A variety of practical and philosophical objections to these principles undermine whatever intuitive appeal cost-benefit analysis might have.[5] To mention one that is not commonly remarked on: for cost-benefit analysis to be decisive in regulatory matters, one must assume some form of social ownership of the resources used to purchase these products. To see why, consider the common complaint against cost-benefit analysis that it puts a dollar value on everything, including human life—human life, it is often said, is priceless. Economists immediately pounce on this by pointing out that if we treat every human life as having infinite value, that would imply that all resources should be spent on life-saving devices and activities. Obviously, they say, this is absurd, and so we have to take into account the opportunity costs of the resources involved. So far so good. Clearly, we have to consider the other uses to which these resources could be applied. This, however, assumes that "we" own the resources in question and that "we" have to come up with a sensible plan to use them. This makes sense and is unobjectionable enough when what is at issue is the expenditure of public funds (e.g., on highway design and construction). However, in safety regulation of consumer products, this way of thinking presupposes that society, or more exactly, the state, has an ownership claim on all the resources in question, at least in the first instance, since it gets to decide how the relevant resources are to be distributed by deciding what characteristics the product should have.

To make this more specific, consider the lawnmower safety standard introduced by the CPSC in 1979. Warren Prunella and William Zamula prepared an internal report for the CPSC that estimated the benefits of its lawnmower safety standards at $262 million annually, with the costs coming in at $189 million.[6] This was intended to justify the imposition of this standard. Kip Viscusi subjects the cost and benefit estimates to devastating criticism and arrives at figures for which the costs outweigh the benefits. All this takes place under the supposition that cost-benefit analysis is the decisive consideration, but that in turn assumes that the state is entitled to decide how the resources in question are to be disposed of. As argued in chapter 2, modern liberals believe that the state has an ownership claim on the resources used to produce these lawnmowers, as well as the resources used to purchase these lawnmowers, which allows them to determine the terms and conditions of disposition. In other words, it entitles the government to say that lawnmowers have to be sold with various safety devices. Although his philosophical commitments are unknown, Viscusi's objection to the lawnmower standard, based as it is on cost-benefit analysis, can be understood as a common ground or convergence argument from modern liberal principles about social ownership.

Finally, not only must one not presuppose any contentious philosophical or methodological principles, one must also eschew any arguments that depend on general assumptions about how markets work—or do not work—that are not widely shared. Such arguments appear on both sides of the political spectrum. Sometimes classical liberals argue in favor of a private ordering on the assumption that markets always, or almost always, work really well. This proposition (or is it an attitude?) is clearly behind the following passage from David Hamilton:

> The producer, in order to remain in business, must respond to the dictates of the consumer in the marketplace. If he should

produce shoddy, he will find few buyers. If he should cheat the consumer by fraud or deception, the consumer will pass him by on the next round of purchases...Failure by the producer to obey the dictates of the sovereign consumer is tantamount to signing his own economic death warrant. (1962, 329–30)

Is each of these statements true? One is tempted to say that they are sometimes true and sometimes not, but that is not quite correct. As stated, they are universal propositions and as universal propositions they are all false. Still, it is possible to say that similar propositions, restricted to some markets, are true, or approximately true. Alternatively, if the phrase, "In some markets" were appended to the beginning of the above passage, these statements would be true. To be sure, that does not say very much; in particular, it does not say enough to warrant a classical liberal conclusion about a particular market.[7] Empirical details about a particular market are needed to make the case, and once those details are given, the need for the general assumption that markets work well drops out.

Mirror images of these arguments can be found on the other side. Some arguments in favor of regulation proceed upon the supposition that consumers are helpless pawns of large corporations. This view was widely held in the 1960s and is nicely illustrated in the following quotation from Richard Barber: "the individual buyer besieged by advertising, deceived by packages, confronted with an expanding range of highly complex goods, limited in time...is simply not qualified to buy discriminately and wisely" (1966, 1204). Barber presents the consumer as confused and overwhelmed; Ralph Nader has a much darker view. According to him, the consumer movement has documented "that consumers were defrauded, injured and manipulated not by the corner gyp market but by the largest business entities in the world: the U.S. blue-chip business firms" (1973, 2). It is hard to know what to make of statements like this, indeed it is not at all clear what is being asserted. Surely, Nader does not mean this happens all the time to everyone, that is, in every transaction. So, is it most of the time? What does "most" mean? More than 50 percent? That is the ordinary meaning of the term. So, now Nader is saying that more than 50 percent of all transactions between U.S. blue-chip firms (how is this class to be determined?) and their customers are either fraudulent, involve injury to the consumer, or manipulate the consumer. That also seems implausible. But perhaps this is not a charitable reading. Maybe the idea is not that half or more of all transactions involve fraud, but just many more transactions than the ordinary person would think. Well, how many more? And who is the ordinary person? For Nader, the latter are the dupes of modern corporations that need to be saved from fraud, injury, and manipulation by him and his followers. This sort of vague, malevolent, and conspiratorial thinking is unlikely to be rationally persuasive to those who are undecided about the proper role of government in any given area or to those classical liberals who are willing to make exceptions to their general strictures against government involvement. To be fair, those people are not Nader's intended audience; he is writing to inspire people, especially young people, to action. But, to be fairer still, these claims are simply intellectually irresponsible without supporting documentation that rises above the anecdotal, which of course Nader does not and cannot supply. This is why Nader is (unfairly) regarded by classical liberals as the poster child for modern liberalism. As a general proposition, sometimes markets work well and sometimes they do not. Conversion arguments on either side cannot presume any less—or any more—than that. That has got to be the background assumption in any conversion argument, and of course it does not say very much. Details about the workings of particular markets are needed.

So what do conversion arguments look like? There may be no general characterization that fits all of them. They are intended to be "close to the surface" in the sense of not presupposing (at least in any obvious way) any deeper, more controversial principles. They are also intended to be the kind of argument that those without firm commitments to abstract principles about the scope of government could accept, as well as to appeal to those on the other side who are willing to make exceptions to whatever general principles to which they are inclined to subscribe. Some patterns will appear in the conversion arguments that follow in this chapter and the next three. Specifically, modern liberal conversion arguments appeal to moral defects that existed in the context of a private ordering at the time a regulatory regime was introduced to deal with those defects. The classical liberal conversion counterarguments typically argue that the regulatory regime installed to deal with those problems is worse, in some all-things-considered way, than what would exist if that regime were dismantled or at least radically altered in a classical liberal direction. These arguments could concede (though they need not) that government regulation was a sensible way to deal with a range of problems that existed at the time but that the regulatory regime in question is no longer appropriate or necessary.

Common ground arguments that appeal to classical liberal principles have been shown in the preceding chapters to be inadequate. If the conversion arguments and counterarguments of this chapter and the next two are plausible, reasoned disagreement about the modern liberal regulatory agenda can be said to persist. The larger purpose of chapters 6 through 10 is to show that there is genuine and persistent reasonable disagreement about the modern liberal regulatory agenda. Thus far, all that has been shown is that modern liberals are not able to offer the kinds of arguments in favor of their regulatory agenda that classical liberals, qua classical liberals, can accept. If it also turns out that modern liberal conversion arguments can be reasonably resisted as well, then reasonable disagreement can be said to persist—at least as long as there continues to be reasonable disagreement about the various modern liberal principles that support these agenda items. It is a safe bet that those disagreements will persist indefinitely. It is doubtful that any of the discussions that follow will lead to *epoche* regarding the individual elements of the modern liberal regulatory agenda, still less that *ataraxia,* either in general or in regard to government regulation, can be realized. Modern liberalism and classical liberalism have been defined as attitudes, that is, dispositions to offer arguments for and against, respectively, various forms of government intervention. To achieve *epoche* about elements of the modern liberal regulatory agenda and *ataraxia* about the entire modern liberal regulatory agenda, then, would be to cease to be a modern liberal or a classical liberal, as those terms have been defined here—one simply would not care. For the vast majority of both modern liberals and classical liberals, that is not in the cards. But it should be possible to see that those on both sides have reasonable beliefs. Undoubtedly, some of those beliefs will appear to some readers to be more reasonable than their contraries, depending on where one's sympathies lie. As long as it is possible to understand the reasoning of those on the other side and to see how or why that reasoning might look persuasive, it will be fair to conclude that there is persistent reasonable disagreement about what to believe. That in turn can motivate the search for reasoned agreement about what to do. That is both necessary and sufficient motivation for the main argument of chapter 11. Let us turn, then, to the agenda, beginning with regulation of the employment relation.

In this chapter, chapter 8, and the first section of chapter 9 we consider the main federal regulations governing the employment relation. This chapter discusses (1) the Fair Labor Standards Act, which mandates a minimum wage and overtime pay, (2) the Equal Pay Act, which requires equal pay for equal work, (3) the Family and Medical Leave Act, which requires employers to grant unpaid leaves of absence for medical reasons or for the birth or adoption of a child, and (4) the three main laws (the Norris-LaGuardia Act of 1932, the National Labor Relations Act of 1935, and the 1947 Taft-Hartley Amendments to the NLRA) that set the basic terms and conditions under which collective bargaining takes place. Chapter 8 considers conversion arguments for and against laws prohibiting discrimination based on race, color, national origin, religion, sex, age, and disability. Chapter 9 begins with a consideration of conversion arguments for and against the Occupational Safety and Health Act of 1970. It then discusses conversion arguments for and against consumer product and service health and safety regulation, which includes medical products, nonmedical products, and occupational licensure. Finally, chapter 10 discusses arguments about land use regulation, specifically, the Endangered Species Act and section 404 of the Clean Water Act.

Minimum Wage and Overtime Pay

The Fair Labor Standards Act (29 U.S.C. § 201) sets a federal minimum wage for covered employees, though states may require a higher minimum. It also requires time and a half pay for overtime work (typically over forty hours per week), and regulates child labor. When minimum wage laws were first being considered at the state level in the early twentieth century, various rationales were offered for them, some quite extravagant. For example, Edwin O'Hara, chair of the Industrial Welfare Commission of the state of Oregon, maintained that low wages, which he believed a minimum wage law would cure, were responsible for not only demoralization and physical impairment, they also undermined ambition, caused moral strain, induced the decay of patriotism and were responsible for various domestic evils, including even the spread of infections and contagious diseases![8] A more commonly cited and much more defensible reason for a legally mandated minimum wage was that it would mitigate or prevent what was called "sweating." (Indeed, until this day, it is routinely alleged that violators of this law run "sweatshops.") In the early twentieth century, women and children who worked outside the home were paid very low wages, in part because they lived in circumstances in which they were not the sole source of their support. This is why they were able to continue to work despite the fact that they were not getting what was necessary to sustain themselves on their own. In the case of women, it is virtually certain that another reason for their low pay was that they were routinely denied opportunities to work in other occupations. This resulted in them being crowded into certain lines of work, which increased the supply of labor, resulting in a lower price for unskilled labor. Immigration and population growth are two other factors that undoubtedly depressed wages at the low end of the wage spectrum. Historically, this has considerably weakened the bargaining position of low-income workers. Reformers opined that what was required to rectify this situation was a mandatory minimum wage law that could provide them with a "living wage," as it was called, then and now. This argument was summed up neatly by Thomas Powell in a contemporaneous law review article:

> The purpose and result of minimum wage legislation is to ensure that those who give their whole strength to an employer receive enough from that employer to maintain that strength, that there is a public interest in having in industry support itself instead of relying on outside subsidies. (1917, 19)

"Outside subsidies" in 1917 would be resources provided by other family members to sustain the women and children who were the objects of reformers' solicitude. These days, it would also include resources provided by the state, in the form of transfer programs, such as Temporary Assistance to Needy Families (TANF), the Food Stamp Program, the Housing Choice Voucher Program (section 8 subsidized housing), the Low-Income Home Energy Assistance Program (LIHEAP), and so on and so forth. Employers of subminimum wage employees are in effect free riding on the taxpayers, just as in earlier times, they were free riding on the support provided by other family members. The appeal to a principle to the effect that employers of workers at the bottom of the income ladder should not be free riding on the backs of other family members or on the state is intuitively plausible. A minimum wage law might also be thought to be a second or third best solution to the problem of assuring covered workers a guaranteed minimum income. The idea is to offer those willing to participate in the labor force an economic floor below which society refuses to allow them to fall. Robert Nozick (1993, 27) states that a minimum wage is a way of symbolizing our concern, as a society, for the poor. Finally, such a legally mandated minimum would also serve as a check on the power of capital owners to impose highly exploitative terms on would-be employees by virtue of the former's superior economic power.

Alternatively, one might argue for a minimum wage law on the basis of a principle to the effect that no one should make less than what it takes to support himself or herself (a "living wage"); perhaps that principle articulates some ethical version of Marx's labor theory of value. Any of these arguments would support some legally mandated minimum wage above the market-clearing rate. It should be noted that these arguments assume that the legally mandated minimum wage is above the market-clearing rate; otherwise, it has no economic effect.

There are, however, many good reasons to oppose minimum wage laws, namely, all the standard reasons that economists are fond of citing: they throw out of work people whose marginal cost at a legally mandated minimum exceeds the marginal value of their contribution. As a corollary, a minimum wage also forecloses employment opportunities that would otherwise exist for unemployed workers whose productivity is less than the minimum wage. Third, and perhaps most importantly, it retards human capital formation among the most disadvantaged and least productive members of society, a group which prominently includes young people just entering the labor force. Fourth, a legally mandated minimum wage, or an increase in the minimum wage, need not even make recipients who stay employed better off. Employers have ways to compensate for increases in direct labor costs in ways that are detrimental to workers' interests. They can make jobs they offer less expensive by making them less attractive along other margins. For example, they can reduce or eliminate bonuses or commissions, change the hours of work, lay off workers more readily when business conditions deteriorate, decrease the amount of job training, increase the pace of work, shorten or eliminate breaks, or reduce employee discounts, to name but a few options.[9] Finally, minimum wage laws disproportionately burden employers who hire minimum wage employees and cannot easily switch their capital to other lines of production, substitute capital for labor, or move operations overseas. Indeed, to the extent that minimum wage laws, or statutory increases in the minimum wage, achieve their intended effect of raising the income of these workers, it is at the expense of their employers, many of whom are not plutocrats and faceless corporations but are instead small businesspeople of modest means. Thus these direct burdens of the minimum wage are borne not by society at large or even by the capitalist class as a whole but are instead thrust upon a minority of capitalists who have chosen to employ their capital in lines that use significant amounts of unskilled labor.

This observation turns the second part of Powell's complaint aired above on its head. He asks why others (through "outside subsidies") should have to support workers whose firms will not pay them a living wage. One could equally ask why the owners of these firms, unlike other owners of capital who can substitute capital for labor or take their capital and flee to another line of production or to a subminimum wage country, should have to pay these workers more than the marginal value of the latter's contribution. Others who bear the direct costs of the minimum wage are those who are forced out of their jobs or are never hired in the first place because their marginal value is less than the legally mandated minimum. Why they should have to bear the brunt of the costs of an increase in the minimum wage is never explained. All of these considerations do not prove that minimum wage laws ought to be abolished or that they should never have been instituted in the first place, though that may well be true. Rather, they serve as reasons for favoring the elimination of a legally mandated minimum or at least as reasonable grounds for doubting the conclusion of any conversion argument for a minimum wage law, at least if it is above the market-clearing rate and thus has some effect.

These considerations against minimum wage laws can be softened by noting that classical liberals need not oppose restrictions on child labor, since children are incapable of entering into binding labor contracts, owing to their age. This does not mean that child labor should be prohibited; it does not take an economist to understand the benefits of child labor to the family economy in general and the well-being of the children themselves in certain circumstances. Concerns about exploitation of child labor (by parents, as much as by employers), however, are real and legitimate, and liberals of all persuasions can be sensitive to them. In addition, both classical liberals and modern liberals can oppose legal barriers to entry to a range of occupations ranging from hairdresser to taxicab driver. These barriers to entry drive up market rates for protected occupations and drive down market rates for other kinds of labor as those with skills but no license are forced to compete for other jobs (typically unskilled), thereby increasing the labor supply for other jobs and lowering the wage at which the market clears.

Equal Pay for Equal Work

In 1942, the National War Labor Board urged employers to equalize pay between women and men doing the same, or substantially the same, work. Compliance was voluntary and sporadic. After the war, wage differentials between men and women persisted, and in 1963 President Kennedy signed into law the Equal Pay Act (EPA), which, according to the language of the act, prohibited discrimination

> between employees on the basis of sex by paying wages to employees in such establishment at a rate less than the rate at which he pays wages to employees of the opposite sex in such establishment for equal work on jobs the performance of which requires equal skill, effort, and responsibility, and which are performed under similar working conditions, except where such payment is made pursuant to (i) a seniority system; (ii) a merit system; (iii) a system which measures earnings by quantity or quality of production; or (iv) a differential based on any other factor other than sex. (29 U.S.C. § 206(d))

The EPA was incorporated into the Fair Labor Standards Act (FLSA); the principal difference between the other provisions of the FLSA and the EPA is that the former exempts, but the latter does not, executive, administrative, and professional personnel. Indeed, most litigation involving the FLSA concerns who is and who is not exempt from its overtime provisions (Banks and Cohen 2005).

The moral argument for equal pay for equal work is fairly straightforward and is based on simple considerations of fairness. If, as seems reasonable, fairness consists of treating like cases alike, then fairness requires equal pay for equal work. If, as also seems reasonable, employers should treat employees fairly, it follows that they should be paid equally for equal work. In addition, wage rates have an expressive dimension, signaling not only the economic value of the labor provided but also the worth, or possibly just the economic worth, of the person who provides the labor. Or at least it is taken that way by those on the short end of these inequalities. Mandating equal pay for equal work is a way of addressing that perceived slight to these workers.

What is the conversion argument against the Equal Pay Act? It is difficult to imagine what such an argument might look like. On the face of it, it violates no widely accepted moral precept, and it would seem to be not particularly costly to administer. There is no obvious economic rationale for violating it. If markets are working properly, unequal pay for equal work should not exist, at least to any appreciable extent. This does not mean, however, that there is no conversion argument against it. To see what such an argument might look like, it is necessary to examine the motivations for the act and how it has been wielded in the courts.

Part of the motivation for passage of the EPA was the fairness argument just alluded to. The existence of a more generic wage gap between men and women was another, equally important, factor. The wage gap is calculated by dividing the median annual earnings for women by median annual earnings for men. At the time of the act's passage in 1963, women made on average 58.9 percent of what men earned, and while the gap has narrowed since then, it has not been substantially eliminated. To the extent that the wage gap was explainable by women failing to receive equal pay for equal work, the EPA was intended to shrink it, but it did not have that effect. After passage of the act in 1963, the wage gap hovered between a low of 57.6 percent (1966) and a high of 60.2 percent (1976 and 1980) before beginning a more or less steady narrowing trend in 1982 (i.e., women's income as a percentage of men's income steadily increased). By 2006, however, that figure had risen to only 76.9 percent, about .6 of a percentage point a year.[10] Many factors have been cited to explain the wage gap, but women not getting paid equally for equal work cannot be one of them, or at least not an important one—unless one assumes that after it was passed, the EPA was not enforced, an unlikely possibility, given that attorney's fees are recoverable under the act (29 U.S.C. § 216(b)), and given that these cases should be the low-hanging fruit for the plaintiffs' bar. Charge statistics from the EEOC are another indicator, albeit imperfect, of the effect of the act, or the lack thereof, on the wage gap. Since 1992, the EEOC has resolved on average 1,085 EPA cases per year, with total settlements averaging $4.025 million per year.[11] This represents a tiny fraction of all the cases resolved by the EEOC. Over the same period, on average, the EEOC, which handles complaints of discrimination based on sex, race, disability, age, and so on, has resolved 80,358 cases per year, with total settlements averaging $203.73 million per year.[12] This means that EPA cases represent 1.35 percent of the EEOC's yearly caseload and 1.97 percent of the total settlement dollars. It might be that the EPA has about the same effect as a minimum wage law that sets the legal minimum below the market-clearing rate, namely, almost no effect at all.

The EPA is regarded by some modern liberals as a timid first step toward a regime of comparable worth, and this is where the conversion argument against it might be found. Under comparable worth, pay is determined by a system of job evaluations that take into account the different factors that contribute to the value of the work done, such as the amount of skill, training, and responsibility involved in the job. The case for comparable worth starts with the assumption that the wage gap is largely explained by gender bias, which is alleged to be pervasive and deeply rooted. Labor markets systematically undervalue work traditionally done by women because it is done by women. As Paula England explains, "this type of sex discrimination occurs when the sex composition of jobs influences what employers are willing to pay those who do the jobs, whether this influence is conscious or unconscious" (1984, 28). In other words, the idea is that women are concentrated in certain occupations, and those occupations are relatively low paid because the factors determining pay rates are systematically undervalued by employers due to gender bias. For example, defenders of comparable worth claim that secretaries' literacy skills and childcare workers' teaching skills are undervalued because of gender bias. The unpleasantness of putting up with sexual harassment in the office and in dealing with the dirty diapers down at the local daycare center are systematically underestimated because of gender bias. And so on and so forth.

To correct these biases, proponents of comparable worth believe that job evaluations should be done that compare jobs traditionally done by women to other jobs, either those traditionally done by men or those in which no gender predominates. Comparisons are then made along a number of different dimensions, such as knowledge and skills, mental and physical demands, accountability, and the pleasantness or unpleasantness of working conditions. Scores are then assigned based on the importance of the various dimensions to the jobs in question. Ultimately, this allows dissimilar jobs to be compared as to their "true" (or intrinsic) worth to the employer, if not to society at large (Paul 1988, 24). If a regime of comparable worth were to be instituted, proponents believe, secretaries would not be making less than truck drivers and gardeners would not be making more than nurses. Or, to take one of the most commonly cited examples, people who take care of zoo animals would not make more than people who take care of small human animals.

Critics of comparable worth attack the key proposition that the wage gap is largely explained by gender bias. They maintain that other factors explain most of the gap.[13] For example, some accounts of size of the gap are based on the definition of full-time employment as thirty-five or more hours a week, which overlooks the fact that full-time working women work 9 to 10 percent fewer hours than full-time working men. Being married and having children have a large and differential impact on earnings. Thomas Sowell (1984, 92) has pointed out that the wage gap between single women and single men is a mere 9 percent. Anna Kondratas found that

> the pay gap between married men and unmarried men is about the same as between men and women overall. Married men earn far more than unmarried men and married men with children earn even more than married men without children.... Married women, on the other hand, earn far less than single women, and married women with children earn less than married women without. (1986, 3)

Other factors implicated in the wage gap include types of educational experience. For jobs requiring a college education, men are more likely to major in the sciences and engineering, where demand is relatively high and supply relatively low. By contrast, women are more inclined to major in literature, art history, and in the case of many feminists, women's studies, where job prospects are, how shall we say, not bright. A second important factor is gaps in labor force participation that occur when women leave the workforce to bear and raise children. Furthermore, women often have limited geographical mobility, a greater demand for flexible hours, and are more inclined to shun outdoor work that requires heavy lifting. Of course, feminist proponents of comparable worth see all these factors as stained with sexism, but that just indicates that their real complaints are not against the wage gap but instead against the underlying factors that produce it. A regime of comparable worth treats the symptoms, not the disease.

Critics can allow that some of the wage gap is explicable in terms of gender bias, but if most of it is not, the case for instituting a regime of comparable worth is weakened in exact proportion to how ambitious it is, since implementing any scheme of comparable worth would involve major changes in how pay is determined for various jobs and is fraught with other difficulties. One is that there really are no objective criteria by which to assess the "intrinsic" value of jobs nor is there any objective way to weight the relevant criteria. How important are knowledge and skills in comparison to level of responsibility in a given job? The idea that there are objective answers to questions such as these is pure fantasy. Bias and other irrelevant factors, unrestrained by market forces, would be given a freer hand without the discipline provided by the market. As Steven Rhoads says in his study of a comparable worth scheme introduced by the state of Minnesota for government workers,

> the three cases surveyed here, cases central to the proponents' argument for successful comparable-worth implementation, provide no examples anywhere of objective job evaluation. The guide for local government implementation...says that job evaluation measures duties against objective criteria, but the guide provides no such criteria. Instead, it lists sixty-six possible criteria and tells localities that they can decide themselves what they value most....Not even the consultants think their methods are objective. There is no agreement on factors to be included, on how they should be weighed or even on how factors...should be measured once decided upon. (1993, 220–21)

It is not difficult to guess the profile of the big winners under the regime of comparable worth instituted in Minnesota: feminists willing to argue relentlessly about the sexism inherent in any dimension along which they themselves happen not to excel. As Rhoads put the point more diplomatically, "in Minnesota, some of the biggest gainers were those who were prepared, who had articulate, forceful representatives on the committees, and who were skillful and assiduous in filling out the questionnaires" (1993, 220–21). Another problem, depending on how ambitious a scheme is implemented, is that raising wages would encourage an oversupply of workers in occupations traditionally dominated by women. That in turn would cause unemployment in those occupations, just as minimum wage laws cause unemployment among the unskilled, and it would permit hiring decisions to be made more frequently on the basis of irrelevant factors, such as physical appearance. Finally, a regime of comparable worth could require a massive new bureaucracy to administer, since it requires an indefinitely large number of types of jobs to be assessed, and it demands constant interference with the verdict of the market.

Comparable worth had some popularity back in the 1980s but in recent years enthusiasm for it has waned. One can only speculate on why this is so. One reason might be that pressures from international competition have made comparable worth a luxury policymakers believe is currently unaffordable—especially if no one's wages are going to be lowered when such a regime is instituted, which of course is the usual promise. Another possible explanation is that business owners and the policymakers they influence appreciate the truly radical nature of the doctrine of comparable worth and the enormous changes it would force in employment practices. It has been left off the modern liberal regulatory agenda in part because of these radical implications and in part because of its association with a form of sectarian feminism to which not all modern liberals would subscribe. In this respect, it is unlike title VII of the 1964 Civil Rights Act or the Family and Medical Leave Act of 1993, which modern liberals pretty much unanimously support.

However, it is arguable that some of the principles of comparable worth have been smuggled into enforcement of the EPA, and this is where a conversion argument against the EPA might be found. Almost no two jobs are exactly equal in every respect; for example, the act itself speaks of "equal work on jobs...which are performed under similar working conditions" (29 U.S.C. § 206(d)). Thus the courts have been required to develop criteria for "substantial equality."[14] This is where the first step on the slippery slope to comparable worth is taken. In their article "Comparable Worth and the Equal Pay Act," Mayer Freed and Daniel Polsby explain concisely how this happens:

> in the absence of "smoking gun" evidence, a court will be able to decide whether the difference in the two jobs is merely a pretext for illicit discrimination only by asking whether, in the absence of discrimination, the employer would have paid the incumbents of the two jobs differently; the only intelligible procedure by which to answer this question is to evaluate the employer's conduct against some standard of reasonableness. But in order for a court to evaluate an employer's decisions...there must be something like an objective and intrinsic value to a given job apart from what employers are willing to pay for the performance of the job. (1985, 143)

Once comparable worth principles are in play, it is open to plaintiffs' attorneys to argue that the dimensions along which the relevant jobs differ embody sexist stereotypes that systematically undervalue what women bring to the table. If it is reasonable to object to the doctrine of comparable worth, it is correspondingly reasonable to object to the EPA. Thus the conversion argument against the EPA.

The fears expressed in the preceding paragraph are probably overblown, however. As Freed and Polsby themselves point out, "there is widespread agreement that comparable worth may not be seriously entertained as a basis for liability under Title VII of the Civil Rights Act of 1964."[15] The only question then becomes whether the courts have bought the argument sketched above as an interpretation of the EPA. It appears that this has not happened; as the statistics cited above indicate (see above page 206), charges of EPA violations amount to only 1.35 percent of complaints handled by the EEOC. The courts seem to have taken the view that it would be easier for a rich man to enter the kingdom of heaven than for a woman to squeeze the doctrine of comparable worth through the eye of the needle of the EPA. There may be some other conversion argument against the EPA, but it is difficult to imagine what it might be.

Family and Medical Leave

The requirement that employers allow employees to take unpaid leave was instituted with the passage of the Family and Medical Leave Act of 1993 (29 U.S.C. § 2601). Its purpose was to protect the jobs of workers who have to take time off to care for family members who are ill or for the birth or adoption of a child (29 U.S.C. § 2601(a)–(b)). The rationale for it is that it is unjust, or at least unfair, that someone should lose her job for any of these reasons. It applies equally to men and women to assure equal protection under the law and to prevent discrimination against women in the workplace (29 U.S.C. § 2601(b) (4)). Prior to the passage of this act, people, especially women, could be let go if they wanted to take an unpaid leave of absence to care for a sick family member or for the birth or adoption of a child. The proposition that people should not be fired for this sort of thing is difficult to object to (though libertarians probably would), and that is what the law prohibits.

But, not all injustices perpetrated by employers on employees can be rectified by state action, at least not without imposing burdens that, broadly construed, outweigh the benefits of the policy. Mandated family leave imposes real and serious burdens on some employers who are unable to replace workers who take extended leaves of absence (up to twelve work weeks in any twelve-month period). In addition, other employees have to take up the slack for those on extended leave, which can have further undesirable consequences. A third problem is that it hurts the employment prospects at the margin for those who, ex ante, are most likely to avail themselves of the policy. Finally, like any such policy, it is subject to abuse, a phenomenon about which little has been heard. If abuse of the policy constitutes an injustice and if employment law without mandatory family leave permits injustices (e.g., firings) to occur, then injustice in this area is inevitable, and it is by no means obvious on which side the injustices and other bad consequences weigh most heavily.

It is worth noting that many larger companies had such a policy in place prior to passage of the Family and Medical Leave Act and thus would likely continue to have such a policy in the absence of a law requiring it. And, smaller firms often made accommodations on an ad hoc basis. This leaves only two kinds of firms who would fire employees: (1) those for whom allowing unpaid leave imposes very large burdens and (2) firms managed by the morally obtuse. The relative size of these two groups is unknown, but these observations raise an obvious question: "How much injustice does this law actually prevent?" The burdens and injustices imposed by the law on some employers are real, but so too are the burdens and injustices imposed on employees under a laissez faire alternative. Reasonable people can disagree about whether the costs, broadly construed to include the injustices permitted or encouraged by the law or its absence, outweigh the benefits, also broadly construed.

Notice that the recognition that there are injustices on each side suggests that a simple cost-benefit analysis carried out in terms of dollars is inadequate. The "costs" of injustices on both sides have to be included in some manner to determine whether or not the policy is, for lack of a better word, "choiceworthy." But, to put a dollar value, say in terms of willingness to pay, on the alternatives seems inappropriate because some of the values involved are moral values and some are not, which suggests the values at stake are incommensurable. Choices still have to be made, but there is something perverse about attaching a dollar value to injustices so they can be traded off against other values, even if those trade-offs have to be made in the final analysis. Perhaps the perversity lies in the fact that it is not perceived injustice (which could be characterized in terms of preferences ultimately cashed out in terms of willingness to pay) that gets (or should get) put in the balance scale but actual injustice. This may explain why there seems to be something wrong with trying to make incommensurable values commensurable. There are some difficult philosophical issues in here, but a conversion argument must remain silent about them if it is to avoid being mired in philosophical disputes about incommensurability—here about how injustices are to be weighed against each other and against other inconveniences.[16]

It might be useful by way of contrast to examine another restriction on the employment relation that is easier for classical liberals to accept. Employers are forbidden from dismissing employees who must serve on juries (28 U.S.C. § 1875). Like military service, though on a much smaller scale, citizens are called upon to provide an essential service for the liberal state and in a way that is burdensome not only to them but also to their employers. If the latter were permitted to fire employees who were called upon to serve on juries, it would greatly increase the burdens that these employees would have to shoulder and would be undeniably unjust. Instead, the law spreads some of the burden onto employers by requiring that the jobs of employees called to serve on juries be kept open. The most salient differences with family leave are instructive, however: jury duty is legally required; service on juries is typically of brief duration; exceptions and exemptions are permitted for certain employment situations; prospective jurors are not in a position to abuse the policy. Under the circumstances, it would be much more difficult than in the case of mandated family leave for classical liberals to maintain skepticism about whether the burdens the law imposes on employers and other employees outweigh its benefits, all things considered. No grand principle of justice should be needed to get nearly any classical liberal to agree that employers should not be able to fire employees who are called to serve on a jury. Reasoned agreement can be reached at a much less abstract level, though it requires classical liberals to countenance an exception to their general principle about freedom of contract. The agreement is reasoned because there is an easily imagined argument for the policy, which contains a lower-level principle to the effect that firms should not be able to fire employees whom the state occasionally needs, and whose presence it insists on, to discharge essential functions (or something to that effect). Such a principle need not be supported, at least in the context of this argument, by any deeper philosophical argument. The persistent search for ever more abstract principles, much praised and encouraged in philosophical and legal circles, is like the propensity to drink too much in that it encourages querulousness among the participants and prevents reasoned agreement from emerging.

Regulation of Collective Bargaining

There are two laws that are of particular importance in the regulation of relations between and among management, unions, and workers: the Norris-LaGuardia Act of 1932 (29 U.S.C. § 101 et. seq.)

and the National Labor Relations Act of 1935 (29 U.S.C. § 151 et. seq.), also known as the Wagner Act. The latter was significantly amended in 1947 by the Taft-Hartley amendments. The Norris-La-Guardia Act did two main things: (1) it explicitly permitted workers to organize, to bargain collectively, and to strike, (2) it prohibited the courts from enforcing so-called yellow dog contracts; these were contracts which required, as a condition of employment, that an employee not join a union or resign his membership, if he were a member. The idea behind these contracts is that when unions tried to organize workers, employers took them to court and got an injunction based on the union's tortious interference with a contractual relation. This was an extremely effective anti-union tool, which the Norris-LaGuardia Act took away. The National Labor Relations Act as amended (hereafter the NLRA) also guaranteed workers the legal right to organize, to bargain collectively, and to go on strike. In addition, it stipulated that a union that was certified by a majority vote of the affected workers would be the exclusive bargaining agent for all these employees. It also (1) specified procedures (including a secret ballot) that must be followed when a union seeks to represent workers, (2) empowered the National Labor Relations Board (NLRB) to settle jurisdictional disputes among unions, and (3) prohibited both companies and unions from engaging in certain so-called "unfair labor practices." In these ways, it set the general framework within which workers could exercise their rights to organize and to bargain collectively.

Classical liberals could accept some of these provisions of the NLRA, or something very much like them, to the extent that they either explicitly acknowledge rights that workers already do have or should have, or to the extent that they simply specify a framework within which those rights can be exercised. States have chartering laws that allow businesses to incorporate as limited liability corporations. These laws define the legal framework within which business is conducted, in the course of which they confer a benefit on businesses, namely, limited liability. These provisions of the NLRA perform a parallel service for organized labor.

But, other provisions of the act, as well as the Norris-LaGuardia Act's prohibition on the enforcement of yellow dog contracts, are more troublesome from a classical liberal perspective, since they imply important limitations on freedom of contract that cannot be clearly justified by any analogy with chartering laws. Two of these provisions stand out: one is the exclusive representation clause (§ 159(a)), and the other is section 158(a), which describes prohibited "unfair labor practices." Let us consider the latter first. Employers are not

(1) to interfere with, restrain, or coerce employees in the exercise of the rights guaranteed in section 157 of this title;

(2) to dominate or interfere with the formation or administration of any labor organization or contribute financial or other support to it...

(3) [to discriminate] in regard to hire or tenure of employment or any term or condition of employment to encourage or discourage membership in any labor organization; Provided, That nothing in this subchapter, or in any other statute of the United States, shall preclude an employer from making an agreement with a labor organization... to require as a condition of employment membership therein...

(4) to discharge or otherwise discriminate against an employee because he has filed charges or given testimony under this subchapter;

(5) to refuse to bargain collectively with the representatives of his employees... (29 U.S.C. § 158(a)(1)–(5))

All of these clauses require interpretation, which the NLRB has done through its various rulings over the years, and there is much that classical liberals might find objectionable in their interpretations. Let us put detailed questions of statutory interpretation to one side, however, and focus on the main idea behind (1) through (5). What numbers (1) through (5) collectively say is that employers must remain neutral if workers choose to organize themselves or if a labor union tries to organize them, and they must accept the results of an election if the workers in its firm choose to unionize. Numbers (1) and (2) require employers to remain neutral on the question of whether or not workers should be represented by a union; it also prohibits company-dominated unions. Number (3) requires employers to remain neutral in the terms and conditions of employment between union and nonunion members. It has also been understood to prohibit yellow dog contracts themselves and not just their enforcement by the courts. Finally, number (3) explicitly permits contracts to require union membership as a condition of employment. (§ 159(a)—the exclusive representation clause—requires it.) Number (4) prohibits retaliation, and number (5) just prohibits the employer from categorically refusing to bargain with the employees' duly elected representatives.[17]

It is easy to see what a conversion argument would look like for these provisions. If a worker could be molested, fired, demoted, or docked in pay for union activity or as retaliation for reporting the firm to authorities, or not hired unless she agreed not to join a union, or pressured into joining a company union, workers' rights to organize and bargain collectively would be a sham. To make this case, there is no need to invoke any philosophical principle to the effect that a right to X entails a right to whatever a person needs to exercise effectively his or her right to X. Nor is there any need to reach for and specify any principle about inequality in bargaining power and then argue that there is an inequality in bargaining power in this case that has crossed the specified threshold. Once we reach that level of abstraction or generality, reasonable disagreement will break out like a case of hives. The conversion argument just sketched does not go beyond an appeal to common sense on this particular issue. The main idea behind this argument is simply that workers will not be able to effectively exercise their right to bargain collectively unless employers are forced to give them some space in which to make that decision. What, then, is the conversion argument against (1) through (5)? There may be one, but I am unable to articulate it. If other classical liberals are similarly struck dumb, they could arguably make an exception to their general principle of freedom of contract. This is not to deny the existence of any argument against these provisions of the NLRA. There are, for example, libertarian arguments against making any exceptions in this context. Some are made fairly directly from first principles (notably, freedom of contract), but there is also an argument in Epstein (1983) that depends on common law principles, and at the deepest level, the utilitarianism of Epstein and others in the law and economics movement.[18] Still, the basic point is that there may be a good argument against these features of the Norris-LaGuardia Act and the National Labor Relations Act; it is just not a conversion argument and thus not likely to command assent from modern liberals, those liberals who antecedently have no opinion on this question, or classical liberals who wear their principles lightly.

Of course, unfair labor practices as specified in (1) through (5) require interpretation to be applied in particular cases, and it is open to classical liberals of an anti-union persuasion to object to those interpretations. But on the basic idea of allowing workers to organize free of employer interference, it is hard to find a persuasive argument against this, at least close to the surface where conversion arguments are found.

The other restriction on employers imposed by the NLRA—the exclusive representation clause—is much more contestable. It says, "representatives designated or selected for the purposes of collective bargaining by the majority of the employees in a unit appropriate for such purposes, shall be the exclusive representatives of all the employees in such unit for the purposes of collective bargaining" (29 U.S.C. § 159). In other words, the union does not represent only those who voted for it; they also represent those who voted against it. This clause effectively removes the question of exclusive representation from the bargaining table. Prior to the passage of this act, exclusive representation was in theory open to negotiation but in fact was virtually unheard of in the private sector. In a 1992 article, Charles Baird makes the classical liberal case against the exclusive representation clause of the NLRA concisely:

> it is important to recognize that under the principle of exclusive representation, created by federal statute, the minority (all workers who do not vote in favor of the winning union) are put to a choice between submitting to the will of the majority regarding the sale of their individual services or losing their jobs. That is governmentally imposed coercion, pure and simple. The fact that workers can opt out of the unwanted representation services of a certified union by quitting their jobs does not mitigate the coercion. If an individual owns his own labor, and has a further right to enter into contracts with any willing buyer of that labor on terms that are mutually acceptable, then exclusive representation overrides those rights.... And since exclusive representation exists solely by virtue of federal statute, the federal government, not any private party, is the source of the coercion. On its face, this is government action: government gives powers to the majority that they otherwise would not have. (Baird 1992)

Because of this clause, workers who were not union members could either be forced to join the union within thirty days of their employment at the firm (a union shop agreement) or pay an agency fee (an agency shop agreement) to the union. Unions and their supporters justified this on the grounds that it prevented nonunion workers from "free riding" on the union's bargaining power with employers. They would benefit from the contract without paying any of the costs. But of course the free riding only occurs because of the exclusive representation clause! If unions represented only voluntary members, nonmembers would not be covered by collective bargaining agreements; there would be nothing to require employers to pay them as much as they paid the union workers, though this assumes the repeal of section 158(a)(3). There is no public good here, much less a public goods problem; the good is excludable by contract. Of course, defenders of unions might argue that the company would pay nonunion employees as much as or even more than union employees as a way of undercutting the union, but that ignores the possibility of negotiating an exclusive representation clause or tying it to excludable private goods, such as grievance arbitration, restrictive work rules that make it possible for union workers to do almost nothing and get paid for it (in other words, "featherbedding"), and possibly other benefits (e.g., a gold-plated health insurance package) as well.

The free rider issue to one side, union shop and agency shop contracts create further problems from a classical liberal perspective. Union dues and agency fees are used for purposes other than collective bargaining, contract administration, and grievance adjustment. One such purpose is purely partisan political activity. This appears to infringe upon First Amendment rights of free speech and free association. In *Machinists v. Street,* Justice Black, quoting James Madison and Thomas Jefferson, objected to this implication of the exclusive representation clause on exactly these grounds:

> if [using forced dues for politics] is constitutional the First
> Amendment is not the charter of political and religious liberties
> its sponsors believed it to be. James Madison, who wrote the
> Amendment, said...that "the same authority which can force
> a citizen to contribute three pence only of his property for the
> support of any one establishment [of religion], may force him
> to conform to any other establishment in all cases whatsoever."
> And Thomas Jefferson said that "to compel a man to furnish
> contributions of money for the propagation of opinions which
> he disbelieves is sinful and tyrannical." These views of Madison
> and Jefferson authentically represent the philosophy embodied
> in the safeguards of the First Amendment 'Machinists v. Street,
> 367 U.S. 740, 790 (1961), notes omitted.'

This case was part of a long line of cases under the Railway Labor Act (45 U.S.C. § 151) and the NLRA that grappled with the question of the legitimacy of forced union dues in one form or another. Not only do unions use dues for partisan political activity, they also use those dues for expenses unrelated to collective bargaining, contract administration, and grievance adjustment, such as organizing drives at other firms and perhaps most outrageously, legal fees to defend union officials against charges of corruption. If the only concern is to eliminate the so-called "free rider problem," these costs should not be chargeable to those who do not voluntarily join the union. The courts have been moving toward this position, though they have not fully embraced it, in a line of cases culminating in *Communications Workers of America v. Beck,* 487 U.S. 743 (1988). The main outstanding issue is how unions can collect these agency costs, specifically, whether they can collect full union dues and then rebate everything except the agency costs to dissenting workers, who must apply for it, or whether they must collect only agency fees from the outset. The amounts involved are not trivial; as Charles Baird points out, in *Beck* "the trial court held that 79 percent of the money exacted from the dissenting workers would have to be refunded, with interest, because that was the percentage of dues used for impermissible purposes. That percentage was upheld throughout the litigation" (Baird 1992). This decision has the potential to be an enormous blow to the political power of unions, though it has yet to be fully enforced by the executive or legislative branches. These two facts are apparently not unrelated.

A second restriction on employers that classical liberals would object to is that employers were forbidden from saying anything at all to workers that might influence them, but the Supreme Court later overturned that on free speech grounds *(N.L.R.B. v. Virginia Elec. & Power Co.,* 314 U.S. 469 (1941)). The act now says that "the expressing of any views, argument, or opinion, or the dissemination thereof... shall not constitute or be evidence of an unfair labor practice under any of the provisions of this subchapter, if such expression contains no threat of reprisal or force or promise of benefit." This meant that an employer could discuss, for example, general economic conditions in his industry perhaps offering some speculation about what might happen in that industry if costs cannot be controlled, but he could not threaten to shut down his factory and move it to Mexico unless the workers at his factory moderated their demands or voted against the union. Nor could he promise a wage increase if the workers would vote for no union representation or to decertify the union. Classical liberals would object to these restrictions. More generally, there seems to have been an effort on the part of the NLRB to minimize any substantive direct communication between management and workers. All communication has to go through the union, even prior to a certifying election. This seems hard to defend, much less to defend by a conversion argument.

Under the heading of "unfair labor practices" unions were originally subject to prohibitions that paralleled those imposed on businesses (except of course they could promise workers benefits for joining the union, and they were exempt from antitrust laws), but the Taft-Hartley amendments added many more prohibitions, including prohibitions on secondary boycotts, common situs picketing, jurisdictional strikes, and closed shop agreements. A closed shop agreement requires an employer to hire only union members. Closed shop agreements were permitted under the original Wagner Act but were prohibited under the Taft-Hartley amendments. Those amendments also permitted states to pass so-called "right-to-work" laws, which prohibit exclusive representation clauses. Currently, twenty-two states have such laws.[19]

In non-right-to-work states, union shop and agency shop agreements continued to be permitted (§ 158(a)(3) and § 159(a)). In the unfair labor practices listed in section 158, the language is often exceedingly vague and open to interpretation by the NLRB, making it difficult to formulate, much less defend, any conversion arguments pro or con. The same is true of the other limitations on freedom of contract stated in this section of the act. So, what can be said about them from either a classical liberal or modern liberal perspective? Some historical background is in order at this point. In the first third of the twentieth century, laws were passed that gave unions special privileges and immunities. For example, they are immune from antitrust laws (15 U.S.C. § 17), and they do not pay taxes (26 U.S.C. § 501(c)(5)). Some of the provisions of the NLRA (and to a lesser extent, the Norris-LaGuardia Act) gave them additional privileges and immunities. The rationale for these is that there had been an important difference in bargaining power between employers and employees, to the disadvantage of the latter. The elected branches of government decided to put their thumbs on the scale to correct this imbalance in bargaining power. Or, to switch metaphors, once again the government got out their road graders to level the playing field. This bargaining power rationale was fairly explicit in the "Findings and Statement of Policy" section of the NLRA:

the inequality of bargaining power between employees who do not possess full freedom of association or actual liberty of contract and employers who are organized in the corporate or other forms of ownership association substantially burdens and affects the flow of commerce, and tends to aggravate recurrent business depressions, by depressing wage rates and the purchasing power of wage earners in industry and by preventing the stabilization of competitive wage rates and working conditions within and between industries. Experience has proved that protection by law of the right of employees to organize and bargain collectively safeguards commerce from injury, impairment, or interruption, and promotes the flow of commerce by removing certain recognized sources of industrial strife and unrest, by encouraging practices fundamental to the friendly adjustment of industrial disputes arising out of differences as to wages, hours, or other working conditions, and by restoring equality of bargaining power between employers and employees. (29 U.S.C. § 151)

The heart of the act, however, is sections 159 and 158; the former is the exclusive representation clause, which classical liberals would oppose on grounds of freedom of contract, free speech, and freedom of association. By contrast, modern liberals would be inclined to favor it because, as they see it, it redresses in part the imbalance in bargaining power between labor and management. Section 158 is more ambiguous; it lists all of the unfair labor practices (by both employers and unions) and stipulates various other limitations on freedom of contract. Some of the clauses in this section were part of the Taft-Hartley amendments, which were intended to redress what some saw as an imbalance in labor's favor that had developed in the years subsequent to the passage of the original NRLA. The upshot is that Congress, the NLRB, and, to a lesser extent, the judiciary all saw themselves as engaged in a balancing act whose ultimate purpose was to bring about a rough parity of bargaining power between labor and management—and, it should be noted, to reduce industrial strife, up to and including violence. Given that different people had widely divergent views about where the equilibrium point was to be found, it would be surprising, indeed remarkable, if the law as it finally evolved got it right, if the latter notion is at all meaningful. After all, the underlying question is about what is fair, and as anyone who has had a sibling as a child can attest, that question is inherently contestable. For these reasons, there are unlikely to be any conversion arguments for or against any of the provisions of section 158 of NLRA beyond the argument sketched above in favor of (something like) the unfair labor practices identified in (a)(1)–(5).

Conversion Arguments

Antidiscrimination Law

Discrimination on the Basis of Race, Color, Religion, and National Origin

Beginning with the Civil Rights Act of 1964 (42 U.S.C. § 2000e), the federal government outlawed discrimination in hiring, promotion, and termination based on a variety of different grounds. Originally, forbidden grounds were limited to race, color,[1] religion, sex, and national origin. Later, age and disability status were included in separate statutes. Let us begin with race, color, religion, and national origin. Race is by far the most important of these, but we shall consider the others along with race, since these categories raise no new or special issues. By contrast, sex discrimination does raise a special issue, namely, sexual harassment, so it will be treated separately, as will age and disability discrimination.

The history and development of antidiscrimination law applied to race is complex and directly relevant to how it should be assessed. Originally, title VII of the 1964 Civil Rights Act was conceived of as prohibiting employers from taking race into account in making decisions to hire, fire, or promote workers. The emphasis was on prohibiting different treatment because of, or on the basis of, these factors—*disparate treatment,* as it came to be called.[2] The argument for this was fairly straightforward and difficult to fault: historically, people—especially white males—in a position to make employment decisions were motivated by the belief that members of other races, notably African Americans, but also members of various nationalities and religious groups (e.g., Chinese, Irish, Catholics, Jews), are socially inferior to whites, and thus these decision-makers were motivated by racial, ethnic, or religious animus. Or, they were motivated by the belief that these races or nationalities are not intelligent, industrious, or more generally, competent, enough to do certain jobs (racial or ethnic stereotyping). The falsity of these stereotypes is almost as self-evident as they were pervasive. Making prejudicial decisions about something as important as employment on the basis of such stereotypes or because of animus toward members of protected groups is morally pernicious, and, so the argument goes, should be made illegal. On the face of it, it is difficult to find good reasons to object to this law as it was initially construed.

However, in a 1971 case, *Griggs v. Duke Power,* 401 U.S. 424 (1971), and in subsequent cases, the Supreme Court interpreted the 1964 Civil Rights Act in such a way as to expand dramatically its scope and reach. It ruled that hiring and promotion practices and policies having a disparate negative impact on protected workers were prima facie suspect. Duke Power required workers who wanted to transfer to certain departments or to be promoted to have a high school diploma and to make certain scores on broad aptitude tests. Since African Americans did worse on these tests and had a lower percentage of high school graduates, these requirements had a negative *disparate impact.* The Court held that, absent a showing that such requirements are necessary to perform the job, disparate impact counts as unlawful discrimination. Since Duke Power was not able to make this showing, the Court ruled for the plaintiff. The practices that were struck down had discriminatory effects. As the Court said, "The Company contends that its general intelligence tests are specifically permitted by § 703(h) of the Act [note omitted]. That section authorizes the use of 'any professionally developed ability test' that is not 'designed, intended or *used* to discriminate because of race...' (Emphasis added.)" (401 U.S. 424, 433). No one charged that Duke Power had intentionally failed to promote or hire someone because of his race. Indeed, when Duke Power first instituted this requirement, African Americans were prohibited under any circumstances from even applying for these more coveted positions. That is, no disparate treatment was alleged or proved, but the tests and other requirements had a disparate impact and were thereby ruled discriminatory.

Currently, the way the law is interpreted, any time a company with fifteen or more employees has job requirements, uses tests, or has other hiring or promotion practices that have a negative disparate impact on minorities, it is risking a discrimination lawsuit from disappointed job applicants or from minorities passed over for promotion. For example, suppose that 12 percent of the relevant population is African American and the use of a test or job qualification results in hiring only 6 percent African Americans. This test or job qualification has a (negative) disparate impact on African Americans, which can serve as a basis for a lawsuit. The company can still use the test or qualification, but it faces certain hurdles. It can argue that the definition of the reference population that serves to define the disparate impact should be restricted to those with certain job-related qualifications or to those who actually applied for the position, or it can contest the definition of the firm's workforce (e.g., does the workforce include employees at other divisions of the firm located elsewhere). Perhaps most importantly, the company can argue that the test or qualification that produced the disparate impact is "job-related and consistent with business necessity." This can defeat a claim of discrimination based on disparate impact. For example, if one is hiring physicians, applicants must be licensed to practice medicine, and if this requirement has a disparate impact on a protected minority population, that requirement would nevertheless be legally acceptable.

The notion that practices that have a disparate impact are prima facie discriminatory has had some perverse effects. The case for requiring an applicant to have a license to practice medicine if she is applying for a job as a physician is self-evident. However, it is often very difficult or expensive to establish that a test or requirement satisfies the business necessity test, in part because there is a tangle of legal opinions about how to interpret this.[3] Consequently, it is often rational for large or high-profile companies to drop the practice before it is challenged and hire or promote by the numbers as best they can so as to ward off a disparate impact lawsuit. Or, they can continue to use the practice that has a disparate impact and bundle it with a more subjective screening device (e.g., an interview) and use the latter to get the numbers to "come out right." That is, employers have instituted what I have elsewhere called "defensive preferential hiring" to avoid lawsuits based on disparate impact (Arnold 1998, 135–37). Although the government does not mandate defensive preferential hiring, they clearly encourage it by the way title VII of the Civil Rights Act has been interpreted to allow hiring practices with disparate impact to serve to get a lawsuit started. Further incentive to "hire by the numbers" comes from the Equal Employment Opportunity Commission (EEOC), which is empowered to bring lawsuits against employers on grounds of discrimination. The EEOC follows the "80 percent rule."[4] This rule says that if the percentage of women or minorities a firm hires is at least 80 percent of their percentage in the relevant reference population, the firm will not be subject to an investigation and a possible disparate impact lawsuit. Rather like the Jews marking their homes with the blood of the lamb to be spared the wrath of God (Exod. 12), rational firms hire enough people from protected groups so that the EEOC passes over their businesses. Alternatively, some firms (especially some units of government) have responded to these pressures by redesigning their tests and other selection criteria to remove the disparate impact or to pass the "business necessity" test, but this is often difficult and/or costly to do.

The way that title VII of the 1964 Civil Rights Act has been interpreted has created important internal tensions within the act. The key provisions of the act governing employment are 42 U.S.C. § 2000e–2(a):

> (a) Employer practices
> It shall be an unlawful employment practice for an employer—
>   (1) to fail or refuse to hire or to discharge any individual, or otherwise to discriminate against any individual with respect to his compensation, terms, conditions, or privileges of employment, because of such individual's race, color, religion, sex, or national origin; or
>   (2) to limit, segregate, or classify his employees or applicants for employment in any way which would deprive or tend to deprive any individual of employment opportunities or otherwise adversely affect his status as an employee, because of such individual's race, color, religion, sex, or national origin.

This clearly prohibits disparate treatment, but it has also been interpreted to ground a presumptive challenge to businesses practices that have a disparate impact. This, along with administrative decisions by the EEOC, have encouraged defensive preferential hiring among large or visible firms as a way of avoiding antidiscrimination lawsuits (often class action suits).

However, defensive preferential hiring seems on its face to be inconsistent with the just-quoted section of the Civil Rights Act, as well as with section 703(j) of title VII, which says,

> nothing contained in this subchapter shall be interpreted to require any employer...to grant preferential treatment to any individual or to any group because of the race, color, religion, sex, or national origin of such individual or group on account of an imbalance which may exist with respect to the total number or percentage of persons of any race, color, religion, sex, or national origin employed by any employer...in comparison with the total number or percentage of persons of such race, color, religion, sex, or national origin in any community.

Despite these provisions of the law, preferential hiring programs have flourished; this is affirmative action in hiring as it is currently practiced and is central to the modern liberal regulatory agenda in employment law.[5]

In retrospect, it is not difficult to understand how and why the law evolved in the way that it did. Disparate treatment goes to motive—someone in authority is discriminating against an applicant because he believes that applicant is inferior to others because of race, color, and so on, or because he simply does not want to associate (or have other employees or customers of his firm associate with) people in the protected groups. That is, the motive is stereotype or animus. But motive is easy to hide or disguise, as every modern-day bigot knows, especially if he has had to say the pieties in a diversity workshop the way most people sing hymns in church. The law would have little effect in improving the economic condition of disadvantaged minorities if it were to be wielded only against firms with signs in the window saying "No Irish or Chinamen Need Apply" or against employers incautious enough to make jokes about minorities in a job interview. The attraction of interpreting discrimination in terms of disparate effects of hiring or promotion policies is obvious: looking to the effects of these practices avoids the need to uncover motives, and it forces businesses to use only those tests and requirements that they can demonstrate are "job-related and consistent with business necessity." Moreover, it could be argued that (defensive) preferential hiring partially compensates for subtle, indeed possibly subconscious, prejudices that infect the hiring process.[6] This is not stiff-armed redistribution, since the business necessity defense is always available; the appeal of allowing that defense is that it ostensibly gives considerations of merit pride of place in employment decisions, if a firm has good reasons to use practices that discriminate unintentionally, that is, if they have good reasons to use practices that, whatever the motives, have a negative impact on protected groups. The crucial issue is who bears the burden of proof, and modern liberals could argue that it is unfair that workers bear it, or at least that it is fairer that the burden be borne by employers, who have the resources, than by those seeking employment, who typically do not.

How might classical liberals reply, that is, what sort of counterargument might they offer? Two distinct responses suggest themselves. One is to take a hard line and argue that title VII should be repealed. On this view, the employment-at-will doctrine should govern without exceptions based on race, et cetera. Both disparate treatment and practices having disparate impact would therefore be legal. Call this the "libertarian response." The second reply makes an exception to the employment-at-will doctrine for disparate treatment discrimination but draws the line at disparate impact. Let us consider the latter position first. It might be argued that discrimination by disparate treatment offends business rationality, since it is not in a firm's financial interests to close itself off to the talents and abilities of workers in protected classes. If persons doing the hiring in firms with over fifteen employees (the only firms covered by the act) are indulging in their "taste" for discrimination, then, unless the person doing the hiring is the firm's owner, the latter faces a principal-agent problem that the law helps him or her address. If, however, the firm's owner is doing the hiring and wants to indulge in disparate treatment discrimination, he would indeed be prohibited by law from doing this, and his right to contract freely with others would be thereby limited. However, discrimination by disparate treatment is simply difficult to defend from a moral point of view, and because of the historical salience of discrimination on the basis of race (and to a lesser extent, gender, religion, and national origin), a classical liberal might be willing to countenance an exception to a general right to freedom of contract. After all, reasonable classical liberals already allow an exception in the case of the law that forbids employers from firing people called for jury duty or military service, and there may be other exceptions they could countenance as well.

The main problem with contemporary antidiscrimination law, on this classical liberal account, arises from the legal suspicion that is cast on employment practices, especially in large or high-visibility firms, that have a disparate impact on members of protected groups. This feature of antidiscrimination law is the main impetus behind affirmative action in the form of preferential treatment and, as such, is central to the modern liberal regulatory agenda. It involves de facto restrictions on freedom of contract and creates real burdens on affected firms, namely firms that believe they might be subject to disparate impact lawsuits and so engage in defensive preferential hiring to ward off such suits. This involves taking race or other factors into account to get the numbers to come out right. One obvious objection to this practice is that it violates a widely accepted and morally defensible ideal of color blindness (or neutrality with respect to other protected class characteristics) in hiring practices. Many employers and their agents actively believe in this sort of neutrality—in part, it can be conceded, in response to the ideals of the original civil rights movement. It is an affront to their moral integrity to put them in a position of having to violate their moral beliefs on a regular basis to avoid lawsuits, especially when they are arguably violating the law as it is written in order to ensure that they are in compliance with the law as it has been interpreted. The social hypocrisy implicit in the existing legal regime grates on the moral sensibilities of many managers pressured to make decisions on grounds that violate this ideal.

The contrast with ordinary disparate treatment discrimination is instructive in this context: retaining the right to treat people differently simply on the basis of race, et cetera is difficult to defend, especially since it is either an expression of animus toward members of the protected group or grounded in baseless stereotypes. To claim that a prohibition on such practices is an affront to the moral integrity of bigots is either a worthy affront or a bad joke. By contrast, adherence to a color (or gender/religion/nationality)-blind standard is morally defensible, and the harm done to the moral integrity of those administering a defensive preferential hiring program is barely attenuated if outsiders believe, perhaps correctly, that there are legitimate exceptions to that standard.

A second objection is associated with the burden of proof problem that motivates defensive preferential hiring. To see what this is, some more historical background is in order. In 1989, a majority of the Supreme Court seemed to have some doubts about affirmative action—especially defensive preferential hiring—as it had developed over more than two decades. Their ruling in *Ward's Cove Packing, Inc. v. Antonio,* 490 U.S. 642 (1989), significantly lessened the pressure on firms to hire by the numbers by loosening and reassigning the burdens of proof in disparate impact cases. There were three important changes or clarifications made by *Ward's Cove:*[7]

(1) The plaintiff must identify a specific employment practice that has a disparate impact; she cannot focus on the "bottom line" percentages of minorities and non-minorities within the firm or within any of its divisions. This requirement does attenuate the incentives to hire by the numbers to avoid lawsuits. Case law had been unclear on this point, and this ruling settled that issue decisively.

Perhaps the most important changes wrought by *Ward's Cove* were related to the business necessity defense that companies could offer once disparate impact had been established. In this connection, the Court set out two conditions:

> (2) The company need only articulate a legitimate business basis for the challenged practice; it need not prove that the practice is strictly necessary for the operation of the business.[8]

For example, fast food restaurants may require basic literacy and numeracy skills, which could have a disparate impact on minorities. They could do this even though their cash registers automatically calculate change, and even though there are little pictures of the food on the buttons of the register. Nevertheless, satisfaction of a basic literacy and numeracy requirement could probably survive the "legitimate business function test." The restaurant could argue that the requirements of very basic literacy and numeracy skills allow them to screen out people who would be unlikely to perform well and could never be promoted, even though they do not actually have to have those skills to do the job and even if the prospective employee has no interest in being promoted. Though the employer has the burden of production (i.e., to produce a reason and any relevant evidence for the test or requirement) and cannot say just anything, the Court suggests that the burden is not onerous:

> there is no requirement that the challenged practice be "essential" or "indispensable" to the employer's business to pass muster: this degree of scrutiny would be almost impossible to meet, and would result in a host of evils we have identified above. (490 U.S. 659 (1989))

As the Court made clear in its discussion of these evils, the chief evil was defensive preferential hiring, or as it is more commonly known, "hiring by quotas." As the Court said,

> the only practicable option for many employers would be to adopt racial quotas, ensuring that no portion of their workforces deviated in racial composition from the other portions thereof; this is a result that Congress expressly rejected in drafting Title VII. [This] would "leave the employer little choice...but to engage in a subjective quota system of employment selection." (490 U.S. 652 (1989))

(3) The plaintiff must be given the opportunity to show that the challenged policy is not reasonably necessary for the operation

of the business. In practice, about the only way this can be done is to show that there is another employment practice the employer could have used which would have less disparate impact on minorities. This practice has to be roughly comparable in terms of its effectiveness and costs. To put it another way, the plaintiff has the burden of persuasion.

There was widespread agreement that this case effectively overturned *Griggs*. Though disparate impact cases could still go forward, it imposed a heavier burden on the plaintiff to establish disparate impact, since a mere imbalance in the bottom line numbers would be insufficient. Perhaps more importantly, it relaxed the "business necessity" defense that employers could use to override the claim of disparate impact: though the Court pretended that "legitimate business function" is simply a clarification of "business necessity," it is clearly a different—and lower—standard. In terms of larger social policy, it significantly attenuated the incentives businesses had to hire or promote by the numbers, since their chances of being successfully sued on these grounds were greatly diminished because of the heavier burden of proof that plaintiffs bore and the relative ease with which the latter's case could be rebutted. Had Congress not intervened, it is likely that this decision would have all but eliminated defensive preferential hiring programs in the private sector, with the exception of firms that do business with the federal government, who are required by executive order to submit elaborate affirmative action plans, complete with minority hiring goals and timetables.[9] But, the *Ward's Cove* standards were not nothing; they would have prevented the use of tests and requirements as mere pretexts to mask disparate treatment discrimination, just as literacy tests and poll taxes were used to deny minorities the right to vote during the pre–civil rights era in the South. If this decision had been allowed to stand, classical liberals who countenance only a disparate treatment exception to the employment-at-will doctrine would have little to which they could object, since it is likely that disparate impact cases would be infrequently threatened, rarely filed, and even more rarely won. The crucial variable in employment discrimination law is not the likelihood of winning but the ease with which a credible threat of litigation can be made, since credible threats can induce settlement before a case even gets filed.

The legislative response to *Ward's Cove*, however, was to overturn it. Liberal Democrats and the civil rights lobby had been content to let the courts do the heavy lifting in encouraging preferential hiring by the decision in *Griggs* and its progeny. When the Supreme Court became uncomfortable with what it had wrought and redefined the rules in *Ward's Cove,* proponents of preferential treatment correctly believed they had enough political muscle to restore the status quo ante, as it existed in the aftermath of *Griggs* and prior to *Ward's Cove.* The 1991 Civil Rights Act did exactly that. The details need not concern us at this point (we return to them in chapter 12), but the basic thrust of the act was to reestablish the *Griggs* standards for the business necessity defense. As the law currently stands, the *Griggs* standards have been fully affirmed and reinstituted, and the incentive to hire by the numbers remains palpable.

Classical liberals object to the *Griggs* standards as reaffirmed in the 1991 Civil Rights Act. As indicated above, some do so primarily on moral grounds relating to a color (and gender/religion/nationality)—blind standard, but others object on the related, though more general, grounds that it limits the freedom of business owners or their agents to hire the most qualified employees, as they judge qualifications (subject to the disparate treatment exception). Are these objections well-taken? If, "well-taken," means "provide reasonable grounds for objecting to the law as currently interpreted," it seems hard to deny. The color-blind standard has intuitive plausibility, even if in the end it should not apply in the present circumstances. As to the more general proposition that business owners or their agents should be free to hire the most qualified employees, as they judge qualifications, subject to a disparate treatment exception, that too is a reasonable supposition. What makes this principle reasonable is that it is an application of the intuitively plausible principle that people should be hired, promoted, or fired according to merit, as merit is defined in and through the market. Subject to certain exceptions and failures to be noted below, having a system in which the owners of private property in the means of production, disciplined by market forces, make these decisions (or delegate them to hired hands) is the most practical way to implement that basic principle. In the case of smaller firms owned by one individual—the so-called classical capitalist firm—this is fairly obvious. The classical capitalist firm is structured so that the provider of capital, the central contracting agent for all inputs (including labor) and the residual claimant are one and the same individual. This means that they have every incentive to hire according to perceived merit, which does not mean that they do not make mistakes, hire their relatives (which usually comes to the same thing), or let prejudice interfere. The first two are inevitable in any system, and the latter is addressed, to the extent that it can be addressed, by the disparate treatment exception. There are real limitations, however, to how much the law can accomplish.

Disparate impact is another matter. Employment practices that have a disparate impact are not legally acceptable unless they can pass the business necessity test as codified in the 1991 Civil Rights Act. This sets a standard that is very difficult to meet, but practices that cannot pass this test may nonetheless be justifiable by success in the market and thus meritocratically justified.[10] The situation is more complicated in the large, open corporation, where stockholders hire boards of directors who in turn hire managers, who in turn set hiring policies. Principal-agent problems can arise at different levels and are dealt with through a variety of control and monitoring mechanisms. A central feature of capitalist systems, however, is that market pressures have a tendency to select out the most efficient policies and procedures, including hiring policies, which are then spread mostly by imitation.[11] Any particular organization might be beset by inefficiencies, including failures to hire the best people, but on a system-wide basis and absent exogenous pressures (e.g., pressures to hire by the numbers to avoid disparate impact lawsuits, or, on the other side, a general climate of prejudice or a propensity to stereotype certain groups), the policies and procedures that predominate in a free enterprise system tend to produce better meritocratic results, as defined by the market, than the alternatives. This is consistent with the proposition that the state might be able to tweak the system to make it do better in this regard (i.e., to be more efficient), as for example when it outlaws disparate treatment discrimination. The use of defensive preferential hiring to avoid policies and procedures with disparate impact is another matter, however, since there is not even a pretense that defensive preferential hiring contributes to efficiency by identifying merit. At least outreach efforts (the noncontroversial form of affirmative action) can lay claim to that virtue.

To summarize this classical liberal reply, affirmative action as it is currently practiced violates a color-blind standard that is morally defensible; it also violates a morally defensible meritocratic hiring principle. (These two principles are, of course, related.) These conversion arguments against contemporary affirmative action practices are defeasible, however, and defensive preferential hiring may be morally preferable at the end of the day, or all things considered. It might be, for example, that the meritocratic principle and the color-blind standard have to give way when they collide with the demands of distributive justice. That, however, involves a philosophical dispute both about the demands of distributive justice and about the priority of those demands over other considerations at the margins. Once the discussion has moved to this plane, however, reasonable disagreement is inevitable, as opposing sides roll out the (probably defective) heavy artillery of grand philosophical and/or legal principles.

The second classical liberal reply—the libertarian reply—is to take a harder line and favor repeal of title VII, which would eliminate even disparate treatment as grounds for a lawsuit.[12] This reply begins with the concession that employment decisions (hiring, promotion, termination) rooted in baseless stereotypes are morally wrong and work an injustice on those negatively affected. It might even be conceded that title VII of the Civil Rights Act was a good idea at the time it was passed and had some positive educative effects, but, so the libertarians charge, it has outlived its usefulness. The main problem now, according to this account, is that at least as far as race is concerned, it has harmed those it was intended to help and has dramatically increased racial friction in the workplace.[13] An omnipresent fact in the contemporary workplace is that any adverse decision against an African American employee can be grounds for a title VII lawsuit based on a claim of disparate treatment. This has a variety of ill effects. Most obviously, it creates an incentive not to hire African Americans in the first place, if a firm can fly under the disparate impact radar of title VII. Second, in many firms, new hires are subject to a probationary period, during which time they can be—and sometimes are—summarily dismissed. After the probationary period, many employers offer some protections against summary dismissal. Those protections and more kick in right away, however, when the new hire is black, because of worries about charges of discrimination. White candidates become marginally more attractive prospective employees, since they can be more easily fired if they do not work out.

A second pernicious effect of the disparate treatment discrimination in title VII is that African Americans tend to be slotted into jobs where their prospects for advancement are diminished relative to nonminorities. They are put in "soft" parts of the corporate hierarchy like public relations, community outreach, and human resources and not in the high pressure "line" jobs. One reason (and it may not be the whole story) why a high-level white manager in the power structure of the firm would do this sort of thing is obvious: if African Americans were put into more demanding and responsible positions and did not work out, firing or demoting them could land both the manager and/or the firm in court. In addition, personnel decisions above the level of the shop floor are often clear enough to insiders but largely opaque to outsiders, which means that proving in court that a dismissal was not informed by forbidden motives can be difficult. Although nominally the burden of proof is on the plaintiff, disparate treatment discrimination is the default explanation for an adverse personnel decision when the paper trail is incomplete or when tacit knowledge is crucial to the decision. Besides, even if the threatened suit is baseless, the high cost of defending against it often makes it reasonable to settle such cases out of court or, even better, to avoid them in the first place by placing African Americans in positions of little real responsibility or not hiring them at all.

So, whites in positions of power and authority in businesses—and they still constitute the power structure—are inclined to make any decision about African Americans with one eye on the company's legal exposure and the other eye on their own legal exposure. The predictable effect of this is to increase the perception of racism on the part of African Americans; that perception is entirely reasonable and not entirely mistaken, but it is partly explainable in terms of the incentives facing white management. African Americans are not given the mentoring (which includes negative as well as positive feedback) nor the opportunities (which includes the opportunity to fail) that whites are given. This makes racial animus or stereotyping an obvious explanation for any adverse decision, including a decision not to promote African Americans to responsible positions, and it thereby reinforces the culture of victimhood that the civil rights establishment has worked tirelessly to keep alive. In the workplace, virtually no one talks about race, and race relations are universally acknowledged to be poor. Whites believe that racial discrimination against African Americans has receded to the status of a minor irritant, while blacks believe it is more virulent than ever. If discrimination on the basis of race were to be permitted, this disagreement might be more easily resolved. It would of course allow racial stereotypes, racial animus, and their ill effects to reassert themselves in some companies, though after a time, the bigots would tend to be drawn only to those firms whose workers and bosses shared their prejudices, and minorities would tend to leave those firms. In other companies, however, this would not happen—in part no doubt due to the educative effects of title VII over a generation and to the current mania for diversity that has become the official justification for preferential treatment programs in the business community.[14] What about those companies where employment decisions are not motivated by stereotypes and/or racial animus? It is tempting to say that in those companies, African Americans would be given the same mentoring and chances to fail as whites, since potential lawsuits are not hovering over the heads of decision-makers. That is probably incorrect, however. Cultural differences between the races tend to make mentoring relationships more difficult to establish, and a residuum of racial prejudice is likely to persist, especially in light of the current valorization of diversity. With some justification, African Americans very often perceive themselves as unassimilable outsiders relative to the extant corporate culture (Cose 1993, 73–91). But, no one has yet explained how a legal prohibition on disparate treatment discrimination will change that. It has apparently not done so up to this point. This may be one of those social problems to which there is no real solution, or at least no solution that can be provided by the law that does not end up making things worse.

To summarize, there are two classical liberal positions on title VII of the 1964 Civil Rights Act. One favors an exception to the at-will employment doctrine for race, religion, and national origin based on disparate treatment. The moral case for this is fairly obvious, and it takes account of the historical facts of discrimination against what are now protected groups. It is a boon for large firms whose owners care only about the bottom line, since it puts legal weight behind good business practice. This position draws the line at disparate impact, however, and favors repeal of the relevant portions of the 1991 Civil Rights Act on the grounds that it encourages defensive preferential hiring by the numbers. The latter is objectionable both because it offends a color-blind standard and a meritocratic principle, both of which have considerable intuitive appeal.

The hard libertarian position endorses these objections to defensive preferential hiring and adds that even disparate treatment should be permitted because that would marginally encourage employers to hire, promote, and fire on the basis of merit, since firms would not be doing what they can to insulate their decisions from lawsuits. Subtle forms of discrimination would remain (in truth, they exist today), but such firms would be under some pressure from their unbiased competitors. Clear-eyed libertarians, of whom there are some, hold out no false hope that racial prejudice would cease to exist—only that it would be reduced at the margins by the workings of a market process that harnesses the draft horse of self-interest much more effectively than plaintiffs' attorneys and the EEOC holding the whip of the law ever could.

Discrimination based on religion or national origin raises no new issues and in any case seems to be much less significant, if EEOC charge statistics are any guide to the prevalence of these forms of discrimination. In the period FY1997–FY2003, the EEOC recorded the following mean annual charge statistics:

Charge	Mean	Percentage
1. Race or color	29,019	36%
2. Sex	24,760	31%
3. National origin	7,701	10%
4. Religion	2,068	3%
5. ADEA	16,796	21%
6. ADA	16,657	21%
7. EPA	1,170	1%
8. Retaliation	20,904	26%[15]

This means that only 13 percent of all charges are lodged against employers on grounds of religious or national origin discrimination, whereas race and sex discrimination accounts for two-thirds of all the charges. The same arguments, both pro and con, that were made regarding racial discrimination can be applied to these forms of discrimination as well, though there seem to be few such charges made on grounds of disparate impact, as opposed to disparate treatment.

Sex Discrimination

Unlike racial discrimination, the law does recognize a class of exceptions to title VII, allowing facial discrimination in cases where sex is a bona fide occupational qualification (BFOQ), though as was noted, the standards are fairly high for this exception. Disparate impact cases have also been pressed, especially in some previously male-dominated occupations, such as law enforcement and firefighting, where selection criteria work disproportionately against women. For example, height and weight requirements were often used by law enforcement agencies, but these were struck down under disparate impact analysis in 1977 (*Dothard v. Rawlinson*, 433 U.S. 321 (1977)). Physical fitness tests for firefighters involving a timed run for one mile and a similar test for transit police were also ruled invalid (*Berkman et al. v. City of New York*, 812 F.2d 52 (2d Cir. 1987) and *Lanning v. SEPTA*, 181 F.3d 478 (3d Cir. 1999), respectively). The same basic arguments and considerations adduced above in regard to racial discrimination, both for and against, apply equally to disparate treatment and disparate impact sex discrimination.

What is distinctive about sex discrimination is the charge of sexual harassment, a form of disparate treatment discrimination that has no exact parallel for the protected classes of race, color, religion, or national origin. In the early years after the passage of the Civil Rights Act, the courts were reluctant to bring sexual harassment under title VII, that is, to construe it as a form of sex discrimination. There were various reasons for this (Mezey 2003, 130–32): First, some judges simply did not see sexual harassment as a form of discrimination because either sex could be harassed by members of the same sex or by members of the opposite sex. Second, the courts were slow to recognize that harassment had real consequences for an employee's terms and conditions of employment. Third, it did not fit the template provided by racial discrimination, where discriminatory behavior was motivated by prejudicial judgments about ability (stereotypes) or animus (in this case, misogyny). Finally, there was the question of employer liability. Judges were reluctant to hold employers liable for the actions of a plaintiff's coworkers or even supervisors. Nevertheless, in a series of cases, the courts came to recognize sexual harassment as a form of sex discrimination, culminating in the 1986 case of *Meritor Savings Bank v. Vinson*, 477 U.S. 57 (1986).

Two prior cases at the appellate level set the stage for *Meritor*. In *Barnes v. Costle*, 561 F.2d 983 (D.C. Cir. 1977), the D.C. Circuit Court ruled that Paulette Barnes's complaint of sexual harassment was a form of sex discrimination under title VII. Barnes's supervisor had offered her benefits pertaining to her employment in exchange for sexual favors, and when she turned him down, he retaliated by abolishing her job. The court found that but for her gender, she would not have faced this dilemma, and it clearly had an effect on the conditions of her employment. This form of sexual harassment came to be known as quid pro quo harassment. In exchange for sexual favors, the employer or a supervisor is offering the employee a benefit or threatening some negative consequence. Quid pro quo harassment is not the only form of sexual harassment, however. In *Bundy v. Jackson*, 641 F.2d 934 (D.C. Cir. 1981), Sandra Bundy claimed that her coworkers and supervisors made repeated sexually charged comments to her (including requests for sexual favors), thereby creating a hostile and offensive workplace environment. Initially, her complaint was dismissed because there were no adverse job-related consequences for her refusal to "be a good sport" about these comments and requests. But on appeal, the D.C. Circuit Court ruled that the creation of a hostile or offensive environment was a form of sex discrimination actionable under title VII.[16]

Meritor Savings Bank v. Vinson involved elements of both forms of harassment. Mechelle Vinson testified that her supervisor, Sidney Taylor, had propositioned her and that although she initially refused, she eventually capitulated because she feared losing her job. She claimed she was forced to submit to his advances during the day as well as during the evening, though the fact that she admitted having sex with Taylor forty to fifty times during the three-year period in question raised some eyebrows. In affirming the circuit court's ruling in favor of Vinson, however, the Supreme Court held that Taylor had created a hostile workplace environment, which was a form of sex discrimination under title VII.

An important player in the evolution of sexual harassment law has been the EEOC. Unlike court rulings, its guidelines do not have the force of law, but sometimes the courts look to the EEOC for guidance. In 1980, the EEOC promulgated guidelines on sexual harassment that the courts have subsequently endorsed. Those guidelines say,

> (a) harassment on the basis of sex is a violation of section 703 of title VII. \1\ Unwelcome sexual advances, requests for sexual favors, and other verbal or physical conduct of a sexual nature constitute sexual harassment when (1) submission to such conduct is made either explicitly or implicitly a term or condition of an individual's employment, (2) submission to or rejection of such conduct by an individual is used as the basis for employment decisions affecting such individual, or (3) such conduct has the purpose or effect of unreasonably interfering with an individual's work performance or creating an intimidating, hostile, or offensive working environment. (29 *C.F.R.* § 1604.11(a) [1999])

The second part of the third condition has been the subject of much judicial attention as judges have attempted to define what counts as an "intimidating, hostile or offensive working environment." Distinctions had to be drawn and criteria articulated. The courts at various levels got out their chains, theodolites, and plumb lines to survey the boundaries of acceptable behavior between the sexes in the modern workplace. They also grappled with the issue of vicarious employer liability, which resulted in various compromises between judges who wanted to assess strict liability and those who did not. Specifically, in two 1998 Supreme Court rulings, *Faragher v. City of Boca Raton,* 524 U.S. 755 (1998), and *Burlington Industries v. Ellerth,* 524 U.S. 742 (1998), the Court held employers vicariously or strictly liable (i.e., whether they knew about it or not) when sexual harassment by supervisory personnel resulted in a tangible employment action (i.e., a benefit or harm). If no tangible employment action ensued, the defendant/employer has available a two-pronged affirmative defense, namely, (1) that the company had a policy against sexual harassment and a mechanism to address complaints and (2) the complaining party did not take advantage of that mechanism. In the case of nonsupervisory personnel engaged in harassment, a negligence standard applies.[17]

To summarize, as case law and EEOC guidelines have developed over the years, two forms of sexual harassment are now recognized: quid pro quo harassment and hostile environment harassment. The former involves a threat or promise of a benefit or harm within the employment context in exchange for sexual favors. Hostile environment harassment occurs when the workplace is permeated by sexuality in a way that interferes with the job or which constitutes a hostile or offensive workplace environment, but no demands are made as a condition of employment nor are there any negative consequences attached to not "being a good sport."

Modern liberals, especially those with feminist sympathies, have applauded the recognition of sexual harassment as a form of sex discrimination, though some believe that the courts have not gone far enough in one way or another.[18] The legal arguments for recognizing sexual harassment as a form of discrimination under title VII are somewhat controversial, but our concern is with the moral arguments for making sexual harassment illegal. As with most items on the modern liberal regulatory agenda, conversion arguments for the policy in question are fairly straightforward and close to the surface. Quid pro quo harassment is morally objectionable by almost any modern standard, and it occurs because of power imbalances in the workplace; the idea that the law should turn a blind eye to this sort of behavior is difficult to defend. As to hostile environment harassment, there is also a fairly straightforward argument, based on chivalric respect for women or simply respect for the sensibilities of coworkers, that this sort of behavior is morally reprehensible and should not be tolerated or condoned. This is buttressed by observing the simple unfairness of sexual harassment in all its forms: it is faced mostly by women and perpetrated mostly by men. This is perhaps the main impetus behind the court rulings that sexual harassment is a form of discrimination. But for their gender, women would not be subjected to such treatment.[19] By making sexual harassment illegal and by making employers liable (up to a point) for the actions of their employees, the latter are given a powerful incentive to police the workplace and get their employees to conform their behavior to morally acceptable standards.

There are a number of classical liberal responses to these arguments and observations, all of which can concede the immorality of paradigm cases of the different forms of sexual harassment. The question for classical liberals is which of these forms of sexual harassment, if any, should be legally actionable. In the case of quid pro quo harassment, a neo-Lockean classical liberal argument can be made for making it illegal. Ellen Frankel Paul (1991, 6) has argued that this form of harassment "is analogous to extortion: the harasser extorts property (i.e., the use of the woman's body) through the leverage of fear for her job." Further classical liberal reasons for making quid pro quo harassment illegal is that it helps owners of businesses to solve a principal-agent problem vis-à-vis their supervisors and thereby validates a merit-based principle of hiring, promotion, and termination. In cases where the owner of a firm does the hiring, the law would of course limit the freedom of contract of employers who would exchange jobs or job benefits for sexual favors and thus counts as a nonnegotiable limitation on the at-will employment relation. However, even that limitation might be defensible on the basis of principles of contract law that classical liberals endorse. Although employment-at-will contracts are open-ended in the sense that not all contingencies can be fully ventilated and discussed before the employment agreement is entered into, these contracts are arguably constrained by some epistemically and normatively legitimate expectations, one of which is that sexual favors are not a term or condition of employment (except possibly in Hollywood). Even a libertarian should be persuaded that, if sexual relations are expected as part of the job, employers should make that explicit at the time of hiring, which in turn might make the employer liable for solicitation to commit prostitution.[20] In this way, there could be a convergence or common ground argument from classical liberal principles to a legal prohibition on quid pro quo harassment.

A legal prohibition of only this form of harassment would be unlikely to have large effects, however, for the simple reason that proving such cases is difficult in the absence of other witnesses, which, one can reasonably speculate, will often be the case. The real action in sex discrimination cases is in the third category specified in the EEOC guidelines—hostile environment harassment, the prize archaeological find in *Meritor*. As the guidelines make clear, this third category is actually a disjunction, one of which is a set of behaviors that "has the purpose or effect of unreasonably interfering with an individual's work performance," and the other of which is a set of behaviors that "creat[es] an intimidating, hostile, or offensive working environment." It is at least possible that a set of behaviors could satisfy one of these disjuncts without satisfying the other, but it is the latter onto which feminists have locked their radar.

There is a classical liberal case to be made that neither of these forms of sexual harassment should be legally actionable. It begins by looking at Supreme Court attempts to define the proscribed conduct. Although the Court tried to do this in 1986 in *Meritor Savings Bank v. Vinson*, it found it necessary to return to the problem in 1993 in *Harris v. Forklift Systems, Inc.*, 510 U.S. 17 (1993). An extensive quotation from this decision is necessary to see what the definitional problems are. In explaining the proscribed conduct, the Court said,

> this standard, which we reaffirm today, takes a middle path between making actionable any conduct that is merely offensive and requiring the conduct to cause a tangible psychological injury. As we pointed out in *Meritor*, "mere utterance of an...epithet which engenders offensive feelings in a employee,"...does not sufficiently affect the conditions of employment to implicate Title VII. Conduct that is not severe or pervasive enough to create an objectively hostile or abusive work environment—an environment that a reasonable person would find hostile or abusive—is beyond Title VII's purview....
>
> But Title VII comes into play before the harassing conduct leads to a nervous breakdown....
>
> We therefore believe the District Court erred in relying on whether the conduct "seriously affect[ed] plaintiff's psychological wellbeing" or led her to "suffe[r] injury." Such an inquiry may needlessly focus the factfinder's attention on concrete psychological harm, an element Title VII does not require. So long as the environment would reasonably be perceived...as hostile or abusive...there is no need for it also to be psychologically injurious.
>
> This is not, and by its nature cannot be, a mathematically precise test. We need not answer today all the potential questions it raises...But we can say that whether an environment

is "hostile" or "abusive" can be determined only by looking at all the circumstances. These may include the frequency of the discriminatory conduct; its severity; whether it is physically threatening or humiliating, or a mere offensive utterance; and whether it unreasonably interferes with an employee's work performance. The effect on the employee's psychological well being is, of course, relevant to determining whether the plaintiff actually found the environment abusive. But, while psychological harm, like any other...relevant factor, may be taken into account, no single factor is required. (*Harris v. Forklift Systems, Inc.,* 510 U.S. 17, 21–23 (1993)

The problems with this elucidation of the standard are both numerous and obvious. First, the standard applies to conduct that "create[s] an objectively hostile or abusive work environment—an environment that a reasonable person would find hostile or abusive." The first part is plainly circular as an explication of what counts as "an intimidating, hostile, or offensive working environment." Moreover, as Justice Scalia noted regarding this passage:

"Abusive" (or "hostile," which in this context I take to mean the same thing) does not seem to me a very clear standard—and I do not think clarity is at all increased by adding the adverb "objectively" or by appealing to a "reasonable person's" notion of what that vague word means." As a practical matter, today's holding lets virtually unguided juries decide whether sex-related conduct engaged in (or permitted by) an employer is egregious enough to warrant an award of damages. (Scalia, concurring, ibid.)

Second, the standard creates problems when the fact finder looks at the factors (in the context of all the circumstances, of course) that the Court recommends for consideration:

the frequency of the discriminatory conduct; its severity; whether it is physically threatening or humiliating, or a mere offensive utterance; and whether it unreasonably interferes with an employee's work performance....But, while psychological harm, like any other...relevant factor, may be taken into account, no single factor is required.

Each of the key terms in this passage is either question-begging ("discriminatory conduct"), vague ("unreasonably interferes," "psychological harm"), subjective ("humiliating," "offensive"), or in need of a metric ("frequency," "severity," "physically threatening") to be applicable. But, the Court was getting tired that day anyway, since it said, "we need not answer today all the potential questions [the standard] raises," thereby leaving open the possibility that it would revisit the issue at a later date when they had some more thoughts on the matter, perhaps after they saw how their policy was working. It is hard work making social policy for an entire nation, even if one needs to reach agreement with only four other people on what it should be.

A perhaps unintended consequence of these and related rulings, beginning with *Meritor,* is that forms of verbal behavior become legally actionable forms of harassment for all protected categories, which has obvious free speech implications. As Eugene Volokh (1997) has argued, this includes political statements, religious proselytizing, sexual jokes (even nonmisogynistic ones), and legitimate art.[21] All can be potentially harassing. As Volokh notes, the Court does not require that harassing speech be constitutionally unprotected (e.g., fighting words, obscenity, pornography), so the current limitations are essentially undefined. In addition, because different jurisdictions have different protected categories, speech is restricted not only for the EEOC's flagship categories of race, religion, sex, national origin, age, and disability (including obesity), but also, in some jurisdictions, sexual orientation, political affiliation, citizenship status, marital status, and personal appearance (Volokh 1997, 628).

Once speech, or at least otherwise constitutionally protected speech, becomes legally actionable title VII harassment (discrimination) in the workplace, classical liberals—and indeed, civil libertarians of every race, color, sex, religion, and national origin—are going to get off the bus. If, however, harassing speech were disallowed as a form of discrimination, this means that some people will suffer—indeed will endure uncompensated suffering—from an "intimidating, hostile, or offensive working environment," at least until they decide to quit. In some cases, possibly many cases, injustices will have been done, but, classical liberals would maintain, this is a price worth paying to keep the thought police in their barracks and out of the workplace. If, as civil libertarians believe (and on this issue classical liberals are all, conveniently, civil libertarians), speech—or at least constitutionally protected speech—should entitle one to a "Get Out of Jail Free" card in sexual harassment cases, the case for hostile environment harassment collapses, since so much of the latter is verbal behavior.

By contrast, many modern liberals would maintain that classical liberal concerns about a "chilled" workplace environment are overblown, and to the extent that these concerns are legitimate, they are simply a price that should be paid to discourage what is, by widely shared contemporary standards, morally obtuse behavior. It is easy to see how different people would be willing to accept different trade-offs between discouraging hostile environment harassment on the one hand and a chilled workplace environment and frivolous lawsuits on the other.

Age Discrimination

The Age Discrimination in Employment Act (ADEA) of 1967 outlawed discrimination against older workers, somewhat arbitrarily defined as those over the age of forty. The crucial clause in the law is the following:

(a) Employer practices
   It shall be unlawful for an employer—
   (1) to fail or refuse to hire or to discharge any individual or otherwise discriminate against any individual with respect to his compensation, terms, conditions, or privileges of employment, because of such individual's age;
   (2) to limit, segregate, or classify his employees in any way which would deprive or tend to deprive any individual of employment opportunities or otherwise adversely affect his status as an employee, because of such individual's age. (29 U.S.C. § 623)

As always, there are some exceptions built into the law. When age is a bona fide occupational qualification (BFOQ), when the affected persons are law enforcement officers, firefighters (29 U.S.C. § 623(j)), or high-level executives (29 U.S.C. § 631), facial discrimination is permitted. Putting these complications to one side, no one seriously maintains that discrimination against those over forty is practiced for its own sake or as an expression of animus toward older people. After all, the people who are alleged to practice this form of discrimination aspire to be in the protected group some day. In this respect, age is not like gender or race. Men are not going to become women, and whites are not going to become black. As postmodernists would say, old people are not...the Other. However, it has been charged, stereotypical thinking about older workers infects management's personnel decisions, especially in hiring. For the latter reason, one of the main purposes of the act was to keep age discrimination based on these stereotypes out of the hiring process (29 U.S.C. § 621(a)(1)). Firings and layoffs are also covered, since biased thinking can affect these decisions as well. As it has worked out, however, only 9 percent of ADEA cases deal with refusals to hire; the vast majority (75 percent) are about firings or terminations (O'Meara 1989, 13). The relative paucity of disparate impact cases probably explains this, at least in part.

To see why, consider cases in which firms find it financially advantageous to let higher paid, older workers go and replace them with younger workers who are paid less. This often happens when a firm is purchased by another firm, which wants to bring in its own people, including recently or newly hired people whom they have trained or are training.[22] An established firm would be very shortsighted to dismiss its own older workers routinely and as a matter of (written or unwritten) policy, if only because younger workers would see the handwriting on the wall and put out their resumes at or before their peak productivity years. But when a business is purchased, the acquiring firm may find this sort of layoff financially necessary or desirable, even if it raises some eyebrows among its own employees. Employees who have been let go under these circumstances have sued on grounds of both disparate treatment and disparate impact discrimination. Regarding the former, the Supreme Court held in *Hazen Paper Co. v. Biggins,* 507 U.S. 604 (1993), that "when the employer's decision is wholly motivated by factors other than age, the problem of inaccurate and stigmatizing stereotypes disappears. This is true even if the motivating factor is correlated with age under a disparate impact interpretation of discrimination under the ADEA" (507 U.S. 604, 611). Thus, in this case, the Court held that these workers were not being treated differently because of their age.

This passage, as well as others in this decision, also seemed to rule out disparate impact age discrimination, if there is a legitimate business reason to let an employee go. Prior to *Hazen,* there had been division in the lower courts about the applicability of disparate impact analysis in ADEA cases, with some appellate courts allowing claims of disparate impact claims to go forward and others disallowing it. The majority opinion in *Hazen,* however, seemed to signal that the Supreme Court would not countenance disparate impact discrimination on the basis of age. In a surprise move, however, the Court recently ruled that disparate impact claims could go forward, but such claims can be rebutted as long as there is a "reasonable factor other than age" (RFOA) that explains the employers' decision, which creates an exception that exactly parallels the exception recognized in *Hazen* that neutralizes a claim of disparate treatment discrimination. In the instant case, *Smith et al. v. City of Jackson, Mississippi et al.,* 544 U.S. 228 (2005), the Court held that

> the RFOA provision provides that it shall not be unlawful for an employer "to take any action otherwise prohibited under subsectio[n] (a)... where the differentiation is based on reasonable factors other than age discrimination..." 81 Stat. 603...It is, accordingly, in cases involving disparate-impact claims that the RFOA provision plays its principal role by precluding liability if the adverse impact was attributable to a nonage factor that was "reasonable."

RFOAs, then, could be used to rebut both disparate treatment and disparate impact claims. This is unlike decisions involving other protected categories, such as race and gender, where a "business necessity" test has to be passed. Why is this? It is hard to avoid the inference that this was a compromise between different factions on the Court. Some justices probably wanted disparate impact claims to be actionable under the ADEA, just as they are for other forms of discrimination under title VII of the 1964 Civil Rights Act. Other justices likely wanted to restrict the ADEA to disparate treatment. Subtle and fine-grained distinctions between the ADEA and title VII had to be drawn—so subtle and fine-grained that they probably do not exist. The bottom line seems to be that the RFOA requirement for layoffs is about as easy to satisfy as the "legitimate business function test" for hiring criteria enunciated in the now-defunct *Ward's Cove* standard; this means that disparate impact cases are likely to be stalled out, and disparate treatment will probably continue to be the main avenue of ADEA litigation. In short, unlike under title VII, illicit motive will have to be proved.

What, then, is the argument for the ADEA, where discrimination is understood in terms of disparate treatment? Presumably, the same type of argument in support of other forms of antidiscrimination law would apply here. This (conversion) argument starts with the principle that it is unjust to deny someone a job, demote, fire, or otherwise adversely affect someone's employment situation on the basis of stereotypical judgments, which are really prejudices, about the relevance of what are in fact irrelevant characteristics from the point of view of worker productivity. A further premise is that age is just such a characteristic. An additional premise is needed to the effect that the problem of age discrimination in employment is sufficiently widespread and serious to warrant a law prohibiting it. (Not every injustice can be the basis for a law.) Congress made such a finding, based on a report from the secretary of labor.[23] Thus the argument for the ADEA, which prohibits discrimination on the basis of age for those over the somewhat arbitrarily designated age of forty. The argument can be made vivid by a cursory examination of some successful suits under the ADEA, where employees who have given long and dedicated service have been unceremoniously dumped on the street by their employers. In these and like cases, it is difficult to maintain that firms should be able to dismiss employees whose only disqualification is that they are over the age of forty. Such decisions are based on groundless stereotypes that link age with characteristics that either increase costs or reduce the benefits of the employment relation for the employer.

How might a classical liberal reply? What might a classical liberal case against the ADEA look like? As it pertains to hiring, there is the obvious point, generalizable from other types of antidiscrimination law, that hiring an older person is hiring a potential lawsuit, if things do not work out. A probationary period effectively does not exist, and if the person is dismissed, it had better be justifiable to a third party. Individual managers, as well as the firms that employ them, can be sued in ADEA and other cases involving antidiscrimination statutes. It is hard to overestimate the significance of this for risk-averse managers, which includes most managers, who spend an inordinate amount of time and effort figuring out ways to avoid getting blamed if and when things go wrong. As before, younger prospective employees look to be a safer hire, all else equal. Putting that problem to one side, to make a case against the ADEA, classical liberals would have to deny that age discrimination is widespread, or they would have to maintain that discriminatory practices can be justified. For the sake of argument, let us assume that age discrimination is widespread (or would be widespread if the law did not exist). How might it be argued that discriminatory practices can be justified and thus that age discrimination should not be legally prohibited?

The argument starts with the observation that ageist stereotypes have some basis in fact and that it can be too costly to find out if the individual worker has or lacks some adverse characteristic of interest that correlates with age. Negative stereotypical characteristics imputed to older workers that are associated with reduced value to the firm include (1) a much shorter prospective career with the firm (whether they are current or prospective employees), (2) a tendency not to work as hard, (3) a decline in creativity, and (4) a diminished willingness to take on new tasks or learn new skills. Sometimes, older workers are blamed for a more general vampire-induced malaise within the firm for which the proposed cure is "fresh blood" or "young blood."

How plausible are these stereotypes? One kind of case where the correlation between age and an undesirable characteristic is quite plausible is prospective length of service. Employers are reluctant to hire or promote a worker in his sixties if the person hired or promoted has to undergo expensive specialized training. The costs of that training would have to be recouped over time, and the firm might reasonably guess that a significantly younger worker will likely give more years of service than an older worker in his sixties. It may turn out to be false; the younger worker might leave the firm after a few years, and the older worker might have stayed longer. Nevertheless, in the absence of contrary evidence, it is reasonable to suppose that workers in their sixties are likely to be with a firm for a shorter period of time than significantly younger workers. Moreover, as Sara Rix has pointed out, "existing research suggests that older adults learn less in training than younger workers, make more errors in training, and take longer to master the training material" (Rix 1994, v).

The case of jobs that impose physical demands is another clear example, since strength, stamina, and other physical capabilities clearly decline with age, even if there is considerable variation between individuals with respect to their rate of decline. But what about the other correlations, which are most relevant for mid-level management, professional, and technical workers—the people most likely to charge that they have been discriminated against because of their age, especially in cases of terminations? Do these correlations exist? In their meta-analytic study, Harvey Sterns and Michael McDaniel (1994) find little evidence that they do: "In sum, regardless of whether supervisory ratings or production criteria are used to define performance, the conclusion remains the same: the relationship between age and job performance is weak" (31).

The authors qualify this conclusion in a number of ways, however. Few of the studies that were done before the ADEA took effect included significant numbers of workers over the age of sixty-five, perhaps because mandatory retirement rules sharply limited their numbers. Even those studies that include relatively large numbers of workers over the age of sixty-five are likely to be biased, however, because of retention effects. In other words, those who do not retire at age sixty-five tend to be more productive than those who do retire at sixty-five, thereby creating an unrepresentative sample of older workers (Sterns and McDaniel 1994, 33).

Although the rate at which individuals decline, both mentally and physically, varies considerably, there can be no doubt that such decline occurs at some point. The ADEA is predicated on the assumption that when productivity declines because of the negative characteristics associated with age (e.g., increased shirking, decreased willingness to take on new challenges, declining creativity), the worker will have reached the point where she retires voluntarily—and if she does not, then an employer can simply fire her for cause. As we know in the case of professional athletes, politicians, and Supreme Court justices, however, not everyone knows when it is time to retire, and it is not hard to understand why. All of the characteristics associated with high productivity are, not coincidentally, seen as virtues. People are naturally reluctant to admit that whatever (few) virtues they possess have diminished. That problem to one side, perhaps the main problem with this assumption behind the ADEA is that it presumes that worker productivity is more or less directly observable (either by the worker, the employer, or both), when often it is not. It is a general characteristic of joint, or team, production that individual contribution can only be imperfectly measured and monitored (Alchian and Demsetz 1972, 778–79). Capitalist organizations have found a number of ways to deal with this general problem. How has it been handled in the past in the context of aging workers?

Prior to the passage of the ADEA, the most common way was by a policy that imposed mandatory retirement, usually at age sixty-five. With the passage of the ADEA and subsequent legislation, this common practice was outlawed. Why was such a policy commonplace? One hypothesis is that this widespread policy was based on groundless stereotypes about declining worker productivity after the age of sixty-five. But there are other possible explanations. Economists operate under the presumption that widely used practices in the business community have some efficiency rationale, even if those who use it cannot articulate it. The reason for this, as noted earlier (see note 11), is that market pressures have a tendency to select out the most efficient policies and procedures, including hiring policies, which are then spread mostly by imitation. The presumption may be false in any particular case, but economists try to discern some efficiency rationale for widely used policies and procedures. If such a rationale can be found, it will explain the persistence, though perhaps not the genesis, of the practice. The presumption of efficiency functions like the presumption of order among early modern astronomers, who believed that the planets behaved according to relatively simple laws, and it was their job to find them.

What, then, might be the efficiency rationale for mandatory retirement? Generally speaking, over the course of a lifetime, a worker's productivity will rise, plateau, and then decline. If productivity could be more or less directly observed, firms could deal with this by simply matching pay to productivity over the course of a workers' career, but they cannot, so they do not. Instead they have a mandatory retirement rule. Why? This question was addressed in a famous article by Edward Lazear in 1979. After canvassing and rejecting a number of alternative explanations, Lazear offers the following hypothesis to explain this widely used policy: Employees are paid less than their marginal value product early in their careers and more later in their careers. This gives the worker an incentive to avoid shirking and other forms of opportunistic behavior throughout most of his career because in order to recoup the wages "withheld" early in his tenure, he must continue to be employed with the firm long enough to be paid more than his marginal value product, which is what he is paid in the latter part of his career. Lazear says, "by deferring payment a firm may induce a worker to perform at a higher level of effort. Both firm and worker may prefer this high wage/high effort to a lower wage/lower effort path that results from a payment scheme that creates incentives to shirk" (Lazear 1979, 1264). A mandatory retirement rule is a crucial link in a larger employment scheme. It serves as a stop-loss device to prevent the worker from being overpaid indefinitely. The theory is that at a certain point, the underpayments from earlier in a career have been fully compensated for, and continuing to employ the worker at that wage or salary beyond that point results in a net loss to the firm. To fill in this story, it is worth noting that this method of compensation gives the younger employee an incentive to acquire knowledge and skills relevant to the job, some of which are firm-specific but some of which are not. This knowledge and these skills are often acquired at the employer's expense, which serves as a commitment signal from the employer to the employee. The former is less likely to fire without good cause an employee on whom they have just spent a lot of money to train. Over time, the firm can recoup its investment, and the worker can be assured of getting the returns to both specific and nonspecific human capital assets he has acquired at company expense. Reputation effects give the firm a further incentive not to renege on its end of the deal by laying off a worker between the time that he starts earning more than his marginal value product and the mandatory retirement age. Which is not to say that it does not happen, but if this were a companywide policy, the firm would have a hard time keeping workers at the front end from leaving the firm in mid-career or as soon as they had acquired additional relatively non-specific human capital at the employer's expense. Other devices firms use to bind themselves to their end of the bargain and/or to mitigate the negative consequences for older workers who are let go are early retirement or severance pay packages, defined benefit pension plans, health insurance for those who retire early, and programs to help laid-off workers find new jobs.

There are other advantages to a bright-line mandatory retirement rule, which have disappeared since the ADEA prohibited it. If a firm judges that an older employee has worn out his welcome, a paper trail has to be created to document his misdeeds and/or declining produc-tivity, both to justify to him why he is being dismissed and to lay the groundwork for a legal defense in case he charges that his dismissal was due to age discrimination. All potentially very ugly. But, under a mandatory retirement regime, he would generally have to do some-thing really egregious (e.g., steal from the firm, essentially stop work-ing on the job) to warrant termination before mandatory retirement. Furthermore, under a rule of mandatory retirement, his prospects for postseparation employment are better, should he choose to continue working, since there is no stigma attached to separation from his longtime employer. Furthermore, as he approaches mandatory retire-ment, the employee, if he is considering postretirement employment, has an incentive to avoid shirking and to keep his knowledge updated and his skills sharp, especially knowledge and skills that are not firm-specific. Under a system in which his job is made more secure by the ADEA, these incentives are diminished, and if Lazear is right, he can continue to be overpaid for his services until he decides it is time to retire or until he dies.

Of course, if market conditions take a turn for the worse, all bets are off, and a firm does what it has to do to stay afloat, which may mean laying off older workers, which the ADEA does not prohibit if it is done properly. When a business is purchased by another firm, typically the purchasing firm believes that it can do a better job with the assets of the purchased firm than the current management team, which is why they purchased the firm in the first place. To do so, however, requires that changes be made, and sometimes the management of the acquiring firm judges that those changes require layoffs. Blanket judgments are not uncommon, even if they are not infallible, but the courts have been reluctant to substitute their judgment for the judgment of managers in these situations.

The Lazear hypothesis about mandatory retirement is an illustration of a more general point about longer-term (or "relational") contracts in a free enterprise system. The economics of contracts and organizations takes seriously the problems posed by the following four more or less permanent features of the economic environment: (1) economic actors are faced with informational asymmetries; (2) they have a propensity for opportunistic behavior; (3) many assets have characteristics that are most valuable only in the context of a particular contractual relationship (sometimes called, "asset specificities"); (4) complete, costlessly enforceable long-term contracts cannot be written.[24] This creates expropriation hazards, that is, the possibility that one party to an exchange can capture some of the value of that exchange that would otherwise go to the other party. The challenge for the economist is to explain how exchanges are crafted to deal with these problems. The Lazear hypothesis about mandatory retirement is a good example of this: it explains the widespread existence of this practice in an economic environment characterized by large firms who use long-term at-will employment contracts supplemented by a mandatory retirement policy and one or more of the other policies mentioned above. In some sense, this hypothesis complements the explanation in terms of stereotypes, so it is not as if the two are competing explanations. The only difference is that the defenders of the ADEA maintain that the stereotypes that ground mandatory retirement are baseless and irrational, whereas the economic explanation denies this, maintaining only that the stereotypes have some validity even if they are not perfect predictors of future performance, which is hard to monitor anyway. In addition, and this is crucial for the economic explanation, mandatory retirement limits the amount workers would be overpaid relative to their productivity.

In rebuttal, it might be pointed out that the economic environment has changed dramatically over the past four decades and a policy of mandatory retirement at sixty-five is no longer efficient for a variety of reasons: the nature of work has changed to become less physically taxing, general health and life expectancy have improved, and lifetime employment at one firm is now the exception and not the rule. Just so. In a different economic environment, such as what exists now, different policies might well be more efficient and would have likely evolved in the absence of the ADEA. The preceding is not an argument in favor of mandatory retirement at this time, though it might be right for employees of some firms (e.g., those, like university professors, whose jobs must be pried from their cold, dead hands); instead, it is an illustration of the general point that policies that handle the expropriation hazards of the employment contract can emerge and become widespread in a free enterprise system in which people are free to make whatever contractual arrangements are mutually beneficial. What exists today has been significantly shaped by an exogenous factor, namely, the ADEA. One can only speculate about what would have emerged if the ADEA had never been passed or what would emerge if the ADEA were to be repealed. It would probably be a quite variegated set of policies, depending on the industry or the context. To summarize, the classical liberal would argue that the ADEA is a bad idea in part because it legally forbids a policy (mandatory retirement) that was mutually beneficial for (some) employers and employees and in part because it blocks or retards the evolution of private solutions to the fundamental challenge of relational employment contracts faced by firms and their older workers whose value to their employers will inevitably decline.

This points to a general problem for many aspects of the debate between modern liberalism and classical liberalism that warrants a brief digression. As noted, widely used policies or practices in the business community typically have some efficiency advantage. No policy is perfect, however, and a consistent application of any policy will lead to a wrong decision across some range of cases. For example, a highly productive older worker is forced out by a mandatory retirement policy that makes no apparent sense in his case, that is, he is let go under a policy that looks to be both unfair and unwise. If this happens frequently enough, modern liberal politicians, responding to constituent pressures and to their own better instincts, address this as moral problem, typically by applying direct pressure to the moral wound. Hence we get the ADEA and probably some other regulatory regimes as well. Then the economists come along and explain the efficiency rationale for the original policy, and they also point out some of the inefficiencies of the statist solution.

The economists' arguments utterly fail to impress modern liberals, who believe that sometimes inefficiencies have to be accepted as the price of moral progress. But, of course, the efficiencies of the original policy prevent certain moral problems from arising in the first place, and the inefficiencies of the statist solution can be represented as new moral problems, though not by economists, since that is not their job. For example, the Lazear hypothesis explains a policy of mandatory retirement as an effective way to prevent shirking by both older and younger workers, which is a moral problem, since it involves a misrepresentation of what the worker is doing for the firm. But it has a downside when older, but still productive, workers are forced to retire. The ADEA is passed to deal with that problem, but it has its downside, too, namely, it permits older workers to retire on the job while continuing to get paid a high salary. The employer is harmed, and opportunities for younger people are foreclosed.[25] So, there is a moral downside to the ADEA. Both the old regime and the new regime permit moral problems to occur. Thus a "Mexican standoff" ensues, with each side pointing its moral six-guns at the other side.

For a final complication, suppose that the law is in place but that general economic conditions have changed so that a mandatory retirement policy is no longer adaptive, that is, it is no longer an efficient response to the original problems of long-term relational contracting, but the policy has hung on as a matter of habit in most firms. Classical liberals believe that since the problem is an inefficiency of some sort, there is money to be made in solving it by crafting a policy solution that results in a Pareto improvement for the affected parties. (Hence the rhetorical taunt they fling at the feet of modern liberals: "If you're so smart, how come you're not rich?") They believe that eventually the market will solve the problem, conceived of as either a moral problem or as an efficiency problem, if it can be solved at all without making things worse, which it sometimes cannot be. Modern liberals deride this is as blind faith in the free market, whereas classical liberals maintain that there is ample evidence from past experience that voluntary arrangements can be worked out to resolve problems such as this. In this way, the standoff continues, at least at the level of ideas. Differing judgments about the incidence and seriousness of the moral problems that attend market and statist approaches or policies make these debates peculiarly resistant to resolution. In this way and for these reasons, reasonable disagreement persists.

Discrimination on the Basis of Disability

Another group protected by antidiscrimination law is workers with disabilities, who are protected by the Americans with Disabilities Act of 1990 (42 U.S.C. § 12101). Arguably the most ambitious and complex of the antidiscrimination statutes, title I of the ADA, which deals with employment, prohibits discrimination against qualified individuals on account of disability. Other provisions deal with state and local government activities, including public transportation (title II), and public accommodations provided by the private sector (title III). The most high-profile title is title III, which mandates modifications, both reasonable and unreasonable, to physical facilities used by the public. This title will not be discussed in this book, in part because the same issues are raised by title I and in part because of space limitations. In addition, this aspect of the ADA could be treated as part of the modern liberal transfer agenda, since it involves a forced transfer of resources from owners of businesses to the disabled. This is a good illustration of the fact that the line between regulation and transfer is to some extent arbitrary.

As it pertains to the employment relation, which is part of the modern liberal regulatory agenda as here defined, the key proviso holds that, "no covered entity shall discriminate against a qualified individual with a disability because of the disability of such individual in regard to job application procedures, the hiring, advancement, or discharge of employees, employee compensation, job training, and other terms, conditions, and privileges of employment" (42 U.S.C. § 12112). There are a number of complications in this law that are not present in title VII of the 1964 Civil Rights Act. Perhaps the most important concerns membership in the protected class. While there have always been some disputes around the edges of what counts as membership in a protected class under title VII (transsexuals, mixed-race individuals), this becomes a major point of contention in applying the ADA, since if a person does not fit the definition of "disabled," he or she has no standing under the ADA to sue. On the face of it, however, the definition is quite broad:

the term "disability" means, with respect to an individual—
(A) a physical or mental impairment that substantially limits one or more of the major life activities of such individual;
(B) a record of such an impairment; or
(C) being regarded as having such an impairment. (42 U.S.C. § 12102(2))

As the EEOC explains, "*Major Life Activities* means functions such as caring for oneself, performing manual tasks, walking, seeing, hearing, speaking, breathing, learning, and working."[26] The second category includes people who have recovered from an impairment (including alcoholism/substance abuse, though current alcoholics and substance abusers are not protected) or who have been misclassified as having impairments. The third category includes people who are perceived as impaired by society, such as burn victims (Perritt 1991, 27), whether or not they are actually functionally impaired in some way.

The definition is not so broad, however, as to include those whose impairment has been substantially mitigated by assistive devices. So, for example, someone who is nearsighted and wears corrective lenses is not counted as disabled under the ADA nor are diabetics whose diabetes is under control. Even without including these people, the act estimates (at 42 U.S.C. § 12101(a)(1)) that at the time of passage, 43 million Americans counted as disabled according to the legal definition. Finally, there is a miscellany of excluded conditions, that is, specific, named conditions that are simply not deemed to be disabilities: homosexuality and bisexuality (§ 12211(a)), transvestism (§ 12208), transsexualism, pedophilia, exhibitionism, voyeurism, gender identity disorders not resulting from physical impairments, other sexual behavior disorders, compulsive gambling, kleptomania, pyromania, and psychoactive substance use disorders resulting from current illegal use of drugs (§ 12211(b)). What all these have in common is that they are medically and/or morally dubious conditions, which if they were not excluded, risk making the law look ridiculous.

However, only "qualified individuals with a disability" can sue under the ADA; a qualified individual with a disability is defined as someone "with a disability who, with or without reasonable accommodation, can perform the essential functions of the employment position that such individual holds or desires" (42 U.S.C. § 12111(8)). So, the idea is that if a person can do the job, that is, if he is qualified for the job, and has a disability but that disability is irrelevant to the performance of the job, he cannot be discriminated against. (In this respect, it is like racial discrimination, since race is an irrelevant factor, too.) For example, one cannot discriminate against a software engineer who uses a wheelchair. If the person's disability is relevant to being able to do the job but if the employer can make reasonable accommodation (e.g., by installing assistive devices) so that the person can do it, then that person is also a "qualified individual with a disability." Finally, if a person has no disability as defined by the

ADA (e.g., she is nearsighted but wears corrective lenses) or if no reasonable accommodation will permit her to perform the job (e.g., no blind bus drivers), then she is also not a "qualified individual with a disability." There are further complications, such as what counts as a "substantial limitation" and a "reasonable accommodation," but a discussion of these can be postponed for now.

Let us consider the findings and purpose of the act (§ 12101) as it pertains to employment, since that is where the premises of the main conversion argument for the ADA are likely to be found. Congress found that the disabled are an insular and discrete minority, which has been subjected to discrimination in a variety of contexts (employment, public accommodations, etc.). The ultimate goals of the act in the employment context are the usual ones of economic improvement (in this case, economic self-sufficiency for the disabled) and equal opportunity. The act is explicit about bringing to bear the full weight of the federal government to achieve those ends. Prior to passage, most states had a law banning discrimination in employment against the disabled, so title I of the ADA was more about imposing a national standard and getting the federal government involved in helping the disabled (Colker 2005, 70). Its complex provisions are intended to force employers to reexamine their prejudices and find ways to integrate the disabled into the life of the firm, which in turn is intended to integrate the disabled more fully into the larger society. The power of the state is to be used to change that way of thinking and "to provide a clear and comprehensive national mandate for the elimination of discrimination against individuals with disabilities" (42 U.S.C. § 12101). The integration just alluded to was also part of the rationale for the Civil Rights Act of 1964, which was intended to integrate more fully minorities and women into society.

A point of contrast with title VII of the 1964 Civil Rights Act, however, is that the ADA is much more likely to impose financial burdens on employers than is title VII. Though the latter might require the installation of an occasional women's restroom or the setting aside of an area for Muslims to say their daily prayers, complying with the antidiscrimination provisions for protected groups under title VII typically does not impose substantial financial burdens on employers. By contrast, the ADA can do that—employers may have to install a variety of assistive devices or make major or minor architectural changes to their facilities. They can be forced to make "reasonable accommodations" that do not impose "undue hardship" (24 U.S.C. § 12111(9)–(10)). How big a burden does this impose? Thomas DeLeire says, unfortunately, there is little evidence about the costs of accommodation. The evidence at hand comes from the President's Job Accommodation Network (JAN)...[which] reports that the median accommodation under ADA costs $500 or less. [Another] study found that the average cost of an accommodation is very low—approximately $900—and that 51 percent of accommodations cost nothing

...According to JAN, 12 percent of accommodations cost more than $2,000 and 4 percent cost more than $5,000. (DeLeire 2000, 22–23)

Stein (2000) finds similarly modest title I compliance costs. These are not the costs associated with changes in public accommodations, which fuel much of the outrage toward the ADA.[27] Still, there are often costs (and not all of them are financial) associated with hiring the disabled, and the ADA forces employers to bear them. To summarize, the case for the ADA in employment is very similar to the case for title VII: it is based on the idea that discrimination rooted in prejudice toward, or stereotypes about, the disabled is wrong, and the force of law should be used to stop or prevent it, as much as possible.

What is the classical liberal view of title I of the ADA? They are inclined to oppose it on a variety of grounds. One of the purposes of the act was to facilitate the employment of the disabled, who have traditionally experienced very high rates of unemployment. The available data on the effects of the ADA on the employment rate of the disabled are not encouraging, however. Daron Acemoglu and Joshua Angrist found a modest post-ADA *decline* in the relative employment of people with disabilities aged twenty-one to thirty-nine, which, they argue, is attributable to the ADA (Acemoglu and Angrist 2001, 945). DeLeire (2000, 22) found a 7.8 percent decline in the relative employment rate of disabled men in the period from 1990 until April 1995, which spans the date that the ADA went into effect. How might the ADA explain these declines in employment rates? One obvious explanation is that prospective compliance costs make employers more reluctant to hire the disabled. The cost data cited by DeLeire and Stein, though modest, might be inaccurate or misleading.[28] One reason is that these figures do not give aggregate totals for ADA-mandated expenditures on employees. As Walter Olson has pointed out,

the numbers shed no light on the aggregate costs of accommodation,...only suggesting that many of the accommodations were cheap. Counting lots of trivial adjustments can readily result in such a finding even if the aggregate burdens of accommodation are high....In the 1982 survey, individual accommodations apparently reached into the tens of thousands of dollars, with 2 percent exceeding $20,000. (Olson 1997, 109)

There are also nonmonetary costs associated with reasonable accommodation that might figure into employers' thinking when they contemplate hiring the disabled. As Blanck and Weighner Marti explain,

> workplace accommodations may themselves be stigmatized (Bell 1997; EEOC 1997; Mancuso 1990; Parry 1993). Employers view certain accommodations (such as reasonable time off and restructuring the work environment) as burdensome because they involve modifications of the managerial and social aspects of the workplace rather than the physical aspects (Hantula and Reilly 1996). Prejudiced attitudes may cause employers to perceive employees who utilize such accommodations as being less capable or responsible and as a result less deserving of promotions (Carling 1994; Moore 1995). Coworkers may view employees who take more breaks or who work in private areas as enjoying special privileges (Carling 1994). These perceptions lead to a loss of morale in the workplace (Key 1997). (Blanck and Weighner Marti 2000, 365)

These costs would not be reflected in the cost data cited by Acemoglu and Angrist (2001), DeLeire (2000), and Stein (2000).

Charge statistics from the EEOC provide more bad news for those who hoped that the ADA would have a positive effect on employment among the disabled. Typically, when an antidiscrimination law is passed, the pattern is for claims of wrongful discrimination in hiring to predominate in the early years as the law takes effect; eventually charges of wrongful discrimination in dismissal come to predominate. For example, regarding title VII of the 1964 Civil Rights Act, Donohue and Siegelman (1991, 1015) found that hiring charges exceeded termination charges by 50 percent in 1966, but by 1985 termination cases outnumbered hiring cases by a ratio of 6 to 1. As explained by Steven Willborn, one plausible hypothesis that accounts for this pattern is that

> in the early years, members of the protected group use the law to gain entry into good jobs from which they historically had been

excluded. As a result, in those early years, one would expect to see mostly cases alleging hiring discrimination. Eventually, however, obvious barriers to entry would be reduced and members of the protected group would begin to use the law to protect their status in those good jobs. As a result, over time one would expect to see cases alleging improper discharges to outnumber hiring discrimination claims. (2000, 113)

When it comes to the ADA, charge statistics do not bear out this pattern, however. Instead, discharge cases have been much higher than hiring cases right from the start. Willborn (2000, 111) estimates the ratio of discharge to hiring cases at between 10 to 1 and 14 to 1. Discrimination in hiring is less likely to be alleged because of the heterogeneity of the disabled as a group. Disparate treatment is as always hard to prove, at least if employers do not make jokes about the disabled in a job interview with a disabled person. As for disparate impact, tests or employment criteria that might have a disparate impact vis-à-vis one type of disability would have no disparate impact vis-à-vis another type of disability, so disparate impact suits are less likely to be filed.[29] By contrast, if an employee with a disability is discharged, he has little to lose by alleging discrimination. These facts taken together would seem to create a relatively strong disincentive to hire the disabled in the first place, since the likelihood of charges being filed with the EEOC is much greater after an offer of employment has been made than if it is not made at all.

Other factors also make the disabled less attractive as job applicants. Probationary periods are an effective and widely used personnel practice (Holzer 1987; Groshen and Loh 1993), but, as in the case of other protected groups, there are effectively no probationary periods for disabled workers, since the latter can contest any decision to terminate on grounds of illicit discrimination. As a general rule, the credibility of threatened legal action is directly proportional to the degree of indeterminacy in the statutory language, which is substantial in the case of title I of the ADA.[30]

A peculiarity of title I of the ADA is that it prohibits prospective employers from inquiring whether a job applicant actually has a disability (that would be viewed as prima facie discriminatory), but if and when a conditional offer of employment is made and the prospective employee reveals his or her disability, the law requires the employer to enter into an "interactive process" with the prospective employee to determine the appropriate reasonable accommodation that might be made for the disability—with the possibility left open that no reasonable accommodation may be found and the offer withdrawn. (Apparitions of plaintiffs' attorneys hover ghost-like over the interactive process, daring any employer or hiring officer to withdraw an offer because no reasonable accommodation can be made.) As stated in the *Code of Federal Regulations,* "this process should identify the precise limitations resulting from the disability and potential reasonable accommodations that could overcome those limitations" (29 *C.F.R.* § 1630.2(o)(3) [1991]). The government is not asking employers to pretend that the guide dog a blind person brings to a job interview is merely a pet who likes to wear a harness; not all disabilities are readily apparent, especially those relating to mental illness. However, many of them are or they can be inferred from other facts disclosed in an interview; those applicants will be further disadvantaged by the law because employers will be reluctant to make them an offer without knowing how far they will have to extend themselves in the ensuing "interactive process" to find a "reasonable accommodation." The uncertainties involved make it sensible to go around that particular minefield by hiring another candidate whom the employer infers has no disabilities. In this way, the act encourages the very behavior it prohibits. All of these considerations suggest that the ADA is unlikely to have had much effect on reducing unemployment among the disabled, a primary aim of title I, and indeed this may explain in part why unemployment rates among the disabled have increased.

Finally, there is a question of how much actual discrimination actually takes place. Complaint resolution statistics from the EEOC indicate that a significant majority of all complaints are found to be not meritorious.[31] There are two ways in which this can happen: administrative closure and a finding of no reasonable cause. In 2003, a representative year, the EEOC resolved 16,915 ADA complaints. Of these 17.7 percent were administratively closed. Administrative closures occur when the charging party cannot be located or does not respond to EEOC communications, or withdraws the charges without benefits, or the EEOC determines it does not have jurisdiction. If at any time in the process a complainant wants to sue, he or she needs a right-to-sue letter from the EEOC, and such letters are not issued in cases of administrative closure. The other no-merit category is the finding of no reasonable cause, which in 2003 accounted for 60.6 percent of the charges. As Zink and Gutman explain the finding of "no reasonable cause," the EEOC has investigated the charges and concluded that there is no reason to believe discrimination has occurred. The charging party still has a right to go to court, and a right-to-sue letter is issued...the finding of no reasonable cause has consistently averaged in the 60% range across the last eight years. (Zink and Gutman 2005, 112)

This means that no-merit resolutions occur in 75 percent to 80 percent of all cases. The fact that a right-to-sue letter is needed if a plaintiff wants to sue means that the charge statistics give an accurate picture of all allegations of ADA discrimination that fail at the level of EEOC review. Unfortunately, statistics are not readily available for how many "no reasonable cause" charges subsequently succeed in the courts, though it is likely to be relatively small.

The EEOC breaks out complaints by disability category, and these statistics are suggestive. One might suppose that the largest categories would be people with sensory losses (the blind, the deaf, etc.) and paraplegics, but that is not the case. Over the period July 26, 1992, to September 30, 2005, the largest category (after "Other Disability" at 20.8 percent) is "Orthopedic and Structural Impairments of the Back" at 13.1 percent, followed by "Regarded as Disabled" at 11.1 percent.[32] Back problems are self-diagnosed, and the primary symptom is pain, or more exactly, reports of pain. Not coincidentally, back problems are frequently alleged in workers' compensation cases as well. Lower-back pain is not well understood medically, and it turns out that across a range of cases, orthopedists, chiropractors, and televangelists all get about the same cure rate. These observations should not be taken to imply that there is no real discrimination against the disabled; it is instead to make a point that is almost never made in polite company, namely, that there is a lot of fraud and bad faith in ADA cases (as well as workers' compensation cases) aided and abetted by attorneys with a moral disability. Facing that fact, as well as the fact that there is a very high rate of nonmeritorious EEOC cases, make it both possible and necessary to ask if the benefits to the disabled of the ADA are worth its very substantial costs, both financial and moral, that are imposed on the rest of society. On this point, there could be reasonable disagreement.

One final problem concerns how cases alleging title I violations are handled in the courts. Critics have charged that the courts at all levels, starting at the top, have eviscerated title I of the ADA.[33] The key case is *Sutton v. United Airlines,* 527 U.S. 471 (1999). It involved twin sisters who were excluded from consideration for employment as overseas airline pilots for United Airlines because they did not have uncorrected visual acuity of 20/100, though with eyeglasses, their vision was 20/20 or better. They sued under title I of the ADA, and the case went all the way to the Supreme Court. The Court agreed with the trial judge, who ordered summary judgment for the defendant. Speaking for the Court, Justice O'Connor asserted (527 U.S. 471, 482–87) that prospective employees are to be evaluated not in their hypothetical uncorrected state but in their condition when corrective measures have been taken. According to the law, then, the plaintiffs were not disabled. Their vision problem did not "substantially limit one or more of the major life activities," the Court reasoned, on the grounds that working as a commercial airline pilot on overseas routes is not a major life activity (527 U.S. 471, 490–94). (One can see how a line drawing problem can come up here as the types of jobs from which a person is excluded by her disability gets broader.) This creates a "Catch-22" situation in the sense that if a person's disability is not too serious, he or she does not count as a "disabled person" in the eyes of the law. But, if the disability is serious enough, then it is likely to turn out that no reasonable accommodation for the disability can be made, and thus the person is not a "qualified individual with a disability." This and similar rulings had the effect of narrowing the scope of the law significantly. Many fewer people have standing to sue than would otherwise be the case, though whether the number is below the target figure of 43 million cited by Congress is anyone's guess.

Justice O'Connor, who wrote the opinion in *Sutton,* offered an elaborate internal argument for construing the statute in this way, but there may have been other factors at work. Although Justice White wrote the majority opinion in *Ward's Cove Packing, Inc. v. Antonio,* Justice O'Connor joined in that opinion. As discussed early in this chapter (see above, n3; also see chapter 12, n12), one of the problems *Ward's Cove* sought to address was the fact that employment tests and other screening devices are often difficult to validate, that is, to show that they accurately "capture" all (or nearly all) and only the right people. In the aftermath of *Griggs,* this made the business necessity test a difficult one to pass, and it motivated employers to engage in defensive preferential hiring (i.e., to hire by the numbers) to reach safe harbor from title VII lawsuits. The decision in *Ward's Cove* reduced that incentive considerably by, in effect, weakening the business necessity test. All that the employer was required to do was

to articulate a legitimate business basis for a challenged test, requirement, or practice. The problem with interpreting the ADA in a way
that construes disability status broadly is not that it would encourage preferential hiring by opening the door to disparate impact suits.
(Disabilities are too heterogeneous for that to be a realistic worry.)
Rather, the problem is that it would subject a lot of plausible but difficult to validate employment criteria to judicial scrutiny on a charge
of disparate treatment discrimination—scrutiny that these criteria
might not survive, despite their common sense appeal. The effect of
the decision in *Sutton* was to exempt those criteria from judicial scrutiny by denying the plaintiffs standing as disabled persons. As Ruth
Colker, one of the Court's harshest critics on this issue, has said in
commenting on *Sutton,* "by concluding at the preliminary stage of the
case that the plaintiffs did not qualify as 'disabled' under the ADA,
the Court avoided the harder question of whether the employer could
reasonably require visual acuity of 20/20 without the use of corrective lenses" (Colker 2005, 105). To which one can imagine Justice
O'Connor saying, "Just so. That's exactly what we want to do. We
don't want juries, or even worse, *judges,* deciding the proper level
of visual acuity for overseas airline pilots." (The fact that Supreme
Court justices make social policy does not mean they always do it
badly.) The effect of this decision and its progeny (viz., *Kirkingburg
v. Albertson's, Inc.,* 527 U.S. 555 (1999), and *Murphy v. United Parcel
Service, Inc.,* 527 U.S. 516 (1999)) was to direct trial judges to grant
summary judgment for the defendant in any case where a person's
impairment does not prevent him from doing a whole host of different kinds of jobs. There is a broader rationale that could be offered in
support of the Court's construal of what counts as disabled in these
contexts: sometimes people have impairments that only prevent them
from doing a specific job or a narrow range of jobs, but those impairments do not affect their ability to do other jobs. The Court is in effect
telling these individuals to make some accommodation to their own
disabilities by not demanding that employers revise their employment criteria for some jobs or make other accommodations when
these individuals are perfectly capable of performing other, sometimes closely related, jobs. They are being told to find another type
of job—and the way the courts do this is to tell these individuals that
they are not disabled according to the law.

The ADA, on this construal, is primarily for qualified individuals whose disabilities either have very pervasive effects on major life
activities and thus potentially exclude them from a wide range of jobs

unless and until accommodations are made, or it is for people whose disabilities are not job-relevant but make them objects of stigmatization by employers or by the general public. As the Court sees it, these are the people the ADA is supposed to help. Whatever Congress intended, the parallels with title VII are striking.

Whether or not the disabled, as the Court defines them, are actually being helped by the law is another matter entirely. If the law significantly deterred employers who would otherwise have discriminated against the disabled from discriminating against them in hiring, one would expect the unemployment rate among the disabled to be declining, but the data do not support that. In fact, unemployment rates have been increasing. What about unjust dismissals? The number of unjust dismissals the law prevents is unknown, but the fact that 75–80 percent of all the ADA charges filed with the EEOC end up classified as no-merit resolutions is suggestive. On the other side, there are very real costs associated with the law that go beyond the costs of reasonable accommodations for the disabled. They include the wasted time and effort expended in the enforcement apparatus (EEOC, courts, attorneys) to adjudicate or settle nonmeritorious claims, as well as the social and moral harm done when disaffected employees who are fired are encouraged, as they are under current law, to try to extort money from their former employers by threatening legal action as they go out the door.

All of these considerations taken together explain why classical liberals are inclined to oppose title I of the ADA and favor its repeal. What would happen if it were abolished? As always, no one really knows, but some informed speculation is possible. In the absence of title I, it would be possible for an employer to have a frank discussion with a prospective employee about the extent of his disability, the costs of addressing it, and how it would be paid for. This would in turn make it more likely that the disabled person would actually be hired. Some modern liberals would object to any suggestion that the employee might be required to pay for any accommodating measures, since it is a fixed point in some versions of modern liberal political philosophy that people should not bear any financial responsibility for unchosen circumstances.[34] Classical liberals could agree but would turn this around and ask why employers should have to bear the financial burden, especially since they must also bear nonfinancial burdens associated with hiring the disabled. Indeed, it seems that the fairest way to pay for these accommodations would be for taxpayers to foot the bill. (There may even be a public goods argument in here for help-ing the disabled in the employment context.) Richard Epstein (1992, 493–94) describes one way this might work. In this way, helping the disabled in the employment arena would move the problem off the modern liberal regulatory agenda and onto their transfer agenda—an agenda where they might get some reasoned agreement from classical liberals to help those to whom fate has not been kind.

Conversion Arguments

Health and Safety Regulation

Occupational Safety and Health Regulation

Regulation of the employment relation increased dramatically with the passage of the Occupational Safety and Health Act of 1970 (29 U.S.C. § 651 et seq.), which created the Occupational Safety and Health Administration (OSHA). Workplace health and safety have long been a concern of government, but it was only with the passage of this act that the federal government assumed a major and guiding role. Prior to that, occupational safety and health had been a province of the various states, some of which did a better job than others. As explained in chapters 2 and 3, the historical foundation for government involvement in this area is the common law of torts. As the Industrial Revolution gained momentum, the common law approach to industrial accidents and injuries proved inadequate because workers injured on the job were repeatedly left uncompensated and without recourse for their injuries. The key factors causing problems were the application of various principles of tort law (viz., the fault requirement, the fellow servants rule, and the defenses of contributory negligence and assumption of risk), as well as the expense and difficulty of settling factual issues. These factors conspired to deprive injured workers of meaningful relief. As a result, state governments instituted mandatory workers' compensation insurance, which dispensed with the question of fault and paid more promptly, in exchange for which workers received smaller payouts than they might have received through the tort system. By the late 1960s, however, this legal regime for dealing with workplace injuries and deaths was deemed inadequate. Workers' compensation is essentially reactive, compensating injured workers after the fact. Modern liberal politicians and the unions that supported them came to favor a more proactive approach. What they wanted, and what they got, were agencies with the power to compel firms to abide by safety and health standards promulgated by the government. Violators could be fined and even shut down in extreme cases for noncompliance. The two main agencies that deal with health and safety issues are the Mine Health and Safety Administration and the Occupational Safety and Health Administration. In what follows, OSHA is discussed, but the same arguments apply equally to the MHSA.

The argument for creating OSHA is remarkably thin; both the Senate and House committee reports cited some apparently alarming statistics about occupational injuries and illnesses. For example, the "Background" section of the House Education and Labor Committee Report (1971, 844) says, "the on-the-job health and safety crisis is the worst problem confronting American workers, because each year as a result of their jobs, over 14,500 workers die." Is that a lot or a little? Without some kind of context, it is hard to say. In the Senate Report (1971, 141–42), the Committee on Labor and Public Welfare cited this and other accident statistics, including the numbers of people killed or disabled, the number of man-hours lost due to accidents, and the estimated financial costs of all of this. It also claimed that the number of disabling injuries per million man hours worked had increased by 20 percent between 1958 and 1970. It further asserted that every twenty minutes a new and potentially toxic chemical substance is being introduced into industry and that the linkages between occupational exposure to these chemicals and chronic illnesses are continually being discovered. Finally, the inadequacy of state programs and voluntary efforts in combatting the "grim current scene" in workplace injuries and accidents was cited. The Senate Report (1971, 144) said that there are significant variations among states in terms of the strength of their laws protecting workers and the vigor with which they are enforced.

What is missing in all this is any attempt to argue for the proposition that the creation of a federal government bureaucracy with a mandate to address these problems would have a nontrivial positive effect on the health and safety of the U.S. workforce, that is, that it would reduce the rates of occupational deaths, injuries, and illnesses below what they would have been in the absence of the law. Perhaps it seemed obvious to supporters of the law that if the federal government were to force businesses to abide by health and safety standards set by experts at OSHA, accidents and occupational disease would decline. Nichols and Zeckhauser (1977, 51) report that one of the bill's sponsors in the House expected a 50 percent reduction in accident rates by 1980! But, there should have been some skepticism about this based on, if nothing else, the relatively small budget of the agency and the relatively small number of agency employees. This was an extremely ambitious undertaking with the potential to affect (in the 1970s) 60 million workers at 5 million business establishments (Nichols and Zeckhauser 1977, 41). OSHA's budget in 1975 was $102.3 million (in 1975 dollars), with a staff of 2,435 FTE (full-time equivalent) employees.[1] As of 2004, 135 million workers at 8.9 million sites were potentially subject to OSHA regulations.[2] The budget for OSHA in 2007 is about $486 million (in 2007 dollars) and the number of (FTE) employees is actually down to 2,150, of whom only 1,100 are inspectors.[3] In constant dollars, OSHA's budget has remained relatively unchanged over the years, this despite the fact that millions more workers are now covered. Although OSHA has a larger enforcement budget than any other safety regulatory agency, it has fewer inspectors than some insurance companies that sell workers' compensation insurance (Cornell, Noll, and Weingast 1976, 499). It would be foolish to assume that most businesses would comply with the law if the standards OSHA promulgated were to impose significant costs on individual firms. And if they were not going to impose significant costs, it is not clear why the agency would be needed in the first place. According to the public record, however, there was never any serious attempt to discuss this or any other objection to the proposal nor was there any discussion of alternative ways the problems of worker health and safety might be addressed.[4] Finally, while there are some vague references to it being cost effective, it is doubtful that supporters would have changed their minds if it could have been shown that the costs of OSHA would outweigh its benefits, especially if most of those costs were at least nominally borne by employers. Beyond that, it is hard to find anything more definite in the way of an argument from supporters of the law. The naivete is stunning, especially, though not exclusively, in light of what has since been learned.

The classical liberal conversion argument against OSHA starts with an examination of its effectiveness. In *Risk by Choice,* W. Kip Viscusi carefully examined the evidence of OSHA's effectiveness in reducing workplace risks in the years immediately after its creation in comparison to the years immediately preceding its creation. He concluded,

> the overall implication of the evidence is clear-cut. Contrary to widespread belief, risk levels were continuing to decline in the years preceding the establishment of OSHA...Workplace risks have continued to decline by about 2 percent annually, roughly the same rate as before OSHA's existence.[5]

This remarkable conclusion calls out for explanation—an explanation which is crucial to evaluating this element of the modern liberal regulatory agenda. This explanation starts from OSHA's guiding legislative mandate, which was "to assure so far as possible every working man and woman in the Nation safe and healthful working conditions" (29 U.S.C. § 651(b)). The way this is to be achieved is by giving the secretary of labor the power to set standards affecting occupational safety and health in the workplace (29 U.S.C. § 655). The standards are to be enforced by the agency, which issues citations to the offending business. Moreover, the statute contains a "general duty clause," which requires that

(a) Each employer—
    (1) shall furnish to each of his employees employment and a place of employment which are free from recognized hazards that are causing or are likely to cause death or serious physical harm to his employees;
    (2) shall comply with occupational safety and health standards promulgated under this chapter. (29 U.S.C. § 658)

The secretary of labor was required to set standards for every industry. Obviously, this is an enormous undertaking, and it would have taken decades to build up the expertise de novo in the government to do this. To avoid this problem, the agency simply adopted the national consensus standards of ANSI (American National Standards Institute) and NFPA (National Fire Protection Association) as their own. In this way, in only one month after OSHA began operation, it was able to pump over 4,000 new regulations into the *Federal Register* (29 *C.F.R.* part 1910 [1974]).

The problem with this approach is that many of the ANSI/NFPA standards were vague, aspirational, or merely suggested guidelines. Far from being pro-industry nonstandards, some of these standards were very stringent, and their enforcement by OSHA brought down some richly deserved ridicule onto government enforcement officials for the unreasonableness or inappropriateness of the standards. (This is where the stories about port-o-potties for cowboys and life vests for bridge painters working over dry riverbeds came from.) In addition, most of these standards were addressed to readily visible safety hazards, whereas health risks from toxic and hazardous substances, which are arguably much more important risks, were addressed only as an afterthought (Viscusi 1983, 11). The standards themselves were treated as rules with which all firms were supposed to be in compliance. Violators were to be issued citations that "shall describe with particularity the nature of the violation, including a reference to the provision of the chapter, standard, rule, regulation, or order alleged to have been violated. In addition, the citation shall fix a reasonable time for the abatement of the violation" (29 U.S.C. § 658(a)). The requirement that any violation be abated raises the issue of compliance costs.[6]

How do compliance costs figure into the act and its enforcement? Notice that the guiding mandate of the act—"to assure so far as possible every working man and woman in the Nation safe and healthful working conditions"—might appear to be ambiguous on the cost issue. In other words, it might be argued (and indeed was argued by employers) that OSHA should be constrained by what is economically possible in the sense that they could institute only those standards whose benefits outweighed their costs. After all, employees themselves may end up paying these costs through lower wages. The courts disagreed with this reading, however; they ultimately read this guiding mandate and the associated general duty clause to mean that, while workplace standards do not have to eliminate all risks (safe working conditions are not necessarily risk-free working conditions), the standards nevertheless do not have to be cost-effective or pass any other test used in cost-benefit analysis. Here is how that understanding of the law emerged.

Originally, OSHA took the view that as long as there was some health or safety benefit, however speculative, to be gained from tightening a standard, the standard should be tightened. Like an angry homeowner with a frustrating task and a very long-handled socket wrench, they wanted to tighten the bolts as tight as they would go. This understanding of the act was rejected, however, in the Supreme Court's decision invalidating OSHA's benzene exposure standard. The Court said,

> the Court of Appeals was correct in refusing to enforce the 1 ppm exposure limit on the ground that it was not supported by appropriate findings. OSHA's rationale for lowering the permissible exposure limit from 10 ppm to 1 ppm was based, not on any finding that leukemia has ever been caused by exposure to 10 ppm of benzene and that it will not be caused by exposure to 1 ppm, but rather on a series of assumptions indicating that some leukemia might result from exposure to 10 ppm

and that the number of cases might be reduced by lowering the exposure level to 1 ppm. . . . [the act] did not give OSHA the unbridled discretion to adopt standards designed to create absolutely risk-free workplaces regardless of cost. (*Industrial Union Dept. v. American Petrol. Inst.*, 448 U.S. 607, 608, 614 (1980))

However, in the famous cotton dust case decided a year later, the Court explicitly rejected the proposition that the act required that any OSHA standard must be cost-effective or pass some other business-tested, economist-approved cost-benefit test. As the Court said,

in effect then, as the Court of Appeals held, Congress itself defined the basic relationship between costs and benefits by placing the "benefit" of the worker's health above all other considerations save those making attainment of this "benefit" unachievable. Any standard based on a balancing of costs and benefits by the Secretary that strikes a different balance than that struck by Congress would be inconsistent with the command set forth in 6 (b)(5). (*American Textile Mfrs. Inst. v. Donovan* 452 U.S. 490, 509 (1981))

The only nod to feasibility, other than technological feasibility, that OSHA has been willing to make is that if the implementation of a standard would put a company out of business, they would stay their hand. Arguably, that too would make the benefit unachievable.

The deeper problem is that the guiding mandate of the act and the general duty clause (29 U.S.C. § 651 (b) and 29 U.S.C. § 655 (a)(1), respectively) make the federal government ultimately responsible for the nation's occupational safety and health. The standards it sets are supposed to address any kind or any pattern of occupational injuries or illnesses that it is technologically feasible to address. Costs do not matter within the limits set out by the Court in the two above-referenced decisions. The language of the guiding mandate and the general duty clause cannot be plausibly read in any other way. Worker health and safety must be the primary concerns, as here understood, regardless of cost, though if improvements in health or safety mandated by OSHA are purely speculative, the latter has exceeded its mandate. Even if a worker gets injured or sick because of her own negligence or carelessness, OSHA still bears some responsibility, if there is some standard the application of which could have prevented the problem. The mournful cry of trucks and heavy equipment backing up bears witness to this. As the Senate Committee Report (1971, 149) says, "this legislation would be seriously deficient if any employee were killed or seriously injured on the job simply because there was no specific standard applicable to a recognized hazard which could result in such a misfortune." This means that once a hazard is recognized, a standard is supposed to be put in place. In fact, however, workers themselves bear much of the responsibility for workplace accidents, but OSHA ignores this. Perhaps it is because behavioral standards applicable to workers would be hard to enforce, but there may be another reason to put the entire burden on employers and not employees. If OSHA actually were to propose behavioral standards, it would be an explicit admission that some of the responsibility for workplace accidents does not lie with the firms OSHA regulates and/or OSHA itself. One can easily imagine shouts from Congress and labor unions that OSHA would be "blaming the victim" for industrial accidents, which of course is exactly what they would be doing if they were to recognize that workers are sometimes responsible for industrial accidents. The larger point is that the open-ended mandate with which Congress created OSHA has produced a situation in which they have every incentive to create more and more standards to cover more and more potential injuries and illnesses, pretty much regardless of cost. Telling evidence of this was revealed in late 1999 and early 2000 when OSHA suggested that employers might be responsible for health and safety conditions for employees who work out of their own homes.[7] The idea of OSHA inspectors inspecting people's homes to see if their bathrooms had, for example, safety handrails installed next to the toilets set off howls of protest in the telecommuting community. Labor Secretary Herman beat a hasty retreat when word of this got out. The fact that they would even think about this sort of thing is indicative of the mentality within OSHA and the incentive structure that fosters it. The enabling legislation sets forth a vague but impossible to meet standard that permits and indeed requires the agency to promulgate more and more standards in a vain attempt to achieve an unachievable goal. This is one reason to favor abolishing it.

The fact that OSHA creates, and has every incentive to create, lots of standards does not mean that it actually enforces them. The more stringent standards that OSHA imposes often have very high compliance costs, so the effectiveness of the standards depends on the economic incentives to comply. Those incentives in turn depend on the chances that a business will be inspected, violations found, and a significant fine attached. However, these chances, as well as the fines, turn out to be rather low. According to recent figures, federal and state inspections total about 96,000 annually.[8] However, there are about 111 million workers subject to OSHA's jurisdiction. This means that there is one inspection for every 1,156 workers annually. Since some of these are follow-up inspections, this figure probably overstates the likelihood that a worker will see an inspector in any given year. Indeed, the probability that a firm will see an OSHA inspector in any year is roughly 1 in 100, which, some critics have pointed out, means that the average worker is more likely to see Halley's comet than an OSHA inspector in any given year. Each inspection yields an average of about two violations for which the average penalty is under $700. Overall cost of violations is about $1.34 per covered worker. None of these figures should be surprising in light of the enormous size of the U.S. economy compared to the size of the budget and workforce at OSHA. Under the circumstances, it would be surprising if OSHA had much effect on workplace health and safety.

The classical liberal case for abolishing OSHA set forth here is buttressed by a consideration of how the risks associated with workplace accidents and illnesses are handled by a private ordering. The best available theory to explain how these risks are handled is the Compensating Differentials theory. It begins with the prosaic observation that people voluntarily accept risks in exchange for some benefit. This is true in life generally as well as in the workplace. People engage in all manner of risky recreational behavior (e.g., skydiving) for the enjoyment they get out of it. They also accept jobs with a higher risk of injury in exchange for some benefit, such as the intrinsic or status rewards that go with the job (being a member of a S.W.A.T. team, being a paramedic) or more commonly, greater pay. Sometimes, the risk premium is explicitly attached to the job by contract, but often it is not. The Compensating Differentials theory explains some wage differentials by reference to these risks, and it attempts to measure those differentials. It depends on a number of assumptions that are only approximately true (Viscusi 1983, 41): (1) workers have full relevant information about the risks they face, (2) insurance functions adequately, (3) there are no externalities, i.e., no altruistic concerns by others for the workers' well-being.

Under these assumptions, the theory holds that wage differentials would accurately reflect the risks of injury, illness, and death associated with various jobs. As is usually the case with economic models, however, the assumptions are literally false. Workers are not fully informed about the risks they take on the job; insurance markets do not always function adequately; the interests of others are implicated when a worker is injured or killed. Still, these assumptions are close enough approximations to the truth to make it worthwhile to examine the empirical evidence for the Compensating Differentials theory. We return to problems created by the falsity of the assumptions later.

Viscusi (1983, 42–45; ch. 6) attempted to confirm the Compensating Differentials theory in a study of the perception of blue-collar workers about the risks they face and the wage premiums they receive. He found that workers who believed they faced dangerous or unhealthy working conditions receive on average $900 a year (in 1980 dollars) more than they would otherwise receive. To calculate the per unit cost of the risk, it is necessary to know the base rate of worker fatalities and serious injuries; the figure for fatalities is about 1 in 10,000 per year and for serious injuries about 1 in 25 (where "serious" is defined as missing at least one day's work). As a result, the implicit value that many workers place on their own lives is around $2 million or more (again, in 1980 dollars).

More recent figures tend to confirm this general picture. Wage premiums for job risks are $34 billion for the 4,900 job-related fatalities each year and $77 billion for the approximately 1.5 million nonfatal injuries and illnesses, for a total wage premium of $111 billion (Viscusi, Vernon, and Harrington, 2005, 834). By themselves, these figures do not mean much, but when compared to the incentives created by OSHA, they take on greater significance. Total yearly fines from OSHA typically average under $26 million, though in recent years under President George W. Bush they have ratcheted up considerably (e.g., $149 million in 2002). Even at the higher figures, the discrepancy between the incentives provided by the market and the incentives provided by OSHA is staggering. As Viscusi, Vernon, and Harrington say,

> overall, the financial cost per worker [for OSHA violations] is only $1.34. A useful comparison is that market forces, through compensating differentials, in combination with workers' compensation premiums, imposed costs in excess of $1,234 per worker. Quite simply, OSHA's enforcement effort is too modest to create truly effective financial incentives for safety. (Viscusi, Vernon, and Harrington, 2005, 851)

The size of the risk premium employers must pay workers to get them to do certain jobs directly affects the willingness of firms to take actions to reduce those risks, since to the extent that they can reduce the risks of on-the-job injuries, they can also reduce the risk premium they must pay. They make capital investments or investments in training up to the point where the marginal benefit (reduction in the risk premium) is equal to the marginal cost (of the safety equipment, etc.). Given that there will always be some risks associated with employment, defenders of government intervention need to tell a story about why it is not a good idea to let the market, as supplemented by workers' compensation insurance or something like it, handle the general problem of health and safety in the workplace, as it handles other problems.

One place this story might begin is with the literal falsity of the assumptions underlying the Compensating Differentials theory. Let us consider each of these foundational premises in more detail. Typically, workers are given information about the hazards of their jobs, but often this information is incomplete, or it is not processed properly. Regarding the former, classical liberals can provisionally concede that there is a role for government in addressing the information problem, if information is a public good. If this creates a genuine public goods problem that cannot be solved by a tying arrangement, then on their view, government should provide the good and pay for it with tax revenues. If there is no public goods problem, then they could simply make an exception in this case (i.e., use a conversion argument) on the grounds that they should not be too fastidious about their principles when the issue is providing information about workplace safety. And indeed, the government has an organization devoted to developing exactly this sort of information, NIOSH—the National Institute for Occupational Safety and Health. Not only does it do research but it also recommends standards. Classical liberals have no problem with either activity, so long as whatever standards it recommends do not have the force of law.

Let us consider now the information-processing problem. It is widely documented in the psychology literature on risk perception that people tend to overestimate the expected harm (probability times the disutility) of low-probability catastrophic events, such as nuclear power plant disasters, but underestimate the expected harm of relatively high-probability events or conditions, such as coronary artery disease.[9] Might there not be a justification for government-imposed standards based on the documented infirmities of judgment that afflict workers and indeed almost everyone? Probably not. One reason is that the low-probability risks of catastrophe are likely to be covered by the risk premium. The risk premium reflects perceived risk, not actual risk. So, if workers tend to overestimate the expected harm of low-probability workplace disasters, they will require a wage premium that is greater than it "should" be. That might offset the underestimation of higher-probability adverse events, though that is speculative. If not, there might be a prima facie case for government regulation of these higher-probability risks, since they tend to be underestimated. With regard to these risks, however, the problem is that the (perception of) expected harm of an adverse event is only one factor in an individual's decision to accept or reject a risk. Another factor is his or her attitude toward risk, sometimes called his or her degree of risk aversion, and that varies considerably across individuals. Young people are notorious for having relatively low levels of risk aversion compared to their elders. Wealthier people tend to be more risk averse than poor people, and so on. (More on this latter point shortly.) The main difficulty with the idea that government experts could more accurately judge which risks should not be taken is that there is no practical way to disentangle workers' underestimation (let us suppose) of the expected harm for higher-probability job risks from their attitudes toward risk that is, their degree of risk aversion. This means that there is no assurance that regulators would not be simply imposing their own values—in this case, their own degree of risk aversion—onto others. This problem becomes acute if workers are fully informed of the job risks they face.

Finally, let us consider the problem about negative effects on third parties. This is sometimes called the externalities problem. The charge is that the wage risk premium does not really take into consideration persons other than the employee, notably family members, who are affected by workplace accidents and deaths, and government regulation of workplace hazards compensates for that. To some extent, this is correct, though workers themselves do consider how their decision to take a certain job will affect their families, and they sometimes buy additional life insurance. Still, some of the loss to family members is uncompensated, especially when the worker dies. As far as fatalities are concerned, however, there may be not much that OSHA can do. According to Thomas Kniesner and John Leeth,

> the BLS [Bureau of Labor Statistics] also found that 40 percent of recent workplace fatalities were from transportation accidents (almost half the fatal transportation accidents were highway accidents), and about 20 percent of workplace fatalities were

from assaults and other violent acts...In other words, only 40 percent of workplace fatalities were caused by dangers thought by most to be unique to the workplace, such as the classic example of falling into a machine. The leading causes of work-related deaths in recent years, transportation accidents and assaults, are unlikely to be reduced much by OSHA inspections.

The self-employed [e.g., farmers] face a much higher chance of dying at work than wage and salary workers, which also has consequences for the effectiveness of OSHA. Although the self-employed are now about 9 percent of the workforce, in the period studied by the BLS they suffered about 20 percent of all workplace fatalities. (1995, 48)

All this suggests that OSHA cannot have a significant effect on death rates in the workplace; OSHA's effect on nonfatal accident rates will be discussed at the end of this section.

There are others besides family members who are affected by disabling accidents and fatalities, namely those whose altruistic preferences are contravened when workers are allowed to take certain risks. Many modern liberals are probably in this group, including, presumably, the members of Congress who supported the creation of OSHA. One source of these altruistic preferences might lie in the relationship between wealth and attitudes toward risk. It has been widely documented that the wealthier a person is, the more risk averse he or she tends to be, ceteris paribus. Consequently, the less wealthy a person is, the less risk averse he or she tends to be, again ceteris paribus. This means that relatively poor people are inclined to take risks (especially occupational risks that are tied to higher income) that relatively well-to-do people would shun. A common enough observation. The willingness to use the force of law to impose altruistic preferences on the relatively disadvantaged may be a form of risk egalitarianism. Specifically, it might be held that, at least in the workplace, people should not be subjected to some unreasonable risks no matter what the expected payoff, where unreasonable risks are defined either in relative or absolute terms. This is not as implausible as it first appears. Throughout most of the Industrial Revolution, workers faced what many people today would regard as appalling and unconscionable risks, and Third World workers often face similar risks today. The problem, however, is to define an unreasonable risk. It might be uncharitable to insist that "unreasonable" must be defined by reference to the approximate level of risk aversion of the average modern liberal, but the problem with any principle that would emerge from a philosophically adequate account of (un)reasonable risk is that it would not command the kind of widespread assent that is required for a conversion argument to succeed. One might argue for this principle on deeper philosophical grounds—general egalitarian grounds, perhaps—but by then classical liberals, as well as others without abiding egalitarian commitments, will have reached their stop and gotten off the bus.

What is the classical liberal alternative to OSHA, since they favor its abolition? There are a number of possibilities. One is to rely entirely on workers' compensation insurance (hereafter, WCI) to provide relief to workers injured on the job. Risk or experience rating, in which a firm's safety record affects its premiums, is done for most firms that have WCI, and it gives them an incentive to take safety into account, as do the wage premiums they have to pay to get workers to take occupational risks. In nearly all states, employers are required to purchase WCI. The only exceptions are Texas, South Carolina, and New Jersey. Mandatory WCI creates a number of problems for which there is no easy solution, however. The main problem with requiring all firms to provide WCI for their employees is that, in a free market, not all firms will be able to get coverage.[10] Some, for various reasons, use practices that are unusually hazardous for their particular industry; others may simply have a poor safety record; still others may be too small to provide useful data for experience rating, or they may be so small that any reasonable premium would not cover the insurance company's administrative costs. The way these firms have been handled in a mandatory workers' compensation regime is to put them into an assigned risk pool, which is funded by the insurance companies who are writing policies in that state. The extent of a firm's responsibility to the pool is determined by its market share in that state. Deficits in this pool are common, and in an unregulated market, they would be compensated for by increasing rates among the firms that can get coverage. The problem is that insurance rates are heavily regulated and political pressures suppress them, often in both the assigned risk pool and in the regular market. When rates are suppressed, insurers first drop coverage of firms with the worst experience rating; these firms are then forced into the assigned risk pool. If rates continue to be suppressed or are suppressed further, insurance companies will continue this practice until ultimately they become reluctant to write new policies or renew existing ones, forcing still more firms into the assigned risk pool. The cycle continues, until, like a great summer party, nearly everyone ends up in the pool, many involuntarily. For example, in 1992, 79.9 percent of Louisiana firms were in the assigned risk pool. Percentages were even higher in Rhode Island (88.6), and Maine (90.6). Nationally, the problem was less dramatic; in the early 1960s, the assigned-risk market accounted for no more than 3.2 percent of all premiums nationally, but by 1992, that figure had increased nearly nine-fold to 28.5 percent. The cycle comes to an end only when enough insurance companies simply stop writing WCI policies so that the state has to undertake some sort of bailout in which only economists who study these issues can figure out who is subsidizing whom.

The classical liberal solution, of course, is to do away with the mandate and rate regulation of WCI. This of course raises the question of what would happen to workers who are injured if their firm has not purchased a voluntary WCI policy, perhaps because no insurance company would sell them one. The state of Texas provides an interesting model of what might emerge, since it allows firms to opt out of workers' compensation insurance. Businesses do not, however, opt out in large numbers; only about 44 percent of all employers are so-called nonsubscribing firms, and they employ only 20 percent of the Texas workforce (Butler 1996, 410). Richard Butler describes the situation of many of the larger firms that opt out of WCI as follows:

> firms that opt out of workers' compensation are able to direct their workers to the employers' occupational medical centers, rather than let workers choose their own treating physicians. Many firms that I spoke with saw this as one of the significant benefits from opting out of workers' compensation. Also, most employees working in opt-out firms are covered by workplace injury agreements that often replicate workers' compensation-like medical and indemnity coverage. This reduces the likelihood of a worker filing a suit and the likelihood of winning a suit should it be filed (because damages would tend to be limited to pain and suffering and the proportion of wages not replaced by the employer's injury agreement). Finally, many (larger) firms in Texas instigated significant safety plans when they opted out in order to further avoid the risk of injury. (1996, 406)

WCI is the exclusive remedy only for subscribing firms. This means that workers injured in nonsubscribing firms can sue, but they have to prove employer negligence (unless they can sue the manufacturer of faulty equipment under products liability law). The interesting wrinkle in the Texas law is that the statute explicitly eliminates the common law defenses of contributory negligence, assumption of risk, and the fellow servants rule. In the run up to passage of compulsory WCI in states other than New Jersey, South Carolina, and Texas, many states limited or eliminated these three defenses by statute, but all those changes were rendered moot with the passage of compulsory WCI (Fishback and Kantor 2000, 28, 93, 94, 116n16, 118n31, 131, 138).

As their name implies, the Texas Association of Responsible Non-subscribers (TXANS) represents many nonsubscribing firms in the state of Texas. As they explain on their Web site,

> TXANS defines a responsible nonsubscriber program as a program that specifically includes:
> • A workplace safety program designed to meet the unique needs of the nonsubscribing business.
> • A well documented responsible nonsubscriber occupational injury benefit plan that establishes the provision of workplace injury benefits.
> • A program that communicates the program's elements to employees.
> • Benefit funding, which is typically secured through insurance or a combination of self-funded and insured benefits.
> • Employer/employee selection of quality medical providers to provide exceptional care for employee injuries.
> • A program to manage benefit claims.
> • Programs to prevent and address disputes in a manner that is fair to both employees and employers.[11]

Not all nonsubscribing firms are members of TXANS, however. According to its executive director, their members employ about one half of the estimated 1.8 million employees of nonsubscribing firms.[12] TXANS members tend to be larger businesses, and they typically provide a higher level of benefits than do small employers. This means that a little less than 1 million workers have no recourse when they are injured, other than what the tort system and the plaintiffs' bar can provide. However, employers who opt out of WCI cannot avail themselves of the standard common law defenses of contributory negligence, assumption of risk, and the fellow servants rule, which in the past served as their Kevlar. Nonsubscribers who are not members of TXANS are very often small contractors, employing day laborers. There is a case to be made that employees of these firms have voluntarily assumed three risks—not just the risk of injury but also the risk of having to prove negligence to a jury in the event they are injured and the risk that their employer will have so few assets as to be effectively judgment-proof. But, as economists are fond of pointing out, the alternative may be no job at all. So, for our purposes, there are four categories of businesses in the state of Texas: (1) those with WCI; (2) members of TXANS, (3) nonmembers of TXANS who are financially sound, meaning they have enough assets to pay a large liability judgment, and (4) small, judgment-proof firms. The fact that many businesses choose to remain in WCI even though they can opt out suggests that they find the entire package worth their while. They gain immunity from tort suits but there is no requirement that they be proved negligent, so they have to pay even when workers act irresponsibly. Members of TXANS have virtually the same coverage as is provided by WCI. Among the nonmembers of TXANS, there is no way of estimating the size of (4) relative to (3), though we know it is some fraction of 900,000 workers. There is also no way of estimating the marginal costs, both financial and moral, of allowing (4) to exist, in comparison to the alternative in which WCI is mandatory (and the firms that cannot afford it do not exist), but it should be clear that there can be reasonable differences of opinion about which alternative is more costly, all things considered.

To summarize, classical liberals believe there is a viable alternative to the command-and-control regime imposed by OSHA. It involves letting market forces, suitably supplemented, handle risks in the workplace. The risk premiums incorporated in the wages of relatively dangerous jobs are significant enough for employers to pay attention to workplace safety—much more significant than the incentives provided by OSHA's mostly empty threats about penalties. As to the suitable supplements, the Texas experiment is instructive. It allows for workers' compensation insurance, but it also permits firms to opt out. The most important thing the state does is to eliminate by statute the standard defenses against tort actions that employers have used in the past to prevent recovery of damages. Finally, there could also be a significant role for government in the provision and dissemination of information about occupational risks.

Is there anything that can be said on behalf of OSHA, as currently constituted? Surely these standards and the associated inspection regime have had some noticeable positive effect over the years. In the aggregate, however, it does not seem so. As Viscusi, Vernon, and Harrington (2005, 858) point out, "the general consensus of the econometric studies is that there is no evidence of a substantial impact of OSHA." On the other hand, narrower studies do seem to show some effect, though the evidence is mixed.[13] There is one carefully done study by Gray and Scholz on the impact of OSHA enforcement on workplace injuries at 6,842 manufacturing plants from 1979 to 1985 that indicates more significant effects:

> the results confirm that inspections with penalty have significant effects on both the frequency and severity of injury rates of the inspected plant. These effects continue for up to three years after the inspection, with the largest impact taking place in the first and second year after the inspection. The imposition of a penalty apparently triggers greater attention to safety in the plants, with cumulative effects that permanently reduce the level of injuries....
>
> Our analysis supports the conclusion that specific deterrence from enforcement actions can be effective in changing business behavior in ways that advance the goals of regulatory statutes. Specifically, we find a significant negative relationship between OSHA inspections that impose a penalty and the change in injuries at the penalized plant over subsequent years. In our analysis, an inspection imposing a penalty reduces injuries by 22% over a three-year period, and reduces lost workdays by 20%. This relationship holds even after testing and controlling for potential biases resulting from fixed effects, serially correlated injuries, and endogenous inspections. (Gray and Scholz 1993, 197, 199)

The problem, of course, is that OSHA only inspects a small fraction of even the relatively dangerous workplaces in the nation.

Finally, Bardach and Kagan (1982, 93–99) cite a number of direct salutary effects of OSHA regulations in the copper smelting, coal mining, automobile, and nursing home industries. As for indirect effects of OSHA, perhaps the most important one, as these authors point out, has been to enhance the power and status of industrial hygienists and other compliance officers within the corporate hierarchy. Without the threat of OSHA inspections and fines, they have less power over production managers, who are responsible for day-to-day operations. It would be a mistake, however, to think that if OSHA were abolished, everything else would remain the same. For example, with OSHA no longer threatening and fining firms for safety violations on the few occasions when they come around, insurance companies might become more proactive about workplace safety programs.[14] In addition, if the Texas model were adopted, firms of any size that opted out of WCI would have a significant incentive to operate safely. They could be sued for negligence, and they are without the body armor provided by the traditional common law defenses.

Workplace health and safety conditions were serious problems— around the turn of the twentieth century. The government response was to mandate WCI, which, despite its problems, might have been a good idea at the time and indeed might be a good idea now. When the regulatory regime of OSHA was installed, however, it was in the midst of a long-term secular decline in workplace accidents and injuries. It is at least arguable that, when everything is considered, whatever good it has done has been outweighed by the problems it has caused and the costs it has imposed.

Consumer Product Health and Safety Regulation: The Food and Drug Administration

There are primarily four government agencies concerned with regulation of the health and safety characteristics of consumer products. The Consumer Product Safety Commission (CPSC) regulates the health and safety characteristics of most consumer products. The National Highway Traffic Safety Administration (NHTSA) and the Federal Aviation Administration (FAA) regulate automotive and aviation products, respectively. Finally, the Food and Drug Administration (FDA) regulates medicines and medical devices, as well as some food products; other food products (e.g., meat inspections) are regulated by the Department of Agriculture. Other federal agencies that have regulatory powers related to health and safety include the Environmental Protection Agency (EPA), the Bureau of Alcohol, Tobacco and Firearms (ATF), and a host of other agencies too numerous to mention. A discussion of all these regulatory regimes goes beyond what could be accomplished here, so we shall restrict our attention to the two regimes that have the largest impact and are central to the modern liberal regulatory agenda: the regulatory regime of the FDA and that of the CPSC. Of these two, the regulatory footprint of the FDA is by far the largest: it has approximately 10,000 employees, a budget of over

$1 billion, and it regulates consumer products estimated to be worth over $1 trillion dollars (Miller 2000, xvii). Let us begin with this organization and the regulatory regime it enforces for therapeutic drugs.

The FDA was officially created in 1927, but its roots go back at least to the Pure Food and Drug Act of 1906 and the Meat Inspection Act of the same year. These were the first federal efforts to regulate food and drugs that go beyond what is provided for in the common law. Both acts were responses to problems in the food supply and problems in the marketing and sale of medical products.[15] Specifically, the Meat Inspection Act (administered by the Department of Agriculture) was a response to Upton Sinclair's exposé of the meat-packing industry in *The Jungle*. More generally, in the latter half of the nineteenth century and into the early twentieth century, food products were often mislabeled, and no one knew the effects of the chemicals being used as additives and preservatives. On the medical side, so-called patent medicines were not actually medicines that were patented; instead, they were medicines whose makers refused to list their ingredients! Most of these so-called medicines were ineffective at best and positively harmful at worst. Although some states had passed laws against the worst practices, not all of them did, and many of these laws were only indifferently enforced. Tort law was not very helpful in curbing any of the abuses because at the time, plaintiffs were required to prove fault or negligence (Friedman 1973, 351–52). Since claims of efficacy for medicines could be neither proved nor disproved, there was no way to hold companies responsible for these claims made on behalf of their products unless one could show that they knew, or should have known, that the claims were false. The doctrine of privity of contract, which requires that a purchaser of a product must have a contractual relationship with the seller in order to bring suit, also played a role in insulating manufacturers from facing the consequences of their bad behavior. This prevented lawsuits against the manufacturer of all sorts of defective products, including medical products, since they were sold through retailers. This doctrine was gradually worn away in the twentieth century, however, beginning with *MacPherson v. Buick Motor Co.,* 217 N.Y. 382 (1916). This gave birth to modern products liability law, which does not require privity of contract. The important point for what is to follow is that in the early twentieth century, the common law was incapable of addressing the abuses of the food and drug manufacturers.

Partly in response to this, the 1906 act provided criminal penalties for adulteration and mislabeling of food and medicine, and
amendments in 1912 criminalized false and misleading claims
about efficacy. The act did not require drugs to have government
approval nor were doctors' prescriptions required for drugs to be
purchased. In 1937, however, 108 people, many of them children,
died as a result of consuming a liquid form of sulfanilamide (a sulfa
drug). Though the manufacturer, Samuel Massengill, was found
guilty of gross negligence under tort law in Tennessee, the tragedy
spurred the passage of the 1938 Federal Food, Drug, and Cosmetic
Act (21 U.S.C. § 301 et seq.), which the FDA was to administer.
Perhaps the most important provision of this law was the requirement that firms had to have prior government approval before they
could market or sell a new drug. A firm had to submit a new drug
application (NDA), which explained the proposed use(s) of the
drug and provided documentation that the drug was "safe." The act
also contained an obscure paragraph on labeling, which the FDA
subsequently interpreted to require that some drugs could not be
purchased unless they were prescribed by a physician.[16] That interpretation was codified in the law in an amendment to the 1938 act
passed in 1951. The 1938 act also gave the FDA power to regulate
cosmetics and medical devices. Amendments to the act passed in
1962 (codified at 21 U.S.C. § 355(d)) went much further, requiring
that new drugs be proved effective as well as safe; or to be more
precise, there had to be substantial evidence that the drug is effective. In addition, it changed the default mode of FDA action from
approval to disapproval. In other words, prior to these amendments a drug was approved unless the FDA disapproved it within
sixty days. After the Kefauver-Harris amendments of 1962, the drug
could not be sold until it was approved. Partly as a result, and partly
because the increasingly elaborate hurdles new drugs had to clear,
the approval process got much longer and much more expensive.
These amendments also required preclearance of all human testing,
and they gave the FDA the power to regulate drug and device advertising and manufacturing.

The two most important features of the current drug regulatory
regime are (1) the requirement that some drugs (the list of which
is now determined by the FDA) can be sold only by prescription,
whereas other drugs can be sold "over the counter," and (2) the
requirement that all new drugs be proved safe and effective according to FDA standards. The former has been a boon to physicians

over the years, as patients have had to schedule a doctor's visit to get medicines that, under other regulatory regimes (including the regime in place in 1938), they could simply purchase at a pharmacy. It also diminished the role and importance of the pharmacist. Prior to the 1938 act, anyone could purchase any nonnarcotic therapeutic drug directly from a pharmacist, but shortly after the passage of the act this changed. (Actually, there were very few therapeutic drugs at the time; pharmacists sold mostly patent medicines and home remedies.) The FDA's motive for more or less creating this regulation out of thin air might have been a concern for patient safety. They might have believed that some drugs were safe enough to be sold on the market but too dangerous to be taken without a doctor's approval and (notional) oversight. Alternatively, they might have thought that it was unsafe for patients to self-medicate and that if they sought advice from pharmacists, pharmacists would in effect be playing the role of the physician and might also have a conflict of interest. Another possible motive is a concern for efficacy. If patients had to seek a doctors' diagnosis, they may be more likely to be cured. But all of this is pure speculation, since regulators left no record of their real motives. At first, the FDA left it up to the manufacturers to decide which drugs would be sold only by prescription, though the FDA could contest the manufacturer's decision in court. In the Humphrey-Durham amendment of 1951, a legal definition of a prescription drug was given (21 U.S.C. § 353(b), (c)), and the designation of which drugs would be sold only by prescription was put into the hands of the FDA.

The postwar revolution in pharmaceuticals that stretched into the 1950s resulted in the FDA getting much bigger, and by 1962 it was ready to take on the larger role that it currently plays. The 1962 amendments were very important because they signaled the completion of a sea change in how the government conceived of its role regarding medical products. The 1906 act moved certain categories of misbehavior from tort law to criminal law and federalized this form of misbehavior, but the scope and purpose of government activity in this area did not change. The 1938 act, however, signaled a more significant change in the government's approach to medical products. The requirement that drugs be shown to be safe and the requirement that a patient have a prescription for some medications made it more difficult for consumers to be in charge of their own medical care. When it came to new drugs, however, physicians were not thought to be qualified to judge safety either. Under the circumstances, and especially given the historical circumstances of the use of patent medicines and outright quackery, it was only natural to suppose that a specialized, independent, nonpolitical government agency should assure drug safety. Taken together, these changes implied that the FDA had taken on the role of guarantor of the safety of all drugs and medical devices.

In 1962, the thalidomide tragedy occurred in Europe. It largely missed the United States because an FDA examiner, Dr. Frances Kelsey, was not convinced of its safety and refused to approve it. (Dr. Kelsey's concerns were with certain neurological side effects, not with phocomelia, the condition of being born without arms or legs, which is now associated with the drug.) This tragedy gave new impetus to what would become the 1962 amendments to the 1938 act, though the latter already prohibited the marketing of drugs whose safety had not been established. Nevertheless, the 1962 amendments can be seen as an attempt to plug the remaining gaps in a regulatory system designed to guarantee drug safety and efficacy: it changed the default decision from approval to disapproval, required preclearance of human subject testing, and gave the FDA regulatory control of manufacturing.

Perhaps the biggest change these amendments brought about was the assignment to the FDA the task of assuring drug efficacy as well as safety. The reason they had not done this before is of some independent interest. A 1911 Supreme Court case (*U.S. v. Johnson,* 221 U.S. 488 (1911)) involved a product whose label suggested or implied that it was effective in curing cancer. Regulations in force at the time prohibited that sort of advertising, so the shipper of the product was indicted and tried for violating the law. The Supreme Court found in favor of the shipper, however, on the grounds that the 1906 statute only covered such properties as ingredients, strength, purity, et cetera. Claims about efficacy were opinion, not fact, reasoned Justice Holmes, who wrote the majority opinion, and as such were constitutionally protected (ibid, 497, 498). By the early 1960s, however, this distinction was no longer tenable. Not only had legal distinctions been drawn between commercial and noncommercial speech, claims of efficacy could be tested empirically, and that was required for new drugs by the 1962 amendments. Actual proof of efficacy—whatever that might mean—was not required, but there had to be "substantial evidence that the drug will have the effect it purports or is represented to have" (U.S.C. § 355(d)(5)). It also demonstrated that the FDA did not believe that doctors were capable of determining, through their own clinical experience, the efficacy of the drugs they were prescribing. Their clinical observations were unscientific; the drug manufacturers, checked by the FDA, had to establish evidence of efficacy. What developed over the years, as a result of cooperation between the FDA and the drug companies, was the modern, large-scale, controlled clinical trial by which new drugs are now routinely tested for both safety and efficacy.

As a result of the 1962 amendments, the mandate to determine the efficacy of drugs created a huge task for the FDA, since they had to certify the efficacy of all the drugs, which numbered in the thousands, that had been approved since 1938 (Temin 1980, 128–32). Drugs approved prior to 1938 were "grandfathered in," but the law required testing of drugs approved between 1938 and 1962. The FDA contracted out the study of all these other drugs to the National Research Council of the National Academy of Sciences. They in turn formed thirty panels of six experts each, all of whom were physicians with academic affiliations. To assess the efficacy of these drugs, they used information provided by the drug companies and published studies, if there were any, but they refused to allow the drug companies to make presentations or question their summary of the evidence. In addition, the panel was allowed to use their "informal judgment," which meant their own personal clinical experience with the drug. In effect, then, six experts were deciding for the entire country whether or not a drug already approved for its safety was also effective. For many of these drugs, there really was not much scientifically rigorous information about efficacy, even from the drug companies. So, they had to rely on, as Justice Holmes put it in *Johnson*, "opinion." The way it worked out, then, was that these panels were permitted, and indeed required, to substitute their own clinical judgment for that of (other) practicing physicians.

The final hole to be plugged was the class of grandfathered drugs, that is, drugs that had been in use prior to 1938 and were sold over the counter. (The law had also set up a review process for the new over-the-counter drugs.) The FDA clearly wanted to certify the grandfathered drugs as effective or get them pulled from the market, but the statute did not seem to permit that. They argued, however, that although these drugs did not have to have an approved NDA, they were subject to all the other laws, including the law on misbranding. To find out if these drugs were misbranded, they had to be subjected to a review, which they were, and some were pulled. By the mid-

1960s the FDA had assumed complete responsibility for the safety and efficacy of all medicines and medical devices.

What argument might be offered for this highly paternalistic regulatory regime? Recall that it has two defining features: (1) new therapeutic drugs must be demonstrated safe and effective to an independent government agency, and (2) most drugs can only be dispensed with a doctor's prescription, which certifies that a knowledgeable professional believes that the drug in a certain dosage is appropriate treatment for the patient's condition. Much of the case for the FDA rests on the bad behavior, both real and imagined, of the drug manufacturers. The fundamental problem is that issues of drug safety and efficacy are often not clear cut. Drug companies can make claims of safety and efficacy that are hard to prove or disprove. They are inclined to hype their products, sometimes just lying to consumers. Even when they do not lie, they have a tendency to distort the truth in ways that are beneficial to them and detrimental to the interests of consumers.[17] But, sometimes they are right that the safety concerns about their products are unwarranted and that the latter really are efficacious, even if it is hard to prove. About these matters, there can be reasonable disagreement about what the evidence shows. A person takes a drug for some medical condition and shortly thereafter has some kind of physical problem. Was the drug a causal factor in producing the problem or would the problem have developed anyway? A person has a medical problem, takes a medication, and the problem goes away. Did the drug cure it? Or did something else cause the problem to go away? Often it is hard to know. Safety and efficacy are two sides of the same coin, since they both involve questions of causation. Sometimes, answers to those questions are reasonably clear but oftentimes they are not.

In light of these basic facts about the drug market, one obvious argument for the current regime appeals to the relative ignorance of the consumer about safety and efficacy. Consumers simply do not know enough to judge the safety and efficacy of therapeutic drugs and suffer a further disadvantage because they have a health problem, which makes them vulnerable. Besides, consumers are unable to process and evaluate whatever scientific information producers might make available, so it is not as if the problem could be solved by requiring manufacturers to provide accurate information. After all, they do provide such information, but in a font size that only Tom Thumb can read. A specialized and impartial agency has to do this.

Indeed, doctors, as well as patients, are ill-equipped to assess safety, and the former are only slightly better at assessing efficacy, based on their clinical experience. Medical products are simply too important to people's well-being to allow them to take products that have not been demonstrated to the satisfaction of independent experts that they are safe and effective. While the government cannot ensure the safety and efficacy of all consumer products, they can do it for prescription drugs. Finally, the doctor's prescription ensures that the medication being taken is appropriate to the condition from which the person suffers. There are, of course, many things that could be done to improve the FDA and its operations, but this basic regulatory structure is the most effective way to ensure the safety and well-being of all consumers of therapeutic drugs. This is a fairly straightforward argument for the current regulatory regime for medical products. It relies on no deep or controversial theories or political principles and is close to the surface, as conversion arguments usually are. What might classical liberals say in response?

Critics of the current regulatory regime could concede that the creation of the FDA was a rational response to problems in the markets for food and medical products in the early twentieth century.[18] Hilts (2003, 25) reports that at one time there were over 15,000 of them, many of them concocted by fly-by-night operations. Labels contained no list of ingredients nor did they have to provide any evidence for the grandiose claims made for these products.[19] In the late nineteenth century and early twentieth century, the nature of the market and the relatively undeveloped state of tort law meant legal institutions could provide little help. Privity of contract still reigned. Statutes passed by the states that were specifically addressed to these problems were indifferently enforced. However, both the markets in medical drugs and devices and tort and contract law are very different now; in light of those differences, critics charge, a much less paternalistic medical regulatory regime would be most appropriate. But why should major changes be made? Would it not be safer to just leave the current regime in place? The answer is "no," and this brings us to the critics' most serious charge against the FDA: it has been a major force in retarding progress in medical science and has been directly or indirectly responsible for literally thousands of unnecessary deaths.

In 1994, it is estimated that at least 106,000 hospital patients died from adverse reactions to "safe," FDA-approved drugs. This excluded errors in drug administration, noncompliance, overdose, drug abuse, therapeutic failures, and merely possible adverse drug reactions (Lazarou et al. 1998, 1200–5). Part of the mission of the FDA is "to protect the public health by ensuring that…drugs are safe and effective" (21 U.S.C. § 393(b)). Based on the wording of their mission, they have failed. These drugs are not safe. Of course, defenders of the FDA would make the obvious point that no drug is completely safe, and no review process can prevent all adverse drug reactions, since there are individual variations in how patients respond to medication; this means that some adverse events are inevitable. Once that is acknowledged, however, the question is no longer one of what procedures will guarantee that all drugs are "safe and effective," since that is plainly impossible. Setting an impossible goal in enabling legislation for a bureaucracy is an invitation for it to expand its mission indefinitely and to permit it to exercise its power arbitrarily—always bad things from any liberal point of view. Instead, the question becomes how much mortality and morbidity a regulatory regime will permit. On this score, the FDA has not done well. A variety of evidence supports this contention.

One concerns the approval time for new drugs. There are different estimates about the length of the approval process for new drugs. The FDA's own Web site shows a steady decline in what they call the New Drug Approval Time, from over thirty months in 1986 to a little over fifteen months in 2000—almost a 50 percent reduction. The New Drug Approval Time is defined as the amount of time from the first NDA submission to NDA approval.[20] This figure is highly misleading, however, since it does not include the investigational stage of the drug approval process. This stage, which starts when an Investigational New Drug Application [INDA] is filed, includes the time period during which all the clinical trials demanded by the FDA are done. Those trials are getting bigger and more expensive. In 1980, the typical drug underwent about thirty clinical trials involving about fifteen hundred subjects. By the mid-1990s, the typical drug had to undergo more than sixty clinical trials involving nearly five thousand subjects (Miller 2000, 20–21). By the FDA's own estimate, when the clinical trials stage is factored in, the entire approval process takes about nine years.[21] Another estimate (by the Tufts Center for the Study of Drug Development) gives a figure of ten to fifteen years.[22] Not all of this is the agency's fault. Sometimes the NDA is incomplete or backed by trials of dubious methodology, and it has to be returned to the drug company, in which case it is the company's fault.[23] In addition, it is arguable that the agency has been periodically underfunded by Congress. As in the case of OSHA, the elected branches of government often indulge in symbolic action when passing laws and creating agencies but then are unwilling to spend the money necessary for the agency to fulfill its mandate. Whatever the source of the delays, however, inordinately lengthy approval times have been a significant problem. These delays have had a number of important negative consequences. The most obvious is that people die or do not get relief from suffering that they would have gotten if the drug approval process were shorter. This is sometimes called "the drug lag problem," and after the 1962 amendments, it became serious, as delays got longer and longer.

The drug lag problem has led to increased mortality and morbidity. One of the most striking cases concerns a family of heart medications known as beta-blockers. Although the first of these drugs, propranolol, was approved in 1968 (three years after it was approved in Great Britain), the FDA delayed the approval of other beta-blockers. As Dale Gieringer tells the story,

> finally, in November 1981, the FDA announced its approval of a new beta blocker, timolol, for an innovative indication, the prevention of second heart attacks. The FDA's action was based on a study published seven months earlier, showing that timolol could reduce mortality from second heart attacks by enough to save an estimated 6,500 to 10,000 lives per year in the United States. [According to FDA estimates: *Wall Street Journal,* November 27, 1981, 5] At this rate, it can be estimated that some 4,000 to 5,800 preventable deaths occurred during the seven months required by the FDA for its purportedly expedited approval. However, as noted by Wardell [1978], there had been clinical evidence for the efficacy of beta blockers in preventing second heart attacks as early as 1974. The total cost of this seven-year delay could then be put at some 45,000 to 70,000 lives—several times greater than all the casualties resulting from thalidomide and other major new drug disasters (Gieringer 1985, 190).[24]

After many years and mounting criticism, this problem has been partially addressed by various reforms. Some of the most important of these reforms include: (1) ANDAs (abbreviated new drug applications), (2) hiring more staff funded by user fees, which were permitted by the Prescription Drug User Fee Act of 1992, (3) parallel tracking, treatment INDs, and accelerated development status for new drugs that treat life-threatening conditions. Each of these requires a bit of explanation. (1) Prior to the passage of the Hatch-Waxman Act of 1984, makers of generic drugs had to submit independent evidence of the safety and efficacy of bioequivalent drugs that they were going to manufacture when a patent on a patented drug expired. This meant repeating many of the clinical trials that had been done by the initial patent holder. This made many drugs uneconomical to produce as generics. The 1984 act removed that requirement and allowed drug manufacturers to get approval on proof of bioequivalence alone. (2) In 1992, Congress permitted the FDA to impose user fees on drug manufacturers to hire more staff and clear up the backlog of NDAs. This has been reauthorized every five years, and although fees have gone up, it has reduced the delays in getting the NDAs through the system. (3) As a result of pressure from AIDS activists in the late 1980s, the FDA allowed drugs that showed some promise of treating life-threatening conditions to short-circuit the approval process in limited ways. Still, long delays persist.

Distinct from the delay problem is the cost problem. The elaborate requirements that must be met for a NDA to be approved, as well as the delays just discussed, significantly increase the total cost of developing a drug. Estimates of the latter vary, but two recent estimates put the cost of developing a drug at $802 million in 2000 dollars (DiMasi et al. 2003, 173) and upwards of $1 billion (Adams and Brantner 2005, 13). These figures are arrived at by factoring in the costs of investigational work on products that do not pan out. This enormous cost makes it unprofitable for drug companies to develop drugs to treat relatively rare conditions, so-called "orphan drugs." Twenty-one years after the passage of the 1962 amendments, the problem was officially recognized when Congress passed the Orphan Drug Act (21 U.S.C. § 360aa–360ee). How much mortality and morbidity occurred during this time period because orphaned drugs were not developed due to the high cost of the FDA-mandated approval process is difficult to say, but it was undoubtedly not nothing. Nevertheless, Congress eventually did act. Instead of simplifying the approval process, however, the government now subsidizes the development of any drug for which there are 200,000 or fewer patients in the United States (regardless of how many patients there are worldwide) by giving grants to defray the costs of testing and tax credits for development costs. They also grant the maker a special kind of monopoly; specifically they will not approve any other drug that can be used to treat the same condition for a period of seven years, even if the other drug were to be developed to treat some other condition. The drug companies have gamed the system, slicing and dicing their patient populations to get under the 200,000 figure, and they have been able to ignore not only overseas patients but also the expected growth in the patient population in the United States. AZT, for example, got orphan drug status even though sales were easily projected to be in the billions. In these and other ways, drugs that would have been produced anyway got orphan status, and competitor drugs that might treat other conditions are kept off the market for seven years. The drug company's incentives are to file for orphan drug status for those drugs near the borderline of the qualifying criteria that are least likely to need the program. How many truly orphaned drugs get produced as a result of this program is hard to say. Whatever the figure and regardless of how many new orphan drugs are invented or discovered, there is no doubt that fewer drugs are produced and marketed than would otherwise be the case if the approval process were not as expensive as it is. This is sometimes called, "the drug loss problem."

What is true of therapeutic drugs is true of medical devices. These range from tongue depressors to Magnetic Resonance Imaging (MRI) machines. The FDA divides these into three classes. Class I devices (e.g., tongue depressors) are subject only to Good Manufacturing Practices regulations and some reporting requirements. Class II devices are subject to specific performance standards as well. Examples of Class II devices include powered wheelchairs, infusion pumps, and surgical drapes. Class III devices are those that support or sustain human life or that present risk of serious injury or illness if they malfunction, such as heart-lung machines. This class also includes new devices for which there are no substantially similar products on the market. For all Class III devices, a premarket approval (PMA) is required. As the FDA explains it, "PMA approval is based on a determination by FDA that the PMA contains sufficient valid scientific evidence to assure that the device is safe and effective for its intended use(s)." Elaborate regulations have been developed to specify what is required for a PMA.[25] Though the approval process can be shorter than it is for a new drug, the FDA demands documentation about safety and effectiveness before granting a PMA. This has led to various horror stories, such as the one involving the Sensor Pad, which is two sheets of plastic that sandwich a silicone lubricant. This device makes it easier for women to perform breast self-examinations. Because there was nothing like it on the market, the FDA classified it as a high-risk

Class III device, and demanded extensive documentation of its safety and effectiveness—documentation that the inventor was in no financial condition to supply. Eventually, this problem got some public exposure, and the FDA backed down and, after ten years, they finally approved it.[26] The problem of "device loss" and "device lag" exist, just as they do for drugs.

A more radical criticism aims at the double-blind clinical trial process used to determine efficacy, at least when patients have a life-threatening condition. Central to this process is the use of placebos in Phase II and Phase III clinical trials on a random selection of patients. Critic Steve Walker explains the fundamental problem vividly as follows:

> How do you take a rational person and get that person to enroll in a double-blind, randomized clinical trial?...How do you get people to do that? You give them no other choice. They're not lives worth saving. They're lives worth using. If you can't get into the trial, they can't use your life. They need two piles of bodies.[27]

It will not do to give access to the drug to those who have been denied admission to the trial, since patients (and their doctors) will find ways to game the system to get denied admission into the trials. The basic problem is that, when one's life is at stake, no one wants to get the placebo, even if, as in the case of developmental cancer drugs, 94 percent of them do not work. Nor do drug companies have any interest in selling their drugs prior to approval by the FDA, since any adverse event could be used to argue against approval. Finally, under current law, patients cannot waive liability for negligence.[28]

There is one final problem the FDA is responsible for that warrants some discussion: its attempt to suppress the exchange of information about off-label uses of prescription drugs. Until a few years ago when the courts reined them in, the FDA's control over product labeling led them to prohibit manufacturers from advertising so-called "off-label" uses of prescription drugs to physicians (Randall 1991, 11). When drugs are approved, they are approved only for certain uses or conditions, but physicians can legally prescribe the drug for any condition they deem appropriate. In other words, the FDA cannot tell doctors what drug to prescribe for what condition. When clinical experience revealed a new use for the drug, the FDA tried to prevent manufacturers from advertising that to other physicians or to the general public without going through the regulatory approval process for the new use, which may very well not be cost-effective, especially if the drug is no longer under patent. Although they do not have to reestablish the safety of the drug for the new use, they do have to establish efficacy, which is the most costly and time-consuming phase of the clinical trials. Two examples: amoxicillin is now a standard treatment for stomach ulcers, since it was discovered that many stomach ulcers are caused by a bacterium (*H. pylori*). It has never been approved by the FDA for this use, and because it is no longer under patent, it probably never will be, due to the expense of the clinical trials. A doctor would be negligent, however, if he did not consider antibiotics when treating stomach ulcers. To take another example, aspirin can reduce the risk of heart attack. For years, the FDA suppressed this information because no drug company would undertake the clinical trials necessary to get this over-the-counter drug approved for this use. In recent years, they have relented and allowed some advertising regarding this use, but it is reasonable to suppose that thousands of people would have been spared fatal heart attacks if this information had been widely available when the substantial evidence accumulated about the efficacy of a low-dose aspirin regimen for reducing the risk of heart attack. More generally, because of FDA efforts, information about off-label uses has not been disseminated as widely as it could be.

Why do physicians prescribe off-label? Sometimes, discovery of an off-label use is serendipitous. Another reason is that best practices are simply ineffective with some patients, who then request or demand that their physicians try something else. Off-label uses also occur with "orphan populations," that is, populations for whom the drug has not been evaluated (e.g., children). Finally, in the case of terminal patients, they have less, sometimes nothing, to lose by trying something different. Although off-label prescribing varies widely, it is most common in treating AIDS, cancer, pediatric illnesses, and skin disorders.[29] The FDA, however, has sought to keep control over the uses of therapeutic drugs. As noted above, mission creep is built into their legislative mandate, which is to assure the U.S. public of safe and effective medical products. To control as best they can the uses of prescription medication, they have tried to shut down avenues of communication between those who learn about new uses for previously approved drugs (physicians and researchers who have discovered off-labels uses) and those who could use that information (other physicians and the general public). The FDA was apparently so worried about inflated or misleading claims made by drug companies on behalf of various products that they even prohibited manufacturers from disseminating offprints of peer-reviewed journal articles and copied pages from the latest textbooks to physicians, as well as less controlled clinical information, about new off-label uses. Eventually, the courts reined in the FDA by striking down the restrictions on peer-reviewed journal articles and textbooks as a violation of the commercial free speech rights of the manufacturers, but they still get to impose other restrictions on disseminating this information.[30] They have even permitted advertising to the general public but only fairly recently. Admittedly, clinical information may often not rise above the level of anecdote and drug companies would undoubtedly hype their products if the "results" of off-label prescribing were permitted to be more widely disseminated. But the liberal remedy (both classical and modern) for undesirable speech is always more speech, not censorship. More on this shortly.

All of the problems detailed above could be ameliorated by thoughtful and intelligent reforms of the FDA, undertaken internally or as a result of external pressure. But there are serious limits to how far reforms can go as long as the mission of the FDA remains what it is, as stated at 21 U.S.C. § 393(b): "the [Food and Drug] Administration shall...protect the public health by ensuring that...drugs are safe and effective [and by providing]...reasonable assurance of the safety and effectiveness of devices intended for human use." This part of the mission statement is what requires the agency to be ultimately responsible for the safety and efficacy of all drugs and medical devices, and that is where the problem lies.

To see why, notice that there are two types of errors that can be made in approving drugs, Type I and Type II errors. Type I errors involve approving a drug that will end up causing net harm to society (however one calculates the costs and benefits of a drug). For example, a drug saves the lives of some people with a life-threatening condition, but it kills more people than it saves. That would be a Type I error. Type II errors involve rejecting a drug that will end up causing a net benefit to society. A Type II error can also occur when the government demands more testing, which causes delays that unnecessarily increase the costs (not only financial but also in mortality and morbidity from the condition the drug is intended to treat). As the ultimately responsible party for the safety of all drugs and medical devices, the FDA has asymmetric incentives regarding these errors. Specifically, it has very strong incentives to avoid Type I errors and relatively weaker incentives to avoid Type II errors. The reasons for this are obvious. Type I errors produce identifiable victims. They also produce unwanted media attention, and on many occasions, congressional hearings where regulators are called upon to explain their decisions and where their motives and integrity are impugned. Richard Merrell, former chief counsel for the FDA, has said,

> it is always safer for agency officials to prevent the marketing of products that entail physical risk—regardless of what benefits they provide. No FDA official has ever been publicly criticized for *refusing to allow* the marketing of a drug. Many, however, have paid the price of public criticism, sometimes accompanied by an innuendo of corruptibility for approving a product that could cause harm. (Quoted in Shapiro, 1979: 813–14n86)

Former FDA commissioner Alexander Schmidt was also clear about FDA incentives, stating,

> in all of FDA's history, I am unable to find a single instance where a Congressional committee investigated the *failure* of FDA to approve a new drug. But, the times when hearings have been held to criticize our approval of new drugs have been so frequent that we are not able to count them.... The message of FDA staff could not be clearer. Whenever a controversy over a new drug is resolved by its approval, the Agency and the individuals involved will be investigated. Whenever such a drug is disapproved, no inquiry will be made. The Congressional pressure for our *negative* action on new drug applications is therefore intense.[31]

By contrast, the victims of Type II errors are merely statistical in the sense of not being personally identifiable. If the FDA rejects a drug that would save lives or demands more tests or otherwise delays the approval of a drug that ultimately gets approved, the unknown victims, their families, and their physicians are none the wiser. They die or suffer in ignorance. Let a Type I error occur, however, and the heat is on. Of course, the greedy drug companies are ultimately to blame in the news media morality plays where someone always has to wear the black hat and twirl the mustache, but the FDA can always be roped in as an accomplice for bowing to industry pressure to approve the NDA. Type I errors bring unwanted attention to the FDA and make the lives of everyone involved at the agency more difficult. The goal should be to minimize the sum of the two types of errors, but the asymmetric incentives leads to more Type II errors than there should be.

Critics of the FDA sometimes overstate the problem by claiming that there are no incentives for regulators to avoid Type II errors, but that is not quite correct. The regulators and the drug company scientists are aware of the possibility of Type II errors, and to the extent that they are good scientists, they want to avoid them. Regulators will also come under pressure from those in the drug industry with whom they deal with on a regular basis, and they will be on the receiving end of whatever pressures the drug companies themselves can bring to bear to approve drugs more quickly.[32] Finally, they have to worry about economists breathing down their necks about Type II errors. All these pressures are more easily resisted, however, since the consequences of resisting them for the individual scientist or decision-maker are less dire than pressure brought to bear when Type I errors are made. Again, the heart of the problem lies in the ultimate responsibility that the FDA has for the safety and efficacy of all medical products. In a system in which no one has that responsibility, this asymmetry would not exist.

To illustrate, consider an area where the government does not assume ultimate responsibility for people's safety: the use of automobiles. Although NHTSA orders auto manufacturers to install various safety devices and lawsuits reveal the grisly calculations that lie behind some design decisions, no one doubts that the lion's share of responsibility for auto accidents lies with the individual driver. Drugs are not like that, however, since people are not at fault for adverse drug events. They do not "do" anything; they are just patients. By contrast, even though NHTSA sets safety standards for automobiles, they typically do not get blamed when people are hurt or killed. Nor do the manufacturers—with some spectacular exceptions. Compare the language of the enabling legislation for the NHTSA:

> The purpose of this chapter is to reduce traffic accidents and deaths and injuries resulting from traffic accidents. Therefore it is necessary—
>
> (1) to prescribe motor vehicle safety standards for motor vehicles and motor vehicle equipment in interstate commerce; and
>
> (2) to carry out needed safety research and development. (49 U.S.C. § 30101)

Notice that the purpose is to *reduce* traffic accidents, et cetera. They are not to ensure that every automobile is "safe." Such language would be instantly recognized as demanding the impossible or as being simply meaningless.

How, then, can this bias in favor of preventing Type I errors and against preventing Type II errors in the drug approval process be corrected? Indeed, there is a broader question about all the problems with the FDA discussed above. None of them amounts to anything unless there is a feasible alternative to the current regulatory regime that does better. Otherwise, these criticisms are like the old socialist criticisms of capitalism—criticisms that ultimately carried no weight because those who offered them could not articulate a socialist alternative and explain how it would avoid the problems of capitalism.

As noted earlier, critics can concede that the creation of the FDA might have been a rational response to problems in the food, drug, and cosmetic industries at the time. The question now is whether it should continue to exist as currently constituted. The case against the FDA as currently constituted is incomplete if it consists of nothing more than excoriating the agency for the statistical deaths and morbidity it is responsible for. What is the alternative? Actually, there are many possible alternative regulatory regimes for therapeutic drugs, but all classical liberal versions have in common features that (1) decentralize decision-making to the point where no one agency, public or private, bears ultimate responsibility for the efficacy of new drugs and (2) reduce reliance on compulsion. One reform is to repeal that part of the 1962 amendments which requires that there be substantial evidence of effectiveness.[33] The reason for this is that although substantial evidence of effectiveness can be gathered, it is often very expensive in terms of time and money to do so. That fact is responsible for much of the drug lag and drug loss problems, as well as the high cost of prescription drugs, under the current regime. Phase II and Phase III clinical trials are the largest and most time-consuming part of the preapproval process and are intended to gather evidence of effectiveness. If drugs had to be approved for safety only, drug lag time would decrease significantly, as would costs, leading to the introduction of more drugs at lower prices. Type II errors would decline since some efficacious drugs would be approved even though the evidence to substantiate their efficacy would be ambiguous. It is true that so-called "innocuous drugs," which could and probably would be approved under such a regime, can present a hazard, if patients are taking them instead of efficacious medications. However, if there is already on the market a drug known to be effective in treating the condition, the patient would be taking it, or would have already taken it and found it did not do him any good; if there is no substitute, at least for him, then literally no harm is done by taking an innocuous drug.

In this instance, some plausible speculations can be made about what would happen if a major reform were to be instituted, but they remain speculations. Ordinarily, that is all that can be done, and it puts the reformer at an apparent disadvantage because there is no way of knowing with much assurance what would happen if the reforms were instituted. But in this case there is a natural ongoing experiment that has obvious implications for what would happen if the efficacy requirement were eliminated. That natural experiment is the current practice of off-label prescribing. This is done with drugs that have been approved for safety but have not been approved for efficacy in treating medical conditions not listed on the label. The off-label use of prescription drugs (which have been designated as "safe") is essentially unregulated. How, then, is information about off-label uses gathered and filtered? Peer-reviewed journal articles, rooted in clinical experience, are a major source of information, which in turn are reviewed and compiled for standard reference compendia such as *AMA Drug Evaluations, the American Hospital Formulary Service Drug Information,* and [USP's] *Drug Information for the Healthcare Provider* (Tabarrok 2000, 36). Another standard reference work is the *U.S. Pharmacopeia Drug Information,* which uses expert committees to compile and evaluate the dosing, indications, interactions, pharmacology/pharmacokinetics, and side/adverse effects of drugs for both labeled and off-label uses.[34] In the absence of FDA efforts to control the flow of information about prescription drugs, which includes the suppression of information about off-label uses, it is likely that other intermediaries will form to gather, process, and compile information relevant to assessing the efficacy of drugs. There is a kind of inconsistency in the current regulatory regime in that evidence of efficacy is required for first use but not subsequent use(s).[35]

On this proposal, companies could still avail themselves of FDA certification for efficacy for first or on-label use. On the one hand, the FDA has enormous resources, embedded institutional knowledge, and a good reputation, at least for its evaluation of clinical testing; dismantling it would be foolish. On the other hand, removing its stranglehold on certifying the efficacy of new drugs is not. That is the main bottleneck in the current system, and removing it would likely result in an increase in the flow of new drugs and therapies, since it would be much easier and less costly to get new products to market. Type II errors would decrease because there is no one entity responsible for making sure that drugs are efficacious. If certification of efficacy were not mandatory and monopolized by the FDA, alternative certifying agencies might come into existence. Competition, it is reasonable to suppose, would make the certification process more efficient.

What about safety? How would that be handled? There are a number of different possibilities. Michael Krauss (1996) has proposed allowing but not requiring FDA certification of safety as well as efficacy. Would this turn back the clock to the bad old days of the early twentieth century? Krauss doubts it. Markets for prescription drugs are much more sophisticated now than they were a hundred years ago. As always, tort and contract law would have to deal with bad outcomes, but that is the case now with off-label prescribing and all other aspects of the patient-physician relationship. Tort law, which barely existed until the late nineteenth century (Friedman 1973, 350–51), has developed considerably over the past century and has done so in ways that are relevant to the drug industry. Specifically, the common law negligence standard operates today in off-label prescribing. The same standard would apply even if drug companies did not have to get (safety) certification prior to marketing. This means that manufacturers could be sued for design defects (i.e., for putting a drug on the market that never should have been marketed because of safety defects, such as failure to do preclinical animal testing and Phase I human testing), and they would be liable for manufacturing defects and failures to warn about risks and side effects, as they are now. It is easy to imagine a role for government in setting labeling standards, as they do with toxic chemicals; this in turn might (partially) insulate manufacturers from suits based on a failure to warn. Though not part of Krauss's proposal, it might also be appropriate for the government to require that drug manufacturers have liability insurance, which would keep fly-by-night operations out of the market and also give someone an incentive to monitor the behavior of drug companies. Self-monitoring is generally insufficient and inefficient. A novel feature of Krauss's proposal is that he would give tort immunity for design defects in drugs that had been certified safe by the FDA. Physicians now have tort immunity when prescribing an FDA-approved drug for on-label use but not for off-label use (and that would continue under Krauss' proposal). Krauss would extend tort immunity for design defects to manufacturers whose drugs are FDA-approved for safety.

Once the FDA is no longer ultimately responsible for the safety of all medical products, the bias in favor of making Type II errors to avoid making Type I errors would further diminish. If someone is to blame, the FDA need not be implicated and thus would not feel compelled to make sure it did not happen again—by doing things that increase Type II errors. If blame were to fall on anyone, it would fall on the drug companies and any alternative certifying agency they might have used. Finally, it is likely that the use of FDA-approved drugs (for both safety and efficacy) would be the norm, though not universal. Krauss says,

> note that these new [i.e., non-FDA-certified] drugs would likely fill very urgent medical needs: the relative tort protection provided by FDA certification means that physicians would likely need good reasons for utilizing non-FDA approved drugs or devices if there exists FDA-certified alternative treatments. (Krauss 1996, 478)

As Krauss points out in a footnote to this passage, the kind of good reasons he has in mind are superior reported efficacy for some patients (especially those with life-threatening conditions), enhanced safety, or lower price (due to the high costs of FDA certification) for low-income patients. The latter possibility would undoubtedly cause egalitarian radar to be switched on, since it means the poor could end up getting drugs that are inferior to drugs purchased by people who are better off. Pursuing the ramifications of this possibility would require a deep foray into health care financing from which a safe return is doubtful.

There are other intermediaries in the market for prescription drugs that would probably play an important role in assuring the safety and efficacy of medical products. The most important of these are the HMOs and insurance companies who pay the bills. As Henry Miller has observed,

> [p]rofound changes have resulted from the evolution of various nongovernmental entities into *de facto* drug-vetting, standard-setting organizations. The newest and most potent of these are managed-care organizations, which exercise their influence

through large-scale purchasing, monitoring, formularies, and drug utilization reviews.…[Computerized systems] perform overall integration of the medical record for case management. A physician can be prevented from prescribing medication if, for example, according to computerized monitoring of his decisions, the drug is inconsistent with a patient's listed diagnosis; excessive in dose, frequency, or length of administration; or likely to interact dangerously with another medication the patient is taking.…In a sense the HMO has become a second gatekeeper between the manufacturer and the patient. (Miller 2000, 29)

The motivation for all of these proposed changes is to break the monopoly power of the FDA. That monopoly power is responsible for a host of ills in the current regulatory regime: the bias toward Type II errors, the inordinate delays, the overregulation of medical devices, and, in part anyway, the high cost of prescription drugs. This proposal also decentralizes decision-making and makes maximum use of local knowledge, here knowledge of the patient's condition, other therapies that have been tried, attitude toward risk, goals, et cetera, in making medication decisions. Decentralizing decision-making to the level where highly particular knowledge is to be found is behind the classical liberal inclination to privatize many functions that the state has assumed over the past century; it is not some blind, ideologically driven faith in the free market, as their opponents have caricatured them.

The other crucial element of the contemporary drug regulatory regime is the requirement that patients get a prescription for drugs of any consequence. Classical liberals would urge that this requirement be dropped, with some possible exceptions. One concerns antibiotics. Bacteria that standard broad-spectrum antibiotics attack can mutate into drug-resistant strains, which has become an increasingly serious problem in recent years and has obvious public health ramifications. The government can help stem that tide by requiring patients to seek the counsel of their physicians before treatment, though that does not guarantee that patients will finish all the medication, which is the standard problem. Daniel Polsby (1998, 218–20) has made a public goods argument for this that classical liberals could support, and he has offered other, related classical liberal arguments for regulating criminogenic and teratogenic drugs.[36] It might also be wise to continue to require a prescription for drugs that are truly dangerous when used as directed or for some patients. This little bit of paternalism could have big payoffs. But most drugs are not like that, and many other drugs could be legally sold at a pharmacy without the requirement of the doctor's prescription. The role of the pharmacist would be enhanced, which would allow patients to tap into a reservoir of knowledge and expertise that very frequently surpasses the physician's when it comes to therapeutic drugs. Americans traveling abroad are often amazed at how easy it is to get medications that are available only by prescription in this country. Any drug can be misused (usually by not following dosing instructions), but that is not why the current regulations are in place. Instead, it is part of a larger culture of paternalism fostered by the FDA in the 1940s and 1950s that is becoming increasingly outmoded as consumers become more knowledgeable and more involved in their own treatment. Part of the rationale for scaling back the number of drugs requiring a prescription is that it would reduce costs by eliminating the need to visit the doctor, but it would also make clear the enhanced responsibility that each of us has for his or her own health.

Notice that none of the arguments advanced above in favor of reducing the role of government make any direct appeal to the positive intrinsic value of autonomy or the negative intrinsic value of paternalism. Such arguments could be made (and often are made when classical liberals preach to the choir), but they are likely to be unimpressive to those, such as modern liberals, who do not value liberty as much as classical liberals do. This is not a criticism but simply a recognition of an important difference between classical liberal and modern liberal values. Instead, the arguments in this section have been broadly consequential in nature, and while not conclusive— they depend on predictions about what would happen—they are at least plausible enough to provide reasonable grounds for doubting the proposition that the existing modern liberal regulatory regime for medical products should remain in place.

Nonmedical Consumer Product Health and Safety Regulation

Public goods arguments for and against nonmedical consumer product safety regulation were discussed in chapter 6. Conversion arguments in this section build on that discussion. The Consumer Product Safety Commission (CPSC) was created by the Consumer Product Safety Act of 1972 (CPSA). In addition to implementing and enforcing the 1972 act, the CPSC is responsible for enforcing various other safety laws passed by Congress, including:

1. The Flammable Fabrics Act of 1953 (15 U.S.C. § 1191). This law was passed in response to some tragedies in which a number of people were badly burned when their sweaters ignited.
2. The Refrigerator Safety Act of 1956 (15 U.S.C. § 1211), which requires that refrigerators can be opened from the inside. This law was passed in response to tragedies involving children suffocating in abandoned refrigerators.
3. The Hazardous Substances Labeling Act of 1960 (15 U.S.C. § 1251), which regulates labeling of hazardous household products. Amendments to this law extended additional protections to children.
4. The Poison Packaging Prevention Act of 1970 (15 U.S.C. § 471), which provided for child-resistant packaging of hazardous substances.

Although most of this legislation was opposed by industry, there was no concerted opposition to these laws. It is morally difficult to oppose their core provisions, even if the standards as written are open to criticism, and classical liberals ought to be able to find public goods arguments (about the kind of society in which we want to live) or conversion arguments to justify them. The Consumer Product Safety Act is another matter, however. It is here that the issue about the safety of nonmedical consumer products is joined with modern liberals. Classical liberals are inclined to believe that the CPSC should be abolished. Modern liberals, however, are inclined to favor retaining this organization, though they are by no means committed to defending each product recall or every safety standard promulgated by the CPSC. It is worth pointing out that the stakes in this debate are probably lower than they used to be. In 1981, the act was amended in a way that gave more prominence to voluntary standards at the expense of mandatory standards. As explained in the *Code of Federal Regulations* (16 *C.F.R* § 1031.2 [1999]),

Congress amended the Consumer Product Safety Act, the Federal Hazardous Substances Act, and the Flammable Fabrics Act, to require the Commission to rely on voluntary standards rather than promulgate a mandatory standard when voluntary standards would eliminate or adequately reduce the risk of injury addressed and it is likely that there will be substantial compliance with the voluntary standards. (15 U.S.C. § 2056(b), 15 U.S.C. § 1262(g)(2), 15 U.S.C. § 1193(h)(2))

Still, the agency can set mandatory standards and, perhaps more importantly, it can issue recalls of what it deems unsafe products.

The main purpose of the act is "to protect the public against unreasonable risk of injury associated with consumer products" (15 U.S.C. § 2051). There is a problem, of course, in defining what counts as an unreasonable risk. The agency is required to take the costs of compliance into account, though they are not required to base their decisions on cost-benefit analysis, so an unreasonable risk cannot be defined solely in those terms. It is an inherently vague notion, and at no point has the CPSC or Congress made any effort to define it or clarify it beyond saying that costs and benefits need to be considered. For now, let us leave this problem.

As a practical matter, how do they proceed? Although there are a variety of ways for the CPSC to discover products that "create an unreasonable risk of injury," a significant source of information is the National Electronic Injury Surveillance System (NEISS), which gathers data from a sampling of hospital emergency rooms. They get some sense of what products are involved in the most injuries and act accordingly. Critics have complained that the NEISS does not take into account the number of products in use, the frequency with which those products are used, or the role of the consumer in causing the accident. A heavily used product whose associated injuries are largely caused by consumers may get flagged and become the subject of Commission action. The ways in which the latter can act, that is, the policy instruments at their disposal, are voluntary and mandatory standards, bans, recalls, and, in extreme cases, seizures. The recall is the most frequently used Commission tool, followed by the setting of mandatory standards. Since its inception in 1972, the Commission has issued recalls on over 4,000 products and has promulgated 288 mandatory standards on items ranging from bicycles to wood stoves.[37] Perhaps the main reason that recalls are the favored policy tool is that the CPSC is permitted to bypass the normal rule-making process, which is cumbersome and time-consuming (as detailed at 15 U.S.C. § 2058). This allows it to move quickly and with some flexibility. Recalls are permitted when (1) there is "a failure to comply with an applicable consumer product safety rule…" or (2) "a product defect…creates a substantial risk of injury…" or (3) "an unreasonable risk of serious injury or death" (15 U.S.C.§ 2064(a)(1); (a)(2); § 2064(b)(2)). Numbers (2) and (3), especially (2), are the predicates for most commission recalls. CPSC recalls and standards are generally obeyed, unlike OSHA rules and regulations. Easier enforcement probably explains why.

How might one argue for this regulatory regime? In *Consumer Safety Regulation*, Peter Asch (1988, 48–59) discusses market failure considerations that contribute to the case for regulation. Specifically, information about product safety is sometimes a public good. It can be jointly supplied and nonexcludable. Under the circumstances, as Asch says,

> the argument for public intervention…is completely clear. We can improve social welfare either by subsidizing private firms to a point such that it becomes profitable to produce and distribute the information, or by having the government itself do the job. (Asch 1988, 51)

We know from chapter 5 that this does not follow: it is necessary to show that the provision of safety information creates a genuine public goods problem for which there is no private sector solution via a tying arrangement. Waiving that difficulty, it is often thought, especially by the public, that vendors have every incentive to provide consumers with too little information about product hazards (cf. Cornell, Noll, and Weingast 1976, 465). However, this ignores the tort system, which penalizes nondisclosure of hazards ("failure to warn"). But, there is no guarantee that the incentives provided by the tort system will be good enough, either in general, or in all product markets. A related problem is that of asymmetric information made famous in Akerlof's (1970) explanation of the "lemons problem" in used car markets. As applied to safety, the problem is this: suppose that some products in a given market are relatively safer than others but that consumers are unable to distinguish the safer ones from the riskier ones. Assuming that the safer products are more expensive to produce, even if consumers would be willing to pay the extra cost, the safer units will not be produced because all units will sell at the same price—the lower price. Thus, all the products in that market will be relatively risky.

Arguments that appeal to failures in the market for safety information as a justification for government involvement suffer from two infirmities, however. One is that it is likely that there will always be reasonable disagreement about how badly a given market for safety information must fail to warrant government involvement. Those who make these arguments do not believe that each and every market failure warrants government interference. Any such judgment depends on a host of factors, including the probability and seriousness of threatened harm, the deterrent effect of the tort system, and the extent to which markets for information can solve the problem. Not to mention any ideological predilections. Those such as Asch who talk about market failure justifications for regulatory intervention admit that the point at which government involvement is "indicated" is inherently contestable (Asch 1988, 56). Second, and more importantly, these considerations are not enough to justify the mandatory standards and bans that the CPSC imposes. At most, they justify mandatory provision, or government provision, of safety information. Weightier considerations are required to bring down the heavy hand of government on the market for consumer goods.

A place to find those considerations is in the empirically demonstrated irrationality of consumers. In modeling consumer behavior, economists assume that consumers have complete and transitive preferences and that their choices maximize expected utility. The problem with this picture is not that it is an idealization rather than a literal description of empirical reality. Instead, the problem is that there is good evidence that people do not even approximate this ideal and indeed deviate from it in systematic and consequential ways.[38] For example, Kahneman and Tversky have shown that people have bias toward certainty, that is, they are inclined to choose options whose outcome is known with certainty over options with uncertain outcomes, even if the options have the same expected utility. People's choices also depend heavily on framing effects (i.e., context), but the determinants of context in the case of consumer choice are largely unknown, though advertising may play an important role. Probability judgments are often arrived at by following a few well-defined but objectively erroneous heuristics. Finally, people frequently underestimate personal risks ("it can't happen to me") because they believe they are more in control of events than they really are.[39]

These findings put the modern liberal demand for the government-sponsored paternalism of the CPSC in a new light. The axiom of economists, endorsed by all classical liberals, is that consumers are the best judges of what is in their own best interests; the corollary to that axiom is that paternalistic action by the state is merely the imposition of some people's values on others. But now it looks like modern liberal distrust of ordinary people's judgment, especially when it pertains to judgments under uncertainty, is well justified, and the issue of paternalism does not reduce to a mere imposition of some people's values on others. It will not do to say that regulators are people too and thus are subject to the same failings. That may or may not be true of them when they go to the local Walmart, but as experts, that is, when they are on guard down at the CPSC, they can be expected to get these things right. The bottom line is that if people are allowed to make these choices on their own, they will make many of the mistakes detailed by psychologists over the past quarter century. An agency devoted to preventing people from making a range of mistakes about product safety can only be helpful. The only question is how helpful they can be.

What is the classical liberal counterargument? On their view, there are two main problems with the agency as currently constituted. Let us return to the problem of defining an unreasonable risk. On the face of it, the policy instruments (recalls, standards, bans, and seizures) the CPSC has at its disposal would seem to be particularly ill-suited "to protect the public against unreasonable risk of injury associated with consumer products." The reason is that, in the ordinary sense of the term, a risk is unreasonable if accepting that risk is ill-suited or irrelevant to some end or purpose that the person who might run that risk has. Since the ends that people have and the circumstances in which people find themselves vary widely, an unreasonable risk for one person may be quite reasonable for someone else. For example, it might be an unreasonable risk for a family with small children to have medicines in containers without childproof caps, but running this risk may be perfectly reasonable for an elderly couple with grown grandchildren and arthritic hands. The policy instruments of the CPSC are uniform in their effects, however, so they are ill-suited to managing the relative nature of unreasonable risks. Perhaps, however, this is not the best way to construe the notion of an unreasonable risk. Maybe an unreasonable risk is a risk that it is not in someone's best interests to run, whatever that person's ends are. On that understanding, a defect in manufacturing or design would probably count as an unreasonable risk (and could be handled by the tort system), but beyond that, it would seem to be hard to know what would qualify. Diminishing or eliminating a risk always has costs, and it is unclear at what point the marginal costs of safety improvements exceed their marginal benefits. What makes this especially troublesome is if costs are conceived of as opportunity costs, that is, the benefits of forgone alternative uses of the resources in question. For example, if lawnmowers were stripped of some mandated safety devices and design features, the cost savings might be used by the consumer to purchase something more valuable to her than the added safety these devices and design features provide, perhaps even some other product that would lower her risk of serious injury in some other area. However irrational consumers are, at some point, the marginal costs of additional safety in any given product outweigh the marginal benefits, and the agency's guess about where that point is is just that—a guess. They have no special insight into how consumers value safety, or even how they would value it, if they were not prone to the breakdowns of human reasoning discovered by the psychologists of risk perception. Surely not all variations in the purchases of different items with different levels of risk attached are to be explained by faulty reasoning. In practical terms, then, it seems that an unreasonable risk is any risk the agency decides people should not assume. Regardless of how badly consumers reason under conditions of uncertainty, the charge that the CPSC is merely impos-ing the values of those in the bureaucracy on the general population begins to look more plausible.

This problem is exacerbated when one examines the CPSC's use of its most commonly employed policy instrument, the recall. The fol-lowing passage of the CPSA provides for that authority and specifies the conditions under which it is to be deployed:

> if the Commission determines…that a product distributed in commerce presents a substantial product hazard and that action under this subsection is in the public interest, it may order the manufacturer or any distributor or retailer of such product to take whichever of the following actions the person to whom the order is directed elects:
> (1) To bring such product into conformity with the require-ments of the applicable consumer product safety rule or to repair the defect in such product.
> (2) To replace such product with a like or equivalent prod-uct which complies with the applicable consumer product safety rule or which does not contain the defect. (15 U.S.C. § 2064(d))

"Defect" is a term of art in this context, and its meaning does not coincide with the legal meaning of the term. It is basically whatever the CPSC says is a defect. However, the most important term in this provi-sion is "substantial product hazard," which is defined as follows:

(a) For purposes of this section, the term "substantial product hazard" means—

(1) a failure to comply with an applicable consumer product safety rule which creates a substantial risk of injury to the public, or

(2) a product defect which (because of the pattern of defect, the number of defective products distributed in commerce, the severity of the risk, or otherwise) creates a substantial risk of injury to the public. (15 U.S.C. § 2064(a))

As Viscusi (1984, 62) has pointed out, defining a "substantial product hazard" as a product "defect" that "creates a substantial risk of injury" is close to being circular. This vague language invites the arbitrary exercise of power, always bad from any liberal point of view. In addition, it creates difficulties for businesses, since the CPSC gives no firm guidelines about the conditions under which it will issue a recall. This makes investment decisions riskier. A firm can be ruined by a CPSC recall that could not be anticipated. Past recalls provide little guidance because of the ad hoc nature of the recall decision. Moreover, as Stuart Madden (1980–81) has argued, there is little doubt that the Commission uses the recall as a way of getting around the rules and regulations they must follow to issue standards and to ban products—rules and regulations which are burdensome and time-consuming but are designed to prevent the Commission from acting capriciously. As in the case of antitrust law, there is no "known and settled law" by which firms can guide their conduct. There are only after-the-fact assessments of penalties.

The second difficulty with the CPSC is that it may very well be on balance ineffective. One obvious measure of effectiveness would be a decline in the home accident death rate over and above the "natural" rate of decline. Death rates have declined steadily throughout the twentieth century, in part because of technological developments, but more fundamentally, because society has gotten richer. Because safety is valued, richer means safer—safer jobs, safer consumer products, and less hazardous activities of other kinds. The market-driven demand for safety increased throughout the twentieth century. The following table tabulates home unintentional injury-deaths. Rates are per 100,000 persons. Representative years are given from 1930 to 1965 to give the reader a sense of the long-term secular trend. Thereafter, figures are given for each year. A column has been added to give the change from the previous year. A five-year rolling average death rate has also been added, beginning in 1965. A rolling average smooths out year-to-year fluctuations.

Prior to 1992 there was no national surveillance system that provided reliable counts of work-related unintentional-injury deaths. The National Safety Council made an estimate of the national total based on data from state workers' compensation authorities and vital statistics. Beginning in 1992, however, the Bureau of Labor Statistics published a national count based on its Census of Fatal Occupational Injuries program. Because this count was somewhat lower than the NSC's estimates had been, some deaths that had been classified as work-related had to be reallocated to the home and public classes. As a result, home accidental injury-deaths increased steadily from 9.4 in 1992 to 12.7 in 2004.[40]

The conclusion to be drawn from these statistics is that it is possible that the CPSC has had no real effect on accidental death rates in the home, but it may have—there is just not enough evidence to say. If the CPSC is effective, one would expect to see declines in death and injury rates related to products for which the agency has mandated standards, subject to a two caveats. One is that consumers may switch to other products as a result of design changes forced by the CPSC (e.g., because of increased costs), and those deaths and injuries would have to be included. Second, there may be a "lulling effect" that comes with the use of safer products. Accidents are always due to a combination of factors, and if consumers are more negligent in their use of product because they believe it is safe, injuries may decline less than they otherwise would or even increase.[41] Those caveats noted, what has been the effect of standards set by the CPSC? Kip Viscusi has done a careful evaluation of the effects, as best as they could be determined, of the following safety standards and/or products: (1) mattress flammability, (2) child-resistant bottle caps, (3) crib regulations, (4) swimming pool slides, (5) carpets and rugs (flammability), and (6) bicycles. He summarizes his findings as follows:

> neither the total accident data nor the product-specific data point to any major success by the agency. This finding is particularly surprising in as much as my analysis focused on some prominent CPSC regulations. Although some kinds of injuries have diminished, available data do not enable us to identify any favorable effects of the standards or any shifts from decreases in risk that were already occurring. (Viscusi 1984, 85)

Table 9.1 U.S. Home Unintentional Injury-Deaths (per 100,000)

Year	Death Rate	Change from Previous Year	5-Year Rolling Average	Year	Death Rate	Change from Previous Year	5-Year Rolling Average
1930	24.4			1975	11.6	−0.6	12.36
1935	25.2			1976	11.0	−0.6	12.00
1940	23.9			1977	10.6	−0.4	11.58
1945	25.3			1978	10.3	−0.3	11.14
1950	19.2			1979	10.0	−0.3	10.7
1955	17.3			1980	10.0	0.0	10.38
1960	15.6			1981	9.5	−0.5	10.08
1965	14.7		14.92	1982	9.2	−0.3	9.8
1966	15.1	+0.4	14.84	1983	9.1	−0.1	9.56
1967	14.7	−0.4	14.76	1984	9.0	−0.1	9.36
1968	14.0	−0.7	14.64	1985	9.1	+0.1	9.18
1969	13.7	−0.3	14.44	1986	9.0	−0.1	9.08
1970	13.2	−0.5	14.14	1987	8.8	−0.2	9.00
1971	12.8	−0.4	13.68	1988	9.3	+0.5	9.04
1972	12.7	−0.1	13.28	1989	9.1	−0.2	9.06
1973	12.5	−0.2	12.98	1990	8.6	−0.5	8.96
1974	12.2	−0.3	12.68	1991	8.8	+0.2	8.92

*Adapted from: *Injury Facts*, 2005–2006 ed., 36–37.

These criticisms of the CPSC are telling in light of the fact that there is a classical liberal alternative already in place, which was described in the second section of chapter 6. Tort and contract law are components of that alternative; another component consists of private standard setting agencies, such as the American National Standards Institute (ANSI), the National Fire Protection Association (NFPA), the American Society for Testing and Materials (ASTM) and Underwriters Laboratories (UL). These and other private certifiers provide an independent assurance of product safety. Safety information is also available from other organizations such as Consumers'

Union for ordinary consumer goods, the Emergency Care Research Institute (ECRI) for hospital products, and from a host of other, more specialized entities.

Tort and contract law handle safety issues related to consumer products, that is, product liability, under one of three legal standards: negligence, breach of implied warranty, and strict liability. The negligence standard holds a manufacturer responsible for a product defect if he knew or should have known that the product is defective, either in manufacturing, design, or marketing ("failure to warn"). It employs a "reasonable person" standard in determining what the manufacturer should have known. That standard is in turn determined by a cost-benefit test, so that, for example, if a manufacturer can prevent some serious harms at very low cost, his failure to do so constitutes negligence.[42] Breach of implied warranty applies when the product is unfit for its intended use or a reasonably anticipated use. This is a somewhat stricter than the negligence standard. The strictest standard of all is strict liability under which there is no fault requirement. All that is necessary is a defective product that is "unreasonably dangerous." Strict liability also supersedes any contractual limitations, such as those in the Uniform Commercial Code. This theory behind the strict liability standard is a relatively recent development in tort law, and it has come to predominate in products liability law. A number of considerations account for this: (1) It reflects a moral judgment to the effect that if someone has been injured by a defective product, whether or not the manufacturer is at fault, the injured party should be compensated by someone (else); (2) Any jury awards against the manufacturer will be rolled into the price of the product, which means that the cost of injuries is spread among all the users of the product; (3) The manufacturer is in the best position to reduce the total costs of accidents through changes in product design, marketing, or manufacturing.[43]

The actions of the injured party are treated differently under the three theories; historically, under a negligence standard, if the user was at all negligent in the use of the product, that would bar recovery; this doctrine is known as contributory negligence. In many jurisdictions, the harshness of this doctrine led to a judicially or legislatively imposed doctrine of comparative negligence, which allows juries to apportion responsibility between the parties in a way they think appropriate. So, a manufacturer might be held two-thirds liable and a user one-third liable for injuries received in connection with the use of some product. Compensation from the manufacturer to the injured party would be reduced accordingly. The test is less severe for the injured party under implied warranty, but in the case of strict liability, the actions of the injured party do not bar recovery for injuries at all, except in extreme circumstances, namely, when the injured party knew about the risks associated with the defect and did not act prudently in accepting those risks (assumption of risk). This has been construed fairly narrowly by the courts. People who get hurt misusing products end up getting compensated, pretty much no matter what their own contribution to the accident was. Tort law differs from jurisdiction to jurisdiction but it is a fair generalization to say that in most jurisdictions, the current standard for product liability is strict liability, with some modifications.

The current consumer product regulatory regime, which involves the CPSC, is essentially an overlay on this classical liberal alternative of products liability law together with private, voluntary standards. Even if the CPSC's standards have been ineffective, surely, it might be argued, recalls and bans must have had some positive effects. Consider some of the really nasty products the CPSC has banned: lead-based paints, various compounds containing respirable asbestos, and lawn darts (16 *C.F.R.* 1303–6 [1999]), whose very name suggests something inordinately dangerous. These are outdoor toys about a foot long with an elongated pointed tip and weigh a quarter to a half a pound. Though it is not immediately apparent because of the way they are constructed, lawn darts present a risk of skull puncture for younger children and indeed some deaths and injuries due to lawn darts have been reported. It is uncertain if the tort system would have dealt with the problem of lawn darts as expeditiously as the CPSC did. In general, the latter is more proactive than the tort system, not just in banning products (of which there have been only a few), but also in recalling products. Surely, it will be argued, they have done *something* right. Classical liberals can admit that the CPSC does some good, but then the question becomes whether or not the benefits are worth the opportunity costs. If the effect of the CPSC were large, say if it reduced the death rate of home accidents by 50 percent or even 15 percent, it would be hard to maintain skepticism about the need for the agency, unless one were to appeal to libertarian or other classical liberal principles, which is forbidden by the terms of the debate at this juncture. But the effects, if any, are nowhere near that large. Then costs do become an issue, and reasonable people can disagree about whether the costs of the CPSC, considered in terms of (1) the cost-effectiveness of the regulations,

(2) the businesses ruined, (3) other financial costs imposed, (4) the useful products taken off the market or altered for the worse in other respects that consumers value, (5) the lulling effects of apparently safer products, and (6) the safety consumers could have purchased in other products, are, all things considered, worth it. About this there could be reasonable disagreement.

Finally, even if one wants to argue that adults should be able to choose whatever level of safety they desire, there is the issue of products used by children. Parents may or may not be good at choosing the "right" level of safety for their children. Might not government bureaucrats do a better job, at least in part, by way of mandatory standards and recalls? The answer is by no means obvious. Many of the CPSC's actions have been directed at products used by children (see Viscusi's investigation of various standards), though most of those efforts have not been very successful. The larger problem is that the products themselves are not more or less risky. Instead, the riskiness of the product comes from its interaction with users, who vary widely in the amount of common sense they possess and/or adult supervision that accompanies their use. It is tempting to think about this on a case-by-case basis. Banning lawn darts was probably a good idea, but mandating swimming pool slide standards, indeed mandating most of the standards the CPSC has imposed, have not been good ideas. The problem is that there is no principled way to legislate good sense and apt discretion on the part of government bureaucrats.[44] Either one has a government bureaucracy to police consumer products or one does not. At the very least, there is reasonable disagreement about whether or not this is one we should have.

Occupational Licensure

Nearly one thousand occupations are regulated by one or more of the fifty states, though only 490 of these require government-sanctioned licenses (Young 1987, 4). Licensed occupations include high-profile occupations such as medicine, dentistry, and the law, but other occupations have also been licensed in one or more states, including barbers, beekeepers, cosmeticians, cotton classers, embalmers, falconers, ferret breeders, lightning rod salesmen, septic tank cleaners, tattooists, taxidermists, threshers, tourist guides, and tree surgeons.[45] There is considerable variation among the various states in the number of occupations that require a license. California requires licenses for one hundred and seventy-eight different occupations, while Kansas requires licenses for only forty-seven (Kleiner 2006, 100–1). Obviously, it is not possible to examine the details of all licensing regulation in the United States; we shall restrict our attention to medicine, in part for historical reasons. Medicine was one of the first occupations to be licensed in modern times, and the rationale for it is best understood in historical context. Moreover, a conversion argument for medical licensure is fairly straightforward and easily generalizable to other contexts—at least those in which health and safety concerns figure prominently.

In his classic book *The Social Transformation of American Medicine,* the sociologist Paul Starr tells the story of the growth and development of American medicine from colonial times to the present. Support within the profession for licensing, as we know it today, started in the 1870s and 1880s (Starr 1982, 102). Throughout much of the nineteenth century, anyone could practice medicine; education and training were spotty at best. Medical schools were essentially for-profit proprietary institutions in which local physicians gave lectures and were entirely supported by student fees. One hundred medical schools would accept any man who paid tuition. Only 20 percent required a high school education or more, and only one required a college degree (Barry 2004, 6). As late as 1877, no medical school in the United States used a laboratory for instruction, and there was little to no clinical education in hospitals (Barry 2004, 47). To graduate from Harvard Medical School, a student need only pass a majority of his examinations (Starr 1982, 114). Moreover, there were different schools of thought about the nature and causes of disease and other ailments, ranging from allopathy (what is now mainstream medicine) to homeopathy, osteopathy, eclecticism, and, at the extreme, Christian Science. It is not that the allopaths knew what they were doing and all the others were quacks. Whatever their persuasion, the treatments of most physicians most of the time either helped their patients fortuitously, had no effect, or did more harm than good. That began to change in the late nineteenth century with developments in medical science in Europe and subsequently in the United States.

The first true research hospital in the United States, at Johns Hopkins University, was founded in 1889; the medical school opened four years later. The latter required a college degree for admission, instituted a four-year curriculum and residency programs, and recruited distinguished faculty from across the country and around the world (Starr 1982, 115). For that to become the model for medical education across the country, as influential medical educators wanted it to be, the proprietary schools had to be driven out of business. By 1905, the American Medical Association was in a position to do this. Every state had some form of licensing, which was controlled by the state chapter of the AMA (Starr 1982, 112). In 1904, the national association established a Council on Medical Education, and in 1906 representatives of the Council visited and graded all the medical schools in the nation. Schools were given a grade of A, B, or C. Those given a grade of A were deemed acceptable; those graded B were thought to be salvageable if certain changes were instituted, but those given a grade of C were eventually pressured into folding or merging with better schools. That pressure was ultimately exerted through the licensing power held by the AMA. As Starr says, "even though no legislative body ever set up either the Federation of State Medical Boards or the AMA Council on Medical Education, their decisions came to have the force of law" (Starr 1982, 121).

Interestingly, the results of these visits were not made public at the time, since professional ethics forbade physicians from criticizing each other in public. Although state medical boards began the winnowing process around 1906, it was not complete until after the publication of the Flexner Report in 1910. To get around the prohibition on criticizing physicians, the Council on Medical Education invited an outside group, the Carnegie Foundation for the Advancement of Teaching, to produce an independent report on the state of medical education in the United States. Abraham Flexner headed up the task force, which revisited every medical school in the country. As a representative of the Carnegie Foundation, medical school administrators believed that part of Flexner's mission was philanthropic, which encouraged them to paint in lurid colors the inadequacies of their programs in hopes that they could elicit funds from the foundation (Starr 1982, 118–121). It turned out that Flexner had other ideas. In an impressive display of Divine Justice visited on medical school administrators, the Flexner report of 1910 was highly critical of the state of medical education at many of these institutions, which made it politically feasible for licensing boards to move against them and close many of them down. This had the effect of further consolidating the power of the Federation of State Medical Boards. Fundamentally, the problem was that advances in medical science had not been matched by changes in medical education. State medical boards took the lead in forcing that change.

Students of occupational licensure, especially economists with classical liberal sympathies, have largely ignored this story and instead have been content to point out that occupational licensure laws consistently reduce competition in the professions by restricting the supply of practitioners, which in turn raises or props up their incomes. This leads to the inference, amply supported by other evidence, that this is the main motivation for professionals to advocate occupational licensure.[46] In the case of physicians, satisfying the substantial education requirements is extremely costly, and fulfilling these requirements effectively prevents aspiring doctors from practicing their trade much before the age of thirty. A minor theme in this literature is that these requirements as embodied in licensure laws provide inadequate assurances of quality of care.

The history and economics of occupational licensure for physicians sets the stage for a consideration of the conversion arguments in favor of and in opposition to laws requiring medical practitioners to be licensed. These arguments were hinted at in chapters 3 and 6 and can be easily summarized. The main conversion argument in favor of occupational licensure laws for health professionals is that they provide consumers of medical services with an assurance of minimum quality in the care they receive. The need for this arises because of informational asymmetries between providers and those who hire them, namely, consumers. Specifically, the latter are incapable of adequately judging the competence of providers, and occupational licensure assures the consumer that the provider has a minimum level of competence.

As might be expected, economists have formalized this simple idea. The seminal paper is Akerlof's 1970 "lemons" paper referred to above. The basic idea of Akerlof's paper is that when consumers have difficulty making qualitative distinctions among products or services, there is a tendency for the average level of quality to be lower than what would emerge in a perfectly competitive market. This was formalized and directly applied to the case of occupational licensure by Leland.[47] The latter considers various free market responses, such as the emergence of specialized firms who sell information about the quality of service providers, but since information "has some of the aspects of a public good" (Leland 1980, 268), a suboptimal amount will be provided. Classical liberals would be unimpressed, since not all public goods create public goods problems; besides, there is no assurance that the government provides anything close to the optimal amount of information through occupational licensure, especially since they are a monopoly provider. Leland also considers the possibility that informed intermediaries would arise to bundle the service with some sort of quality guarantee and sell it to the public—in other words, retailers—but he rejects this on the grounds that information about the quality of medical services is difficult or impossible for middlemen to obtain (Leland 1980, 269). However, this article was written before the rise of health maintenance organizations (HMOs) and preferred provider organizations (PPOs), who are perfectly competent to evaluate physicians and the services they provide and indeed do so regularly. They have, in effect, become the retailers of medical services.

The central feature of occupational licensure is the legal exclusion of nonlicensed providers. This is what classical liberals object to. Milton Friedman represents, only to dismiss, the paternalistic argument in favor of this when he says,

> in practice, the major argument given for licensure by its proponents is...a strictly paternalistic argument...Individuals, it is said, are incapable of choosing their own servants adequately, their own physician or plumber or barber. Most of us, therefore, are incompetent and we must be protected against our own ignorance. This amounts to saying that we in our capacity as voters must protect ourselves in our capacity as consumers against our own ignorance by seeing to it that people are not served by incompetent physicians or plumbers or barbers. (Friedman 1962, 148)

This argument is not as weak as Friedman thinks it is, at least as it applies to physicians, for two reasons. One is that licensure could be represented as solution to a Ulysses and the Sirens problem (Elster 1979, 36–47), whereby we bind ourselves to a certain course of action to avoid temptation. In this instance, the temptation is to purchase low-cost medical care, which presumably would be more likely to produce bad health care outcomes. As voters, we may not know exactly what level of competence we want to be assured of, but we do know that we want someone who is knowledgeable to make that judgment. Perhaps more importantly, modern liberals would argue that the elimination of licensing requirements would lead to more bad outcomes for the poor, since they would be more likely to patronize low-cost, low-quality health care providers. After all, not everyone is insured, and some people have very thin coverage. Without occupational licensure laws to protect the public, so the argument goes, these citizens would be more likely to be harmed by seeking out inexpensive but ill-trained providers.

The classical liberal counterargument was foreshadowed in chapter 6. Most insured medical care these days takes place under the aegis of an insurance company in one way or another. They have an interest in seeing to it that the physicians they pay do not get them dragged into court on malpractice charges, so there is some motivation for these firms to monitor and weed out incompetent practitioners. But what about practitioners who are not monitored by health insurance companies? It was suggested in chapter 6 that it would be appropriate for the state to require that all practitioners, whether affiliated with a provider organization or not, to carry liability insurance, which, as a practical matter they all do anyway. This would in turn require regulation of insurance companies since otherwise the requirement that practitioners carry liability insurance could be easily evaded, but that would be a small concession. In the absence of occupational licensure, insurance companies that provide liability policies would either develop the expertise to evaluate physicians in house or farm it out to private certification agencies. The rationale for this liability insurance requirement would be to ensure consumers that physicians and other health care providers are not policing themselves, always a bad idea. This of course is exactly what they currently do, since the state typically grants a monopoly on the certification of health care occupations to provider-dominated groups. Juvenal famously understood the folly of this when he asked, "Quis custodiet ipsos custodes?"

The main motivation for eliminating the state monopoly on certification (i.e., licensing) is to make health care more affordable and more efficiently delivered. Less extensively and expensively trained professionals, equipped with sophisticated diagnostic software, could handle routine healthcare problems much more efficiently and cost-effectively, and the main beneficiaries would be those with little or no health insurance. Classical liberals could concede (but need not) that licensing made sense in the early part of the twentieth century when developments in medical science outstripped developments in both medical education and in tort law, though whether the Johns Hopkins model should have been the template for medical education is at least debatable. It is difficult to know what would have happened if the state had not intervened. Classical liberals would maintain, however, that whether or not medical licensure was historically justified, it no longer is. Of course, modern liberals would reply that a much more effective way to ensure health care for the poor is to institute a single-payer system of some sort, in other words, some more aggressive form of socialized medicine than currently exists. That may well be true, but once the dispute about occupational licensure becomes part of the larger debate about the delivery and financing of health care, a long and inconclusive debate will be well underway. Reasonable disagreement is inevitable.

Similar arguments on both sides apply in the case of other professions that directly affect health and safety such as pharmacy, architecture, and engineering. Once we extend our gaze beyond these and similar professions, however, it becomes clear that occupational licensure serves no other function than as a barriers-to-entry device that restricts the supply and increases the incomes of licensed practitioners. For example, to be a licensed cosmetologist, one must complete 1400–1600 hours of training and take a practical exam. Training costs run anywhere from $6,500 to $10,000.[48] Bad outcomes mean at most bad hair days, hardly a serious health hazard. Indeed, cosmetology licensure laws have been applied to practitioners of African hair-braiding and other forms of natural hairstyling, despite the fact that hair-braiding is not taught in cosmetology schools nor is it tested on the practical exam. In a string of cases beginning in the early 1990s, the public interest law firm, Institute for Justice, litigated challenges in a number of states to cosmetology licensing laws that prohibited the unlicensed practice of hair-braiding.[49] They have been largely successful, but the fact that numerous states have moved against the mostly minority women who offer this service is emblematic of the mindset in the state bureaucracies—controlled by licensed providers—that license various occupations. Competing private certification agencies might come into existence to provide consumers with quality assurances. The worst that could happen is that these competing certification agencies would all be dominated by practitioners more interested in protecting fellow professionals than in serving the public. Which is essentially what we have now, except that there is no competition.

In all occupations in which there are substantial health and safety consequences for malpractice, it is possible for classical liberals to admit (though many of them will not) that occupational licensure made sense at some point in time. Markets for professional services, however, have become much more sophisticated, and there is no longer any good reason to give currently licensed practitioners the power to set standards and impose requirements on those who want to sell their services to the public. The temptation to make such standards and requirements mere barriers to entry whose main effect is to raise the income of provider groups is overwhelming. It is a temptation that mere mortals, as well as physicians, should not be expected to resist.

Conversion Arguments

Land Use Regulation

Land use regulation that cannot be construed as a substitute for or supplement to the common law includes most prominently the Endangered Species Act of 1973, which imposes restrictions on what property owners can do with property on which an endangered plant or animal species has been found, and section 404 of the Clean Water Act of 1972, which gives the federal government the power to regulate wetlands. The differences between modern liberals and classical liberals on these regulatory regimes are rooted in philosophical differences about the nature and sources of property rights. Recall from chapter 2 that modern liberals believe that the state has some sort of priority of ownership of what is otherwise private property. In consequence, land use regulation can be justified as the exercise of the state's (or perhaps society's) ownership rights in productive assets—at least so long as the state does not usurp too many of the rights and privileges of ownership (so that ownership is private in name only) and so long as the process from which such regulations emerge is tolerably open and democratic. The point here is perfectly general. Much of the modern liberal regulatory agenda is quite unproblematic, given this modern liberal conception of social ownership. Regulation is simply the exercise of ownership rights by the state in the name of society. This may explain why modern liberals have felt little need to justify any of the items on their agenda as the latter have emerged from the regulatory process. Absent a convincing philosophical argument for this conception of public ownership, however, justifying the modern liberal regulatory agenda to classical liberals requires an argument that either makes no presuppositions about social ownership in the first instance or one that accepts, for the sake of argument, the classical liberal view on this.

Classical liberals, by contrast, believe that ownership of productive assets lies in the first instance with private parties, either on Lockean grounds, on more consequentialist grounds, or simply as a matter of custom. In either of the first two cases, their philosophical commitments imply a heavier burden on those who would restrict those rights by regulation. Conversion arguments are a way to overcome this philosophical impasse, or rather to bypass it, insofar as these arguments require each side to hold in abeyance its deeper views about the locus of property rights in the first instance. The purpose of this chapter is to consider conversion arguments for and against these two main forms of federal land use regulation that modern liberals are inclined to favor and that classical liberals are inclined to oppose.

The Endangered Species Act

The Endangered Species Act of 1973 (16 U.S.C. § 1531 et seq.) is a complex piece of legislation requiring the cooperation of literally dozens of government agencies in addition to private landowners. The two most important agencies in implementing the ESA are the Fish and Wildlife Service (FWS) and the National Marine Fisheries Service (NMFS). The former is housed in the Department of the Interior and the latter in the Department of Commerce. Each of these agencies is entitled to list species as endangered or threatened, though most listings are done by the FWS: "The term 'endangered species' means any species which is in danger of extinction throughout all or a significant portion of its range" (16 U.S.C. § 1532(6)); "The term 'threatened species' means any species which is likely to become an endangered species within the foreseeable future throughout all or a significant portion of its range" (16 U.S.C. § 1532(20)). Although most listings are done by the FWS, private parties may petition to list a species or have the status of a species changed (16 U.S.C. § 1533(b)(3)(A)).

Three sections of the original act do most of the work: 16 U.S.C. § 1533 states the mechanics of the listing process and requires the development of a plan to recover an endangered or threatened species. Because the federal government owns or controls so much land, especially in the West, 16 U.S.C. § 1536 details a consultative process that the secretaries of the Departments of Commerce and Interior must engage in when other federal agencies (e.g., the Bureau of Land Management, the U.S. Forest Service) are involved. 16 U.S.C. § 1538 spells out the actions prohibited by the act on private land, including what it means to "take" a member of an endangered species: "The term 'take' means to harass, harm, pursue, hunt, shoot, wound, kill, trap, capture, or collect, or to attempt to engage in any such conduct" (U.S.C. § 1532(19)). Under 16 U.S.C. § 1538(a)(2), plant species are subjected to less stringent protection than animals. Though takings of members of endangered plant species on federal lands are prohibited, incidental destruction of plants on private property is not forbidden unless it is deliberate or in knowing violation of the law.

Because of various problems with the act and its implementation, the ESA has been amended at least ten times.[1] Perhaps the most important amendments were passed in 1978. They required the secretary of the interior to designate a species' critical habitat whenever it listed a species as endangered.[2] Critical habitat is defined by reference to specific areas occupied by the species at the time of listing. It is not coextensive with the entire range of the species, which might be quite large. The secretary can take economic factors into account in designating critical habitat (16 U.S.C. § 1533(a)(3)) but not in the decision to list. Conflicts with other government agencies, specifically a conflict over the Tellico Dam in Tennessee and the Grayrocks Dam and Reservoir in Wyoming, led to some other provisions in the 1978 amendments. Construction on the Tellico Dam was halted to preserve a tiny minnow-like fish known as the snail darter. The FWS also determined that the Grayrocks project threatened the habitat of the whooping crane on the Platt River. The FWS's action halting work on the Tellico Dam was upheld in *Tennessee Valley Auth. v. Hill,* 437 U.S. 153 (1977). The Supreme Court opinion, written by Chief Justice Burger, said, "the plain language of the Act, buttressed by its legislative history, shows clearly that Congress viewed the value of endangered species as 'incalculable'" (*Tennessee Valley Auth. v. Hill,* 437 U.S. 153, 187 (1977)).

Arguably, this was Burger's way of telling Congress to fix the law. Outrage in Congress over the implications of the act for the Tellico and Grayrocks projects (into which the federal government had already put enormous resources) led to changes in the law that permitted some compromise. Specifically, these amendments created the Endangered Species Committee, quickly dubbed by the press, "the God Committee," which was authorized to exempt federal projects from the provisions of the act, if they judged that the economic and social benefits of the project outweighed the biological consequences of the exemption.[3] Basically, the Committee could authorize incidental "takings" of members of endangered species by the relevant federal agency, provided the latter's actions did not lead to the species' extinction and provided that mitigation measures were taken to lessen the impact on the affected species (16 U.S.C. § 1536(e)).

The next major change in the law came with the 1982 reauthorization of the ESA.[4] This reauthorization relaxed some of the listing requirements, and it required the secretary to issue a preliminary finding on listing within ninety days, to be followed by a critical habitat listing. A major complaint against the act, as originally formulated, was that it treated federal government agencies differently from the way it treated private parties. Unlike federal agencies, the ESA required no consultative process between the FWS or NMFS and private landowners nor did it make any provision for incidental takings. All takings of endangered species were prohibited. However, legal counsel for the FWS advised that, absent a taking (i.e., a dead body), nothing could be done by the government to protect an endangered species on private property. Hence the motivation to "shoot, shovel, and shut up." The 1982 amendments made some efforts to fix these problems. A new section, 16 U.S.C. § 1539, was created, which permitted incidental takings, provided that a habitat conservation plan (HCP) was submitted and accepted and provided that whatever incidental takings occurred did not threaten the species as a whole. In theory, this allowed landowners to use their land for their own purposes while protecting endangered species. In practice, however, the expense and delay involved in developing HCPs and getting them approved put them beyond the reach of nearly all small to medium-sized landowners. For large landowners, the more land that was subject to the HCP, the more likely it would turn out that multiple endangered species would be implicated. Besides, the habitat modifications that landowners were most interested in—development—remained strictly limited.

Case law effectively allowed even some animal species to be haled into court as defendants. In a series of cases originating in Hawaii,[5] the plaintiffs successfully argued that populations of feral goats and sheep, which were maintained by the state of Hawaii for the purpose of sport hunting, had illegally harmed an endangered bird species, the palila, by destroying seedlings of the vegetation upon which the birds exclusively depended for food and nesting, though there was no showing that the birds could not have found other habitat. In these cases, the courts allowed to stand the FWS's expansive definition of "harm" within the statutory definition of a "taking." As the secretary of the interior defined it in the *Code of Federal Regulations:*

> "Harm" in the definition of "take" in the Act means an act that actually kills or injures wildlife. Such act may include significant habitat modification or degradation where it actually kills or injures wildlife by significantly impairing essential behavioral patterns, including breeding, feeding or sheltering (50 *C.F.R.* 17.3 [2002]).

This means that habitat modification, including interference with breeding behavior, counts as a form of injury to wildlife. In a related case that attracted national attention, *Babbitt v. Sweet Home Chapter of Communities for a Great Oregon* the Supreme Court affirmed the secretary of the interior's understanding of "harm," which allowed the FWS to (continue to) impose logging restrictions in the Northwest and the Southeast to protect the habitats of the spotted owl and the red-cockaded woodpecker, respectively.

This expansive conception of harm was responsible for a number of horror stories. Randy Simmons recounts the story of North Carolina landowner Ben Cone's encounter with the FWS regarding the red-cockaded woodpecker:

> in North Carolina, Ben Cone had 1,560 acres of his 7,000 acres of land taken by the ESA to provide habitat for the red-cockaded woodpecker. He still owns the land, of course, but no timber may be harvested within a half-mile radius of each colony of woodpeckers. In addition, each colony must be protected from the controlled burning Cone does to improve wildlife habitat on his property, so now he has to rake and bushhog around each nest tree before burning because a burned tree would constitute a taking under the ESA.
>
> In addition to increased management costs, Cone has suffered a loss of land value. He had the 1,560 acres appraised in 1993 and found that, absent the woodpeckers, the estimated value of the hunting leases, timber, and pine straw was $2,230,000. With the woodpeckers, the land was worth just $86,500, or 96 percent less. The twenty-nine birds therefore cost Cone $73,914 each, a cost he alone has borne. (Simmons 1999a, 320–21)

Habitat Conservation Plans provide no real solution, since the government can still prevent people from using their property in the way that is most valuable to them. Indeed, Cone was offered an HCP by the Fish and Wildlife Service that would have allowed him to harvest timber on all the land except for the acreage devoted to woodpecker habitat. That, of course, was exactly the problem as Cone saw it.

Charles Mann and Mark Plummer have documented problems with two high-profile HCPs: the Balcones Canyonlands Conservation Plan (BCCP) in Texas and Southern California's Natural Communities Conservation Plan (NCCP) (Mann and Plummer 1995a; 1995b). These were ambitious regional conservation plans designed to protect the habitats of endangered bird species: the golden-cheeked warbler and black-capped vireo in Texas and the coastal California gnatcatcher in Southern California, respectively. Beginning in 1989 in Texas, nearly a dozen agencies and groups, ranging from environmentalist organizations to developers to local, county, and state government agencies, met to hammer out a plan to set aside preserves for the threatened warbler and vireo that would pass muster with the FWS. As boom times returned to the Austin area, land values began to climb, and when Travis County tried to pass a bond issue to finance the county's land purchases, it failed on a close vote, and the plan was defeated. Shortly after that, the project coordinators met with the FWS to present them with an alternative: they would fund a much larger preserve 200 miles to the southwest near the Rio Grande River. The price was to permit takings of vireos in Travis county—takings which would probably lead to the disappearance of the bird in the Austin area, though it would not cause the extinction of the species. The FWS said no because it would restrict the vireo's range. The fallout was substantial: after the golden-cheeked warbler and the black-capped vireo were listed as endangered species, property values in Travis County, Texas declined $359 million (Wilkinson 1993, 15); one landowner alone suffered a decline in the appraised value of her land from $830,000 to $38,000 (Adler 1995, 3). As Mann and Plummer said,

> behind the battle in Austin and wherever else economic growth encounters a listed species, federal biologists have been transformed into economic mandarins, with the power to govern projects ranging from fence posts to highways to dams. They have the power to make compromises in the name of Native American hospitals, shopping malls, orange growers, or even developers; or not to make them in the name of beetles, butterflies or birds.... Although that position is mandated by the Endangered Species Act, it has never been accepted by the people whose lives are governed by the law. (Mann and Plummer 1995b, 208)

To protect themselves, ranchers and other property owners surveyed their land and submitted the results to the FWS. If there was no suitable habitat for the vireo or if that habitat had been unoccupied by the birds for at least three years, the FWS would issue what was called a "bird letter," which permitted the landowner to develop his or her property without interference from the FWS. Bird letters increased property values up to 25 percent, and those who could not get them suffered as a result (Mann and Plummer 1995b, 201–2). The upshot was predictable: in a habitat version of "shoot, shovel and shut up," landowners stripped their land of every tree and every bit of vegetation that might serve as vireo habitat so that they could get a bird letter.

Southern California's Natural Communities Conservation Plan (NCCP) began when a developer, the Fieldstone Company, purchased 2,300 acres in San Diego County in 1988.[6] It subsequently learned that the sage scrub vegetation was a habitat for the coastal California gnatcatcher, a bird that was likely to be listed in the near future as an endangered species. Fieldstone created an HCP before the species was listed, but the FWS did not approve it. The company then learned that the western portion of its property was full of Del Mar manzanita, an endangered plant species, so the plan had to be modified again. Eventually, project manager John Barone learned that there were thirty-six potentially listable species on the company's property. Other developers and the state got involved, and six years and countless revisions later, a coordinated HCP for the entire Southern California area—6,000 square miles—was worked out. The FWS did not participate: "They were at worst obstructing and at best delaying the process by withholding information and guidelines" (Burgess 2001, 125). Development is proceeding and the various habitats are protected, but costs have been astronomical, given land values in Southern California. These are not isolated incidents.[7]

Some of these problems with the implementation of the law requiring HCPs were finally addressed through Department of Interior policies under the leadership of former Arizona governor Bruce Babbitt. Three policies have been implemented to mitigate these and related problems: (1) Safe Harbor, (2) Candidate Conservation Agreements, and (3) No Surprises. Safe Harbor was designed for landowners interested in protecting endangered species on their land; they were reluctant to do so because they feared being subject to section 9's "no takings" provision or the costs of working up an HCP. Under Safe Harbor, if a landowner agreed to take proactive measures to preserve species on their property, he or she would be assured that if other endangered or threatened species migrated to their property, the landowner would not face additional restrictions or costs. Candidate Conservation Agreements provide the same assurances for habitats of species proposed for listing. The No Surprises policy applies to approved HCPs, which include incidental take permits. As a result of No Surprises, landowners can be assured that no additional restrictions on the use of their property will be imposed, nor will any additional financial contributions be required. These policies mitigate the disincentives to destroy endangered species and their habitats.

It is possible to dismiss these cases as merely anecdotal; every law has its perverse consequences, though the injustices that have been visited on these property owners are quite real. Recently, however, more systematic empirical work has been done to substantiate the hypothesis that land use regulations, such as those imposed by the ESA, negatively affect species conservation efforts on private lands. In one study, Jeffrey Michael and Dean Lueck examined the rate of pre-emptive habitat destruction for red-cockaded woodpeckers (RCWs).[8] Because RCWs tend to nest in older trees, landowners at risk to being subjected to critical habitat designation were more likely to harvest trees prematurely. According to another study, the listing of the endangered Preble's meadow jumping mouse led some landowners to make their land more hospitable to to the species, but that was offset by other landowners making their land less hospitable to the mouse.[9,10] On its own terms, the ESA seems to have been less than successful.

Even for a government program, the ESA was poorly thought out and executed. It has been repeatedly amended to deal with an array of problems its implementation created. What are the moral arguments for and against it? The "Findings" section of the act provides some of the resources for an argument in favor of it. It states:

> The Congress finds and declares that—
>
> (1) various species of fish, wildlife, and plants in the United States have been rendered extinct as a consequence of economic growth and development untempered by adequate concern and conservation;
>
> (2) other species of fish, wildlife, and plants have been so depleted in numbers that they are in danger of or threatened with extinction;
>
> (3) these species of fish, wildlife, and plants are of esthetic, ecological, educational, historical, recreational, and scientific value to the Nation and its people;
>
> (4) the United States has pledged itself as a sovereign state in the international community to conserve to the extent practicable the various species of fish or wildlife and plants facing extinction. (16 U.S.C. § 1531(a))

All of these findings make it clear that the primary aim of the ESA is to preserve biodiversity; it also suggests that biodiversity is a public good. Accordingly, the most promising line of argument for it is a public goods argument. Recall from chapter 6, however, the problem with a public goods argument for the ESA is that the costs of sustaining or maintaining biodiversity are distributed in a way that classical liberals would reject: those who benefit pay almost nothing, and those who pay (by being subject to a regulatory taking) do not benefit. The obvious solution, from a classical liberal perspective, would be for the state to use tax dollars to purchase the land or to purchase conservation easements from private landowners and developers. There is no way to estimate the costs of this, though it is clear that they would be enormous, especially near urban areas where land prices are high. If taxpayers had to foot the entire bill to purchase the land or conservation easements on which each and every endangered species is found, it is doubtful that the ESA would enjoy whatever support it currently has.

Recently proposed legislation does address some of these problems that classical liberals have with the ESA as currently constituted. The Endangered Species Recovery Act of 2007 (H.R. 1422) proposes to allow landowners tax credits for habitat protection and habitat restoration on privately owned lands.[11] The aggregate amount of tax relief is limited, however, to a total of $400 million, and there are the inevitable exclusions and limitations that go with any such bill. As of this writing, it has not been passed into law.

Are there any conversion arguments for the ESA? Those based on the principles of deep ecology are nonstarters, since those principles are philosophical and thus cannot be used in conversion arguments; nor will they persuade classical liberals or those without firm commitments on the proper scope of government for the simple reason that they do not persuade most people. The principles of deep ecology are so far removed from what most people are willing to accept that there is little hope of converting those who do not already share those convictions. Ascribing independent intrinsic value (i.e., value that is logically independent of human beings) to ecosystems has a strangeness to it that makes any argument that depends on it something only a philosopher (or a religious mystic) could love—and not even most of them. Deep ecologists are the Bishop Berkeleys of the environmental movement. As Hume said of Berkeley's arguments for the unreality of matter, "they admit of no answer and produce no conviction" (Hume 1975 [1777], 155n1). However, it would not be difficult to formulate a conversion argument in defense of protecting some high-profile celebrity megafauna species such as bald eagles, wolves, and grizzly bears, but the ESA is comprehensive in its reach, calling for the preservation of each and every endangered species, no matter how inconsequential, within the borders of the United States. This includes a whole host of species that the vast majority of people do not know about or care about. One could, of course, appeal to the instrumental value of biodiversity for human beings and their purposes, but that guides the discussion back toward public goods.

By contrast, the argument against the ESA as currently constituted is fairly straightforward and close to the surface: even with the recent Department of Interior's policies of Safe Harbor, Candidate Conservation Agreements, and No Surprises, there is no assurance that landowners could not have enormous costs imposed on them to save the habitat of endangered species. None of these policies ensure that there will be no more cases like that of Ben Cone. If the ESA imposed only minor burdens on landowners, the case for demanding compensation for every regulatory taking would be less than compelling, since it would presuppose a Lockean conception of private property rights that only classical liberals are inclined to accept. Or, if the only property owners affected were wealthy landowners and corporations, the charge that this regulatory regime is unfair could be shrugged off. But the ESA is not like that; it has imposed substantial burdens on the large and small property owners alike—burdens for which they have not been compensated by those who have benefited from the preservation of these species. Moreover, it is not only property owners who have been harmed. Jobs disappeared in the Pacific Northwest at a much faster rate than they otherwise would have because of attempts to save the habitat of the spotted owl.[12] The benefits of biodiversity flow to everyone in the nation, indeed to everyone on the planet. The latter benefit but do not pay, whereas the affected landowners and others pay but do not benefit, at least on net. One does not have to be a modern liberal to find this deeply unfair, but it helps.

The problem goes to the very heart of the ESA. As the Supreme Court said in *Tennessee Valley Auth. v. Hill,* 437 U.S. 153, 187 (1977), "the plain language of the Act, buttressed by its legislative history, shows clearly that Congress viewed the value of endangered species as 'incalculable.'" This means that species preservation has infinite value and cannot be traded off against virtually anything. The act does contain narrow classes of exceptions (16 U.S.C. § 1539): a person may defend himself (but not his property) against a member of an endangered species, Native Americans can continue to hunt or fish endangered species for subsistence purposes, indigenous Alaskans can still carve scrimshaw, and so on. But the thrust of the act, as the Court correctly found, prohibits trade-offs. As a practical matter, of course, some trade-offs are made, but the absolutist character of the act has been barely diminished.

There is no doubt that the ESA answers to a real and legitimate problem: biodiversity has declined, and habitat destruction by humans is a primary cause. In "Modern Extinctions in the Kilo-Death Range," Nott et al. say, "regional extinction rates are typically three orders of magnitude higher than background rates deduced from the fossil record…Habitat loss is widely thought to be the predominant cause of extinction" (Nott, Rogers, and Pimm 1995, 17). This theme is echoed in countless publications, ranging from the popular to the scholarly. Still, there is something odd about assigning infinite value, even at the level of aspiration, to biodiversity. There is a useful parallel with air and water pollution, first suggested in chapter 6, that is worth considering. Modern life cannot proceed without permitting some air and water pollution, though it is easily possible for either or both to get out of hand to the point where the state should step in and regulate them. Classical liberals could agree to this on the grounds that clean air and clean water are public goods that create genuine public goods problems, and because only the state can effectively address these problems, it is up to the state, through the democratic process, to determine how clean each should be. Indeed, any sensible liberal could agree to this, whatever his or her commitments are about property rights. Similarly, it seems that modern society cannot really function without some loss of biodiversity, despite the lofty sentiments expressed in the Findings section of the ESA. Biodiversity does appear to be a public good, and at some level of its loss, a genuine public goods problem exists. The difficulty is to find the right state solution to it.

An important disanalogy, at least in the case of air pollution, is that nearly everyone who benefits from activities that cause pollution is also harmed by that very pollution and its associated costs. Automobile owners in the Los Angeles basin know that part of the price they pay for the convenience of owning and operating an automobile is the somewhat dirtier air they breathe, and the higher taxes and motor vehicle operating costs (including higher gasoline costs) they must endure. These costs serve as a democratic check on standard setting and enforcement by the state, since if the state imposes standards that are too strict (i.e., whose costs are too high), popular pressure will be brought to bear against those doing the imposing through the democratic process. The costs of the ESA, by contrast, are largely borne by a small minority of the population, and to the extent that they are reflected in the prices of other goods and services (e.g., homes and land), they are invisible.

It is a safe bet that the extinction of plant and animal species (some caused by human activity, some not) is going on at this very moment in various places throughout the United States. After all, species loss is an entirely natural phenomenon, and natural history has witnessed catastrophic species loss in the past that dwarfs what is taking place today and that had nothing to do with human activity. The really hard question is how much of this loss that is currently caused by human activity should be permitted. The law seemingly avoids this question by answering, "none of it." This in turn requires that government bureaucrats be given significant discretionary power—inevitably exercised with some measure of arbitrariness (e.g., as illustrated in the Balcones Canyonlands Conservation Plan) to impose uncompensated regulatory takings on landowners. The arbitrary exercise of discretionary power by unelected bureaucrats is always a bad thing from any liberal perspective. There is no obvious answer to the really hard question. Economic factors have to be taken into account, which, as economists are fond of reminding us, is just another way of saying that other values have to be taken into account. Making the sort of trade-offs prohibited by the ESA cannot be avoided, but it is now being done by unelected bureaucrats exercising their own judgment as they see fit; that, coupled with the sheer unfairness of the burdens it imposes, are the key premises in the main conversion argument against the act as currently constituted.

Section 404 of the Clean Water Act

The Clean Water Act of 1972, as amended in 1977, contained a section (404) on dredging and navigable waters (codified at 33 U.S.C. § 1344). This section gives the secretary of the army, through the chief engineer of the Army Corps of Engineers, the authority to require permits to discharge dredge or fill material into the navigable waters of the United States. On the face of it, this part of the CWA looks relatively straightforward: one can easily imagine how the discharge of dredge or fill material might render otherwise navigable waters (public property, by convention) unnavigable or might create an environmental hazard, such as pollution, if the dredged or fill material dumped into the navigable waterways were toxic. A public goods argument and/or an argument based on common law negative externalities in favor of these provisions looks easy. In 1975, however, an environmental organization, the Natural Resources Defense Council, successfully sued the Army

Corp of Engineers to get them to take jurisdiction over all wetlands in the nation, relying on a creative understanding of the meaning of the term "navigable waters of the United States" to bring wetlands under the Corps' jurisdiction. According to this lower court decision, "Congress by defining the term 'navigable waters' in section 502(7) of the Federal Water Pollution Control Act Amendments of 1972...to mean 'the waters of the United States, including the territorial seas,' asserted federal jurisdiction over the nation's waters to the maximum extent permissible under the Commerce Clause of the Constitution. Accordingly, as used in the [Clean] Water Act, the term is not limited to the traditional tests of navigability" (*NRDC v. Callaway*, 392 F. Supp. 685, 686 (D.D.C. 1975)).

So, "navigable waters," within the meaning of the statute as interpreted by the courts, do not really have to be navigable after all. By some estimates, this would give the Corps regulatory authority over some 270 to 300 million acres of land in the United States, at least 80 million acres of which are private property (*Rapanos v. United States* 547 U.S. 715 (2006), Scalia, J., dissenting; Lewis 2001, 4; Riggs and Freeman 2002, 53). In light of this decision, it became clear that a lot of regulation would have to take place at the wholesale level, which indeed is what happened. Using guidelines developed by the Environmental Protection Agency (EPA), general permits are routinely issued on a nationwide or regional basis for minor encroachments such as road crossings, utility line backfills, and bank stabilization projects. For larger projects not fitting the criteria for a national or regional permit, an individual permit is required. These permit applications are subject to a high degree of scrutiny, similar to that imposed by the ESA.[13] As David Sunding explains, the Army Corps of Engineers is guided by the following considerations:

(1) Does the applicant have no practicable alternative that would avoid impacts to the waters of the United States, and has the applicant minimized unavoidable impacts?

(2) Does the mitigation proposal adequately compensate for any adverse impacts of the project?

(3) Does the project contribute to significant degradation of the aquatic ecosystem?

(4) Is the state where the activity is to take place satisfied that the project is consistent with state water quality standards and coastal zone management plans?

(5) Is the project contrary to the public interest? (Sunding 2003, 30–31)

Of necessity, representatives of the Corps must exercise consider-able discretion in the approval process. Number (5) especially can be used to create all manner of mischief for owners of private property.

One of the most contentious issues in the enforcement of section 404 is the definition of wetlands covered by the law. Although as indicated above, the D.C. Circuit Court adopted an expansive definition, later decisions by other courts, including those by the Supreme Court, have redefined it more restrictively. In 1997, an appellate court held that the government actually had to demonstrate the connection with interstate commerce and could not simply declare it so (*United States v. Wilson,* 133 F.3d 251 (4th Cir. 1997)). In 1998, another federal appeals court overturned the so-called Tulloch Rule, which effectively prohibited the dredging of wetlands *(National Mining Association v. U.S. Army Corps of Engineers,* No. 97–5099 (D.C. Cir., 1998)). The prohibition embodied in the Tulloch Rule was based on the theory that some of the material removed in the dredging process would inevitably fall back into the wet-land, so that the dredger, being unable to wipe his chin as it were, was actually doing some filling into a so-called "navigable waterway," which meant dredging could be regulated.[14] The court did not buy it, ruling that the Corps had exceeded its statutory authority.[15] In *Solid Waste Agency of Northern Cook Cty.(SWANCC) v. Army Corps of Engineers,* 531 U.S. 159 (2001), the Supreme Court invalidated the Corps' attempt to assert juris-diction over isolated wetlands that might be visited by migratory birds, who presumably crossed state lines in the course of doing their business. However, in *United States v. Riverside Bayview Homes, Inc.,* 474 U.S. 121 (1985), the Court did agree that wetlands directly adjacent to navi-gable waterways were within the Corps' jurisdiction. Finally, in 2006 in *Rapanos v. United States,* 547 U.S. 715 (2006), the Court squarely faced the issue of how closely a wetland has to be related to or connected to a genuinely navigable waterway to be subject to the act. Writing for a plu-rality of four justices (Scalia, Thomas, Roberts, and Alito), Justice Scalia was ready to return to a more restrictive meaning of the term, "waters of the United States," which would rule out everything but waterways that actually were navigable, their immediate tributaries, and directly adjacent wetlands. However, the swing voter, Justice Kennedy, was not persuaded. He believed that there only had to be "a significant nexus" between the wetland and some (actually) navigable waterway for the Corps to assert jurisdiction. In his concurrence, he said,

wetlands possess the requisite nexus, and thus come within the statutory phrase "navigable waters," if the wetlands, either alone or in combination with similarly situated lands in the region, significantly affect the chemical, physical, and biological integrity of other covered waters more readily understood as "navigable." When, in contrast, wetlands' effects on water quality are speculative or insubstantial, they fall outside the zone fairly encompassed by the statutory term "navigable waters." (*Rapanos v. United States*, 547 U.S. 715, at 780 (2006))

Well, that certainly clarifies the scope of the law. This was Justice Kennedy's contribution to the semantic eutrophication of the meaning of "navigable waters."

At the end of the day, the question at issue is not a metaphysical one of coming up with a stylized definition of "navigable waters," or indeed even "wetlands." (The latter term, by the way, is not even mentioned in the statute.) The central question is instead a social policy question of how much of the surface area of the United States should be subject to the permitting process run by the Army Corps of Engineers. There seems to have been a judicial usurpation of legislative authority, which resulted in thrusting upon the Army Corps of Engineers vast regulatory powers not included in the actual legislation; this judicial usurpation was done in such a way that the courts had to revisit repeatedly the question of the scope of the Corps' authority. The statute as written is about as useful as a divining rod in answering that question. It never occurred to these judges at any level to tell the legislature, in effect: "You want to regulate wetlands? Pass a law."

That problem to one side, what argument can be given for section 404 of the CWA as it has been interpreted by the courts? In discussions of the benefits of wetlands, it is customary to distinguish functions from values.[16] Functions compose the processes that occur in wetlands, whether or not they are valued by human beings. "Values" refer to characteristics of, or processes that occur in, wetlands that human beings happen to value. Let us begin with the functions or processes that occur in wetlands:

1. Wetlands moderate the volume and velocity of water that enters them. This includes storm runoff but also seasonal flooding. Wetlands permit spatial spreading of flow.
2. By maintaining contact between groundwater and surface water, wetlands serve as an interface to allow surface water to replenish groundwater and vice-versa.
3. Water detention in wetlands reduces the kinds and amounts of dissolved and suspended substances in water. In this way,

wetlands diminish eutrophication by removing part of the
nutrient load from the water.

4. Various plant forms, fish, mammals, and birds inhabit wetlands.

When human beings come into contact with wetlands, they often
conform their activities to these processes in ways they find advantageous: wetlands prevent erosion and flooding of land humans find
valuable; they help replenish groundwater in times of drought; since
water quality (a value term) is defined by reference to the quantity and
variety of suspended and dissolved substances, wetlands enhance
water quality by reducing eutrophication; finally, wetlands produce
fish, mammals, and birds that have commercial and aesthetic value.
Two-thirds of U.S. shellfish and commercial sports fisheries rely on
coastal marshes for spawning, and 35 percent of endangered species
are wetland-dependent (Parenteau 1991, 308).

Because of the peculiar qualities of water, the first three of these
benefits are public goods (or their absence is a public bad). Fish,
birds, and mammals, as well as various plant species, are not public
goods, though the biodiversity they represent is. One could construe
(the absence of) all four of these benefits as public goods problems
that only state action can effectively solve. However, as was noted in
chapter 6, the problem with section 404 of the CWA is that the kind
of state solution it imposes is not one that classical liberals could
accept, because of the distribution of the costs: those who benefit are
not burdened and those who are burdened do not benefit.

The other side of the coin is that sometimes people modify the land
to suit their needs, as when wetlands are drained and converted to
agricultural uses. Indeed, for many years the policy of the federal government was to eliminate wetlands. The Swamplands Acts of 1849,
1850, and 1860 transferred millions of acres of wetlands to the states
to be drained for agricultural purposes. Flood control, mosquito control, and other government projects also destroyed wetlands, though
it appears that drainage for agricultural purposes was the main impetus behinds wetlands conversion:

> The Department of Agriculture estimates that annual wetland
> conversions were as high as 800,000 acres per year in the con-
> tinental U.S. before 1954. In the 1950s, for a variety of reasons,
> net wetland conversion slowed to an estimated 458,000 acres
> per year, but America's stock of wetlands was still diminishing

rapidly. By 1954, wetland acreage in the lower 48 states had dropped by more than 30 percent since the nation's founding. (Adler 1999, 12)

Conversion to agricultural uses is now prohibited by the Food Security Act of 1985 (16 U.S.C. § 3801 et seq.). Though cropland converted before 1985 was grandfathered in, the opportunity cost of convertible wetlands has fallen on some private landowner or other. It is difficult to know the extent of the burden property owners face. In explaining the apparent success of section 404, William Lewis says,

in fact, the Section 404 program has succeeded in protecting wetlands not mainly through the denial of permits, but rather through the preference of potential permit seekers to stay away from wetlands in order to avoid delay caused by permitting and to escape potentially costly mitigation that might be extracted from them through permitting. (Lewis 2001, 130–31)

Of course, it is hard to see how a property owner can "stay away" from wetlands if he finds that he happens to own some, or if the criteria for wetlands are shifting or in dispute, but those problems to one side, the mitigation issue is important in light of the "No Net Loss" policy. Subject to various qualifications and exceptions, this policy requires that the loss of wetlands be offset by the restoration of damaged or former wetlands or the creation of new wetlands. That is part of the permitting process, and can impose real burdens on property owners.

It is hard to see what a conversion argument for section 404 would look like. By contrast, a conversion argument against this part of the CWA is fairly straightforward: it parallels exactly the conversion argument against the ESA. Like the ESA, section 404 of the CWA imposes substantial uncompensated burdens on owners of private property, and that is unfair. There is also something odd and unmotivated about the official "No Net Loss" policy that successive administrations have followed. It is clear that some wetlands serve purposes and functions that are extremely valuable, but that does not explain why the total number of acres of wetlands in the United States should remain constant—just as there is no discernible reason why the number of extant species should never decrease. The fundamental problem with both the Endangered Species Act and section 404 of the Clean Water Act is nicely captured in a national survey commissioned by the Fish and Wildlife Service and carried out by Belden and Russonello, Inc., in 1996: 87 percent of those surveyed find it personally important that biodiversity be maintained; 77 percent support the expenditure of more federal tax dollars for that purpose, but only 48 percent are themselves willing to pay more taxes for that purpose (Lewis 2001, 42n1). *Res ipsa loquitur.*

The upshot of this discussion of both section 404 of the 1972 Clean Water Act and the 1973 Endangered Species Act is that public goods arguments are probably the only arguments that might succeed. The peculiar properties of water make some of the benefits of the preservation of some wetlands public goods, though the "No Net Loss" policy, even at the level of aspiration, is not well motivated. The same problem afflicts the Endangered Species Act, which has a similar policy regarding biodiversity and species disappearance. The problem in both cases, however, is that the state solutions to these possible public goods problems embodied in the respective existing regulatory regimes would be rejected by classical liberals because of the distribution of the costs. The unfairness of that burden is the key premise in conversion arguments against these two regulatory regimes. Moreover, it is difficult to see how one could mount conversion arguments in their favor. Given that arguments based on the principles of deep ecology are not available, these two items of the modern liberal regulatory agenda are not supported by arguments that could command wide assent.

Imposing Values

Deciding on the Proper Scope of Government

Arguments for and against the modern liberal regulatory agenda have been exhaustively considered in the preceding chapters. One purpose of this extended consideration has been to show that there is persistent reasonable disagreement about most of this agenda. There are conversion arguments, which are more or less compelling, for all these items, with a few exceptions. The two land use regulatory regimes as currently constituted—those imposed by the Endangered Species Act and section 404 of the Clean Water Act regulating wetlands—are difficult to defend by a conversion argument and cannot be defended by a public goods argument, at least absent some compensation for property owners subject to regulatory takings under these acts. Those regulatory takings can and have imposed enormous costs on private parties for the benefit of everyone. The simple unfairness of these impositions makes them very difficult to defend. Those elements of the modern liberal regulatory agenda to one side, there are decent conversion arguments for all the other elements on that agenda, even if classical liberals do not find them compelling. This is the modern liberal vision of the proper role of government, as it pertains to the regulation of private property rights. On their view, government, in the form of the relevant laws and regulatory bureaucracies, acts as a counterweight to powerful private interests, which for various reasons are apt to do things that are not in the public interest. All the problems in the regulatory bureaucracies are problems of detail that can be solved by hiring better people, writing better rules, or even modifying legislation.

By contrast, classical liberals favor dismantling nearly all of these regimes, as currently constituted, and they have conversion arguments to support their views. There are some exceptions, that is, some regulations that some classical liberals could accept: (1) legal prohibitions on disparate treatment discrimination on the basis of race, and so on, and quid pro quo sexual harassment; (2) a law requiring equal pay for equal work; (3) core provisions of the National Labor Relations Act relating to the right to unionize; (4) an FDA, though stripped of its authority to preapprove every new drug; (5) perhaps some regulation of consumer products affecting children; (6) some statutory changes to tort law; and that's about it. Not all classical liberals could be so persuaded.

Libertarians, especially those in the natural rights tradition, would hold their ground, but if some of the modern liberal conversion arguments of the last four chapters are good ones and if there really are no good classical liberal conversion counterarguments, other classical liberals could be persuaded to make some exceptions and accommodations. Whether those exceptions and accommodations can be rendered consistent and coherent is of course another question, which must be left for another time. Nevertheless, even with the maximum concessions made by these relatively moderate classical liberals, the changes envisioned would be enormous. Endangered species, with the possible exception of a few celebrity megafauna, would be on their own. Damp ground all over the United States would be safe from the Army Corps of Engineers. There would be no mandatory minimum wage, or legally mandated time and a half overtime pay; no mandated family and medical leave. Affirmative action in the form of preferential hiring policies would either be permitted but not encouraged, or legally forbidden, depending whether a disparate treatment exception remains when title VII is swept away; no legal prohibitions on age discrimination, hostile environment sex discrimination, or discrimination on the basis of disability. No OSHA, no CPSC, no occupational licensure. And, at this point, modern liberals would add, "and the life of man, solitary, poor, nasty, brutish, and short." The differences are indeed dramatic. These moderate classical liberals are moderate only by comparison to their stiff-necked libertarian friends. Their disagreements with modern liberals are many, varied, and profound.

In light of these disagreements, what is to be done, as Lenin might ask? After all, at the end of the day, someone's values, someone's vision of the proper scope of government, is going to be imposed on the polity, and indeed the twentieth century has witnessed the imposition of modern liberal values and the modern liberal vision, at least insofar as regulation and transfer policies are implicated. (In tax policy, the record has been more mixed.) This raises the question of whether this imposition has been politically and morally legitimate in the face of persistent reasonable disagreement about the wisdom of those agendas. Disagreements about the proper scope of government do not of course exhaust the kinds of disagreements that can arise in a modern polity. For example, the level of military spending and acceptable levels of air pollution must be decided on, but in cases such as these the question of the proper scope of government is not at issue. Both classical liberals and modern liberals agree that government needs to decide this sort of thing, and assuming a fair and open debate and a commitment to democracy, those who come up short have no legitimate grounds for complaint—even if they think some issue was wrongly decided. However, when the question concerns the proper scope of government, as it does in areas covered by the modern liberal regulatory agenda, it seems that more is required. In these areas, disagreement is not merely about the details of the law or about what level of resources should be committed to a government function that is widely agreed to be legitimate, but instead there is disagreement about whether it is legitimate for the government to intervene in a private ordering in the first place. That disagreement is more fundamental. Liberalism by definition favors limited government, so the question of how limited government should be has special salience for liberals of all persuasions in a way that it does not for, say, totalitarian socialists. This suggests that in this internal debate among liberals, there is a special burden on whatever side ends up having its way and imposing its values and imposing its vision of the proper role or scope of government on the polity.

Thus the question arises about whether the imposition of the modern liberal regulatory agenda has been politically and morally legitimate in light of the persistent reasonable disagreement about its wisdom and morality.

The purpose of this chapter is to provide a framework for answering this question. To this end, what is needed are principles by which to judge whether the imposition of someone or some group's values, more specifically, someone or some group's vision of the proper scope of government, is legitimate. These principles would apply to the various regulatory regimes but should also apply to other aspects of the dispute between modern liberals and classical liberals in tax policy, transfers, and indeed in any other area that implicates the question of government's proper role. These principles can be used to evaluate the legitimacy of the imposition of the modern liberal regulatory agenda on contemporary U.S. society and would provide guidance to classical liberals about how to proceed, should they ever be in a position to impose their values. Although the requirements to be discussed below will appear to be excessively demanding, "intellectual," and unsuitable for the rough and tumble world of politics, at the end of this chapter, I shall offer some preliminary suggestions about why these appearances are misleading. Chapter 12 extends these suggestions by applying these principles or requirements to selected elements of the modern liberal regulatory agenda in a way that demonstrates their reasonableness.

To begin the search for these requirements, recall from chapter 5 the situation of liberals vis-à-vis the anarchists regarding the provision of national defense. Someone's collective values regarding national security are going to be imposed; that is unavoidable. Assuming the liberals have the votes and the guns to enforce it, it will be their collective values. Anarchists living in that society may or may not share any principles or values, either substantive or procedural, with liberals that would allow agreement about national defense to be reached on common ground. If there is no common ground in the form of shared principles, then reasoned debate and disagreement could still occur, in the sense that those on each side could give their reasons for what they believe, but it would be pointless since there is no way for either side to get a toehold in the belief structure of the other side. All that would remain is the question of how liberals are to treat the anarchists. They are constrained in that treatment only by their own principles of practical reasoning and morality. The situation is apparently more hopeful in the dispute between modern liberals and classical liberals if only because there are some shared commitments, including most notably, a commitment to limited constitutional government, to democracy, and as I shall suggest, a commitment to reason, or more exactly, to the process of giving reasons. Let us consider each of these commitments in more detail, beginning with the first two.

All liberals are committed to limited, constitutional government in the sense that all liberals believe that certain aspects of social life are off limits to state action. These limitations are embodied in the personal and political rights discussed in chapter 1. Classical and modern liberals also agree on the legitimacy of democratic governance. The grounds of that commitment are various. Modern liberals who are social contract theorists (e.g., Rawls 1971) find it in the actual, tacit, or hypothetical consent of the governed. Modern liberal descendants of the founders of Utilitarianism (e.g., Goodin 1995) believe in democracy as the instrumentality best suited to maximize social utility. For other modern liberals (e.g., Gutmann and Thompson 1996; Fishkin 1991), the source of their commitment is found in the conviction that collective democratic deliberation, within the limits set by personal and political rights, has intrinsic value and/or tends to produce the best outcome, however that is to be understood.[1] Whatever the source of their commitment to democracy, modern liberals are committed to the proposition that democratic procedures should be used to determine the proper scope of government in tax, transfer, and regulatory policy, as long as personal and political rights are not infringed upon. To see why, recall the argument from chapter 2 for the proposition that modern liberal attitudes about tax policy and spending policy presuppose social ownership of productive assets, that is, they presuppose the proposition that society, as principal, has at least a partial prior ownership claim on the productive assets of a society for which the state acts as agent. The idea is that modern liberals believe that the amount and distribution of the tax burden and the ways in which tax revenues can be spent are matters of state discretion within very broad limits; tellingly, tax cuts themselves are viewed as a form of spending—"tax expenditures"—as they are often called. This presupposes a priority of ownership of productive assets by the state. That priority is cashed out in one or more of three ways: first, in a state of nature, society would have an enforceable morally legitimate claim on some of people's income and wealth. In other words, there is a kind of primordial moral obligation to share that can be backed by coercive power. Second, the extraction of revenue from individuals by the state need not be conceived of as an exchange for which the state must provide something of comparable value in return, since that revenue did not belong to the individual in the first place. Finally, it is up to the state to decide how to slice and dice all the incidents of ownership identified by Honoré at the beginning of chapter 3, guided by whatever considerations modern liberals think are most salient (e.g., considerations of distributive justice). This means that management rights and rights of disposition, which are the main incidents that implicate the regulatory agenda, are matters for the state, as society's representative, to decide. This is implicit in one aspect of the way the modern liberal regulatory agenda has been imposed. Specifically, the state does not compensate individuals or businesses when a regulatory regime restricts management rights, disposition rights, or any of the other rights associated with full liberal ownership. Much of the modern liberal regulatory agenda has been imposed through the democratic process. To be sure, there are important practical limitations on the exercise of state power in these matters. Nevertheless, what these considerations about social ownership of productive assets show is that, from a modern liberal point of view, the imposition of the modern liberal regulatory agenda through the democratic process is both necessary and appropriate; after all, society has limited ownership rights in these assets in the manner just explained.

Classical liberals are also committed to limited, constitutional government and to democratic governance. Rights define the limits of limited government (about which more shortly). What about democracy? Some classical liberals are social contract theorists whose commitment to democracy is grounded in some sort of consent or agreement (e.g., Locke [1690] 1988; the Founding Fathers; Buchanan 1975). Others follow Hayek, whose commitment to democracy is to be found in the fact that democratic governance is the most effective check on the abuse of state power (Hayek [1944] 1972, 71). This is essentially a conservative justification of democracy. The question then becomes whether classical liberals can agree to the use of democratic procedures to decide the proper scope of government in regulatory, tax, and transfer policy. The answer is not straightforward.

Libertarians would object to using democratic procedures to decide these questions because they believe that property rights and freedom of contract are as stringent and inviolate as any other rights, that elected representatives should no more vote on limitations on property rights not embodied in the common law than should they vote on, for example, limitations on the right of freedom of thought and expression. For some libertarians, the use of democratic procedures might be legitimate in determining the scope and burdens of national defense, penalties and procedures in the civil and criminal justice systems, and possibly some other areas, but not for deciding questions about property rights, including income rights. This means that traditional questions about tax policy (e.g., the progressivity, if any, of the income tax), transfer policy (e.g., welfare), and regulatory policy (e.g., minimum wage law) should not be subject to democratic deliberation. An obvious source for this view might be some doctrine of natural rights. Other classical liberals are less doctrinaire. To the extent that classical liberalism is understood as a propensity to argue against government intervention in a private ordering, that propensity may be more or less strong, or, alternatively, it may be more or less easily restrained by countervailing considerations. One obvious countervailing consideration is the simple recognition of how far the existing state is from the minimal state, as celebrated in libertarian thought.

Consider, for example, Richard Epstein's version of classical liberalism, as articulated in *Simple Rules for a Complex World* (1995). Instead of hard and fast rules prohibiting various regulatory, tax, and transfer regimes, Epstein proposes various limitations on the kinds of such regimes that may be imposed. For example, regarding regulation, he says,

> Any form of regulation thus requires compensation in cash for the losses inflicted (1) unless the regulation is necessary to prevent the kinds of losses that neighbors could enjoin under ordinary tort law principles...or (2) unless some compensation *in kind* is furnished to the party whose property is taken. (Epstein 1995, 132)

The idea behind (1) is that compensation is not owed when the state's police power is legitimately exercised to prevent or redress torts; the idea behind (2) is that sometimes regulation can simultaneously impose burdens and confer benefits, as in the case of residential zoning laws. Such regulations are permissible, according to Epstein's version of classical liberalism, because landowners are compensated for the regulatory taking and thus are not made worse off because their property values increase, or at least do not decrease, because building factories and other commercial establishments has been prohibited.

Regarding taxation, he says,

> The reason for taxation in this large and complicated world is that we can never achieve unanimous consent about the funding of necessary public services, such as national defense and the maintenance of law and order. The same form of necessity that undergirds the control of monopoly—a massive coordination problem—again overrides a system that allows only for voluntary exchanges. (Epstein 1995, 137)

He believes that these considerations lead directly to a flat tax. In relating these points about taxation and regulation to the libertarian ideal, he says,

> The subsequent discussions of necessity, eminent domain, and taxation, then, marked a strategic retreat from a strong libertarian position that imposes obligations on individuals only for wrongful conduct....The supplemental rules of necessity, taxation, and eminent domain are not designed to redistribute income or wealth...Rather, these principles are all designed to overcome coordination problems that block socially desirable solutions. (Epstein 1995, 140)

Finally, Epstein recognizes the inevitability, if not the legitimacy, of transfer programs. The problem with current transfer programs is that those who shoulder the burdens are not the same as the group that imposes them:

> Redistribution no longer represents a collective acknowledgment of a collective social responsibility. Instead, a political majority...requires group A to provide benefits to group B. It is, as Leo Durocher said, a case of, "Let's you and him fight." The separation of financial responsibility from political control inexorably leads to an excessive level of benefits and to poorly designed programs...*if* there must be public redistribution, then it must be financed out of general revenues collected from the same group of individuals that votes the program into place. (Epstein 1995, 145)

Like a conservative sex educator who has been told he must discuss birth control methods, Epstein would prefer to preach abstinence, but he is willing to discuss second-best measures to safeguard the public fiscal health, if democratic polities are going to ignore his advice and go ahead and redistribute. State-funded redistribution is going to take place by means of transfer programs instituted through the democratic process. And, in fact, the same is true of regulation. Whether current regulatory regimes persist or are altered fundamentally will be decided through the democratic process. That is unavoidable. Indeed, regulation is itself a form of redistribution in that someone or some group almost always benefits at the expense of others. Epstein is simply calling for better alignment between these two groups across the board in matters of taxation, regulation, and transfers.

Other classical liberals may have other ideas about where and how to draw the line on the question of the proper scope of government regulation. For example, some may be willing to be guided by the kinds of conversion arguments canvassed in chapters 7 through 10. To allow property rights to be restricted even when their exercise does not involve the violation of the rights of others is to treat property rights as nonfundamental. In a democracy, nonfundamental questions are decided through the political process instead of through the judiciary. The openness to conversion arguments among nonlibertarian classical liberals indicates a willingness to stay the impulse to argue against government intervention in a private ordering and to admit, in effect, that in any particular case, the impulse may be wrong and should be resisted—if and only if, however, good reasons can be found.

There are also historical and pragmatic reasons for classical liberals to permit these questions to be decided democratically. From the time of the Founding up until the early twentieth century, U.S. society was arguably a classical liberal society, though not exactly a libertarian one. Many of the current restrictions and limitations on property rights were previously unthinkable. Nevertheless, large-scale historical forces (including statist ideologies, as well as industrialization and the transition from an agrarian to an urban/suburban society) operating in the last quarter of the nineteenth century and the first half of the twentieth century transformed the state in ways that permanently broadened the scope of what could be decided through the democratic process. However property rights were viewed by the Founders, the state now treats them as purely conventional; if classical liberals want to roll back the scope of government, they have no real choice but to do it piecemeal and through the democratic process.

Other considerations point in the same direction. Consider the following thought experiment. Suppose that a majority of the Supreme Court were to announce one day that they had been up all night reading *Anarchy, State, and Utopia* and were largely convinced by its main argument. Suppose further that they intended this announcement to send a signal to libertarians to prepare to sack the modern welfare-regulatory state, perhaps by hiring Hun lawyers to file lawsuits. This would undoubtedly provoke a constitutional crisis comparable to the one faced in 1937 when Roosevelt pushed his plan to pack the Supreme Court, and it is very likely that some way would be found to make the Court back down. Although this is a tactical or practical point, it is not merely that. Imposition of the libertarian vision of government in this manner would be widely regarded as illegitimate—and at a certain point what is regarded as illegitimate really is illegitimate.

Finally, classical liberalism in its nonlibertarian guise is founded on a darker conception of human nature and the human condition than both modern liberalism and libertarianism. This is reflected in Hayek's defense of democracy as a limitation on the use of state power, the basic idea being that it is less likely for state power to be exercised in truly disastrous ways if it is limited by democratic accountability. The scope of this observation is perfectly general and thus should be applied by classical liberals to their own ideas. If they are going to roll back the modern welfare-regulatory state, indeed even if they are only going to correct what, from their point of view, are its worst abuses, their fallibilism constrains them to admit that if things go badly, the changes made should not be too difficult to reverse. This means that whatever changes are instituted have to be done piecemeal and in a way that is broadly consensual.[2] Besides, these classical liberals (just like their modern liberal counterparts) believe that in a fair fight, reason is on their side, that they can persuade enough people, including some nondogmatic modern liberals, of the wisdom of their views— presumably by conversion arguments—to allow them to impose their vision of the proper role of government. For all these reasons, these nonlibertarian classical liberals can allow the proper scope of government to be decided by the democratic process.

By contrast, all liberals can agree that questions about the scope and implications of personal and political rights cannot be subject to the democratic process. These questions have to be taken off the table. However, both modern liberals and at least the nonlibertarian classical liberals are committed to the view that the proper scope of government in tax, transfer, and regulatory policy should be decided through the democratic process and thus by the elected branches of government. For modern liberals, this commitment to democratic decision-making is rooted in their doctrine of social ownership of productive assets. Society, or perhaps the state, has an (limited) ownership claim on productive assets in the first instance. This means that the (democratic) state gets to decide the contours of the various rights, terms, and conditions that constitute private ownership; they can alter the rules, within very broad limits, without compensation to the nominal private owners. Classical liberals are divided on the issue of democratic decision-making on scope-of-government questions, exclusive of personal and political rights. Libertarians, at least in the natural rights tradition, would deny that this is an appropriate venue for democratic decision-making. For them, these questions are a matter of fairly stringent rights—property rights and a right to freedom of contract to be exact—and those rights have to be upheld and enforced by the courts. Nonlibertarian classical liberals take a more nuanced view and can allow revisions in the definition of property rights in particular cases, though they may, in the manner of Epstein, impose some constraints on the types of outcomes they deem legitimate. This commitment to democratic decision-making about the proper scope of government is rooted in (1) their willingness to make exceptions to the libertarian conception of ownership rights in the face of compelling or at least persuasive conversion arguments, (2) their willingness to admit that they might be mistaken and that the implementation of their views could visit real hardship on the polity, and (3) their commitment to the process of giving reasons, coupled with an optimistic assessment of their chances for success in making their case in the democratic marketplace of ideas. Let us call this requirement, shared by modern liberals and nonlibertarian classical liberals, to decide questions about the scope of government through the democratic process the *democracy requirement*. At this point, libertarians, at least those in the natural rights tradition, have to be read out of the debate. Only the nonlibertarian classical liberals remain to carry on the dialogue with modern liberalism. But how?

Public Justification

A commitment to reason provides the beginnings of an answer. All liberals are committed to the process of giving reasons for their view of the proper role of government. Respect for persons as reasoning beings—an important liberal value—is the penultimate source of this commitment. The deepest sources of that commitment are undoubtedly various. Extracting those sources for Kantians, Utilitarians, Rawlsians, Communitarians, Deliberative Democrats, Civic Republicans, Social Contract Theorists, Natural Rights Theorists, and Hayekians, to mention just some of those who support liberal institutions, would take us too far afield. Whatever the sources, in the context of the debate among liberals about the proper scope of government, this commitment requires giving reasons for expanding or contracting that scope. Call this the *public justification requirement*. What does it involve? It might involve conversion arguments, convergence arguments from the other side's first principles, or even, in theory, common ground arguments. Suppose, however, that none of these types of arguments can be given. For instance, modern liberals might believe that the current regime of affirmative action, which involves preferential treatment programs, is required by the demands of distributive justice as they see it, but they might be willing to concede that it may not be supportable by any other type of argument. In other words, they might be perfectly well aware that their argument presupposes a philosophically contentious principle of distributive justice, such as Dworkin's principle about equal concern and respect, that their interlocutors do not accept.[3] Call these *principled sectarian arguments*. These of course are the arguments philosophers typically make to each other and to a broader public when addressing public policy questions. Could the public justification requirement be satisfied by a principled sectarian argument? After all, the fact that others reject it because they reject the principle on which it is based does not mean that the argument is not a good one.

While that is no doubt true, there are a number of reasons why principled sectarian arguments cannot be used as part of a public justification. One is based on the fact that there will often be good conversion counterarguments against the program or regulatory regime in question, as was the case with nearly all of the items on the modern liberal regulatory agenda. Those counterarguments provide reason to doubt the conclusion of any principled sectarian argument. (Reflective equilibrium cuts both ways.) Perhaps more importantly, principled sectarian arguments cannot be rationally persuasive for those who have different principled views on the issue in question. For example, classical liberals will not be impressed by arguments against cutting income tax rates that point out that society has better things to spend its money on than giving it to the rich. That clearly and directly presupposes that this money belongs to society in the first place, an assumption classical liberals will not grant. Similarly, modern liberals are not going to be impressed by an argument against title VII of the 1964 Civil Rights Act that says that employers have an absolute moral right to discriminate on the basis of race when hiring because they own their businesses. This presupposes very stringent private property rights in productive assets and a very stringent right to freedom of contract, rights that modern liberals doubt exist. These respective demurrals are quite reasonable because the first principles presupposed by these arguments on either side are almost certainly mired in philosophical disputes, the resolutions of which are, how shall we say, a long way off.

Finally, the most compelling reason against allowing principled sectarian arguments to satisfy the public justification requirement is that offering such an argument fails to show respect for one's interlocutors. One knows—or should know—beforehand that those on the other side will not accept a principled sectarian argument, at least absent a proof of the philosophical principle involved. Assuming that one has the political power to implement one's views—and that is the assumption in this context—offering an argument that one knows the other party will reject out of hand is an expression of intellectual contempt, since it does not even try to get reasoned agreement from those on the other side. It is a sad truth that much of the debate on both sides has been carried on in this spirit. One of the attractions of conversion arguments is that they seek reasoned agreement whatever the deeper philosophical commitments of both sides might be. Basic respect for persons as reasoning beings—an important liberal value—requires that one make an honest effort to persuade, and principled sectarian arguments are just not honest in this context. Just as when a teenager is prohibited from doing something she wants to do, a parent owes her an explanation that she can understand, so too do modern liberals owe an explanation to their classical liberal counterparts, and indeed to anyone, when they are going to impose their values in a way that affects the scope of government, and it has to be an explanation that they might accept. Of course, the same considerations apply if classical liberals are imposing their values by altering the scope of government. In either case, eschewing principled sectarian arguments is a way of recognizing those on whom one's values are imposed as reasoning beings, as ends in themselves, as individuals with their own values, their own conception of the good life they are seeking to advance, and their own philosophical commitments, if any. This does not mean that those being imposed upon must agree with or accept the argument. Those doing the imposing only have to give reasons that might be rationally persuasive, even if in the end they do not in fact persuade.

But to whom is the argument addressed? Certainly not just classical liberals, since some of those affected, and thus some of those who have an interest, are neither classical nor modern liberals. Ideally, this justification would have to be given to all the people in the polity who are going to be affected by the proposed change in the scope of government—it is their behavior, their situation, that will be affected by what the state does. In a modern democratic polity this is of course impossible. Those doing the imposing cannot go around to every affected businessperson and explain to him or her why, for example, the state requires that workers be paid a minimum wage or why OSHA inspectors are going to inspect his or her facilities. Since "Ought" implies "Can," substitutes have to be found. The most obvious substitutes for the set of people affected are their representatives in the legislature, who themselves may or may not be classical liberals. On one theory of republican government, these representatives "stand in for" the people they represent. Some of those thus represented are classical liberals, but many of them have no discernible principles regarding the proper scope of government—and, frankly, the vast majority of the public fits this description. The fact that the vast majority of citizens have no discernible commitment to any principles about the proper scope of government is yet another reason to avoid principled sectarian arguments, since the acceptance of the relevant sectarian principle by those affected (an acceptance which might be heavily "dispositional") cannot be assumed, especially if it is their ox that is about to be gored. For example, making the above argument against tax cuts for the wealthy in a way that presupposes social ownership of productive assets or making the argument against title VII on the grounds that employers should be free to discriminate against people on the basis of race are simply not going to be rationally persuasive to those who are neither classical liberals nor modern liberals. What about common ground arguments? These arguments presuppose only general principles that all liberals subscribe to, and it is a safe bet that most people in the United States, and indeed in all advanced, industrialized democracies, are liberals and subscribe, if only dispositionally, to commonly held liberal principles.[4,5] However, as chapter 6 shows, common ground arguments for the modern liberal regulatory agenda are not going to work, so they are ruled out. What about convergence arguments, that is, arguments that go from distinctively classical liberal premises (e.g., strict property rights, freedom of contract) to modern liberal conclusions? These will be persuasive for classical liberals, but it is unlikely that they would convince those without firm convictions (i.e., principled convictions) about the proper role of government in the contested areas. That leaves only conversion arguments. Therefore, with regard to arguments in favor of the modern liberal regulatory agenda or the classical liberal counteragenda, only conversion arguments can satisfy the public justification requirement. This is as it should be: conversion arguments presuppose no deep principles and are the sort of argument that ordinary citizens and their legislators are likely to reach for in order to justify some concrete measure in tax, transfer, or regulatory policy that they favor.

The conception of public justification employed in this chapter is different from other conceptions of public justification discussed in the contemporary philosophical literature.[6] A brief aside on some of those differences is warranted. One important one is that the object of public justification is not the liberal political order *per se,* but only a small fragment of it, a particular regulatory regime, for example. For the purposes of the disputes under consideration in this book, the liberal political order can be taken for granted. We leave it to others, who are more ambitious in their aims and less modest in their claims, to grapple with the larger question of how the liberal political order itself can be justified, especially to those with highly divergent views and values. A second difference, perhaps equally important, is that this conception of public justification is not a "success" concept in the sense that it requires actual or hypothetical agreement (e.g., by ideally rational agents). On the account of public justification defended in this chapter, a regulatory regime (or tax policy or transfer program) may be publicly justified, even if others are not persuaded and even if the regulatory regime, tax policy, or transfer program cannot, in the final analysis (whatever that might mean), be successfully defended.

Are there any substantive requirements that a conversion argument must meet to count as a public justification for altering the scope of government? This question will be addressed in detail in the next section. For now, there are some formal or procedural requirements for public justification that need to be identified and defended. Since the rationale for requiring a conversion argument is respect for persons as reasoning beings, committing any of the traditional fallacies of informal logic (e.g., an ad hominem argument) is prohibited, as indeed are nearly all the types of arguments politicians make when someone turns a camera on them and asks them to explain in thirty seconds what they think about some proposal. The real work of deliberative democracy has to take place among legislators and between the executive and the legislature.[7] Politicians can be given a pass on what they say to the public, especially since, for the most part, the public is not paying attention anyway. It is when they are dealing with the people's representatives that they have to show some respect for those on the other side as reasoning beings.

Another plausible procedural condition for public justification is that those imposing their values on others must take seriously the arguments offered by those who are opposed to what they are doing. What does that involve? At a minimum, it requires an effort to address the arguments of those on other side, which requires, also at a minimum, that those arguments not be misrepresented. Straw man arguments of the most extravagant sort abound in politics on all sides of an issue, and their repeated use in political deliberation is a great sin. The case for making an effort to understand what can reasonably be said against a proposal and then to address those reasons, was made most eloquently by John Stuart Mill in *On Liberty:*

> Complete liberty of contradicting and disproving our opinion, is the very condition which justifies us in assuming its truth for purposes of action; and on no other terms can a being with human faculties have any rational assurance of being right.... The steady

habit of correcting and completing his own opinion by collating it with those of others, so far from causing doubt and hesitation in carrying it into practice, is the only stable foundation for a just reliance on it: for, being cognisant of all that can, at least obviously, be said against him, and having taken up his position against all gainsayers—knowing that he has sought for objections and difficulties, instead of avoiding them, and has shut out no light which can be thrown upon the subject from any quarter—he has a right to think his judgment better than that of any person, or any multitude, who have not gone through a similar process. (Mill [1859] 1978, 19–20)

Mill practiced what he preached; in chapter 4 of *On Liberty* he considers two important objections to his own Harm Principle, one of which caused him to reformulate it (Mill [1859] 1978, 78–80). Part of this passage seems mistaken, however. Mill suggests that considering what can be said against an opinion does not cause "doubt and hesitation." The opposite seems to be true; a dispassionate consideration of the conversion arguments and counterarguments of chapters 7 through 10 may not result in suspension of belief (*epoche*), but it should result in some doubt and hesitation about whatever side one is antecedently inclined to favor. In his essay, "Of Miracles," Hume got it about right when he said, "a wise man...proportions his belief to the evidence...He considers which side is supported by the greater number of experiments [arguments]: to that side he inclines, with doubt and hesitation; and when at last he fixes his judgement, the evidence exceeds not what we properly call probability" (Hume [1777] 1975, 110–11). In the current case, that would mean diminishing one's convictions to the extent that the best argument on the other side looks plausible or cannot be easily refuted.

One cause of that diminution is that both sides have to engage in informed speculation about what would happen if alternative classical liberal laws and institutions were to be put in place of an existing modern liberal regulatory regime. This speculation amounts to telling stories about what one believes would be likely to happen if changes in a classical liberal direction were made. Typically there will not be a lot of evidence on which to base this speculation, though these stories are not completely groundless. Consider for example how the current practice of off-label prescribing bears on the question of what would happen if the FDA did not have to certify efficacy. Still, any story about what would happen if a regulatory regime were changed in a classical liberal direction will be partly, and maybe largely, speculative. Now it might be thought that only classical liberals have to engage in this speculation, that is, only they have to try to tell plausible stories for which there is little direct evidence about the effects of their favored changes. This would seem to place them at a permanent disadvantage vis-à-vis their modern liberal counterparts who defend existing regulatory regimes. But that is not quite correct. Modern liberal conversion arguments for the status quo depend just as crucially, though often only tacitly, on speculation about what would happen in the event that classical liberal laws and institutions were put in place. After all, modern liberals believe that the existing regulatory regimes are preventing outbreaks of various social ills that would exist in the absence of current regulations; if they do not believe that, they would not favor the existing regulatory regime. So, whether they acknowledge it or not, they are committed to comparative claims about what would happen if a classical liberal alternative were put in place.[8] After all, these regimes were put in place to deal with perceived social problems, which were quite real at the time, but those problems might not recur if these regimes were eliminated or changed. For example, the fact that the FDA successfully addressed a social problem about the content and purity of food and drugs a hundred years ago does not mean that this problem would recur if drugs did not have to be certified safe and effective by the FDA today. Tort law provides protections that did not exist in 1906 when the Pure Food and Drug Act was passed and in 1938 when the Federal Food, Drug, and Cosmetic Act was passed.

To take another example, some classical liberals are inclined to believe that racial prejudice has abated to the point where repeal of title VII would not have much effect on the scope of employment opportunities for African Americans relative to the current regime. Or, they believe that affirmative action programs as encouraged and practiced under title VII are simply not effective at achieving their ends; modern liberals are inclined to disagree. Justice O'Connor recently seemed to side with modern liberals. In a title VI case involving the University of Michigan's law school admissions process, she found racial preferences were consistent with the law, but she asserted that eventually these preferences would be unnecessary:

> Finally, race-conscious admissions policies must be limited in time. The Court takes the Law School at its word that it would like nothing better than to find a race-neutral admissions formula and will terminate its use of racial preferences as soon as practicable. The Court expects that 25 years from now, the use

of racial preferences will no longer be necessary to further the interest approved today. (*Grutter v. Bollinger et al.*, 539 U.S. 306 (2003))

Although there is much more to the dispute over title VII, or in this case title VI, than just the factual question about what would happen if it were repealed, that is undoubtedly an important part of the disagreement. Gathering evidence relevant to this factual dispute may be possible, but whatever evidence is gathered is likely to be indirect and less than conclusive. Still, some speculation about what would happen under a classical liberal regime is required for modern liberals, if they are to take their opponents seriously. In large measure, this is what taking one's opponent seriously amounts to. In this way, comparative institutional analysis becomes an essential component of any responsible discussion of the proper scope of government. Moreover, the fact that both sides must engage in counterfactual speculation is a reason for diminishing the certitude with which each side holds its respective beliefs.

Modern liberals might admit that in principle all this is correct, but when it comes to the question of actually making changes in existing institutions, caution favors the status quo. Radical change in existing regulatory regimes might look attractive in theory, but such changes will upset established expectations and may have large unintended negative consequences. This is, of course, a deeply conservative argument, which is ironic since modern liberalism historically has had a well-deserved reputation for innovation at the boundaries between state and civil society. The proper response to this argument, however, depends on the context. In some instances, the gains from regulatory reform in a classical liberal direction might be too slender or too speculative to warrant change. For example, there might not be very much to be gained from abolishing occupational licensure for physicians, especially if laws could be changed to allow other, less well-trained professionals (e.g., nurse practitioners) to take over some of the more routine tasks. Second, there are some cases in which regulatory reform should be done in stages and piecemeal, as Karl Popper might put it. Minimum wage laws and antidiscrimination laws are obvious candidates for incremental change. More generally, if the case for regulatory reform is good enough, the expertise of those with more intimate knowledge of particular regulatory bureaucracies and the problems they face needs to be brought to bear. Finally, sometimes staying with the existing regulatory regime is not a form of "playing it safe." To take the most dramatic example, people are dying every day because the existing medical products regulatory regime demands evidence of efficacy. More generally, all the existing regulatory regimes have significant downsides that classical liberal alternatives apparently lack. Of course, the converse is true as well. Those in a position to make changes have to move in a direction they think is best. "Playing it safe" has risks, as does institutional change.

To summarize, there are a number of conditions that must be met for a regulatory regime, or a change in a regulatory regime, to be publicly justified. First, the argument in its favor cannot be a sectarian argument and indeed must be a conversion argument. (Chapters 5 and 6 demonstrate that common ground arguments cannot succeed.) Only conversion arguments are sufficiently atheoretical so that they could be found persuasive by nearly any liberal, classical or modern. Although a (good) conversion argument may not successfully persuade those inclined to disagree, the case must nevertheless be made if respect is to be shown to those persons. For the same reason, public justification requires that those offering the conversion argument do not commit any of the traditional informal fallacies. Furthermore, public justification also requires that the views of those on the other side be taken seriously. Essentially, this involves gathering whatever evidence one can (however indirect it might be) that is appropriate to a comparative institutional analysis of the relevant alternatives.

The Problem of Faction and Its Relevance

The preceding section identifies the kind of argument that has to be made—a conversion argument—and the other considerations that have to be taken into account if the public justification requirement is to be met. Those considerations are mostly formal or procedural: they talk about the type of argument that should be offered and the epistemic virtues that are supposed to be exhibited. But what does the substance of these arguments look like? In other words, are there any substantive requirements that must be met in the course of offering a conversion argument in favor of some regulatory regime or in favor of some fundamental change to a regulatory regime? In fact there are. One place to begin a search for them is with a conception of the role of government that all liberals share. All liberals can agree that the main purpose of government is to create a framework within which people, either individually or collectively, can pursue their conception of the good life. There has been a dispute about whether that includes anything very substantive. Advocates of liberal neutrality say no; liberal perfectionists say yes.[9] Regardless of who is right about this question, many things are required of government if it is to discharge this task, and much of the disagreement between modern liberals and classical liberals concerns what those things are. Nevertheless, both sides can agree that one of the main impediments, perhaps the most important impediment, to the realization of their respective visions of the good society, or at least good government, is the undue and improper influence that some groups exercise over the use of state power. I shall argue that this agreement, thin though it may appear to be, can serve as the basis for an additional requirement that must be met for some vision of the proper scope of government to be legitimately imposed on a liberal polity.

For modern liberals, two overlapping groups, variously organized, are the main problem: the business community (or maybe just the big business community) and the relatively advantaged, or as they are more commonly called, "the Rich." There is no need to demonize these groups or to hold them responsible for all of society's problems, though some modern liberals do. But, according to modern liberal analysis, the baleful influence of these two groups is felt almost everywhere in government: in tax policy, the democratic process, assistance to the least advantaged, regulatory issues, the use of government-owned assets, and corporate welfare. Let us briefly consider each of these in turn.

The United States has one of the least progressive taxation systems in the contemporary industrialized world. The Republican Party has had great success at the ballot box by promising to cut taxes—and they have delivered on that promise. Most of the benefits of these tax cuts, go to the top nth percent of the population, however, where "n" is some fairly small number. The wealthy have poured resources into the political process, in part anyway, to ensure this result. Tax cuts have in turn kept the government from getting the resources necessary to help the least advantaged, as well as others to whom fate has not been kind. For example, whatever the virtues of free trade, tens of thousands of people have lost their jobs as a result of it, and the federal government has done very little to help. It is a fixed point in modern liberal political thought—maybe even their North Star by which they navigate—that the state has an obligation to help those who have been disadvantaged, especially (though perhaps not exclusively) if it has been through no fault of their own.

This is an important motivation for much of the modern liberal transfer agenda, but it is also a motivation for many items on their regulatory agenda as well. Employment law is a good illustration of this. Modern liberals believe that workers are at a permanent disadvantage relative to employers because of systematic differences in economic power that favor the latter. Regulation of the employment relation can redress, or at least address, some of these imbalances. Wage and hour legislation, mandated family and medical leave, the ground rules of collective bargaining, and antidiscrimination law have all been justified on the grounds that they redress to some extent power imbalances between employers and employees that favor the former at the expense of the latter. For example, if employers did not have some economic power over employees, employees who suffer discrimination could simply quit and go somewhere else, but because of the fear of protracted unemployment and because of their roots in their communities, doing so is usually not simple or easy. The state addresses this problem by forbidding discrimination, not only in hiring but also in promotion, termination, and in any of the terms or conditions of employment.

Turning to other forms of regulation, the phenomenon of regulatory capture is common, though not universal. Regulatory agencies are often captured by the firms they are supposed to regulate. Job offers to regulators and campaign contributions to politicians who oversee these regulatory regimes are the main conduits by which businesses make their influence felt. Their influence has been particularly palpable in agencies at the state level that provide economic regulation (e.g., rate regulation of insurance and utilities). The EEOC and the health and safety regulatory agencies seem to have been less subject to regulatory capture, and indeed they have often operated in an adversarial mode relative to the industries they regulate. The business community has been able to have some influence, however. It has supported inadequate funding and budget cuts for these regulatory agencies, which is highly effective in hamstringing them. As for government-owned assets, sweet-heart deals have been common for grazing, timber, oil, gas, and mineral leases, and for segments of the electromagnetic spectrum. And, if modern liberals are being honest, they will admit that powerful public sector unions (e.g., teachers' unions) have exploited the government's position as monopoly suppliers to win wage concessions that private sector unions can only envy. Finally, there is corporate welfare. The federal government provides a staggering array of subsidies to businesses. As the Cato Institute defines it, "corporate welfare consists of government programs that provides unique benefits or advantages to specific companies or industries."[10] According to that definition, in 2004, $90 billion was spent on sixty-five corporate welfare programs.

The great puzzle or difficulty for modern liberalism is to figure out a way to minimize or moderate the influence of the rich and the business community on the exercise of state power in all its manifestations within the context of a democracy. Restraining that influence is a necessary, though not a sufficient condition for a fuller realization of their vision of good government. Some believe that campaign finance reform is a good place to start. (More on this shortly.)

Classical liberals have a different set of villains, though there is some overlap with those of modern liberalism. The most important fact of twentieth century political life in their view is the vast expansion in the scope of government activity. This is true regardless of how one measures it. One important result of this trend has been the creation of an enormous game of musical chairs with the wealth produced in U.S. society. In this world of threats to currently held assets (through taxation and regulation) and opportunities to seize the assets of others (e.g., through subsidies), groups with a common interest organize and try to influence the process to avoid getting harmed or to gather unto themselves more than their share of the benefits of social cooperation—or both. All this is a familiar enough story, but what is distinctive about the classical liberal perspective on this is that there are no "good" interest groups, no groups anointed by history, or by their downtrodden or marginal status, or even by their age, vying for their share—a fair share—of the pie. This is because nearly all of what the government is doing with these resources is beyond its proper scope, according to classical liberals. Whether it is agribusiness supporting the Agriculture Department's Market Access Program, which gives millions of tax dollars to exporters of agricultural products to pay for their overseas advertising campaigns, or the AARP fighting to keep the way the Consumer Price Index is determined because it is the basis for calculating cost-of-living adjustments (COLAs) for Social Security, it is all illegitimate. The problem, as they see it, is not to figure out a way to restrain some groups, to reduce the share of the pie that some groups get, so that other groups can get more. That is the central problem for modern liberalism, but not for classical liberalism. Instead, the problem for the latter is to figure out a way to shrink dramatically the size of the pie, both relatively and absolutely, that the state divides up in the first place. There are a few basic legitimate functions of government, almost entirely having to do with the enforcement of rights and the provision of public goods, that need funding—and just about everything else is illegitimate. The basic problem is not limited to the transfer agenda; it concerns tax policy and the regulatory agenda as well. This point warrants some elaboration.

The main problem with the current tax system, according to classical liberals, is that the tax base and the tax rates are determined entirely through the political process with no effective check, either constitutional or legislative. This confers enormous power on elected officials, which they have exercised with impunity. Once tax rates reach a certain absolute level, a tax break can mean a great deal to its beneficiaries. Politicians are in a position to confer these tax breaks on some, which means the burden falls more heavily on others. This is why the tax code is so complex and riddled with loopholes. A politician may not be able to get some pork barrel spending program for his district, but he might be able to get a tax break for organized groups that have supported him, some of which are business groups. The only limits are those imposed by the political process itself. That process does put an effective upper limit on taxation, and sometimes the political winds blow the tax code in a direction that classical liberals approve of, as for example when the degree of progressivity of the income tax declines because of cuts in the top marginal rate. Still, most of the changes in the tax code, produced by a conspiracy of sorts between interest groups and politicians, are intended to benefit some at the expense of others and have no purpose other than that. There is insidious corruption in all of this, but the tax code is arguably the most valuable asset owned by the political class, and it would require a Herculean act of self-restraint for them to refrain from selling it off piecemeal. Modern liberals would concur with this analysis, except for the favorable judgment about the occasional decline in the degree of progressivity of the tax code. They are inclined to believe that considerations of distributive justice should shape the tax code, as well as spending programs for the benefit of the least advantaged.

Let us turn now to regulation. As the preceding four chapters make clear, classical liberals oppose nearly all of the modern liberal regulatory agenda. Grounds for this opposition are various. Libertarians who believe in natural rights argue straight down from their political principles regarding property rights and freedom of contract. Other classical liberals oppose this agenda on other grounds, which were articulated in the classical liberal conversion counterarguments of chapters 7 through 10. Sometimes, the complaint is that a particular regulatory regime simply does not have its intended effect. For example, OSHA and the CPSC seem not to have done much good. In other instances, these regulatory regimes have unintended bad consequences that arguably would be eliminated or significantly diminished if the classical liberal alternative were in place. The drug loss and drug lag problems would probably be much smaller if the FDA no longer monopolized the drug approval process. Employees from protected groups would no longer have limited immunity for incompetence on the job nor would they be able to extort money from their employers if and when they are shown the door. Occupational groups would no longer be able to charge a premium for their services because they have restricted the supply of practitioners. Not all classical liberal complaints against the modern liberal regulatory agenda can be represented as complaints about the misuse of state power to benefit some at the expense of others, but most of them can.

As a first approximation, the predators in the classical liberal vision of current U.S. society are the organized interest groups, and the prey are the unorganized taxpayers and consumers. This picture is misleading, however, for two reasons. First, there are the temporarily "virtuous lobbyists," representing the temporarily virtuous interest groups. A story from the 1970s illustrates this point. Sometimes interest groups seek to have the government impose safety regulations on products they manufacture because they know that it will be more difficult or expensive for foreign manufacturers to comply with those standards. In one case, the trade association for U.S. bicycle manufacturers proposed design standards that would have effectively excluded foreign-made bicycles from the U.S. market (Cornell, Noll, and Weingast 1976, 493–94). The CPSC was unaware of this until it was brought to their attention by an organized consumer group. The CPSC repealed the standard and started over but only because of pressure from this interest group. A lot of the lobbying that goes on prevents bad things from happening, including the imposition of bad regulations, whose primary effect is to benefit some interest group at the expense of others, usually consumers. Whatever their motives— and they are usually self-interested—these lobbyists are indeed doing the Lord's work when they prevent some organized interest group from capturing economic rents through the regulatory process. A second reason why this picture is misleading is that it suggests that predators and prey are distinct groups. A taxpaying consumer might be a founding member of a particularly bloodthirsty interest group. Consider, for example, Archer Daniels Midland (ADM) and its chairman, Dwayne Andreas. Some believe these two to be the all-time winners in the corporate welfare version of the Publishers' Clearinghouse Sweepstakes. Many times has the government come around to the ADM household with the oversized check. As James Bovard explains,

> ADM and its chairman Dwayne Andreas have lavishly fertilized both political parties with millions of dollars in handouts and in return have reaped billion-dollar windfalls from taxpayers and consumers. Thanks to federal protection of the domestic sugar industry, ethanol subsidies, subsidized grain exports, and various other programs, ADM has cost the American economy billions of dollars since 1980 and has indirectly cost Americans tens of billions of dollars in higher prices and higher taxes over that same period. At least 43 percent of ADM's annual profits are from products heavily subsidized or protected by the American government. Moreover, every $1 of profits earned by ADM's corn sweetener operation costs consumers $10, and every $1 of profits earned by its ethanol operation costs taxpayers $30. (Bovard, 1995)

Andreas probably pays a hefty amount in income taxes, but he more than makes up for it in the salary and benefits package a grateful board of directors has given him as chairman of the board at ADM. It is as if the James gang's grand tour of the banks of the Old West and the Midwest had corporate sponsors. Those sponsors would have gladly paid Jesse and Frank handsomely. Classical liberals are uniformly sympathetic to the public choice analysis of government, which attempts to explain the workings of government and the attendant use of state power to enrich some at the expense of others by modeling government actors and lobbyists in the same way economists model consumers, entrepreneurs, firms, and capital providers. Interest groups are analogized to consumers, who "demand" legislation from politicians. The latter are like the entrepreneurs who give the consumers what they want, sometimes even anticipating what they might want and then selling them on the idea. The bureaucracies through which the goods are supplied are analogized to the firms. Finally, the taxpayers are like the capitalists, in the sense that they provide the resources that the political entrepreneurs use. Unfortunately, the political process is a money-losing operation for the taxpayers, except for public goods such as national defense that they get, usually at inflated prices; for the rest of it, what taxpayers receive in exchange for their taxes are vague promises that their lives will be improved.

One would expect modern liberals to be fundamentally sympathetic to the public choice analysis of government spending. After all, this picture paints their favorite villains in a particularly bad light. Powerful special interests, accountable to no one, put their hands in the till and then stuff their pockets with subsidies and tax breaks (which from a modern liberal point of view are equivalent). Modern liberals have not embraced this analysis of government as wholeheartedly as one might expect, however. One reason might be that it portrays government and government service too bleakly. Both are modeled as merely another venue through which individuals pursue their self-interest with scant regard to the public interest. Since modern liberals view government as the chief instrumentality to correct the defects of the free market—the latter, on their view, runs entirely on self-interest (and on some accounts, greed)—it is not surprising that they find public choice analysis incomplete at best. They are inclined to believe that this analysis cannot apply to all state actors (modern liberal politicians and bureaucrats) and their political supporters (i.e., themselves). Still, when it comes to most of the things that the contemporary state does that modern liberals disapprove of, public choice explanations are attractive, even compelling.

What emerges from this overview are overlapping but different visions of what is wrong with modern society, at least insofar as it is traceable to government. In modern parlance, the problem is the untoward influence of special interests. In the language of James Madison, it is the problem of faction, as discussed in *Federalist* 10. At this juncture, it would be helpful to review Madison's analysis of the problem of faction, his proposed solution, and its contemporary relevance.

As Madison defines it, a faction is "a number of citizens, whether amounting to a minority or majority of the whole, who are united and actuated by some common impulse of passion, or of interest, adverse to the rights of other citizens, or to the permanent and aggregate interests of the community" (Hamilton, Jay, and Madison [1787–1788] 2000, 54). The problem of faction, as it manifests itself in a democracy, is that, "our governments are too unstable; that the public good is disregarded in the conflicts of rival parties; and that measures are too often decided, not according to the rules of justice, and the rights of the minor party; but by the superior force of an interested and overbearing majority" (Hamilton, Jay, and Madison [1787–1788] 2000, 54). Madison goes on to discuss some of the more particular sources of the problem, including differences of religious opinion and the pursuit of preeminence and power by ambitious men. But the most powerful and durable source of the problem is the "various and unequal distribution of property." This accounts for the differences in interests. As examples, Madison cites creditors and debtors, landed interests, moneyed interests, mercantile interests, and manufacturing interests. A lot of what government does (and has been doing since the time of the Founders) is to referee the conflicts among these groups.

According to Madison, there are only two methods of dealing with the problem of faction: remove its causes or control its effects. The former requires either the destruction of liberty or giving everyone the same opinions, passions, and interests. The destruction of liberty is the cure that is worse than the disease. As to giving people the same opinions, given the fallibility of human reason, that is not possible. Passions and interests of necessity differ because of the diversity of faculties (i.e., talents and abilities) in humankind and the "various and unequal distribution of property" to which this diversity of faculties gives rise. The only viable option, then, is to control the effects of faction. So far so good; both classical liberals and modern liberals would concur with Madison's analysis of the problem. Fundamentally, there is no completely satisfactory solution to the problem of faction, and this too is something that modern liberals and classical liberals could agree on. But, some things can be done to control its effects.

Madison's solution is embedded in the Constitution and the historical circumstances of the nation's founding. It consists of a number of different elements. One is the republican principle, which shuns direct democracy in favor of rule by elected representatives. Direct democracy, according to Madison, would be gasoline on the fire of the problem of faction. Second, the republic should be large and have a federal structure. The latter requires a division of labor among different levels of government; state and local governments have a different purview from that of the national government. Besides, the existence of state governments was a "fact on the ground" that had to be taken into account. Following some suggestive observations by Hume, Madison believed that a large republic would multiply the number of factions and make it more difficult for them to coalesce into a temporary majority that could and would ignore the public good and the rights of the minority. Communication and concerted action would be much harder to effectuate if the number of factions were greater. A large number of citizens also make direct democracy infeasible.

Finally, and this is where the Founders borrowed heavily from Montesquieu, the guiding principle of the structure of the federal government was to be separation of powers within a system of checks and balances. The legislative, executive, and judicial branches were to be separate and independent, with each branch endowed with mechanisms to block or limit the actions of the others. One of the most important of these was the principle of judicial review, by which actions of the legislature and president were subject to review by the courts to judge their compatibility with the Constitution. This principle was not fully articulated until *Marbury v. Madison,* 5 U.S. 137 (1803), though some believe that it was implicit in the structure of the Constitution. The basic motivation for all these features of government was to constrain the power of the elected branches as a way of mitigating the problem of faction.

The problem with Madison's solution, according to the modern liberal reading of history, was that the price was too high. The Constitution as originally conceived hamstrung the government and hampered it in its response to new needs and new problems that arose over the course of the nineteenth century and into the twentieth century. Fortunately, from the perspective of modern liberalism, beginning in the late nineteenth century and culminating in the New Deal, a variety of forces conspired to erode the barriers erected by the Founders against a more activist government, that is, a government with a broader scope or purview. Among those forces were modern liberal ideas and the ideas of their predecessors in the Progressive Movement. Unfortunately, these and other developments allowed the problem of faction to become more pronounced and virulent. As tax revenues rose and government expanded its scope, the stakes got higher. There was more to be gained and more to be lost from whatever the government did or did not do. In addition, as technology advanced, the costs of organizing interest groups and the costs of communication among them fell through the floor. Both political parties have become little more than a collection of different interest groups, or in Madison's term, "factions." The result, as Madison said, is that "the public good is disregarded in the conflicts of rival parties; and that measures are too often decided . . . by the superior force of an interested and over-bearing majority" (Hamilton, Jay, and Madison [1787–1788] 2000, 54).

Although other factors were clearly at work, modern liberals have to accept some responsibility for this situation because they have

consistently and successfully advocated a larger role for government—a role that goes far beyond what the Founders and contemporary classical liberals envision. The ship of state cannot take on
the tasks imposed by the modern liberal transfer, regulatory, and tax
agendas without acquiring the barnacles of the interest groups on its
hull. Modern liberals would say, indeed they would have to say, that
this is a price worth paying, even as they hatch schemes to reduce
that price. On their view, these changes in the scope of government
have allowed government to address major social problems that a
private ordering has proved incapable of handling or handling well,
though whether government efforts are still necessary is a matter of
speculation, as this book has shown. Besides, it is not as if under
a classical liberal regime, the problem of faction would disappear.
Recall that the deepest source of the problem of faction is the unequal
distribution of property. Classical liberals are content to allow enormous inequalities in wealth and income, and those inequalities are
part of the problem, indeed a big part of the problem, according to
both Madison and modern liberalism. However, classical liberals
would argue that any attempt to reduce those inequalities as a way
of eliminating the problem of faction will not succeed because it will
simply raise the threat level, and thus the incentive to act, for those
with the most resources to commit to the fight. If Madison is right in
his analysis of the sources of the problem of faction, the problem is
an enduring feature of a liberal polity. The main question is how to
mitigate it, given that Madison's solution is no longer viable for the
reasons explained above. And, it is not as if modern liberals are bereft
of ideas about how to do that.

The Transparency Requirement

As noted earlier, many modern liberals believe that campaign
finance reform is a good place to start. Public financing of presidential campaigns has been in place since 1976, funded by a voluntary
checkoff on tax returns. Some modern liberals believe it should be
extended to Congress. This is supposed to insulate candidates from
the special interest money. If the government funds campaigns, so
the theory goes, candidates can focus on articulating their vision
of the public interest. There are at least four problems with this
proposal, two practical and two moral. One practical problem is
how to determine who gets funding and who does not. Currently,

the threshold is fairly high for presidential candidates to qualify for government money. According to the Federal Election Commission's Web site:

(1) In order to qualify for matching funds, a candidate in the primary elections must first raise over $5,000 in each of 20 states (i.e., over $100,000), consisting of small contributions ($250 or less) from individuals.

(2) General election nominees must agree not to accept any private contributions (from individuals or PACs, for example).

(3) Candidates must promise not to spend more than $50,000 of their own money on their campaign.

(4) Recipients of public funds must adhere to a limit on total spending.[11]

Minor or new party candidates must receive at least 5 percent of the vote to be eligible for funding, though like major party candidates, they can opt out of the system and spend their own money. The two major parties also get taxpayer funding for their conventions. Together, these provisions make it more difficult for marginal voices to be heard and enhance the prospects of incumbents. Of necessity, elected politicians write the rules or choose those who do, and they are not about to write themselves out of a job; instead they are going to configure the rules to help incumbents (i.e., themselves) stay in power.[12] Second, it is difficult to see how private money can be kept out of the political process. First Amendment considerations constrain what the law can do, and within those constraints, efforts to keep special interest money out of politics have thus far been complete and utter failures; it is often said that money in politics is like water in that it will eventually seek its own level.[13]

Presidential candidates can choose to opt out of federal funding. In the past, nearly all of them accepted federal monies, but in 2008 it might turn out that at least one major party candidate will decline. Participation by taxpayers is low and has consistently declined since the late 1970s.[14] If public financing were expanded to cover Senate and House races, other public monies would have to be used. The moral problem with this is two-fold: first, it would force people to subsidize points of view they disagree with, sometimes vehemently. If unions are rightly prohibited from using agency fees from nonunion members for political activity, it is hard to see why politicians should be permitted to use taxpayer money for the same purpose.[15] Second, most people, and that includes classical liberals, modern liberals, and those in between, believe that many of society's most pressing problems have been directly caused by politicians, though of course they differ about which politicians are to blame. Rewarding them by funding their practice of what Madison called the "vicious arts" with tax dollars is something that a substantial majority will rightly regard as profoundly immoral and simply will not fly politically.

What will fly politically, however, is a requirement of disclosure. Almost everyone seems to think that is a good idea. Candidates for public office are now required to submit full and complete disclosure about the sources of their campaign funds. The popular theory behind this is that if Senator X or Representative Y has to disclose that he gets campaign contributions from a certain industry or labor union, that would embarrass him or her in the eyes of the voters if he or she votes for a bill that has no discernible purpose other than to benefit that industry or union. What works in theory, however, often does not work in practice. Disclosure requirements seem not to have had much effect, which perhaps explains their popularity with the political class. Most of the time, the politicians take the money and vote the way the faction wants them to vote without any embarrassment whatsoever. On the other side, it has been said in Texas that if an elected official cannot take a man's money and vote *against* him, he simply does not belong in politics. Besides, the voters are not paying attention, either at the time a given bill is under consideration or at the next election. Only the interest groups are paying attention. Disclosure requirements help them, that is, the interest groups, discover to whom (else) the politicians owe favors, and of course the "wrong" vote may cause them to reassess their support for that person. A second difficulty with a disclosure requirement is that it provides an almost overwhelming temptation for partisans on both sides, especially those in the media, to overlook the arguments for and against the measure under discussion and to direct all attention to following the money. This is supposed to tell us why the elected official is supporting or opposing a bill, but of course it may not. Causation often goes in the other direction; the elected official gets financial support from a particular industry or labor union because he is antecedently disposed for other reasons to favor the interests of the faction in question. Or, on some occasions, he actually believes some proposal which benefits an organized group that supports him is a good idea. This is probably more common than most cynical observers are inclined to believe. If all one knows about a measure is which groups support it and which groups oppose it, one has very little idea about whether or not the measure is a good one, whatever one's predilections are on the modern liberal/classical liberal dispute. To address the actual reasons for and against a measure requires more intellectual effort to understand the issues and the arguments pro and con. For the average politically engaged citizen, not to mention for the average journalist, it is far easier to avoid expending that effort by following the money. For the average citizen, who has at most a rudimentary knowledge of government and politics, there is no incentive at all even to discover who benefits. Indeed, as a way of commandeering journalists and politically engaged citizens to consider the reasons for and against legislation, it might be a good idea to prohibit the disclosure of a legislator's sources of campaign contributions. Political debate was more robust and issue-driven when Richard Nixon was receiving cash campaign contributions in a black satchel.

Still, there seems to be something to the idea of discovering and disclosing who benefits from a particular measure and to what extent. Indeed, if policies are to be evaluated by their consequences, broadly understood, identifying those who benefit and the extent to which they benefit would seem to be essential. This is broader than identifying the interest groups who favor or oppose the measure. Government policies have both intended and unintended beneficiaries; a full accounting of who benefits has to include both. To take one example from regulatory policy, the intended beneficiaries of affirmative action are women and minorities who would otherwise suffer discrimination. Unintended beneficiaries include incompetent or underperforming women and minorities who remain employed only because it is too difficult to fire them. It is difficult to know how many of them there are, but their existence can be acknowledged. Other unintended beneficiaries are the diversity consultants who ply their trade to corporate and educational clients and the lawyers on both sides who are hired to try these cases. In transfer policy, the intended beneficiaries of, say, the food stamp program, are the poor it is supposed to help. The unintended beneficiaries are the farmers whose income is increased because they sell more food, the bureaucrats who administer the program, and the brokers in poor neighborhoods who illicitly turn food stamps into cash. In tax policy, the mortgage interest deduction is intended to help homeowners by allowing them to deduct interest payments from their taxable income, but the main unintended beneficiaries are the mortgage banking industry, which supplies the loans, and the home construction industry, which builds new houses. Both groups are able to sell more of their product at a higher price because consumers are buying their products with tax-free dollars. The identification of unintended beneficiaries and victims, at least in a categorial way, might lead to measures that will minimize their numbers.

The distinction between intended and unintended beneficiaries of any piece of legislation contains some hidden complexities that warrant elucidation. One problem concerns whose intentions determine the designation of the intended beneficiaries. "The legislators who support the bill" is an obvious answer that will not do for a couple of reasons. One is that different legislators intend to help different individuals or groups by supporting the bill, so it is unclear which ones should count as the intended beneficiaries on this criterion. Perhaps most importantly, sometimes the so-called unintended beneficiaries are exactly the people legislators want (i.e., intend) to help. Home-buyers might be the intended beneficiaries of the mortgage interest deduction, but legislators might have voted for the home mortgage deduction because they wanted to help their supporters in the mortgage banking industry or the home construction industry. To find the so-called intended beneficiaries, it is necessary to look at the explicit purposes of the law in question. Many laws as recorded in the U.S. Code have opening sections devoted to findings and purposes. This is one place to look for the intended beneficiaries—they are intended by the legislation to benefit from the law. Although it is odd to talk about laws, as opposed to people, as having intentions, it makes sense at a certain level. Besides, the contrast between intended and unintended beneficiaries is established usage in the public choice literature on rent-seeking. The intended beneficiaries are those whose interests are the publicly stated targets of the legislation, whereas the unintended beneficiaries are those who are not explicitly mentioned but are often the real targets of the legislators' solicitude. For example, there are import quotas on sugar, which are intended to help the sugar beet farmers in the Upper Midwest and the sugar cane growers in Louisiana, Florida, and Hawaii. The unintended beneficiaries, however, include Archer Daniels Midland. Because the price of sugar is kept up by the import quota, soft drink manufacturers find it cost effective to buy high-fructose corn syrup, a sugar substitute, from ADM. ADM, then, is an unintended beneficiary of the sugar import quota; it makes enormous profits selling high-fructose corn syrup to the soft drink industry, but it is not mentioned as an intended beneficiary of the legislation, either in the law itself or in the public justification that is offered in support of the law, where the virtues of the Midwestern sugar beet farmers, and Cajun, Latino, and Hawaiian sugar cane growers are extolled and their hardships painted in vivid colors.

Not all of the unintended beneficiaries of a piece of legislation are the objects of legislators' solicitude. For example, perhaps the main unintended beneficiaries of the laws prohibiting the use of recreational drugs are the drug dealers and producers, but it would take a darkly conspiratorial mind to believe that those who oppose drug legalization do so at the behest of the drug dealers and drug producers' trade associations, who are funneling campaign contributions to these politicians.[16] Diversity consultants did not exist before antidiscrimination laws were passed, and yet they reap windfalls from antidiscrimination laws because they are hired at inflated fees to conduct "diversity workshops" so that large employers can demonstrate their bona fides when they are haled into court, as they inevitably will be at some point, to defend themselves against a charge of race or sex discrimination.

A final complication in the distinction between intended and unintended beneficiaries is that the intended beneficiaries may not actually benefit from the government action or benefit as much as they would appear to benefit. Two brief examples: the mortgage interest deduction allows people to buy mortgages with cheap dollars, but that makes it possible for sellers to raise their prices. Home-buyers are not made better off, or not made as well off as they would appear to be. Similarly, the high cost of a college education prompts government to increase the availability of student loans, which in turn encourages colleges and universities to raise their prices. In this way, federal dollars fan the flames of inflation in higher education. No one can say for sure exactly how these things work themselves out; many factors are in play, including especially the relative elasticity of demand for the product or service in question.

Just as there are intended and unintended beneficiaries, so too there are intended and unintended victims of government action.[17] Recall that one of the lessons of chapter 6 is that many elements of the modern liberal regulatory agenda cannot be represented as public goods. That is not necessarily a criticism, since they might be justified on other grounds. Nevertheless, for something to be a public good, it is necessary that the vast majority of the members of the group would judge that the collective benefits of the good outweigh its collective costs, and they would further judge that the individual benefits of the good outweigh their proportionate share of the costs. These conditions are very stringent; most government activity does not produce public goods. This means that most government action will result in someone or some group suffering net harm, where net harm is understood very broadly to include whatever on balance negatively affects someone's interests relative to the status quo ante. That fact alone is not morally problematic. For example, an employer might be fined because he violated some sensible OSHA standard or some union worker with a poor work ethic may never recover when her job is eliminated because the government has signed a free trade agreement. As these examples illustrate, there is no presumption that victims do not deserve the treatment they get. The larger point is that true transparency requires not only that the beneficiaries of government action be identified but that the victims—those whose interests are on balance negatively affected—be identified as well. As some of the above examples illustrate, a transparency requirement is not biased against modern liberalism, since classical liberal reforms would hurt some people in the near term and indeed in the long term as well. True public goods, where (nearly) everyone is a net beneficiary, are not easy to find once one moves beyond the goods of national security and the security produced by the criminal and civil justice systems. Most government action will produce net benefits for some and net harms for others. A deeply dishonest feature of contemporary public political discourse by politicians on both sides of the political spectrum is the bald-faced denial of that fact regarding nearly every piece of legislation. Whether from the Left or the Right, government policies and programs are typically represented as Pareto improvements when they really are not. Examples are too numerous to mention.

How does all this differ from cost-benefit analysis or even Utilitarianism? A number of ways: first, there is no demand that for some group's vision of the proper role of government to be legitimately imposed, the benefits must outweigh the costs or that the proposed policy be the most cost-effective of any alternative. It just says that, whatever the benefits and whoever the beneficiaries are, they should be identified, whether or not they are intended. Same with the costs and the victims. Second, there is no requirement of commensurability for benefits and harms, either in terms of ability to pay or anything else. The pluses and minuses of any proposal might be quite heterogeneous and incomparable and include moral values such as fairness. This says nothing about how they are to be weighed. All that is required is that they be identified.

Although it seems unobjectionable enough to require that the beneficiaries and victims of government action or policy, both intended and unintended, be identified, there are at least two objections that might be raised to it. One is moral; the other is practical. Perhaps the most obvious moral objection to some transparency requirement is that, if observed, it could hinder moral progress, specifically, progress toward a more just society. Many of the items on the modern liberal regulatory agenda, as well as the classical liberal counter-agenda, can be represented as answering to the demands of justice; those demands often conflict with the self-interest of the citizenry or a sufficiently large and powerful part of it. A critic might charge that if a certain policy or program is what justice demands, why does it matter if some transparency requirement has been met or not? Indeed, it might have greater prospects for success if the unintended victims are not publicly identified, since the latter may be roused to political action to prevent reform.

However, this overlooks the fact that what justice demands is very often controversial, if only because principles of justice are controversial. Men and women of high intelligence and good will can differ profoundly about which principles are correct or most defensible. Moreover, even if there were agreement about principles, which there is not, there can be reasonable disagreement about how principles are to be applied.[18] If the principles are mistaken or incorrectly applied, it is fair to say that those instituting the policy are doing no more than coercively and unjustifiably imposing their own preferences on society at large, since there is in fact no larger purpose being served. This is true even if their intentions are wholly honorable. Though some economists falsely reduce all beliefs about what justice demands to preferences, they are right about those cases in which the principles are in fact false or are misapplied. To maintain that all that matters are the demands of justice is to be insensitive to the uncertainties and controversies that attend discovering what justice demands. Besides, arguments that appeal to abstract principles of distributive justice are principled sectarian arguments that have been ruled inadmissible by the public justification requirement.

A second reason why it matters that some transparency requirement be met is that the best argument in favor of some policy very often will crucially depend on controversial empirical claims about beneficiaries and victims that need to be substantiated. A full airing of the argument will expose its proponents to challenges on the facts, which they may or may not be able to sustain. Legislators are not omniscient and often operate with a relatively crude understanding of the effects of a law. Consider proposals to increase the minimum wage, often advanced on the grounds of fair treatment to minimum wage workers. Unintended beneficiaries include union members whose wages are tied directly or indirectly to the minimum wage. Unintended victims include young people who are denied employment, possibly even let go from a job they currently hold, to the extent that the demand for unskilled labor is downward sloping. An honest effort to identify the unintended beneficiaries and victims of this policy may cause some legislators (most notably, those who feel free to do the right thing, as they see it) to conclude the gains associated with raising the minimum wage do not offset the costs, broadly construed. But, they might conclude that the gains do outweigh the losses. Gains and losses may also include moral considerations, such as considerations of fairness, as they see it. Regardless of the outcome, both sides will have a better understanding of what the state is doing.

A more practical objection to a transparency requirement is that it is often difficult to know who all the beneficiaries and victims of a piece of legislation really are. Intended beneficiaries and victims are usually easy enough to identify, at least in a general way, especially in the case of government subsidies. For example, the National Flood Insurance Program (NFIP) is intended to help homeowners who live in flood plains by permitting them to purchase subsidized flood insurance from the government. The intended victims are simply the taxpayers who provide the subsidy, though NFIP has adopted various stratagems to hide the extent of the subsidies (Arnold 2000, 6–8, 18–19). Those stratagems should be prohibited. It may be difficult to know at the outset the extent of the benefits and costs, but estimates can be made, and more importantly, once the program is underway, it is possible to update the numbers affected and the dollar and/or moral value of the benefits. Finally, attention to the intended beneficiaries and victims forces legislators to ask hard questions about whether the transfer program, tax change, or regulation will actually work, that is, have its intended effect. For example, it appears that no one thought carefully about whether OSHA would actually do any good, given its paltry budget and staffing. The intended victims were businesses that would have to spend money to comply with the law. It should not take an economist to realize that many firms would simply wait to address violations of OSHA safety regulations until they were issued a citation, and for many firms, that would be waiting for Godot. A lot of cheap symbolism and useless programs could be avoided if honest attempts were made to determine the actual effects of legislation on its intended targets.

It is in the case of the unintended beneficiaries and victims that a transparency requirement would have the most impact. To say that these beneficiaries and victims are unintended does not mean they are not foreseen. Application of the doctrine of double effect depends on being able to identify the foreseen but unintended consequences of actions, and indeed a lot of what economists do is to discover the foreseeable but unintended consequences of actions and policies in a systematic way. Consider first unintended beneficiaries. Two questions have to be addressed: First, who are they? That is, what types of people and what types of businesses will be positively affected? The second question concerns the extent of the effect, that is, how much do they benefit? Sometimes both questions are relatively easy to answer, but sometime they are not. For example, government employees are typically foreseen but unintended beneficiaries of government action, since people have to be hired to administer transfer programs, staff regulatory bureaucracies, and even administer increasingly complex provisions of the tax code. The impact on this group is relatively easy to calculate, since the extent to which they benefit is readily apparent. The taxpayers should probably be counted as unintended victims, since their interests are on balance harmed, unless a genuine public goods problem is being solved. In the case of tax policy and transfer programs, the unintended beneficiaries who are not government employees are sometimes harder to determine. The line from sugar import quotas to profits for Archer Daniels Midland's high-fructose corn syrup operations is relatively short and direct, but sometimes the connection between government programs and unintended beneficiaries is less direct. It is at this juncture that attention to the interest groups supporting the bill can be a helpful guide to identifying other unintended beneficiaries of the legislation. If the independent grocers' trade association is backing a bill, it is likely that they are unintended beneficiaries, though that fact alone cannot be used as a reason to oppose the legislation. After all, the latter may be a good idea that should be implemented. Still, transparency requires that the unintended beneficiaries be "outed" and that some estimate be made about the extent to which they will benefit. Of course, not all unintended beneficiaries are members of organized interest groups. Unintended beneficiaries of antidiscrimination laws include marginal employees who would be fired but for their employers' fears of lawsuits. They do not have a lobby (unless they are unionized), their numbers are hard to determine, and the extent to which they benefit is unknown. That fact does not preclude the need to identify them, however, and bring to bear whatever evidence can be gathered at a reasonable cost to estimate their numbers and the extent to which they benefit.

Unintended victims are more difficult to identify, even in a cat-egorial way. Public choice theory teaches that the main unintended victims of rent-seeking are two unorganized groups: taxpayers and consumers. Consumers pay higher prices for consumer products sub-ject to protectionist measures and regulatory interventions. Which consumers are harmed and the extent to which they are harmed is often difficult to determine, but as with the unintended beneficiaries, that does not preclude making an effort to identify them. Those who actually pay taxes are the unintended victims of special tax breaks for various interest groups, though the extent to which they are harmed is often difficult to ascertain because of the counterfactuals involved.[19] A serious attempt to identify the unintended victims of government action addresses a major failing in government over the past half cen-tury: many tax, transfer, and regulatory programs have had significant unintended negative consequences that, by most any accounting, have outweighed whatever good those programs had done. These consequences are foreseeable, however, at least in a rough way. A small example: A number of years ago, Congress put a hefty excise tax on various expensive items, including automobiles, jewelry, aircraft, and yachts valued at over $100,000, as a way of raising revenue from the rich. The tax was projected to raise $31 million in its first year, but it only raised $16 million. Moreover,

> according to a study done for the Joint Economic Committee, the tax destroyed 330 jobs in jewelry manufacturing, 1,470 in the aircraft industry and 7,600 in the boating industry. The job losses cost the government a total of $24.2 million in unemploy-ment benefits and lost income tax revenues. So the net effect of the taxes was a loss of $7.6 million in fiscal 1991, which means the government projection was off by $38.6 million.[20]

To repair the damage, Rep. Patrick Kennedy (D-RI) proposed a 20 percent tax credit for purchasers of U.S.-built luxury yachts, though the credit was capped at $2 million. If the yacht builders did not have a lobbying group before all this happened, it is a safe bet that they have one now, and campaign contributions from their trade associa-tion are probably flowing in as this is being written. There may be no way to know the exact shape of the demand curve for U.S.-made yachts and other luxury goods, but it is reasonable to suppose it is fairly steep. After all, they are luxury goods and not necessities. There is no evidence that this fact was taken into account when the tax was imposed. A bigger and more important example comes from welfare policy, where generations of dependent recipients were created as a by-product of a well-intentioned effort to end poverty. There is little doubt that many of these people were harmed on balance by antipoverty programs. In this instance, they were both the intended beneficiaries and the unintended victims of the program.

How serious an effort, or to be more exact, how expensive an effort, must be made to identify the beneficiaries and victims, both intended and unintended, of government action? The answer economists give when one pulls the little string on their backs, "until the marginal benefits of the information equal the marginal costs of gathering it," will not do because there is no obvious way to quantify the benefits legislators would receive from having this information. There probably is no general answer to this question. Even a modest attempt to implement this transparency requirement would represent a noticeable improvement over the current situation in which neither unintended beneficiaries nor unintended victims are even acknowledged. As postmodernists might say of both groups, but especially of the unintended victims, theirs is a narrative worthy of being heard.

Not only must the beneficiaries and victims be identified, it is also necessary to explain the manner in which their interests are affected. There is a tendency to think of benefits and costs in financial terms, but that does not exhaust the ways in which people can be helped or hurt by government programs. Fair treatment for some and unfair treatment for others are predictable effects of antidiscrimination laws, as well as of the repeal of such laws. Enhanced safety for some employees somewhere and major costs for businesses that hire them can be the effect of the implementation of the Occupational Safety and Health Act. Increased uncertainty is a harm facing business firms or their executives who must deal with OSHA inspectors, CPSC bureaucrats contemplating recalls, or Justice Department lawyers who must approve a merger or acquisition. There are different and probably incommensurable ways in which beneficiaries and victims are helped or harmed, and that has to be made clear in a transparent account of the effects of a law or policy.

All these points are clearly illustrated in the war on drugs (which is not part of the modern liberal regulatory agenda or the classical liberal counteragenda). In discussing the war on drugs, Ethan Nadelmann (1988, 13–14) has remarked that when the size of the set of unintended victims and unintended beneficiaries becomes large, relative to the size of the intended beneficiaries and victims, something has gone seriously wrong. Consider first the intended beneficiaries of the drug war. Some people are going to use recreational drugs and will develop a drug abuse problem whether recreational drugs are legal or not, but there are other potential drug abusers who are deterred from using recreational drugs because they are illegal. Members of this subset and those close to them are the main intended beneficiaries of the war on drugs; these are the people the war on drugs is supposed to help. Nadelmann made an attempt to estimate the size of this group, an estimate that was sharply criticized by James Q. Wilson (1990, 24). There is no need to put a dollar value on these benefits, and neither of them did. The unintended beneficiaries of the drug war include the drug dealers and producers, who are able to make huge profits because their product is illegal. Other unintended beneficiaries are the law enforcement personnel who are hired to prosecute the war on drugs (e.g., personnel in the DEA and the D.A.R.E. program), additional prison guards hired to staff prisons housing drug law offenders, and the police departments that are able to capture the drug dealers' assets through asset forfeiture laws. The intended victims of the war on drugs are the very same drug dealers and producers who are also the unintended beneficiaries of the current policy. Unintended victims are the taxpayers who must fund the drug war, crime victims who are victimized because of the high price of illegal drugs, drug users who are harmed by adulterated drugs, and drug users who are arrested and incarcerated even though their drug use harms no one, including themselves. Even though it is difficult to estimate the size of most of these groups, there is evidence to support the basic contention of those opposed to the war on drugs about the size of the unintended beneficiaries and victims, at least relative to the size of the intended beneficiaries and victims. This in turn supports the widely shared, though by no means unanimous, view that the war on drugs should be seriously reevaluated.

It is difficult to formulate precisely the transparency requirement, but the basic idea is clear enough: if legislators wish to change (increase or decrease) the scope of government, an intellectually serious and responsible effort should be made to identify the beneficiaries and victims, both intended and unintended, of the legislation and to explain the manner in which they either benefit or are harmed. The greater the potential effect of the change, the heavier the responsibility is to work this out. All this has to be done in a public context, such as in a Senate or House committee report or in legislative debate, because the targets of this requirement are other legislators who represent the interests of those who do oppose or would oppose the change, either on grounds of principle or simply because they are about to take a hit to their interests. Such arguments can also be conceived of as directed to those who have not made up their minds about where they stand.

To summarize, as part of an argument that satisfies the public justification requirement, a serious effort must be made to identify the intended and unintended beneficiaries and victims of any proposal for or against a change in the scope of government. This is the *transparency requirement,* and it should be satisfied in as detailed a way as is feasible. Although satisfaction of the public justification requirement requires satisfaction of the transparency requirement, for ease of reference, in what follows I shall treat these as separate requirements. There are, therefore, at least three requirements that must be met for the legitimate imposition of someone or some group's values on a liberal democratic polity: the democracy requirement, the public justification requirement, and the transparency requirement. The arguments for each of these requirements are perfectly general and thus would apply to issues or disputes about ownership of public property, tax policy, and transfer programs, as well as government regulation.

Thus far little has been said about how these requirements might be implemented. On the face of it, they seem to require that political battles be fought according to the Marquess of Queensbury rules, and yet politics is not like that. Every few years, the world is treated to video clips of parliamentary disputes, often in Asian democracies, that feature real fisticuffs, which are not conducted in accordance with the Queensbury rules. In politics, sucker punches, real and figurative, abound. It is true that the preceding is a normative investigation designed to identify some conditions that must be met for someone's or some group's values to be legitimately imposed on the polity, but unless some plausible mechanisms can be sketched to describe how these requirements might be implemented, they lack practical force or significance. To put the same point in different terms, it might be objected that satisfaction of all three requirements is an impossibly strict standard that could never be met. Since "Ought Implies Can," these requirements should be rejected.

To address this objection, let us consider the ways in which these requirements have been or might be satisfied in regard to the modern liberal regulatory agenda. The democracy requirement will usually not be a problem, since much of the modern liberal regulatory agenda has been implemented through the democratic process. Title VII of the 1964 Civil Rights Act, for example, was imposed by the Congress and signed into law by the president, as was the Americans with Disabilities Act of 1990. This requirement does rule out judicially imposed major changes in the scope of government, however, which creates a problem for disparate impact and hostile environment sex discrimination, as we shall see in the next chapter.

Implementation of the first part of the public justification requirement also creates no insuperable problems. Those who have the political power, that is, the votes, to implement their vision of the proper scope of government have reasons for doing what they intend to do; respect for their opponents as reasoning beings requires only that they give those reasons in the form of a conversion argument. This is often done in committee reports or in the floor debate. If they cannot be bothered to do that, they can hardly claim to have imposed their values legitimately. Besides, conversion arguments are perfectly suited to those not philosophically inclined, which includes nearly all practicing politicians.[21]

The second and third parts of the public justification requirement do appear to be utopian, however. After all, many politicians are personally dishonest, so asking them to avoid being intellectually dishonest is akin to expecting someone with poor personal hygiene to be well-dressed. The difficulty in meeting this requirement is not as great as it might first appear, however. There is no need for all politicians to be intellectually honest all the time. All it takes is one intellectually honest committee report or one intellectually honest legislator to make the case on the public record. Or, there may be institutional mechanisms that could be implemented to hire intellectual beat cops (or riot police) to patrol the debates on the floor of the legislature. Lawyers of course would be ill-suited for this role. As Socrates said of the Sophists, their job is to make the weaker case appear the stronger and the stronger case appear the weaker. Professional academics would also likely be poor candidates because of their penchant for getting sidetracked into methodological disputes that get them really excited but routinely cause everyone else's eyes to glaze over. Clearly, what is needed is a corps of modern-day Pyrrhonian skeptics, trained to ensure that the best arguments—or at least decent arguments—for and against various legislative proposals are ventilated. Some philosophical training might well be appropriate, though the thought of hiring scores of professional philosophers to police debate in the legislature is either amusing or frightening.

Besides, they are ill-suited for such a role because of their penchant for using the nightstick of abstract philosophical principle to thrash those with whom they disagree.

The transparency requirement also creates apparent difficulties in implementation. It would undoubtedly be argued that it is unreasonable to expect those with an agenda they want to impose to point out the weaknesses or drawbacks to what they are doing, which is what they would be doing if they identified the unintended beneficiaries and victims of the proposal. That may well be true, but there is nothing in the requirement as stated that demands that those doing the imposing must detail those unintended beneficiaries and victims. This is, or should be, the job of the opposition in the deliberations. And they do not have to do it alone. Ironically, the interest groups have an important and useful role to play in this connection. Interest groups opposed to the legislation have every incentive to identify both unintended and intended victims, as well as unintended beneficiaries. They can pass that information on the legislators who will actually vote on the bill, as indeed they do now. Of course, they will overstate the harms and understate the benefits, but the liberal remedy for dubious or dishonest speech is always more speech. Nevertheless, the best argument for the feasibility of these requirements is a detailed examination of the record of how some of the elements of the modern liberal regulatory agenda have been imposed. If it can be shown that some of these items have been legitimately imposed, or could have been imposed had proponents or opponents done what could be reasonably expected of them, that would make the dismissal of these requirements as utopian unwarranted. This is the burden of the next and final chapter.

TWELVE

Applications

Chapter 11 argues that multiple criteria must be satisfied for any element of the modern liberal regulatory agenda to be legitimately imposed, at least if there is persistent reasonable disagreement about that element. The application of these criteria to all of the regulatory regimes for which there are such disagreements is obviously too large a task to be accomplished in a book that has already gone on too long. Selected regimes can be investigated in some detail, however, to see if they have been legitimately imposed. This chapter does that for three high-profile regulatory regimes, specifically those created by (1) elements of title VII of the 1964 Civil Rights Act, (2) the Occupational Safety and Health Act of 1970, and (3) the 1938 Federal Food, Drug, and Cosmetic Act, together with the 1951 and 1962 amendments. A recurring theme in the following discussion is that the legislature frequently abdicated its responsibility to define the proper scope of government activity. In most cases, that responsibility was assumed by the courts.[1] Sometimes, it was thrust upon the courts by inadequately drawn legislation, but at other times, activist judges took advantage of vague legislative guidelines to define standards themselves. A related dereliction of duty was the failure of legislators to identify unintended beneficiaries and victims of the laws they were passing. Sometimes modern liberal politicians were culpable, but at other times, their counterparts in the opposition failed to do their job. Let us begin, however, with one of the few success stories, that is, a case in which a regulatory burden was legitimately imposed: the prohibition on racial discrimination, where "discrimination" is understood in terms of disparate treatment, as embodied in title VII of the 1964 Civil Rights Act.

The Antidiscrimination Regulatory Regime

Racial Discrimination

Title VII of the 1964 Civil Rights Act was passed by the legislature and signed by the executive, and thus satisfies the democracy requirement. The conversion argument for it, as it applies to race, is clear and straightforward, and versions of it were made repeatedly on the floor of the House and Senate during debate.[2] Discrimination in hiring on the basis of race is morally objectionable. It was, however, a pervasive phenomenon in U.S. society, especially in the South. Racial prejudice, combined with strong private property rights and freedom of contract conspired to permit it, and that is what title VII outlawed. The victims and beneficiaries of the law, both intended and unintended, were reasonably clear and transparent to everyone at the time. Intended victims of the new law included racially prejudiced employers and their hiring agents whose freedom would be circumscribed by the law. So too were less-qualified white males whose situation would be negatively affected by the passage of the law. Intended beneficiaries included racial minorities, most especially black Americans, who would get jobs for which they otherwise would not have been hired. Every law and regulatory regime has unintended beneficiaries and victims, and this one is no exception. The primary unintended beneficiaries of this law were those hired to enforce it, including, most notably, plaintiffs' attorneys and EEOC bureaucrats. Taxpayers might have to be counted as unintended victims, though the indirect benefits that accrue to them, including benefits that come from improved efficiency in labor markets, would have to be offset against the increase in taxes required to fund the bureaucracy and the associated legal costs borne by the state.

The main concerns about unintended victims, however, were voiced by southern legislators who opposed the bill (*Cong. Rec.,* 88th Cong., 2nd sess., (1964): 2560, 2574, 2576, 2605, 8500). They believed it was a "quota bill" that would unfairly penalize qualified whites (and unfairly benefit less qualified blacks). These legislators worried that, as a practical matter, there would be no way for firms to avoid the charge of discrimination in hiring except by instituting quotas. In other words, they were concerned that hiring practices that had a negative disparate impact on minorities would be counted as a form of discrimination under the law. In answer to a question about the definition of discrimination, Sen. Hubert Humphrey, the Senate's leading supporter of the bill, addressed this concern. He clearly indicated that he understood "discrimination" in terms of disparate treatment (what, at the time, was called "intentional discrimination") only, not in terms of disparate impact. He said to one of the bill's opponents that, "if the Senator can find in Title VII...any language which provided that an employer will have to hire on the basis of percentage or quota related to color, race, religion, or national origin, I will start eating the pages one after another because it is not there."[3]

An interpretive memorandum on title VII inserted into the *Congressional Record* by Senators Clark and Chase was even more explicit:

> There is no requirement in Title VII that an employer maintain a racial balance in his workforce. On the contrary, any deliberate attempt to maintain a racial balance, whatever such balance may be, would involve a violation of Title VII because maintaining such a balance would require an employer to hire or refuse to hire on the basis of race. (Ibid., 7213)[4]

On the House side, there is an explicit denial that quotas are permissible from Rep. John Lindsay (ibid., 1540). Although the term "disparate impact" was not used, the concept was thoroughly discussed; a shared understanding of what "discrimination" meant in the context of this bill emerged, and it did not include disparate impact.

As Herman Belz has pointed out, many supporters of the bill would have preferred to interpret "discrimination" to include both disparate treatment and disparate impact, but in order to get the support of northern and midwestern Republicans, they had to stipulate that "discrimination" was to be understood narrowly to mean only disparate treatment. As Belz says,

> the southern critics' arguments forced the supporters of Title VII to accept anti-preferential provisions and to assert their disapproval of quotas more clearly and emphatically than they otherwise might have. These professions...can be accepted as genuine, without denying that supporters were aware of, and were probably willing to accept, *de facto* quotas that might result from administrative and judicial enforcement of the law. (Belz 1991, 27)

For modern liberals enamored of the "Madisonian moment" and the virtues of deliberative democracy, this incident is a shining Madisonian moment and a clear illustration of the virtues of deliberative democracy. Opponents of the bill forced a clarification that very likely would not have otherwise occurred. Though as Belz indicates, supporters of the bill would have been happy to understand "discrimination" more broadly, the need to get the votes of some Republicans forced a clarification that resulted in a narrower shared understanding of the term. So that there would be no subsequent misunderstanding, this was codified at 42 U.S.C. § 2000e–2(j):

nothing contained in this subchapter shall be interpreted to require any employer...to grant preferential treatment to any individual or to any group because of the race, color, religion, sex, or national origin of such individual or group on account of an imbalance which may exist with respect to the total number or percentage of persons of any race, color, religion, sex, or national origin employed by any employer...in comparison with the total number or percentage of persons of such race, color, religion, sex, or national origin in any community...or in the available work force in any community.

The fact of the matter, of course, is that it did not turn out that way when the law was enforced. In a story that was told in chapter 8, beginning with *Griggs v. Duke Power,* 401 U.S. 424 (1971), the courts interpreted title VII in a way that clearly violated this shared understanding of "discrimination." Proponents of title VII cannot be responsible for that, even if in the event they were pleased by what the courts wrought. They had done their job; the courts just did not do theirs. By acting in this way, the courts violated the democracy requirement and arguably the transparency requirement as well. They created large classes of unintended beneficiaries and victims in defiance of the shared understanding achieved in the legislative process. To summarize, the democracy, public justification, and transparency requirements were all satisfied in the debate on title VII of the 1964 Civil Rights Act, insofar as title VII is interpreted to prohibit racial discrimination, understood in terms of disparate treatment, in hiring. Neither the democracy requirement nor the transparency requirement was satisfied on the disparate impact interpretation of discrimination, however, when the judiciary imposed the latter on society at large.

There are two more incidents related to preferential hiring programs that have to be considered. One is the attempt by Sen. Sam Ervin to dismantle these programs in 1972, and the other is the legislative response to the Supreme Court's ruling in *Ward's Cove* in the Civil Rights Act of 1991. In the 1972 debate on amending title VII, Senator Ervin tried to end preferential hiring, as well as minority set-asides, which were imposed by executive order and monitored by the Office of Federal Contract Compliance.[5] This was the first straight up or down vote on preferential treatment programs in the Congress, and Ervin's amendments were defeated. The democracy requirement was thereby satisfied, albeit after the fact, but the public justification requirement was not. The latter demands an intellectually serious conversion argument in support of it, and criticisms of it require an intellectually serious response. Senator Jacob Javits responded to Senator Ervin's charge that preferential treatment programs are inconsistent with the shared understanding title VII as it was passed in 1964. Javits's argument consisted of the following observations (*Cong. Rec.*, 90th Cong., 2nd sess., (1972): 1664–65): the Third Circuit Court of Appeals had upheld a preferential hiring program imposed by the Nixon administration on government contractors, and so the executive branch was legally entitled to do it. Moreover, the courts had ordered hiring and promotion by the numbers in other cases. Senator Ervin's amendment would have prevented both. This is why it should be defeated. Senator Harrison Williams added that the amendment would "deny the judicial and executive branches of Government all power to remedy the evils of job discrimination" (ibid., 1676).

These are not serious replies. Senator Williams's claim is simply false, since the judiciary still had the power to order injunctive and make-whole relief in disparate treatment cases, which it did on occasion, and Senator Ervin's proposal would not have prohibited that. The latter deserved a more adequate response, whether or not he or any other opponent would have been persuaded. Senator Javits's argument amounts to nothing more than saying that preferential treatment programs are currently legal, a point that Senator Ervin not only conceded but which he himself used as a key premise in his argument in favor of his amendment! After all, he wanted to change the law, and a reply that simply cites the current law is a completely inadequate response. Besides, an intellectually serious (and intellectually honest) conversion argument in favor of the new understanding was readily available; supporters just failed to use it. (See chapter 8, p. 227.) Instead, they simply kept up the pretense of, "no quotas to see here folks, just move along."

Over the next twenty years, preferential hiring programs became ubiquitous as the scope of government contracting grew and as private individuals and the EEOC successfully pressed disparate impact lawsuits. Then came the *Ward's Cove* decision. As explained in chapter 8 (see above, pp. 229–31), a majority of the Supreme Court seemed to have some doubts about affirmative action in the form of defensive preferential hiring. Their ruling in *Ward's Cove Packing, Inc. v. Antonio*, 490 U.S. 642 (1989), significantly lessened the pressure on firms to hire by the numbers by loosening and reassigning the burdens of proof in disparate impact cases. Indeed, it is not too much of an exaggeration to say that they effectively reinstituted the original understanding of title VII. The congressional response was to overturn this ruling by passing the 1991 Civil Rights Act. This reimposed the *Griggs* standards and gave legislative sanction to preferential hiring programs, thereby satisfying the democracy requirement, but did the legislative debate on this bill satisfy the public justification and transparency requirements?

Recall that to meet the public justification requirement, a conversion argument has to be given that does not commit any of the traditional fallacies and takes seriously the views of those on the other side. This involves gathering whatever evidence one can that is appropriate to a comparative analysis of the relevant institutional alternatives. That in turn involves identifying the intended and unintended beneficiaries and victims (the transparency requirement).

To see whether these requirements were met, it is necessary to explain the implications of the act for title VII. They can be grouped under four headings:[6]

(1) *The use of statistics.* The act did not clarify how statistics were to be used to establish disparate impact. In particular, the question of what population should be used to calculate the percentage of minorities who would have been hired or promoted in the absence of the suspect practice remained contestable. The courts prefer data from actual applicants, and these are best from the plaintiff's point of view, but sometimes such data is unavailable, in which case they have allowed general workforce and even general population data to establish the prima facie case of disparate impact discrimination (e.g., when the jobs in question are either unskilled or can be quickly learned). Regarding general workforce and general population data, there is also a question of how to define the geographical area from which the population is to be drawn. The size of that area can be variously defined by reference to the immediate neighborhood, the city in which workers or potential workers live, or even the Standard Metropolitan Area (Perritt 1992, 130–31).

(2) *The particularity requirement.* The new law did follow *Ward's Cove* in requiring the plaintiff to identify a particular employment practice that produces disparate impact unless "the elements of the respondent's decisionmaking process are not capable of separation for analysis" (42 U.S.C. § 2000e–2(k)(1)(B)(i)). So, if an employer uses a test and an interview to make hiring decisions but leaves it to the discretion of the hiring officer how to weight these requirements, the two requirements would be treated as one practice for purposes of

proving disparate impact. The particularity requirement, subject to the above-noted exception, was a concession to opponents of the bill, who argued that failure to insert this provision would make the act a (relatively pure) "quota bill." After all, if a firm's bottom-line numbers were enough to establish a prima facie case of disparate impact discrimination and if business necessity would be hard to establish, the incentives to hire by the numbers to avoid litigation would be substantial.

(3) *The business necessity defense.* The act said that for a challenged hiring practice, policy, or procedure that produced disparate impact to be sustained, it has to be "job related for the position in question and consistent with business necessity" (42 U.S.C. § 2000e–2(k) (1)(A)(i)). An interpretive memorandum was inserted into the *Congressional Record* that said that these concepts were to be understood as enunciated in *Griggs* (102nd Cong., 1st sess., (1991): 28680). That tightened the job-relatedness requirement so that an employer had to demonstrate that the disputed hiring practice or qualification had a direct bearing on job performance, and "demonstration" is defined so that the respondent has the burden of production and the burden of persuasion (42 U.S.C. § 2000e (m)). There is also some suggestion (though this is a matter of some dispute) that the challenged practice or qualification must be relevant only to the ability to do the job for which the person is being hired. No longer could an employer reject someone because he believed that the applicant would be unlikely to progress and be promoted in the firm. This interpretive memorandum on this point has more weight than usual because the 1991 Civil Rights Act was specifically passed, at least in part, to overturn the understanding of "business necessity" articulated in the *Ward's Cove* decision.[7]

(4) *Alternative practices.* Alternative practices with lesser disparate impact come into play if the plaintiff establishes that there is a comparable alternative hiring practice or qualification that has less disparate impact than what the employer is using, and the employer was informed about it but failed to use it. If all those conditions are met, disparate impact is proved and the plaintiff wins. However, there is no requirement that the plaintiff produce an alternative with less discriminatory impact. After all, if the offending practice or qualification has a disparate impact and fails the business necessity test, it has to go; the plaintiff has no obligation to suggest an alternative.

There are many other provisions in the 1991 law, but they are tangential to the concerns of this book. What is crucial and undeniable is that Congress clearly sanctioned the disparate impact theory of discrimination, but how did it fare in meeting the demands of the public justification and transparency requirements? The latter demands identification of the intended and unintended beneficiaries and victims of the legislation; the former demands a serious argument be made to the effect that the benefits of the legislation outweigh the costs, all things considered.

Opponents of the bill, who bear the main burden in identifying unintended victims (and beneficiaries), raised concerns relevant to these two requirements when they argued that the bill was "a quota bill." For example, Senator Helms made reference to a June 3, 1991, *Newsweek* article in which representatives of Fortune 500 companies admitted to hiring by quotas (*Cong. Rec.,* 102nd Cong., 1st sess., (1991): 22526). The Bush administration had objected to earlier versions of the bill on exactly these grounds. The concern about quotas is primarily a concern about the existence and fate of unintended victims and beneficiaries of the proposed legislation, namely, more qualified nonminority candidates who would not be hired as a result of a company's defensive preferential hiring program and less-qualified minority candidates who would be hired in their place.

How did proponents of the legislation respond to these concerns? The short answer is, "Not well." Senator Kennedy said, "it is not an issue of quotas...current laws do not force employers to provide preferential treatment to any employee or applicant" (ibid., 22547–48). Of course the bill does not *force* employers to hire by the numbers; it just makes them vulnerable to lawsuits if they do not. Senator DeConcini clearly stated the potential problem (viz., that employers would use quotas defensively), but his response was simply to deny that it was a quota bill and then to disparage President Bush's concerns by attacking his motives (ibid., 28868–69). Much was made of the fact that the "leading" opponent of the bill was the Republican nominee for governor of Louisiana, David Duke, former Ku Klux Klansman and barely disguised racist. Debate in the House was equally dismal, consisting mostly of denials that it was a quota bill and an attack on the motives of the bill's opponents.[8]

Proponents of preferential treatment may object that too much is being made of what was essentially a nondebate by the time the bill reached the floor. The real work on these bills is done in committees and in private meetings among legislators. Regarding the latter, the public justification requirement demands that the arguments be made in full public view, which is what the *Congressional Record* records. The idea behind this requirement is that if legislators are going to impose burdens on some members of the population to benefit others, they have to do it in public to the representatives of the people who are being imposed upon. A case can be made for permitting committee reports to count, since these too are part of the public record. Two committees of the House of Representatives, the Education and Labor Committee and the Judiciary Committee, issued substantive reports.[9] Although the minority reports from each committee raised the question of whether the law would encourage hiring by the numbers as a way of avoiding disparate impact lawsuits, the majority reports did not address this concern, or they just dismissed it out of hand.[10] In sum, the lack of respect shown to opponents of the bill was made abundantly clear.

Perhaps more importantly, if one looks at the actual provisions of the amendments to title VII, it is clear that each of the relevant features of the bill identified above *increases* the incentives to hire less-qualified minorities at the expense of more qualified nonminorities:

(1) *The use of statistics.* The fact that the use of statistics to establish disparate impact was never completely clarified in the language of the statute is significant. The reference class against which the population of those hired is to be measured may only be established if the case comes to trial. As previously noted, data on the protected class status of all those who actually applied for the job is best, but sometimes that is not available, and proxies are used (Perritt 1992, 126–28). An employment practice that does not have a disparate impact on minorities if the reference class is the Standard Metropolitan Area may well have a disparate impact if the reference class is defined as those living in the immediate vicinity of the factory. What all this means is that even if an employer seeks to avoid disparate impact employment practices, he may not know whether he has used any until and unless he is haled into court. This, together with other uncertainties in the law, gives employers an incentive to hire as many minorities as possible, which presumably is just what some proponents of the law wanted. However, this point was not made in congressional debate on the bill. No one got up on the floor of the House or Senate and said, "We're going to leave the determination of the reference class in disparate impact suits up to the courts, since that will increase employer uncertainty about the application of the law.

We seek to have as many employers as possible hire as many minorities as possible, and the best way to achieve this is to create real indeterminacy in the law so that businesses and their legal counsel will be unable to assess accurately their legal exposure."

(2) *The particularity requirement.* The impact of the particularity requirement is uncertain. Originally, some members of Congress wanted to dispense altogether with the requirement that plaintiffs in disparate impact suits identify the particular practice or practices which caused a disparate impact. All the plaintiff would have to show is that the "bottom line" numbers were not right; a challenged firm would be left with only the business necessity defense. Given the stringent way the business necessity test had been interpreted, employers would have virtually no choice but to institute quotas to stay out of court. Opponents of the bill objected, so the compromise language of the law required that the plaintiff identify the practice that caused the disparate impact, but it allowed an exception: if the decision-making process did not permit disaggregation, it could be treated as a single practice. It is hard to know if this exception gutted the particularity requirement and significantly encourages quotas without knowing if it is usually possible to disaggregate decision-making processes that resulted in offers of employment. Congress made no effort to find out what the effect of this provision would be. Once again, Congress showed little interest in materially important matters of fact regarding the consequences of the act.

(3) *The business necessity defense.* The tightening of the business necessity defense by requiring that the employer "demonstrate"[11] that the qualification or hiring practice have a direct bearing on job performance and by restricting acceptable requirements to those directly relevant to the job clearly increased the incentive for firms to hire by the numbers. But, the interpretive memorandum's reference to *Griggs* hardly clarified the concept of business necessity, since the Supreme Court's decision in that case did not really define "business necessity"; the Court has had to revisit the issue repeatedly, though Congress was displeased with what it did when it last laid hands on the statute, which resulted in the *Ward's Cove* standards. Once again, Congress deliberately chose language that is highly indeterminate. The effect of this can only be to increase employer uncertainty, further strengthening the incentive to use hiring quotas as a prophylaxis against title VII litigation. No effort was made to determine how common disparate impact practices were or how feasible it would be for companies to devise race or

gender-neutral alternatives. Given the premises of proponents of legislation about the important negative cultural and educational effects of discrimination against women and minorities (understood in terms of disparate impact), it would be very common for facially neutral hiring practices to affect their prospects negatively. And by 1991, it was clear that it would be difficult to validate tests and hiring practices in a way that would satisfy the business necessity defense.[12] To say that the resulting legislation "is not a quota bill" is just disingenuous.

It is important to remember what is at stake. It is reasonable to suppose that proponents of this legislation favored preferential hiring policies (a term they would probably prefer to the more emotionally loaded "quota"), and they were crafting the law to encourage employers to adopt them. Now, there are a number of arguments in favor of preferential hiring. Some are principled sectarian arguments that appeal to principles of distributive or compensatory justice, but there is also a conversion argument for preferential hiring, which was sketched on page 227 of chapter 8. There may be other possible conversion arguments but—and this is the crucial point— neither that argument nor any other was offered. To the extent that they recognized the issue at all, they simply denied that the bill encouraged preferential hiring by denying that it was a quota bill. This is not an argument; it is an evasion of their responsibilities as legislators.

Why were proponents of the legislation not more forthcoming about their intentions? Two obvious reasons suggest themselves. First, many Americans, including many voters, think preferential hiring is just wrong. Members of Congress might be reluctant to vote in favor of this bill if it were publicly recognized as a major piece of public policy encouraging a kind of preferential hiring that many Americans think is just wrong and not merely a technical correction of some Supreme Court decisions. For this to be a factor, one need not suppose that voters were listening to the debate; legislators' political opponents almost certainly were listening or would consult the record before the next election. Second, squarely facing this issue would have required, as a practical matter, rewriting 42 U.S.C. § 2000e–2(a), which states, "it shall be an unlawful employment practice for an employer—(1) to fail or refuse to hire or to discharge any individual...because of such individual's race, color, religion, sex, or national origin."

Rewriting this section would have involved explicitly exempting discrimination against some groups; those (privileged) groups would then have to be identified and defined. It would have also required rewriting the first sentence of subsection (j) of 2000e–2, which now reads, "nothing contained in this title shall be interpreted to require any employer...to grant preferential treatment...." The requisite change would involve dropping the first three words of this sentence—or simply repealing this provision in its entirety. If proponents of the new act wanted to be honest about the fact that they were encouraging preferential hiring, they would have revised or repealed these sections to make it clear that only some forms of discrimination are legally prohibited. This would have made explicit the race- and gender-conscious intent of the relevant sections of the amended version of title VII as they construed it, and it would have exempted from litigation companies that engaged in the "right" kind of discrimination. The fact that they did not make these changes makes their lack of intellectual honesty transparently clear. It also makes it clear that they failed to meet the public justification and transparency requirements, whether the main victims and beneficiaries of the act are conceived of as intended or unintended.

Finally, while opponents of the bill, such as Rep. Armey, did their job by calling attention to the unintended victims and beneficiaries of the bill, President Bush and his administration failed to do theirs. They knew it was a quota bill, and yet Bush signed it anyway in a vain attempt to curry favor with the civil rights establishment and the African American community. It is easy to be cynical about the legislative process, which is often compared to making sausages; critics of that process are said to be naive about "how things are done." Nevertheless, a normative assessment of public policy must make judgments on the process, the outcome, or both. That is what is being done here, and a negative assessment is unavoidable.

Sexual Harassment

The inclusion of sex or gender as a prohibited grounds for discrimination was something of an afterthought, put in the bill as a poison pill intended to make the legislation unacceptable to the majority in Congress. Instead, it got swept along with the other provisions, making it into the final version of the law that eventually passed. It would be easy to object that the inclusion of sex as a protected category was done without a full and fair discussion that meets the public justification and transparency requirements. That objection can be resisted, however, on the grounds that the same considerations that apply to race also apply to gender. Baseless stereotypes and gender animus (misogyny) were common enough phenomena to warrant giving proponents of the act a pass on their failure to discuss it. But, this parity highlights the problem with recognizing one form of sex discrimination—hostile environment harassment. Before discussing the latter, a word needs to be said about quid pro quo harassment. Recall that this form of harassment occurs when sexual favors are demanded in exchange for some employment benefit. This is not, we have supposed, a matter about which there is persistent reasonable disagreement between modern liberals and at least some classical liberals, since there are convergence and conversion arguments for making it illegal that classical liberals could accept. Indeed, it is hard to imagine any conversion or convergence argument against making it illegal, though of course there are burden-of-proof questions that need to be addressed, and there are principled sectarian (i.e., libertarian) arguments against it. Recall, however, that the criteria spelled out in chapter 11 for legitimately imposing values only come into play when there is persistent reasonable disagreement about the proper scope of government, and we have assumed for the sake of argument in this instance that there is not persistent reasonable disagreement about whether quid pro quo sexual harassment should be illegal.

Returning to hostile environment harassment, the case against recognizing it as a form of sex discrimination was made in chapter 8. Basically, it comes down to the chilling effect on the workplace environment and freedom of expression that this prohibition brings in its train. This is consistent with a recognition that paradigm cases of hostile environment harassment are morally objectionable; it is just that there is no way to prohibit those instances without also prohibiting innocuous speech and creating a chilling environment. Those on the other side would argue that the value of discouraging the kind of behavior that no reasonable person thinks is morally acceptable outweighs the inconveniences just alluded to. About these matters there can be reasonable disagreement.

What there should not be any disagreement about, however, is the proper venue for this social policy question to be discussed and debated. It should be a matter of legislative debate and determination, but of course that is not what happened. The courts took it upon themselves to construe hostile environment harassment as a form of sex discrimination, thereby violating the democracy requirement, since there was no discussion of hostile environment harassment in the run up to the passage of the Civil Rights Act. Suppose, contrary to fact, that the courts had refused to recognize either quid pro quo harassment or hostile environment harassment as forms of sex discrimination. If there really had been a consensus for outlawing quid pro quo harassment (and there probably was), it is likely that the legislation would have been quickly enacted, since there are obvious political points to be scored by sponsoring and/or supporting such legislation and an obvious political price to pay for opposing it. (On this point, compare the legislative response to *Ward's Cove,* which was much more contentious.) The chances of passing such a bill would approach near certainty, if Congress were to exempt itself from being covered by the law, as it often does. The case is less clear for hostile environment harassment, since civil libertarian opponents would undoubtedly bring up the inherent difficulties in defining the prohibited conduct, which is mostly speech, though it is possible that the legislature might reach agreement on a policy that is about the same as what was laid down by the courts, flawed though it may be. The difference is that it would have been imposed by the legislature after a full debate in which the issues referred to above would have been fully ventilated—and if those issues were not discussed, it would have failed to meet the public justification requirement, the transparency requirement, or both.

The Occupational Safety and Health Regulatory Regime

Recall from chapter 9 the legislative history of the Occupational Safety and Health Act. Supporters of the bill correctly regarded its passage as a fait accompli. Though the act was passed by the legislature and signed into law by the executive, and thus the democracy requirement was satisfied, the public justification requirement was not. House and Senate committee reports recited some out-of-context occupational health and safety statistics and simply asserted that state and voluntary efforts were inadequate to address the problems of occupational health and safety. This hardly rises to the level of an argument to justify the proposition that the creation of OSHA would lead to significant improvement in workplace health and safety. The transparency requirement was also not satisfied. As John Mendeloff has pointed out, the most striking characteristic of the testimony and the congressional commentary was their idealism and their silence on the costs of regulation. In the whole legislative history, I found only two brief statements by Republican conservatives that point out that intervention can do more harm than good. In contrast, the idea that even one injury or fatality is too many is frequently repeated, along with assertions about the infinite value of human life. (Mendeloff 1979, 20)

The refusal to discuss the costs this regulatory regime might impose has the effect of avoiding an assessment of the extent to which people (in this case, businesses) would be negatively affected by the legislation. Of course, the fact that businesses would have to pay to bring their workplaces into compliance was obvious to everyone, but there was no interest at all in how much this would cost or even in the question of setting the parameters to address this question. Again, to quote Mendeloff, "Congressional aversion to hinting at the existence of costs and the possibility of trade-offs is, of course, not unique to the OSH Act. All proponents minimize costs of action, just as opponents minimize the costs of inaction. Yet even other recent safety legislation has not been this oblique in its references to costs" (ibid., 21).

The paltry budget and relatively small staff proposed for OSHA is further evidence of a failure to address seriously the question of whether the act would measurably affect occupational health and safety. As explained in chapter 9, OSHA's budget in 1975 was $102.3 million (in 1975 dollars), with a staff of 2,435 FTE (full-time equivalent) employees.[13] Around that time, the bill had the potential to affect 60 million workers at 5 million business establishments (Nichols and Zeckhauser 1977, 41). As of 2004, 135 million workers at 8.9 million sites were potentially subject to OSHA regulations.[14] The budget for OSHA in 2007 is about $486 million (in 2007 dollars) and the number of (FTE) employees is actually down to 2,150, of whom only 1,100 are inspectors.[15]

It is the job of the opposition to bring these questions about costs to light, but in an exercise of speaking truth to (union) power, Republican opponents chose to focus on the relatively unimportant procedural questions of whether the Labor Department would set standards, do inspections, and hear appeals on various rulings or whether those tasks should be divided among different agencies. The Labor Department had the reputation of being a worker-friendly bureaucracy, so the burning question for opponents was whether the Labor Department should be judge, jury, and executioner or whether a regime of separation of powers and checks and balances was advisable. Evidently, they all forgot that someone needed to carry the water bucket for the business community and ask the more fundamental question, "Is this really a good idea?"

The failure of the transparency requirement to be seriously addressed is further evident in light of the two key Supreme Court rulings relating to OSHA: the benzene standard case (*Industrial Union Dept. v. American Petrol. Inst.*, 448 U.S. 607 (1980)) and the cotton dust standard case (*American Textile Mfrs. Inst. v. Donovan*, 452 U.S. 490 (1981)). Recall that in the benzene standard case, the Court held that the act "did not give OSHA the unbridled discretion to adopt standards designed to create absolutely risk-free workplaces regardless of cost" (448 U.S. 607 (1980)). In the cotton dust standard case, however, they rejected the proposition that the act required that any OSHA standard must be cost-effective or pass some other, business-tested, economist-approved, cost-benefit test. Based on the text of the statute, these two decisions look to be a reasonable interpretation. To see why, recall that OSHA's guiding legislative mandate was "to assure so far as possible every working man and woman in the Nation safe and healthful working conditions" (29 U.S.C. § 651(b)). Moreover, the statute contains a "general duty clause," which requires that "each employer...furnish each of his employees employment and a place of employment which are free from recognized hazards that are causing or are likely to cause death or serious physical harm to his employees." (29 U.S.C. § 658). As the Court correctly noted, these clauses did not mean that employers had to create a risk-free workplace, but they also did not require that any regulations pass a cost-benefit test. These two cases gave OSHA inspectors a long enough leash to get onto the front porch of telecommuters' homes in 2000 before Labor Secretary Herman jerked their chain. Outside of the parameters set by the Court, the inherent vagueness in these two key clauses of the statute makes the Court's interpretation about as good as any other. So, it is not as if the Court had usurped legislative prerogatives. However, the mere fact that each of these cases even made it to the Supreme Court is evidence that the statutory language was vague enough to violate the transparency requirement. Whose interests are going to be harmed by this bill and to what extent are those interests going to be harmed? Based on the statutory language prior to these two decisions, there was no way even to hazard a guess of an answer to that question. Vague and aspirational identification of the intended beneficiaries and the extent to which they are supposed to benefit usually means that the victims (both intended and unintended) cannot be easily identified, nor can the extent to which the victims' interests are harmed be estimated. It is a common device used to paper over differences and get everyone on board, but that does not excuse it. According to the legislative record, no one stood up to ask the very simple questions about the scope of the bill that the Supreme Court ended up having to answer. There are, of course, limitations on what can be known about the effects of legislation such as this; no one could be expected to foresee, for example, the total yearly financial costs that the OSH Act would impose on the business community, but there was nothing to prevent the Congress from explicitly creating a framework to address this, such as the one the Supreme Court was forced to create in these two decisions. Or some other framework, if that is what they wanted.

Finally, it should not have been difficult to foresee that there would be a substantial class of unintended victims of this legislation. Legislators should have asked someone in a position to know how the act would be implemented, since any bureaucracy created by the act would have inadequate expertise for the foreseeable future to develop adequate standards; they might have discovered that ANSI and NFPA standards would be imposed in a blanket fashion and that these would undoubtedly be completely inappropriate across a range of cases. It is hard to resist the conclusion that the OSH Act of 1970 was a "feel good" measure intended to symbolize the compassion of members of Congress for the plight of workers injured on the job.

The Medical Products Regulatory Regime

Recall that the three key features of the current medical products regulatory regime that classical liberals object to are (1) the requirement that patients get a prescription from a doctor to take most medications and (2) the requirement that new drugs be approved by the FDA for safety and (3) the requirement that there be evidence that new drugs are efficacious for the on-label condition for which they were being prescribed. These are the three main sources of the government paternalism that inform the current medical products regulatory regime. Let us begin with the safety requirement. Recall that the 1938 Federal Food, Drug, and Cosmetic Act was given impetus by the sulfanilamide tragedy in which over 100 people, many of them children, died from a drug that used diethylene glycol (today used as antifreeze) as a base. In light of that tragedy, it was not surprising that the act required that new drugs be proved "safe." This safety requirement ultimately demanded some interpretation, both because a determination had to be made about how "safe" drugs needed to be and because drugs were discovered that had clear therapeutic value but also had negative side effects. In 1938, there were very few drugs extant, and most of them were botanicals. The suggestion that legislators should have foreseen the complications posed by the existence of side effects and, perhaps more importantly, the resultant bias created by the law in favor of making Type II errors and against making Type I errors is probably unreasonable. The transparency requirement cannot demand an unachievable degree of foresight; all that can be asked is that reasonably foreseeable unintended beneficiaries and victims be identified, and it is at least arguable that the additional statistical mortality and morbidity produced by the bias against making Type I errors in safety judgments was unforeseeable.

Matters are rather different in the case of the prescription drug requirement. That requirement was not part of the original 1938 Federal Food, Drug, and Cosmetic Act. Instead, it was part of some regulations promulgated by the FDA to implement the act. The story of how this was done is of some independent interest as an illustration of how a government bureaucracy can impose its will without legislative authorization, thereby violating the democracy requirement. In hearings and testimony on the 1938 bill, the issue of personal responsibility for medical decisions was thoroughly discussed under the heading of self-medication. As Peter Temin says,

> this [self-medication] was stated publicly to be the aim of the FDA in proposing and supporting the legislation. Self-medication was to be improved and facilitated, not hampered. Campbell, the chief of the FDA, said forcefully in Senate hearings at the start of the legislative process: "There is no issue, as I have told you previously, from the standpoint of the enforcement of the Food and Drugs Act, about self-medication. This bill does not contemplate its prevention at all. If it did a single short section in the measure could have been drawn up to that effect. But what is desired...is to make self-medication safe." (Temin 1980, 45)

Campbell later said, "all of the provisions dealing with drugs...are directed toward safeguarding the consumer who is attempting to administer to himself."[16] The House report on the bill reiterated Campbell's point: "the bill is not intended to restrict in any way the availability of drugs for self-medication. On the contrary, it is intended to make self-medication safer and more effective."[17]

Basically, the act said that drug labels had to contain directions for use, recommended dosages, and warnings of possible dangers (e.g., relating to misuse and/or side effects). A conversion argument for that provision is fairly straightforward. However, certain drugs were exempted from this labeling requirement, namely, those that were sold by prescription. These were medicines for which "representations or suggestions contained in the labeling thereof with respect to the conditions for which such drug or device is to be used appear only in medical terms as are not likely to be understood by the ordinary individual."[18] Concerns were also expressed that some drugs were dangerous, either for everyone or for people with certain medical conditions. As the FDA understood this regulation (which they themselves promulgated), this required that the patient obtain a prescription from a physician. They never explained why that was the case, however. They could have required that directions for use be offered in language ordinary people could understand, and/or they might have required these drugs to be purchased from a licensed pharmacist, who could provide counseling. That would have sufficed to provide proper warnings and explanations of how the drug should be taken or administered. It is difficult to avoid the inference that the real rationale behind the prescription requirement was a concern about efficacy. It is likely that the FDA was trying to discourage self-medication, not out concern for safety but out of a paternalistic concern for efficacy. This makes a certain amount of sense; prior to the invention of the sulfa drugs, most medications treated symptoms, not the underlying conditions. Efficacy in treating symptoms was easy for the patient himself or herself to judge, though it is always possible to confuse correlation with causation. But, if the drug addresses the underlying condition, then the diagnosis of that condition becomes critical, and that is something the layperson is not in a good position to do. Requiring patients to see a physician before taking any drug that might address an underlying condition makes a certain amount of sense. Assuming the FDA knew all this, that would explain an otherwise puzzling regulation. But this is all speculation, since there is no documentary evidence to support it.

In any case, all these drugs that were exempted from the basic labeling requirement had to have a label on them saying they were to be sold only by prescription written by a licensed physician (or dentist or veterinarian). If the drug were subsequently sold without a prescription, the manufacturer or the pharmacist could be sued by the FDA for mislabeling or misbranding them. This meant that a whole class of drugs could not be sold without the authorization of a physician, which represented an important step toward the current paternalistic medical products regulatory regime. In this way, a major restriction on freedom of choice in therapeutic drugs was imposed on the U.S. public by an unelected bureaucracy. At first, the manufacturers were able to designate which drugs were to be sold by prescription, but this led to considerable confusion, since different manufacturers of the same drug could designate their drugs differently. They also could be sued by the FDA if the latter did not agree with their decision about whether the drug should be sold only by prescription. Later, this method of designation was eliminated, and prescription drugs were given a statutory definition (21 U.S.C. § 353(b)), but it was up to the FDA to enforce it though companion regulations. The important point for our purposes is that this was done solely on the initiative of the Food and Drug Administration. Congress passed no law requiring a prescription for these medications.

The distinction between prescription and nonprescription (over-the-counter) drugs was, however, legally codified in 1951 in the Humphrey-Durham amendment to the act. The story of how this came about is revealing. Originally, both the House bill (H.R. 3298) and the Senate bill (S.1186) gave the administrator of the Federal Security Agency (at the time, the parent agency of the FDA) decision-making authority about which drugs would require a prescription, subject to statutory guidelines, though there were some differences of detail between the two bills.[19] The bill that ultimately passed, however, formally removed the administrator from the decision-making process. The law simply defined the categories of drugs that require a doctor's prescription:

> (1) A drug intended for use by man which—
>   (A) because of its toxicity or other potentiality for harmful effect, or the method of its use, or the collateral measures necessary to its use, is not safe for use except under the supervision of a practitioner licensed by law to administer such drug; or
>   (B) is limited by an approved application under section 355 of this title to use under the professional supervision of a practitioner licensed by law to administer such drug;
> shall be dispensed only
>   (i) upon a written prescription of a practitioner licensed by law to administer such drug. (21 U.S.C. § 353(b))

The second category (B) refers to new drugs that were being investigated by researchers. What is most interesting about both House and Senate reports, however, is that nowhere in the thirty-seven pages of the House Report or in the twelve pages of the Senate Report is there any attempt to justify the requirement that some drugs be sold by prescription only. That was taken for granted at the outset, probably because it had already been codified in regulations issued by the FDA immediately after passage of the 1938 act. This is one of the reasons why it is so important that changes in the scope of government be done democratically and after a full and open debate. If it is done surreptitiously by a government bureaucracy, the temptation is to accept it as a fait accompli.

The 1951 Humphrey-Durham amendment and its precursor FDA regulations had profound effects. The intended beneficiaries were patients who were forced—against their will but in their presumed best interests—to seek the guidance of a physician. Though there is no way of judging the size of this group, it is not the empty set, since people who self-medicate would undoubtedly make mistakes that physicians would prevent, and there would probably be more of them than the number who would be misdiagnosed by physicians. It is not clear who the intended victims of this legislation are; perhaps it is the manufacturers whose sales are hurt by the prescription drug requirement. But, the law created myriad unintended beneficiaries and victims. At the top of the list of unintended beneficiaries were physicians, who now held in their hands prescription pads of gold. Self-medication for any but the most inconsequential ailments was effectively forbidden by law, and the beatification of doctors had begun. By 1951, the revolution in therapeutic drugs was well under way, and the power this law conferred on physicians should have been evident to members of Congress, but no mention was made of this in either of the committee reports. The main unintended victims of the law were consumers who would have to pay higher prices because they had to make an unnecessary visit to a physician to get a prescription for conditions they could correctly self-diagnose. Many medical conditions are obvious to those who have them and require no particularly dangerous treatments. Pharmacists are perfectly capable of advising people about safety, dosing, and side effects, which they currently do anyway. Pharmacists were also unintended victims of this amendment, which is ironic because both Humphrey and Durham were pharmacists by trade. The role of the pharmacist was much diminished by this legislation and the precursor regulations issued by the FDA. Prior to the regulations imposed by the FDA in the aftermath of the 1938 act, consumers could purchase any nonnarcotic drug a pharmacist would sell them, and the latter served as an important information resource for consumers.[20] Their role in health care delivery has been substantially reduced by the prescription drug requirement.

Ironically, the problems about restricting the right of self-medication and the problem of higher prices were almost recognized in a minority House report signed by Representatives Leonard Hall, Joseph O'Hara, and John Bennett.[21] They objected to the provision of the bill reported out of the House committee that gave the administrator of the FSA the power to determine which drugs would be prescription drugs. Even though that power would have been constrained by statute, the final decision would have been his; these legislators expressed concern that this put too much power in one person's hands. They believed that the administrator would make more and more drugs "prescription only." It was even theoretically possible that aspirin could be designated a prescription drug.[22] This would severely constrain the right of self-medication, which, they pointed out, the 1938 act sought to strengthen. Finally, on the cost issue, their report said:

> thousands of articles of a medicinal or remedial nature are now lawfully available to the people and may be purchased without the expense of a prescription—doctor fees and prescription prices at the drugstore. The undersigned believe that the bill as reported will increasingly over the years restrict the number and nature of drugs available to the public on over-the-counter sale, and thus will gradually and substantially increase the cost of medication. (Ibid., 31)

The irony is that Hall, O'Hara, and Bennett explicitly supported the statutory recognition of a distinction between prescription and nonprescription drugs (ibid., 28); they just objected to the mechanism by which the distinction was to be made—on approval of the FSA administrator. Instead, they favored a statutory definition of what counted as a prescription drug. In the event, their view prevailed because it echoed the Senate version of the bill sponsored by Senator Humphrey that ultimately passed. Their fears were also realized, however, as the right of self-medication was significantly constrained and the cost of getting medications rose, the latter occurring at least in part because of the prescription drug requirement. It is just that the reason was not that the administrator had too much power; instead, it was because so many drugs fit the statutory definition of a prescription drug.

The initial change in the scope of government activity occurred in 1938 when the act prevented people from buying drugs that might not be safe. There is an easy conversion argument in favor of this part of the act, which was sketched in chapter 9 (see pp. 292–93), and the problem with it, namely, that it creates a bias against Type I errors and in favor of Type II errors, is one that legislators probably could not be expected to foresee. That problem only became evident after passage of the 1962 amendments when the FDA took on comprehensive responsibility to assure the public that all medications are "safe and effective." Not coincidentally, that is when the drug and device loss and lag problems became particularly noticeable, but in 1938, that problem was probably not foreseeable.

Shortly after the passage of the 1938 act, the scope of government activity changed again when the FDA promulgated its regulation regarding prescription drugs. That is when this aspect of the modern drug regulatory regime was instituted, and that is when the democracy requirement was violated. The fact that it was later codified by legislation in the 1951 Humphrey-Durham amendment reveals that its backers realized that it was of dubious legislative provenance. Indeed, the House (majority) Report says, "at present, the restrictions on dispensing 'prescription' drugs are not specifically stated in the statute" (ibid., 3), which is just a polite way of saying that the FDA had just made it up. This failure of the democracy requirement probably explains why the transparency requirement failed to be met when the Humphrey-Durham amendment was passed in 1951, since the distinction between prescription and nonprescription drugs was taken for granted by that time. In both the House and Senate reports, there was much talk of "strengthening" the 1938 act and of "closing loopholes" in it, but no one thought to question the distinction the FDA had drawn between prescription and nonprescription drugs, which they were about to codify in the law.

The final paternalistic component of the contemporary medical products regulatory regime is the Kefauver-Harris amendments of 1962, which, among other things, required drug companies to provide "substantial evidence of effectiveness" for a drug to be approved. As was just noted, much of the drug (and device) loss and lag problems are traceable to this requirement, and it too has contributed significantly to the high cost of medicines. Phase II and Phase III clinical trials, which gather evidence of efficacy, are the most expensive and time-consuming part of the drug approval process. This means that the unintended victims include those who suffer a greater incidence of mortality and morbidity because of the delay in approving drugs or because they lack the financial resources to pay the higher costs of medicines that have to go through extensive and expensive clinical trials to establish "substantial evidence of effectiveness." As chapter 9 demonstrates (see pp. 295–96), this is a substantial number of people. Were these unintended victims identified?

To answer this, it is worth noting that the Senate committee report recognized that claims of efficacy are often contestable; what works for some patients does not work for all patients, and there is the more fundamental question of causation and correlation, which well-designed clinical trials can address at different confidence levels. The Senate Report says,

> the term "substantial evidence" is used to require that therapeutic claims for new drugs be supported by reliable pharmacological and clinical studies. When a drug has been reliably tested by qualified experts and has been found to have the effect claimed for it, this claim should be permitted even though there may be preponderant evidence to the contrary based upon equally reliable studies....What the committee intends is to permit the claim for this new drug to be made to the medical profession with a proper explanation of the basis on which it rests.[23]

The bill further recognizes by implication the possibility of off-label prescribing, which it does not prohibit, though if the drug is to be marketed for off-label uses, that is, if off-label uses are to become on-label uses, the manufacturer has to submit test results to establish "substantial evidence of effectiveness." The general point is that the committee report recognized the complexities involved in establishing efficacy. However—and this is the crucial point—nowhere in the committee report was there a recognition of the implications of this for increased mortality and morbidity or its implications for the cost of prescription drugs. Safety can be established relatively easily and quickly; what is harder is efficacy. Getting evidence of this delays the introduction of new medicines and devices and thus increases mortality and morbidity, and of course costs. The deep irony of this is that Estes Kefauver, whose name the bill bears, started his hearings in 1959 to investigate the high prices of prescription drugs and to expose the greed of the drug companies. He got fixated on the latter and proposed an amendment, which did not make it into the final bill, to force the licensing of patented drugs after three years to other manufacturers, who would then be required to pay a royalty not to exceed 8 percent of sales. Kefauver fully supported the efficacy requirement, however.

Of all the senators on the committee, he should have taken the lead in investigating the effect on drug prices of this requirement. In an addendum to the report, Kefauver, along with some other senators, complained mightily about the failure of the bill to address the exorbitant profits of the drug companies, but no mention was made of the increased costs and decreased availability of prescription drugs that would attend the imposition of an efficacy requirement demanded by him and other members of the legislative branch (ibid., 37–50). Nor was this issue brought up in the remarks of Senators Dirksen and Hruska, who opposed the forced licensing provision championed by Kefauver (ibid., 52–63).

This is not to suggest that an efficacy requirement was unwarranted. The drug companies made extravagant claims of efficacy for their products that were unsupported by the evidence. Prior to the Kefauver-Harris amendments, they did not have to substantiate these claims, as long as their products were safe. (They had Justice Holmes to thank for that.) Moreover, the drug companies engaged in a variety of dubious practices to promote their products to physicians and to the general public (Young 1992, 408–22). (Pharmacists were out of the loop because of the Humphrey-Durham amendment.) Tort law may well have been inadequate to handle the inevitable problems that accompanied the revolution in therapeutic drugs. Some sort of efficacy requirement might well have been justified, all things considered. The basic problem was that when this bill was being written, not all things were considered. Specifically, no one asked about the delays that would be introduced by requiring clinical trials to establish "substantial evidence of effectiveness" or about the added costs of this requirement. This did not require clairvoyance; just a little thoughtfulness. The conclusions to be drawn from this discussion of the medical products regulatory regime administered by the FDA are these: the requirement that drugs be shown to be safe was likely legitimately imposed, since the bias problem this created was probably unforeseeable. The prescription drug requirement, first imposed by the FDA immediately following the passage of the 1938 Federal Food, Drug, and Cosmetic Act and later codified by the Humphrey-Durham amendment in 1951 was not legitimately imposed because it violated the democracy requirement in 1938 and the transparency requirement in 1951. Finally, the requirement that there be substantial evidence of effectiveness, imposed by the Kefauver-Harris amendments in 1962, was also illegitimate because it violated the transparency requirement.

In the 1942 film *Casablanca,* the police captain played by Claude Rains raids the nightclub owned by Humphrey Bogart's character, and with a straight face Rains tells Bogart that he is "shocked...shocked" to find that gambling (in which he participates) is taking place in the back rooms of the nightclub. It is a fair challenge to ask if the criticisms of the political actors made in this chapter are of the same sort. Are we to be "shocked" that politics is taking place in the halls of Congress and elsewhere in Washington? That people in positions of power and authority are not honest? The obvious response to these rhetorical questions is to point out that our investigation is normative, that the intent is to establish what ought to be, not what is. Alternatively, this investigation can be conceived of as attempting to discover evaluative principles or standards by which to judge the political morality of the actions of key actors who determine the actual scope of government activity. Besides, compared to the institutional reforms urged by other political philosophers, the institutional implications of chapter 11 are relatively modest.[24]

Moreover, it would be unduly cynical to absolve these individuals of any moral responsibility for the manner in which they do their jobs simply because they are politicians. Besides, some of them have performed admirably. In response to objections raised by some southern senators, Hubert Humphrey forcefully denied that title VII could be used to pressure employers to use preferential hiring programs to avoid getting sued for discrimination. He could have dismissed their concerns as motivated by prejudice or tinged with racism, but he did not do that. This stands in stark contrast to what was said in Congress about President George H. W. Bush's concerns about the implications of the 1991 Civil Rights Act—concerns he lacked the political courage to act on when the bill came to his desk. Sponsors of the bill attacked his motives and linked him with the racist David Duke. These ad hominems are perhaps less an expression of the coarsened rhetorical environment than they are a reflection of the fundamental dishonesty of the 1991 Civil Rights Act, whose main effect was to pressure companies into hiring by the numbers while maintaining the legal fiction that this type of hiring is prohibited by law. On that very bill, Rep. Dick Armey clearly laid out the case for the proposition that the proposed bill was a quota bill, a case that his opponents simply ignored. Justice Byron White, the author of the majority opinion in *Ward's Cove Packing Co., Inc. v. Antonio,* 490 U.S. 642 (1989), effectively overturned *Griggs v. Duke Power,* 401 U.S. 424 (1971), the latter being among the most egregious violations of legislative intent in recent

U.S. history. For all intents and purposes, he brought the law back into line with the congressional understanding of "discrimination" in 1964, which is why Congress passed the 1991 Civil Rights Act. In ruling on the Endangered Species Act in the Tellico Dam case (*Tennessee Valley Auth. v. Hill,* 437 U.S. 153 (1977)), Chief Justice Burger said, "the plain language of the Act, buttressed by its legislative history, shows clearly that Congress viewed the value of endangered species as 'incalculable'" (ibid., at 187). Arguably, this was his way of telling Congress to fix the law, which they did, though not entirely satisfactorily. By contrast, Justice Kennedy, in *Rapanos v. United States,* 547 U.S. 715 (2006), refused to overturn the creative understanding of the term "navigable waters" promulgated by the D.C. Circuit Court (in *NRDC v. Callaway,* 392 F. Supp. 685, 686 (D.D.C. 1975)), which violated the democracy requirement in the regulation of wetlands. After all, if Congress wanted to regulate wetlands, they could pass a law to do that. Nothing in the language of section 404 of the Clean Water Act warranted the D.C. Circuit's decision. Once again, they just made it all up. Finally, the Court did the best it could with the vague and ambiguous language of the Occupational Safety and Health Act of 1970 in the benzene exposure standard case (*Industrial Union Dept. v. American Petrol. Inst.,* 448 U.S. 607 (1980)) and the cotton dust standard case (*American Textile Mfrs. Inst. v. Donovan* 452 U.S. 490 (1981)). Apparently, at the time of the passage of the Occupational Safety and Health Act, no one considered the fundamental questions of the scope and implications of the act that the Court ended up having to address in these decisions. When modern liberals were not pushing these scope decisions off onto the courts and when the courts were not appropriating these issues for themselves, they were endowing unelected bureaucrats in the executive branch with broad discretionary powers that no friend of democratic accountability should be comfortable with. Mid-level bureaucrats in the Fish and Wildlife Service and the Army Corps of Engineers make decisions that have an enormous financial impact on hundreds, even thousands of people.

Fundamentally, the requirements discussed in the preceding chapter are really quite modest in their demands on elected officials. Not everyone in the majority has to step up and address the public justification and transparency requirements. It is just that someone has to do so at some point. They do not have to take principled positions. Indeed, the conversion arguments that are demanded of them are deliberately unprincipled, in the sense that political philosophers use the term. Much of the real work of legislation takes place in committee, and it is there that the public justification and transparency requirements can be addressed. Few people read those reports anyway, but as a matter of showing respect to those with whom they disagree and to those who will be negatively affected, it is appropriate to ask of elected officials and their staffs to address in a serious way the criticisms and proposals of their opponents. Both houses of Congress have elaborate rituals of personal respect for their opponents; it does not seem too much ask of them that they show a similar respect for their opponents' intellects.

Debate about the proper scope of government is a permanent feature of life in a democracy and has special salience for liberals of whatever persuasion, because of their belief in limited government. Finally, just as contending armies routinely believe that God is on their side, so too do people (including politicians) with modern or classical liberal sympathies believe that reason is on their side. Each side believes that their ideas on the proper scope of government are correct, or at least better than the other side's. This means they should be open to suggestions to institutionalize the democracy, public justification, and transparency requirements. How this should be done is best left to those with a more intimate knowledge of the machinery of government. Finally, if political actors on both sides were to take seriously the opinions and arguments of those who oppose them, rancor would likely diminish, and they would be able to escape Mill's charge that "some, whenever they see any good to be done, or evil to be remedied, would willingly instigate the government to undertake the business, while others prefer to bear almost any amount of social evil rather than add one to the departments of human interests amenable to governmental control."

Notes

1. See chapter 4 of *Utilitarianism*, "Of What Sort of Proof the Principle of Utility Is Susceptible," (Mill [1861] 1957, 44–51).
2. For a discussion of epistemic sincerity and insincerity, see Gaus (1995, 139–140).
3. Shapiro (2007) is a sustained convergence argument for the proposition that modern liberals of diverse philosophical persuasions should support free market institutions such as privatized pensions and health care.
4. This is a major theme of volume two of Hayek's *Law, Liberty and Legislation* (1976), which is subtitled "The Mirage of Social Justice."
5. This is the thrust of Adam Thierer and Clyde Wayne Crews Jr.'s 2003 book, *What's Yours Is Mine: Open Access and the Rise of Infrastructure Socialism*.
6. The most important decision on this was *Cipollone v. Liggett Group, Inc.*, 505 U.S. 504 (1992). For a general discussion of preemption by product labeling statutes, see Schaffer (1996) and Smith and Gabor (1996).
7. I suspect that a similar conclusion could be sustained against critiques of the existing order found in the writings of anarchists such as Murray Rothbard, but I am aware of no one who has made this case. This suspicion is, of course, just that, and it may be possible to allay it, but that too is another debate that must be left for another time.
8. This reads out of the debate, most famously, John Rawls. In *A Theory of Justice* Rawls initially maintained that the implications of his principles for the choice between a capitalist economic system and socialist one depended on empirical questions about which he had little to say. Toward the end of his life, however, Rawls changed his mind and maintained that only what he called a "property owning democracy" or a form of liberal socialism would satisfy his two principles of justice (2001, 135–40). However, he never specified a system of property rights in the means of production for either of these systems nor did he address any of the other burden-of-proof questions raised in the text. He was making very radical proposals that, at this time, have virtually no chance of being implemented. These problems,

coupled with Rawls's obliviousness to the failure of "actually existing" socialism around the world, justifies reading him out of the debate that is the subject of this book.

9. Not all communitarians reject the liberal label. Michael Walzer and Charles Taylor identify themselves as liberals in Gutmann (1992). One of the medium-sized debates of the late 1980s and early 1990s concerned the liberal credentials of communitarians. For a good overview, see Buchanan (1989). Feminists are all over the map, ranging from libertarian to left-wing radical, and they are angry with almost everyone else. For reasons about to be explained, some of them can be characterized as modern liberals and some as classical liberals. The next section begins with a more general characterization of liberalism, which by implication reads some of the more radical feminists out of the debate that is central to this book.

10. These are listed at the beginning of chapter 3 and are systematically discussed throughout that chapter. Freedom of contract is arguably implicit in a right of self-ownership and/or ownership of one's labor. Freedom of contract serves as a point of departure for classical liberals in the sense that they maintain that there is a presumption in favor of it.

11. This preliminary characterization follows, with some modification, John Gray's characterization of liberalism in his synoptic overview of liberal political thought and institutions (1995, 45–55). Notice also that, in accordance with the stipulation defended in the last section, socialists who claim liberal credentials have been read out of the debate.

12. See, for example, Plant (1988; 1991 184–213, 253–292), Copp (1992, 23–61), Jacobs (1993, 141–189), Gewirth (1996, 38–44), and Sterba (1998, 41–76).

13. This is not the issue, which is also dead or almost dead, of whether there is a third way between capitalism and communism. That question is about the possibility of a different form of socialism (specifically, market socialism), whereas the issue referred to in the text is whether there is a way to coordinate production that does not rely on either central planning or markets. Albert and Hahnel (1978; 1987; 1991) have attempted to outline such an alternative, but it is very difficult to see how it could actually work. This objection is carefully developed in Prychitko (1988, 132–39). For the debate on market socialism, see Schweickart (1993), Roemer (1994a; 1994c), Arnold (1994), and Pierson (1995).

14. One other related difference is about whether advanced industrial countries should bargain to impose environmental and labor regulations on developing countries in exchange for opening borders to trade. This is sometimes justified on grounds of fairness to domestic producers, but it is also justified by the kinds of arguments that are used to support imposing these restrictions on domestic firms.

15. On the debate about supply-side economics, see the articles in Fink (1982). Though some might object that the preceding

paragraphs paint too rosy a picture about the degree of consensus among economists, there is no denying that there has been important growth in economic knowledge over the past thirty to forty years, and that growth has attenuated the ideological character of many of the disputes about economic policy. Whether this provides a model for liberals seeking agreement about the proper role of government in other areas raises some interesting methodological questions that cannot be pursued here.

16. Libertarians in the natural rights tradition would favor state provision of public goods such as national defense and (possibly) the public goods produced by the criminal and civil justice system but not on the grounds about to be discussed. Instead, they would favor these on the grounds that the purpose of government is to give legal expression to people's natural rights.

17. This account of public goods is based on Head (1974, 167–172), though he characterizes the first condition in terms of joint supply rather than joint consumption. There are some subtle differences in the ways that public goods have been characterized in the literature. For a discussion of these differences, see Cullity (1995).

18. The classic statement of the public goods problem can be found in Olson (1965, ch. 1). For an entrée into the large literature by economists on this problem, see Cowen (1988) and Cowan and Crampton (2004). Public goods will be discussed in more detail in chapters 5 and 6.

19. Olson (1965, 60–62) discusses a number of ways this can happen. On tying arrangements, see especially Demsetz (1970). Many of the articles in Cowen (1988) discuss private solutions to public goods problems or to what appear to be public goods problems.

20. Olson calls these "privileged groups" (Olson 1965, 49–50) and observes that a public good will be provided for a privileged group of rational individuals. The standard hypothetical example of this that is often cited is the lighthouse: it might be worth it for one shipping company to pay the entire costs of erecting and operating a lighthouse, even if other shippers could free ride on the provision of services by the lighthouse. It is worth noting that many economists since Mill have used this as an example of a public good that everyone could agree the government should provide (e.g., Samuelson 1964, 151, 159), since no group of shippers is a privileged group, in Olson's sense. Ronald Coase actually investigated how lighthouse services were provided in Great Britain, however, and found that they were private sector operations in which fees were collected at nearby ports (Coase 1974, 357–376). This involved a tying arrangement where the private excludable good was the use of the port facilities.

21. Some of the ideas discussed in the text under this heading are suggested by John Roemer (1994b, 312–313). Roemer does not, however, draw the parallels with public goods that are identified in what follows in the text. See also Gaus (1999, 179–181).

22. The inflation must be high and the corruption rampant for these to be genuine public bads. The effects of low inflation are slight, subtle, and widely scattered, and of course the Keynesians have argued that low inflation can be a good thing, on balance. Not so for high inflation. In the case of low levels of public corruption, the latter may actually produce a public good. Government officials, especially at the state and local level, sometimes combine a low level of mendacity with an even lower level of intelligence. When their schemes are exposed and they are hauled off to jail, public enjoyment of the spectacle is both nonrivalrous and nonexcludable.

23. Henceforth, for ease of exposition, the terms "public goods" and "public goods problem" will be taken to include public bads and public bads problems, unless confusion threatens.

24. As Kirk (1954, 43) describes conservatives, they have "an inclination to tolerate what abuses may exist in present institutions out of a practical acquaintance with the violent and unpredictable nature of doctrinaire reform."

25. See, for example, the essays in Meiners and Morriss (2000).

26. Some classical liberal economists adopt a broader conception of externalities in arguing against various forms of government intervention, but that is best construed as part of a strategy of arguing for classical liberal policies on the basis of principles that modern liberals are inclined to accept—principles that take an expansive view of what counts as an externality. That is, they are convergence arguments.

27. See Epstein (1998, 187–213) for a classical liberal attempt to deal with these and related problems. One problem that the above account glosses over is that the common law changes over time and not always in ways that classical liberals approve of. Moreover, modern liberals might favor dramatically expanding the scope of torts as a way of giving legal backing to a wide variety of community norms. This means that the attempt in the text to distinguish the externalities that classical liberals believe the state should deal with from those that it should ignore by reference to the common law is a first approximation in addressing what is in reality a more complex issue. Nevertheless, it is a useful first approximation in distinguishing how classical liberals and modern liberals think about the proper role of the state in dealing with negative externalities.

28. Even in this area there is some enthusiasm for private provision of the good. See, for example, Benson (1990; 1998), who favors private provision of some protective services.

Chapter 2

1. Rate regulation often involves explicit subsidies and regulation of entry and exit. For example, local telephone companies are

required to provide service to rural subscribers at unprofitable rates. This was offset by allowing higher prices in other areas and by legal barriers to entry for potential competitors (Viscusi, Vernon, and Harrington 2005, 539–40). See Asch and Seneca (1985, 62) on entry and exit regulation.

2. This was done in the Transportation Act of 1920, ch. 91, 41 Stat. 456. See Epstein (1998, 298–300) for a discussion of the problems with the original Interstate Commerce Act of 1887 and how it led to the Transportation Act of 1920.

3. For a concise discussion of the three acts, see Stone (1977, chs. 1–2).

4. U.S. Bureau of the Census, *Statistical Abstract of the United States: 1999,* table no. 394, 240.

5. For a discussion of trucking and airline deregulation in the larger context of deregulation in the United States and the United Kingdom, see Swann (1988, 168–72).

6. There is evidence that widespread literacy in Scotland was partly responsible for the Scottish Enlightenment (Herman 2001, 25–27).

7. For two very different versions of this argument, see Galston (1989) and Guttmann (1989).

8. Among philosophers, see, for example, Dworkin (1984, 207–8, 269–71), Rawls (1971, 277–78), Ackerman (1980, 208), and Haslett (1997).

9. See McCaffery (1994a; 1994b) for interesting arguments to the effect that modern liberals and conservatives (i.e., classical liberals) should both support abolishing the inheritance tax in favor of a version of a consumption tax. In the language of chapter 1, this would be a convergence argument.

10. For this sort of analysis of the causes and consequences of the Great Depression, see Rothbard (1963); for a more general analysis along these lines, see Ikeda (1996).

11. Sometimes this is held out as an ideal toward which society should move. See, for example, Friedman (1962, 87). However, even among libertarians, it is difficult to find explicit defenses of this proposal, though see Narveson (1988, 275–78) for an exception. For more on libertarian views on education, see the articles collected in Rickenbacker (1974).

12. Friedman, perhaps the most famous classical liberal advocate of partial privatization, discusses the externalities of education at some length in his classic paper on education (Friedman 1955), which served as the basis for the chapter on education in *Capitalism and Freedom* (1962, 83–107) in which he advocates vouchers. He adds to the list of externalities mentioned in the text a negative externality that a lack of education might be responsible for: increased crime among young people. For a libertarian argument based on natural rights and not externalities for at least some public funding of education, see Lomasky (1987, 173–81).

13. For an account of the standard justification for rate regulation and antitrust law which is nonetheless sensitive to its limitations and the objections to it, see Samuelson and Nordhaus (1992, 338–53). See also Asch and Seneca (1985, ch. 14). The main criterion for a natural monopoly is that production by a single firm minimizes the costs of production (Viscusi, Vernon, and Harrington 2005, 401). Commonly cited examples include rail service in smaller communities, residential water and sewer services, and retail electricity.

14. The seminal articles in this literature are Stigler (1971) and Peltzman (1976). See also Stigler (1975) for a careful case study of the ineffectiveness of rate regulation in electric utilities. For a summary of various theories of regulation and more complete references to the literature, see Viscusi, Vernon, and Harrington (2005, 375–96).

15. See Stone (1977, 45) and Viscusi, Vernon, and Harrington (2005, chs. 8–9) for an articulation of the incipiency-of-monopoly rationale for antitrust law, which was popular among supporters of the Federal Trade Commission Act and seems pervasive today outside of classical liberal circles.

16. See the cases discussed in Armentano (1990), which also gives a clear general statement of one classical liberal view of antitrust.

17. See Wagner (1989, 72–88) for an elaboration on this point.

18. For an explanation of this observation as it pertains to estate taxes, see McCaffery (1994a).

19. The data in this table are derived from two charts. One is from the *Wall Street Journal*, "A Rich Tax Debate," Featured Article, Editorial page, January 22, 2002. Available at http://www.opinionjournal.com/editorial/feature.html?id=95001783. The other is from the National Taxpayers Union Foundation, http://www.ntu.org/main/page.php?PageID=6, (accessed May 22, 2008). Both are reprinted by permission.

20. The benefits of tax shielding do not accrue entirely to the consumers of these services. Providers capture some of the benefits by raising prices. When tax shielding for certain categories of goods and services is instituted, the demand curve shifts to the right, since consumers are paying for these services with cheaper dollars. The public choice analysis is that provider groups are the driving force behind tax shielding.

21. In *Justice as Fairness: A Restatement* (2001, 74–78), Rawls goes to considerable lengths to clarify his meaning in these passages from *A Theory of Justice* (1971). I owe this point to Samuel Freeman.

22. See, for example, Tollison and Wagner (1982).

23. Blum and Kalven (1954 [1978], 90–92) point out that a flat tax with an exemption for the first X dollars of income will effectively be a progressive tax. They call this a degressive tax and observe that the larger the exemption, the greater the effective degree of progressivity. As long as classical liberals favor exempting some income from taxation, they cannot represent themselves as opposed to all forms of progressive taxation.

24. Shugart (1997) consists of a collection of essays illustrating this point in considerable detail. See also Gross (1995).

25. Health care for the poor is not provided by social insurance because recipients do not have to pay premiums to receive care. Programs such as Medicaid are straight-up transfer programs.

26. Fishback and Cantor (2000, 120–42) argue that workers' compensation insurance came about because it was in the interests of all the affected parties, not just the workers.

27. For a representative sample of modern liberal political philosophers who take this view, see Walzer (1983), Ackerman (1980), Dworkin (1981a; 1981b), and Rawls (1971). Some recent work in political philosophy attempts to distinguish inequalities that should be eliminated or reduced from those that should not. The distinction is usually drawn on the basis of unchosen versus chosen inequalities. On this view, the state should eliminate or dramatically reduce inequalities due to bad luck (e.g., physical and mental handicaps, on-the-job injuries, natural disasters), but inequalities due to personal or individual choices should be permitted to stand. Social insurance programs can then be justified on the grounds that they redress inequalities due to bad luck. Seminal articles on "luck egalitarianism," as it is sometimes called, include Dworkin (1981a; 1981b) and Arneson (1989; 1990). Important criticisms of luck egalitarianism can be found in Anderson (1999).

28. Although the benefit formulas are progressive, lower-income groups tend to die at a younger age than their more affluent counterparts, they tend to work more years, and the funding of the system is regressive in that there is a flat payroll tax with a ceiling on the wages taxed. Whether old-age social insurance programs are on balance progressive or regressive intragenerationally is the subject of some controversy. See Shapiro (2007, 161–63) and the references cited therein for a discussion of this point.

29. Etzioni and Brodbeck (1995, 3). For a discussion of whether communitarian values can justify Social Security, see Shapiro (2007, 184–88).

30. For a defense of these claims, see Marmor, Mashaw, and Harvey (1992). For a critique of some of these programs, see Murray (1984).

31. One of the major changes wrought in the welfare system in light of the Personal Responsibility and Work Opportunity Reconciliation Act of 1996 has been to alter the character of this commitment by giving a fixed amount to the states for welfare in the form of block grants, over which the latter have considerable discretionary control. Modern liberals have rightly pointed out the importance of this feature of welfare reform as expressive of a change in the nature of society's commitment to the poor.

32. For a discussion of correlated risks in disaster insurance, see Arnold (2002, 15); for correlated risks in unemployment insurance, see Schmidtz and Goodin (1998, 162–64).

33. Rappaport (1992) suggests that the market was in the process of developing a way of contracting around these difficulties within the framework of the common law at about the time state-mandated workers' compensation programs were instituted, so the private sector might have developed a solution to this problem given enough time. It is a commonplace among classical liberals to claim that, given enough time, someone will craft a private sector solution to a given social problem that will be superior to what the state could do. Such claims are obviously hard to verify or falsify.

34. For representative classical liberals who believe the state has some role to play in this area, see Hayek (1960, 257–58, 285–86) and Friedman (1962, 190–93). For the libertarian rejection of welfare, see Nozick (1974, 150–83), Narveson (1988, 245–74), and Machan (1985; 1995).

35. See Olasky (1996) and David Schmidtz's contribution to Schmidtz and Goodin (1998). For discussions of the historical record of mutual aid societies, see Olasky (1992) and Beito (1990).

36. This proposition is defended in detail in Epstein (1997). See also Goodman and Musgrave (1992).

37. In the absence of tax breaks for health care premiums, it is likely that most health insurance plans would discontinue coverage of routine care because overutilization would make such coverage prohibitively expensive. If routine health care were paid for out of pocket, it is likely that people would no more insure themselves for it than they would insure for routine automobile maintenance.

38. The Cato Institute (http://www.cato.org) has been a forum for classical liberal critiques of the existing system and proposals for alternatives. See their Web site for online papers and references to literature in print.

39. Shapiro (2007, 151–94) has a very interesting argument for the claim that modern liberals should favor a scheme that resembles Chile's. His argument is a convergence argument from modern liberal principles to ostensibly classical liberal policies.

40. In Arnold (2002, 22–27), I explain why this is so. This article offers a critique of existing disaster insurance programs in a way that intended to appeal to both modern and classical liberals, that is, it is a conversion argument.

41. For an introduction to this basic public choice critique, see Wagner (1989) or Mitchell and Simmons (1994).

42. Much of this grows out of the Austrian critique of central planning. See Lavoie (1985) for a summary of that critique. The seminal Austrian work on the business cycle is Hayek (1935). For a mature statement of his views, see Hayek (1979). An up-to-date version of the Austrian theory of the business cycle can be found in Horwitz (2000, 121–28). Of course, economists of the Austrian school are not the only ones who maintain that the visible hand

of the state is a major factor in the explanation of the business cycle. Most famously, Milton Friedman has argued for this view. See, for example, Friedman (1970, 20–26; 1976, 213–37).

Chapter 3

1. The list to which this note is appended is adapted from Becker (1977, 19).
2. There is a dispute about the reach of the takings clause for the other incidents of ownership, which was inaugurated by Richard Epstein's *Takings* (1985). More will be said about this below in the discussion of incident #7, the right to security.
3. For a comprehensive discussion of these theories, see the articles in the December 1985 issue of the *Journal of Legal Studies,* especially the overview article by Priest (1985).
4. I argue in Arnold (1994, 201–5) that this problem would be serious and endemic to market socialist firms in which the state owns the capital firms employ.
5. For brief histories of employment law, see Hill (1987, ch. 1) and Rothstein et al. (1994, ch. 1).
6. Although these programs can be conceived of as regulations imposed on the employment relation, they are first and foremost social insurance (i.e., transfer) programs. As such, a discussion of them is beyond the scope of this book.
7. Employment law also includes a variety of other forbidden grounds for firing employees, such as serving on a jury, voting, refusal to perform unlawful acts, reporting illegal activity, and so on. None of these has anything like the impact of antidiscrimination statutes on the workplace.
8. Regarding the first two, in most states, workers' compensation insurance rates are heavily regulated and insurance companies are compelled to fund otherwise uninsurable risks. Participation is mandatory in all states except three. More on workers' compensation insurance in chapter 9.
9. A concise summary of twentieth-century labor law can be found in Justice (1983, ch. 1).
10. For a good example of a modern liberal who understands some of the systemic problems with regulation, see Sunstein (1997).
11. U.S.C. § 1539(a)(2). See also Rohlf (1989, 82–86). The prohibition on "taking" members of endangered species has created the perverse incentive to "shoot, shovel, and shut up" when a landowner discovers endangered species on his property; Congress subsequently tried to address this problem through amendments to the ESA. More on this in chapter 10.
12. Classical liberal economists and politicians often argue against government regulations on the basis of cost-benefit analysis,

however. These arguments could be construed as convergence arguments from modern liberal premises, which in this case assume partial state ownership in the first instance. They can also be construed as straightforward utilitarian arguments, which are especially favored by economists with classical liberal sympathies. They believe that the total costs of these regulations are so far out of balance with the total benefits that modern liberals— indeed even socialists—ought to agree that they are a bad idea. The dialectical situation is further complicated by the fact that many modern liberals reject cost-benefit analysis on more philosophical grounds (e.g., incommensurability of values).

13. See Goodman and Musgrave (1992, ch. 11) and Jensen and Morrisey (1999). In 1968, there were five health care mandates. Now there are over a thousand. See also Epstein (2000, ch. 6) and Shriver and Arnett (1998).

14. For a comprehensive discussion of these two acts, see Hazen (1996, chs. 1, 2, and 9).

15. Other laws that have this as their main purpose include the Public Utility Holding Act of 1935, the Investment Company Act of 1940, the Investment Advisers Act of 1940, and the Securities Investor Protection Act of 1970. For a brief discussion of all of these acts, see Allen and Herring (2001, 20–22).

16. An exception to this general claim is rate regulation of workers' compensation insurance, which is justified by the various goals of this form of insurance. Thomason et al. (2001, 8–17) identify four such goals: adequacy of coverage, affordability, delivery system efficiency, and the promotion of workplace safety. As these authors point out, these goals are sometimes in conflict with one another.

17. For a discussion of the goals of insurance regulation generally, see Lereah (1985, 4–5, 43–53). See also Joskow (1973).

18. For analytical purposes, the term "price controls," as it is used here, does not include rate regulation of traditionally regulated industries such as public utilities and insurance. The latter was just discussed and the former were discussed at the beginning of chapter 2.

19. *Federal Trade Commission v. Standard Education Soc.,* 302 U.S. 112, 116 (1937).

20. In Arnold (2002, 22–26) I explain how the private sector could overcome the problem of correlated risks in catastrophe insurance. The proposal for banks outlined here parallels the suggestion made there.

21. In recent years the states have had the authority to permit price maintenance agreements, which they have exercised by passing so-called fair trade laws.

22. Epstein (1998, 92) discusses two alternative classical liberal policies: one is to prosecute price-fixing cases; the other is the common law approach, wherein collusive agreements are held to be legally unenforceable. See also Epstein (1995, 125).

23. For histories of occupational licensure, see Kleiner (2006, 19–26), Young (1987, 9–14), Rubin (1980), Hogan (1979), and Lieberman (1970).
24. Other arguments in favor of licensing are discussed in chapter 9. See below, pp. 323–24.
25. For a brief discussion of the literature on this point, see Young (1987, 49–52). See also Friedman (1962, ch. 9).
26. See Nozick (1974, ch.9). Indeed, it is possible to see exactly why Nozick's formulation is overstated. The community—or the state—has at most (partial) income rights in individuals; it lacks all the other incidents of ownership that slaveholders have.
27. On surrogacy arrangements, see Anderson (1993, 168–89) and the references cited therein.
28. See, for example, Richards (1982, 94–127). For organ sales, see Feinberg (1988, 171) and G. Dworkin (1994).
29. See, for example, Cohen (1998) on organ sales and McElroy (1994) on surrogacy arrangements.
30. See, for example, Sunstein (1997a; 1997b; 1996), Lessig (1995), Sher (1999), and Anderson (1993). This shift in modern liberal opinion seems to have occurred because of the gravitational influence of a body of communitarian thought that has emerged in the past two decades or so. Influential early communitarian works include Sandel (1982), Taylor (1979), and MacIntyre (1984). Although one gets the impression that communitarians generally have modern liberal, or at least left-wing, sympathies on policy issues, their writings are typically too vague or ambiguous about the traditional question of the proper role of the state in civil society to get a clear sense of where they stand on this. For an elaboration of this point, see Buchanan (1989). There is a vast literature on the meaning of liberal neutrality as a political value or ideal and how it might be justified. For an entrée into this literature, see Wall and Klosko (2003). This involves philosophical disputes that are not directly relevant for present purposes. The questions at issue here—whether it is appropriate for government to regulate lifestyle choices and why—arise at a lower level of abstraction than the philosophical debate about the meaning and warrant of liberal neutrality.
31. See Viscusi (2002, chs. 4, 5) and the studies cited therein. In addition, it is now abundantly clear that a considerable percentage of the proceeds of these settlements go for purposes unrelated to smoking. As Viscusi (2002, 56) notes, "reports in 2001 by the National Conference of State Legislatures and the General Accounting Office estimated that only 5 percent to 7 percent of the money was being targeted to tobacco programs, such as those for smoking prevention and cessation."
32. For modern liberal arguments in favor of extensive government regulation of tobacco use, see Goodin (1989). The observations in the text should not be taken to suggest that modern liberals favor prohibition of either drugs or tobacco. It seems that most liberal academics (whether classical or modern) believe that the drug

war has been lost and favor some form of legalization or decriminalization. For modern liberal arguments in support of this, see Reiman (1994) and Husak (2003). For classical liberal arguments, see Narveson (1994) and Shapiro (2003). A major exception is the classical liberal James Q. Wilson, who believes that most recreational drug use should continue to be illegal. See Wilson (1990). As a general proposition, it may be that modern liberals would oppose any bans on ostensibly private behaviors, even if they agree that it is appropriate for the state to discourage such behaviors, either through regulation or taxation.

33. The explanatory power of this model and its influence on the contemporary state is explored in detail in Nolan (1998).

34. See note 30 for references on liberal neutrality. For a critique of Sunstein's views on norm management, see Arnold (2000).

35. I adopt this term from my article "Postmodern Liberalism and the Expressive Function of Law" (2000). They are so-called because of the importance they attach to the expressive dimension of law and its role in constructing a social narrative. In this book, I treat postmodern liberalism as a subspecies of modern liberalism.

36. This is not the only ground on which modern liberals might oppose state paternalism. For other arguments against state paternalism that modern liberals have used, which include appeals to the value of autonomy, see, for example, Feinberg (1971, 115–16), G. Dworkin (1972, 82–84), and Daniels (1985, 157–58).

37. It is worth noting that some classical liberals favor drug legalization, or at least oppose drug prohibition laws, on the very same kind of grounds as those who favor continued criminalization. Specifically, they believe that drug prohibition laws are a major cause of crime associated with drugs. See, for example, Nadelmann (1987) and Friedman and Friedman (1984, 137–41).

38. See, for example, Will (1983) and Kirk (1954).

39. This question is addressed indirectly in Carey (1998), a collection of essays about the debate between libertarians and conservatives on the proper role of government.

40. Indeed, some public choice theorists seem to treat everything the government does, aside from providing public goods, as transferring resources between largely nonoverlapping groups. This allows them to represent most governmental activity, from taxation to regulation to overt transfer programs, as a vast game of musical chairs that politicians, bureaucrats, and interest groups play with citizens' income and wealth.

Chapter 4

1. For an overview of economists' contribution to the study of competition policy using game theory, see Phlips (1995).

2. See, for example, Viscusi, Vernon, and Harrington (2005, chs. 19–23).
3. Much of the remainder of *The Triumph of Conservatism* is dedicated to substantiating this picture in detail. For a monograph-length study that supports this hypothesis in the railroad industry, see Kolko (1965).
4. For a classical liberal statement of this position on antitrust, see Armentano (1990). On the public choice analysis of the relationship between interest groups and the state in general, see Buchanan, Tollison, and Tullock (1980); for its application to regulation, see Stigler (1971) and Peltzman (1976).
5. Important factors in producing this wave of deregulation were technological developments in telecommunications. Explaining deregulation, as well as regulation, is a challenging task for economists. For a summary and survey of comprehensive theories of the supply of and demand for regulation, see Viscusi, Vernon, and Harrington (2005, 375–396).
6. Recall from chapter 3 that regulation of insurance rates is generally about imposing floors, not ceilings, on prices as a way of restraining insurance companies from risking insolvency through imprudent portfolio management.
7. For a discussion of these issues from a classical liberal perspective, see Thierer and Crews (2003).
8. The relative rarity of natural monopolies has been remarked on by numerous economists over the decades. As noted in chapter 2, Yale Brozen (1980) has documented this in detail for the U.S. economy in the twentieth century.
9. Technological innovations in a variety of contexts have repeatedly undercut a wide range of market failure arguments for regulation, including those based on claims of monopoly. For illustrations, see the essays in Klein and Foldvary (2003).
10. This opposition has not been completely uniform, and some classical liberals have come to be favorably disposed to some aspects of antidiscrimination law when "discrimination" is construed narrowly. (More on this in chapter 8.) On the other hand, other classical liberals have opposed these laws. For example, Milton Friedman opposed the forerunners of antidiscrimination law in the early 1960s. See Friedman (1962, 111–15).
11. Mandatory workers' compensation laws and unemployment insurance could be conceived of as falling under this heading, but for reasons indicated in chapter 2, they are forms of social insurance and thus are categorized as transfer programs. The main regulatory issues in workers' compensation insurance concern rate regulation. On this, see Fishback and Kantor (2000) and Thomason, Schmidle, and Burton (2001).
12. These and other reasons to prefer the common law over statutory law in environmental matters are discussed in Schoenbrod (2000, 17–19) and Morriss (2000, 136–38, 142–45).

13. 42 U.S.C. § 9607(a); see also Dixon (2000, 1n2).
14. A number of writers have drawn a distinction between our preferences as consumers and our preferences as citizens. See Sagoff (1988, 27–29), Ackerman and Heinzerling (2002, 1573), and Anderson (1993, 209–10). This serves an environmentalist agenda to the extent that people's preferences as citizens endorse environmental values and are accorded a privileged status.
15. Feinberg's argument (1974, 56) for preserving endangered species appeals to the interests of future generations. For appeals to the independent value of biodiversity, see, for example, Rolston (1985).
16. In recent years, the main criminal element involved in legalized gambling has been the politicians who sponsor the enabling legislation and configure regulation of the gaming industry. Bribes, payoffs, and a variety of other scandals have accompanied the legalization of gambling in the various states with depressing regularity; scandals also plague state-run lotteries. Because of the enhanced power it confers on politicians to enrich themselves at the public's expense, even libertarians should probably have reservations about legalized gambling.

Chapter 5

1. There is a large literature on this topic. Rhodes (2000) contains a good bibliography of twentieth-century writings on coercion. The locus classicus of contemporary discussions is Robert Nozick's 1969 paper, "Coercion." I am indebted to Scott Anderson for guidance through this literature.
2. Different classical liberals have different conceptions of coercion. See, for example, Nozick (1969), Gorr (1988), Kelley (1998), and Lester (2000). Although the use or threat of violence is at or near the core of different classical liberal conceptions of coercion, there is disagreement about what else, if anything, is contained in the concept. For example, in "moralized" conceptions of coercion, such as Nozick's (1969), the violence or threat thereof must be wrongful for it to be genuinely coercive, which has the odd implication that legitimate state action is noncoercive. Nonmoralized conceptions, however, do not include this requirement (cf. Lester 2000, 72). However this dispute is ultimately resolved, there is widespread agreement among classical liberals that low wage offers and offers to work under undesirable health and safety conditions are not coercive.
3. Kelley (1998, 48–54) develops this line of argument without endorsing it. Zimmerman (1981) has an account of coercion that might have the implication that these workers are coerced, depending on the relevant empirical facts.
4. It is an interesting comment on their respective cultures that Americans run for public office whereas Britons stand for public office.

5. What about the state's unwillingness to enforce contracts between private parties that alienate fundamental personal and political rights? For example, one cannot sell oneself into slavery or sell one's right to vote. The state's treatment of these rights as inalienable could be construed as simply a limitation on the right to freedom of contract. The same is true of the state's unwillingness to enforce an unconscionable contract. (I owe these points to Samuel Freeman.) Undoubtedly, many classical liberals favor making such contracts unenforceable, though not all of them do. For example, some libertarians believe that all rights are alienable. This does not affect the claim in the text that classical liberals would resist construing legal rights in employment law as fundamental inalienable rights. All, or nearly all, classical liberals would oppose that.

6. Nozick (1974, 90–95). Govert den Hartogh (2002, 87–90) criticizes Nozick's rejection of the principle and argues in favor of it as a principle of nonvoluntary obligation that can, under certain circumstances, be enforced.

7. This is a common theme in the writings of Murray Rothbard. See, for example, Rothbard (1978). Indeed, it is implicit in the writings of other anarchists of the most diverse persuasions. As the historian James Joll ([1964] 1966, 30) has observed, "the fundamental idea that man is by nature good and that it is institutions that corrupt him remains the basis of all anarchist thought."

8. Goldman (1911, 56) defines anarchism as follows: "ANARCHISM:—The philosophy of a new social order based on liberty unrestricted by man-made law; the theory that all forms of government rest on violence, and are therefore wrong and harmful, as well as unnecessary."

9. Though typically public goods problems are framed in terms of financial costs, this observation about opportunity costs needs to be factored into the definition of a public goods problem in some way. Arguably the two types of costs are equivalent in some sense, but as the above example makes clear, both should be mentioned in the definition. The most obvious way to do so is to make the second condition a conjunction, so that it now reads, "(2) each individual in that population believes that the benefits of having the good outweigh the opportunity cost and her share of the financial cost of the good."

10. Intentional objects are the contents of preferences, beliefs, and other mental states. The existence of something as an intentional object, or as a component of an intentional object, does not imply its existence in reality. If Ernest is hunting unicorns, that does not imply that unicorns exist. This feature of intentional objects makes it possible to talk freely about societies, communities, and so on, while sidestepping the question of whether or not they are real.

11. Though not mentioned by name, it is clear to anyone familiar with Rothbard's work that he is the individualist-anarchist whom

Nozick has in mind as the foil in part I of *Anarchy, State, and Utopia*. There are rumors that Nozick had long phone conversations with Rothbard when composing this part of the book, but those rumors cannot be confirmed.

12. I defend this requirement in more detail in chapter 11 in the section titled "Public Justification."

Chapter 6

1. See Lewis (1999, 14). It is easier to monitor the number of units shipped than the number of units on which an operating system has been installed.

2. A variation on this proposal can be found in Krauss (1996, 474–82). Krauss's alternative will be discussed in chapter 9.

3. Why not simply privatize the FDA? One obvious reason is that the FDA has a good reputation for certifying drug safety and efficacy, which privatization might compromise, if it were sold to, for example, the Pharmaceutical Research and Manufacturers of America (PhRMA).

4. Information about the workings of the CPSC in what follows comes from Viscusi (1984).

5. One reason to make such large assumptions is that in the event that they are false, a modern liberal defender of this regulatory agency could argue that what is needed to make them true is a larger budget and expanded powers for the agency. Of course, at some point the costs outweigh the benefits, and a public goods problem no longer exists, but locating that point for the largely hypothetical preferences of the vast majority of the population appears to be an insoluble problem. In the face of such a problem, it is best to proceed in the manner of economists who must deal with an intractable problem, namely, assume that it has been solved.

6. The belief (is it a mere assumption?) that private standard setting is too lax because the standard setting agencies are captives of the industries for which they set standards is, as Cheit (1990, 5–14) shows, inaccurate and greatly oversimplified. There are some systematic differences between government standards and private standards, and the two types interact in subtle and complex ways. See Cheit (1990, ch. 1).

7. See below, chapter 9, pp. 316–18.

8. This possibility is just that, a possibility, and as suggested in the text, it depends not merely on the incidence of medical malpractice in the free market alternative but on how much undisciplined medical malpractice goes on under the current regulatory regime. Physicians are notoriously protective of their own, and discipline by state professional boards is widely regarded as lax. This laxity

might be in part explained by the fact that because they act as representatives of the state, they have a monopoly on certification—a monopoly they would not enjoy under a free market alternative. But that is just speculation.

9. To be accredited by regional accrediting associations, however, private school teachers must meet some objective qualifications (e.g., a bachelor's degree with a subject area major), but they do not require an education degree and state certification. See, for example, page 3 of the "Nonpublic School Standards for Accreditation 2004," of the Southern Association of Colleges and Schools, available at http://www.sacscasi.org/region/standards/nonpublic2004.pdf (accessed June 14, 2005). Perhaps most importantly, these accrediting agencies cannot force compliance; they can only deny accreditation.

10. This claim has to be qualified because of the implications of accreditation for colleges and universities. If colleges and universities hired many faculty members without terminal degrees, for example, they would probably lose accreditation from the independent accrediting agencies, which means they would also be denied access to federally guaranteed student loans, a serious kink in the air hose to their diving bell.

11. Information in this paragraph is presented in summary form in Rohlf (1989, 13–17).

12. Coursey (2001, 201–2) discusses problems with all these measures. For example, public expenditure levels partially reflect manipulation by special interest groups, bundling with other issues, and so forth. Contingent valuation surveys do not require that people actually put up their own money; they are just asked how much they would be willing to pay. Moreover, these surveys have proved very sensitive to how the questions are framed, so sensitive that the amount that people are willing to pay for species preservation are orders of magnitude apart, depending on how the question is framed. Still, the evidence generated by these surveys has some value, as Coursey's discussion demonstrates.

13. Both statutes require a permit for any change in the use of the land or for any development to go forward, a permit which may, in the end, be denied. Details of the permitting process and the substantial regulatory burdens thereby imposed are given in chapter 10. See below, chapter 10, pp. 332–33 and 341–43.

14. "Might be defensible" is the proper term, since some classical liberals believe that the values that the ESA and CWA intend to realize can be produced by the private sector via a tying arrangement. See, for example, Simmons (1999a) and Brown and Layton (2001).

15. One complication in the case of the Kesterson NWR is that the selenium pollution arrived via a drainage system built and operated by the U.S. Bureau of Reclamation, a government agency! Without that system, the farmers' pesticides would never have

reached Kesterton (Simmons 1999b, 518). There is a question, not easily resolved, about who is ultimately responsible for the pollution in this case—the farmers, the government, or some combination of the two.

16. Http://thomas.loc.gov/cgi-bin/query/z?c103:H.R.1388.IH (accessed May 13, 2008).

17. There is evidence that enormous resources, including land, would be required for the goals of the ESA to be truly realized. See Noss (1992; 1994). There is also evidence that, at the level of individual taxpayers, the public is simply not willing to pay the costs this would entail. See below, chapter 10, pp. 345–46.

18. There are also negative effects on employed workers, such as reduced benefits and more difficult working conditions; these are discussed in detail the next chapter. See below, chapter 7, pp. 203–4.

19. Other reforms classical liberals might favor are discussed in chapter 9. See below, ch. 9, pp. 282–84.

20. This is only one argument, and probably not the most important argument, in favor of the various antidiscrimination laws. Arguments from considerations of justice are probably more important and come more readily to mind. These will be discussed in chapter 8, pp. 228–29.

21. This and other problems with the ADA are discussed in Hudgins (1995). More on this topic in chapter 8.

Chapter 7

1. There are of course exceptions. For example, James P. Sterba (1998, 41–76) has argued that libertarians should support part of the modern liberal transfer agenda, namely, welfare for the poor.

2. If Mill is counted as a modern liberal, then there is at least one counterexample to this general proposition, but arguably Mill cannot be accurately characterized as either type of liberal. A good illustration of the general proposition about the lack of comprehensive principles concerning the proper role of government in modern liberal thought can be found in the writings of the legal theorist Cass Sunstein. Sunstein favors a wide range of government interventions and is clearly a modern liberal as characterized here, but it is very difficult to discern any general principle about the proper role of government to which Sunstein subscribes.

3. For example, in an important ruling on affirmative action, *Grutter v. Bollinger et al.,* 539 U.S. 306 (2003), Justice O'Connor said, "the Court expects that 25 years from now, the use of racial preferences will no longer be necessary to further the interest approved today."

4. In what follows, there are a few exceptions to the dialectical structure outlined above. Specifically, there are three cases in which there really are no good classical liberal conversion counterarguments,

or at least none that this author can think of. Arguments from first principles are available, however, for those who wish to maintain their ideological purity. For the rest, conversion on that point should seem reasonable, at least until some classical liberal formulates a persuasive conversion counterargument.

5. Practical objections include problems with assigning a dollar value to goods not typically traded on any market, such as benefits to the environment. Standard philosophical criticisms of cost-benefit analysis are that it ignores distributional issues and that it considers our valuations only as consumers and not as citizens. The former point is made by Buchanan (1985, 9–10), the latter by Sagoff (1988; 1995) and Ackerman and Heinzerling (2002).

6. Information on the lawnmower standard, including the estimate of Prunella and Zamula, comes from Viscusi (1984, 94–96).

7. Sometimes, economists with libertarian sympathies make arguments against government intervention based on such assumptions. Doctrinaire members of the so-called "Austrian School" seem to argue in this way on a priori grounds. See, for example, von Mises (1966) and Rothbard (1977).

8. O'Hara (1916, iii–iv), as quoted in Nordlund (1997, 15).

9. Wagner (1989, 113–14). Wessels (1981, 4–16) has a good discussion of these stratagems. For a dissenting view on the effect of increases in the minimum wage on the employment rate, see Card and Kreuger (1994; 1995). For important methodological and substantive criticisms of Card and Kreuger, see Hammermesh (1995) and Neumark and Wascher (1995).

10. Institute for Women's Policy Research, Fact Sheet #C350, February 2008, http://www.iwpr.org/pdf/C350.pdf (accessed May 14, 2008).

11. "Equal Pay Act Charges," http://www.eeoc.gov/stats/epa.html, and http://www.eeoc.gov/stats/epa-a.html (accessed May 14, 2008). These Web pages note that the figures include concurrent charges with title VII, ADEA, and ADA filings, so there is no way to know how many of the EPA charges are stand-alone.

12. "All Statutes," http://www.eeoc.gov/stats/all.html, and http://www. eeoc.gov/stats/epa-a.html (accessed May 14, 2008).

13. A concise, if somewhat dated, presentation of these factors can be found in Paul (1988, 46–51).

14. See, for example, *Thompson v. Sawyer*, 678 F.2d 257, 271–72 (D.C. Cir. 1982); *Shultz v. Wheaton Glass Co.*, 421 F.2d 259, 265 (3d Cir.), *cert. denied*, 398 U.S. 905 (1970). See also 29 *C.F.R.* § 800.120 (1983): "There is evidence that Congress intended that jobs of the same or closely related character should be compared in applying the equal pay for equal work standard."

15. Freed and Polsby (1985, 135). They reference the following case law in support of that contention: *Lemons v. City and County of Denver*, 620 F. 2d 228, 229 (10th Cir.), *cert. denied*, 449 U.S. 888 (1980); *Brennan v. City Stores, Inc.*, 479 F. 2d. 235, 238 (5th Cir. 1973); *Francoeur v. Corroon & Black Co.*, 552 F. Supp. 403, 406–7 (S.D.N.Y. 1982).

16. For a collection of essays on philosophical problems concerning the (in)commensurability of values, see Chang (1997).

17. There is a separate affirmative obligation (§ 158(d)) for employers to bargain in good faith. This imposes additional burdens on employers; what follows in the text does not apply to this obligation, which would be rejected by classical liberals, in part owing to the difficulty of defining "bargaining in good faith."

18. See especially the discussion of yellow dog contracts in Epstein (1983, 1370–71), and the discussion of unfair labor practices in section 4 of that essay on pages 1386–1403.

19. However, workers employed in the railway and airline industries and various federal enclaves are not protected by right-to-work laws even if they live and work in right-to-work states. National Right to Work Legal Foundation, Inc., http://www.nrtw.org/rtws.htm (accessed May 15, 2008).

Chapter 8

1. Although section 2000e begins with definitions of fourteen different terms, neither "race" nor "color" is defined. Given the experience of South Africa and Nazi Germany grappling with this question, that omission was probably wise. In its Compliance Manual on race and color discrimination, the EEOC does make some effort to distinguish race and color. It says, "the courts and the Commission read 'color' to have its commonly understood meaning—pigmentation, complexion, or skin shade or tone. Thus, color discrimination occurs when a person is discriminated against based on the lightness, darkness, or other color characteristic of the person. Even though race and color clearly overlap, they are not synonymous. Thus, color discrimination can occur between persons of different races or ethnicities, or between persons of the same race or ethnicity." (Notes referring to case law have been omitted.) *EEOC Compliance Manual,* sec. 15: Race and Color Discrimination, http://www.eeoc.gov/policy/docs/race-color.html#III (accessed May 15, 2008).

2. The law does allow a narrow class of exceptions, the so-called "bona fide occupational qualification." Arthur Gutman describes it this way: "However, there are conditions under which facial discrimination is legal, and the defense for legal facial discrimination is termed bona fide occupational qualification (BFOQ). It is a statutory defense in Title VII that has been used primarily for facial exclusion based on sex. It may also apply to religion and national origin, but never to race or color. It is also a statutory defense in the Age Discrimination in Employment Act (ADEA). To succeed in the BFOQ defense, the respondent must prove it is reasonably necessary to exclude all or most members of a given

class…The key point for present purposes is that BFOQ implies a threat to business survival" (Gutman 2005, 26).

3. See Epstein (1992, ch. 11), Gutman (2005), and Malos (2005).
4. *Uniform Guidelines on Employee Selection Procedures* (1978) 29 *C.F.R.* Section 1607.4D (1989).
5. Another aspect of modern affirmative action in employment concerns firms that do business with the federal government and have more than fifty employees or government contracts worth more than $50,000. These firms are required to submit elaborate affirmative action plans, complete with minority hiring goals and timetables within which those goals are to be achieved. This is required by Executive Order 11246, signed into law by Lyndon Johnson in 1965. See 30 *Federal Register* 12319. See also note 9 below.
6. This idea is developed in Rachels (1979).
7. The three summary points listed below are adapted from Perritt (1992, 91–92).
8. Some critics of *Ward's Cove* claimed that this weaker requirement would permit employers to discriminate because of customer preference or employee morale. These concerns are specious, however, since a person denied a job or promotion or fired for this reason could sue under the disparate treatment construal of discrimination.
9. Classical liberals need not object on behalf of government contractors to the requirement of "hiring by the numbers." This is simply one of the requirements for bidding on government contracts. If a firm has a moral problem with that, it can simply refuse to bid on these contracts. As I have argued elsewhere (1998, 154–55), however, classical liberals can object to this policy on behalf of the nation's taxpayers, even if they cannot do so on behalf of the affected contractors.
10. Part of the reason for this is that validating employment tests and other hiring criteria is often difficult and expensive, even if they make intuitively good business sense. See the above example about basic literacy and numeracy requirements for employees in fast food establishments. For more general discussions of the problems involved in validating tests and criteria, see the references cited in note 3.
11. This general evolutionary hypothesis was first applied in economics by Armen Alchian (1950). Along with Ronald Coase's "The Nature of the Firm" (1937), it has spawned an enormous literature on the economics of contracts and organizations. A seminal work in that literature is Oliver Williamson's *The Economic Institutions of Capitalism* (1985). For more on the transactions cost efficiencies of capitalist organizations in the context of the employment relation, see Arnold (1994, chs. 4, 5). See especially the last section of chapter 5, "The Employment Relation in a Free Enterprise System."

12. A much more elaborate libertarian argument for abolishing title VII than what follows, which is based on the law and economics approach pioneered by the Chicago School, can be found in Epstein (1992, 159–266).

13. The main racial group to which this applies is African Americans. The problems about to be described seem to be less prominent in the case of other protected minorities and women. Perhaps this is because, in the light of the prominent historical injustices suffered by African Americans, both members of that minority group and the judicial system are more likely to ascribe racial animus and/or stereotyping to an employer than a parallel animus or stereotyping in cases involving members of other protected groups.

14. The extent to which contemporary management genuinely believes in the value of diversity is unclear. As diversity consultant David Jamieson said, "CEOs have learned to speak PC [political correctness] so well we can't tell if they are genuinely interested in diversity or not." Quoted in Lynch (1997, 19). One is reminded of Mill's observations about belief in the teachings of Christ among the Victorians: "They are not insincere when they say that they believe these things. They do believe them, as people believe what they have always heard lauded and never discussed.... The doctrines in their integrity are serviceable to pelt adversaries with; and it is understood that they are to be put forward (when possible) as the reasons for whatever people do that they think laudable.... The doctrines have no hold on ordinary believers—are not a power in their minds. They have an habitual respect for the sound of them, but no feeling which spreads from the words to the things signified, and forces the mind to take them in, and make them conform to the formula. Whenever conduct is concerned, they look round for Mr. A and B to direct them how far to go in obeying Christ" (Mill [1859] 1978, 40). In the present case, of course, Mr. A and Ms. B are the firm's legal counsel.

15. Zink and Gutman (2005, 105). Percentages add up to more than 100 percent because some cases involve charges of discrimination on multiple grounds.

16. There was some suggestion of quid pro quo harassment as well. "The appellant in this case asserts some claims encompassed by the *Barnes* decision, arguing that her rejection of unsolicited and offensive sexual advances from several supervisors in her agency caused those supervisors unjustifiably to delay and block promotions to which she was entitled" *Bundy v. Jackson,* 641 F.2d 934 (D.C. Cir. 1981).

17. *Faragher v. City of Boca Raton,* 524 U.S. 755, 806–809 (1998); *Burlington Industries v. Ellerth* 524 U.S. 742, 760–63 (1998).

18. See, for example, Mezey (2003, ch. 5).

19. Though in *Oncale v. Sundowner Offshore Services,* 523 U.S. 75 (1998), the Court also held that hostile environment sexual harassment could occur between persons of the same sex. In this

case, it was a group of men sexually harassing another man. The reader does not want to know the details.

20. On the other hand, many libertarians favor legalizing prostitution.

21. Volokh (1997) contains dozens of jaw-dropping instances of political correctness run amok; he argues that this sort of thing is inevitable, given the problems with the Court's standard alluded to above.

22. This is a common theme in the case law discussions found in Gregory (2001) and elsewhere in this literature.

23. See Department of Labor (1965). This finding was incorporated into the act at 29 U.S.C. § 621(a).

24. These four facts are central to the problems of relational contracts and are systematically discussed in Williamson (1985). See also Arnold (1994, 111–21).

25. Higher education seems to have had more than its share of this problem. Professors who were hired in the 1960s were supposed to retire in the 1990s, thereby opening up more slots for younger faculty. When mandatory retirement was eliminated, many of these faculty members stayed on the job but did more and more of their work "at home."

26. EEOC (2004) § 1630.2-i. There is some dispute about including "working" as a major life activity, or at least some controversy about how broadly "working" is to be understood. As the courts have interpreted it, having an impairment that prevents a person from doing one specific job or a narrow range of jobs does not make one disabled. This interpretation has broad ramifications, which are discussed shortly.

27. Opponents of the ADA take grim satisfaction in gawking at the moral train wrecks produced when government enforcement engines plow into small businesses. See, for example, Olson (1997).

28. Jolls (2000, 277–79) also discusses this possibility.

29. A further reason why disparate impact lawsuits are less likely to be filed is discussed below.

30. Indeterminate terms, or terms that have been legally contested, in title I include: "disability," "major life activity," "substantially limiting," "qualified," "essential functions," "direct threat," "reasonable accommodation," and "undue hardship." Like a brilliant array of colors, these terms appear on the palette of plaintiffs' attorneys when they paint their portraits of Grave Injustice at trial.

31. The statistics that follow come from Zink and Gutman (2005, 112–14). In fairness, it should be noted that title VII charges have a similarly low rate of favorable outcomes for complainants.

32. Http://www.eeoc.gov/stats/ada-resolutions.html.

33. The case for this claim is made in detail in chapter 4 of Colker (2005) titled "The Face of Judicial Backlash."

34. This assumes that people are in no way responsible for their disabilities, which of course is false across an unknown range of cases. Putting that problem to one side, the idea that people should

not be held responsible for their unchosen circumstances and the inequalities thereby produced is known as "Luck Egalitarianism." In two important articles, Ronald Dworkin (1981a; 1981b) offered the first systematic defense of Luck Egalitarianism, which has since become a topic of much discussion in contemporary political philosophy. Not all modern liberals are Luck Egalitarians, however.

Chapter 9

1. Http://www.aflcio.org/issues/safety/memorial/upload/_26.pdf (accessed May 18, 2008).
2. Http://www.osha.gov/as/opa/oshafacts.html (accessed May 18, 2008).
3. Ibid.
4. See Subcommittee on Labor (1971), which reprints the House and Senate committee reports (141–181, 831–876). See also "Statement of the Managers on the Part of the House," and the parts of the floor debates reprinted in Bureau of National Affairs (1971, 125–139, 297–313).
5. Viscusi (1983, 30, 31). How can this be squared with the finding of the Senate that the number of disabling injuries per million man hours worked had increased by 20 percent between 1958 and 1970? The answer is that Viscusi examined a number of different measures of risks, including death rates and workdays lost. See Viscusi (1983, 30, 31). See also Nichols and Zeckhauser (1977, 40). Later in this section, I shall discuss more recent evidence that is favorable to OSHA.
6. The alternative to mandating abatement would be to impose a tax for violations; this is the economists' preferred solution but of course is politically impossible. See Mendeloff (1979, 24–31).
7. "OSHA Covers At-Home Workers," *Washington Post*, January 4, 2000.
8. Figures in the remainder of this paragraph come from Viscusi, Vernon, and Harrington (2005, 848–851).
9. The literature on how people actually reason under conditions of risk and uncertainty is voluminous; Kahneman and Tversky (1979) and Kahneman, Slovic, and Tversky (1982) are two of the most widely cited works in this literature. The seminal study of people's perceptions of risks of fatalities is Lichtenstein et al. (1978).
10. Detailed information in the remainder of this paragraph comes from Thomason, Schmidle, and Burton (2001, 44–46, 258–260). Note that the general problem about to be described would characterize the classical liberal alternative to occupational licensure defended in chapter 6 (pp. 172–76).
11. "TXANS and Responsible Nonsubscription," http://txans.org/history.htm (accessed May 18, 2008).

12. Personal communication from Steve Bent, Executive Director, TXANS.

13. Viscusi, Vernon, and Harrington (2005, 858–861) summarize about a dozen studies bearing on this question.

14. This is the obverse of the familiar "crowding out" problem that occurs whenever the government takes over what had been the responsibility of the private sector. Organized responses to social problems in the private sector tend to wither when government assumes responsibility for those problems. This means that it is difficult to predict what would happen if government were to disband OSHA and withdraw from problems of health and safety in the workplace.

15. These problems are described in graphic detail in Hilts (2003, 11–55).

16. A concise history of the act and the amendments can be found in Temin (1980, 38–57). Temin explains how the FDA tied that obscure paragraph about labeling to a chair and tortured it to get it to say that some drugs could not be legally sold without a prescription. The development of the regulatory distinction between prescription and over-the-counter drugs is discussed in detail in chapter 12. See below, pp. 408–13.

17. This is a theme, perhaps the major theme, of Philip J. Hilt's (2003) history of drug regulation and the FDA.

18. Not all of them do. In a very interesting study, Ronald Hamowy (2007, 103–138) argues in detail that critics of the food and drug industries at the time vastly overstated the threats and dangers to the public from adulterated foods and patent medicines. Harvey Washington Wiley, an early crusader for food and drug laws, comes in for particularly heavy criticism in Hamowy's account of the era.

19. For a history of the early U.S. patent medicine market, see Young (1961).

20. Http://www.fda.gov/cder/reports/reviewtimes/default.htm#Approval%20Time (accessed May 19, 2008).

21. Http://www.fdareview.org/approval_process.shtml (accessed May 19, 2008).

22. Http://csdd.tufts.edu/NewsEvents/RecentNews.asp?newsid=4 (accessed May 19, 2008).

23. In the early days after the 1962 amendments, NDAs were rejected without explanation. Now the FDA is willing to work more closely with the drug companies to get their applications into proper shape.

24. Of course, physicians could have prescribed propralonol off-label to prevent second heart attacks, but in this first decade after the 1962 amendments, physicians were reluctant to prescribe off-label. So, it is unclear how many of these additional deaths can be laid at the doorstep of the FDA.

25. See http://www.fda.gov/cdrh/devadvice/pma/ (accessed May 19, 2008).

26. "F.D.A. Seeks More Testing of a Device to Detect Breast Cancer," *New York Times*, September 4, 1994.
27. Quoted in Kerry Howley, "Dying for Life-Saving Drugs," *Reason*, August/September 2007, 30.
28. Ibid.
29. See Tabarrok (2000, 26) for estimates of the frequency of off-label prescribing.
30. See *Washington Legal Foundation v. Friedman*, 13 F. Supp. 2d 51 (D.D.C. 1998) and *Washington Legal Foundation v. Henney*, 202 F.3d 331 (D.C. Cir. 2000).
31. Alexander Schmidt, "The FDA Today: Critics, Congress, and Consumerism," speech delivered on October 29, 1974, before the National Press Club, Washington, D.C. Quoted in Grabowski (1976, 76).
32. For a detailed look at how the industry influences (and fails to influence) the FDA, see Hawthorne (2005, 143–166). As Hawthorne's discussion makes clear, the common assumption that drug manufacturers can apply great pressure to regulators to get them to approve a drug that does not merit approval is a myth.
33. This is a common element in the proposals of Krauss (1996) and Klein and Tabarrok (2004). For the latter, see their Web site: http://fdareview.org/. A less radical proposal that has classical liberal features is that of Miller (2000). Considerations of space prevent a full discussion of all these proposals.
34. Klein and Tabarrok (2004, 60). This article describes other ways doctors get information about the efficacy of off-label uses of prescription drugs.
35. Klein and Tabarrok (2003) used a sequential online survey to conduct structured interviews with approximately 500 physicians about off-label prescribing. Nearly all favored permitting it. However, a majority favored FDA efficacy requirements for first use, though a significant minority did not. Klein and Taborrak discuss the objections that some in the majority raised to dropping the efficacy requirement for first use. Readers who are skeptical of dropping the efficacy requirement should consult this article.
36. Criminogenic drugs are those that increase the likelihood that a person will commit a violent crime. Anabolic steroids, some amphetamines, and crack cocaine are arguably criminogenic. Teratogenic drugs, such as thalidomide, are those that increase the likelihood of birth defects. See Polsby (1998, 209–18).
37. See http://www.cpsc.gov/businfo/reg1.html for a list of standards and http://www.cpsc.gov/cpscpub/prerel/prerel.html for a list of recalled products (accessed May 19, 2008). Many of the standards they have promulgated are relevant to the other laws the CPSC is charged with implementing.
38. A fuller discussion of these findings and their relevance to consumer behavior regarding product safety can be found in Asch (1988, 70–82).

39. A seminal work in this literature is a collection of essays edited by Kahneman, Slovic, and Tversky (1982). See also Gilovich, Griffin, and Kahneman (2002).
40. Personal communication (May 22, 2008) from Alan Hoskin, Manager of the Statistics Department, National Safety Council.
41. The lulling effect for automobile safety has been demonstrated by Peltzman (1975) and for job safety by Viscusi (1979).
42. This is the so-called Hand Formula, named for Judge Learned Hand. The Hand Formula states that a defendant is negligent when his burden (B) of taking loss avoidance is less than the probability of a harm (p) times the degree of loss (L).
43. These propositions, especially (1) and (3) may not be true or they may be true of only a restricted range of cases. The claim advanced here is only that these propositions are, in effect, pre-suppositions of a regime of strict products liability.
44. The problem of "regulatory unreasonableness" as it might be called, is discussed in detail in a very interesting study of the phenomenon by Bardach and Kagan (1982).
45. This list was compiled from Starr (1982, 103), Rottenberg (1980, 2), Gellhorn (1976, 6), and Young (1987, 4).
46. See, for example, Starr (1982, 230), Friedman (1962, 137–160), Young (1987, 49–52), Svorny (1992; 2004). Indeed, Svorny (2004) consists of a compendium of economists' pronouncements on this theme. See also Rottenberg (1980, 7–9).
47. See Leland (1979; 1980). The gist of the argument is stated infor-mally at Leland (1980, 267).
48. Http://www.beautyschoolsdirectory.com/faq/howpay.php (accessed May 19, 2008).
49. Information on these cases can be found on the Institute for Justice's Web site: http://www.ij.org/economic_liberty/index.html (accessed May 19, 2008).

Chapter 10

1. For a listing of these amendments, see http://www.fws.gov/laws/lawsdigest/ESACT.HTML.
2. Prior to the 1978 amendments, the FWS had been informally des-ignating critical habitat, though it was mostly a matter of drawing lines on maps and informally advising government agencies and landowners what they could and could not do. Personal commu-nication from FWS biologist, John Fay, July 11, 2008.
3. How one weighs the "economic and social benefits" against the "biological consequences" of the project is pretty mysterious. Interestingly, the "God Committee" voted against completing the dam, but it did so on the mundane grounds that proponents failed to show that the economic benefits of the dam outweighed its

costs. The dam was built anyway after Tennessee senator Howard Baker attached an amendment to a public works bill requiring its completion (Paul 1987, 30).

4. The summary of changes that follows in this and subsequent paragraphs is drawn from Burgess (2001, 13–19).

5. *Palila v. Hawaii Department of Land & Natural Resources,* 471 F.Supp. 985 (D.Haw.1979); *Palila v. Hawaii Department of Land & Natural Resources,* 639 F. 2d 495 (9th Cir. 1981); *Palila v. Hawaii Department of Land & Natural Resources,* 649 F. Supp. 1070 (D.Haw.1986) *Palila v. Hawaii Department of Land & Natural Resources,* 852 F.2d 1106 (9th Cir. 1988).

6. Information on the NCCP can be found in Mann and Plummer (1995a). See also Burgess (2001, 123–25).

7. See Jonathan Adler, "Money or Nothing: the Adverse Environmental Consequences of Uncompensated Land Use Controls," *Boston College Law Review* 49(2) (March 2008), 321–22 for a discussion of at least six other cases in which perverse incentives led landowners to destroy habitat that might attract members of endangered species.

8. Dean Lueck and Jeffrey A. Michael, "Preemptive Habitat Destruction Under the Endangered Species Act," *Journal of Law and Economics* 46(1) (April 2003), 27–60. Lueck and Michael estimate (ibid., 33n27) the cost of maintaining habitat for one colony of RCWs to be a minimum of $200,000 in foregone timber harvests.

9. Amara Brook, Michaela Zint, and Raymond De Young, "Landowners' Responses to an Endangered Species Act Listing and Implications for Encouraging Conservation," *Conservation Biology* 17(6) (December 2003), 1638–49.

10. These and other studies of habitat destruction are discussed in Adler, "Money or Nothing: the Adverse Environmental Consequences of Uncompensated Land Use Controls," 326–30.

11. A copy of the proposed bill can be found at http://www.govtrack. us/congress/bill.xpd?bill=h110–1422 (accessed May 19, 2008).

12. There were persistent rumors at the time that the main agitators on behalf of the spotted owl in the Pacific Northwest were marijuana farmers, who were concerned that opening the old growth forests for lumbering would expose their crops to the authorities. This illustrates a pervasive problem with land use regulation, namely, its susceptibility to being hijacked to serve other interests and other agendas.

13. For a detailed explanation of the steps involved in the permitting process, see Parenteau (1991, 332–39).

14. William Lewis (2001, 11) claims that the Tulloch Rule was aimed at excavations intended to drain wetlands and at not dredging operations *per se.* According to Lewis, the intent of the Tulloch Rule was to prevent any alteration of any wetland. This was part of a "No Net Loss" policy regarding wetlands that has been official government policy in successive administrations. As Lewis himself notes, "even activities on a small scale must meet the

test... of avoiding degradation of wetland function" (Lewis 2001, 11n7).

15. In response, the Corps has revised its regulations to conform to this ruling while maintaining most of its regulatory authority over dredging. See 33 *C.F.R.* § 323 (1993); 40 *C.F.R.* § 232 (1999).

16. The discussion that follows is based on Lewis (2001, 42–64).

Chapter 11

1. Others who are left of center (communitarians, civic republicans, some feminists) would deny that they are liberals because of their philosophical disagreements with liberalism. See, for example, Sandel (1982), Pettit (1997), and the writings of many of the feminists cited in Haslanger and Tuana (2006). However, according to the broad and very weak characterization of liberalism presented in chapter 1—where liberalism involves a commitment to equal liberty, democratic governance, and the more or less free market— most of these writers would count as modern liberals, despite their philosophical disagreements with those who proudly wear the liberal label. Whatever those disagreements, they nevertheless remain committed to equal liberty and democratic governance. What about the market? As is the case with modern liberals, they are reluctantly committed to it and have about the same misgivings about it as their more orthodox modern liberal counterparts.

2. As an illustration, consider the legislative response to the *Kelo* decision, in which the Court permitted private property to be condemned by local governments and sold to private developers (*Kelo et al. v. City of New London et al.,* 545 U.S. 469 (2005). In response to this decision, which was excoriated across the political spectrum, legislative prohibitions on takings for economic development were enacted in a number of state legislatures. The National Conference of State Legislatures tracks this legislation. See http://www.ncsl.org/programs/natres/EMINDOMAIN. htm (accessed May 20, 2008).

3. See Dworkin (1977) for the application of this principle in his argument supporting the special admissions program at University of California at Davis (the *Bakke* case).

4. Not everyone is a liberal, however. There are always a few anarchists around, and increasingly in Western societies, there are Islamist theocrats who reject core liberal ideas and values. For both groups, conversion arguments are at least possible, though talk of conversion to Islamist theocrats is not likely to be well received. There may well be nothing to discuss with either group, which means that the only questions that remain are moral and practical questions about how they ought to be treated—as long as liberals remain in a position to impose their views and values.

5. Those dispositions might be deeply buried and require a great deal of prompting to be manifested. Public ignorance about the basic principles of liberal, capitalist democracies is widespread and has been widely remarked on. However deep and pervasive that ignorance is, there are obviously some political changes that would be widely regarded by a large segment of the electorate as morally and politically illegitimate—even if they did not feel particularly strongly about it.

6. For a brief introduction to the issues surrounding public justification in this sense, see Fred D'Agostino, "Public Justification," in *The Stanford Encyclopedia of Philosophy* (Summer 2003 Edition), ed. Edward N. Zalta, http://plato.stanford.edu/archives/sum2003/entries/justification-public/ (accessed May 20, 2008).

7. James Fishkin (1991), and Ackerman and Fishkin (2004), have made various proposals over the years to get greater public involvement in public policy deliberations. Though I am skeptical of the feasibility of these proposals, as well as of their ultimate value in producing good policy, the conception of public justification defended here might be altered to accommodate greater participation by average citizens.

8. In some cases, the classical liberal alternative involves repealing a law (e.g., title VII of the 1964 Civil Rights Act), but there is always more to it than that. Informed speculation about how a private ordering would handle whatever social problem the regulatory regime was originally designed to handle is required. Modern liberals would have the burden of showing that there is reason to believe that this disfavored alternative would be worse, in some all-things-considered sense. Of course, classical liberals have a corresponding burden. The burden of proof is the epistemological version of original sin in the sense that everyone has it.

9. For a useful collection of essays on liberal neutrality and perfectionism, see Wall and Klosko (2003).

10. Cato Institute, *Cato Handbook on Policy,* 6th ed., 2005, 334. The online version can be found at http://www.cato.org/pubs/handbook/hb109/ (accessed May 20, 2008).

11. Http://www.fec.gov/pages/brochures/checkoff.shtml (accessed May 20, 2008).

12. See, for example, "Campaign Finance Measure Approved: House Bill Would Cap '527' Donations, Used Largely by Democrats," *Washington Post,* August 2, 2006.

13. In *Unfree Speech,* Bradley Smith (2001, 88–105) discusses other practical problems with government financing of political campaigns.

14. In 1978, 28.6 percent of taxpayers contributed but by 2005, only 9.12 percent of filers chose to contribute. The decline has been fairly steady over the time period in question. These figures come from the Federal Election Commission. See http://www.fec.gov/press/bkgnd/Fund_Status_05_07a.pdf (accessed May 20, 2008).

15. See the passage quoting Madison and Jefferson in Black's opinion in *Machinists v. Street* quoted on page 218 of chapter 7.

16. However, it was recently revealed that some Indian tribes that owned lucrative casinos funded a political campaign to prevent legalized gambling operated by other Indian tribes. Ironically, this campaign was headed up by former Christian Coalition chairman Ralph Reed, who brought out his fundamentalist Christian troops to oppose the new casinos. See "Tribe Sues Abramoff, Reed Over Casino Closure," *Washington Post,* Wednesday, July 16, 2006.

17. It might be objected that the term "victim" is morally loaded in a way that biases the discussion. However, the term does not always have a moral connotation, as for example, when we speak of victims of natural disasters. Although it admittedly has some misleading connotations, there seems to be no widely used alternative; let us stipulate, then, that "victims," as the term is used in this context, are simply people whose interests are on balance negatively affected by a government action or policy.

18. For example, there is disagreement over whether Rawls's two principles of justice, as originally formulated, imply that the economic system of advanced industrial democracies should be free market capitalism or some form of socialism. For an argument in favor of the former, see Shapiro (1995). For arguments in favor of the latter, see Clark and Gintis (1978); Doppelt (1981); Di Quattro (1983); Schweickart (1978).

19. A further exception: members of some subset of the taxpayers are (intended or unintended) beneficiaries of some government action. The extent to which they benefit can outweigh their share of the costs.

20. George Will, "Tax Break for the Yachting Class," *Jewish World Review,* October 28, 1999, at http://www.jewishworldreview. com/cols/will102899.asp (accessed May 20, 2008).

21. As the next chapter illustrates, the committee reports often exhibit relatively high-quality argumentation. Fiery rhetoric is largely absent; respectful disagreement is the rule, not the exception, and facts and evidence are carefully marshaled. But, as we shall see, floor debate is often more intellectually disreputable.

Chapter 12

1. Any statute has to be interpreted by the courts and by that fact alone, the courts will be involved in defining the proper scope of government. As long as this is done at the margins, the democracy requirement is not violated. Nevertheless, at some point, the indeterminacy of the legislation is so great or the courts' interpretations are so at variance with the text of the statute or the

shared understanding of the legislature that it is fair to say that the democracy requirement has been violated.

2. Belz (1991, 22–27) contains a useful summary of the debate, including citations to the *Congressional Record* where this conversion argument was made.

3. Ibid., 7420. Humphrey did, however, admit (6000) that he was "disturbed" by a ruling by the Illinois Fair Employment Practices Committee that invoked a precursor of disparate impact theory to rule that a minority had been the victim of discrimination.

4. On the same page, the memorandum explicitly denies the disparate impact interpretation of discrimination, though not by that name.

5. In 1965, President Lyndon Johnson established minority set-aside programs for government contracts by issuing Executive Order 11246. This created the Office of Federal Contract Compliance and led to the establishment of defensive preferential hiring programs by government contractors. The imposition of minority set-asides by executive order violated the democracy and transparency requirements, but a full discussion of minority set-asides goes beyond the scope of what can be accomplished here. For more on these programs, see Arnold (1998, 147–53).

6. The discussion that follows is drawn from Perritt (1992, 128–36).

7. For an account of that understanding, see chapter 8, p. 230.

8. See, for example, Rep. Jack Brooks remarks on the quota question at *Cong. Rec.*, 102nd Cong., 1st sess., (1991),13523–24.

9. H.R. Rep. No. 40–1, 102nd Cong., April 24, 1991 (Education and Labor Committee) and H.R. Rep. No. 40–2, 102nd Cong., May 17, 1991 (Judiciary Committee).

10. The minority report of the Education and Labor Committee (ibid.) raises the issue on pages 125–39. See especially page 138. See also Rep. Dick Armey's remarks on pages 162–64. The minority report of the Judiciary Committee (ibid.) also raises this issue on pages 56–60. The majority report of the Education and Labor Committee summarily dismisses these concerns on page 44, and the Judiciary Committee's report simply fails to address the issue. Compare this cavalier treatment of what is perhaps the central civil rights issue of this bill with both reports' careful discussion of the issue of the recovery of expert witness and attorney's fees, which goes on for many pages.

11. Recall that "demonstrate" is a term of art in this context; it means that the employer has the burden of production and persuasion in establishing business necessity. See 42 U.S.C. § 2000e (m).

12. For a thorough discussion of this point and an entrée into the empirical literature on the difficulties in validating testing in a way that would satisfy the business necessity defense, see Epstein (1992, 206–26, 236–41).

13. Http://www.aflcio.org/issues/safety/memorial/upload/_26.pdf (accessed May 21, 2008).

14. Http://www.osha.gov/as/opa/oshafacts.html (accessed May 18, 2008).
15. Ibid.
16. Quoted in Temin (1979, 96). For further assurances that the thrust of the act was to protect and enhance self-medication and not to restrict the sale of drugs, see Williams's (1947, 163–65) discussion of the legislative history of the act.
17. "Federal Food, Drug, and Cosmetic Act," House Report No. 2139, 75th Cong., 3rd sess. (1938): 8.
18. U.S. Food and Drug Administration, "Promulgation of Regulations under the Federal Food, Drug, and Cosmetic Act," 3 *Federal Register* 3168 (December 28, 1938).
19. "Amending Section 503(b) of the Federal Food, Drug, and Cosmetic Act," H.R. Rep. No. 700, 82nd Cong., 1st sess. (1951): 1. "Amending Sections 303(c) and 503(b) of the Federal Food, Drug, and Cosmetic Act," S. Rep. No. 946, 82nd Cong., 1st sess. (1951): 2–3.
20. See Temin (1980, 22–23). It is difficult to know how the role of the pharmacist would have evolved in the absence of the prescription requirement. Although it is likely that they would have played a more important role in the health-care delivery system than they currently do, they probably would have shied away from making diagnoses, if only because that would have increased their exposure to lawsuits. Based on this problem about liability, it is easy to envision a conversion argument for state-imposed guidelines regarding what pharmacists are and are not permitted to say to their customers about the drugs they sell.
21. "Amending Section 503(b) of the Federal Food, Drug, and Cosmetic Act," H.R. Rep. No. 700, 82nd Cong., 1st sess. (1951): 28–32.
22. See the testimony of the FSA administrator quoted in the Minority Report of the House (ibid., 30).
23. "Drug Industry Act of 1962," S. Rep. No. 1744, 87th Cong., 2nd sess. (1962): 16.
24. As noted in chapter 1 (see note 8), John Rawls believes that justice requires either what he calls a "property owning democracy" or a "liberal socialist regime" (2001, 136–40). Other mainstream political philosophers seem to believe that whatever redistribution the government is currently doing is at least an order of magnitude less than what it should be. To take another example, many philosophers believe in the desirability of a "single-payer" health care system. All of these represent very large changes to the existing order—much larger than the changes suggested here.

References

Acemoglu, Daron, and Joshua D. Angrist. 2001. "Consequences of Employment Protection? The Case of the Americans with Disabilities Act." *Journal of Political Economy* 109:915–57.

Ackerman, Bruce A. 1980. *Social Justice in the Liberal State*. New Haven, Conn.: Yale University Press.

Ackerman, Bruce A., and James Fishkin. 2004. *Deliberation Day*. New Haven, Conn.: Yale University Press.

Ackerman, Frank, and Lisa Heinzerling. 2002. "Pricing the Priceless: Cost-Benefit Analysis of Environmental Protection." *University of Pennsylvania Law Review* 150:1553–84.

Adams, Christopher P., and Van V. Brantner. 2005. "Spending on New Drug Development." Available at SSRN: http://ssrn.com/abstract=869765.

Adler, Jonathan. 1995. Testimony before the Committee on Environment and Public Works, U.S. Senate, July 12.

———. 1999. "Swamp Rules: The End of Federal Wetland Regulation?" *Regulation* 22(2):11–16.

———. 2008. "Money or Nothing: the Adverse Environmental Consequences of Uncompensated Land Use Controls." *Boston College Law Review* 49(2):301–66.

Akerlof, George. 1970. "The Market for 'Lemons': Qualitatitive Uncertainty and the Market Mechanism." *Quarterly Journal of Economics* 84:488–500.

Albert, Michael, and Robin Hahnel. 1978. *Unorthodox Marxism*. Boston: South End Press.

———. 1987. "Socialist Economics." *Socialist Review* 17:87–104.

———. 1991. *The Political Economy of Participatory Economics*. Princeton, N.J.: Princeton University Press.

Alchian, Armen. 1950. "Uncertainty, Evolution and Economic Theory." *Journal of Political Economy* 58:211–21.

Alchian, Armen, and Harold Demsetz. 1972. "Production, Information Costs, and Economic Organization." *American Economic Review* 62:777–95.

Allen, Franklin, and Richard Herring. 2001. "Banking Regulation Versus Securities Market Regulation." Working Paper 01–29, Wharton Financial Institutions Center, University of Pennsylvania. http://fic.wharton.upenn.edu/fic/papers/01/p0129.html (accessed May 3, 2008).

Anderson, Elizabeth. 1988. "Values, Risks, and Market Norms." *Philosophy & Public Affairs* 17:54–65.

———. 1993. *Value in Ethics and Economics.* Cambridge, Mass.: Harvard University Press.

———. 1999. "What is the Point of Equality?" *Ethics* 109:287–337.

Armentano, Dominick T. 1990. *Antitrust and Monopoly.* New York: Holmes & Meier.

Arneson, Richard. 1989. "Equality of Opportunity for Welfare." *Philosophical Studies* 55:77–93.

———. 1990. "Liberalism, Distributive Subjectivism, and Equal Opportunity for Welfare." *Philosophy and Public Affairs* 19:158–94.

Arnold, N. Scott. 1990. *Marx's Radical Critique of Capitalist Society.* New York: Oxford University Press.

———. 1994. *The Philosophy and Economics of Market Socialism.* New York: Oxford University Press.

———. 1998. "Affirmative Action and the Demands of Justice." *Social Philosophy & Policy* 15:133–75.

———. 2000. "Post-Modern Liberalism and the Expressive Function of Law." *Social Philosophy & Policy* 17:87–109.

———. 2002. "The Role of Government in Responding to Natural Catastrophes." In *Liberty and Hard Cases*, edited by Tibor Machan, 1–34. Stanford, Calif.: Hoover Institution Press.

Asch, Peter. 1988. *Consumer Product Safety.* New York: Oxford University Press.

Asch, Peter, and Rosalind Seneca. 1985. *Government and the Marketplace.* New York: Dryden Press.

Babbitt, Bruce. 1994. "The Triumph of the Blind Texas Salamander and Other Tales from the Endangered Species Act." *E Magazine* 5:54–55.

Bain, Joseph. 1959. *Industrial Organization.* New York: Chapman.

Baird, Charles W. 1992. "The Permissible Use of Forced Union Dues: From *Hanson* to *Beck. Policy Analysis*, no. 174 (July 24). Washington, D.C.: Cato Institute. Available online at http://www.cato. org/pub_display.php?pub_id=1034&full=1 (accessed May, 15, 2008).

Bakunin, M. [1882] 1970. *God and the State.* Translated by B. Tucker. New York: Dover.

Banks, Cristina, and Lisa Cohen. 2005. "Wage and Hour Litigation: I/O Psychology's New Frontier." In *Employment Discrimination Litigation: Behavioral, Quantitative, and Legal Perspectives*, edited by Frank J. Landy, 336–70. San Francisco: Jossey-Bass.

Barber, Richard. 1966. "Government and the Consumer." *Michigan Law Review* 64:1203–38.

Bardach, Eugene, and Robert A. Kagan. 1982. *Going By the Book: The Problem of Regulatory Unreasonableness.* A Twentieth Century Fund Report. Philadelphia: Temple University Press.

Barnett, Randy. 1998. *The Structure of Liberty: Justice and the Rule of Law.* Oxford: Clarendon Press.

———. 2004. *Restoring the Lost Constitution: The Presumption of Liberty.* Princeton, N.J.: Princeton University Press.

Barry, John M. 2004. *The Great Influenza: The Epic Story of the Deadliest Plague In History.* New York: Penguin Paperbacks.

Baumol, William J., and Janusz A. Ordover. 1985. "Use of Antitrust to Subvert Competition." *Journal of Law and Economics* 28:247–65.

Becker, Lawrence. 1977. *Property Rights.* London: Routledge and Kegan Paul.

Beito, David. 1990. "Mutual Aid for Social Welfare: The Case of American Fraternal Societies." *Critical Review* 4:709–36.

Bell, C. G. 1997. "The Americans with Disabilities Act, Mental Disability, and Work." In *Mental Disorder, Worker Disability, and the Law*, edited by R. J. Bonnie and J. Monahan, 203–19. Chicago: University of Chicago Press.

Belz, Herman. 1991. *Equality Transformed: A Quarter Century of Affirmative Action.* Bowling Green, Ohio: Social Philosophy and Policy Center; Transaction Publishers.

Benson, Bruce. 1990. *The Enterprise of Law: Justice Without the State.* San Francisco: Pacific Research Institute for Public Policy.

———. 1998. *To Serve and Protect: Privatization and Community in Criminal Justice.* Foreword by Marvin E. Wolfgang. New York: New York University Press.

Berlin, Isaiah. 1969. "Two Concepts of Liberty." In *Four Essays on Liberty*, edited by Isaiah Berlin. New York: Oxford University Press.

Blanck, Peter, ed. 2000. *Employment, Disability, and the Americans with Disabilities Act: Issues in Law, Public Policy, and Research.* Evanston, Ill.: Northwestern University Press.

Blanck, Peter, and Mollie Weighner Marti. 2000. "Attitudes, Behavior, and ADA Title I." In *Employment, Disability, and the Americans with Disabilities Act: Issues in Law, Public Policy, and Research*, edited by Peter Blanck, 356–84. Evanston, Ill.: Northwestern University Press.

Bloch, Farrell. 1994. *Antidiscrimination Law and Minority Employment.* Chicago: University of Chicago Press.

Blum, Walter, and Harry Kalven. [1954] 1978. *The Uneasy Case for Progressive Taxation.* Chicago: Midway Reprints. University of Chicago Press.

Bovard, James. 1995. "Archer Daniels Midland: A Case Study In Corporate Welfare." *Cato Policy Analysis* No. 241. Washington, D.C.: Cato Institute. Reprinted at http://www.cato.org/pub_display.php?pub_id=1100 (accessed May 20, 2008).

Brook, Amara, Michaela Zint, and Raymond De Young. 2003. "Landowners' Responses to an Endangered Species Act Listing and Implications for Encouraging Conservation." *Conservation Biology* 17(6):1638–49.

Brown, Gardner, and David F. Layton. 2001. "A Market Solution for Preserving Biodiversity: The Black Rhino." In *Protecting Endangered Species in the United States: Biological Needs, Political*

Realities, Economic Choices, edited by Jason Shogren and John Tschirhart, 32–50. Cambridge: Cambridge University Press.

Brozen, Yale. 1980. *Is Government the Source of Monopoly? and Other Essays*. San Francisco: Cato Institute.

——. 1982. *Concentration, Mergers, and Public Policy*. With the assistance of George Bittlingmayer. New York: Macmillan.

Buchanan, Allen. 1985. *Ethics, Efficiency, and the Market*. Totowa, N.J.: Rowman and Allenheld.

——. 1989. "Assessing the Communitarian Critique of Liberalism." *Ethics* 99:852–82.

Buchanan, James M. 1975. "The Samaritan's Dilemma." In *Altruism, Morality, and Economic Theory*, edited by Edmund S. Phelps, 71–85. New York: Russell Sage Foundation.

——. 1975. *The Limits of Liberty: Between Anarchy and Leviathan*. Chicago: University of Chicago Press.

Buchanan, James M., Robert D. Tollison, and Gordon Tullock. 1980. *Toward a Theory of the Rent-Seeking Society*. College Station: Texas A&M University Press.

Buchanan, James, and Richard E. Wagner. 1977. *Democracy in Deficit*. New York: Academic Press.

Bureau of National Affairs. 1971. *The Job Safety and Health Act of 1970: Text, Analysis, and Legislative History*. Washington, D.C.: Bureau of National Affairs.

Burgess, Bonnie B. 2001. *Fate of the Wild: The Endangered Species Act and the Future of Biodiversity*. Athens: University of Georgia Press.

Butler, Richard J. 1996. "Lost Injury Days: Moral Hazard Differences between Tort and Workers' Compensation." *The Journal of Risk and Insurance* 63:405–33.

Caplan, Arthur. 1997. *Am I My Brother's Keeper?* Bloomington: University of Indiana Press.

Card, David, and Alan Krueger. 1994. "Minimum Wages and Employment: A Case Study of the Fast-Food Industry in New Jersey and Pennsylvania." *American Economic Review* 84:772–93.

——. 1995. *Myth and Measurement: The New Economics of the Minimum Wage*. Princeton, N.J.: Princeton University Press.

Carey, George, ed. 1998. *Freedom and Virtue: The Conservative/Libertarian Debate*. Wilmington, Del.: Intercollegiate Studies Institute.

Carling, P. 1994. "Reasonable Accommodation in the Workplace for Persons with Psychiatric Disabilities." In *Implications of the Americans with Disabilities Act for Psychology*, edited by S. M. Bruyere and J. O'Keefe, 103–36. Washington, D.C.: American Psychological Association.

Carlton, Dennis W., and Robert H. Gertner. 2002. "Intellectual Property, Antitrust, and Strategic Behavior." NBER Working Paper 8978, June.

Cato Institute. 2001. *Cato Handbook For Congress 2001*. Washington D.C.: Cato Institute.

———. 2005. *Cato Handbook on Policy*, 6th ed. Washington, D.C.: Cato Institute. Available online at http://www.cato.org/pubs/handbook/hb109/.

Caves, Richard. 1967. *American Industry: Structure, Conduct, Performance*. Englewood Cliffs, N.J.: Prentice Hall.

Chamberlin, Edward. 1938. *The Theory of Monopolistic Competition*. Cambridge, Mass.: Harvard University Press.

Chang, Ruth, ed. 1997. *Incommensurability, Incomparability, and Practical Reasoning*. Cambridge, Mass: Harvard University Press.

Cheit, Ross. 1990. *Setting Safety Standards*. Berkeley: University of California Press.

Clark, Barry, and Herbert Gintis. 1978. "Rawlsian Justice and Economic Systems," *Philosophy & Public Affairs* 7:302–25.

Coase, Ronald. 1937. "The Nature of the Firm." *Economica* 16: 386–405.

———. 1960. "The Problem of Social Cost." *The Journal of Law & Economics* 2:1–44. Reprinted in *The Firm, the Market, and the Law*, edited by Ronald Coase, 95–156. Chicago: University of Chicago Press.

———. 1974. "The Lighthouse in Economics." *The Journal of Law & Economics* 17:357–76. Reprinted in *The Firm, the Market, and the Law*, edited by Ronald Coase, 187–213. Chicago: University of Chicago Press.

Coate, Malcolm B., Richard S. Higgins, and Fred S. McChesney. 1995. "Bureaucracy and Politics in FTC Merger Challenges." In *The Causes and Consequences of Antitrust*, edited by Fred S. McChesney and William F. Shugart II, 213–30. Chicago: University of Chicago Press.

Cohen, Lloyd. 1998. "Increasing Supply, Improving Allocation, And Furthering Justice And Decency In Organ Acquisition And Allocation: The Many Virtues Of Markets." *Graft* 1:122.

Colker, Ruth. 2005. *The Disability Pendulum: The First Decade of the Americans with Disabilities Act*. New York: New York University Press.

Conrad, Alison M., and Frank Linneham. 1995. "Formalized HRM Structures: Coordinating Equal Employment Opportunity or Concealing Organizational Practices?" *Academy of Management Journal* 38:787–820.

Copp, David. 1992. "The Right to an Adequate Standard of Living," *Social Philosophy & Policy* 9 (Winter): 231–61.

Cornell, Nina W., Roger G. Noll, and Barry Weingast. 1976. "Safety Regulation." In *Setting National Priorities: The Coming Decade*, edited by Henry Owen and Charles L. Schultze, 457–504. Washington, D.C.: The Brookings Institution.

Cose, Ellis. 1993. *Rage of a Privileged Class*. New York: Harper Collins.

Coursey, Don. 2001. "The Revealed Demand for a Public Good: Evidence from Endangered and Threatened Species." In *Protecting Endangered Species in the United States: Biological*

Needs, Political Realities, Economic Choices, edited by Jason Shogren and John Tschirhart, 200–25. Cambridge: Cambridge University Press.

Cowen, Tyler, ed. 1988. *The Theory of Market Failure: A Critical Examination*. Fairfax, Va.: George Mason University Press and the Cato Institute.

Cowen, Tyler, and Eric Crampton, eds. 2004. *Market Failure or Success: The New Debate*. Northampton, Mass.: Edward Elgar.

Crandall, Robert W., and Clifford Winston. 2003. "Does Antitrust Policy Improve Consumer Welfare? Assessing the Evidence." *Journal of Economic Perspectives* 17 (Fall): 3–26.

Cullity, Garrett. 1995. "Moral Free Riding." *Philosophy & Public Affairs* 24 (Winter): 1–34.

D'Agostino, Fred. 2003. "Public Justification." *The Stanford Encyclopedia of Philosophy* (Summer 2003 Edition), edited by Edward N. Zalta. http://plato.stanford.edu/archives/sum2003/entries/justification-public/.

Daniels, Norman. 1985. *Just Health Care*. Princeton: Princeton University Press.

DeLeire, Thomas. 2000. "The Unintended Consequences of the Americans with Disabilities Act." *Regulation* 23(1):21–24.

Demsetz, Harold. 1970. "The Private Production of Public Goods." *Journal of Law & Economics* 3 (October): 293–306. Reprinted in *The Theory of Market Failure: A Critical Examination*, edited by Tyler Cowan, 111–26. Fairfax, Va.: George Mason University Press and the Cato Institute.

Department of Labor, Secretary of Labor. 1965. *The Older American Worker: Age Discrimination in Employment*. Washington, D.C.

DiMasi, J. R., W. Hansen, and H. G. Grabowski. 2003. "The Price of Innovation: New Estimates of Drug Development Costs." *Journal of Health Economics* 22:151–85.

DiQuattro, Arthur. 1983. "Rawls and Left Criticism." *Political Theory* 11:53–87.

Director, Aaron. 1964. "The Parity of the Economic Marketplace." *Journal of Law and Economics* 7:1–10.

Dixon, Lloyd. 2000. *The Financial Implications of Releasing Small Firms and Small-Volume Contributors from Superfund Liability*. Santa Monica, Calif.: Rand.

Donohue, John J. III, and Peter Siegelman. 1991. "The Changing Nature of Employment Discrimination Litigation." *Stanford Law Review* 44:983–1033.

Doppelt, Gerald. 1981. "Rawls's System of Justice: A Critique From the Left," *Noûs* 15:259–309.

Dunn, Charles W. 1938. *Federal Food, Drug, and Cosmetic Act: A Statement of its Legislative Record*. New York: G. E. Stechert.

Dworkin, Gerald. 1972. "Paternalism." *Monist* 56:64–84.

——. 1994. "Markets and Morals: The Case for Organ Sales." In *Morality, Harm, and the Law*, edited by Gerald Dworkin, 155–61. Boulder, Colo.: Westview.

Dworkin, Ronald. 1977. "Why Bakke Has No Case." *New York Review of Books*, 24, no. 18 (November 10).

———. 1981a. "What is Equality? Part I: Equality of Welfare." *Philosophy & Public Affairs* 10:185–246.

———. 1981b. "What is Equality? Part II: Equality of Resources." *Philosophy & Public Affairs* 10:283–345.

———. 1984. *A Matter of Principle*. Cambridge, Mass: Harvard University Press.

———. 1987. "What Is Equality? Part III: The Place of Liberty." *Iowa Law Review* 73:1–55.

———. 2000. *Sovereign Virtue*. Cambridge, Mass.: Harvard University Press.

Eads, George, and Peter Reuter. 1985. "Designing Safer Products: Corporate Responses to Product Liability Law and Regulation," 1–32. Rand Paper Series, Institute for Civil Justice. Santa Monica, Calif.: Rand Corporation. Originally published in *Journal of Products Liability* 7 (1984): 263–94.

Elster, Jon. 1979. *Ulysses and the Sirens: Studies in Rationality and Irrationality*. Cambridge: Cambridge University Press.

———. 1983. *Sour Grapes*. Cambridge: Cambridge University Press.

———. 1985. *Making Sense of Marx*. Cambridge: Cambridge University Press.

England, Paula. 1984. "Socioeconomic Explanations of Job Segregation." In *Comparable Worth & Wage Discrimination: Technical Possibilities and Political Realities*, edited by Helen Remick, 28–46. Women in Political Economy Series. Philadelphia: Temple University Press.

Epstein, Richard A. 1983. "A Common Law for Labor Relations: A Critique of the New Deal Legislation." *Yale Law Journal* 92:1357–1408.

———. 1985. *Takings*. Cambridge, Mass.: Harvard University Press.

———. 1992. *Forbidden Grounds*. Cambridge, Mass: Harvard University Press.

———. 1993. *Bargaining With the State*. Princeton, N.J.: Princeton University Press.

———. 1995. *Simple Rules for a Complex World*. Cambridge, Mass.: Harvard University Press.

———. 1997. *Mortal Peril*. New York: Addison-Wesley.

———. 1998. *Principles of a Free Society*. Reading, Mass: Perseus Books.

———. 2000. "Antidiscrimination in Health Care: Community Ratings and Preexisting Conditions." In *American Health Care: Government, Market Processes and the Public Interest*, edited by Roger Feldman, 201–28. Oakland: Independent Institute.

EEOC (Equal Employment Opportunity Commission). 1997. *EEOC Compliance Manual: EEOC Guidance on the ADA and Psychiatric Disabilities. FEP Manual (BNA)*, 63, 70:1281.

Etzioni, Amitai, and Laura Brodbeck. 1995. *The Intergenerational Covenant: Rights and Responsibilities*. Washington DC: The Communitarian Network.

Feinberg, Joel. 1971. "Legal Paternalism," *Canadian Journal of Philosophy* 1 (September): 105–24.

——. 1974. "The Rights of Animals and Unborn Generations." In *Philosophy and Environmental Crisis*, edited by W. T. Blackstone, 43–68. Athens: University of Georgia Press.

——. 1984. *The Moral Limits of the Criminal Law. Vol. 1, Harm to Others*. New York: Oxford University Press.

——. 1985. *The Moral Limits of the Criminal Law. Vol. 2, Offense to Others*. New York: Oxford University Press.

——. 1986. *The Moral Limits of the Criminal Law. Vol. 3, Harm to Self*. New York: Oxford University Press.

——. 1988. *The Moral Limits of the Criminal Law. Vol. 4, Harmless Wrongdoing*. New York: Oxford University Press.

Fink, Richard H. 1982. *Supply-Side Economics: A Critical Appraisal*. Frederick, Md.: University Publications of America.

Fishback, Price V., and Shawn Everett Cantor. 2000. *A Prelude to the Welfare State: The Origins of Workers' Compensation*. Chicago: University of Chicago Press.

Fishkin, James. 1983. *Justice, Equal Opportunity and the Family*. New Haven, Conn.: Yale University Press.

——. 1991. *Democracy and Deliberation: New Directions for Democratic Reform*. New Haven, Conn.: Yale University Press.

Freed, Mayer, and Daniel Polsby. 1985. "Comparable Worth in the Equal Pay Act." *University of Chicago Law Review* 51 (Fall 1984): 1078–111. Reprinted in *Labor Law and the Employment Market: Foundations and Applications*, edited by Richard A. Epstein and Jeffrey Paul, 134–67. New Brunswick, N.J.: Transaction Books.

Friedman, Lawrence. 1973. *A History of American Law*. New York: Simon & Schuster.

Friedman, Milton. 1955. "The Role of Government in Education." In *Economics and the Public Interest*, edited by Robert A. Solo, 123–44. New Brunswick, N.J.: Rutgers University Press.

——. 1962. *Capitalism and Freedom*. Chicago: University of Chicago Press.

——. 1970. *The Counter-Revolution in Monetary Theory*. London: Institute of Economic Affairs.

——. 1976. "Wage Determination and Unemployment." In *Price Theory: A Provisional Text*, revised ed. Chicago: Aldine.

——. 1978. *Tax Limitation, Inflation and the Role of Government*. Dallas: The Fisher Institute.

Friedman, Milton, and Rose Friedman.1984. *Tyranny of the Status Quo*. San Diego: Harcourt, Brace, Jovanovich.

Frolich, Norman, and Joe A. Oppenheimer. 1992. *Choosing Justice: An Experimental Approach to Ethical Theory*. Berkeley: University of California Press.

Galston, William. 1989. "Civic Education in the Liberal State." In *Liberalism and the Moral Life*, edited by Nancy L. Rosenblum, 89–102. Cambridge, Mass: Harvard University Press.

Gaus, Gerald F. 1995. *Justificatory Liberalism*. Cambridge: Cambridge University Press.

———. 1999. *Social Philosophy*. Armonk, N.Y.: M. E. Sharpe.

Gellhorn, Walter. 1976. "The Abuse of Occupational Licensing." *University of Chicago Law Review* 44:6–27.

Gewirth, Alan. 1996. *The Community of Rights*. Chicago: University of Chicago Press.

Gieringer, Dale H. 1985. "The Safety and Efficacy of New Drug Approval." *Cato Journal* 5:177–201.

Glovich, Thomas, Dale Griffin, and Daniel Kahneman. 2002. *Heuristics and Biases: The Psychology of Intuitive Judgment*. Cambridge: Cambridge University Press.

Goldman, Emma. 1911. *Anarchism and Other Essays*; with biographic sketch by Hippolyte Havel. 2nd rev. ed. New York: Mother Earth Publishing.

Goodin, Robert. 1988. *Reasons for Welfare*. Princeton, N.J.: Princeton University Press.

———. 1989. "The Ethics of Smoking." *Ethics* 99:574–624.

———. 1995. *Utilitarianism as a Public Philosophy*. Cambridge: Cambridge University Press.

Goodman, John C., and Gerald L. Musgrave. 1992. *Patient Power*. Washington, D.C.: Cato Institute.

Goodman, Nelson. [1955] 1965. *Fact, Fiction, and Forecast*, 2nd ed. Indianapolis, Ind.: Bobbs Merrill

Gorr, Michael. 1988. *Coercion, Freedom, and Exploitation*. New York: Peter Lang.

Grabowski, Henry G. 1976. *Drug Regulation and Innovation: Empirical Evidence and Policy Options*. Washington, D.C.: American Enterprise Institute.

Gray, John. 1995. *Liberalism*, 2nd ed. Minneapolis: University of Minnesota Press.

Gray, Wayne B., and John T. Scholz. 1993. "Does Regulatory Enforcement Work? A Panel Analysis of OSHA Enforcement." *Law & Society Review* 27:177–214.

Gregory, Raymond. 2001. *Age Discrimination in the American Workplace: Old at a Young Age*. New Brunswick, N.J.: Rutgers University Press.

Groarke, Leo. 1990. *Greek Skepticism: Anti-Realist Trends in Ancient Thought*. Montreal: McGill-Queen's University Press.

Groshen, Erica L., and Eng Seng Loh. 1993. "What Do We Know about Probationary Periods?" In *Industrial Relations Research Association Series: Proceedings of the Forty-fifth Annual Meeting*, edited by John F. Burton Jr., 10–19. Madison, Wisc.: Industrial Relations Research Association.

Gross, Martin L. 1995. *The Tax Racket*. New York: Ballantine.

Grossman, Sanford J., and Oliver D. Hart. 1986. "The Costs and Benefits of Ownership: A Theory of Vertical and Lateral Integration." *The Journal of Political Economy* 94:691–719.

Gutek, Barbara A., and Margaret S. Stockdale. 2005. "Sex Discrimination in Employment." In *Employment Discrimination Litigation: Behavioral, Quantitative, and Legal Perspectives*, edited by Frank J. Landy, 229–55. San Francisco: Jossey-Bass.

Gutman, Arthur. 2005. "Adverse Impact, Judicial, Regulatory, and Statutory Authority." In *Employment Discrimination Litigation: Behavioral, Quantitative, and Legal Perspectives*, edited by Frank J. Landy, 20–46. San Francisco: Jossey-Bass.

Gutmann, Amy. 1989. "Undemocratic Education." In *Liberalism and the Moral Life*, edited by Nancy L. Rosenblum, 71–88. Cambridge, Mass: Harvard University Press.

——, ed. 1992. *Multiculturalism and 'The Politics of Recognition.'* Princeton, N.J.: Princeton University Press.

Gutmann, Amy, and Dennis Thompson. 1996. *Democracy and Disagreement*. Cambridge, Mass.: Belknap Press of Harvard University Press.

Hall, Maximilian J. B. 1993. *Banking Regulation and Supervision*. Hants, England: Edward Elgar.

Hamilton, Alexander, John Jay, and James Madison. [1787–1788] 2000. *The Federalist Papers*. Great Minds Series. Amherst, N.Y.: Prometheus Books.

Hamilton, David B. 1962. *The Consumer in Our Economy*. Boston: Houghton Mifflin.

Hammermesh, Daniel 1995. "Comments: What a Wonderful World This Would Be." *Industrial and Labour Relations Review* 48:835–38.

Hamowy, Ronald. 2007. *Government and Public Health in America*. Northampton, Mass.: Edward Elgar.

Hantula, D. A., and N. A. Reilly. 1996. "Reasonable Accommodation for Employees with Mental Disabilities: A Mandate for Effective Supervision?" *Behavioral Sciences and the Law* 14:107–20.

Harrington, Michael. 1962. *The Other America: Poverty in the United States*. New York: Macmillan.

Harsanyi, John. 1980. "Can the Maximin Principle Serve as a Basis for Morality? A Critique of John Rawls's Theory." In *Essays on Ethics, Social Behavior, and Scientific Explanation*, edited by John Harsanyi. Dordrect, Holland: D. Reidel.

Hartogh, Govert den. 2002. *Mutual Expectations: A Conventionalist Theory of Law*. Law and Philosophy Library, vol. 56. The Hague: Kluwer Law International.

Haslanger, Sally, and Nancy Tuana. 2006. "Topics in Feminism." *The Stanford Encyclopedia of Philosophy* (Summer 2006 Edition), edited by Edward N. Zalta. http://plato.stanford.edu/archives/sum2006/entries/feminism-topics/ (accessed May 20, 2008).

Haslett, D. W. 1997. "Distributive Justice and Inheritance." In *Is Inheritance Legitimate?*, edited by G. Erreygers and T. Vandevelde, 133–55. Berlin: Springer-Verlag.

Hawley, Ellis W. 1966. *The New Deal and the Problem of Monopoly.* Princeton, N.J.: Princeton University Press.

Hawthorne, Fran. 2005. *Inside the FDA: The Business and Politics Behind the Drugs We Take and the Food We Eat.* Hoboken, N.J.: John Wiley & Sons.

Hayek. F. A. 1935. *Prices and Production,* 2nd ed. London: Routledge and Sons.

———. 1937. "Economics and Knowledge." *Economics* 4:33–54.

———. [1944] 1972. *The Road to Serfdom.* Chicago: Phoenix Books. University of Chicago Press.

———. 1945. "The Use of Knowledge in Society." *American Economic Review* 35:519–30.

———. 1960. *The Constitution of Liberty.* Chicago: University of Chicago Press.

———. 1972. *A Tiger by the Tail: A 40-years' Running Commentary on Keynesianism,* compiled and introduced by Sudha R. Shenoy. London: Institute for Economic Affairs.

———. 1976. *Law, Liberty, and Legislation, vol. 2: The Mirage of Social Justice.* Chicago: University of Chicago Press.

———. 1978. "Competition as a Discovery Procedure." In *New Studies in Philosophy, Politics, Economics, and the History of Ideas,* edited by F. A. Hayek, 179–90. Chicago and London: University of Chicago and Routledge and Kegan Paul.

———. 1979. *Unemployment and Monetary Policy: Government as Generator of the 'Business Cycle.'* San Francisco: Cato Institute.

Hayward, Gregory D., Jason F. Shogren, and John Tschirhart. 2001. "The Nature of Endangered Species Protection." In *Protecting Endangered Species in the United States: Biological Needs, Political Realities, Economic Choices,* edited by Jason Shogren and John Tschirhart, 1–20. Cambridge: Cambridge University Press.

Hazen, Thomas L. 1996. *The Law of Securities Regulation.* Hornbook Series. St. Paul, Minn.: West Publishing.

Head, John G. 1974. *Public Goods and Public Welfare.* Durham, N.C.: Duke University Press.

Herman, Arthur. 2001. *How the Scots Invented the Modern World.* New York: Three Rivers Press.

Higgs, Robert. 1995. *Hazardous to Our Health? FDA Regulation of Health Care Products.* Oakland: Independent Institute.

High, Jack, and Thomas DiLorenzo. 1988. "Antitrust and Competition, Historically Considered." *Economic Inquiry* 26:423–35.

Hill, Andrew D. 1987. *Wrongful Discharge and the Derogation of the At-Will Employment Doctrine.* Philadelphia: Industrial Research Unit, Wharton School, University of Pennsylvania.

Hilts, Philip. 2003. *Protecting America's Health: The FDA, Business, and 100 Years of Regulation.* New York: Borzoi Books, Alfred A. Knopf.

Hobhouse, L. T. [1911] 1964. *Liberalism*. Introduction by Alan P. Grimes. Oxford: Oxford University Press.

Hogan, Daniel B. 1979. *The Regulation of Psychotherapists*, Vol. 1. Cambridge, Mass.: Ballinger.

Holcombe, Randall. 1995. *Public Policy and the Quality of Life*. Westport, Conn.: Greenwood Press.

Holzer, Harry J. 1987. "Hiring Procedures in the Firm: Their Economic Determinants and Outcomes." In *Human Resources and the Performance of the Firm*, edited by Morris M. Kleiner et al., 243–74. Madison, Wisc.: Industrial Relations Research Association.

Honoré, A. M. 1961. "Ownership." In *Oxford Essays in Jurisprudence*, edited by A. G. Guest, 107–40. Oxford: Oxford University Press.

Horwitz, Steven. 2000. *Microfoundations and Macroeconomics: An Austrian Perspective*. New York: Routledge.

Hudgins, Edward L. 1995. "Handicapping Freedom: The Americans with Disabilities Act." *Regulation* 18 (2). Available online at http://www.cato.org/pubs/regulation/reg18n2e.html.

Hume, David. [1777] 1975. *Enquiries Concerning Human Understanding and Concerning the Principles of Morals*, 3rd ed., edited by L. A. Selby-Bigge. With text revised and notes by P. H. Nidditch. Oxford: Oxford University Press.

Husak, Douglas. 2003. "Four Points About Drug Decriminalization." *Criminal Justice Ethics* 22 (Winter/Spring): 21–29.

Ikeda, Sanford. 1996. *Dynamics of the Mixed Economy*. London: Routledge.

Jacobs, Lesley. 1993. *Rights and Deprivation*. Oxford: Oxford University Press.

Jencks, Christopher. 1966. "Is the Public School Obsolete?" *The Public Interest* 2 (Winter): 18–28.

Jensen, Gail A., and Michael A. Morrisey. 1999. "Employer-Sponsored Health Insurance and Mandated Benefit Laws." *The Milbank Quarterly* 77:1–21.

Joll, James. [1964] 1966. *The Anarchists*. The Universal Library, UL 191. New York: Grosset and Dunlap.

Jolls, Christine. 2000. "Accommodation Mandates." *Stanford Law Review* 53:223–306.

Joskow, Paul. 1973. "Cartels, Competition, and Regulation in the Property-Liability Insurance Industry." *The Bell Journal of Economics and Management* 4:375–427.

Justice, Betty W. 1983. *Unions, Workers, and the Law*. Washington, D.C.: Bureau of National Affairs.

Kahneman, Daniel, and Amos Tversky. 1979. "Prospect Theory: An Analysis of Decision Under Risk." *Econometrica* 47 (1979): 263–91.

Kahneman, Daniel, Paul Slovic, and Amos Tversky, eds. 1982. *Judgment Under Uncertainty: Heuristics and Biases*. Cambridge: Cambridge University Press.

Kaysen, Carl, and Donald F. Turner. 1959. *Antitrust Policy; an Economic and Legal Analysis.* Cambridge, Mass.: Harvard University Press.

Kelley, David. 1998. *A Life of One's Own: Individual Rights and the Welfare State.* Washington, D.C.: Cato Institute.

Key, L. E. 1997. "Co-Worker Morale, Confidentiality, and the ADA." *DePaul Law Review* 46:1003–42.

Kirk, Russell. 1954. *A Program for Conservatives.* Chicago: Henry Regnery Company.

Klein, Daniel, and Fred Foldvary, eds. 2003. *The Half-Life of Policy Rationales: How New Technology Affects Old Policy Issues.* New York: New York University Press.

Klein, Daniel, and Alex Tabarrok. 2003. "Do Off-Label Drug Practices Argue Against FDA Efficacy Requirements? Testing an Argument by Structured Conversations with Experts." Independent Institute Working Paper Number 47. Independent Institute: Oakland, Calif.

———. 2004. "Who Certifies Off-Label?" *Regulation* 27(2):60–63. Available online at http://www.cato.org/pubs/regulation/regv27n2/v27n2-8.pdf.

Kleiner, Morris M. 2006. *Licensing Occupations: Ensuring Quality or Restricting Competition?* Kalamazoo, Mich.: W. E. Upjohn Institute for Employment Research.

Kniesner, Thomas J., and John D. Leeth. 1995. "Abolishing OSHA." *Regulation* 18(3):46–56.

Kolko, Gabriel. 1963. *The Triumph of Conservatism.* New York: Glencoe, the Free Press.

———. 1965. *Railroads and Regulation: 1877–1916.* Princeton, N.J.: Princeton University Press.

Kondratas, Anna. 1986. "Comparable Worth: Pay Equity or Social Engineering?" The Heritage Lectures No. 63, February 5, 1986.

Krauss, Michael. 1996. "Loosening the FDA's Drug Certification Monopoly: Implications for Tort." *George Mason Law Review* 4:458–83.

Kymlicka, Will. 2002. *Contemporary Political Philosophy: An Introduction*, 2nd ed. New York: Oxford University Press.

Landy, Frank J., ed. 2005. *Employment Discrimination Litigation: Behavioral, Quantitative, and Legal Perspectives.* The Professional Practice Series. Eduardo Salas, series editor. San Francisco: Jossey-Bass.

Lavoie, Don. 1985. *Rivalry and Central Planning.* New York: Cambridge University Press.

Lazear, Edward. 1979. "Why Is There Mandatory Retirement?" *Journal of Political Economy* 87:1261–84.

Lazorou, Jason, Bruce Pomeranz, and Paul Corey. 1998. "Incidence of Adverse Drug Reactions in Hospitalized Patients: A Meta-analysis of Prospective Studies." *Journal of the American Medical Association* 279:1200–5.

LeComte, Eugen, and Karen Gahagan. 1998. "Hurricane Insurance Protection in Florida." In *Paying the Price*, edited by Howard Kunreuther and Richard J. Roth Sr., 97–124. Washington, D.C.: National Academy of Sciences, Joseph Henry Press.

Leland, Hayne. 1979. "Quacks, Lemons, and Licensing: A Theory of Minimum Quality Standards." *Journal of Political Economy* 87:1328–46.

——. 1980. "Minimum-Quality Standards and Licensing in Markets with Asymmetric Information." In *Occupational Licensure and Regulation*, edited by Simon Rottenberg, 264–84. Washington, D.C.: American Enterprise Institute for Public Policy Research.

Lereah, David A. 1985. *Insurance Markets: Information Problems and Regulation*. New York: Praeger.

Lessig, Lawrence. 1995. "The Regulation of Social Meaning." *University of Chicago Law Review* 62:943–1045.

Lester, Jan. 2000. *Escape from Leviathan: Liberty, Welfare, and Anarchy Reconciled*. New York: St. Martin's.

Lewis, Ted G. 1999. *MicroSoft Rising*. Los Alamitos, Calif.: IEEE Computer Society.

Lewis, William E., Jr. 2001. *Wetlands Explained: Wetland Science, Policy, and Politics in America*. New York: Oxford University Press.

Lieberman, Jethro K. 1970. *Tyranny of the Experts*. New York: Walker and Company.

Liebowitz, Stan J., and Stephen E. Margolis. 1999. *Winners, Losers & Microsoft: Competition and Antitrust in High Technology*. Oakland: Independent Institute.

Locke, John. [1690] 1988. *Second Treatise of Government*. In *Two Treatises of Government*, edited by Peter Laslett. Cambridge Texts in the History of Political Thought. Cambridge: Cambridge University Press.

Logomasini, Angela, and David Riggs, eds. 2002. *The Environmental Source 2002*. St. Louis: Competitive Enterprise Institute.

Lomasky, Loren. 1987. *Persons, Rights, and the Moral Community*. New York: Oxford University Press.

Lueck, Dean, and Jeffrey A. Michael. 2003. "Preemptive Habitat Destruction Under the Endangered Species Act," *Journal of Law and Economics* 46(1):27–60.

Luper-Foy, Steven, and Curtis Brown, eds. 1994. *Drugs, Morality and the Law*. New York: Garland.

Lynch, Frederick R. 1997. *The Diversity Machine*. New York: Free Press.

Machan, Tibor. 1985. "Moral Myths and Basic Positive Rights." *Tulane Studies in Philosophy* 33:35–41.

——. 1989. *Individuals and Their Rights*. LaSalle, Ill.: Open Court.

——. 1995. *Private Rights and Public Illusions*. New Brunswick, N.J.: Transaction Books.

Machovec, Frank M. 1995. *Perfect Competition and the Transformation of Economics*. London: Routledge.

MacIntyre, Alasdair. 1984. *After Virtue.* Notre Dame, Ind.: University of Notre Dame Press.

Madden, M. Stuart. 1980–81. "Consumer Product Safety Act Section 15 and Substantial Product Hazards." *Catholic University Law Review* 30:195–248.

Malos, Stan. 2005. "The Importance of Valid Selection and Performance Appraisal." In *Employment Discrimination Litigation: Behavioral, Quantitative, and Legal Perspectives*, edited by Frank J. Landy, 373–409. San Francisco: Jossey-Bass.

Mancuso, L. L. 1990. "Reasonable Accommodations for Persons with Psychiatric Diabilities." *Psychosocial Rehabilitation Journal* 14:3–19.

Mann, Charles C., and Mark L. Plummer. 1995a. "California vs. Gnatcatcher." *Audubon* 97 (January-February): 38–48, 100–104.

———. 1995b. *Noah's Choice: The Future of Endangered Species.* New York: Alfred A. Knopf.

Marmor, Theodore, Jerry Mashaw, and Philip Harvey. 1992. *America's Misunderstood Welfare State: Persistent Myths, Enduring Realities.* New York: Basic Books.

Mason, E. S. 1939. "Price and Production Policies of Large-Scale Enterprise." *American Economic Review*, supplement (March): 61–74.

McCaffery, Edward J. 1994a. "The Uneasy Case for Wealth Transfer Taxation." *Yale Law Journal* 104:283–365.

———. 1994b. "The Political Liberal Case for Wealth Transfer Taxation." *Philosophy & Public Affairs* 23:281–312.

McElroy, Wendy. 1994. "Breeder Reactionaries." *Reason.* December. Available online at http://www.reason.com/news/show/29569. html (accessed September 29, 2008).

Meiners, Roger E., and Andrew P. Morriss, eds. 2000. *The Common Law and the Environment: Rethinking the Statutory Basis for Modern Environmental Law.* Lanham, Md.: Rowman and Littlefield.

Mendeloff, John. 1979. *Regulating Safety: An Economic and Political Analysis of Occupational Safety and Health Policy.* Cambridge, Mass.: MIT Press.

Mezey, Susan Gluck. 2003. *Elusive Equality: Women's Rights, Public Policy, and the Law.* Boulder, Colo.: Lynne Rienner.

Mill, John Stuart. [1859] 1978. *On Liberty*, edited by Elizabeth Rapaport. Indianapolis, Ind.: Hackett Publishing.

———. [1861] 1957. *Utilitarianism*, edited by Oskar Piest. Library of Liberal Arts. Indianapolis, Ind.: Bobbs-Merrill.

Miller, Henry I. 2000. *To America's Health: A Proposal to Reform the Food and Drug Administration.* Stanford, Calif.: Hoover Institution Press.

von Mises, Ludwig. 1966. *Human Action: A Treatise on Economics.* Chicago: Henry Regnery.

Mitchell, William C., and Randy T. Simmons. 1994. *Beyond Politics: Markets, Welfare and the Failure of Bureaucracy.* Boulder, Colo.: Westview Press.

Moore, J. A. 1995. "Can the ADA Work for People with Mental Illness?" *Journal of the California Alliance for the Mentally Ill* 6:25–26.

Morriss, Andrew P. 2000. "Lessons for Environmental Law from the American Codification Debate." In *The Common Law and the Environment*, edited by Roger E. Meiners and Andrew P. Morriss, 130–57. Lanham, Md.: Rowman and Littlefield.

Moss, David A. 1999. "Courting Disaster? The Transformation of Federal Disaster Policy Since 1803." In *The Financing of Catastrophic Risk*, edited by Kenneth A. Froot, 307–51. Chicago: University of Chicago Press.

Murray, Charles. 1984. *Losing Ground: American Social Policy 1950–1980*. New York: Basic Books.

———. 1988. *In Pursuit of Happiness and Good Government*. New York: Simon & Schuster.

———. 1997. *What It Means to Be a Libertarian*. Broadway Books: New York.

Nadelmann, Ethan. 1987. "Drug Prohibition in the United States: Costs, Consequences, and Alternatives." *Science* 245:939–46.

———. 1988. "The Case for Legalization." *The Public Interest*, no. 92 (Summer): 3–31.

Nader, Ralph, ed. 1973. *The Consumer and Corporate Accountability*. New York: Harcourt, Brace, Jovanovich.

Narveson, Jan. 1988. *The Libertarian Idea*. Philadelphia: Temple University Press.

———. 1994. "Drugs and Responsibility." In *Drugs, Morality and the Law*, edited by Steven Luper-Foy and Curtis Brown, 3–24. New York: Garland.

National Safety Council. 2006. *Injury Facts*, 2005–2006 Edition. Itasca, Ill: National Safety Council.

Neumark, David, and William Wascher. 1995. "The Effects of New Jersey's Minimum Wage Increase on Fast Food Employment: a Reevaluation Using Payroll Records." National Bureau of Economic Research Working Paper No. 5214. Cambridge, Mass.: National Bureau of Economic Research.

Nichols, Albert, and Richard Zeckhauser. 1977. "Government Comes to the Workplace: An Assessment of OSHA." *The Public Interest* 49:39–69.

Nolan, James L. 1998. *The Therapeutic State*. New York: New York University Press.

Nolan, Virginia, and Edmund Ursin. 1995. *Understanding Enterprise Liability: Rethinking Tort Reform for the Twenty-First Century*. Philadelphia: Temple University Press.

Nordlund, Willis. 1997. *The Quest for a Living Wage*. Westport, Conn.: Greenwood Press.

Noss, Reed F. 1992. "The Wildlands Project: Land Conservation Strategy." *Wild Earth*, Special Issue: 10–25.

——. 1994. "Building a Wilderness Recovery Network." *George Wright Forum* 11:17–40.

Nott, M., E. Rogers, and S. Pimm. 1995. "Modern Extinctions in the Kilo-Death Range," *Current Biology* 5:14–17.

Nozick, Robert. 1969. "Coercion." In *Philosophy, Science, and Method: Essays in Honor of Ernest Nagel*, edited by Sidney Morgenbesser, Patrick Suppes, and Morton White, 440–72. New York: St. Martin's.

——. 1974. *Anarchy, State, and Utopia*. New York: Basic Books.

——. 1993. *The Nature of Rationality*. Princeton, N.J.: Princeton University Press.

O'Hara, Edwin V. 1916. *A Living Wage By Legislation: The Oregon Experience*. Salem, Ore.: State Printing Department.

Olasky, Marvin. 1992. *The Tragedy of American Compassion*. Washington, D.C.: Regnery Gateway.

——. 1996. *Renewing American Compassion*. New York: Free Press.

Olson, Mancur. 1965. *The Logic of Collective Action*. Cambridge, Mass: Harvard University Press.

Olson, Walter. 1997. *The Excuse Factory*. New York: Free Press.

O'Meara, Daniel P. 1989. *Protecting the Growing Number of Older Workers: The Age Discrimination in Employment Act*. Philadelphia: Wharton School, Industrial Research Unit.

Parenteau, Patrick A. 1991. "Wetlands Regulation Under Section 404 of the Clean Water Act." In *Natural Resources Law Handbook*, edited by Baynard Baur et al. Rockville, Md.: Government Institutes, Inc.

Parry, J. W. 1993. "Mental Disorders under the ADA: A Difficult Path to Follow." *Mental and Physical Disabilities Law Reporter* 17:100–12.

Paul, Ellen Frankel. 1986. "Moral Constraints and Eminent Domain: A Review Essay." *George Washington Law Review* 55:152–79.

——. 1987. *Property Rights and Eminent Domain*. New Brunswick, N.J.: Transaction Publishers.

——. 1988. *Equity and Gender: The Comparable Worth Debate*. New Brunswick, N.J.: Transaction Publishers.

——. 1991. "Bared Buttocks and Federal Cases." *Society* 28, no. 4, May/June.

Peltzman, Sam. 1975. "The Effects of Automobile Safety Regulation." *Journal of Political Economy* 83:677–725.

——. 1976. "Toward a More General Theory of Regulation." *Journal of Law & Economics* 19 (August): 211–40. Reprinted in Stigler (1988).

Perritt, Henry H. 1991. *Americans with Disabilities Act Handbook*. New York: Wiley Law Publications.

——. 1992. *Civil Rights Act of 1991: Special Report*, Employment Law Library. New York: John Wiley and Sons.

Pettit, Philip. 1997. *Republicanism: A Theory of Freedom and Government*. Oxford: Clarendon Press of Oxford University Press.

Phlips, Louis. 1995. *Competition Policy: A Game Theoretic Perspective*. Cambridge: Cambridge University Press.

Pierson, Christopher. 1995. *Socialism after Communism*. University Park: Pennsylvania State University Press.

Plant, Raymond. 1988. "Needs, Agency, and Moral Rights." In *Responsibility, Rights and Welfare: The Theory of the Welfare State*, edited by J. Donald Moon, 55–76. Boulder: Westview.

———. 1991. *Modern Political Thought*. Oxford: Basil Blackwell.

Polsby, Daniel. 1998. "Regulation of Foods and Drugs and Libertarian Ideals: Perspectives of a Fellow-Traveler." *Social Philosophy & Policy* 15:209–42.

Posner, Richard. 1972. *Economic Analysis of the Law*. Boston: Little, Brown.

———. 1996. *Law and Legal Theory in England and America*. Oxford: Clarendon Press, Clarendon Law Series.

Powell, Thomas Reed. 1917. "The Constitutional Issue in Minimum-Wage Legislation." *Minnesota Law Review* 2 (December).

Priest, George L. 1985. "The Invention of Enterprise Liability: a Critical History of the Intellectual Foundations of Modern Tort Law." *Journal of Legal Studies* 14:461–528.

Prychitko, David L. 1988. "Marxism and Decentralized Socialism." *Critical Review* 2:127–48.

Rachels, James. 1979. "What People Deserve." In *Justice and Economic Distribution*, edited by John Arthur and William H. Shaw, 150–63. Engelwood Cliffs, N.J.: Prentice Hall.

Randall, Teri. 1991. "FDA Scrutinizes 'Off-Label' Promotions," *Journal of the American Medical Association* 266(1):11.

Rappaport, Michael. 1992. "The Private Provision of Unemployment Insurance." *Wisconsin Law Review* 61:61–129.

Rasmussen, Douglas, and Douglas Den Uyl. 1990. *Liberty and Nature: An Aristotelian Defense of Liberal Order*. LaSalle, Ill.: Open Court.

Rawls, John. 1971. *A Theory of Justice*. Cambridge, Mass.: Belknap Press of Harvard University Press.

———. 2001. *Justice as Fairness: A Restatement*, edited by Erin Kelley. Cambridge, Mass.: Belknap Press of Harvard University Press.

Reich, Charles B. 1964. "The New Property." *Yale Law Journal* 73:733–87.

Reiman, Jeffrey. 1994. "Drug Addiction, Liberal Virtue, and Moral Responsibility." In *Drugs, Morality and the Law*, edited by Steven Luper-Foy and Curtis Brown, 25–48. New York: Garland.

Rhoads, Steven E. 1993. *Incomparable Worth: Pay Equity Meets the Market*. New York: Cambridge University Press.

Rhodes, Michael R. 2000. *Coercion: A Nonevaluative Approach*. Value Inquiry Book Series 92. Amsterdam: Rodopi.

Richards, David A. J. 1982. *Sex, Drugs, Death, and the Law: An Essay on Human Rights and Overcriminalization*. Totowa, N.J.: Rowman and Littlefield.

Rickenbacker, William, ed. 1974. *The Twelve-Year Sentence*. LaSalle, Ill.: Open Court.

Riggs, David, and Allison Freeman. 2002. "The Clean Water Act." In *The Environmental Source 2002*, edited by Angela Logomasini and David Riggs, 45–58. St. Louis: Competitive Enterprise Institute.

Riley, Jonathan. 1998. *Mill on Liberty*. Routledge Philosophy Guide-Book Series. London: Routledge.

Rix, Sara. 1994. *Older Workers: How Do They Measure Up? An Overview of Age Differences in Employee Costs and Performances*. Washington, D.C.: American Association of Retired Persons.

Robinson, Joan. 1933. *The Economics of Imperfect Competition*. London: Macmillan.

Roemer, John. 1994a. "The Morality and Efficiency of Market Socialism." In *Egalitarian Perspectives*, edited by John Roemer, 287–302. Cambridge: Cambridge University Press.

——. 1994b. "A Future for Socialism." In *Egalitarian Perspectives*, ed. John Roemer, 303–32. Cambridge: Cambridge University Press.

——. 1994c. *A Future for Socialism*. Cambridge, Mass.: Harvard University Press.

Rohlf, Daniel J. 1989. *The Endangered Species Act: A Guide to its Protections and Implementation*. Stanford, Calif.: Stanford Environmental Law Society.

Rolston, Holmes III. 1985. "Duties to Endangered Species." *Bioscience* 35:718–26. Reprinted in *Philosophy Gone Wild: Environmental Ethics*, edited by Holmes Rolston III, 206–220. Buffalo, N.Y.: Prometheus.

Romano, Roberta. 2002. "Empowering Investors: A Market Approach to Securities Regulation." In *Entrepreneurial Economics: Bright Ideas from the Dismal Science*, edited by Alexander Tabarrok, 177–242. New York: Oxford University Press.

Rothbard, Murray. 1963. *America's Great Depression*. Princeton, N.J.: Van Nostrand.

——. 1977. *Power and Market*, 2nd ed. Menlo Park, Calif., and San Francisco: IHS & Cato Institute.

——. 1978. *For a New Liberty*, rev. ed. New York: Collier Books, Macmillan.

Rothstein, Mark, Charles B. Craver, Elinor P. Schroeder, Elaine W. Shoben, and Lea S. VanderVelde. 1994. *Employment Law*. Hornbook Series. Vols. 1 & 2. Minneapolis, Minn.: West Publishing.

Rottenberg, Simon. 1980. "Introduction." In *Occupational Licensure and Regulation*, edited by Simon Rottenberg, 1–10. Washington, D.C.: American Enterprise Institute for Public Policy Research.

Rubin, Stephen. 1980. "The Legal Web of Professional Regulation." In *Regulating the Professions*, edited by R. D. Blair and S. Rubin, 29–60. Lexington, Mass.: Lexington Books.

Sagoff, Mark. 1988. *The Economy of the Earth*. Cambridge Studies in Philosophy and Public Policy, Douglas MacLean, series editor. New York: Cambridge University Press.

———. 1995. "Free Market Versus Libertarian Environmentalism." *Critical Review* 6:211–30.

Samuelson, Paul. 1964. *Economics*, 6th ed. New York: McGraw Hill.

Samuelson, Paul A., and William D. Nordhaus. 1992. *Economics*, 14th ed. New York: McGraw Hill.

Sandel, Michael J. 1982. *Liberalism and the Limits of Justice*. New York: Cambridge University Press.

Schaffer, Michelle. 1996. "Pre-emption by Product Labeling Statutes." *For The Defense* 19:15–20.

Schmidt, Alexander. [1974] 1976. "The FDA Today: Critics, Congress, and Consumerism." Speech given at the National Press Club, Washington, D.C., October 29, 1974. Quoted in H. Grabowski, *Drug Regulation and Innovation*, 76. Washington, D.C.: AEI Press.

Schmidtz, David. 1991. *The Limits of Government*. Boulder, Colo.: Westview.

Schmidtz, David, and Robert E. Goodin. 1998. *Social Welfare and Individual Responsibility*. New York: Cambridge University Press.

Schoenbrod, David. 2000. "Protecting the Environment in the Spirit of the Common Law." In *The Common Law and the Environment*, edited by Roger E. Meiners and Andrew P. Morriss, 3–24. Lanham, Md.: Rowman and Littlefield.

Schumpeter, Joseph. 1942. *Capitalism, Socialism, and Democracy*. New York: Harper and Row.

Schweickart, David. 1978. "Should Rawls Be A Socialist?" *Social Theory and Practice* 5:1–28.

———. 1993. *Against Capitalism*. Cambridge: Cambridge University Press.

Senate Committee on Labor and Welfare. 1971. "Report on the Occupational Safety and Health Act of 1970." Report No. 91–1282. Reprinted in *Legislative History of the Occupational Safety and Health Act of 1970*. Prepared by the Subcommittee on Labor of the Committee on Labor and Public Welfare, U.S. Senate. Washington, D.C.: Government Printing Office.

Shapiro, Daniel. 1995. "Why Rawlsian Liberals Should Support Free Market Capitalism" *Journal of Political Philosophy* 3 (March): 58–85.

———. 2004. "The Moral Case for a Market-Based Retirement System." In *Social Security and Its Discontents* edited by Michael Tanner, 89–108. Washington, D.C.: Cato Institute.

———. 2007. *Is the Welfare State Justified?* New York: Cambridge University Press.

Shapiro, S. A. 1979. "Limiting Physician Freedom to Prescribe a Drug for Any Purpose: The Need for FDA Regulation." *Northwestern University Law Review* 73:801–72.

Sher, George. 1999. *Beyond Neutrality*. New York: Oxford University Press.

Shogren, Jason F., and John Tschirhart, eds. 2001. *Protecting Endangered Species in the United States: Biological Needs, Political Realities, Economic Choices.* Cambridge: Cambridge University Press.

Shriver, Melinda L., and Grace-Marie Arnett.1998. "Uninsured Rates Rise Dramatically in States with Strictest Health Insurance Regulation." *Heritage Foundation Backgrounder* No. 1211.

Shugart, William F. *Taxing Choice.* 1997. New Brunswick, N.J.: Transaction Publishers.

Siegan, Bernard. 1972. *Land Use Without Zoning.* Lanham, Md.: Lexington Books.

Simmons, Randy T. 1999a. "The Endangered Species Act: Who's Saving What?" *The Independent Review* 3:309–26.

———. 1999b. "Fixing the Endangered Species Act." *The Independent Review* 3:511–36

Smith, Adam. [1776] 1976. *An Inquiry into the Nature and Causes of the Wealth of Nations.* Chicago: University of Chicago Press.

Smith, Bradley A. 2001. *Unfree Speech.* Princeton, N.J.: Princeton University Press.

Smith, Scott A., and Janell M. Gabor. 1996. "Preemption by Federal Agencies in Toxic Tort Litigation." *For the Defense* 19 (May): 21–25.

Soule, Edward. 2003. *Markets and Morality.* Lanham, Md.: Rowman and Littlefield.

Sowell, Thomas. 1984. *Civil Rights, Rhetoric or Reality?* New York: Morrow.

Starr, Paul. 1982. *The Social Transformation of American Medicine.* New York: Basic Books.

Starr, Tama. 1996. "The 7.63% Solution." *Reason* (February): 30–35.

Stein, Michael A. 2000. "Employing People with Disabilities: Some Cautionary Thoughts for a Second-Generation Civil Rights Statute." In *Employment, Disability, and the Americans with Disabilities Act: Issues in Law, Public Policy, and Research*, edited by Peter Blanck, 51–67. Evanston, Ill.: Northwestern University Press.

Sterba, James. 1998. *Justice for Here and Now.* New York: Cambridge University Press.

Sterns, H. L., and Michael McDaniel. 1994. "Job Performance and the Older Worker." In *Older Workers: How Do They Measure Up? An Overview of Age Differences in Employee Costs and Performances*, edited by Sara Rix. Washington, D.C.: American Association of Retired Persons.

Stigler, George. 1971. "The Theory of Economic Regulation." *Bell Journal of Economics and Management Science* 2:3–21. Reprinted in *Chicago Studies in Political Economy*, edited by George Stigler. Chicago: University of Chicago Press.

———. 1975. "What Can Regulators Regulate?: The Case of Electricity." In *The Citizen and the State: Essays on Regulation*, edited by George Stigler, 61–77. First published in *The Journal of Law & Economics* 5 (October 1972).

Stigler, George, ed. 1988. *Chicago Studies in Political Economy.* Chicago: University of Chicago Press.

Stone, Alan. 1977. *Economic Regulation and the Public Interest.* Ithaca, N.Y.: Cornell University Press.

———. 1982. *Regulation and its Alternatives.* Washington, D.C.: Congressional Quarterly Press.

Subcommittee on Labor, Committee on Labor and Public Welfare, U.S. Senate. 1971. *Legislative History of the Occupational Safety and Health Act of 1970.* Washington: Government Printing Office.

Sunding, David. 2003. "An Opening for Meaningful Reform." *Regulation* 26(2):30–35.

Sunstein, Cass 1993. *The Partial Constitution.* Cambridge, Mass.: Harvard University Press.

———. 1996. "On the Expressive Function of Law." *University of Pennsylvania Law Review* 144:2021–56.

———, ed. 1997. *Free Markets and Social Justice.* New York: Oxford University Press.

———. 1997a. "Social Roles and Social Norms." In *Free Markets and Social Justice*, edited by Cass Sunstein, 32–69. New York: Oxford University Press.

———. 1997b. "Incommensurability and Valuation in the Law." In *Free Markets and Social Justice*, edited by Cass Sunstein, 70–107. New York: Oxford University Press.

———. 1997c. "Preferences and Politics." In *Free Markets and Social Justice*, edited by Cass Sunstein, 1–31. New York: Oxford University Press.

Sunstein, Cass, and Richard Thaler. 2003. "Libertarian Paternalism is not an Oxymoron." *University of Chicago Law Review* 70:1159–1202.

Svorny, Shirley. 1992. "Should We Reconsider Licensing Physicians?" *Contemporary Economic Policy* 10(1):31–38.

———. 2004. "Licensing Doctors: Do Economists Agree?" *Econ Journal Watch* 1(2):279–305.

Swann, Dennis. 1988. *The Retreat of the State.* Ann Arbor: University of Michigan Press.

Tabarrok, Alexander T. 2000. "Assessing the FDA via the Anomaly of Off-Label Drug Prescribing." *The Independent Review* 5:25–53.

Taylor, Charles. 1979. *Hegel and Modern Society.* Cambridge: Cambridge University Press.

Temin, Peter. 1979. "The Origin of Compulsory Drug Prescriptions." *Journal of Law and Economics* 22:91–105.

———. 1980. *Taking Your Medicine: Drug Regulation in the United States.* Cambridge, Mass.: Harvard University Press.

TXANS (Texas Association of Responsible Non-Subscribers). 2007. *An Overview of Nonsubscription to Workers' Compensation in Texas.* Austin: Texas Association of Responsible Nonsubscribers. Available at http://txans.org/images/ceworkshop407.pdf (accessed May 18, 2008).

Thierer, Adam, and Clyde W. Crews, Jr. 2003. *What's Yours Is Mine: Open Access and the Rise of Infrastructure Socialism.* Washington, D.C.: Cato Institute.

Thomason, Terry, Timothy P. Schmidle, and John F. Burton, Jr. 2001. *Workers' Compensation: Benefits, Costs, and Safety under Alternative Insurance Arrangements*. Kalamazoo, Mich.: Upjohn Institute for Employment Research.

Tollison, Robert D., and Richard E. Wagner. 1982. *Balanced Budgets, Fiscal Responsibility and the Constitution*. Studies in Law and Economics. Washington, D.C.: Cato Institute.

U.S. Bureau of the Census. 1999. *Statistical Abstract of the United States*.

U.S. Congress. 1964; 1972; 1991; *Congressional Record*.

U.S. Food and Drug Administration. 1938. "Promulgation of Regulations under the Federal Food, Drug, and Cosmetic Act." 3 *Federal Register* 3168 (December 28, 1938).

U.S. House of Representatives. 1938. "Report on the Federal Food, Drug, and Cosmetic Act." Report No. 2139, 75th Congress.

———. 1951. "Amending Section 503(b) of the Federal Food, Drug, and Cosmetic Act." House Report No. 700, 82nd Congress.

———. 1971. House Education and Labor Committee. "Report on the Occupational Safety and Health Act." Report No. 91–1291. Reprinted in *Legislative History of the Occupational Safety and Health Act of 1970*. Prepared by the Subcommittee on Labor of the Committee on Labor and Public Welfare, U.S. Senate. Washington, D.C.: Government Printing Office.

———. 1991. House Education and Labor Committee. "Civil Rights and Womens Equity in Employment Act of 1991." Report No. 40–1, 102nd Congress, April 24.

———. 1991. House Judiciary Committee. "Civil Rights Act of 1991." Report No. 40–2, 102nd Congress, May 17.

U.S. Senate. 1951. "Amending Sections 303(c) and 503(b) of the Federal Food, Drug, and Cosmetic Act." Senate Report No. 946, 82nd Congress.

Van Fraassen, Bas C. 1980. *The Scientific Image*. Oxford: Clarendon Press.

Viscusi, W. Kip. 1979. *Employment Hazards: An Investigation of Market Performance*. Cambridge, Mass.: Harvard University Press.

———. 1983. *Risk by Choice*. Cambridge, Mass: Harvard University Press.

———. 1984. *Regulating Consumer Product Safety*. Washington, D.C.: American Enterprise Institute.

———. 2002. *Smoke-Filled Rooms: A Postmortem on the Tobacco Deal*. Chicago: University of Chicago Press.

Viscusi, W. Kip, John N. Vernon, and Joseph E. Harrington, Jr. 2005. *Economics of Regulation and Antitrust*, 4th ed. Cambridge, Mass.: MIT Press.

Volokh, Eugene. 1997. "What Speech Does 'Hostile Work Environment' Harassment Law Restrict?" *Georgetown Law Journal* 85:627.

Wagner, Richard E. 1989. *To Promote the General Welfare*. San Francisco: Pacific Research Institute for Public Policy.

Wall, Steven, and George Klosko, eds. 2003. *Perfectionism and Neutrality: Essays in Liberal Theory*. Lanham, Md.: Rowman and Littlefield.

Walzer, Michael. 1983. *Spheres of Justice*. New York: Basic Books.

Wardell, W. 1978. "Are These Requirements Enough or Too Much?" In *The Scientific Basis of Official Regulation of Drug Research and Development*, edited by A. F. De Schaepdryver, L. Lasagna, F. H. Gross, and D. R. Laurence. Proceedings of the 7th International Congress of Pharmacology.

Weingast, Barry R., and Mark J. Moran. 1983. "Bureaucratic Discretion or Congressional Control? Regulatory Policymaking by the Federal Trade Commission." *Journal of Political Economy* 91:765–800.

Welch, Finis 1995. "Comments." *Industrial and Labour Relations Review* 48:842–49.

Wessels, Walter J. 1981. *Minimum Wages, Fringe Benefits, and Working Conditions*. Washington, D.C.: American Enterprise Institute.

Wilcox, Clair. 1955. *Public Policies Toward Business*. Chicago: Irwin.

Wilkinson, Cynthia M. 1993. "Endangered Species or Endangered Rights?" Paper presented at the Third Annual Texas Water Law Conference, October 28, in Austin, Texas.

Will, George F. 1983. *Statecraft as Soulcraft: What Government Does*. New York: Simon & Shuster.

Willborn, Steven L. 2000. "The Nonevolution of Enforcement under the ADA: Discharge Cases and the Hiring Problem." In *Employment, Disability, and the Americans with Disabilities Act*, edited by Peter Blanck, 103–15. Evanston, Ill.: Northwestern University Press.

Williams, Edward B. 1947. "Exemption from the Requirement of Adequate Directions for Use in the Labeling of Drugs." *Food, Drug, and Cosmetic Law Quarterly* 2:155–72.

Williamson, Oliver. 1985. *The Economic Institutions of Capitalism: Firms, Markets, Relational Contracting*. New York: Free Press.

Wilson, James Q. 1990. "Against the Legalization of Drugs." *Commentary* 89 (February): 21–28.

Young, James H. 1961. *The Toadstool Millionaires*. Princeton: Princeton University Press.

——. 1992. *The Medical Messiahs: A Social History of Health Quackery in Twentieth-Century America*. Princeton, N.J.: Princeton University Press.

Young, S. David. 1987. *The Rule of Experts*. Washington, D.C.: Cato Institute.

Zimmerman, David. 1981. "Coercive Wage Offers." *Philosophy & Public Affairs* 10:121–45.

Zink, Donald, and Arthur Gutman. 2005. "Statistical Trends in Private Sector Employment Discrimination Suits." In *Employment Discrimination Litigation: Behavioral, Quantitative, and Legal Perspectives*, edited by Frank J. Landy, 101–31. San Francisco: Jossey-Bass.

Index

Ackerman, Bruce, 3, 53, 423n8,
     425n27, 448n7
Adler, Jonathan, 334–35, 345,
     446n7, n10
adverse selection, 99, 111
Age Discrimination in
     Employment Act of 1967,
     78, 185, 245–55
agency shop, 217–18, 220
agreement, reasoned, 5–8,
     11–13, 16
Akerlof's "lemons problem," 311,
     323
American National Standards
     Institute (ANSI), 171, 272
American Society for Testing
     and Materials (ASTM),
     171
*American Textile Mfrs. Inst. v.
     Donovan* (cotton dust
     standard), 274, 417
Americans with Disabilities Act of
     1990, 78, 185, 256–67
     linguistic indeterminacies,
          441n30
     purpose of the act, 258
anarchism, anarchists, 25, 147–48,
     162–63, 350
Andreas, Dwayne, 371
antidiscrimination laws, 78
     as producing a public good,
          186–87
     See also Age Discrimination
          in Employment Act of
          1967; Americans with
          Disabilities Act of 1990;
          Civil Rights Act of 1964;
          Civil Rights Act of 1991
antitrust, 39, 120–24, 424n13, n15

classical liberal view of, 46–48,
     101, 424n16, 431n4
modern liberal view of, 41–42,
     44, 101
Archer Daniels Midland (ADM),
     371
arguments
     common ground, 6–7, 12, 16,
          123, 131, 133
     convergence, 7, 11, 133–34,
          419n3, 422n26
     conversion, 65, 140, 173, 185,
          216, 358–59, 401
     and affirmative action, 233
     and age discrimination,
          247–55
     characterized, 7–8, 10–12,
          134, 190–200
     and disability discrimination,
          258–67
     and drug regulation, 289,
          292–93, 294–308
     land use regulation, 333–36,
          338–40, 345–46
     and nonmedical consumer
          product safety, 311–20
     and occupational licensure,
          323–27
     and OSHA, 270–71, 271–84
     and race discrimination,
          223–24, 227, 228–36
     and sexual harassment, 238,
          240–45
     and unionization, 216, 220,
          221
     practical liberal, 12–13, 135
     practical political, 155
     principled sectarian, 357–60,
          365, 382, 401, 403

477